OUTLINES

OF

UNIVERSAL HISTORY:

IN THREE PARTS;

WITH A COPIOUS INDEX TO EACH PART, SHOWING THE CORRECT MODE OF PRONOUNCING EVERY NAME MENTIONED IN IT.

PART I. ANCIENT HISTORY.
PART II. MEDIÆVAL HISTORY.
PART III. MODERN HISTORY.

BY

JOSEPH J. REED.

PART I. ANCIENT HISTORY.

PHILADELPHIA:
J. B. LIPPINCOTT & CO.
1862.

PREFACE.

The object of this work is to present to the student of history a succinct but connected narrative of events from the earliest period down to the present time. Several works have been written on Universal History, more or less excellent in their way, but suited rather to the advanced pupil and the man of leisure, than to the beginner, and to the man whose opportunities for reading are limited. Some of them are too voluminous, some are too meagre to be useful, and not one of them, so far as the Author is aware, presents a complete system of cotemporary history. The want of a text-book for schools, which shall be sufficiently comprehensive to embrace all that is essential in the annals of each nation, yet not so elaborate as to consume too much of the time or exhaust the patience of the pupil, and which shall at the same time enable him to ascertain with very little effort what has been going on throughout the world at any given epoch, has long been felt. In the course of his own experience, both as a student and a teacher, the Author has frequently had occasion to lament the non-existence of such a text-book; and the knowledge of the fact that history was not taught systematically in our schools, but that sometimes the pupils contented themselves with reading the history of the United States, and that of England, of Greece, and of Rome, and perhaps that of France, sometimes only one or two of these histories, and that they rarely extended their studies to the annals of other nations, determined him to attempt the compilation of a complete summary of the history of the world.

Whatever merit the plan of the present work possesses is, however, due to the Author's wife (formerly Miss Pamelia M. Converse), whose long experience in tuition corresponded with his own as regards the defective mode of teaching history, now so generally practised. The division of the work into centuries, the history of each nation being contained in parallel columns, the pages being so arranged that the heading of the particular century in use shall be always visible, and the system of widening or contracting the column as the nation increased or decreased in importance, are wholly due to her. The Author's own share of the labor has been devoted to the compilation of the details, in the course of which he has found it necessary to abridge the history of every country—a task which has occupied him six years. How far he has succeeded in presenting an accurate and useful, as well as readable, narrative, must be left for the public to decide. In a work in which such a mass of details has been condensed, he can hardly hope to have avoided mistakes; but his object has throughout been to produce a reliable text-book, and for this purpose he has consulted the best ancient and modern authorities. Wherever a point in history is obscure or doubtful, the reader is referred to standard authors, whom he may consult if desirous of further information; and, generally, the Author has named the authorities on which he himself relied. The work is intended not only for the use of schools, but for that of the very numerous class of grown-up persons who have not had opportunities in their youth for prosecuting studies of this kind, but feel the importance of an acquaintance with the world's history, and yet are deterred from seeking it by the idea that to gain even a slight knowledge of it, there is a necessity for consulting a large number of books, many of which, perhaps, are not accessible to them. It is hoped that these "Outlines of Universal History" will supply what is wanted.

The present volume comprises that portion of the world's annals styled Ancient History. It commences with the very earliest traditions of those Asiatic nations which sprang directly from the cradle of our race, and it terminates with the close of the 5th century of the Christian Era. The reason why this last-named period is chosen for drawing the line between Ancient History and that which follows, is, that it was the time when the old civilizations of the heathen world had died out, and their places had become filled by an infusion of new races and new ideas, derived, to a certain extent, from barbarian sources, but mainly from Christianity, which, after undergoing the severest trials and sufferings, had at last risen triumphant over paganism, and was then the dominant influence in Europe. The second volume will comprise Mediæval History, or that of the Middle Ages, a period of one thousand years, which may be called the great transition period between the childhood and the manhood of mankind. In it the great nations of the present day were formed, and the grand ideas which became the basis of modern progress were promulgated; and a proper acquaintance with its details will prepare the way for the study of Modern History (to which the third volume is devoted), which will be but imperfectly understood without a knowledge of the two preceding divisions. One advantage arising from a comprehensive plan of this kind, is that no one nation's history assumes an undue preponderance over another. The pupil cannot be misled into the notion that there are but three or four nations worth troubling his head about, since, if he pay proper attention to the cotemporaneous history, he will find how much the actions of one country have influenced those of others, and that impulses which actuate man at the present day may have been derived from remote antiquity, or from the most distant nations. As in a family, so among the different peoples of the earth, the turbulent conduct of one member impairs the harmony of the others, — a truth which, in these days of steam and electricity, is sensitively recognized in every Exchange almost every hour. Another advantage, or, rather, peculiarity of the present plan, is that the history of each country is extracted from its own annals, and complete in itself: it is, therefore, independent of any other; hence, there is very frequently the repetition of an event; for instance, two accounts of the battle of Marathon will be found, one in the history of Greece, the other in that of Persia, but in each case it is considered from the national point of view.

The introduction into this work of a history of the Christian Church requires some notice. It may seem out of character to class such a history with that of the nations of the earth; but, in truth, in the early ages of the Church, the Christians were a nation in themselves, as regarded the heathen world, and were assailed as such. The bond of union between them was as strong as that which binds the citizens of any land to each other. And when the triumph of the Church over its religious foes was completed, it had its political foes to contend with, and this fully occupied it during the Middle Ages. In that stormy period it triumphed over emperors and kings, over nations and individuals, and was as distinct a power as France or England. In modern times it has had to contend with schismatics, heretics, reformers, and those who would, if they could, destroy it altogether; and it has had as distinct characteristics as any cotemporaneous nation has. It has, in short, been a POWER throughout the last eighteen centuries, and is, therefore, fully entitled to the place in history which is here assigned to it. Perhaps it will be said that Mohammedanism, Budhism, and other religions, have the same claim; but their case will, it is hoped, be found amply disposed of in the history of the respective countries wherein they prevail. Universality is not their characteristic, as it is of Christianity. In treating the history of the Christian Church, the Author has endeavored to confine himself strictly to the statement of facts supported by the best authorities: he has scrupulously avoided all comment of his own, lest by any chance the feelings of others might be wounded. This ought rather to enhance than to detract from the value of his narrative.

With regard to the mode in which the work ought to be used, a glance at the arrangement of it will probably suggest the readiest way to the teacher, — or to the student, where there is no teacher. In Ancient History there are a few leading nations to whom the others were in turn subordinate; as, for instance, first Egypt, then Assyria, then Syria, then Greece, and then Rome. The Author suggests that it would be well to study the histories of these leading countries thoroughly, reading each of the cotemporaneous ones in a less particular manner, yet so that the pupil shall be exercised as to the details thereof *century by century*. But as the principal object of the work is to present a general view of the affairs of the world during each century, and, in so doing, to treat the subject in its entirety, and not with special reference to any one leading nation, care must be taken to impress upon the pupil's mind that, in selecting Egypt, Greece, or Italy, or any other country, as the connecting link, he must not lose sight of the independence of each history; that is to say, for example, the history of Persia is to be studied with reference not merely to Greece and Rome, but also to its own intrinsic importance, and its influence upon the world. To assist the teacher, a few questions have been added at the foot of each column, rather, however, as suggestive of the kind of exercise to which the pupil should be subjected, than as exhaustive of the subject. The varying size and number of the columns devoted to each nation, is an indication of the relative importance of that same nation at any given epoch; thus Italy, in its earliest stage, occupies but a narrow column, but when mistress of the world, she fills nine broad columns. So also may be traced the fall and extinction of empires. A copious index has been added, which is intended as a guide to the pronunciation of names, as well as a reference to particulars; but the system of accenting the names has also been adopted in the text, — a dash being placed over the strongly accented syllables.

In conclusion, the Author desires to bear testimony to the very valuable aid he has derived from the Philadelphia Library, and to the uniform kindness and attention he has received from its accomplished librarian, Lloyd P. Smith, Esq., and his assistants, during the years that he has been engaged upon this work. To him and to the secretary, William E. Whitman, Esq., he is indebted for many valuable suggestions and much information, whereby the work has been materially benefited. Without easy and copious access to a great variety of authorities, it could not have been compiled; but all that was required has been most courteously afforded by these gentlemen, to whom the Author here tenders his best thanks.

PHILADELPHIA, *August*, 1862.

OUTLINES

OF

UNIVERSAL HISTORY.

INTRODUCTION.

History is the record of the actions of mankind, and of the events which have happened in the world. It is the accumulated experience of ages.

When it narrates the actions of men and nations in all countries and times, it is called *Universal History*, or the History of the World.

When it narrates those of any one nation, it is called by the name of that nation; as, the History of Greece, the History of Rome. This is *National History*.

When it relates to the foundation of the Christian religion it is called *Sacred History*, which includes also the early history of mankind, and of the Jewish nation, and is contained in the Old and New Testaments. Those nations which do not believe in Christianity, such as the Hindoos, the Chinese, the Turks, have also what they call Sacred History; but in this work, whenever that term is employed, it will refer solely to the Bible.

When it relates to those events and actions which have influenced mankind generally, and not any one nation in particular, it takes its name from the subject; as, the History of the Church, or Ecclesiastical History — the History of Commerce — the History of Inventions — the History of Civilization.

When it relates to one particular person, it is called *Biography*, or the life of that person; as, the Life of Cæsar, the Life of Washington.

History, in its more extended sense, treats of the causes of the rise and fall of nations, of their habits, manners, religion, policy, and forms of government. It investigates the effects of these on the human race, and traces the progress and the decay of civilization. This branch is more properly styled the *Philosophy of History*. From these materials the student will discover what are the evils which bring on the downfall of a nation, and what are the measures best adapted to promote its happiness and prosperity.

History is also divided into *Ancient* and *Modern*. This is a purely arbitrary division, but is found to be convenient. *Ancient History* comprehends all those events which happened between the creation of Man and the destruction of the Roman Empire in the year of the Christian Era 476. *Modern History* commences from this last-named period, and comes down to the present time. It is usually divided into two periods: the first of which, comprising about 1000 years, is called *Mediæval History*, or the *History of the Middle Ages*; the second is more properly called Modern History.

Chronology treats of the date of the occurrence of each event, and is absolutely necessary to a proper understanding of history.

The chronology of the first ages of the world is very uncertain: the best writers disagree as to the dates of many of the principal events. The system of Archbishop Usher has been that most generally followed, but modern researches have thrown great doubts on the accuracy of many of his dates, especially on those relating to the most early history and the creation of man.

The scope of this work is elementary only, and designed merely to show the general course of history, without going into details; the student, therefore, who desires to obtain more complete information, must himself search the best authorities in order to satisfy his mind on the many doubtful and contested points which occur both in history and chronology.

The course of civilization may be thus stated:

Starting from India and China, it spread into Bactria and Persia, and thence over Southern Arabia to Ethiopia and Egypt. In China, it attained to its height about 2000 years ago, since which period it has been stationary, so that that country presents to us the remarkable spectacle of a primitive people with a primitive language. It then travelled westward to Assyria, Persia, and Egypt, and thence to Greece, where it received a development which has had a permanent influence on the world; for we find that the study of the writings and actions of the poets, philosophers, and statesmen of that country, usually form part of the education of the youth of modern times. The prosperity of Greece was but short-lived. Under Alexander the Great, B. C. 330, it attained its greatest height, but soon after fell before a power which rose up still further west, and was destined to become the subjugator of the then known world. This power was Rome. The civilization of the Romans combined the elegance of Greece with a most extended political and military organization; the arts and sciences were successfully cultivated by the Romans, as is shown in their vast public works — their roads, aqueducts, bridges, temples, etc. When this form of civilization was at its height, and all the world was at peace under the weight of the Roman yoke, the fulness of time had come for the appearance on earth of Him whose teachings were to supersede the ancient faith, and to become the basis of modern civilization. One of the most interesting subjects to which the student of history can turn his attention, is the progress of the Christian religion. He will find that it flourished in spite of persecution and contempt; that although at first forced to hide itself in caves and secret places, its disciples gradually became the powerful of the earth; that it lost its purity as it increased in worldly power; and that there sprang up within it innumerable divisions, which remain to this day, and have caused some of the most sanguinary wars recorded in history.

From the ruins of the ancient civilization arose the modern, which, developing itself in Italy, spread over Western Europe, and was carried over from that continent to America, by the Spaniards, Portuguese, French, and English, in the fifteenth and following centuries. It is fast traversing the mighty continent of North America, where vast fields of development are awaiting it; and it will probably then cross the Pacific, and revisit the old world of the East, under a higher and a nobler form.

Next in importance to Christianity are those inventions and discoveries

Questions. — What is History? — Under what divisions may it be classed? — What is Universal History? — What is National History? — What is Sacred History? — What other kinds of Sacred History are there? — What name does History take, when it refers to any particular subject? — What is it called when it relates to one particular person? — What is it in its more extended sense? — What other division of History is there? — What does Ancient History include? — What does Modern History include? — What is Mediæval History? — What does Chronology treat of? — Is the chronology of the first ages of the world certain? — Do the best writers agree as to the dates of principal events? — What is the design of this work? — State the course of civilization. — What were the obstacles which the Christian religion had to overcome?

which have contributed so powerfully to the progress of civilization in modern times.

The invention of printing, in the fifteenth century, became the means of diffusing knowledge amongst all classes of men, at a comparatively small cost and with little trouble; whereas, prior to that invention, there were no such things as books, but every author's works, even the Scriptures, were in manuscript, and had to be copied by hand.

The invention of gunpowder, coming into general use about the same period, placed the weak on a level with the strong, and put an end to the empire of brute force. Before that time men passed their lives in athletic exercises, to the almost entire neglect of their minds, physical strength being the principal thing required for wielding the battle-axe and spear; but when gunpowder came into use, it was found that weak men, with the modern weapons, were a match for the stoutest knights in armor; consequently, those mail-clad warriors were forced to lay aside their ferocious occupation, and turn to the arts of peace.

The discovery of the mariner's compass enabled the sailor to find out in what direction his ship was moving, and gave him courage to go out of sight of land, instead of keeping close to the shore, as was the case in ancient times.

The discovery of America, and of a passage from Europe to India round the Cape of Good Hope, vastly extended the fields of enterprise, and enlightened mankind as to the true form of the globe.

The invention of the telescope; the discoveries made by Kepler, Galileo, and Newton, in Astronomy and the physical sciences; those made in later times in *Chemistry, Geology, and the other sciences;* and, in the most recent (our own) times, the application of *steam* and *electricity* to locomotion and international communication, have entirely changed the face of society.

These inventions and discoveries constitute the most important events in modern history. The ancients knew little of the sciences; their arts related principally to architecture, sculpture, and the manufacture of articles for domestic use. They attained to only a very moderate degree of excellence in navigation, agriculture, and the means of locomotion and international communication. Their history consists for the most part of wars waged upon their neighbors, usually according to the will of kings, who led their subjects to slaughter, pretty much as the farmer sends his cattle to the market. The history of these kings is in fact that of their subjects, and many nations have little history beside a record of the names of their rulers. This is the case with China, India, Persia, Assyria, Egypt, and Babylon, in ancient times, and with all Oriental nations in modern times. In the middle ages but little progress was made in the arts and sciences; history is then busy with recording wars and cruelty of the most ferocious kind. The ancient civilization had been crushed out by races of barbarians which poured into Europe out of Central Asia, as one wave follows another; but from their invasions the ground-work of modern civilization is derived.

The student will also notice the prominent part which War plays in the history of mankind. It would not be exaggerating to say that four-fifths of the record of man's career are occupied by it. It appears to have hitherto formed part of the Divine plan of the government of the world. Its uses appear to have been principally the keeping the population of the earth within the limits of the means of subsistence; the compulsory propagation of ideas, habits, and languages, amongst nations which would otherwise, possibly, have become stagnant; the punishment of various races, and the extermination of those which had become so thoroughly wicked and depraved, that their longer continuance on earth would have been a curse to the others. It appears also to be a part of the Divine plan that nations shall be subdued or expelled by a more energetic race when they have, for any length of time, occupied their land without making it yield a certain amount of benefit to themselves or their neighbors. War has sometimes been the means of effecting the amalgamation of different races of men, and thereby producing out of them a nation of greater energy and intelligence; and it is an ordeal which every nation has had to go through when it has sought to rid itself of foreign or domestic tyranny, though unhappily such effort has not always been attended with success.

With these introductory remarks, we proceed to the consideration of that portion of the world's history which is styled Ancient, commencing with that period called "the Ante-Historical," because it relates to events which occurred before authentic records were preserved, and because it rests mainly upon tradition.

What inventions and discoveries are next in importance to Christianity?—What is said of the invention of printing?—What of gunpowder?—What of the mariner's compass?—What was the state of art and science among the ancients?—What does their history chiefly consist of?—What is said of war?

PART I.

ANCIENT HISTORY.

ANTE-HISTO-

No date can be assigned to the origin of the globe. The only sources from which we can expect to derive its history, are the Scriptures and the researches of geologists. The Scriptures, however, do not descend into particulars, but merely state, generally, that it was created "in the beginning." After its creation it underwent a variety of convulsions and revolutions, evidently occupying immense periods of time, whereby its surface was gradually fitted for the abode of man; but the description of these wonderful phenomena is the province of geology. We must, therefere, content ourselves with saying, that at the time appointed in the Divine Plan of the Universe, Man made his appearance on this earth. It is reasonable to assume that he was created full grown, with his bodily and mental faculties perfect and ready for use; and that he was placed in some favored region of the earth, where the climate would neither scorch nor freeze him, but was mild and equable, and where the soil would spontaneously yield fruits and plants for his subsistence. This region is described in Scripture as "the garden of Eden," but the only clue given as to its situation is that found in Gen. ii. 10–14, where it is said that four rivers parted from the river that went out of Eden, and that these rivers were named Pison, Gihon, Hiddekel, and Euphrates. No four rivers can now be found on the surface of the earth agreeing in all points with those mentioned; but it is evident that the district here alluded to is Chaldæa. The traditions of the East point to the beautiful vale of Cashmere as the original seat of the human race. It may be collected from Scripture, and from the deductions of philosophy, that man has always existed in society; that the first societies were families; the first form of government patriarchal; that, gradually men became keepers of flocks and herds, and cultivators of corn; that families spread and combined; and that from their union arose monarchies, the next most ancient form of civil government.

Mankind is divided into different races, which vary very much in their intellect and form. These varieties are, according to the ablest writers, three, viz., the Caucasian, the Mongolian, and the Negro. The first includes the people of Western Asia, Europe, and Northern Africa; the second, the people of Eastern Asia and the Indians of America; the third, the tribes with woolly hair and black skin that people Africa. History does not inform us of the origin of these different varieties, but they have existed from the remotest periods of which we have any account. The first, or Caucasian, is that which fills the most prominent place in history; for with that race has originated almost all that ennobles mankind in religion, philosophy, literature, art and science, as the histories of Egypt, Assyria, Greece, Rome, Italy, France, Spain, Germany, England, and the United States of America, testify. The second race is inferior to the first in many respects, but has attained to a considerable degree of civilization, as is shown in the history of China, and of ancient Mexico; though vast tribes of this race have retained to this day their wandering and unsettled habits; the Tartars and the red Indians of North America are instances of this. The third, or Negro race, has not manifested mental development equal to that of the other two races. It has in all ages furnished slaves and servants to the higher and dominant classes of the Caucasian nations, and although amongst some of the communities of Africa ruled over by Negro princes, a knowledge of many of the useful arts is found, yet no settled form of civilization, no literature has ever existed amongst them, and they have, therefore, no station of eminence in the history of the world.

The Chinese, the Hindoos, the Persians, the Egyptians, and some other nations, pretend to carry back the records of their empires far beyond the commonly received date of the creation of Man. Their claims to such remote antiquity, however, are unsupported by historical evidence, and appear to have originated in their vanity, or in the craftiness of their priesthood.

As regards the date of the creation of man, the learned Dr. Hales has given a list of the opinions of 120 eminent historians and chronologers, all of whom differ on the point—some to the extent of 3368 years—the extremes being 6984 and 3616 years before the Christian era. Archbishop Usher computes that the creation of man took place in the year 4004 B. C., a year remarkable in astronomy as an epoch when the great axis of the earth's orbit coincided with the line of the equinoxes, and consequently when the true and mean equinoxes were united. This is the usually received date. Subsequent research has, however, thrown great doubt upon its accuracy. The date suggested by Dr. Hales, viz., 5411 B. C., is more in accordance with the ancient Egyptian, Assyrian, Persian, and Chinese systems. As relates to the period which elapsed between the Flood and the Birth of Abraham, we are by his system enabled to account for many things which are irreconcilable with the shorter period given by Usher. The labors and discoveries of Wilkinson, Clinton, Layard, Rawlinson, Champollion, Lepsius, Bunsen, and others, who have succeeded in deciphering the ancient inscriptions and records of the Egyptians and Assyrians, have proved, almost beyond a doubt, that a much higher antiquity must be ascribed to those nations than that hitherto allowed. The scope of the present work does not admit of the discussion of these difficult and abstruse subjects; we can, therefore, only refer the student, who desires further information, to the works of the learned men above-mentioned.

The Book of Genesis gives us an account of the creation of the first man. He was called "Adam" (or "red"), a name common to both male and female (Gen. v. 2), and of the first woman, who, when first created, was called "Aishah" (from "Aish," a man), but whose name was subsequently changed to "Hhavah" or "Eve," signifying "mother" (Gen. iii. 20). This first pair were placed in a luxurious spot called Eden, where they remained until, on account of their sin, they were expelled and sent forth to wander over the face of the earth. During their sojourn in Eden, they had no children; it was not until after their expulsion that any were born to them. In the course of time they had a numerous progeny. Of their children we have the record of three only, viz., Cain, the first born (whose name signifies "Acquisition"); Abel (or "pain"), the second son; and Seth (the "appointed"). Cain, after the murder of Abel, went eastward into the land of Nod (or "exile"), where he built a city called Enoch. Of the precise site of this city we are ignorant; we may, however, conjecture that it was somewhere to the eastward of the Tigris, where Cain's descendants became the idolatrous race with whom the descendants of the righteous Seth afterwards intermarried (Gen. vi. 2). They became famous as artificers in brass and iron, and as musicians (Gen. iv. 21, 22). The sacred historian gives us the names of eight of Cain's descendants (Gen. iv.), and eight generations from Adam to Tubal-Cain; the last named may have been contemporary with Methuselah. We have also a list of nine in direct line from Adam through Seth to Noah, in whose days the Flood occurred. Through this line of patriarchs the knowledge and worship of the One true God was handed down and preserved; whence they and their children are called "the sons of God" (Gen. vi. 2), but they gradually lapsed into idolatry and wickedness, and united themselves with "the daughters of men," *i. e.*, the descendants of Cain—which occasioned the denunciation of God's wrath by Enoch, recorded in the Epistle of Jude, and its realization in the deluge which occurred in the days of Noah.

It is probable that the inhabitants of the earth, before the flood, attained to a considerable degree of civilization, as, in addition to what is recorded of the descendants of Cain, we find in various parts of the world the remains of architectural buildings of gigantic dimensions, which were erected long anterior to authentic history, and to which an antediluvian origin is universally ascribed. If we suppose (with Dr. Hales) that a period of 2256 years elapsed between the creation of man and the deluge, there would have been plenty of time for the peopling of a large portion of the earth and the formation of empires. That this was the case, is confirmed by the primitive history and traditions of all the Oriental nations.

Bero′sus, the Chaldæ′an historian, gives a list of ten monarchs who reigned in Chaldæa prior to the deluge—the first of whom, Alo′rus, or Chry′sor, was cotemporary with La′mech, the seventh from Adam in Cain's line, in the 1056th year of the world, and (according to Hales) B. C. 4355, the beginning of whose kingdom was probably the union of the sons of God with the daughters of men, referred to in Genesis. After a reign of 100 years he was succeeded by

Alaspa′rus	B. C. 4255
A′milon, of Pantibi′bla	" 4225
Am′menon, of Chaldæa	" 4095
Megalo′rus, of Pantibi′bla	" 3975
Dao′nus, a shepherd of Pantibi′bla	" 3795
Euedores′chus, of Pantibi′bla	" 3694
Amempsi′nus, a Chaldæan	" 3515
Otiar′tes	" 3415
Xisu′thrus	" 3335

In the days of the earliest of these kings (or about the year B. C. 4100), the historian relates that there came from the sea coast a man named Euan′nes,

Can any date be assigned to the origin of the earth?—From what source can we derive its history?—What is said of the origin of Man?—Relate where he was first placed, and what was said of him?—How was mankind divided?—Mention the different races that are named?—What is said of the antiquity of the Chinese and the Hindoos?—What list has Dr. Hales given as to the date of the creation of Man?—Relate what is said of the creation of Adam and Eve?—What is said of their descendants?—What is said of the inhabitants of the earth before the flood?—Who was Berosus?—What does the Chaldæan historian give?

RICAL PERIOD.

who preached the coming of God with his angels, to execute judgment upon the world for its wickedness. This corresponds with the Apostle Jude's statements respecting Enoch, who lived about this time, and is perhaps the same person as Euannes. In the days of Xisuthrus, the last of these princes, happened the great deluge, the particulars of which, as given by the Chaldæan historian, correspond in many respects with those given in Genesis; but it is probable that he borrowed them from that book.

In China we find traditions respecting the reign of three "Celestial" emperors before the time of Fo-hi, (whom many suppose to have been Noah); but these personages probably represent either certain principles, or long periods of time, and not actual men.

The traditions of the Hindoos are extravagant, unintelligible, and utterly unworthy of credit.

The antediluvian traditions of Egypt furnish us with the names of twelve deities, or deified chieftains, who are supposed to have lived upon earth for very long periods of time. Amongst them are found deities corresponding with those afterwards worshipped by the Greeks. The Egyptian priests asserted that the Greeks derived their religion from them. They identified the goddess Deme′ter, or Ce′res, with their own I′sis; Bacchus with Osi′ris; Jupiter with A′mun; and so on. But Isis and Osiris were also identified with Dian′a (the moon), and Apollo (the sun).

Amid the profound obscurity which hangs over the earliest history of Greece, we find traditions of a country called Lecto′nia, inhabited by a people called the Cyclo′pes. This district was submerged by a flood occasioned by the overflowing of the vast sea which anciently covered Southern Russia, and which, owing to some convulsion of nature, burst a channel through the Bos′phorus and Dardanel′les. It occupied that portion of the earth's surface where now is the Grecian Archipe′lago, as well as Greece; the Grecian islands being the remains of that ancient land. Buildings, or constructions, of gigantic dimensions, which tradition attributes to the Cyclopes, are still to be seen in Greece.

This ancient race also inhabited Sicily, but of their origin nothing is known. In the Grecian mythology mention is frequently made of them, and they are numbered among the Ti′tans, the sons of Ura′nus and Ge (heaven and earth). They are described by Homer as a gigantic and lawless race of shepherds, who devoured human beings. Their name implies creatures with circular eyes. The superstition of the ancient Greeks led them to regard volcanoes as the workshops of Vulcan, the God of Fire, and the Cyclopes as his assistants; and Mount Ætna, and other volcanic mountains in Sicily, were considered as their abodes. The Pelasgi were among the earliest inhabitants of Greece. They came from Asia Minor, and settled in the Grecian islands and in the Peloponnesus, whence they spread over Greece, Thessaly, Illyria, and Italy. They are said to have been an agricultural people, but possessed of considerable knowledge of the useful arts. They introduced the worship of Jupiter and Vulcan, and of the Cabi′ri. Whether the Jupiter thus worshipped was an earthly prince or chieftain, cannot now be ascertained; the mythological being to whom the Pelasgi consecrated the grove of Dodo′na, in Epi′rus, had a variety of attributes, and was called the father of gods and men. Some have supposed that he was an Asiatic monarch possessed of very extended dominions and great abilities, who, after death, was deified, or honored as a god. The seat of his empire has been laid in a variety of places; but all is the most vague surmise. The Zeus or Jupiter of the more modern Greek theogony (or "generation of the Gods," which owes its consistency to He′siod, who reduced it to a system) will be more particularly mentioned in the next division of this work — the earliest historical period — where a succinct account of the Greek mythology is given. The Cabiri (a Hebrew word signifying "to be great") were mystic divinities, whose character, attributes, and office are uncertain. Their number has been variously estimated at from two to eight, and they were worshipped with peculiar splendor in the island of Samothrace. It is probable that the name Cabiri (mighty ones) was applied indiscriminately to the powers that presided over the principal operations of Nature. The language of the Pelasgi was, probably, related to the Greek, as the two coalesced in all parts of Greece with facility; but we possess no certain knowledge of it, nor of the habits and civilization of that people. There are in Greece remains of architecture, such as the tomb of A′treus at Myce′næ, which are said to be Pelasgian, and some writers have ascribed a similar origin to the gigantic remains of the Cyclopes, but there is not sufficient evidence in support of these opinions. The Le′leges were another ancient race who inhabited Greece before the Helle′nes; they have frequently been confounded with the Pelasgi, but they were essentially different, being a warlike and migratory race, while the Pelasgi were a peaceful and agricultural people. They inhabited the coasts of Greece, and their chief occupation was piracy. Their origin is unknown. But we may reasonably infer that all these races, varying in habits and character as they did, probably on account of the different circumstances by which their nationality had been moulded, were branches of that great Indo-Germanic family which sent forth from Central Asia, from time to time, vast tribes to people the earth.

One of the most ancient nations in the world is the Iberian, which, even in the remotest antiquity, was found to have dwelt in Spain from a period long anterior to recorded history. The descendants of this people are to be met with, at the present day, in the Basque provinces of Spain, where their language is still heard; indeed, some Spanish writers have fondly contended that it was the primitive language of mankind, so ancient is it, and so little akin to the dialects of surrounding nations.

The traditions of Persia, collected in the Dabista′n, a volume compiled from works of the ancient Ghebers, or fire-worshippers, gives a succession of monarchs and prophets who preceded Kai′omurs. It is said that long before Zoroa′ster, the Persians venerated a prophet called Ma′habad, the father of men, who invented ornaments and weapons, built cities and palaces, and introduced the arts and commerce. That he had thirteen successors of his own family who were the monarchs and high-priests of the country. That the last of them, A′zerabad, abdicated the throne, and retired to a life of solitary devotion. The Empire then became a scene of rapine and murder, until a famous sage named Jy-af′fram was induced to assume the government. He founded the Jya′nian dynasty, the last king of which was Jy′abad, who, after a long and prosperous reign, suddenly disappeared, and the empire fell into confusion. His son, Shah Kūlēev, was then made king. The successors of this last named monarch were prosperous until the days of the last prince of the dynasty, Māhăbōol, who resigned, owing to the depravity of his subjects. His eldest son, Yēssān, founded a new dynasty, which terminated in his descendant, Yēssān Ajūm. At the end of his reign the general wickedness of mankind exceeded all bounds and God made the mutual hostility of the various tribes the means of Divine vengeance. Warfare raged until the human race was nearly extinct. The Creator then called to the throne Kai′omurs (or Gilshah, "lord of the earth"). The descent of this prince is traced to Noah; he is said to have been the grandson of that patriarch. Such is the traditional history of Persia.

Allusion has been made to the classification of the human race into three great divisions, the Caucasian, the Mongolian, and the Negro: to which some writers have added the Mala′yan, or yellow-skinned race, and the aboriginal American. It has been a subject very learnedly discussed, whether these races all sprang from one stock or single pair of human beings, or whether they each had ancestors of their own. Some eminent physiologists have contended that the differences between the races are so striking and so fundamental, that they must have derived their origin from different sources. They maintain, for instance, that the Negro could not have descended from the same ancestors as the Caucasian, and they support their arguments by the assertion, that no length of residence in Africa will convert a Caucasian into a Negro, pointing to the Egyptians, Copts, Mamelukes, Moors, and other nations which have resided there for centuries, as proofs. On the other hand, the advocates of the unity of the origin of mankind support their views by reference to the Bible, and by attributing to climate and other influences operating during very long periods of time, all the varieties which we meet with in the human race. It is not within the scope of this work to discuss the subject, but it is here mentioned by way of suggesting further inquiry on the part of the student, who ought to be informed as to the doubts which have been cast upon the commonly received opinions of the origin of mankind, in order that he may satisfy himself by his own researches, "prove all things, and hold fast that which is good." The valuable works of Prichard and of Blumenbach on the Physiology of Man will afford him ample materials for reflection on this grand subject, which is one of the most interesting that can occupy his attention. Some have feared that such researches militate against the doctrines of Christianity. We think, however, that on investigation it will be found that the great doctrine of human redemption remains unharmed. But the student should be careful to read both sides of the question, and avoid being led away by hasty generalizations.

Who was Euannes? — In whose reign did the flood happen? — What tradition do we find in China? — What is said of the traditions of the Hindoos? — What of those of Egypt? — What is said of the traditions of Greece? — Relate the traditions of Persia? — Who founded the Jyanian dynasty? — What was the relationship between Kaiomurs and Noah? — What addition has been made to the classification of the races of mankind? — What is said of the origin of mankind?

FROM THE EARLIEST PERIOD

EGYPT.

The earliest historical personage we meet with in the history of Egypt is Menes, but chronologists are not agreed as to the date of his reign, some placing it as far back as 3893 B. C., and 3643 B. C., and others at 2188 B. C., a difference of 1700 years! The former are, probably, nearer the truth. All we know of Menes is, that he was the first king who united the provinces of Egypt under one crown; but they had previously existed for a long period as independent kingdoms, of which Thebes was the principal city; and they were in a flourishing and luxurious state. Menes was born at This, a city near Aby′dos (the city of Osi′ris), whence he is called the founder of the Thinite dynasty. He constructed a vast dam, whereby he diverted the course of the Nile and drained the ground on which he afterwards built the famous city of Mem′phis. He fortified this city with immense walls; whence its name, which signifies "the wall with battlements." He also conquered a neighbouring nation called the Lybians; and he is said to have been torn to pieces by a hippopotamus.

His son, Atho′thes I., erected the royal palace at Memphis, which city then became the capital of Upper and Lower Egypt. He is said to have been learned in anatomy and medicine.

Athothes II. was the third king of Egypt, but nothing more is known of him. His successor, Miaba′es, built the Pyramids of Kokome, now in ruins and undistinguishable. Semem′pses, the next monarch, was the last of the dynasty. A severe pestilence afflicted the country in his time. On his death Egypt was divided into Upper and Lower; and was governed by two different dynasties of kings, during a period of 224 years. Of the dynasty (the 3d) which reigned at Memphis, we have records of the following monarchs: — Sesos′tris or Sesorche′res the Great, who is said to have been nearly nine feet high, and is called the Patriarch of the Memphite dynasty; Toi′chros, or A′ses Tekte′ra, to whom the Lybians submitted; Sesorto′sis; Ma′res; Sesorche′res II., his son, the great lawgiver, in whose reign considerable progress was made in medicine, astronomy, geometry, architecture, and the art of writing; An-Soy′phis (Sa′sychis, or Kau′ra), who built the brick pyramid of Dăshōor (the only one which was built of brick), and which became his tomb; Si′rios (or Sahu′ra) whose tomb is in the Northern Pyramid of Abouseer, in the field of Pyramids at Ghizeh; Chnu′bos-Gneu′ros (or Har′karu); Raso′sis; and Biy′res.

A cotemporary dynasty reigned at Thebes, whose names are given by Mane′tho, the Egyptian historian; but as his record contains but little other information, it is needless to cite from it. The student is referred to the works of Bunsen and others for further information on the subject. The differences between the accounts of Manetho, Eratos′thenes, Syncel′lus, Euse′bius, Hero′dotus, and other historians, are very great. We hasten on to more authentic history. It is probable that many of the dynasties reigned at the same time over different portions of Egypt. We have adopted the lines of kings selected by Eratosthenes and confirmed by Bunsen, as the chain of our history.

The 4th dynasty, under Che′ops and his brother Ceph′ren, re-united the provinces of Upper and Lower Egypt on the extinction of the house of Menes. Cheops was an impious and cruel king, and forced his people to build the second largest pyramid, as Cephren did the largest. The brothers ruled for some time conjointly, and some time with Sha′fra, the son of Cheops. The building of the Pyramids cost the lives of upwards of 100,000 men, and caused great suffering, until Mĕnchēres (Men-ke-u′ra, or Myceri′nus) abolished this compulsory labor. The latter is remembered as a good and humane king. He built the third Pyramid of Ghizeh, which is cased with red granite half way up. And he restored the national religious ceremonies which had been abolished by Cheops. It is remarkable that no traces have been found of Cheops and Cephren, who sacrificed thousands to build themselves an immortal tomb; while the remains of Mencheres reposed quietly in their resting place for thousands of years, until recently removed to the British Museum in London, where they now are. He was succeeded by Menche′res II., and the latter by Pam′mes (*Pa Amun*, Tham′pthis, or Amo′sis), a grandson of Cheops in the female line — and a ferocious king who was dethroned by Otho′es, or Aktisa′nes, an Æthiopian, the founder of the 9th dynasty. After the death of the latter the Empire was broken up and divided, and was not re-united until nearly 300 years afterwards. Under this dynasty the arts reached their zenith in Egypt. The 5th dynasty reigned at the same time with the 6th. Of the latter it is recorded that Othoes, the usurper, was slain by his guards, and that a child, six years old, named Apap′pus-Phi′ops (or Pepi-me-ri′-ra), probably a descendant of one of the ancient royal families, was placed on the throne of Memphis. His reign was a very long and peaceful one, and is said to have lasted "one hundred years all but one hour." He was a zealous patron of the arts and sciences. Numerous monuments remain of him; among others is an obelisk without hieroglyphics. Menthno′phis, his grandson, reigned one year, when he was murdered by a conspiracy of the Egyptian princes. His wife was the beautiful and heroic Nito′cris, who reigned after him six years. She completed and adorned the pyramid of Mencheres, and then invited the murderers of her husband to a subterranean banquet; during the feast she turned the waters of the Nile on them by means of a private canal, and drowned them, and afterwards destroyed herself. Her fame, as "the rosy-cheeked queen," long survived her. The Greek historian, Strabo, attributes the foregoing exploit to a female named Rhodo′pis, whom we may identify with Nitocris. He relates that, one day, as she was bathing, the wind carried away her sandal, and laid it at the feet of the king, who was sitting in the Court of Justice in the open air. His curiosity being excited by the singularity of the event, and by the elegance of the sandal, he could not rest until he had discovered the fair owner of it, and made her his queen. In this narrative we may recognize the origin of the well-known story of Cinderella and the little glass slipper.

On the death of Nitocris, Egypt was split up into several small kingdoms, five dynasties of kings reigning at the same time. This was a period of confusion and decay. Of the 7th dynasty, there were seventy kings or chiefs who reigned seventy days, probably forming a council. The 8th dynasty consisted of twenty-eight Memphite kings. Of the other three dynasties, the 9th, 10th, and 11th, little is known.

Achtho′es, the first of the 9th dynasty, was an atrocious tyrant. He became mad, and is said to have been destroyed by a crocodile.

Bunsen gives the following list of kings, which brings us down to the time of A′menem′he I., the founder of the 12th dynasty.

Amyrtai′os	reigned	22 years.
Tosima′res	"	12 "
Enentofina′os	"	8 "
Semphu′crates	"	18 "
Mentu′phis	"	7 "
Meii′res	"	12 "
To′mac-phtha	"	11 "
Soiku′nis	"	60 "
Pete-Athy′res	"	16 "

It has been assumed that the birth of Abraham occurred in the reign of Soikunis, B. C. 2153 years, but great confusion prevails in the chronology of this period.

The ancient Egyptians had no written language. They commemorated public events by painting or carving hieroglyphics, or emblematical figures on their temples, obelisks, and other monuments, the deciphering of which, in recent times, has let in a flood of light upon the ancient history of the country. To Champollion, a French *savant*, who lived at the beginning of the present century, is mainly due the honor of discovering the mode of interpreting these inscriptions. The student will find a concise account of this discovery, and of the nature of hieroglyphics (a word compounded of two Greek words, *ieron* (holy) and *gluphein* (to carve) in a very beautifully illustrated work on the Rosetta stone, recently published by Messrs. Hale, Jones, and Morton of the University of Pennsylvania. In process of time the Demotic (or common) alphabet was brought into use among the people, about the middle of the 7th century, B. C. And after the conquest of the country by the Greeks, the language underwent further modifications until it became what was called the Coptic, a name derived from Coptos, a great city of Egypt, and implying descent from the ancient people of the land. This was the language spoken by the natives in the time of the Ptolemies.

What is said of the reign of Menes in Egypt? — Where was he born? — What dynasty did he found? — Who erected the palace at Memphis? — At the close of what reign was Egypt divided into Upper and Lower? — Give an account of the different dynasties and their kings? — What is said of the 4th dynasty? — Give the account of the pyramids, and of the circumstances attending their erection? — What is said of the beautiful and heroic Queen Nitocris? — What took place at the death of Nitocris? — Who was the founder of the 12th dynasty? — What are hieroglyphics? — Who discovered the mode of deciphering them? — When did the Demotic and Coptic dialects arise?

SYRIA.

Tradition says that Noah, after many years' sojourn among his descendants, grew weary of their iniquities, and, having prophesied their destiny (Gen. ix. 25–27), he went eastward towards China, where he settled and died. Notice is taken of this tradition in the column devoted to the history of that country.

The descendants of his eldest son, Ja'pheth (whose name signifies "enlargement") settled in "the isles of the Gentiles," or the maritime countries of Western Asia and Eastern Europe.

The descendants of Ham, the youngest son, mostly settled in Canaan and the neighboring parts; and if by the word "Cush" we may understand the sea coast of Arabia, they probably settled there, and thence crossed into Africa.

One of the sons of Ham was named Canaan, upon whom a curse was pronounced by the Lord, ordaining that the posterity of Ham, through that son, should be servants to the posterity of Shem and Japheth (Gen. ix. 25–27); whence it has been supposed that Ham was the ancestor of the dark colored races; but this is not stated in Scripture.

The descendants of Shem, the second and favored son of Noah, settled chiefly in Me'sopota'mia, and through two of them, Arpha'xad and He'ber, in the direct line, came Abraham, in whom all the families of the earth were to be blessed.

The patriarchs, descendants of Arphaxad in the direct line, dwelt in Ur of the Chaldees, until the days of Te'rah, the father of Abraham. In the days of Nahor, the father of Terah (B. C. 2363–2283), there lived in the land of Uz a wealthy man named Job, whose sufferings and piety form the subject of one of the most ancient poems extant, viz: The Book of Job (or "enduring enmity," as the name signifies), which beautiful work has been for ages celebrated throughout the East, and now forms one of the books of the Old Testament.

The line of the patriarchs who dwelt in Ur of the Chaldees ends with Terah, the father of Abram, Nahor, and Haran. The birth of Abram is placed by Hales in the year B. C. 2153, and by Usher (the common chronology), B. C. 1990.

After the birth of Abram, Terah removed with his family to Haran, where he died. Abram remained there until he was seventy-five years old, when he left Haran and went into Ca'naan (B. C. 2078), which was then in subjection to Chedorla'omer, king of Elam (or Persia), one of those kings who became masters of portions of the old Assyrian empire. There he acquired great wealth, and appears to have become a personage of very great influence, venerated for his probity and wisdom. But there came a famine in the land, and Abram removed into Egypt, then in its most flourishing state under the kings of the 12th dynasty. Here the "Pharaoh" or king (probably Sesortcheres), became enamored of Sara'i, Abram's wife, which occasioned his (Abram's) expulsion from the country: he thereupon returned to Canaan. Soon after this event the native princes of Syria rebelled against Chedorlaomer. That monarch, with his allies, suppressed the rebellion, and, at the same time, carried off Abram's nephew, Lot, and his cattle (B. C. 2070); whereupon Abram armed his retainers and rescued Lot (see Genesis xiv.).

When Abram was eighty-six years old (B. C. 2067), his son Ishmael was born; and in his one hundredth year was his son Isaac born (B. C. 2053). A few months previously So'dom and Gomor'rah had been destroyed, and the Dead Sea formed.

The account above given refers solely to the line of patriarchs destined to be the progenitors of the Israelites. But the land of Syria itself was peopled by a variety of nations or tribes, sunk in the grossest idolatry and vice. They worshipped and offered up human sacrifices to a deity named Moloch. Those who inhabited the sea coasts became skilful navigators, and world-renowned in after ages under the name of Phœnicians. The names of the A'morites, Pe'rizzites, Jebusites, Hittites, Hi'vites, Amal'ekites, are familiar to every reader of Scripture as those of the inhabitants of that portion of Syria which was called Canaan. The northern portion of Syria was in subjection to the Assyrians, and the southern owned the sway of Egypt for a time. The two great empires of Assyria and Egypt made Syria their battle ground for many centuries.

Give an account of Noah and his descendants? — What is said of Job? — Name Abraham's father and the period of his birth? — At what time did he go to Canaan? — And to Egypt? — Whom did he rescue from the Persians? — What is said of the other inhabitants of Syria?

INDIA.

The origin of the Hindoos, like that of every other ancient nation, is buried in obscurity. That they are not the original inhabitants of India is certain; but at what period they subdued the country, and whence they came, are matters of conjecture. Sir William Jones, the great Oriental scholar, places their advent so far back as 3800 years before the Christian era. It is generally believed that they were Arians, and came from the West and North of the Hi'mala'ya mountains, bringing with them the religion of Brahma. The Bheels, the Khonds, the Puharrees, and other native tribes, were driven into the mountains, or reduced into hopeless servitude, in which condition they exist at the present day. The Pa'riahs, or degraded outcasts of India, are the descendants of the aborigines. Their ancient government was patriarchal, and they still claim to be the proprietors of the land. They are treated with great cruelty, not being allowed to live in towns, or adopt any permanent residence, or to hold intercourse with any but themselves.

The Persians gave the country the name of Hindoosta'n, or country of the Hindoos, but the Hindoos themselves called it, in ancient times, Bhārātā, and sometimes Pu'nya-Bhnim, or the land of virtues. The Greeks gave it the name of India, from the Persian.

The Hindoos were divided into four tribes: 1, the Brahmins, or priests; 2, the Cshatri'ya, or Ketterees, soldiers; 3, the Bhy'se, or farmers and traders; 4, the Su'dra, or mechanics, servants, and laborers. The ancient and sacred language was the Sanscrit; in this their Shasters or holy books are written; but only the learned can now understand it. The Shasters contain their religion and philosophy, and are divided into four Vedas, (a word signifying science,) containing 100,000 stanzas of four lines each.

Arrian's account of the Hindoos, written for Alexander the Great, proves that they have undergone no change for centuries, and they were in his time considered a people of the remotest antiquity. In the early ages their civilization was in advance of other nations. Women were not condemned to live in seclusion, as is now the case, nor were they treated as inferiors: they could hold property, and the fortune which a woman brought to her husband was inherited by her daughters. The laws of Menu provide for their guardianship by the State, and widows are allowed to marry. It was not until a much later period that the dreadful practice of *suttee*, or burning the wife on the death of her husband, came into vogue. It is said to have originated in the fact that husband-murder at one time grew common, and in order to deter the women from committing such a crime, a law was made that they should die with their husbands.

The religion of the Hindoos is that of Brahminism, and admits of no proselytes. For this reason it has remained fixed for countless ages. It inculcates the worship of one Supreme Being, under the name of Brahma. This Being consists of a triple divinity, expressed by the mystic term Om, and distinguished by the names of Vishnu, Brama, and Siva, which represent the creating, the preserving, and the destroying power of the Almighty. It teaches that Vishnu has undergone several incarnations upon earth; also that the human soul after death transmigrates into animals. The Hindoos have a number of inferior deities, and their religion contains a vast number of absurdities, together with many beautiful tenets.

On the conquest of India, the Hindoos established townships, or village communities, which exist at the present day. They also established a system of tenure of land, which has been equally stable. They made slaves of the original inhabitants. The government of the latter was patriarchal, while the civil institutions of the Hindoos were municipal in their character.

The peninsula was portioned out by the conquerors into different States or kingdoms. Ra'ma, their most celebrated hero, founded the kingdom of Oude, and carried his arms as far as Tapro'bane, or Ceylon. Crish'na, almost as famous, was the first king of Magad'ha. Both Rama and Crishna are worshipped as two of the several forms of Vishnu, and the two great epic poems of Ra'maya'na and Ma'habharat, which, together with the sacred books, constitute the chief authorities for the ancient history of India, celebrate the warlike exploits of those renowned heroes of antiquity. Many wonderful tales are told of Rama, and his name twice repeated is the ordinary salutation among all classes of Hindoos.

What is said of the origin of the Hindoos? — Of the natives? — Of the Pariahs? — Who gave the name of the country Hindoostan? — What is the religion of the Hindoos? — What did the Hindoos establish after the conquest of India? — Who were Rama and Crishna?

CHALDÆA, BABYLONIA, AND ASSYRIA.

The dwelling of the sons of Shem was "from Mesha, as thou goest unto Sephar, a mount of the East," but these nomadic tribes extended themselves over a large portion of Asia. It is probable that the seat of the patriarchal government of such families and tribes as remained faithful to the ancient worship of The One God, was "Ur of the Chaldees;" and here dwelt in succession the descendants of Arphaxad whose name occurs third in the list of the sons of Shem (Gen. x. 22), for seven generations, until the days of Terah, the father of Abraham.

Meanwhile there were springing up around them nations given to idolatry and impiety, which rejected the patriarchal authority. Of these, the chief was that ruled over by the founder of Bab′ylon and Nin′eveh, the famous Ni′nus, or Bel, of Eastern history, surnamed Nimrod (or, the rebel), who founded his empire on the banks of the Euphrates. There, on the plains of Shinar, commenced the erection of the tower of Babel (intended probably for astronomical purposes as well as a rallying point and watch tower), so celebrated in the traditions of the East. Around this tower grew up the city of Babylon; but it dwindled to a small town during the 1000 years which elapsed between the first and second Assyrian Empires. The great city, so often spoken of in later times by the prophets, was almost entirely rebuilt by Nebuchadnezzar, according to the expression attributed to him: "Is not this great Babylon that I have built for the house of the kingdom, by the might of my power, and for the honor of my majesty?" (Daniel iv. 30.) It was adorned with splendid edifices by Semi′ramis and Nito′cris.

The memory of Nimrod has been preserved in the poems and traditions of the East. He was worshipped in after ages as the God, Bel, and deified by the Greeks under the name of Ori′on. His death is placed by Dr. Hales in the year B. C. 2456.

Of his successors, we know but little more than their names, and the periods during which they are said to have reigned. Adopting the dates given by Dr. Hales, we have

	B. C.
Evecho′us, or Chos′ma Be′lus, who began his reign	2456
Porus	2448
Nechu′bus	2413
A′bius	2370
[In the reign of this prince is placed the carrying off of Job's camels by the Chaldeans (Job i. 17), B. C. 2337. Job himself at this time inhabited the land of Uz, probably the north of Arabia.]	
Onibal′lus	2322
Zinzi′rus (whose reign lasted until B. C. 2237)	2282

After this, the first Assyrian empire, founded by Nimrod, fell to pieces, and was divided among various chieftains, who probably predominated over each other according to their valor or abilities. A period of a thousand years elapsed before the second Ninus, of Assyrian history, re-united the various provinces of the ancient empire under one sceptre. In the year B. C. 2233, the Chaldæans commenced a series of astronomical observations which were recorded for many centuries, and were sent by Callis′thenes to Aristot′le 1900 years afterwards.

During these thousand years, the countries which formerly constituted the old empire became independent kingdoms. Kaiomurs, or Kai-A′murath, made himself master of the greatest part of Persia, Bactria, Khorassan, and the eastern portion, and transmitted it to his successors; while in the western portion we read of Am′raphel, King of Shinar (Mesopota′mia), and Chedorla′omer, King of Elam (Persia). (See Gen. xiv.) In the year B. C. 2082, these kings, with their allies, subdued the land of Canaan. Twelve years afterward (2070), they suppressed a rebellion there, on which occasion they encountered Abraham, and were defeated by him.

The languages spoken by the Assyrians and the Babylonians were not identical, but were sufficiently alike to prove that they were derived from an origin common to them, and to the Hebrew, Chaldee, and Syriac languages. They are all termed Semi′tic, from having been spoken by the descendants of Shem.

Who dwelt in Ur?—Who was the founder of Babylon and Nineveh?—Who was worshipped as the God Bel, and deified by the Greeks under the name of Orion?—When did the first Assyrian empire, founded by Nimrod, fall to pieces?—Who made himself master of the greatest part of Persia?—When did the battle of the four kings against five, recorded in Gen. xiv., take place?—What is said of the languages of the Assyrians and Babylonians?

PERSIA.

In that region, named Balkh, lying north of the Hindoo Koosh Mountains, existed an empire which extended over those countries now called Caubul, Khorassan, Persia, and Northern India. It probably was identical with that ancient Assyrian Empire which existed in the most remote period. It was peopled by the A′rians, a vast nomadic tribe occupying the region of Artacoa′na (now Herat), who were the occupiers and subjugators of Persia and India. The name given to this empire by its inhabitants was Iran:—the name "Persia," given to it in the Bible, and by Greek and Roman writers, is derived from Fars, or Phars, one of its provinces.

The first dawn of the authentic history of this country commences with the celebrated chieftain, Kai′omurs (or Kai Amurath), who, on the dissolution of the empire founded by Nimrod, B. C. 2190, established an independent kingdom at Balkh (said by Asiatics to be the most ancient city in the world). He became the founder of the dynasty of Persian kings, known as the "Paishdadians" (or, distributers of justice). In his time, Zerdoosht (or Zoroaster), said to have been king of Bactria, taught a pure and simple religion (subsequently styled the Magian, from the Persian word *mag*, a priest), in opposition to the prevailing idolatrous worship of the sun, moon, and stars; but he was not the author of this religion; he himself attributed it to Kaiomurs, whence his followers were called Kai-omursians. Zoroaster taught that God existed from all eternity: that the universe was governed by two principles, Hormuzd, the agent of good, and Ahriman, the agent of evil: that each had a creative power, and owing to their actions upon all things, there was a mixture of good and evil in all: but Hormuzd, being alone eternal, must ultimately prevail. He decreed the public worship of fire as the emblem of God. The Persians, however, before the time of Zoroaster, reverenced fire as one of the elements, though we do not find that they preserved it in temples, or worshipped it. Zoroaster also appointed the public reading of his great work, the Zend-a-vesta (or living word). It should be stated that there is more than one Zoroaster in history, and that great difficulties attend the fixing of the exact period of the great author of the Magian religion. After a reign of thirty years, Kaiomurs was succeeded by his grandson, Hooshung, B. C. 2160.

Hooshung was distinguished for justice and wisdom, and is said to have invented many useful arts. He was the first who constructed aqueducts in Persia, and he built the city of Susa. He was also the author of a work on "Eternal Wisdom." His son, Ta′hamurs, succeeded him, and extended his empire by conquests in the East. Tahamurs was an illiterate man, as he learned to read and write from some of the prisoners taken by him in his wars. During his reign, which is placed between the years B. C. 2070 and 2040, the worship of images came into use in Persia. He was succeeded by his nephew, the famous Giamschid′ (or Jemsheed), the founder of Istakhar′, or Perse′polis, and the lawgiver of Persia. He divided his subjects into four classes: 1, the priests and learned men; 2, writers and keepers of records; 3, soldiers; 4, artificers, husbandmen, and tradesmen. He also introduced the solar year, and ordered the first day of it, when the sun entered Aries, to be celebrated by a splendid festival. The early part of the reign of this prince was very prosperous, but at length his prosperity affected his mind. He fancied himself a God, and endeavored to compel his subjects to worship him, which so excited their disgust that they rebelled, and called in the Aramæan prince, Zohak, when Giamschid was dethroned and expelled, and the dynasty of Kaiomurs came to an end, B. C. 2010. There are various accounts of Zohak; the Persian annalists have indulged in a variety of fables concerning him—so much so, indeed, that his whole history has by some authors been deemed a myth. He is represented as having been a ferocious cannibal, and his name is even yet held in execration. His agents pursued the unfortunate Giamschid through India and China until they arrested him, when the dethroned prince was placed between two boards, and sawn asunder with the bone of a fish. The career of Zohak was brought to an end by the patriotism of a blacksmith of Isfahan, named Kawah, who roused the people to revolt, and expel the tyrant. A period of very great obscurity in the history of Persia here begins. The same events are recorded as having occurred in the 8th century B. C.

What was identical with the ancient Assyrian Empire?—Who were the Arians?—Whence comes the name Persia?—Who was the founder of the Paishdadian dynasty?—Who was Zoroaster?—What did he teach?—Who built the city of Susa?—Of what work was he the author?—What is said of his successor?—Of Giamschid?—Of Zohak?—Who was Kawah?

CHINA.

There is little doubt that China was peopled by Turanian (or Tartar) tribes. According to tradition, the founders of the State, one hundred families in number, descended from the mountains of Kul-cum, on the lake of Khu-khu-nor, north-west of China, and settled in the provinces of Chen-see, Le-ong, and Ho-nan. It is said that these emigrants were Noah and his friends, who fled from the rebellion and idolatry of his descendants to this remote region.

Some suppose Fo-hi, the first emperor of China, to be identical with Noah. Chinese historians relate that Fo-hi fixed his residence at Hwa-seu, in Chen-see, and founded the city of Chin-too, in Ho-nan. This corresponds with the tradition above mentioned. He was a beneficent ruler, introducing many excellent laws and institutions, and died generally regretted.

His successor, Shin-nung (or, the divine husbandman), taught agriculture and medicine, and established fairs for the convenience of trade. He is said to have reigned 140 years, and was succeeded by Hwang-te (the yellow emperor), who followed the course of his predecessors in improving his country. His grave, as well as that of his son and successor, Shaou-Haou, an inglorious and negligent prince, is shown to this day.

Chuen-hueh, who succeeded him, was a beloved and revered prince, and, in his time, the empire is said to have been as extensive as it is at the present day. Chinese historians notice that a remarkable conjunction of five of the planets took place in his reign.

Te-kuh, his son, established schools, but introduced polygamy. Te-kuh's eldest son, Te-che, was a vicious prince, who was dethroned by the nobility, and his brother, Yaou, the most celebrated of all the Chinese emperors, was called to the throne in the year B. C. 2357.

Yaou is described as the most perfect of men, who diffused happiness wherever he went. He commenced his reign by regulating the astronomical year. In his time, China was devastated by a fearful deluge, which nearly destroyed the country, but one of the principal historians of China, Ming-tsze, says that this deluge happened long before, and had not quite subsided in the time of Yaou. This emperor associated with him in the government a man of the people, named Shun, renowned for his piety. He was a husbandman and fisherman, yet displayed great genius in draining marshes and cutting canals. Yaou is said to have reigned 120 years, and died B. C. 2238, leaving his kingdom to Shun, whose wise sayings are recorded in the ancient Chinese book called "the Shoo-king." Having founded a hospital for the aged, Shun died B. C. 2208, at Ming-teaou, and was succeeded by Yu, the founder of the Hea dynasty, which ruled China for 540 years. This last was an excellent prince, and was called "Ta" (the great). He died B. C. 2198, and was succeeded by his son, Te-ke, who died B. C. 2188. Tae-kang, who succeeded, was dethroned for his cruelty, and Chung-kang was placed on the throne B. C. 2159.

Chung-kang loved his people, and was anxious to improve their condition. He invited them to observe the defects of the government, and to suggest improvements, but died before he could effect much. Te-seang (B. C. 2146), his son, was a humane but weak emperor, and was dethroned and killed by Keaou and Han-tsuh, B. C. 2119, who massacred his adherents. The empress, however, escaped with her infant son, Shaou-kang, whom she sent away into the mountains, where he remained until she procured him a situation as kitchen-boy in the palace of the Governor of Yu. Here his birth was discovered; he was therefore sent to the desert country of Lo-fun, where his virtues and abilities gained him the affection and respect of the neighborhood, and attracted the attention of the surrounding Governors. The latter formed a party to restore him to the throne, whilst the empress interested many nobles of the Court in his behalf. Combining their respective forces, they defeated and dethroned the usurpers, and placed Shaou-kang on the throne. He reigned peacefully 22 years, and died in the year B. C. 2037. He was succeeded by Te-choo, an excellent prince, who labored to reform the abuses which had arisen during the usurpation of Keaou and Han-tsuh; but his efforts were vain, and the nation continued to degenerate. During the reigns of his successors, Te-hwae and Te-mang, nothing worthy of notice occurred. The same may be said of a large portion of Chinese history. The monotony of the annals and the names render it one very difficult to remember.

Who peopled China?—Whom do some suppose Fo-hi to be?—Relate what the Chinese historians say of him and his successor.—Who established schools and introduced polygamy?—What is said of Yaou and of Shun?—Who was the founder of the Hea dynasty?—Relate what is said of the succeeding Emperors of China.

GREECE.

Of the aboriginal inhabitants of this small but illustrious country, we have no certain information. We have already mentioned the Cyclo′pes who inhabited Lecto′nia, and were afterwards met with in Sicily. Fables describe them as giants and cannibals, having only one eye, placed in the middle of the forehead. The Pelasgic race succeeded the Cyclopean. The Pelasgians emigrated from Asia Minor into Thessaly, whence they spread over Greece and Italy. According to some historians, this migration took place 1883 years before the Christian Era; the date of it is, however, uncertain. From Pelasgus, the mythical ancestor or chief of the Pelasgi, Greece was called Pelas′gia. The Cyclopes and Pelasgi have been mentioned in the Ante-Historical Period.

As the history and manners of the ancient Greeks and Romans would be but imperfectly understood without a knowledge of their mythology, a short sketch of it is here given.

A *Myth* is a legend or fable, embodying, under the form of the actions of a deity or hero, some philosophical truth or religious doctrine. Mythology is the study of the whole body or system of these myths. The earliest myths embodied crude ideas of the origin of nature and of the world. Thus, Cha′os (or confusion) is represented as the oldest of the gods. From him came Ge, or Tithe′a (the earth), Ha′des (hell), Eros (love), E′rebus (darkness), Nux (night). From the two latter came He′mera (day) and Phōs (light). From Tithea came Ou′ranos, or Ura′nus (heaven), and Thalas′sa (the sea); and from Uranus and Tithea came Oce′anus (meaning thereby all the waters and moisture in the world). Here we have a system of cosmogony (or creation of the world,) which is easily understood, if the student will remember that the principles here prefigured under the name of Chaos, Eros, Uranus, Tithea, and so on, are supposed to have the power of generating others. Thus we next find Uranus uniting with Tithea, that is to say, Heaven acting upon the Earth; and from this union spring the Titans (other powers of Nature). The Titans, properly so called, were twelve in number, but there were many other mythological personages to whom the name of Titan was given. The twelve Titans, six males and six females (thus symbolizing the equal influence of the male and female principles in the production of the elements, and the inhabitants of the world,) were—

1. Oce′anus: the god of the water which was believed to surround the earth, and to be the source of all rivers and streams. He is represented as the husband of Te′thys, and the father of all river-gods and water-nymphs. The Greeks regarded the earth as a flat circle encompassed by a river, which river was Oceanus. Out of and into this river, the stars were supposed to rise and set, and on its banks were the abodes of the dead.
2. Cœus.
3. Crius.
4. Hype′rion: married to Thia, and the father of He′lios (the sun), Sele′ne (the moon), and Eōs (the dawn). Thus, he represents the principle which produces light.
5. Jape′tus: married to Asia, the daughter of Oceanus, and the father of Atlas (the mountain, or power which keeps heaven and earth asunder), Prome′theus (or forethought), Epime′theus (or afterthought), and Menœ′tius.
6. Cro′nus: the representative of Time, and identical with Saturn. He married Rhea, and became the father of Hestia, Deme′ter, He′ra, Ha′des, Posei′dōn, and Zeus. Of these, more will be said presently.
7. Thia: married to Hyperion.
8. Rhea: married to Cronus.
9. Themis: (the personification of Order), married to Zeus, and mother of the Ho′ræ (hours), Euno′mia (good laws), Di′ce (justice), Ire′ne (peace), and the Mœræ (shares or fates).
10. Mnemo′syne: (the personification of Memory), the wife of Zeus, and the mother of the Nine Muses.
11. Phœbe: wife of Cœus, and mother of Aste′ria and Leto (or Latona).
12. Tethys: wife of Oceanus, and mother of the Ocea′nides (river-gods).

Who were the Cyclopes?—What race succeeded them?—What is a Myth, and the study of Mythology?—Mention the earliest myths embodied.—Give examples.—What is said of Oceanus?—What did the Greeks suppose the earth to be?—What is said of Hyperion?—Of Japetus?—Cromus?—Thia?—Rhea?—Themis, etc.?

In this manner, the elements of matter and the attributes of mind are deduced from the union of Heaven and Earth. We now come to a more detailed apportionment of these principles among the offspring of the Titans, and human beings make their appearance. Discord breaks out among the Elements.

Uranus is the father of many children beside the Titans. By his wife, Gæa, (the earth), he has the three Cyclopes (*i. e.*, round-eyed beings) Brontes, Ste′-ropes, and Ar′ges; and the He′catonchei′res (or hundred handed), Cott′us, Bria′reus, and Gy′ges. These represent different elements of brute force and violence. Uranus, detesting these Cyclopes and Hecatoncheires, throws them into Tar′tarus, or place of wicked spirits. Gæa, indignant at this, persuades the Titans to rebel against him (that is, the Earth raises up spirits antagonistic to Heaven). Armed with an adamantine sickle, Cronus (Saturn) mutilates Uranus and throws his members into the sea. Thence spring up the three Eri′nyes, or Eume′nides, (avenging deities), Tisi′phone, Alec′to, and Megœ′ra, who pronounce curses on men, and torment them with remorse. From the same source spring the Gigan′tes (giants); the Melian nymphs, who nursed Zeus (Jupiter); and Aphrodi′te (Venus) who rose out of the foam of the sea. That is, the operation of Time (Saturn) on the visible universe brought forth those principles which produce gigantic forms, prone to violence, but capable of remorse, and also of the perception of beauty and love. The Titans then depose Uranus, liberate the Cyclopes and Hecatoncheires, and raise Saturn to the throne. Saturn (or Time) then devours his children, Hestia, Demeter, Hera, Hades, and Poseidōn, all better known by their Latin names, which are as follows: —

Greek.	Latin.	
Hestia	Ves′ta, . .	goddess of fire and heat.
Demeter . . .	Ce′res, . .	" corn and plenty.
Hera	Ju′no, . .	" the air.
Hades	Pluto, . .	god of the lower world and of all metals that come out of the earth.
Poseidōn . . .	Neptu′nus,	" " sea.

To which list we may as well here add the other deities:

Zeus	Ju′piter, .	king of the gods and of heaven.
Aphrodi′te . .	Venus, . .	goddess of beauty and love.
Athenæ, Pallas .	Miner′va, .	" wisdom and war.
Ar′temis . . .	Dia′na, . .	" the moon and chastity.
Hephœs′tus . .	Vulca′nus,	god of fire and of the mechanical arts.
He′lios	Apol′lo, .	" the sun, music, and poetry.
Diony′sus . . .	Bac′chus, .	" wine and festivity.
Ares	Mars, . .	" war.
Her′mes . . .	Mercu′rius,	" eloquence, mischief, and wit; also the messenger of the gods.
Hebe	Juven′tus, .	goddess of youth.
Pan	Pan, . . .	god of forests, pastures, flocks and shepherds.

Of these there are twelve who are styled the great gods of Olympus, viz., 1, Jupiter, 2, Neptune, 3, Apollo, 4, Mars, 5, Mercury, 6, Vulcan, 7, Vesta, 8, Ceres, 9, Juno, 10, Minerva, 11, Venus, 12, Diana. These were sometimes worshipped collectively, as well as singly and separately. They held their court on Mount Olym′pus, in Macedo′nia, which mountain is now called Lacha; and there they occupied themselves with the affairs of the world, and feasted upon ambrosia and nectar.

To resume the allegory. Saturn having devoured his children (that is, Time having swallowed up Fire, Corn, Air, Death, and the Sea), their mother, Rhea (the Earth), conceals the birth of Jupiter (the all powerful who was to become the conqueror of Time) in the Dictæan cave in Crete. When Jupiter is grown up, he, with the assistance of Thetis (a marine goddess), gives Saturn a potion which makes him throw up the children which he had swallowed. United with his brethren, Jupiter makes war upon Saturn and the ruling Titans. The fable is that this contest was carried on in Thessaly: — Saturn and his favorite children occupying Mount Othrys, Jupiter and his party occupying Mount Olympus. Here we have a personification of the contest between the supreme power of heaven (aided by those fertilizing principles which Time had for a while impaired) and Time itself (aided by the destructive principles of brute force and violence). The contest lasts ten years, and the Titans are overcome and hurled down to Tartarus. Heaven and order are triumphant, and the world is subjected to a new system of government. Jupiter becomes monarch of the Universe. He divides his kingdom with his two brothers, Pluto and Neptune, giving to the one the dominion of the world of shadows, or Hades, and to the other that of the sea, retaining to himself that of Heaven, while all three possess equal influence on earth, or rather, the world is a field of operations common to all. Thus the allegory represents the world as acted upon equally by Earth, Air, and Water. Jupiter then becomes the parent of many children. By Metis (prudence) he has Minerva (the goddess of wisdom), said to have been concealed in his head. By Them′is (order) he has the Horæ (seasons), Thallo and Carpo, or, according to some, Eunomia, Dice, and Irene, and the Mœræ (fates), Clotho, Lach′esis, and At′ropos, who spin the thread of life. The latter cuts it when the life of the being is to end. They are the fates who allot to man the duration of life. By Eury′nome (wide-spread law) he has the three Graces, Euphro′syne, Aglai′a, and Thali′a. By Ceres (corn) he has Perseph′one, or Proser′pina (the mysterious fertilizing power of the earth), afterwards carried off by and married to Pluto. By Mnemos′yne (memory) come the nine Muses, said to have been born at Pieria, near Mount Olympus. These muses are: —

1. Calli′ope,	the muse of	epic poetry.
2. Clio,	"	history.
3. Euter′pe,	"	lyric poetry.
4. Melpom′ene,	"	tragedy.
5. Terpsich′ore,	"	choral dance and song.
6. Era′to,	"	amorous poetry.
7. Polyhym′nia,	"	sacred poetry and music.
8. Ura′nia,	"	astronomy.
9. Thali′a,	"	comedy and idyllic poetry.

From Jupiter and Latona (invisible power) come Apollo (the sun) and Diana (the moon). By Juno (the air) he has Mars (war) and Ilithyi′a (the goddess of birth). Hephæstus, or Vulcan (fire) springs from Juno without the co-operation of Jupiter.

By combining these elements a still more numerous progeny of minor deities and demigods is produced: and by bearing in mind the attributes of each, the student will be enabled to explain the allegorical legends of ancient Greece and Rome.

We have yet to notice the Greek myth of the creation of man, which is contained in the legend of Prome′theus. This mythical personage is said to have formed men out of earth and water, to have breathed life into them, and to have given them a portion of all the qualities possessed by animals. Having deceived Jupiter, the latter withheld fire from these mortals, but Prometheus recovered it by stealing it from heaven in a hollow tube. For this crime Jupiter chained him to a rock in Scythia. Prometheus thus bound defied the conqueror, and declared it to be the decree of fate that he (Jupiter) should be dethroned by his own son. Refusing to explain the meaning of these words he was hurled by Jupiter, together with the rock to which he was fastened, into Tartarus. After a long time he returned to the upper world, but was seized and fastened to Mount Cau′casus, where his liver was continually gnawed by an eagle, being renewed as often as devoured. He was ultimately released from his torments, some say by Jupiter, others by Minerva, others by Chiron, who took his place on the rock. In order to punish the mortals whom Prometheus had created, Jupiter caused Vulcan to form Pandora (the all-gifted), the first woman, in order that by her charms she should bring misery on the human race. The gods and goddesses each gave her a gift, or power, whereby to work the ruin of man. Venus gave her beauty, and Mercury gave her boldness and cunning. She was then sent as a wife to E′pime′theus, the brother of Prometheus, bringing with her a box containing all the gifts. Her curiosity was so great that she could not resist opening it; whereupon all the evils incident to humanity poured out of it, and she had only time to shut down the lid and prevent the escape of Elpis (Hope), the gift of Jupiter. In this very beautiful allegory we

Relate the story of Uranus? — And of Saturn? — What was the origin of Venus? — Give the Greek and Latin names of the principal gods and goddesses. — Where did they hold their court? — Continue the allegory of Saturn. — Explain it. — Give an account of the war with the Titans. — What is the meaning of the allegory? — With whom did Jupiter divide his kingdom? — Name some of his children. — Who were the nine Muses, and where were they born? — Relate the legend of Prometheus and Pandora. — What do their names signify?

TO THE 20TH CENTURY B.C. 2000.

GREECE.

have the finest specimen of the highly poetical manner in which the Greeks symbolized the origin of Man, and the evils which afflict the world. Prometheus represents divine forethought, which framed mankind with the knowledge that the monarch of heaven (Jupiter) shall be dethroned by his son; that is, that man shall be rebellious to his Maker. By Prometheus is also symbolized that inventive faculty which enabled man to discover the use of fire, metals, and the various productions of Nature; whereupon he became proud and impious, and was sentenced to punishment in Tartarus (Hell). But he is allowed to remain on earth, chained to the rock of his earthly nature, with an eagle (conscience) preying on his liver, until released from his misery by Minerva (Divine Wisdom). To Epimetheus (that is, as an afterthought), Pandora, or woman, endowed with all graces and gifts, was sent upon earth, but her curiosity leads her to pry into secrets which it was not desirable for her to know. Hence all the evils which have befallen the human race. But God permitted Hope to remain with her, to preserve her and her offspring from despair.

Jupiter was worshipped in Assyria under the name of Bel, Belus, or Baal: in Egypt, under that of Ammon, or Amun; and in Rome, under that of Jove. He has various surnames and epithets, descriptive of his attributes, and the localities in which he exercised his power. It is probable that in all this there is a blending of the exploits of a powerful chief with those recorded of Jupiter. Some authors believe that he was a prince who ruled over a great part of Asia, Egypt, and Greece. Others identify him with Ninus, King of Assyria. He was, in the ancient mythology, as we have seen, the son of Saturn and Rhea. He was the chief of the gods, and was worshipped as the god of rain, storms, thunder, and lightning. The Greeks had various traditions about his birthplace; by one, it was placed at Mount Lycæus, in Arcadia; by another, at Dodona, in Epirus; by a third, in Crete.

Neptune was the brother of Jupiter, and god of the sea. His abode was in the depth of the ocean near Ægæ, in Eubœa (now Negropont). He was the creator of the horse, and rode over the waves in a chariot drawn by horses with brazen hoofs and golden manes. He holds a trident in his hand, and was sometimes accompanied by his wife, Amphitri′te, and by dolphins and sea nymphs. The winds were under the control of Æ′olus, each wind being represented by a subordinate deity: — Boreas was the north wind; Notus, or Auster, the south wind; Eurus, the east wind; and Zephy′rus, the west wind.

Saturn is also represented as a king of Italy, during whose beneficent reign "the Golden Age" lasted. He shared the throne with Janus, who was worshipped as a god with two heads, and was supposed to preside over the beginning of everything. Janus opens the year and the seasons, and, as the porter of heaven, is supposed to look two ways; hence his two heads. The month of January derives its name from him.

Juno has various names, such as Ju′ga, Pro′nuba, Luci′na, etc. She was supposed to watch over every woman from birth to death, and especially over marriage and childbirth. She is represented as the Queen of Heaven, and the housekeeper and controller of finances. The month of June was sacred to her.

Vesta was the goddess of Home, as well as of Fire. The Pena′tes (or household gods,) were inseparably connected with her. So were the Lares, or spirits presiding over the hearth and fireside. On family festivals, sacrifices were offered to Vesta; and, in her temple, the sacred fire was kept perpetually burning by virgins devoted to her service, and thence called Vestal Virgins.

Venus was worshipped in Syria under the name of Astarte, and was called Ashtoreth by the Hebrews. She is also styled Cythere′a, and was specially worshipped in Cythe′ra and Cyprus. The month of April was sacred to her: so were doves, swans, swallows, and sparrows. She is said to have become enamored of Ado′nis, a beautiful youth, the son of Theias, King of Assyria. Adonis died of a wound received from a boar while hunting, and the grief of the goddess was so great that Pluto allowed Adonis to return from the lower world to spend six months every year upon earth with her. By this allegory of Venus and Adonis, which is so beautifully treated by the poets, it is to be understood that the Sun (represented by Adonis,) passes the summer with the productive powers of Nature (Venus), and then returns to the lower world, where he spends the winter (personified by the boar which killed him), to return again to the upper world in the spring. She is usually represented as attended by her son, Cupid (Eros, or sensual love), who is armed with a bow and arrows, and torches. He has golden wings, and his eyes are covered (signifying that he acts blindly).

Diana was worshipped under many titles, such as Cyn′thia, Phœ′be, He′cate, etc. She was the protectress of the young of men and beasts, and the guardian of chastity and modesty. She is represented as a hunter, armed with bow and arrows, and accompanied by her maids, and as the special patron of hunting. She slew Ori′on with an arrow, for offending her modesty. For the same reason she is said to have turned Actæ′on into a stag, whereupon he was devoured by his own dogs. She slew the children of Ni′obe, who boasted that she was superior to Lato′na, and was turned into a stone, which shed tears during the summer. Diana also fell in love with Endy′mion, a youth whose surprising beauty warmed her cold heart as she gazed on him asleep on Mount Latmus, in Ca′ria. She came down and kissed him as he slept, and doomed him to perpetual sleep, in order that she might kiss him nightly without his knowledge. This fable of Endymion and Diana is the subject of much beautiful poetry and sculpture, and is allegorical of the beauty which the moon sheds over Nature while unconscious of her presence.

Vulcan is said to have been the architect of all the palaces in Olympus. He had a workshop there, and forged the thunderbolts of Jupiter. The Cyclops were his workmen. He also made the armor of Achilles; the necklace of Harmo′nia, the wife of Cadmus, which proved fatal to all who possessed it; and the fire-breathing bulls of Æ′etes, King of Colchis. He is represented as lame, in consequence of being thrown down by Jupiter from Heaven on to the Island of Lemnos. He is also said to have been the husband of Venus.

Minerva was the protectress of agriculture. She invented the plough and the rake, and created the olive. She is the patron of science and art, and has various names and surnames. She was the especial deity of Athens, and the friend of heroes and of skill in war. She carried an Ægis, or shield, made of a goatskin covered with scales, having in the middle the terrible head of Medu′sa, the Gorgon, which turned all beholders to stone.

Apollo was said to be the god who punishes, and who affords help. He is the god of prophecy, song, and music; of the Sun; of civil polity, and founding of cities; and the protector of cattle. The famous oracle of Delphi was his.

Mars derives his name from the Etruscan word Mavors. In the Sabine and Oscan languages he is styled Mamers. He is the representative of the sanguinary spirit of war, delighting in battle for the mere sake of cruelty.

Mercury is the god of eloquence, prudence, and skill; the inventor of music, astronomy, gymnastics, measures, weights, and many other useful things. He was employed by the gods on a variety of occasions to execute their commands, and is represented as their messenger, with golden sandals, and wings on his ankles. He was also the charioteer and cup-bearer of Jupiter, and had power to send or take away sleep. He also conducted the dead from the upper to the lower world.

Hebe waited on the gods, and filled their cups with nectar. She was superseded in her office by Ga′nymede, the son of Tros and Callir′hoe. He was the most beautiful of all mortals, and was carried off from Mount Ida by Jupiter to be his cup-bearer.

Pan (or Faunus) was a sensual being, with horns and goats' feet, sometimes dancing, sometimes playing on the shepherd's flute, which he invented. He was fond of noise, and frightening people; hence the word "panic," for sudden fear. He was worshipped principally in Arcadia.

This account of the Grecian mythology would be incomplete without some notice of Hades, or the nether world, whither the spirits of the dead were supposed to go. The entrance to it was through a gate, guarded by Cer′berus, a many-headed dog. The departed spirits had to cross the river Styx, which flowed seven times round the lower world. They were ferried over it in a boat by an old man, named Charon, the son of E′rebus, for which service he was paid by a piece of money placed in the mouth of the corpse. The dead were judged by Minos, Rha′daman′thus, and Æ′acus, and ruled by Pluto, the cruel king of Hades. This region was divided into Ely′sium, or the Ely′sian Fields, where the spirits of the blessed rove — and Tar′tarus, where the wicked undergo their punishment.

What is said of Jupiter? — Neptune? — Amphitrite? — Æolus and the winds? — Saturn? — Janus? — Juno? — Vesta? — What were the Lares and Penates? — The Vestal Virgins? — Venus and Adonis?

What of Diana? — Orion? — Actæon? — Niobe? — Endymion? — Vulcan? — Minerva? — Apollo? — Mars? — Mercury? — Who was Hebe? — Ganymede? — Pan? — What is said of Hades, and the Elysian Fields?

EGYPT.

The reign of Pete-Athy'res terminated the preceding dynasty. The old empire was again united under A'me-nem'he I., the founder of the twelfth and most illustrious dynasty. After he had reigned eight years, he associated with him Sesorte'sen I., and reigned eighteen years more, when he was murdered by one of his servants.

Sesortesen then ruled jointly with Amenemhe II., and it appears from ancient inscriptions that he was a powerful king and a successful warrior. His successor was Sesortesen II., who associated with him his son, Sesortesen III. (the celebrated Sesostris), who is said to have subdued, in nine years, all Western Asia, Europe (as far as Thrace), and Ethiopia and Nubia, where he erected those vast fortifications which have been the wonder of succeeding ages. His successor, Amenemhe III. (known to the Greeks as Mœris), was the builder of those famous works, the Nilometer and the Labyrinth. He also constructed the lake Mœris, and the dyke and canal system of the Fayoom district, by which the irrigation of the country by the Nile was regulated. The pictures still to be seen in the grottoes of Benihassan attest that, under this dynasty, Egypt attained to a high degree of civilization, and excelled in the elegant and useful arts.

Amenemhe III. associated with him in the kingly office Amenemhe IV. Of his successors, Siphtha and Phruo'ro, we know nothing, except that the country degenerated during their reigns.

The last king of the twelfth dynasty was Amun-Timæos, in whose time the weakness of the kingdom offered great temptations to invasion. Accordingly, the shepherd tribes of Arabia, combining together, invaded the country, and took possession of it almost without a battle. These shepherds were termed Hyksos, or shepherd-kings (from the Egyptian words, *Hyk*, a king, and *Sos*, a shepherd). They were guilty of the greatest cruelties while subjugating the country. After completing the conquest of it, they set up as king one of their number, whose name was Sala'tis. He established his court in Memphis, and fortified the eastern parts of the kingdom, especially the city of A'baris. He died after a reign of nineteen years, and was succeeded by another king named Bnon, who reigned forty-four years. After him came Apach'nas, who reigned thirty-six years.

It must be borne in mind that the chronology of this country is but an approximation to the truth, and many events are placed by some writers in one century which other writers would place in a very different epoch. For instance, no point is more disputed than the duration of the rule of the Shepherd Kings, some assigning to it a period less than 300 years, others a period of nearly 1000 years.

The student's attention is called to the fact that the names given by the Egyptian historians to these Shepherd kings are perversions of real names into opprobious epithets. Thus, Salatis means "a liar;" Bnon means "a filthy fellow;" Apachnas, "a convict;" Stan, "the devil;" Jannes, or Aman, "a coward;" and so on. Considerable ingenuity must have been exercised in preserving the real name under the nickname in the hieroglyphics.

Which was the most illustrious dynasty?—Who was the founder of it?—Who was associated with him?—What is said of him?—What celebrated conqueror lived at this time?—Mention the names of the other kings of this dynasty.—Who was the last of the 12th dynasty?—What was the state of the kingdom in his reign?—Who were the shepherd kings?—What is said of them, and of the period of their rule?—And of their names?

SYRIA AND PALESTINE.

Twenty years after the marriage of Isaac and Rebekah, their sons, Esau and Jacob were born (B. C. 1993). And when a famine was in the land, Isaac went to Abim'elech, king of the Philistines at Gerar. There he dwelt, and became rich, and founded the city of Beershe'ba. Soon after this he was called to the burial of his father Abraham, who died at the age of 175 B. C. 1978. (Gen. xxv. 7.)

The marriage of Esau (B. C. 1953), with two Hittite women, was a source of grief to Isaac. And the trick played on him by Jacob, in supplanting Esau, added to his troubles. Jacob was sent away to his uncle Laban, in Padan Aram, in order to escape from the vengeance of Esau, and there he married his cousins, Leah and Rachel, by whom and by their handmaids, Bilhah and Zilpah, he had many children, who became the ancestors of the twelve tribes of Israel.

			B. C.
By Leah he had	Reuben,	born	1915
" "	Simeon	"	1913
" "	Levi	"	1911
" "	Judah	"	1910
By Bilhah "	Dan	"	1909
" "	Naph'tali	"	1908
By Zilpah "	Gad	"	1907
" "	Asher	"	1906
By Leah "	Iss'achar	"	1905
" "	Zeb'ulun	"	1904
" "	Dinah (a daughter)	"	1903
By Rachel "	Joseph	"	1902

After the birth of Joseph, Jacob returned to Canaan, having met and been reconciled to Esau on the way.

During this period the Phœnicians were extending their commerce and colonies. Strictly speaking, the people called by the Greeks "Phœni'cians," were two nations, viz., the Sido'nians and the Philis'tines, the former dwelling in the north, the latter in the south of Canaan. They built many cities, of which A'radus (on an island to the north), and Anta'radus (opposite to it on the main land), Tri'polis (now Tarablus), By'blus, or Bery'tus (now Beyrout), and Tyre (situated in what was subsequently the portion of Asher, the son of Jacob), were the most remarkable. Their language was Semitic, having affinity with the Hebrew.

At what time did the marriage of Isaac and Rebekah take place?—What did Isaac do when there was a famine in the land?—Who did Jacob marry?—Name his children.—What two nations compassed the Phœnician nation?—What cities did they build?—What was their language?

INDIA.

The history of India during this, as in many of the following centuries, is a perfect blank. But much information respecting its early religion and literature is to be found in its ancient poems and religious compositions. Mention has been made of the Vedas. These books have been translated into English by Sir William Jones, Colebrooke, Cary, Wilson, and others, and prove that the Hindoos had peculiar aptitude for philosophical speculation. The word *Brahme* means will, wish, and the propulsive power of creation. "What *is* Brahme?" is the usual theme of their sacred dialogues.—"Brahme is food, mind, and speech." It is "that by which all beings are supported." "Brahme is life, intellect, meditation, and joy. It is "the Universal Soul." The sun and fire were esteemed symbols of the Godhead. The ancient Brahminical sect of Bhrigu worshipped fire; that of the Ribhu retired into solitude to perform penance and worship the Sun. The Brahmins had no idea of God as a Creator and Ruler, their notion being that He is essence eternally diffused; that all visible life is mere illusion, The soul, after death, enters some animal or vegetable form.

What is meant by Brahme?—What were the sects of Bhrigu and Ribhu?—What was the Brahmin's idea of God?—Where does the soul go after death?

ASSYRIA.

Beyond the mere names of three kings we have no record of what was passing at this period in this portion of the world. Great obscurity is spread over the history of Assyria, as well as over Persia, during this and several succeeding centuries.

Mr. Clinton fixes the dates of the accession of these three kings as follows:

	B. C.
On the death of Arale'us, Xer'xes, (or Bale'us,) ascended the throne .	1980
Armani'tes	1950
Belo'chus	1912

The earliest writers on Assyrian history are Cte'sias and Bero'sus; the former of whom founded his history upon extracts from Babylonian annals. But the original works of these authors have not come down to our times. Fragments of them are to be met with in the works of Euse'bius, Abyde'nus, Polyhis'tor, and others, who have more or less founded their histories on the earlier records of those authors, whose works were extant when they formed their compilations.

The religion of the most ancient Assyrians is believed to have been pure Sabianism, or worship of the sun, moon, and stars, (a term derived from the Hebrew word *tsaba*, "a host or army"); and there is strong probability that this form of worship had its origin among the inhabitants of the Assyrian plain. The Fire worship of a later age was a corruption of Sabianism. The symbols and religious ceremonies depicted on the monuments at Khorsabad and Koyunjik prove that it was nearly identical with that system which prevailed in Persia. There can be no doubt that the names of the kings found on the inscriptions at Nimroud represent the most ancient monarchs of whom any records have been discovered on the Euphrates or the Tigris. They all belong to the first Assyrian empire, and between them and the modern Assyrian monarchs elapsed a period of a thousand years, of which we have no particulars. The student should consult the works of Herodotus, Layard, and Rawlinson on the subject. An excellent sketch is contained in Vaux's "Nineveh and Persia."

What is said of the history of Assyria during this century?—What kings are mentioned by Mr. Clinton?—Who were the earliest writers on the history of the nation?—What the religion?—What was Sabianism?—What period elapsed between the first and second empires?

B.C. 2000—1900.

PERSIA.

During this and the succeeding six centuries, Persia appears to have had no independent existence as an empire. Whether Zohak founded a dynasty and kingdom of his own, or was the king of Assyria who subdued the country, or whether Persia was divided into petty kingdoms under Aramæan and Scythian princes, as is probable, does not appear.

The Persian historians extend the reign of their kings over an immense period, and fill up the time with romantic accounts of the exploits of their heroes; but no reliance can be placed on these poetical stories.

According to some historians, Zohak was dethroned by the blacksmith Kâwâh, who placed Fe′ridoon on the throne, and after him followed four other kings; so that, according to them, the Paishdadian dynasty did not terminate until the reign of Kershasp, the fifth monarch from Zohak; but Sir John Malcolm, in his History of Persia (vol. i., p. 210), has proved that Feridoon was the same monarch as the Arba′ces of the Greek historians; and that the reign of the ferocious Zohak, which is said by some Persian historians to have lasted 1000 years, and by others 700 years, represents the period during which the country was ruled by Assyrian princes, whose cruelty is depicted in the stories related of Zohak. The Arbaces referred to lived in the eighth century before the Christian Era, consequently there is here a long gap in Persian history.

Feridoon, who was placed on the throne by Kawah, the blacksmith, was an immediate descendant of Tahamurs. He had escaped from the vengeance of Zohak, and fought bravely under Kawah. His romantic adventures and exploits are favorite themes of Persian poets. His first act on ascending the throne was to convert the celebrated apron of the blacksmith, which had been used as a banner, into the national standard of Persia. As such, it was richly ornamented with jewels; to which every king, from Feridoon to the last of the Pehlivi monarchs, contributed. It was called the *Derufsh-e-Kawanee* (or standard of Kawah), and continued to be the standard of Persia until captured by the Arab followers of Mohammed, at the battle of Kadessia, A. D. 636. Its value amounted to an immense sum of money. There is nothing in Persian history better attested than the story of this apron.

What is said of this and the succeeding centuries of Persia? — What is said of Zohak? — What of Kawah and his apron?

CHINA.

The history of China during this century presents nothing remarkable. The Empire decayed more and more, and the posterity of Yu fell into disrepute. A series of vicious and feeble emperors contributed, by their misgovernment, to bring about this state of things. The people were little better than slaves, having no voice in the government; the mandarins (or nobles), however, appear to have made some efforts to stem the approaching ruin; but it was not until the second century after this that the Hea dynasty was displaced, and a more energetic race of sovereigns placed on the throne.

The names of the Emperors who reigned during this century are:

	B. C.
Te-wang, who began to reign	2014
Te-see, " "	1996
Te-puh-keang, " "	1980
Te-keung, " "	1921
Te-kin, " "	1900

The prefix "Te" signifies Emperor or Commander-in-Chief. The names of the Chinese Emperors are short sentences. They have sometimes two or three names. Those adopted by the Emperor, on his accession, are styled *Kwo-haou*, or "national designations." Epithets called "titles in the ancestorial hall," are also given to them. Thus the founder of the present Mantchoo dynasty of Emperors styled his family the *Ta-tsing*, or "general purity." His son succeeding to the throne took the name of Shun-che, and on his death received for ancestorial name that of She-tsoo-chang-hwang-te. The language of the country is expressed by symbols and peculiar accentuation. It consists of intonated monosyllables, of which there are 487 distinct, which are increased to 1445 by different intonations. It contains 14,000 characters, composed of 216 roots, which express the most simple ideas. By compounding these an immense variety of expressions is obtained; but the language is extremely difficult of acquirement. Strictly speaking, the Chinese language has no grammar; the mutual relation of words is pointed out by their respective positions. Gender, number, case, tenses, moods, etc., are expressed by particles, which either precede or follow the verb. The conversational language differs widely from the written. The Chinese literature is rich in history, philosophy, and poetry, but very defective in natural history, geography, and science, generally.

What is said of the history of China during this century? — What of the language and literature?

GREECE.

So little is known of the history of Greece during this period, that the space allotted to it may be profitably occupied by the consideration of collateral matters with which the student is expected to be acquainted. We may here notice the legend of the flood of Deuca′lion, which strikingly resembles that of Noah in many particulars. Deucalion is described in the mythology as the son of Prometheus and Clym′ene, and as king of Phthia, in Thessaly. When Jupiter resolved to destroy, by a flood, the degenerate race of man, Deucalion and his wife Pyrrha were, on account of their piety, the only mortals saved. On the advice of his father, Deucalion built a ship, in which he and his wife floated in safety during the nine days' flood which destroyed all the other inhabitants of Greece. At last the ship rested on Mount Parnass′us (some say Mount Athos or Mount Othrys), and, when the waters had subsided, Deucalion offered up a sacrifice to Jupiter, and consulted Themis as to how the race of man might be restored. The goddess bade them cover their heads and throw the bones of their mother behind them. They interpreted this expression, "bones," to mean the stones of the earth. They accordingly threw stones behind them; and from those flung by Deucalion sprung up men; from those thrown by Pyrrha sprung up women.

This is an example of the ancient Greek mode of allegorizing; but a far better one (due, however, to a later age) is found in the exquisitely beautiful myth of Cupid and Psyche; and as another opportunity for introducing it may not occur, it is here presented. Psyche (in Greek, "the soul") was the youngest of the three daughters of a king, and her beauty excited the jealousy of Venus. To avenge herself the goddess ordered Cupid to inspire Psyche with love for the most contemptible man that could be found. But Cupid fell in love with her himself, and conveyed her to a secluded retreat, where, unseen and unknown, he visited her every night, leaving her before daybreak. He enjoined her never to inquire who or what he was; but she had the imprudence to mention to her sisters the intimacy she had formed, and they, being jealous of her, made her believe that he was a hideous monster, who came by night because he dared not show himself by day. To satisfy her curiosity she procured a lamp, and drew near him while he was sleeping. To her amazement, she found he was possessed of more than mortal beauty, and in her agitation she let fall a drop of hot oil on his shoulder. Cupid awoke, upbraided her for her suspicions, and departed. Psyche's happiness was gone. She wandered from place to place in search of her lost lover, and at length came to the palace of Venus. The goddess kept her prisoner and treated her as a slave, making her perform the most humiliating tasks. Psyche would have died had not Cupid invisibly supported her; with his aid she accomplished her tasks, and ultimately overcame the hatred of Venus. She became immortal, and was united to Cupid for ever.

This beautiful allegory typifies the influence of Love on the Soul, and how, through suffering, that which was at first sensual becomes purified and exalted, so as to partake, ultimately, of the nature of Divine Love. Or to explain it more fully, the three daughters of a king (God) are, the body, the mind, the soul, (Psyche). The purity of the latter is repugnant to the sentiment of sensual love, which tends to lower it to unworthy objects. The soul is for a time possessed with this unworthy passion, but its spirit of inquiry prompts it to investigate the nature of it, and the charm vanishes. But the soul without love is but half divine. An object on which to bestow the affections is sought for, and through trials and suffering the truth and constancy of the soul is developed, its nature purified, and it then becomes allied to the earthly passion, which it exalts to divinity and renders immortal.

From Deucalion and Pyrrha descended Hellen, Amphic′tyon, Protogeni′a, and others. Soon after the flood of Deucalion (we are not told how soon) In′achus, a native of Argos, led the Argives from the mountains into the plains of the Peloponnēsus (the southern part of Greece). The era of this chieftain is placed by historians in the next century, whence we may conclude that the flood of Deucalion, if it has any historical foundation, took place somewhere about the close of this century.

Hellen, the son of Deucalion, was king of Phthia, in Thessaly. He is the mythical ancestor of all the Hellenes. His sons, Æ′olus and Do′rus, were the mythical ancestors of the Œolians and Dorians; and his grandsons, Achœ′us and Ion, were the mythical ancestors of the Achœans and the Ionians.

Relate the legend of Deucalion and Pyrrha? — Of Cupid and Psyche? — Explain this allegory? — What is said of Inachus? — Who was Hellen? — Œolus? — Dorus? — Achœus and Ion?

EGYPT.

Apachnas was succeeded by Apophis, who reigned 61 years, and Jannes, who reigned 50 years; after him, Archles, who reigned 49 years. The history is very confused, but there is little doubt that contemporary dynasties of the Shepherd kings were reigning in different parts of the kingdom, and that the Egyptians resisted them long with varying success. The period of their rule is called "the Middle Period."

It was during the reign of one of these Shepherd kings that Joseph was sold by the Midianite merchants to Potiphar, "an officer of the king, and captain of the guard." In this situation he gained the confidence of his master by his integrity and abilities, and rose from one step to another, until a combination of favorable circumstances gained him the notice of the king, whose minister he became. His sagacity in foreseeing an approaching famine, and providing against it, and in firmly establishing the king's authority, fully justified the confidence placed in him. Every one is familiar with the exquisitely beautiful story related of him in Genesis. In it allusion is made to the Shepherd race, when Joseph says to his brethren (Gen. xlvi. 34): "Every *shepherd* is an abomination unto the Egyptians."

It seems probable that before, or in consequence of, the invasion of the Shepherds, two separate kingdoms were formed — one at Thebes, the other at Xois — which lasted through the whole of the time that the Shepherds maintained themselves in Egypt. Each of them had peculiar local advantages for the establishment of an independent kingdom. The Thebaid was remote from Memphis, where they fixed their capital, and by retiring into Ethiopia the Egyptian kings could easily place themselves beyond their reach. Xois was protected by the intersecting branches of the Nile, which made it unapproachable by land. The Theban dynasty lasted 453 years, the Xoite 484 years. No name is preserved from the 13th and 14th dynasties, which consisted, the former of 60 Theban or Diospolitan kings, the latter of 76 Xoite kings. The 15th, or Shepherd dynasty, consisted of six foreign (Phœnician?) kings; the 16th, of 30 other Shepherd kings; and the 17th, of 43 Shepherds and 43 Diospolitans. The Shepherds never raised any pyramids or memorials of themselves, although the country they had conquered abounded with them. Their tenure of the land was precisely analogous to that of the Turks in Europe at the present day. They lived encamped in cities, devoting themselves to nothing but war, and living on the tribute paid by the Egyptians.

The confusion and destruction which attended the conquest of Egypt by the Hyksos, have rendered the chronology of this period quite uncertain, beyond the reigns of the six kings of the 15th dynasty. No reliance can be placed on the assigned length of periods, which furnish us with neither names, nor facts, nor monuments, because we have no control over the fictions or errors of historians. A connected chain of history is, therefore, impossible.

What is said of the Shepherd kings in this period? — Of the Theban and the Xoite dynasties? — Of Thebes and Xois? — Of the mode in which the Shepherds occupied the land? — And of the chronology?

SYRIA AND PALESTINE.

The next event in the life of Jacob was the birth of Benjamin, and the consequent death of his beloved Rachel, B. C. 1989. The sale of Joseph by his brethren to the Midianite merchants followed soon after.

The death of Isaac took place B. C. 1873, before the rise of Joseph to power in Egypt. And while the sons of Jacob were growing up, and becoming the fathers of tribes, the children of Esau, in like manner, were forming tribes and nations in Edom (Idumæa) and Northern Arabia. The sacred historian (Gen. xxxvi.) gives a list of "dukes" and kings who descended from them.

About this period, B. C. 1872, Joseph became powerful in Egypt, and was ultimately made the king's chief minister. Thus, when the famine drove his brothers into Egypt for food, he had the power to serve them. He forgave them their cruelty to himself, and settled them and his father in the land of Goshen, B. C. 1863. There Jacob "was gathered unto his people," B. C. 1846, and there his descendants dwelt, and in process of time became very numerous.

There is considerable difficulty in fixing the date of the events recorded in Scripture relative to the time of Joseph, and the exodus of the Israelites. In this work the computation adopted by St. Paul, the Jews, and Josephus, has been used. By this system, 215 years are allotted to the sojourning of Abraham and the patriarchs in Canaan, and 215 years to the sojourning in Egypt. The Septuagint version of the Bible also adopts this chronology, and is the foundation of St. Paul's remark (Gal. iii. 17): "The promise to Abraham preceded by 430 years the giving of the Law." According to the common chronology, the departure of the Israelites out of Egypt took place about the year 1490 B. C. This is founded on the assertion in Exodus xii. 40: "The sojourning of the children of Israel in the land of Egypt was 430 years; and at the end of the 430 years, even on that very day, all the hosts of Jehovah went out from the land of Egypt." But in Exodus vi. 16–19, and Numbers xxvi. 58, mention is made of four generations only, during this 430 years, viz., Levi, Kohath, Amram, and Moses, which seems incredible. The difficulties attending this disputed point are well treated in Kenrick's *Ancient Egypt*, vol. ii., book 3, to which the student is referred.

Mr. Osburn, in his *Monumental History of Egypt* (vol. ii. c. 2), maintains that the patron of Joseph was the king, or Pharaoh (from Phrah, "the sun"), Apophis, or Phiops. Under Joseph's administration the whole realm of Egypt was converted absolutely into the property of the king. Taking advantage of the famine, which his sagacity had provided against, he purchased of the Egyptians, in their distress, their jewels and precious metals, their lands, their cattle, and their persons. Having broken down the power of the native princes and their vassals, Joseph removed them into cities, thus effecting a momentous social revolution, which advanced Egypt many centuries in civilization.

How many sons had Jacob? — Did Isaac live to see the rise of Joseph's power? — Where did the children of Esau form tribes? — When and where did Jacob die? — What is said as to the era of Joseph and of the Exodus?

INDIA.

The heroic legends of the Hindoos are to be found in the ancient poems, called the Ramayana, and Mahabharat, which are to them like the Iliad and the Odyssey to the Greeks. The first details the wonderful exploits of Rama, who has been already mentioned. His greatest achievement was the conquest of the King of Ceylon, a terrible giant, who had carried off his Queen, and kept her prisoner in his castle; this the hero stormed, and rescued the lady. A festival, which used to be kept with great splendor, is still held every year in commemoration of this victory. The Hon. Mountstuart Elphinstone considers this expedition to Ceylon a fable (*History of India*, vol. i., p. 389); but it is strange that a national custom should have sprung up on a purely fabulous basis.

The Mahabharat celebrates the war between the lines of Pandu and of Curu (two branches of the reigning family), for the territory of Hastinapura (probably a place on the Ganges, north-east of Delhi, which still bears the ancient name). In this contest, Crishna takes a leading part. He is the ally of the Pandus, who are victorious, but lose so many men that they abandon the world, and perish among the snows of the Himalaya. Crishna falls in the civil wars of his own country, Gujerat. Mr. Elphinstone considers that the era of Crishna is the fourteenth century B. C.

The ancient Hindoos made considerable advances in astronomy, but they left no complete system. Their priesthood made it subservient to their own purposes, and carefully concealed the original sources of information. Hence the data from which their tables were computed were never quoted, and there is no record of a regular series of observations among them. But there is no doubt they ascertained accurately the mean motions of the sun and moon, and had begun a series of astronomical observations in the 15th century B. C. Their progress in mathematics was equally remarkable, especially in algebra.

Various languages prevailed in India in ancient times. The principal one, spoken by the upper classes, was the Sanscrit. In this language the Vedas, the Institutes of Menu, and the Puranas, are written: hence, it has been called the sacred language; but it was spoken by the lower classes, although in a barbarous dialect. It is now dead (that is, no longer spoken), but it is still much cultivated, and bears striking resemblance to the Greek and Latin languages. The five northern languages of India are those of the Punjab, Canouj, Mithila (or North Berar), Bengal, and Gujerat. They are said to be branches of the Sanscrit. Of the five languages of the Deccan, three of them (viz., the Tamul, Telugu, and Carnata), have an origin distinct from the Sanscrit. The remaining two (the Orissa and Maharashtra, or Mahrãtta), are supposed to be derived from the Sanscrit. As these are spoken in a very large portion of the Deccan, there is every probability that the Hindoos of Northern India conquered it at an early period.

What are the Ramayana and the Mahabharat? — What of the adventures of Rama? — Of the era of Crishna? — Of the ancient Hindoo astronomy, mathematics, and languages? — Why is the Sanscrit called the sacred language?

B.C. 1900—1800.

ASSYRIA.

All the record which has come down to us of this century consists of the names of two kings, Bale′us and Alta′-des, with the dates 1860 B. C. and 1808 B. C., as the commencement of their reigns. When more of the ancient monuments of Assyria shall have been discovered, and their inscriptions deciphered, we may perhaps gain something like a connected narrative; but at present, much is unknown. Colonel Rawlinson, an officer in the British army, has devoted much time to deciphering the cuneiform (or wedge-shaped) inscriptions of ancient Persia and Assyria, and has succeeded in ascertaining the meaning of some hundreds of words. He has come to the conclusion that this ancient language was neither Hebrew, nor Chaldee, nor Syriac, nor any of the known cognate dialects, but that it was of the Semitic family of languages. He includes the Assyrian and Babylonian languages in one category. They were not exactly identical, but so closely allied that the natives of both countries could manage to understand each other. A full account of his discoveries is given by him in his "Commentary on the Cuneiform Inscriptions of Babylonia and Assyria," which also contains a brief notice of the ancient kings of Nineveh and Babylon.

It has been a question disputed among the learned, whether the Chaldæans were a nation, or merely priests and magicians. Herodotus only notices them as a tribe of priests; Diodo′rus speaks of them as a separate caste under Belus, an Egyptian priest; the Book of Daniel refers to them as astrologers, magicians, and soothsayers. On the other hand, the learned Gesenius has shown that Chaldæan was the name of a distinct nation. Strabo also treats them as such; and Cicero positively asserts that they were a people properly so called. Heeren argues that the name was applied to the nomadic (or wandering) tribes generally. Their origin and name have been ascribed to Chased, the son of Nahor (Gen. xxii. 22). Jerome says: "From him came the Chasdim, afterwards called Chaldæi." But it appears that Chased only united the scattered tribes of a pre-existing race, or else, by founding a dynasty, created a nation in the land of Ur, which existed in the days of Abraham, and was distinguished by the name of Ur by the Hebrews.

What is recorded of this century?—What is Col. Rawlinson's opinion as to the Assyrian and Babylonian languages?—Were the Chaldæans a nation?

PERSIA.

In the preceding century we have given the Persian account of Zohak, and the revolution effected by the blacksmith Kawah. But, according to Sir John Malcolm (see his *History of Persia*, vol. i., p. 209), Zohak was the Assyrian king who conquered the country; and the thousand years during which he is said to have reigned, were the period in which it was a province of the Assyrian Empire. The true era of Kawah's revolution is therefore about the 10th century B. C. As there is no authentic history of Persia during this long period, we will refer to the romantic legends which oriental poets have embodied in verse, and which are to the Persians what the poems of Homer and Hesiod were to the Greeks.

Frequent mention is made in Persian history of Turan. This is the ancient and the proper name of the country now called Tartary. The name Turan is said to have been derived from Toor, one of the three sons of Feridoon. It was the appellation by which all the countries between the Jaxartes and the Oxus, and between the Caspian and the boundaries of China, were known formerly to the natives of Persia. Toor was slain in battle by his own nephew, the young king, Manucheher, of Persia. The history of Turan is very disjointed. Mention is made of kings of Turan, who were in fact nothing more than chiefs of wild hordes of Tartars, without a fixed residence. These chiefs are frequently termed Deev, or devils, by the Persian historians; as, the Suffeed Deev, or white devil. We read of Pushung, king of Turan, who led 30,000 warriors into Persia, and of Afra′siab, who appears to have been a very powerful prince, and to have conquered Persia, over which he reigned 12 years.

The three great heroes of Persian antiquity were Sam, Zal, and Roostum, whose exploits are celebrated in the poems of Ferdu′si (the Homer of Persia). The first of these heroes, Sam, was the vizier (principal minister) of Manucheher, the grandson of Feridoon. He was appointed ruler over Seistan, Cabul, and the countries north of the Indus. It does not appear that he performed any extraordinary feats of arms, but was renowned for his wisdom, owing to which he was enabled to save the country on several emergencies. He was the father of Zal, and the grandfather of Roostum.

What is probably the date of Zohak's reign?—What country was called Turan?—Who was Toor?—Who were the three great Persian heroes?

CHINA.

From the accession of Te-kin, in the year B. C. 1900, to the end of the century, the degeneracy and misery of the people increased. In 1879, Te-kung-kea; 1848, Te-kaou; 1837, Te-fa; 1818, Kee-kwei, respectively became emperors.

The last-named prince is described as one of the worst monarchs who ever ruled China. He indulged in the most degrading licentiousness, and beheaded those who remonstrated with him. In his court he had piles of meat and ponds of wine, to which he invited his votaries, and indulged in all kinds of excesses. The most monstrous debauchery was practised in this prince's palace without shame or reluctance. The chief agent in these orgies was his wife, Mo-he, to please whom he built a room coated with jasper, and the furniture whereof was adorned with precious stones. His conduct to his subjects was on a par with his sensuality. He treated them with the most ferocious cruelty, and the execration in which he was held has caused the handing down to posterity of these particulars relating to him. Unfortunately this licentiousness is the leading feature in Chinese history. It is the most revolting of all histories. The most senseless and ferocious tyranny engendered the worst vices among the people, and their history is one of massacres and revolts, murders and civil wars. Now and then a good monarch appears, and for a brief interval the nation thrives, but he is immediately succeeded by an insane tyrant, and all is gloom again.

Some persons have discovered a very great resemblance between the Chinese and the ancient Egyptian Empires. In both, agriculture and astronomy were highly prized, respect for superiors inculcated, parents held in honor, and a hieroglyphic mode of writing adopted. Among the Egyptians the most degrading superstitions prevailed; while the Chinese had a political religion of mere forms. In both nations the worship of the dead was practised. Some have traced the origin of the Chinese to a colony of Egyptians, forgetting that similar causes produce similar effects, and that nations will spontaneously adopt rites and customs similar to those of other people, by the mere impulse of human nature. In the very earliest ages the Chinese were acquainted with many arts now lost.

Who became Emperors in this period?—What is said of the last-named prince?—Of Chinese history?—In what did China resemble ancient Egypt?

GREECE.

The earliest name we meet with in the history of Greece, that has historical reality, is that of In′achus, the son of Oce′anus and Teth′ys, who gave his name to the river flowing round the walls of Argos. He is by some supposed to have been a Pelasgian chieftain. He founded the kingdom of Argos, but the precise era of his reign is very difficult of determination. By those who compute by generations, as given in mythology, it is said to have begun in the year 1986 B. C.; but by others (and among them Mr. Clinton), it is placed in 1803 B. C.

We have already mentioned that Deucalion and Pyrrha had two sons, Hellen and Amphyc′tion. Hellen had three sons: Dorus, Xuthus, and Æ′olus. He gave to those who had before been Greeks the name of Helle′nes, and partitioned his territory among his three children. Æolus reigned in Thessaly; Xuthus in Peloponne′sus; and Dorus, Northern Greece. Xuthus had two sons, Achæ′us and I′on. These gave to their respective subjects the names of Æolians, Achæans, Ionians, and Dorians. Mr. Grote, in his history of Greece, well observes that, as history, these genealogies deserve no notice, but they symbolize intelligibly the first fraternal aggregation of Hellenic men, together with their territorial distribution. But even the ablest Greeks believed in the reality of such eponymous persons as Hellen and Ion.

These eponymous (or name-giving) men meet us in every page of early Greek history, and are perpetually referred to by writers in later ages. To find an eponym (or name-giver) for every conspicuous local name, was the invariable turn of Greek retrospective fancy. Thus, if any locality became famous, some mythical ancestor was discovered to be the originator of its name. The sons of Deucalion are instances of this. As in subsequent ages the Grecian States developed distinct peculiarities of languages and manners, and became known as Ionians, Dorians, Æolians, and Achæans, and the entire nation by the name of Hellenes, the inventive genius of Greece framed a genealogy starting from the sole survivors of the deluge, from whom the immediate eponymous ancestors of the people are represented to have derived their descent. The ancestors, in short, came into existence long after their descendants.

Who was the first king of Argos?—Who were the sons of Deucalion?—Name the mythical ancestors of the different tribes of the Greeks.—What are eponymous men?

THE 18TH CENTURY

EGYPT.

THE death of Joseph, whose administration had so entirely changed the face of Egypt, has been placed in the year B. C. 1792. He died full of honors, as is illustrated by the variety of names given to him by the Egyptians, and which are still to be seen on his tomb at Sakharah, in Egypt. His first title, *Tsaphnath*, signifies "one in communion with the goddess of wisdom;" his next, *Pheh-nuk*, or *Paa-neah*, "one who flees from adultery." His name, *Ei-tsuph* (Joseph), means "he came to save." *Abrech*, or *Hb-resh*, "royal priest and prince." His friend and patron, Aphophis (or Phiops), reigned 61 years. He left Egypt the richest kingdom upon earth. He constructed the beautiful temples and palaces which adorn Memphis, and rivalled in marvellousness the Labyrinth. He located the Israelites in the land of Goshen (*i. e.*, "of herbage," or "flowers"), supposed to have been the Delta. The remains of the institutions of Joseph, established under the auspices of Aphophis, are likewise traceable in the account of the laws and customs of Egypt preserved in Greek tradition. Aphophis was succeeded by his son, Melaneres, who took Thebes from the Upper Egyptians, and reduced all Egypt proper under the rule of the Shepherd kings. He expelled the Upper Egyptians from the entire monarchy. A tablet at Asouan, on the extreme southern limit of Egypt, represents him standing on the symbols of both Egypts, wearing the northern crown, and worshipped as a conqueror. It was sculptured upon the occasion of the cession to him of the last position they had maintained there. Melaneres likewise wrote his own name on the rock at Hamamat, on the occasion of hewing granite from thence. And the inscriptions record that a prince named Atfu, at Chenoboskion, was priest to the pyramid of Melaneres, as well as that of Aphophis and of Saites. The name of Melaneres is not in the Greek lists of Egyptian kings.

The two successors of Aphophis on the throne of Lower Egypt have no place in the genealogies found on the monuments at Karnak or Abydos. During their reigns a race of Aphophean kings reigned at Thebes, and the war of independence against the Shepherd kings commenced, and lasted until far into the next century.

What is said of Joseph's administration?—Of his death?—His titles?—His tomb?—Of the land of Goshen?—Of Aphophis?—Of his successors?—Of the war of independence?

SYRIA.

OF the history of this country during this period, we have little or no account. Tyre and Sidon were flourishing cities, and the Phœnicians visited distant lands in their ships. The land of Canaan was in all probability in much the same state as it was when invaded by Joshua; that is, divided into a number of petty states or tribes under their own rulers or kings. The children of Israel, who had in the previous century emigrated into Egypt, had grown numerous and wealthy in the land of Goshen, allotted to them by the Egyptian king, Aphophis (or Phiops), the Pharaoh of Scripture; and had, from their numbers, become a source of considerable uneasiness to his successors, Melaneres, Jannes, and Asses. "They multiplied, and waxed exceeding mighty;" and, by way of keeping them in subjection, the Egyptians forced them to abandon their pastoral occupations, and make bricks for public buildings. It does not appear that their condition was in any way ameliorated by the struggle for independence which was then going on in Egypt. The Shepherd kings still held absolute sway over them.

It appears to have been the policy of the Shepherd kings to encourage the settlement of Canaanites in Egypt. This policy, inaugurated by Aphophis, was continued by his successors. It was therefore not merely an isolated act of kindness on the part of the Pharaoh, done at the request of Joseph, to locate Jacob and his family in Goshen (the Delta of the Nile); but it was done from a desire to colonize that fertile strip of land with skilful shepherds and husbandmen. We have elsewhere noticed the locality of Goshen (see Egypt). The name is not Hebrew, nor is its meaning certainly known. It is conjectured to mean "herbage," or "flowers." In the Coptic texts there are many words spelt with the same letters, and all denoting one class of objects, that is, objects that grow or vegetate. The kings of the 22d dynasty, who made Bubastis, in the eastern Delta, their northern capital, assumed a name similar to Goshen, represented in the hieroglyphics by an irrigated field, bounded by two canals. Hence the locality of Goshen is ascertained with tolerable certainty. The name "Delta" was given to that portion of Egypt because its shape resembled the triangular form of the Δ of the Greek alphabet.

What was the condition of Canaan?—What became of the children of Israel?—Where was Goshen?—What is the meaning of the name?—And of "the Delta"?

INDIA.

AFTER Rama, sixty princes of his race ruled in succession over his dominions; but as we hear no more of Ayodha (or Oude), it is possible that the kingdom, which was at one time called Coshala, may have merged in another, and that the capital was transferred from Oude to Canouj. Ayodha is not mentioned in the Mahabharat, nor is Canacubya (Canouj), unless, as asserted in Menu, Panchala is only another name for that kingdom. Panchala seems to have been a long, but narrow territory, extending on the east to Nepaul (which it included), and on the west along the Chambal and Banas, as far as Ajimere. We know little else of its early history, except from the Rajpoot writings, traditions, and inscriptions. Canouj was one of the most ancient places in India. It was a city of great extent and magnificence, and its ruins are still to be seen on the banks of the Ganges.

The traditions of the Deccan point to a period when the natives were not Hindoos. By the latter, the aborigines are described as having been, before their civilization, goblins and demons, or foresters and mountaineers. Their language (the Tamul) must have been formed and perfected before the introduction of the Sanscrit; but from the fact of there being a Tamul literature, the people must have been something more than mere foresters and mountaineers. If any credit is to be given to the Hindoo legends, Ravan, who reigned over the southern part of the Peninsula at the time of Rama's invasion, was the head of a powerful and civilized State. Some of the most distinguished Tamul authors were of the despised class called Pariahs; and, as these lived in comparatively modern times, it is evident that the Brahmins had no influence in the land at the time we are speaking of. The common origin of the Sanscrit language with those of the West, leaves no doubt that there was once a connection between the nations by whom they were used; but it proves nothing regarding the place where such a connection subsisted, nor about the time, which might have been in so early a stage of their society as to prevent its throwing any light on the history of the individual nations. Mr. Elphinstone doubts that it spread from a central point (*History of India*, vol. i., p. 98).

What is said of the kingdom of Oude?—Of Panchala?—Of Canouj?—Of the original inhabitants of the Deccan?—Of the Tamul language?—And the Sanscrit?

ASSYRIA.

ON the death of Altades, B. C. 1776, we find the name of Mami'tus recorded as his successor; but between this latter and the accession of the next king is a space of 166 years. Of this period we possess no account.

As regards the exact site of ancient Nineveh, Colonel Rawlinson gives the following opinion:—"Nimroud, the great treasure-house which has furnished us with all the most remarkable specimens of Assyrian sculpture, although very probably forming one of that group of cities which, in the time of the prophet Jonah, were known by the common name of Nineveh, has no claim itself, I think, to that particular appellation. The title by which it is designated on the bricks and slabs that form its buildings, I read doubtfully as Levekh, or Halukh, and I suspect this to be the original form of the name which appears as Calah in Genesis, and Halah in Kings and Chronicles; and which, indeed, as the capital of Calachene, must needs have occupied the same site in the immediate vicinity: and, I may add, that before I had deciphered the name of the city on the slabs of Nimroud, this geographical identification was precisely that at which I had arrived, from observing that the Samaritan version of the Pentateuch employs for the Hebrew Calah the term Lachisa, a form which Babylonian orthography shows to be absolutely the same as the Greek name Larissa, by which Xenophon designated the great ruined capital that was passed by the ten thousand Greeks in their retreat, a few miles to the northward of the Lycus. The real and primitive Nineveh, which is frequently mentioned in the inscriptions, I conjecture to have occupied the site where we now see the high mound opposite to Mosul, surmounted by the pretended tomb of the prophet Jonah; for we have historical proof of this particular mound having been locally termed Nineveh from the time of the Arab conquest down to comparatively modern times; and I think that the ruins a short distance to the northward, which are now termed Koyunjik, were not the true Nineveh itself, but formed a suburb of that capital." Khorsabad was also an immediate dependency of Nineveh. It is popularly termed "the French Nineveh," from the excavations and researches made there by French antiquaries within the last few years.

What king is mentioned during this century?—What does Col. Rawlinson say respecting the site of ancient Nineveh?—The tomb of Jonah?—Koyunjik?—Khorsabad?

B.C. 1800—1700.

PERSIA.

As there is no authentic history wherewith to fill up this period, we devote the space to the exploits (fabulous or otherwise) of Persia's great heroes, Zal and Roostum. Zal was the son of Sam, and was born with white hair, whence his name (which signifies "aged"). Believing that the child was the offspring of some deev (or magician), the father sent it to be exposed on Mount Elburz. There it was nurtured by a simurgh (or griffin) until it was fetched away by Sam. Zal's first adventure, on coming to maturity, was his meeting with the beautiful princess, Rouda′bàh, or Rodah′ver, daughter of Mehrab, king of Caubul, a prince of the race of Zohak. It occurred while Zal was hunting. Coming to the foot of a high tower, he saw a lady of exquisite beauty, on whom he gazed ardently until his passion was returned. As there was no mode of ascending the battlement, the lady loosened her tresses, which fell in ringlets to the bottom of the tower, and enabled Zal to ascend. From this marriage came the great hero of Persia, Roostum.

The exploits of Roostum have been magnified into miracles, and his history is enveloped in romance. One of the principal of his achievements was the capture of the Kullah Suffeed (or White Fort), in the province of Fars. This fort was almost impregnable from its situation. The ascent to it was three miles long, by a very narrow path, and very easily defended. Disguising himself as a dealer in salt, and putting bags upon his camels, with an armed man in each bag, he contrived to gain access to the fort, which he at once stormed and took. This is one of many warlike exploits recorded of the young hero. But the terrible confusion in the Persian annals of this epoch is well illustrated in their making him the companion-in-arms of Kai-Kobad (the De′joces of the Greeks), who lived centuries afterwards. Roostum's greatest exploit was the killing the Deev Suffeed, or White Demon (probably some northern prince), in single combat. He repeatedly defeated Afrasiab, the powerful king of Turan. In one of these battles he vanquished a famous warrior named Peelsoon, in the presence of both armies. The student will find an interesting account of Roostum in Malcolm's *History of Persia*, vol. i., chap. iv.

Mention some of the adventures of Zal.—Of Roostum.—Who were the Tartar chiefs overcome by the latter?—What is said of Kai-Kobad?

CHINA.

The cruelties of Kee-kwei continuing, Ching-tang (a descendant of Hwang-te), who held an hereditary fief of the crown, afforded an asylum to the persecuted; and, being urged on all sides to take up arms, he did so. He defeated Kee-kwei, who surrendered himself prisoner; but on promising reformation, Ching-tang left him in possession of the throne. He was no sooner reinstated than he sought to destroy Ching-tang, who again levied an army, and dethroned him. Kee-kwei fled, and, forsaken by the whole world, died in exile B. C. 1766. His son and successor, the last of the Hea dynasty, Chan-wei, retired to the northern deserts, where he ended his life amongst savages. To the Hea dynasty belongs the merit of having established the curious system of government under which China is now ruled. That it is adapted to the wants of the people, is attested by the fact of its having endured for so many centuries, and survived so many revolutions.

Ching-tang, therefore, ascended the throne (B. C. 1766), and became the founder of the Shang (or "supreme") dynasty. According to Chinese historians, the whole globe trembled, and the stars lost their lustre, on his accession. He appears to have felt or feigned great reverence for God, since he was perpetually invoking the Shang-te (or "Supreme Emperor") in his edicts and discourses. To His interference Ching-tang ascribed his elevation. During his reign occurred a seven years' drought, against which, it seems, the Emperor had provided by laying up grain in the store-houses: whereby we are reminded of the Egyptian minister, Joseph.

Ching-tang was an able man, and was, from his unwearied benevolence, called "the well-beloved sovereign." He died B. C. 1753, and his successor, Taë-kea, was chosen Emperor through the agency of the celebrated minister, E-yin. Taë-kea being prone to vice, E-yin caused him to be confined, with his family, for many years, in the catacombs of his ancestors, until he had reformed. When he had done this, he was restored to the throne. He died B. C. 1721. In the reign of his successor, Wuh-ting, and B. C. 1713, the able minister E-yin died, and was buried with royal honors. He left a worthy disciple, named Kew-tan, who became as illustrious as his master.

What is said of the cruelties of Kee-kwei?—What is said of the Hea dynasty?—Of E-yin?—Of Ching-tang?—And his successors?

GREECE.

Inachus reigned a considerable time at Argos. He had two sons, Phoro′neus and Ægiale′us, the former of whom succeeded his father at Argos (B. C. 1753), and introduced amongst his subjects many social habits. His tomb was still shown in the days of Pausa′nias. Ægialeus established himself in Sicyon, and gave his name to the north-western region of the Peloponnesus. The name of Phoroneus was of great celebrity in the Argeian mythical genealogies, and furnished both the title and subject of the ancient poem called "Phoronis," in which he is styled "the father of mortal men." Phoroneus and Ægialeus were sometimes represented as "autochthonous," or of the original race of men, the one in Argos, the other in Sicyon.

The offspring of Phoroneus, by the nymph Tele′dice, were Apis and Niobe. Hellan′icus, in his Argo′lica, states that Phoroneus had three sons: Pelas′gus, Ia′sus, and Age′nor, who, at the death of their father, divided his possessions by lot. Pelasgus acquired the country near the river Erasinus, and built the citadel of Larissa. Iasus obtained the portion near to Elis. After their decease, the younger brother, Agenor, invaded and conquered the country, at the head of a large body of horsemen. It was from these three persons that Argos derived the three epithets which are given to it in the poems attributed to Homer: *Argos Pelasgikon*, *Iason*, and *Hippoboton* (good for horses). This is a specimen of the way in which legendary persons, as well as legendary events, were got up to furnish an explanation of Home′ric epithets. We may remark as singular, that Hellanicus seems to apply "Pelasgikon Argos" to a portion of Peloponnesus, while the Homeric Catalogue applies it to Thessaly. (See note to p. 83, vol. i., of Grote's *History of Greece.*)

The dominion of Phoroneus extended over the whole of the Peloponnesus, and, on his death, his son Apis succeeded him, and gave the name of A′pia to the country. According to Æschylus, Apis was the son of Apollo. He was a medical charmer, who came across the gulf from Naupactus, purified the territory from noxious monsters, and gave it the name of Apia. But this is poetical fiction, and it still remains a mystery why the Peloponnesus was named Apia. Apis was a harsh ruler, and was put to death by Thelxi′on and Tel′chin. Apis was succeeded in his kingdom by Argos, the son of his sister Niobe, and from this chieftain the Peloponnesus was denominated Argos. About this time, B. C. 1764 (or, according to Usher, 1796), a deluge happened in Attica, which is called the deluge of O′gyges, from the king who is said to have then reigned in that district. Mr. Grote asserts that this was the flood of Deucalion (*History of Greece*, vol. i., p. 194), and that it destroyed most of the inhabitants of the country; but other authors treat the historical personality and the date of Ogyges as perfectly well authenticated. A similar catastrophe happened in Bœotia, during the reign of another Ogyges, owing to the overflowing of Lake Copais.

The most ancient name in Attic archæology is that of Erech′theus. He is said to have been the son of Hephæstos and the earth, and brought up by Minerva, adopted by her as her ward, and installed in her temple at Athens, where the Athenians offered to him annual sacrifices. In Homer's Iliad, the Athenians are styled "the people of Erechtheus." In the Erecthei′on (or temple of Erectheus, on the Acrop′olis of Athens), Erechtheus was worshipped conjointly with Athe′ne (Minerva). He was identified with the god Poseidon (Neptune), and bore the denomination of Poseidon Erechtheus. The Bu′tadæ, one of the most ancient and important families of Athens, boasted that they were lineally descended from him; and one of them, chosen among themselves by lot, enjoyed the privilege and performed the functions of his hereditary priest.

With regard to Greek names, the modern practice is to follow the spelling adopted by the Romans, and in some cases to alter names according to more recent habit; as, for instance, Livius into Livy, Terentius into Terence, Aristoteles into Aristotle. The Greek alphabet contains no *c*, *f*, *h*, *j*, *q*, *v*, *w*, or *y*. The Romans and the moderns have used these letters in translating Greek names into their own languages: thus, Thoukudides has become Thucydides; Odusseus, Ulysses; Eracles, Hercules—the Greek aspirate being rendered by the letter *h*. Mr. Grote has retained the Greek mode of spelling proper names: we prefer, however, employing the mode sanctioned by custom and by the best authors, reference to whom would be difficult under the other system.

What is said of the reign of Inachus?—Who were his sons, and what is said of them?—Who was Apis?—What were the ancient names of the Peloponnesus?—When did the flood of Ogyges occur?—What is the name of the most ancient Attic hero?—Give the particulars of the honors paid to Erectheus.

THE 17TH CENTURY

EGYPT.

The interval between the death of Melaneres and the descent of the Amonian fanatics, under Amo′sis, upon Memphis, includes about eighty years, but is involved in difficulties. A number of kings, descendants of the viceroy appointed by Melaneres, reigned in Upper Egypt. Of the descendants of Mencheres we find the names of Skeniophris and Menthesu′phis II., the latter of whom fell in battle in Ethiopia. The reigns of all of these monarchs were inglorious.

The bursting of the lake of Ethiopia occurred in the time of Joseph. It was an event which appears to have created peace and a good understanding between the rulers of Upper Egypt, Nubia, and Ethiopia, which endured until the religious war broke out respecting the worship of the god Amun-Sa. A set of fanatics, headed by Amosis, a descendant of the Mencherian Pharaohs, marched down the Valley of the Nile, breaking open and plundering the tombs, and defacing the public monuments, especially at Memphis, which city Amosis took. He then assumed the crown, and, after a long interval of anarchy and bloodshed, expelled the Shepherd kings. Manetho says that the expulsion of the Shepherds from Memphis was accomplished by the alliance of the kings of Thebes with the kings of the rest of Egypt. Be that as it may, it is tolerably certain that Amosis became master of a large portion of Egypt. He reigned twenty-five years, amid much turbulence and revolt. A cotemporary dynasty reigned at Xois, in the Delta, whence they were called Xoite kings. They form the 14th dynasty. Amosis founded the 18th dynasty. His successor (according to Mr. Osburn, *Monumental History of Egypt*, vol. ii., p. 171,) was Ameno′phis I., who also reigned for some time jointly with him. According to others, Thothmes I. was the name of the successor of Amosis. But the confusion is so great as to render it impossible to speak with certainty on the subject.

The Exodus of the Israelites, under Moses, is by some authors placed in this century. Dr. Hales computes that it took place B. C. 1648. Mr. Clinton, in B. C. 1625. But Usher places it in B. C. 1491, and Lepsius in B. C. 1330. If the former be correct, then either Amosis or Amenophis was the Pharaoh whose heart was hardened to resist the appeals of Moses.

What is said of the successors of Melaneres?—Of the Amonian fanatics?—Of Amosis?—Of the Xoite dynasty?—Of the Exodus of the Israelites?

SYRIA.

The notices of this country, during this period, by historians, are slight. The descendants of Jacob, settled in Goshen, became exceedingly numerous, so much so, indeed, as to excite the apprehensions of the rulers of the land (either the Xoite kings of the Delta, or of the Pharaoh of Lower Egypt). According to Mr. Osburn (*Monumental History of Egypt*, vol. ii., ch. ix.), the king mentioned in Scripture was Sethos II., and the princess who adopted Moses was Thouoris, the daughter of Sesostris the Great, and wife of Siphtha, the infant king of Xois. We cannot here discuss the chronology of this period. It is so confused that the epoch of the Exodus has not been fixed within three centuries (see "Egypt"). As Moses grew up he refused to be called the son of Pharaoh's daughter (Heb. xi. 24). Having witnessed the oppression under which the Israelites suffered, and in his anger slain an Egyptian, he fled from the fury of the king (Siphtha?), and remained in Midian until the accession of Sethos II. (Osburn, *ubi supra*). This monarch is by some said to be the Pharaoh who refused to let the Israelites depart, and was drowned in the Red Sea in pursuit of them (see Osburn). But, according to others, the Exodus of Moses took place in the time of Amosis, king of Lower Egypt, who was *not* drowned in the Red Sea. The discrepancies are irreconcilable. According to the Jewish historian, Jose′phus (*Contra Apion*, i. 26), Moses was a priest of Helio′polis, and his real name was Osarsiph (*i. e.*, "saved by Osiris," the god of Heliopolis). He afterwards changed his name to Moses. The legend related by Josephus is, that Amenophis, king of Egypt, having been advised to clear the country of lepers, collected 80,000 unclean persons, and located them at the city of Ava′ris. There, Osarsiph, a priest of Heliopolis, induced them to revolt, and, having procured the assistance of 200,000 of the Shepherds, he marched against Amenophis. The king having assembled 300,000 Egyptians, took counsel of them, and withdrew into Ethiopia, together with the whole population of Egypt, "lest he should seem to be fighting with the gods." The legions of Moses then took possession of Egypt, which invasion is called "the invasion of the Solymites" (*i. e.*, spoilers). This is the profane, in opposition to the sacred, account of Moses.

What were the names (according to Mr. Osburn,) of Pharaoh's daughter?—And of the king who refused to let Israel go?—Relate Josephus's legend of Moses.

INDIA.

In the absence of any direct historical information respecting this period of Indian history, we recur to the subject of the four great castes of the people. Mr. Elphinstone (*History of India*, vol. i., ch. v.) thinks that the three superior castes — the Brahmins, the Cshatriyas, and the Veisyas — were not original inhabitants of India, but conquering races: that the Sudras, or servile class, were the subdued aborigines, and that the independent Sudra towns were in such of the small territories into which Hindostan was divided, as still retained their independence, while the whole of the tract beyond the Vindya mountains remained as yet untouched by the invaders, and unpenetrated by their religion. The three upper classes are directed by the law to dwell in the country between the Himalaya and the Vindya mountains, from the eastern to the western ocean. Whether these classes were foreigners, or superior native tribes, cannot now be decided, though the difference between their appearance and that of the Sudras would lead us to believe the former. The great tribe of Yadu, which is the principal, perhaps the only one, which came from beyond the Indus, is the tribe of Crishna, and of the purest Hindoo descent. There is a story of their having crossed to the west of the Indus after the death of Crishna, who, as we have seen, perished in the civil wars of his native land, Gujerat. Were the founders of the Hindoo castes Scythians? It has been supposed by some that the whole Hindoo people sprung from the same root with the Scythians. (See Elphinstone's *History of India*, vol. i., Appendix II.)

The temples of the Hindoos, unlike those of the Egyptians, are not of very great antiquity. The inscriptions found in them confirm the belief that very few are older than the Christian Era; hence, the source from which so much ancient history has been derived, is wanting in the case of India. There is reason to believe that the Hindoos were acquainted with the art of navigation at a very early period. It is mentioned in the Code of Menu, but intercourse with the Mediterranean took place at a still earlier period. It may, however, have been carried on by traders from Egypt and Babylon, and not by natives of India. The first clear accounts of the seas west of India give no signs of trade carried on by Hindoos.

What is supposed to have been the origin of the three superior castes?—What that of the Sudras?—Were the Hindoos originally Scythians?—What of their navigation?

ASSYRIA.

In this century we find only the name of Manchaleus, the commencement of whose reign is stated to have been B. C. 1610. No great reliance is, however, to be placed on these names, which are Greek adaptations of ancient Assyrian titles; and probably the personages indicated thereby existed only in the imagination of the Greek historians. According to Mr. Layard (*Nineveh and Babylon*, abridged, p. 505), no mention appears to be made, in the Assyrian inscriptions, of kings who reigned before the 12th century B. C. But on the monuments in Egypt, of the 18th dynasty, mention is made of Nineveh; so that it is certain that kings of some sort, and having names, did reign over that ancient city. The monuments of Nineveh prove that the Assyrian monarch was a thorough Eastern despot, having complete power over the lives and property of his subjects. Of the gods of Assyria, the names of thirteen have been found:

1. Asshur, the king of the circle of the great gods.
2. Anu, the lord of the mountains, or of foreign countries.
3. (Not yet deciphered.)
4. San.
5. Mer′odach (Mars?).
6. Yav (Jupiter?).
7. Bar.
8. Nebo (Mercury?).
9. Mylit (or Gula), consort of Bel, and mother of the gods (Venus?).
10. Da′gon.
11. Bel (Saturn?), father of the gods.
12. Sha′mach, the Sun.
13. Ish′tar, the Moon.

The religion of the Babylonians was akin to that of the Assyrians, but the names of their deities were not the same. On some of their monuments have been found inscriptions from which it appears that a god, named Marduk, held the same place as Asshur did with the Assyrians. He is styled "the great Lord," "Lord of Lords," "Elder of the gods," etc. Nebu seems to hold the second rank. It may also be conjectured that, in their general plan, the Babylonian palaces and temples resembled those of Assyria. They were erected upon lofty platforms of brickwork. The bricks were usually one foot square by three and a half inches thick, and are supposed to represent multiples of some Babylonian measure.

As to the names of the kings given by the Greek historians?—How many of the principal deities of Assyria are known?—And of Babylonia?—What of the temples?

B.C. 1700—1600.

PERSIA.

The following is a *résumé* of the ancient history of Persia:

It may be divided into distinct periods: the fabulous, the poetical, and the historical. The first includes all prior to Kai-Kobad. The poetical begins with the Kaianian dynasty, and continues until the reign of Ardisheer′ Bab′igan. The historical begins with that monarch, and terminates with the overthrow of his dynasty.

Of the fabulous period, it is impossible to fix the dates with any approach to correctness. The monarchs mentioned in the Dabistan are Mahabad and thirteen successors of the same name (supposed to be the fourteen Menus of the Hindoos); Jy-Affram, who established the Jyanian dynasty, the number of whose successors is not known (the last was named Jyabad); Shah Kuleev, who established another dynasty, of which the last prince was Shah Mahabool, supposed to be the Mahabali of the Hindoos, and, by some, to be the Belus of the Assyrians; Yassan, the founder of the Yassanian dynasty, which ended with Yassan Ajem. The aggregate reigns of these monarchs is estimated at many millions of years. Then came the Paishdadian dynasty of kings, whose reigns (according to Ferdusi) were enormously long. Those of Kaiomurs, Hooshung, and Tahamurs embraced 100 years; that of Jemsheed (Giamschid), 700; that of Zohak, 1000 (the term of the Assyrian conquest); of Feridoon, also 1000; of Manucheher, 120; of Nouzer, 7; of Afrasiab, 12 (conjectured to be the term of the Scythian conquest); of Zoo and Kershasp, the same period, both being cotemporary with Afrasiab, and ruling part of Persia.

In the historical period we are aided by Grecian writers; but the difference between these and Persian authors, from the period of Kai-Kobad (Dejoces) to the invasion by Alexander the Great, is nearly three centuries.

The ancient Persians had made progress in civilization. The female sex was held in great respect, and was assigned a high and honorable position in society by the ordinances of Zoroaster. But the community seldom enjoyed good government or just laws. The power of the sovereign was but faintly acknowledged by the great feudal lords who held lands on tenure of military service; consequently the country was at the mercy of lieutenants (satraps), who farmed the provinces.

Into what portions may the ancient history of Persia be divided?—Give a sketch of the fabulous period.—What is said of the historical?—And of the ancient state of the people?

CHINA.

Wuh-ting died B. C. 1691.

"During the reigns of the successors of Wuh-ting, viz., Tae-kang (B. C. 1691–1666), Seaou-kea (1666–1649), Yung-ke (1649–1637), nothing particular happened, but the vigor of the Shang princes greatly decayed.

"Tae-woo, who ascended the throne in the year B. C. 1637, was greatly grieved at the loss of all authority. Two trees grew up in one night, the stems increased to a considerable thickness in seven days, and in three other days decayed. Greatly astonished at such an extraordinary event, he consulted two of his ministers. E-chi, who was one of them, answered: 'Calamity may be averted by governing virtuously, and by affectionately cherishing the people.' Tae-woo did not forget this lesson, and thenceforth paid no attention to omens, but contented himself with governing well. He erected hospitals, or almshouses, for the aged, where they were very well provided for; prevented the mandarins from oppressing the people; and thus established his authority upon a firm basis—the love of his subjects."

This extract from Chinese history will show that the happiness of the people was entirely dependent on the accidental caprice or fancy of the monarch. Thus, if a miraculous development had not taken place, Tae-woo would have followed in the downward path of his predecessors, but Heaven interfered on behalf of the people, and persuaded him to govern righteously. Of this mixture of childishness and fact is the history of China composed. The Emperor of China is regarded as the common father of an immense family, who does not punish, but corrects. By means of endearing names his tyranny is cloaked; and when he inflicts even the most cruel punishments, he is said to be actuated by the tenderest compassion. He is considered Heaven's vicegerent, and is to be worshipped as such. He is styled Teën-tsze, or "Heaven's Son"; Hwang-te, "august Emperor"; Hwang-shang, "supremely august"; Ta-hwang-shang, "the great supremely august"; Shing-choo, "the holy Lord"; Wan-suy-yay, "the lord of a myriad of years". He wears a robe of yellow, to represent the sun; and the nobles and people prostrate themselves, not only before him, but before a tablet with the inscription, "Wan-suy-yay."

When did Wuh-ting die?—What is said of the reigns of his successors?—Of Tae-woo?—Of the power of the Emperor?—And of his titles?

GREECE.

Argos had four sons; of whom the eldest, Ecbasus, succeeded him in the kingdom of Argos, and was in his turn succeeded by his son, Age′nor; but we know little about them. Agenor's son, Argos Panop′tes, was a powerful prince. On account of his watchfulness and vigilance, he is said to have had eyes distributed all over his body, and to have freed Peloponnesus from monsters and wild animals. According to another fable, Argos was changed into a peacock. Some commentators consider that Argos is an allegorical expression for the starry heavens; hence he is said to have had eyes all over his body.

The descendants of Æolus furnish many names of celebrity in the heroic legends of Greece. The adventures of Ty′ro, the beautiful daughter of Salmoneus, the son of Æolus, formed the subject of one of the dramas of Sophocles. Salmoneus founded a city, which was destroyed by Jupiter on account of the impiety of its founder. Pelias and Ne′leus, both Æolids, contended for the possession of the kingdom of Iolkos, in Thessaly; the former obtained it, and the latter went into Peloponnesus, where he founded the kingdom of Pylos. He married Chloris, the daughter of Amphi′on, king of Orchomenus, by whom he had a beautiful daughter, Pero, who was courted by numberless suitors. But Neleus would only give her in marriage to the man who should bring to him the oxen of Iph′iclus, from Phyl′ace, in Thessaly. These oxen were guarded by a fierce dog, whom no one dared approach. Nevertheless, Melam′pus, a distant relative of Neleus, undertook the exploit, and accomplished it by means of his prophetic powers (see Homer's *Odyssey*, book ii., line 278; xv., 233, 4).

The daughters of Æolus also added to the heroic legends. Can′ace is the subject of deep tragical interest, both in Euri′pides and in Ovid. Iphimedi′a was the mother of the famous Alo′ids (so called from their father, Alo′eus), Otos, and Ephial′tes, who were said to have been nine fathoms in height, and nine cubits in breadth. They made war upon the gods, and piled Ossa on Olympus, and Pelion on Ossa, in order to reach them. But the arrows of Apollo cut short their career. Another daughter, Cal′yce, became the mother of Endymion, whom the goddess Diana threw into a perpetual sleep.

What is said of Argos and his sons?—Of Argos Panoptes?—Of the descendants of Æolus?—Of Tyro?—Of Salmoneus?—Of Neleus?—Of the Aloids?—Of Endymion?

ITALY.

Ital′ia was originally the the name of the land of the I′tali, a name derived by the Greeks from It′alus, a king of the Œnotrians, who at one time occupied the whole of the Peninsula to the south of the Tiber, and Cape Garga′nus. The Oscan name of the country was Vitellium. In the Tyrrhenian or Tuscan language the word Italos signified an ox; hence the Campanian coins have a bull with a human face on them, representing King Italus. The Œnotrians are said to have emigrated into Italy under Œno′trus, one of the sons of Lyca′on, from Arca′dia, seventeen generations before the Trojan war. The Pelasgi were also settled in Italy from a very remote period. The Tyrrhenians were originally Pelasgian; their Etruscan conquerors being of a different race. The earliest inhabitants of the plains of the Tiber were the Si′culi, who were subjugated by a strange people that came down from the Abruzzi, but the name of the conquering race has not survived. They became one people with the vanquished.

The Œnotrians were distinguished into two tribes: the Italietes in the south, and the Chenes in the north, of Italy. The Opicans, Oscans, or Ausonians inhabited the neighborhood of Beneventum. Their language was, like the Pelasgian, akin to the Greek. The aborigines dwelt on the Anio, and were subdued by the Sabines, who are, in the oldest Latin legends, termed Sacrani, Casci, and Prisci. Their language was akin to that element of the Latin language which is not Greek; it resembled the Oscan in some particulars. But the origin of the Latins is very obscure.

In their mythology, Janus, or Dia′nus, was the god of the Sun; Saturn and his wife, Ops, the god and goddess of the Earth. Between Saturn and the Trojan settlement there were only three kings of the aborigines in the legend, viz., Picus, Taunus, and Lati′nus, who were adored as Indige′tes (or "special gods of the country"). Of these gods, an account has already been given in the mythology of Greece (p. 17). Latinus is the same as Lavi′nus, or Lavinius. The Sabelli, or Samni′tes, were another early race of inhabitants of Italy, whose home was at Am′iter′num, in the Apennines, and who gradually subdued the southern portion of the peninsula.

Whence is the name of Italy derived?—What was the Oscan name of the country?—What is said of the Pelasgi?—The Siculi?—The Œnotrians?—The Sabelli?—The Latins?

THE 16TH CENTURY

EGYPT.

THOTHMES I. (or Thothmo′sis,) was one of the heroes of the history of Egypt. According to Manetho, he was the son of Amosis, but the inscriptions prove that he was the sixth descendant of that monarch. His name and fame are co-extensive with the utmost borders of the land, and cover its entire surface. He was the builder of the most magnificent monuments of Egypt. The temples of Semneh, Kummeh, Wady Halfa, Ibrim, and Amada, and the splendid constructions at Karnak, Luxor, and Medinet-Aboo, owe their origin to him. Of the principal events of his reign, the inscriptions on these monuments record many particulars. He made war upon the Shepherds, but was not very successful; he thereupon made treaties of peace with them, which remained unbroken during the rest of his reign. He conquered Nubia and Ethiopia, and appears to have reduced under his sway the princes of Lower Egypt, and a portion of Palestine. He reigned forty-seven years, and died about B. C. 1591. His son, Acher′res (or Thothmes II.), succeeded him, and carried forward the great works which his father had left unfinished: he also built several temples. His reign, which lasted only twelve years, appears to have been disturbed by wars with the black races in the South, and with the foreign colonists in the Delta. The next monarch was Arma′is, the son of Thothmes II. In honor of him the Great Sphinx of Ghizeh was constructed. This was one of the wonders of Ancient Egypt. It was a huge mass of rock, which, partly by sculpture and partly by additions built upon it, has been shaped into the form of a lion, with a man's head. It was dedicated to the god Re-Athom ("the father of the gods") in Heliopolis. Armais appears to have been an unfortunate monarch. We are told in the Greek lists that, after he had reigned five years, he was expelled from Egypt by his brother, Egyptus, and fled to Greece, where he founded the city of Argos, and reigned over the Argives under the name of Dan′aus. This is probably a mistake, for there is an inscription to the effect that in the seventh year of his reign he was engaged in a war with the Phutim, or negro tribes of the Sahara. But the end of his reign was disastrous. He had roused the hostility of the religious fanatics of the South by requiring exclusive honors to be paid to the god Amun, and he was expelled by them from Egypt. These people were headed by a young prince, named Amenophis, who was a negro by birth, but claimed descent from Menes. His followers were worshippers of the Sun, of which deity the king was the priest. One of their first acts was to erase from the temples the name and reliefs of the god Amun, and they endeavored to extirpate idolatry. They committed great devastations among the historical monuments, and consequently rendered the history of the country very obscure.

Amenophis commenced several temples to the Sun; he also founded a noble city at Tel-el-Amarna, in Middle Egypt, where he built a vast temple to the Sun, the ruins of which are among the most considerable in Egypt. He was the first monarch of the Middle Egyptian dynasty: the records of his successors have been obliterated. He was expelled from Thebes by his own followers. Chebres, one of the constructors of the palace of Luxor, is the next name on the list. After him, the son of Armais, Amenophis-Memnon, ascended the throne (B. C. 1528). His reign was eminently peaceful and prosperous; but his success appears to have been mainly owing to the energy and ability of his mother, Queen Tai, who was one of the most remarkable women of Ancient Egypt, and erected some of the most notable monuments of that country. He restored the worship of Amun, and endeavored to repair the mischief done by the Sun-worshippers. Amid the confusion which prevails in the history of this extraordinary country, we find the name of Thothmes III. assigned by some historians to the successor of Acherres, and to him are attributed the temples of Amada, Ombi, and Eilithyia. The paintings in the tomb of Quorneh show that his dominion extended from Nubia to Mesopotamia; and the statistical table at Karnak records a series of expeditions undertaken by him against the Assyrians. He is said to have reigned thirty-five years, and to have been succeeded by his son, Amenophis II. The student who wishes to clear up the difficulty, may consult the works of Lepsius, Wilkinson, Kenrick, Sharpe, Osburn, and others, on the subject. As Egypt was divided into two or more kingdoms, each of whose monarchs was ambitious of recording his exploits, the number of kings on the monuments is easily accounted for.

What is said of Thothmes I.? — Of Acherres? — Of Armais? — Of the Great Sphinx? — Is Armais the same person as the Greek Danaus? — Who were the Phutim? — What of Amenophis and his followers? — Of his successors? — Who was Queen Tai? — Amenophis-Memnon? — Thothmes III.?

SYRIA.

IN the preceding century we have noticed the conflict which prevails between the historical records, as to the exact era of Moses and the Exodus. According to the received chronology, the birth of Moses is placed in the year 1571 B. C. By Dr. Hales it is placed in 1728 B. C. By Mr. Clinton, in 1705 B. C.; and by Lepsius, in 1360 B. C. The readers of Scripture do not require to be reminded of the circumstances attending the Exodus (or going out) of the children of Israel from Egypt. Moses is said to have been 80 years of age when the great movement took place. "A mixed multitude" followed him. Some authors have estimated the number, including women and children, at four millions. There were 600,000 men on foot (Exod. xii. 37), who constituted the strength of the nation. This immense multitude was led forth into Arabia, where they remained, under the leadership of Moses and his brother Aaron, for forty years, until, in short, the men who had come out of Egypt had died, and a younger generation had taken their place. While sojourning in the wilderness, Moses framed the system of laws which the Jews have ever since observed. It is a mixture of religious and political ordinances (contained in the books of Exodus and Leviticus), constituting a theocracy (or religious government), which was administered by the tribe of Levi, specially set apart for that purpose. The high priest was the head of the nation, but, in time of war, leaders of the Israelitish armies were appointed. It is a much-disputed point whether or not Moses instituted a national Senate. At the delivery of the law of Mount Sinai he was attended by a council of seventy elders; and during a rebellion in the wilderness he established one of the same number (Numbers xi.). But this council of seventy is not once distinctly named afterwards, although we read of convocations of the people. Each tribe governed its own affairs as a separate republic under its own chief; but the State at large possessed no legislative power: all great public decrees had to be ratified by "the congregation," or general assembly of the people. This was the system which prevailed before the time of the kings. The student will find an excellent account of the early Jewish polity in Milman's *History of the Jews*, book iii.

What was the date of the birth of Moses? — What is said of the Exodus? — Of the sojourn in the wilderness? — Of the laws of Moses? — Of the ancient Jewish polity?

INDIA.

THE great Oriental scholar, Sir William Jones, supposes that this century was the epoch of the composition of the sacred book called the Yajur Veda. He fixes the date of it at 1580 B. C. There are four Vedas, but the fourth is rejected by many learned Hindoos. Each Veda is composed of two parts. The first, called *Mantra*, consists of hymns and prayers; the second part, called *Brahmana*, of precepts which inculcate religious duties, and of arguments relating to theology. Some of these last are embodied in separate tracts, which are sometimes inserted in the second part above mentioned, and sometimes are in a detached collection, forming a third part, called *Upanishad*. Every Veda likewise contains a treatise explaining the adjustment of the calendar, for the purpose of fixing the proper period for the performance of each of the duties enjoined. The Vedas are not single works, but produced by different authors, whose names are attached to them. They were probably written at different periods, but were compiled in their present form in the 14th century B. C. (Elphinstone's *History of India*, vol. i., ch. iv.). Sir William Jones fixes the date of the compilation in the 12th century B. C.; and all the other European writers who have examined the question, fix the age of the compiler, Vyasa, between the 14th and 12th centuries B. C. The Hindoos themselves unanimously declare him to have lived at least 3001 years before Christ, but we are not acquainted with any evidence for the truth of this.

The primary doctrine of the Vedas is the unity of God; but among the creatures of the Supreme Being are some superior to man, who should be adored, and from whom favors and protection may be obtained through prayer. The three principal manifestations of the Deity — Brahma, Vishnu, and Siva — are rarely named, nor are their incarnations alluded to. There seem to have been no images, and no visible types of the objects of worship. The general tendency of the Vedas is to show that the substance, as well as the form, of all created beings, was derived from the *will* of the self-existing cause. This is not the case with the institutes of Menu, of which more will be said hereafter.

What is said of the epoch in which the Vedas were written? — What are they? — Who was their compiler? — What do they inculcate? — How do they differ from the code of Menu?

ASSYRIA.

DURING this century the following names of kings appear from very doubtful sources, viz.: Manchale'us (died B. C. 1580), Sphe'rus (1580–1560), Mam'ilus (1560–1530), Spare'tus (1530–1490).

Mention is also made of Chushan-Rishathaim, "King of Mesopotamia," who subdued the Israelites, and kept them in subjection eight years; after which he was expelled by Othniel (see Judges iii. 8–11), B. C. 1565–1557. The inscriptions and paintings of Egypt, during this century, also celebrate the expeditions of Thothmes I. and Thothmes III., kings of that country, into Armenia and Mesopotamia, which they subdued. They appear also to have exacted tribute from the Assyrians.

The Assyrian records, says Mr. Layard (speaking of those as yet deciphered), are nothing but a dry narrative of military campaigns, of no importance but to those immediately concerned in them. In this respect they present a remarkable contrast to the historical books of the Jews, which they nevertheless illustrate in an interesting manner. The books of the Old Testament, apart from the deeds of war and blood which they chronicle, contain the most interesting of private episodes and the most sublime of moral lessons. In the Assyrian records, the care with which the events of each king's reign was chronicled is remarkable. They were usually written in the form of regular annals; and, in some cases, as on the great monoliths at Nimroud, the royal progress during a campaign appears to have been described almost day by day. But, as yet, no monuments have been found in Assyria to which an earlier date than the 15th century B. C. can be assigned. They are, on the whole, free from the exaggerated forms of expression, and the magniloquent royal titles, which are found in Egyptian documents of the same nature. They are very minute in describing the amount of the spoil, the two registers, "the scribes of the host," as they are called in the Bible, being seen in almost every bas relief, writing down the various objects brought to them by the victorious warriors: the heads of the slain, the prisoners, the cattle, the sheep, the furniture, and the vessels of metal. (Layard, *Nineveh and Babylon*, p. 508.) Driving away the cattle and sheep of a conquered people, has ever been the custom of Eastern nations who have not altogether renounced a nomadic life, and whose chief wealth consequently consisted in those animals. When Asa, king of Judah, defeated the Ethiopians, "he carried away sheep and camels in abundance, and returned to Jerusalem" (2 Chron. xiv. 15). The Assyrian dominions, as far as we can learn, did not extend much further than the central provinces of Asia Minor and Armenia to the north, not reaching to the Black Sea, though probably to the Caspian. To the east, they included the western provinces of Persia; to the south, Susiana, Babylonia, and the northern part of Arabia; to the west, Lycia, and perhaps Lydia, and Syria was considered within the territories of "the great king." Egypt, and Meroe, in Ethiopia, were the furthest limits reached by the Assyrian armies.

What names of kings are given in this century?—What do the Egyptian inscriptions say of Assyria?—What is the character of the Assyrian inscriptions?—What the limits of the Empire?

PERSIA.

WE may pause here to take notice of the authorities from which the preceding account of Ancient Persia has been taken. Our knowledge of that part of it which precedes the reign of Kaiomurs, the first prince of the Paishdadian dynasty, rests upon the authority of the Dabistan, a book to which we have already referred (p. 11). It is a Persian work, containing an account of twelve religions, written about the close of the 16th century A. C., by a native of Cashmere, called Sheik Mohammed Mohsin, surnamed Fani (or, "the perishable"). It was compiled by him from ancient Pehlivi manuscripts, and from verbal communications which he had with Persians, who, in secret, followed the religion of Zoroaster. One of the books to which he refers is the Dussateer, or, as it is sometimes called, the Temarawatseer, which is still in existence, and in the possession of the priests of the Parsees, or Fire-worshippers of Bombay. The Dussateer is supposed to have been written by fifteen prophets, of whom the first was Mahabad, and the last Sassan, who lived in the time of Khosroo Purveez in the 7th century A. C. According to Mohsin Fani, the primeval religion of Persia was a firm belief in one Supreme God. This was followed by the worship of the heavenly bodies, or Sabianism. To this worship succeeded that of fire, which was first introduced by Hooshung. The followers of Mahabad worshipped the planets, which they typified by images of a very extraordinary nature. The religion of Zoroaster was a great improvement upon the system which then prevailed. We have already noticed its leading tenets: further particulars may be found in the work to which we are so largely indebted, Malcolm's *History of Persia* (see vol. i., chap. vii.).

Besides the ancient books above noticed, there are the Zend-a-vesta, already mentioned, and the fragments of the royal archives of Persia preserved in the Shah Namah. The deeds of the kings of Persia were written in a work styled the Chronicles of that kingdom. To this work the Greek historian, Ctesias, who was at the court of Artaxerxes Mnemon, had access. On the conquest of the country by the Arabs, in the 7th century A. C., most of these ancient books, with countless others, were destroyed. Some fragments, however, were saved and preserved by the Gheber priests. These were collected and given to the poet, Dukiki, to form into an epic poem, which should contain the history of Persia from Kaiomurs to Yezdijird. Dukiki only lived to write a thousand stanzas. He was assassinated by one of his own slaves; and the work was then entrusted to the celebrated Persian poet, Ferdusi, who, under the auspices of Mahmoud, of Ghuznee, in the 11th century A. C., composed the famous poem above mentioned, called the Shah Namah (or, "Book of Kings"). From this work we derive nearly all that the Asiatics know of the ancient history of Persia and Tartary; and we have had to disentangle what is really historical from the poetical redundancy of expression and fables with which it is mixed.

Name the authorities from which the ancient history of Persia is derived.—What is the Shah Namah?—Who was its author?—Where did he live?—Under what celebrated monarch?

CHINA.

THE annals of China during this century are very meagre. The reign of Tae-woo was, as we have seen, a happy one, both for the monarch and for his subjects. Of his successors little can be said, except that their reigns were so inglorious as scarcely to deserve notice. Their names, during this century, were:

	B. C.		B. C.
Chung-tang	1562	to	1548.
Wae-jin	1548	"	1534.
Ho-tan-kea	1534	"	1525.
Tsoo-yih	1525	"	1506.
Tsoo-sin	1506	"	1490.

During the reign of Chung-tang, the barbarians, who appear in after times under the name of Huns, and were always a terror to the Chinese, made great inroads into the empire, and were with difficulty subdued. The frequent inundations of the Hwang-ho (or "Yellow river,") compelled this Emperor to remove his capital to the province of Ho-nan. The Emperors of China have constantly changed the Capital of their Empire: there is no parallel in the history of any other country to the frequency of this change.

The religion of the ancient Chinese was pagan. It was a State religion, which did not consist of doctrines which are to be taught, learned, and believed, but of rites and ceremonies. It was entirely a bodily service, and its ritual was contained in the statistics and code of the Empire. The objects worshipped were chiefly things, but persons were also included. There were three grades of sacrifices: the great, the medium, and the inferior—collectively called the *kiun-sze* (or "crowd of sacrifices"). The objects to which the great sacrifices were offered were four, viz.: *tien*, the heavens, or sky; *ti*, the earth; *tai-miau*, the great temple of ancestors; and the *shie-tsih*, or gods of land and grain. The medium sacrifices were offered to eight objects, viz.: the sun, the moon, the manes of former Emperors (to which has been added Confucius), the gods of heaven, earth, and the passing year. The inferior sacrifices were offered to a number of objects, as, the wind, thunder, rain, mountains, rivers, eminent persons, the North Pole, etc. This State religion is of very ancient date, and has undergone few modifications in its essential features during the long succession of monarchs; and it still retains much of its primitive simplicity. It has been remarked by Mr. Williams (*The Middle Kingdom*, vol. ii., ch. xviii.), that the Chinese religion is distinguished from other ancient systems of religion by the absence of human sacrifices, and the non-deification of vice. In no form is sensuality worshipped: there is no Venus in the list of their deities, nor does their mythology teem with licentious amours, as is the case in the Greek and the Hindoo mythologies. And though the Chinese are a licentious people, they have never endeavored to sanctify vice. In this respect it must be admitted that they present a remarkable contrast to every other nation.

What is said of the Emperors during this century?—Of the removal of the Capital?—Of the ancient religion?—And its superiority over the Greek and the Hindoo?—Of the character of the Chinese?

GREECE.

To this era may be referred the wanderings of Io, a priestess of Juno, if such a personage had historical reality. She is said to have been the daughter of I′asus, the son of Argus Panoptes, who was king of Argos in the preceding century. According to the Greek fiction, Io was changed by Jupiter into a white cow, to avert the jealousy of Juno; but the latter drove her from her native land by the incessant stinging of a gad-fly, which compelled her to wander over many countries. She gave her name to the Ionian Gulf, traversed Asia, and at length arrived in Egypt, where Jupiter restored her to her original form. This myth is referred to in the *Prometheus* of Æs′chylus, and is repeatedly mentioned by the ancient Greek writers. According to the Phœnicians, Io was treacherously carried off from Argos by the crew of a ship, and sold in Egypt; and this system of forcible abduction of women appears to have been practised in this and subsequent ages by both Greeks and Asiatics.

Iasus was succeeded in his kingdom by Croto′pus, Sthen′elas, and Gela′nor. In the reign of the latter, Dan′aus came with his fifty daughters from Egypt to Argos. This is another of the famous romantic stories of early Greece. Danaus and Ægyp′tus were the grandsons of Io. Ægyptus had fifty sons, who were eager to marry the fifty daughters of Danaus, in spite of the repugnance of the latter. To escape from their importunities, Danaus fled with his daughters from Egypt to Argos. Thither he and they were followed by the sons of Ægyptus, who forced him to consent to the marriage; but, on the wedding-night, he furnished each of his daughters with a dagger, and enjoined them to murder their husbands during the hour of sleep. His orders were obeyed by all except Hypermnes′tra, who preserved her husband, Lyn′ceus, thereby incurring the displeasure of her father. He, however, forgave her; and when, by the voluntary abdication of Gela′nor, he became king of Argos, Lynceus was recognized as his son-in-law, and ultimately succeeded him. From Danaus was derived the name of Danai, applied to the Argives and to the Greeks generally.

About the middle of this century, Cecrops founded the city of Athens. He is generally represented in modern histories as an Egyptian, who brought a colony of his countrymen into Greece, but the greater number of the ancient authorities say that he was a native of Attica (Grote, *History of Greece*, vol. i., p. 195). In the fable he is stated to have been the means of deciding the dispute between Neptune and Minerva for the possession of the Acropolis, by testifying that the latter had planted the sacred olive tree there; whereupon the council of gods adjudged the prize to her. Cecrops distributed the inhabitants of Attica into twelve local sections. He also took a census of the population, which he accomplished by the primitive method of commanding each person to cast a single stone into a general heap, and afterwards counting the stones: they were found to number 20,000. He greatly reformed the people by the institution of marriage laws, and abolishing impious sacrifices. The country was named Cecropia, after him. It had previously been called Actæa, from Actæus, who had been king of the country before him, and whose daughter he married. His son, Erysich′thon, succeeded him. It is by no means improbable that Egyptians and Phœnicians settled on the coasts of Greece. It was so in Argos, and may have been the case in Attica.

The heroic pedigree of Arcadia commenced with Pelas′gus, who is said by some to have been the brother of Argus. Lyca′on, the son of Pelasgus, and king of Arcadia, is famous (or, rather, infamous) for his ferocity and impiety. The Greek fable says that Jupiter, in order to witness the misdeeds of Lycaon and his fifty sons, visited them in disguise. On this occasion they killed a child, and served it up to him for a meal, but the god overturned the table, and struck dead the king and all his sons, except the youngest. The town where this occurred received the name of Trapezus (Table-town). Pausa′nias, the Greek historian, relates that Lycaon, at the solemn worship of Jupiter, offered up a child to the god, and made libations with the blood upon the altar; and that, immediately after having done it, he was changed into a wolf. The extraordinary part of the affair is that the historian avows his firm belief in the story. He adds that the sons of Lycaon, instead of being slain, became founders of various towns in Arcadia.

What is said of Io?—Give the two versions of the legend.—Who were the successors of Iasus?—When did Danaus arrive in Argos?—Relate the legend of his daughters.—Give an account of Cecrops.—What dispute did he decide?—What else did he do?—What is said of Pelasgus and Lycaon?

ITALY.

About this period the Gauls, pouring from France into Spain, subdued or expelled the greater portion of the Iberians settled in the north of that country. After a brave resistance they forced their way through the south of France into Italy, and settled in the northern portion of it. They also settled in Corsica, Sardinia, and Sicily. But there is much difficulty in tracing the successive arrival of the races which peopled Italy. The number of them is extraordinary. We meet with Œnotrians, Umbrians, Sabellians, Etruscans, Pelasgians, Latins, Greeks, Siculians, Iberians, Tyrrhenians, Illyrians, Opicans (Ausonians or Oscans), Cascans, Sabines, Marsians, Samnites, Lucanians, Messapians, Ligurians, and Venetians; but, as Niebuhr observes (*History of Rome*, ch. xiii.): "No one can mount up to the fountain-head of these streams by which the tribes of the human race have been borne down; still less can any eye pierce across the chasm which there severs that order of things wherein we and our history are comprised, from an earlier one. That a prior race of mankind has passed away, is a general, popular belief, and it was shared and cherished by the Greek philosophers; but, whilst the latter supposed that a few had been preserved, like embers, from the general ruin, and that from them a new race of mankind had sprung and spread by degrees over the desolated earth, the people regarded the renewal of the life of man as a new creation, as we see exemplified in the Lai (stone men) of Deucalion, and the Myrmidons of Æacus; and the extinct race were deemed to have been rebels against the heavenly powers, led astray by the consciousness of their enormous strength. Thus the Greeks dreamed of the Titans of Phlegra, and the Italians fabled of the Campanian giants. The uniform notion, however, was that the times of the giants were not parted by a gulf from those of the present human race, but that the latter gradually gained the upper hand, whilst the former expired as gradually. The simpleness of the understanding identified this race as the architects of the enormous walls and other works, the epoch of which is removed far beyond the limits to which history reaches back. Yet much may be achieved in the way of investigation by a careful analysis of national legends and traditions." Allusion has already been made (p. 11) to the Cyclopean and other gigantic remains, and to the supposed race of giants which once inhabited the earth (see also Genesis vi. 4). Their existence was believed in down to later ages; as is evidenced in the legends of Polyphemus in the Homeric legends, and the account of Goliath in the Old Testament.

Niebuhr thus traces the movements of the tribes which peopled Italy. The Pelasgians (of whom the Œnotrians, the Morgetes, the Siculians, the Tyrrhenians, the Pencetians, the Daunians, the Liburnians, and the Venetians, were tribes), surrounded the Adriatic with their settlements: they settled also in Sardinia and in Sicily, where they appear as Elymians and Sicelians. They extended their colonies to the Danube. The Ligurians were in possession of Lombardy. They were at this time one of the great nations of Europe, possessing the country from Lake Garda to the foot of the Pyrenees: before this time they had also inhabited Tuscany. The Celts and Germans subsequently poured down from the north across the Alps into Lombardy, and the Ligurians retired behind the Ticino and into the Apennines. The Umbrians and Pelasgians were also driven from their settlements on the Adriatic by these conquering races. This took place about the end of the 7th century B. C. We are anticipating history in this rapid sketch. The irruption into Tuscany forced the Cascans and the Oscans southward. These again were pressed onward by the Sabines upon the Sicelians. The Pelasgians, on the Tuscan coasts, were expelled or subjugated; in Œnotria, they were subdued by the Greeks; in Daunia, by the Oscans; and on the Adriatic, by the Sabellians and Umbrians. The continued progress of the Sabellians subsequently occasioned the Ausonian Opicans to attack the Latins, a people that were sprung from an earlier immigration of other tribes belonging to their own race.

In the space devoted to the history of Italy, during the centuries which intervene between this early period and authentic history, brief notice will be taken of the nations or tribes above enumerated, and of such particulars as are known of their languages and destiny, for which we are mainly indebted to the researches of Niebuhr.

What is said of the Iberians?—Enumerate the races which peopled Italy.—What is said of a prior race of mankind?—Of giants?—What was the fate of the Pelasgians?—What is said of the Ligurians?—Give a sketch of the effects of the invasion of Italy by the Celts and Germans.

B.C. 1600—1500.

BRITAIN.

It is not known who were the first inhabitants of Britain. It is probable that about this period the Gauls or Celts, who emigrated from Eastern Europe into Germany, Italy, and France, found their way also into England. They were of Asiatic origin, as is evidenced by their language and traditions. They gave to England the name of "Albion," which is compounded of two Celtic words: *Alb*, "a mountain," and *Inn*, "an island." The name of "Britain," or Bretagne, was afterwards given to it by the Armorican Celts on the northern coast of France, who immigrated thence into England. This name was latinized by the Romans into "Britannia." Lastly, its present name, "England," or Engelland, was given to it by the Angles, a tribe of Saxons who aided in the conquest of it in the 5th century A. C.

The name of Alb-inn was also given by the Celts to Scotland. When the Cymry, or Cimbri, settled there, they gave it the name of "Celyddon," or "land of forests," which was subsequently changed by the Romans into "Caledonia." The name of Scotland was given to it by the Scuits, or Scots, who, immigrating from the north of Ireland, settled there in the 3d century A. C.

Ireland takes its name also from the Celts, who called it *Er-in*, two Celtic words signifying "the western island." This name was translated by the Greeks into "Ierne," and by the Romans into "Hibernia." It may also mean "the holy island," and by some has been derived from the Persian words, *Eir-in*, which have that meaning. That the ancient Irish were of oriental origin is undoubted, from the nature of their language, from their traditions, and the religious rites which prevailed among them. Traces of the worship of Bel, or Baal, may be found among them, and in the names of places the prefix Bal is of very common occurrence, as in Bal-lyshannon, Bal-lina, etc.

Wales is derived from *Wal*, "the land of the Gaul." The Welsh call themselves "Cymry," an appellation which came into general use in the 5th century A. C. This was latinized into "Cimbri," or "Cambri," whence the Latin name "Cambria." They descend from the Cimmerians, who, under Hu Gadarn, their great leader, immigrated from the banks of the Don into Northern Europe.

Who peopled Britain?—Whence is the name of Albion derived?—Of Britain?—England?—Caledonia?—Scotland?—Ireland?—Wales?—Cambria?—Who were the Welsh?

FRANCE.

In this early period a people called Iberians inhabited the southern portion of France. They were a peaceful and industrious race, who crossed the Pyrenees from Spain, and spread themselves over the province of Aquitaine and the northwest of Italy, at a still more remote period. They spoke the Euscara (Vascon or Basque) language. A division of them settled in Liguria, a name given by them to the country. The origin of this people is unknown, but they are one of the most ancient of nations.

The Gauls (Galli, Gael), a nomade or wandering race, known in after times in Asia Minor as Galatians, came originally from Asia, and spreading themselves over Europe, separated into various tribes, known as Celts, Belgians, Volke, Arecomici, and Tectosages. In the 16th century B. C., the Celts settled themselves on the banks of the Garonne and in the Cevennes. Here they came in contact with the Iberians, whom they drove further south, and crossing the Pyrenees, penetrated into Spain, where they also settled. Another body of Gauls invaded the north coast of Spain, and established themselves there, the province of Gallicia being named after them.

In this remote age the Gauls led a pastoral life: they painted and tattooed their bodies: their weapons were axes and knives made of stone, and arrows pointed with flint; and they used shields of wood. They styled themselves "Celts," the name "Gaul" being that by which other nations, particularly the Romans, distinguished them. "Ii que linguâ suâ *Celtæ*, nostrâ *Galli* appellantur." (Cæsar, *de Bello Gallico*, book i., ch. i.) They must not be confounded with the people of Iberian origin who inhabited the south of France, and who spoke the Vascon, Gascon, or Basque language, such as the people of Aquitaine, and those south of the Garonne; nor with the Armoricans, or Bretons, in the north, who spoke a language analogous to the modern Welsh, and were of Cimmerian origin. Thierry (*Histoire des Gaulois*, vol. i., introduction,) maintains that the last mentioned language was a dialect of the Celtic or Gaulish, and that the Cimmerians themselves were a branch of the great Celtic race, which came originally from Asia.

Who were the original inhabitants of France?—What is said of the Gauls?—What did they style themselves?—What other races inhabited France?—Who were the Bretons?

SPAIN.

The historians of Spain are not behind those of other nations in claiming immense antiquity for their country. Thus it is asserted that Tubal, the son of Japhet, was the first man that peopled Spain after the flood; and it has been contended by some that he landed in Lusitania, where he founded the city of Setubal; and by others, that he settled in Navarre, where he founded the city of Tudela. It has even been gravely stated that Noah came into Spain, and founded the cities of Noela and Noega! to such extravagances will national zeal carry enthusiastic historians. That this beautiful peninsula was known to the ancients at a very early period, is undoubted. Osiris, the Egyptian, is said to have rescued Spain from the tyranny of Geryon, a stranger who had established himself there, and had founded the cities of Girona and Cadiz. Horus, the son of Osiris, also performed sundry exploits against the children of Geryon, as did Hercules in after times.

The most modern researches have proved that Spain was inhabited by the Iberian race long anterior to the dawn of history. The descendants and language of this people still survive in the Vascon or Basque provinces; and, as we have before observed, some zealous Spaniards have endeavored to prove that the Euascaran or Basque language was originally the language of all mankind. In the 16th century B. C., the Celts, pouring down from the Pyrenees, established themselves in the country north of the Ebro, and, mixing with the Iberians, formed the Celtiberian and Lusitanian nations, and the province of Gallicia took its name from them.

The Celts in Spain were distinguished by the Romans into Neriæ, Præsamarci, and Cileni (Pliny, book iii., ch. i.). They occupied more than half the peninsula. The limits of the territory which they occupied may be represented by a line starting from the frontiers of Gallicia, running along the Ebro to the middle of its course, and then following the Idubedian mountains to the Guadiana. (Thierry, *Histoire des Gaulois*, vol. i., p. 7.) The Iberians forced their way through the south of France into the north of Italy. The Ligurians, whom they found there, are supposed to have been of Iberian origin, as the name is derived from *Li-gora*, an Iberian word signifying "mountaineer."

What do the Spanish historians say of the origin of their nation?—And of the Basque language?—What is said of the Celts?—What became of the Iberians?

GERMANY.

While the Egyptian, Assyrian, and Chinese Empires were flourishing in a high degree of civilization, the north of Europe was a wilderness, covered with immense forests and marshes. The Baltic and Euxine Seas also were more extensive than they now are, and there is reason to believe that at a very remote period they overspread the whole of the country now lying between them. It appears probable that the ancient Iberian race were the first inhabitants of Central Europe, but at a period far beyond the range of history. They were gradually dispossessed and driven out by the Gauls, a race originating in Central Asia, who by degrees spread themselves over Scythia, Asia Minor, Thrace, Germany, and France. At what epoch in the world's history this vast movement occurred, we are as yet ignorant. In the 16th century before our era, a division of the same race, which has since been denominated *Celtic*, emerged from Asia, and passed through Russia, Poland, and Germany, on their way to France, planting colonies or settlements as they passed. Another division made their way, under leadership of the three sons of Bor, viz., Wile, We, and Odin, into the far north. These leaders were afterwards deified and worshipped. Fifteen centuries subsequently another chief of the Scythians assumed the name of Odin, and founded an empire in Sweden. Of him we shall speak when we come to treat of the history of Sweden in the first century before the Christian Era. It is this last-mentioned Odin, and his two sons, Thor and Balder, who became the popular heroes and deities of Northern Europe.

The Gauls, who settled in Germany, were the progenitors of those tribes on whom were subsequently engrafted the Cimbri and Teutons, the ancestors of the German people. Of the progress of the Celts or Gauls, notice has been already taken in the columns devoted to France, Spain, and Italy. The student who desires full information on the earliest known and subsequent history of the Celts as a race, is referred to Thierry's *Histoire des Gaulois*, a very learned and valuable work, and to a popular treatise on the same subject by Ritson (*Memoirs of the Celts or Gauls*), which, however, is not always reliable, especially in regard to ancient geography.

What was the condition of Germany in the most ancient times?—Of the Celtic invasion?—Of Odin and his three sons?—Of a second Odin?—Of the history of the Celts?

THE 15TH CENTURY

EGYPT.

There is evidence that forty-three nations owned the sway of Amenophis-Memnon. The celebrated statue which is said by the Greeks to have emitted musical sounds at sunrise, and was called by them "the statue of Memnon," was erected in honor of him. At his death the repressed fanaticism of the Amonians burst forth with tenfold violence, and Egypt was once more convulsed with a religious civil war. His immediate successor was Horus, who appears to have been heir to the throne, but did not acknowledge that he was the son of Amenophis. He styles himself the son of Thothmosis; from which we may infer that he was a fierce enemy of the disc or sun-worshippers, and disapproved of the tolerance shown to them by his father and grandfather. He persecuted the sun-worshippers, and destroyed the works of his grandfather at Karnak. He constructed many fine temples, and was worshipped as a god during his lifetime. The lists assign to the reign of Horus a duration of 36 or 37 years, but there are no monumental data wherewith to verify or contradict it. The German arrangement of the chronology makes Horus the last monarch of the 18th dynasty. Mr. Osburn (*Monumental History of Egypt*, vol. ii., ch. vi.) supposes that Ramessu, the son and successor of Horus, should be considered the last of that line of kings. A review of the condition of Egypt under the 18th dynasty, will show that it is characterized by great national aggrandizement, extensive intercourse with foreigners, and increase of public and private wealth. Corn, which Egypt produced in abundance, appears to have been the principal article of export. And notwithstanding domestic broils and religious discussions, the arts rose to a high state of development. The decorations of the royal palaces appear to have been gorgeous in the extreme; and we may gather from the representations on the monuments that the Pharaohs of Egypt maintained a large collection of rare and fierce animals, such as lions, panthers, leopards, giraffes, gazelles, antelopes, and apes. Probably the savage animals were kept for purposes of hunting.

Ramessu, or Rameses, the son of Horus, was reckoned the founder of the 19th dynasty, but the reason for this does not distinctly appear. It may have been on account of the services he rendered to Egypt by expelling the sun-worshippers, and conquering Middle Egypt, which henceforth became a portion of the dominions of the Theban Pharaohs. His reign was short, not much more than a year and a half. He was succeeded by his son, Sethos I. This monarch appears to have been actuated by the same hatred of the sun-worshippers as his father, for he defaced the inscriptions of that sect, and wrote his own name over them. His great work was the construction of the vast hall in the palace of Karnak, which is 320 feet long, by 164 feet broad. The stone roof was supported by 134 columns, each 40 feet high, and 27 feet in girth. Through the centre of the hall was a broad avenue, on both sides of which were six pillars, each 66 feet high, and 36 feet in circumference. From the paintings on the walls, it has been inferred that Sethos offered up human sacrifices to the god Amun-Ra. Negro captives appear prominently in them, as they do in those inscriptions of the time of Thothmosis, whence it is evident that the black races of Africa were as distinct from the Egyptians of ancient days as they are from the white races of modern times. It is recorded of him that he invaded Canaan, and defeated the Hittites, Ammonites, and Moabites, and to have made successful war upon the Arabs. The termination of the Xoite kingdom dates from the commencement of the reign of Sethos; and it appears that he forced the inhabitants of the Delta to labor at the quarries and on the great works then in course of erection. Of these he completed the palace-temple at Gournou, in Western Thebes, and his own tomb in the Biban-el-Malook, consisting of a vast series of galleries and halls underground, covered with painted reliefs, representing mythic scenes connected with death and judgment. This famous tomb is known as Belzoni's tomb, from its having been discovered and opened by that unfortunate explorer in the year 1819. The student will find a very interesting account of this discovery in the narrative which Belzoni has given of his travels and explorations in Egypt. The reign of Sethos is said to have lasted fifty-five years. His leading characteristic appears to have been fanatical exclusiveness for the worship of Amun: he made all the rest of the gods mere priests and ministers of this his favorite idol.

What is said of the statue of Amenophis?—For what was the reign of Horus remarkable?—What was the condition of Egypt under the 18th dynasty?—Who founded the 19th?—What is said of Sethos I.?—What else is recorded of him?—And of his tomb?—What celebrated traveller explored it?

SYRIA.

On the death of Moses, Joshua, whom he had appointed to carry out the conquest of the land of Canaan, and to locate the tribes of Israel therein, assumed the leadership of the Hebrews. The details of the conquest of Canaan by the combined forces of the twelve tribes of Israel, will be found in the Book of Joshua. The war lasted nearly seven years; during which time, the seven nations of Canaan, viz., the Canaanites (properly so called), the Amorites, the Hittites, the Hivites, the Girgasites, the Perizzites, and the Jebusites, were entirely subdued, though not extirpated; and thirty-one kings fell under the sword. The conquered land was partitioned and allotted to the twelve tribes: those of Reuben, Gad, and half of Manassah, receiving portions on the east of Jordan — those of the other half of Manassah, of Dan, Naphthali, Zebulun, Issachar, Ephraim, Dan, Benjamin, Simeon, and Judah, receiving portions on the west. The tribe of Levi, being set apart for the priesthood, were allotted their portion, not in land, but in tithes, or tenths of the yearly produce of the land; however, forty-eight cities, each with a domain of between 800 and 900 acres, were bestowed upon them. The newly-formed republic remained at peace with external foes during the life of Joshua. After his death, Joshua not having appointed a successor to the supreme authority, the separate republics, under the control of their own chieftains and other local officers, assumed the administration of their own affairs respectively.

We now come to the heroic age of Hebrew history. The imperfect conquest of the country, for many of the ancient inhabitants had been allowed to remain, left many troublesome enemies within its borders, and the Israelites had also powerful adversaries around them. Several wars ensued, in which the Hebrews gained the advantage; but, from intermarrying with their enemies, they were led into apostasy to the national religion, and hence fell under the power of the neighboring nations. Chu'shan Rishatha'im, king of Assyria, subdued the land, and remained master of it for eight years. At the expiration of this period, Othniel, the nephew of Caleb, of the tribe of Judah, drove out the invaders. The land then had rest for forty years (Judges iii. 11). It was next assailed by a confederacy of the Ammonites, Amalekites, and Moabites, under Eglon, king of Moab, who once more inflicted foreign domination upon it. This oppression lasted eighteen years, and was terminated by Ehud, a hero of the tribe of Benjamin, who assassinated Eglon, and expelled the Moabites. After this exploit there was peace for eighty years (Judges iii. 30).

The personages styled *Soph'etim* (or "Judges"), such as Othniel, Ehud, and others who came after them and delivered Israel from oppression, appear, says Milman (*History of the Jews*, vol. i., p. 188), as gallant insurgents, or guerilla leaders, rather than as grave administrators of justice, or the regular authorities of a great kingdom. The office of the Hebrew "Judge" was rather that of a military dictator, raised on an emergency to the command of the national forces. What his judicial functions were, seems very doubtful; nor do we find him exercising authority, or even engaged in war, beyond the boundaries of his own tribe; except in the case of Deborah, who sat under her palm-tree judging the tribes of Israel (Judges iv. 4, 5). Yet even in this case, the convention here mentioned bears the appearance rather of an organized warlike confederacy, to break the yoke of the Canaanites, than of a peaceful judicial assembly: and some of the tribes took no part in the great enterprize projected by the prophetess. The want of union among the people, and the dissoluteness of their manners, are fearfully displayed in certain occurrences which took place "in those days when there was no king in Israel." We allude to the tragedy described in the 19th chapter of the Book of Judges, which produced a civil war, and almost caused the extermination of the tribe of Benjamin (Judges xx.). The mode in which the national loss was repaired is as remarkable as the vengeance taken on the unhappy Benjaminites, but finds a parallel in the conduct of the founders of Rome toward the Sabine women. The city of Jabesh, in Gilead, was devoted to destruction, the men slaughtered, and the women were given to the survivors of the tribe of Benjamin, who were also allowed to carry off the damsels dancing at a festival outside of the gates of Shiloh (Judges xxi. 21–23). The remark of the author of the Book of Judges, "every man did that which was right in his own eyes," (xxi. 25), is a proof of the sad state of the nation.

Who conquered Canaan?—Where is the history of the conquest to be found?—How long did the war last?—What became of the tribe of Levi?—What happened after the death of Joshua?—Who was Othniel?—Ehud?—What were the functions of the "Judges"?—What was done to the tribe of Benjamin?

INDIA.

The authors of the Vedas, though they ascended beyond the early worship of the elements, and the powers of nature, to a knowledge of the real character of the Divinity, and, though anxious to diffuse their own doctrines, did not disturb the popular belief; but, actuated either by their characteristic respect for immemorial usage, or, perhaps, by a regard for the interests of the priesthood (from which the most enlightened Brahmin seems never to have been free), they permitted the worship of the established gods to continue, representing them as so many forms or symbols of the real Divinity. At the same time, they erected no temple and addressed no worship to the true God. The consequence was such as was to be expected from the weakness of human nature: the obvious and palpable parts of their religion prevailed over the more abstruse and more sublime: the ancient polytheism (or, system of many deities,) kept its ground, and was further corrupted by the introduction of deified heroes, who have, in their turn, superseded the deities from whom they were supposed to derive their divinity (Elphinstone's *History of India*, vol. i., p. 164). Thus the theism (or, belief in one God,) inculcated by the Vedas as the true faith, in which all other forms were included, has been supplanted by a system of gross polytheism and idolatry; and, though nowhere entirely forgotten, is never steadily thought of, except by philosophers and divines. The Hindoos are, to a certain extent, believers in the existence of a Supreme Being, from whom all others derive their existence, or rather, of whose substance they are composed; for, according to the modern belief, the universe and the Deity are one and the same. But their devotion is directed to a variety of gods and goddesses, of whom it is impossible to fix the number. Some accounts, with the usual Hindoo extravagance, make the deities amount to three hundred and thirty millions; but most of these are ministering angels in the different heavens, or other spirits who have no individual name or character, and who are counted by the million (Elphinstone, as above). We shall, in the next century, give a sketch of the Hindoo mythology, which has been modified into its present form by the Institutes of Menu and the Puranas.

What is said of the authors of the Vedas?—Of their mode of dealing with the national religion?—Of the fate of their system?—Of the modern belief and mythology of Hindoos?

ASSYRIA.

The following names of kings occur in this century:

Sparetus, who died	1490
Ascatades, reigned	1490 to 1450
Amyntas, "	1450 " 1405
Belochus, "	1405 " 1380

As regards the religious system of the ancient Assyrians, the knowledge which we have hitherto been able to derive from the inscriptions is hardly sufficient to enable us to speak with certainty. Mr. Layard observes (*Nineveh and Babylon*, p. 512), that all we can now venture to infer is, that the Assyrians worshipped one Supreme God, as the great national deity, under whose immediate and special protection they lived, and their empire existed. The name of this god appears to have been Asshur, as nearly as can be determined at present from the inscriptions. It was identified with that of the empire itself, which was always called "the country of Asshur"; it entered into those of both kings and private persons, and was also applied to particular cities. To this allusion is made in Genesis x. 11, 12: "Out of that land (Shinar, or Mesopotamia,) went forth Asshur, and builded Nineveh, and the city Rehoboth, and Calah, and Resen, between Nineveh and Calah; the same is a great city." With Asshur, but apparently far inferior to him in the celestial hierarchy, although called "the great gods", were the twelve other deities, whose names have already been given. These twelve gods may possibly be identified with the Greek deities. They may also have presided over the twelve months of the year, and the vast number of inferior gods, which in one inscription is stated to be four thousand, and over the days of the year, the celestial bodies, and the various phenomena of nature. The Supreme God is sometimes represented under a triune (or, three in one) form, the inferior deities being originally mere names for external things, or symbols and myths. Although in the most ancient and uncorrupted age accepted as such by the ignorant multitude, their true meaning became lost, except to the priests by whom they were turned into a mystery. Asshur is generally typified by a winged figure in a circle: the circle representing infinity, having neither beginning nor end; the wings being emblems of the love and wisdom with which he watched over all things.

What is said of the religion of the ancient Assyrians?—What was the name of their supreme deity?—How was he typified?—How many inferior deities were there?

PERSIA.

We extract the following note from Malcolm's *History of Persia* (vol. i., p. 202), as containing useful information concerning the ancient languages of Persia:

"We are informed, by what are deemed the best Persian authorities, that, when the Arabs invaded that country, they found three languages: the Farsee, Deri, and Pehlivi; from one or other of which, all the various dialects now spoken in Persia are derived. There were, according to some authors, seven languages in Persia; but the Herowee, the Suckzee, the Zawulee, and the Suodee (now obsolete), appear to have been mere vulgar dialects: they were never written: and Moullah Mohammed Saaduck (in whose introduction to a dictionary of the ancient Fars there is a short account of the former languages of Persia,) asserts that 'a word from any of these tongues would have destroyed a stanza.' The Pars, or Farsee, is still (though much mixed with Arabic since the Mohammedan conquest,) the general language of the kingdom. The Deri, we are told, was a polished language, spoken in some of the principal cities of the Empire, and believed by some to have been the Court dialect during the period of the Kaianian dynasty. The word Deri implies eloquent, and is meant to express that in which there is no imperfection. As a proof of the sweetness and elegance of this dialect, we have a tradition from Mohammedan authors, that their prophet declared, that if God had a mandate (command) to issue, which was to proclaim his goodness and mercy, he would deliver it in a gentle tone, and in the Deri language; but when he speaks in wrath, he uses the Arabic tongue. They assert, on the same authority, that Deri and Arabic are the only languages spoken in Paradise. The third language is the Pehlivi, a word to which many meanings have been assigned; but the most probable conjecture is, that it was derived from Pehleh, the ancient name of the countries of Isfahan, Rho', and Doonaw'ar. The Zund is the holy language in which the Zend-a-vesta of Zoroaster is written; and his followers affirm that it can only be known to God, angels, prophets, and enlightened priests. The sacred volume is in this language, but has a Pehlivi translation annexed."

What languages prevailed in Persia at the time of the Arab conquest?—Which is the general language of the kingdom?—What is said of the Deri?—Of the Pehlivi?

CHINA.

The reigns of the Emperors of the Shang dynasty, which are recorded in this century, partake of the same inglorious character as those of the preceding one. The names of the reigning monarchs are:

	B. C.	B. C.
Tsoo-sin . . .	1506	to 1490
Wuh-kea . .	1490	" 1465
Tsoo-ting . .	1465	" 1433
Yang-kea . .	1433	" 1408
Pwan-kang . .	1408	" 1401
Seaou-sin . .	1401	" 1373

It appears that the authority of the Emperor had become reduced almost to a cipher by the mandarins and tributary lords of the different provinces; and the unhappy people were bowed to the earth by the most remorseless tyranny on the part of these turbulent and oppressive feudatories. The first four of the above-mentioned Emperors made few attempts to restrain the proceedings of these petty tyrants. But Pwan-kang was a man of a different stamp: he made a desperate effort to crush the insolence of the mandarins, and to free the people from constant oppression. He removed the capital from Ho-nan, whither it had been removed by his predecessor, Chung-tang, a century and a half previously, and transferred it to the Yin district, in the same province. He also changed the name of the dynasty from Shang to Yin, but notwithstanding this arbitrary alteration, the dynasty is not remembered in Chinese annals by any other name than its original one of Shang (or "supreme"). Pwan-kang had considerable difficulty in reconciling the nation to these changes, although they were intended for its benefit; nor is it easy for us, in the present age, to understand how the mere change of the locality of the Court could have had much effect in repressing the turbulence of the numerous chieftains whose depredations extended over the whole Empire. The province of Ho-nan (*i. e.*, "south of the river") is extremely fertile, and is sometimes called Chung-Hwa (or, "the middle flower"). Kai fung-fu, the capital, is the most ancient city in China. It was there that Fo-hi, the first Emperor, resided. The Empire was divided into eighteen provinces, which received their final organization in the reign of Kien-lung (1736 -1796 A. C.). (Williams's *Middle Kingdom*, vol. i., ch. ii.)

What Emperors reigned during this century?—What is said of Pwan-kang?—Of the province of Ho-nan?—Of the ancient city, Kai-fung-fu?—Of the eighteen provinces?

GREECE.

Attica.—Of Cran'aus, the successor of Erysich'thon, few particulars are known. The ancient inhabitants of Attica were sometimes called Cran'ai, after him. He was dethroned by Amphic'tyon, who, in his turn, was expelled by Erichtho'nius, the same person, apparently, as Erechtheus. These violent changes prove that the people were still in a savage state. Erichthonius is represented to have been the pupil and favored companion of Minerva, and he placed in the Acropolis of Athens the original Palla'dium, or wooden statue of that goddess. He also instituted the festival of the Pan'athenæ'a in her honor; which festival was observed for many ages. Among other things related of him is that he was the first person who taught the art of breaking in horses to the yoke, and who drove a chariot and four (Grote, *History of Greece*, vol. i., p. 196). In the time of Pandi'on, who succeeded Erichthonius, Diony'sius (Bacchus), and Deme'ter (Ceres), both came into Attica. In this myth we may recognize the fact that the cultivation of corn and of the vine came into general use; and rites were instituted in honor of those two deities, especially at Eleu'sis. Pandion had two sons, and two daughters, Procne and Philome'la, of whom are related one of the celebrated tales of Ancient Greece. Procne was married to Te'reus, king of Thrace, who was guilty of violence to Philomela. In revenge, the two sisters murdered Itys, the son of Tereus, and served him up as a meal to his father. For this combination of crimes the three were changed by the gods into birds: Procne into a swallow, Philomela into a nightingale, and Tereus into a hoopoe. (Ovid's *Metamorphoses*, 6; Thucydides, b. ii., 29.)

Sparta, Lacedæ'mon, or Laco'nia.—The earliest names we meet with in the early history of this afterwards illustrious State, are those of Lelex and his wife, Cleochari'a. From them descended Euro'tas, and from him a daughter, Sparta, who became the wife of Lacedæmon, fabled to have been the son of Jupiter and Tayg'ete, the daughter of Atlas. In this manner the Greeks were accustomed to blend the mythical with the real. Amyclas, the son of Lacedæmon, had two sons, Cynor'tas and Hyacin'thus—the latter a beautiful youth, the favorite of Apollo, by whose hand he was accidentally killed while playing at quoits: *i. e.*, he was struck down by a sun-stroke while exerting himself in the game. In after ages the Lacedæmonians observed the festival of the Hyacin'thia, and traced its origin back to this legend; another illustration of the mode in which the early history of Greece was moulded to suit the ideal wants of a subsequent age.

Thebes.—This famous city was the capital of Bœo'tia, a province notorious for the deficiency displayed by its inhabitants in intelligence and taste. The origin of this city is connected with some of the most famous of the Greek legends, and merits particular notice. It has been usually attributed to Cadmus, an emigrant from Phœnicia, who led a body of followers thither in quest of his sister Euro'pa, who had been carried off by Jupiter, who assumed the shape of a bull; she had been taken by him to Crete, where she became the mother of the famous Mi'nos, Rhadaman'thus, and Sarpe'don. Cadmus settled in Bœotia, where he founded the city to which he gave the name of Thebes, after the famous one of that name in Egypt. His choice of the site of Thebes was guided by the oracle of Delphi, which directed him to follow a cow, and begin to build where the animal should lie down. Cadmus obeyed the oracle, and came to the fountain of Arei'a, which was guarded by a fierce dragon. The hero killed the monster, and, at the suggestion of Minerva, sowed its teeth in the earth. Thence sprang up armed men, called Sparti, among whom he flung stones, till they began to assault each other, and all were slain except five. For this, Cadmus was sentenced by Jupiter to eight years' servitude; after which he married Harmo'nia, the daughter of Mars and Venus, presenting to her the famous necklace made by Vulcan, which had been given by Jupiter to Europa (from which it may be inferred that Cadmus had found his sister). All the gods came to the Cadmei'a, the citadel of Thebes, to be present at the nuptials of Cadmus and Harmonia, which are highly celebrated in the mythology. The daughters of Cadmus are all illustrious in fable. They will be noticed hereafter. From the five surviving Sparti descended the five great families of Thebes. Cadmus also introduced an alphabet of sixteen letters.

Argos.—This State calls for no particular notice. Lynceus, and his son, Abas, ruled over it: after them, it was divided into two kingdoms.

What were the principal events in the history of Attica during this century?—Of Sparta?—Of Thebes?—Of Argos?—What was the festival of the Panathenæa?—Relate the legend of Philomela.—Of Hyacinthus.—Of Cadmus, and the origin of Thebes.—Of Jupiter and Europa.—Of Harmonia's necklace.

ITALY.

The name "Abori'gines" was, as we have seen, given to the earlier inhabitants of Latium, and that of Latins to the nation which arose out of the conquest of the Priscans by the foreigners, said to have been the Trojan followers of Æne'as in the 11th century B. C. Ancient writers describe the Aborigines as a horde of uncivilized savages: it is probable that they were the same people as the Sicelians, who were gradually driven south into Sicily. The Latins inhabited the portion of Italy called Latium, near the Tiber. Their chief town was Lavin'ium, where was their common sanctuary and council-seat. Their language (subsequently brought to so high a state of refinement, and the parent of the modern languages of Western Europe,) was the same as that of the Oscans originally: but it became mixed with the Pelasgian and the early Greek, and by degrees assumed the form in which it appeared in the later days of the Roman republic. Words relating to agriculture and to the gentler ways of life agree in Latin and Greek, whilst the Latin words for all objects appertaining to war or the chase are utterly alien from the Greek; which, as Niebuhr observes, was probably owing to the Pelasgian origin of the agricultural serfs. Still, the Pelasgian language was a peculiar one: it was not Greek, although it possessed an essential affinity to it, and the Greeks were indebted to the Pelasgians for many things, especially their theology.

The Œnotrians were Pelasgians, and became in after ages the serfs of the Italian Greeks. The cities of Cortona, Cœre, Ravenna, Spine, Pisa, Ardea, Saguntum, Antium, Circeii, Trachina (or Terracina), Pompeii, and Capreæ, were of Pelasgian origin. Traces of Pelasgian names are also found in such words as Acheron'tia, Argyrip'pa, Sipon'tum, and in places along the whole coast of the Adriatic. The Oscans were an equally important part of the ancient population of Italy. They were the same race as the Opicans and the people styled Ausonians by the Greeks. Their original land was in the neighborhood of Beneventum: they spread over Campania and the southern portion of the Peninsula, and were subsequently conquered by the Sabellians. Yet their language became that of their conquerors, and was one of the roots of the Latin tongue. The Ausonians were probably called, in their native language, "Auruni," or "Aurunci"; the Volsces were of this race. Between the Volsces and the Æquians an intimate connection existed. The Faliscans and the Apulians were also Oscans.

The Romans considered the Sabines a tribe, and not a race. They termed them Sabellians, along with the Marsians, Pelignians, Samnites, and Lucanians. Among themselves these tribes were termed Sabini, or Savini; the Greek word Samnites is evidently derived from Savini. Their original home was Amiternum, in the highest parts of the Abruzzi. Thence they issued in very remote times, and drove the Cascans before them in one quarter, and the Umbrians in another. The tradition runs that these colonies were sent out in pursuance of a religious vow, by which, every twenty years, the cattle were sacrificed or redeemed, and the young men compelled to seek employment abroad. We meet with very frequent mention of the Sabines and Samnites in the course of the history of Italy. The Hernicans were most probably Marsians: their name is said to be derived from the Sabine and Marsian word Hernæ, which signifies "rocks." It is probable that all these tribes were only branches of the Oscan stock, for there was an intimate connection between their languages. Niebuhr says of them (*History of Rome*, ch. vi.): "The strictness of their morals, and their cheerful contentedness, were the peculiar glory of the Sabellian mountaineers, particularly of the Sabines and the four northern cantons. In other respects the character of the several tribes was essentially distinct." Divination was practised by them. Most of them lived in open hamlets; but the Samnites dwelt round the summits of their hills, which they fortified. A federal league existed between them, but it was not adhered to strictly. Their want of union was fatal to them. The absence of a predominant capital, and of the unity consequent upon it, were the principal causes of the downfall of the Sabellians.

The Umbrians were a most ancient people of Italy. According to Thierry (*Histoire des Gaulois*, vol. i., p. 9), they were Celts, who organized themselves under the collective name of "Ombra," or "Ambra" (signifying, in Celtic, "valiant," or "noble"), and crossing the Alps, made themselves masters of Northern Italy.

What is said of the Aborigines?—Of the Latins?—Of the Latin language?—Of the influence of the Pelasgians?—Name the Italian cities of Pelasgian origin.—Who were the Œnotrians?—The Oscans?—The Ausonians?—The Volsces and Æquians?—The Sabines, Marsians, and Sabellians?—What is conjectured respecting the Umbrians?

B.C. 1500—1400.

BRITAIN.

No records exist which throw light upon the history of England, Scotland, or Wales, during this early period. But Ireland has traditions which carry her antiquity back even to a more remote age. How much fable and how little truth there are in them, it is not easy to determine. The early legends of a nation are, however, always interesting, as illustrating the national genius; and by attentively considering them, the student may find a clue to the explanation of many subsequent events of a dubious character. Thus the genius of Greece is powerfully manifested in her mythology and heroic legends: the modern characteristics of the Oriental nations — China, India, Persia—are manifested in their ancient books. So is it with the legends of Ireland, in which there is an undoubted admixture of truth. The bardic historians of that country begin with a purely fabulous personage, named Cesa′ra, a niece of Noah, who, a few weeks *before* the Flood, arrived in Ireland with an antediluvian colony! We are not told whether the Flood extended to her settlements; but the bards say that after her, at different intervals, five or six bands of adventurers colonized the island. About the fourth century after the Flood, Ireland was invaded and conquered by a chief of the race of Japheth, named Par′tholan, who, "landing at Imbersceine, in Kerry, the 14th day of May, on a Wednesday," fixed his residence on an island named Inis-Samer, in the River Erne, in Ulster. Romantic stories are told of Partholan, all of which may be found in Keating's *General History of Ireland*, a work which contains all the fables that the lively fancy of the Irish people has invented respecting their own history. After holding possession of the country for 300 years, the race of Partholan were all swept away by a plague; and the hill of Howth, then called Ben-Heder, was the scene of the most awful ravages of this pestilence. To this colony succeeded another (about the time of the patriarch Jacob), who were called, from their leader, Nemedians, and are said to have come from the shores of the Euxine: they were probably Gauls or Celts. They waged war with those African or Phœnician pirates called Fomorians, and their exploits are favorite topics with the ancient Irish bards. (Moore's *History of Ireland*, v. i., p. 75.)

What is said of the study of national legends?—What is the earliest fable respecting Ireland?—Who was Partholan?—Who were the Nemedians?—The Fomorians?

FRANCE.

In the absence of historical information respecting this period of the history of France, we may turn our attention to the religion and manners of the Celts. They were extremely superstitious and cruel, and resorted to human sacrifices to propitiate their deities. In their public religious ceremonies they prepared huge frames of osier twigs, into which they put men alive, and, setting fire to them, burnt the wretched victims, who were, however, mostly criminals. Impaling on stakes was another favorite torture with them. Their deities had a strong resemblance to those of the Greeks. The names of some of them have been preserved. Teuta′tes (Mercury) was the favorite deity: he was the inventor of all arts, the patron of commerce, and the guide and protector of travellers. He′sus was the god of war: Tar′anis was the king of heaven: a deity styled "the Scythian maid" resembled Diana in her attributes (to her shipwrecked strangers were immolated). That Teutates was identical with Mercury is evident from a passage in Livy (*Romanæ historiæ*, b. xxvi., ch. xliv.): "Near New Carthage, in Spain, was a mount called Mercurius Teutates." This same god was also worshipped by the Phœnicians, under the name of Taau′tus, and by the Egyptians under that of Thoth (Huet's *History of the Commerce of the Ancients*, ch. 7, 8, 47). It is supposed also that he was worshipped by the Germans under the name of Theuth, whence they were called Teu′tones, or Teutons. Their priests were Druids; and Druidism was prevalent among them, not only in France, but in Spain, England, and especially in Ireland; whence their Oriental origin is undoubted. Great doubt exists as to the origin of the term "Druid." Some have derived it from the Greek word *drus*, "an oak": others from the ancient British word, *deruidhon*, "wise men": or from the British words, *derw*, "an oak," and *hud*, "an incantation." A more probable derivation is from the ancient Irish word *Draoid*, "a cunning man." In the Irish version of the Bible this term is used in place of the words "wise men," and magicians"; as in Matthew ii. 1: "The Druids came from the East"; and in Exodus vii. 11: "The Druids of Egypt did in like manner with their enchantments." Their favorite tenet was the transmigration of the soul.

What is said of the religion of the Celts?—Name their principal deities.—What Greek deities do they resemble?—Whence is the name "Druid" derived?—What does it mean?

SPAIN.

The conquest of the country by the Celts had a permanent result: the victors remained the predominant race until subjugated in after times by the Carthaginians. Their history prior to the invasion of the land by the latter is very obscure. The Spanish historian, Mariana, devotes a chapter to an account of the fabulous kings of Spain (*History of Spain*, ch. iii.), from which it would appear that he really believed in a great portion of it. We have already alluded to the legends respecting Tubal and Geryon, Osiris and Horus. The dismal conflict in chronology respecting the eras of these personages is sufficient to invalidate the whole narrative. The Geryon mentioned by the Greeks in "the labors of Hercules," cannot have been the person mentioned by Mariana, as the first undoubted king of Spain, for the historical Hercules lived in the 13th century B. C. The introduction of Osiris into the story is a mistake; but that the Egyptian king, Horus, may have sent an expedition into Spain, is not improbable, though no record of it is found in the Egyptian inscriptions. Mariana confounds him with Hercules, and says that, having slain the three sons of Geryon in single combat, "in the island of Cadiz," Hercules (or Horus) caused vast stones and other materials to be cast into the sea at the mouth of the straits, now called the Straits of Gibraltar; and raised two mounds, known by the name of "the pillars of Hercules": that on the Spanish side being called Calpe; that on the African side, A′byla. All things being thus settled, Horus appointed His′palus king of Spain, and then visited Italy. It is said that the name "Hispania" was derived from this king Hispalus, or from his son Hispa′nus; but this is all bare surmise. Mariana says that on the death of Hispalus, Hercules returned into Spain, where he reigned once more, and lived to a very great age. On his death he was deified, and temples were raised to his honor. It is singular that the Celtic Hercules is described by the Roman author, Lucian, as a decrepid old man, with a very grey beard and wrinkled countenance, drawing after him a multitude of men all tied by the ears. This agrees with the Spanish historian's account: but then the Celtic Hercules must be a different personage altogther from the famous Greek hero.

Was the conquest of Spain by the Celts permanent?—What is said of its legends?—Of Geryon, Horus, and Hercules?—Of the pillars of Hercules?—Of the god of that name?

GERMANY.

From the remotest antiquity down to modern times, the Germans have been divided into tribes and nations, and have never been united by any strong bond. The authentic history of the country does not commence long prior to the first century before Christ; but we have accounts of the occasional outpourings of the various Germanic tribes into other countries, as Greece, Italy, Gaul, Asia Minor. Notice of these incursions will be found in the histories of those countries.

Pliny divides the Germans into three great tribes, viz., the *Ingæ′vones*, the *Hermi′ones*, and the *Istæ′vones*. He places the first of these on the North Sea, the second in the interior of Germany, and the third on the Rhine. He also mentions two other great German nations: the Vendili on the Baltic, and the Peucini on the Danube, in Hungary. These ancient names were lost amid the migrations of the tribes: the Ingævones were subsequently known as Saxons, the Istævones as Franks, and the Hermiones as Goths.

The German tribes have likewise been divided by some authors into *Suevi* and *Non-Suevi* (or High and Low Dutch). Under the denomination of Suevi are comprehended the Suevi, Alemanni, Bavarians, Burgundians, Goths, Alans, Vandals, Gepidæ, all of whom were originally wandering shepherd tribes, consisting of nobles, freemen, and slaves. The Non-Suevi consisted of the Franks, Saxons, Lombards, Thuringians, and Frieslanders, who first practised husbandry, had settled dwellings, and were divided into three classes: one of freemen, the other two of bondsmen, termed Lazzi and Slavi, or Servi. The ancient name "Suev" is still to be traced in the words Sweden, Swabia, Switzerland, which countries were originally peopled by the Suevi. This division is not irreconcilable with those adopted by the Roman historians.

The name "German" is derived from the Latin word *Germanus*, "a brother": its root is in the Persian word *Irman*, "a guest, or companion-in-arms"; but it has been derived from several German words, as *ger*, "a lance", *mann*, "a man"; *heer*, "an army"; *ehre*, "honor"; *gewehr*, "security". All these derivations point to one fact, viz., the high estimation in which honor and valor were held among these rude tribes. The word Celt is supposed to mean "hero", and Cimmerii, "warriors".

When does the authentic history of Germany begin? — How does Pliny classify the Germans? —What tribes were Suevi?—Non-Suevi?—Whence the name German?—Celt?

EGYPT.

The successor of Sethos was Ramses, or Rameses II. His name, written at full length, is Ra-me-rois-sotp-ra, shortened and corrupted by the Greeks into Sesos′tris, the greatest king of Egypt, and the hero of her traditional history. The name of this monarch occurs on the monuments more frequently than that of any other. The number of kings who have inscribed their names on monuments, from the foundation of the monarchy to the Macedonian conquest (in the 4th century B. C.), is 150. The memorials of the reign of Sesostris-Ramses exceed in number those of the whole of them collectively. Different accounts of this renowned monarch have come down to us. In addition to what has been ascertained from the inscriptions, we have the history of him from the great Greek historian, Herod′otus of Halicarnas′sus, who visited Egypt about 440 B. C.; from Diodo′rus Sic′ulus, who was in Egypt about 40 B. C.; and from the Roman historian, Tacitus, who furnishes us with an account of what had been seen and heard there during the visit of Germanicus, the nephew of Tiberius, to that country A. C. 19 (*Annales*, book ii.). We are told that on the birth of Sesostris, his father collected together all the male children who were born on the same day throughout Egypt, and caused them to be brought up under the same roof with him. Their food, studies, and pastimes were all in common, and they were specially trained to the use of arms. This practice appears to have existed in Egypt long before the time of Sesostris. When that prince arrived at manhood he was sent by his father to conquer Lybia (*i. e.*, Western Africa), which task he accomplished. He next made successful war upon the Nubians and the Idumæan Arabs; all which exploits are recorded on the monuments. He built ships of war on the Red Sea: with them he sailed down the entire length of it, subduing the nations that inhabited its coasts. He then entered the Erythræ′an Sea (the Indian Ocean), and pursued his career of conquest along its shores. He returned to Egypt with a vast troop of prisoners. On his arrival at the city of Daphne, on the Nile, he was welcomed by his brother, whom he had appointed viceroy of Egypt during his absence; but while he and his sons were banqueting, the palace was surrounded with faggots, and set on fire. Two of his sons flung themselves into the burning mass; and, over their bodies, Sesostris and the rest of his family rushed through the flames and escaped. Having punished the conspirators, he devoted himself to the construction of ornamental and useful works. The Greek historians inform us that Sesostris set out with an army of 600,000 footmen, 240,000 horsemen, and 27,000 war-chariots, to conquer the world: that he subdued Æthiopia, all Asia from the Red Sea to the mouths of the Ganges, and thence pursued his conquests through Tartary to the Don, overran Thrace, where he nearly lost his army through famine, and thence returned to Egypt. This expedition occupied nine years. The manifest exaggerations on the part of these historians, destroy the credibility of the narrative. They were led astray by the grossly false representations of the Egyptian priests. It should be remembered, too, that the earliest of these histories (that of Herodotus,) was written 1000 years after the death of Sesostris, and the latest (that of the Roman author, Tacitus), 1500 years. Sesostris constructed the new palace of Luxor, the Memnonium of Western Thebes, and the great excavation of Amun, at Abou Simbel, and, from the inscriptions in these edifices, it appears tolerably certain that he never was out of Egypt! (Osburn, *Monumental History of Egypt*, vol. ii., p. 486.) What, then, becomes of the tales of the historians? Sesostris, moreover, dug a number of canals and channels for fertilizing the country, and built in every city a temple to the god that was principally worshipped there. In all these constructions he employed captives, and not Egyptians. He subdued Lower Egypt, and fortified the north-eastern frontier against the Arabs; and it may be inferred that his reign was eminently prosperous. The reign of Sesostris lasted sixty-six or sixty-eight years.

His son, Amenephthis, succeeded him. His reign was short: and he was followed by his son, Sethos II., an infant, under the guardianship of the dowager Queen, Thouoris. As Sethos grew up, he became depraved and impious. Mr. Osburn maintains (vol. ii., ch. ix.) that Sethos II. was the Pharaoh who expelled the Israelites, and was drowned in the Red Sea. To us it appears that that event must be referred to an earlier period. With Sethos II. ended the 18th dynasty.

Who was the successor of Sethos I.?—What is the commonly-received name of Rameses?—What historians have given an account of him?—When did they respectively write?—What were the principal events of his reign?—What is said of his exploits?—Who was his successors?—What is said of Sethos II.?

SYRIA.

The next oppression suffered by the Israelites was that inflicted on them by the Philistines, on which occasion, Shamgar, the son of An′ath, acted the part of a deliverer. He is said to have slain 600 of the enemy with an ox-goad (Judges iii. 31), which was a strong pike, eight feet long, and pointed with iron. The Canaanites in the north had now become a powerful people. Jabin, their king, held his court at Hazor, on the Samach′onite Lake, whence he sent armies to oppress the Israelites. Under the command of Sis′era, these armies subdued the country, and kept it in subjection for twenty years. A deliverer at length appeared in the prophetess Deb′orah, the wife of Lapidoth, of the tribe of Ephraim. She at that time acted as the Judge of Israel (Judges iv. 4). Having formed a plan for the deliverance of her country, she commanded the northern tribes of Israel to assemble, and confided the conduct of the expedition to Barak, the son of Abin′oam, of the tribe of Naphtali. The Israelites were drawn up on the summit of Mount Tabor: thence they descended, and poured suddenly on the army of the Canaanites. The latter were completely routed, and nearly destroyed. Sisera took refuge in the tent of Jael, a woman of the Kenite tribe (the descendants of Hobab, the brother-in-law of Moses). She received him hospitably; but, during his sleep, she killed him by driving a tent-nail through his head. For this deed she was declared "blessed above women", in the hymn of triumph of Deborah and Barak (Judges v.). The proper rhythmical form of this celebrated hymn is not preserved in the English translation of the Bible, but it will be found in Milman's *History of the Jews*, vol. i., pp. 194–197. Another interval of rest of forty years' duration then elapsed before a new enemy appeared. The frequent use of the number forty in Scripture is very striking, and leads us to the belief that it was intended to represent a long, rather than a definite, period. Thus, the flood is said to have been forty days upon the earth. Moses was forty years old when he fled into Midian: he was twice forty (80) when he led Israel out of Egypt: he was thrice forty (120) when he died: the Israelites were forty years in the wilderness: the land had rest for forty years after the exploits of Othniel, and twice forty after that of Ehud; half of forty before the time of Deborah, and forty afterwards: Jesus was forty days in the wilderness: and so on, in many other instances.

We next read of the oppression of the children of Israel by the Midianites, who appear to have been masters of Palestine for seven years. This number, seven, performs as important a part in Jewish history as the number forty. In ancient times, mysterious power was attributed to certain numbers, viz., 3, 4, 7, 9, 12, and 40, from their supposed correspondence with the divine attributes and the powers of nature; and the Jews were not behind the other nations of antiquity in their belief in mystic relationships. This time, the deliverance of Israel from their oppressors was effected by Gideon, the son of Joash, of the tribe of Manasseh. He was one of the most illustrious of the ancient Hebrew warriors. His first exploit was the overthrow of the altar of Baal, or Bel, in the city of Ophrah, for which the citizens demanded his punishment: but his father replied, "Jerub-baal" (*i. e.*, let Baal plead for himself); and Gideon escaped. He was thence called Jerub-baal. Having assembled a force of 22,000 men, he advanced against the enemy, who were encamped on the plain of Jezreël. There he, at the head of 300 chosen followers, each provided with a trumpet, a lamp, and a pitcher, attacked the Midianites in the night, and threw them into confusion. Their whole army took to flight, and was cut to pieces by the rest of Gideon's troops (Judges vi., vii., viii.). The barbarism of the age is shown in the treatment of the town of Succoth, which had refused refreshment to the soldiers of Gideon. The elders of the city were scourged to death with thorns: the inhabitants of Penuel were put to the sword: and the Midianitish princes, Zeba and Zalmunneh, were likewise put to death. The enemy lost 120,000 men by the brilliant victory at Jezreël. The Israelites, out of gratitude, offered to Gideon royal authority, which he declined accepting; but he asked for the golden trinkets which they had taken from the enemy, and with these he made an ephod, or priestly garment, and set up, in his native city, a place of worship distinct from that in Shiloh. Again "the country had quietness forty years in the days of Gideon" (Judges viii. 28).

What is said of Shamgar?—Of Deborah and Barak?—Of Jabin?—Of Sisera and Jael?—Of the number 40, as used in the Bible?—And of other mystic numbers?—Who was Gideon?—Whence the name Jerub-baal?—Relate the particulars of his great exploit at Jezreël, his cruelty, and his idolatry.

INDIA.

The following seventeen are the principal deities of the Hindoo mythology, the only ones universally recognized as exercising distinct and divine functions, and therefore entitled to worship, viz.:

1. Brahma, the creating principle;
2. Vishnu, the preserving principle;
3. Siva, the destroying principle; with their corresponding female divinities, who are mythologically regarded as their wives, but, metaphysically, as the active powers which develop the principle represented by each member of the triad, viz.:
4. Sereswa′ti, goddess of learning and eloquence.
5. Laksh′mi, goddess of abundance and fortune.
6. Parva′ti, called also De′vi, Bhava′ni, or Dur′ga; she is represented as a fury, delighting in carnage and lust.

Then there are:

7. Indra, god of the air and of the heavens.
8. Varu′na, god of the waters.
9. Pava′na, god of the wind.
10. Agni, god of fire.
11. Ya′ma, god of the infernal regions and judge of the dead.
12. Cuve′ra, god of wealth.
13. Car′tikeia, god of war.
14. Ca′ma, god of love.
15. Su′rya, god of the sun.
16. Soma, god of the moon.
17. Gane′sa, the remover of difficulties, who presides over the entrances to all edifices, and is invoked at the commencement of all undertakings.

To these may be added the planets, and many sacred rivers, especially the Ganges, which is personified as a female divinity, and honored with every sort of worship and reverence.

We have already stated that Brahma, Vishnu, and Siva, are three manifestations of the Supreme Deity. Of Brahma, the separate worship is now neglected: there is but one temple to him in India, though he once had preëminence. But Vishnu and Siva, with their various incarnations, now attract almost all the religious veneration of the Hindoos: the relative importance of each is eagerly supported by numerous votaries; and there are heterodox sects of great variety, which maintain the supreme divinity of each, to the entire exclusion of his rival (Elphinstone, *History of India*, vol. i., b. ii.). Of the incarnations of Vishnu and Siva we will speak further on.

Which are the principal deities of the Hindoos?—What other objects are worshipped?—What is the present state of Brahma worship?—Of the votaries of Vishnu and Siva?

ASSYRIA.

Continuing our list of kings, as extracted from the fragmentary history handed down to us by the Greek historians, we find the names of:

	B. C.		B. C.
Belo′chus . .	1405	to	1380
Bellepa′res . .	1380	"	1348
Lam′prides . .	1348	"	1316
Sosa′res . . .	1316	"	1296

The fragments of Berosus handed down to us by Eusebius and Syncellus from Polyhistor, afford us many of the foregoing particulars of Assyrian history. Berosus states that he obtained his information from many authors, whose works had been preserved in Babylon with great care for 10,215 years (as reported by Diodorus). Ctesias says he had access to these ancient records, and states that thirty Assyrian kings reigned previous to Sardanapalus, during 1300 years. Their names, as given, are evidently Greek in their character: if they have any historical reality, their original Assyrian form must have been transformed by the Greek historians.

The student will find a very learned dissertation on the ancient Assyrian chronology in "*Palmoni*," an *Essay on the Chronographical and Numerical Systems in use among the Ancient Jews*, App. pp. 889–895. The object of the essayist is to prove that the ancient chronologies of the Egyptians, Assyrians, and Persians were constructed on a uniform numerical plan, founded on systems of cycles of lunar and solar years: but space does not admit of our doing more than referring to his curious and interesting researches.

If we may credit the historians of Egypt, Sesostris, king of that country, extended his conquests over the greater part of Asia, and subdued (or, rather, plundered) the Assyrians, Medes, Persians, and Bactrians, and carried off captive vast numbers of them. Furthermore, it is alleged that the expedition against them was undertaken in consequence of their revolt against the yoke imposed on them by Thothmes and Amenophis II., the predecessors of Sesostris, from which it may be inferred that contests between the two nations, Egypt and Assyria, had been of frequent occurrence. The Assyrians avoided allusion, on their monuments, to death and funeral rites; while the Egyptians portrayed them on almost every temple and tomb.

Name the kings who reigned during this century.—What are the authorities for the most ancient history of Assyria?—What is said of the Egyptian invasion?

PERSIA.

This country has no recorded history during this and the succeeding five centuries. We therefore devote the space allotted to it to some further notice of its languages, and also of its antiquities.

The probability is that the languages of Persia, before mentioned, were only different dialects of one tongue. The Zund, which approaches nearest to the Sanscrit, may certainly be deemed the most ancient of these dialects or languages: for in the earliest period of which we have any authentic record, it was the language of the learned and religious. Some of the followers of Zoroaster have ascribed its invention to that prophet; but this is impossible; and the existence of such a belief proves nothing more than that, in his lifetime, it was a language unknown to the vulgar.

The Pehlivi was, according to Ferdosi, the language of the Court in the time of the Kaianian dynasty; and probably for a long period afterwards. It is to be observed that, except the religious works of Zoroaster and others, all the books written in Persia, before the Mohammedan invasion, were in Pehlivi; but we never hear of a Deri manuscript—a fact which makes it evident that this term was only used to signify the most polished spoken dialect of the common language of the country; and it might, in that sense, equally apply to the Pehlivi, as to the Farsi or Persian. The latter term, previous to the Mohammedan invasion, probably meant the language commonly spoken; for even at that period, all the books appear to have been written in Pehlivi. The Farsi or Persian language has been subsequently rendered more copious; and in its present form is so mixed with the Arabic and the Pehlivi, that it is no very easy labor to separate the words that belong to the different languages of which it is constructed (Malcolm, *History of Persia*, vol. i., p. 204, note).

We have already mentioned the division of the people into castes by Giamschid (Jemsheed): the division, however, appears to have been almost inoperative, as no fact is stated in the history of Persia which proves the existence of such a system. The division is recorded in a Pehlivi work, called the Binidad, and in the Shah Namah of Ferdusi; also by the authors of the Burhan Kuttah and the Tarikh Tubree.

What is further said of the languages of Persia?—Of the Zund?—The Pehlivi?—The Deri?—The Farsi?—Of Jemsheed's division of the people into castes?

CHINA.

Pwan-kang reigned 28 years (1401–1373). We have already noticed the principal actions recorded of him. His successor, Seaou-sin, subverted the good institutions which his brother had introduced. He was a prince who lived entirely for his own pleasure, and greatly contributed to hasten the ruin of the country. His successor, Seaou-yih, who ascended the throne in 1352, was also an indolent and worthless prince. But, whilst the Shang dynasty decayed, there arose another, the Chow, which very soon restored the Empire to its former lustre. Koo-kang, the patriarch of his family, who was a descendant of the former Emperors, removed from his native country, Pin, to Ke, in Shense province. His good government attracted crowds of people from all quarters to reside under so wise and lenient a ruler. Koo-kang established regular tribunals to facilitate the affairs of government. All his institutions bespeak his great wisdom, and he was a prince so generally beloved that the whole Empire looked up to him. Within a very short time the number of inhabitants in his newly-founded city amounted to 300,000. It does not appear that he set up any claim to the Imperial throne; but it may be inferred that he exercised regal authority, while the indolent and feeble princes of the Shang dynasty were wasting their lives in the luxury and debauchery of their palaces. That so large a number of persons as 300,000 should have removed to Ke in a short time, proves that the gross misgovernment of the country had rendered the rule of the Emperor in other parts of the Empire intolerable. We shall find very frequent instances in the Chinese annals, of governors of provinces attracting, by their wise administration, large masses of the population to their districts, and thereby acquiring power enough either to set up as an independent sovereign, or as Emperor.

Seaou-yih died B. C. 1324. He was succeeded by Woo-ting, who appears to have been a compound of indolence, superstition, and common sense. He had a wise minister, to whom he entirely entrusted the affairs of the Empire, and withdrew himself from the administration of the government. During this reign the first ambassadors arrived from an unknown country, in order to do homage to "the Son of Heaven" (the Emperor).

Who were the successors of Pwan-kang?—Who was the ancestor of the Chow dynasty? What is said of Koo-kang?—Of Woo-ting?—And the first embassy?

GREECE.

Crete.—We must not omit to notice the kingdom founded on this island by Mi′nos (B. C. 1407). This famous lawgiver was so renowned for his justice that the Greeks believed he became one of the judges in Hades after his death; and that his brother, Rhadaman′thus, was appointed to the like office. The grandson of Minos (named, after him, Minos,) was also a king and lawgiver in Crete, and under him the island became a powerful maritime State. He divided the island into three portions, and reigned nine years. The Cretans traced their legal and political institutions to him. It is of him and his daughter, Pasiph′aë, that the story of the Minotaur is related. The Minotaur was said to be a monster, partly man, partly bull, born of Minos' daughter, Pasiphaë, who concealed him at Cnosus, in a labyrinth built by the architect, Dæ′dalus. About the same time, Minos made war upon Attica and Meg′ara, and compelled these States to send yearly seven youths and seven maidens to be devoured by the Minotaur in the labyrinth. Minos appears to have been more angry with Dædalus for constructing the labyrinth, than with Pasiphaë for harboring the Minotaur. Dædalus fled to Sicily, whither Minos pursued him, and was slain. The monster was killed by the Athenian hero, The′seus, who was enabled to find his way out of the labyrinth by means of a clue given to him by Ariad′ne, the daughter of Pasiphaë. Ariadne fell in love with Theseus, and left Crete with him; but, on their arrival at Naxos, he was forced by Bacchus to leave her. Bacchus then married her. The adventures of Ariadne with Theseus and Bacchus have furnished the ancient poets with fine subjects for their genius. These events are more properly referable to the next century.

Attica.—Erechtheus succeeded his father, Pandion, as king of Athens. In his reign the Eleusinian Mysteries (*i. e.*, festivals and solemnities observed at Eleusis in honor of Ceres and her daughter, Proserpine,) were introduced at Athens by Eumolpus (B. C. 1356). The immediate successors of Erechtheus were Cecrops II. and Pandion II., the latter of whom was expelled by the Me-tion′idæ, or descendants of Me′tion, a son of Erechtheus.

Sparta.—Of this State there is little worthy of notice during this century. Cynortas was succeeded by his son, Perie′res, who married Gorgoph′one, the daughter of Perseus, and had issue, Tynda′reus, Ica′rius, Apha′reus, Leucip′pus, and Hippoc′oön. Tyndareus is an important personage in the Greek mythological legends.

Argos.—Abas, the son and successor of Lynceus, founded the city of Abæ, in Phocis. His sons, Acris′ius and Prætus, divided the kingdom between them. The former had a daughter named Dan′ae, who was kept prisoner in a tower by her father, in consequence of a prediction that her son would destroy him. The fable runs that Jupiter, in the form of a shower of gold, visited her. She became the mother of Per′seus; and in consequence of this, her father put her and her child into a chest, and threw them into the sea. They were rescued by a fisherman named Dictys, and the child lived to become one of the most famous heroes of Greece. His adventures are the subject of many a fable and poem. The chief of his fabulous exploits was the cutting off the head of Medusa, one of the Gorgons, whose countenance was so terrible as to turn all beholders into stone. By means of winged sandals, a magic wallet, and a helmet which rendered him invisible, he accomplished his task. He then went to Ethiopia, which was suffering from an inundation and a sea-monster. To appease Neptune and the latter, Andro′meda, the king's daughter, was chained to a rock, in order to be devoured by the monster; but Perseus slew the beast, and released Andromeda. The princess having been promised to Phineus, the wedding was about to take place, when Perseus quarrelled with the bridegroom, slew him, and carried off the bride. He then returned to Argos, where he accidentally killed his grandfather, Acrisius, and thus realized the prediction. He shared the kingdom with his uncle, Prætus, and founded Myce′næ (B. C. 1313).

Corinth, the original name of which was Ephy′ra, was founded (B. C. 1347) by Sis′yphus, the son of Æolus and Euareta. The Greeks say, that on account of his wickedness in this world, he is punished in Hades by being forced to roll up a hill a huge block of marble, which, as soon as it reaches the top, rolls down again. He instituted the Isthmian games, and was a zealous promoter of commerce and navigation.

Who founded the kingdom of Crete?—What is said of Minos and Rhadamanthus?—The Minotaur?—Of Pasiphae?—Of Dædalus?—Of Theseus and Ariadne?—What were the Eleusinian mysteries?—Relate the legend of Danae.—Of Perseus and Andromeda.—Of Sisyphus.—What is said of the history of Attica?—Of Sparta?

ITALY.

It was not until after a desperate, but fruitless resistance, that the Siculi in the north of Italy abandoned their native land to their Gaulish invaders. The battles which they fought with the latter are mentioned in history as the most sanguinary that had as yet been witnessed in Italy (Diony′sius of Halicarnassus, book i., ch. 16). Being at length overcome, they retreated southward, whence they crossed over into the island which has taken from them the name of Sicily. We may fix the year 1364 B. C. as the period when the Gauls became masters of the entire valley of the Po. But the conquerors did not stop there: they pushed their conquests further south, until they reached the mouth of the Tiber; and this river, together with the Nera and the Trento, became the boundary of an Umbrian or Gaulish Empire, which, extending thence to the Alps, embraced more than the half of Italy. Having become the possessors of this beautiful territory, they settled peaceably in it, and organized their State in accordance with the usages of the Gaulish nations. They divided it into three regions, or provinces, determined by the nature of the country. The first, which was named by them Is-Ombria (whence the Latin name "Insubria"), or Low Umbria, included all the level plains in the vicinity of the Po. The second, which they named Oll-Ombria (Olombria), or High Umbria, comprised the two slopes of the Apennines and the rising coast of the upper sea. The third comprised the coast of the lower sea, between the Arno and the Tiber, and received the denomination of Vil-Ombria, or maritime Umbria. Under these circumstances, the Umbrians received a considerable increase of population. They counted, in the provinces of Isombria and Olombria alone, three hundred and fifty-eight great towns, which historians have dignified with the title of cities (Pliny, b. iii., ch. xiv.). Their influence, moreover, extended over all the Italian nations to the extremity of the Peninsula; and they maintained their ascendancy for more than three hundred years. The Insubrians were a very tall and strong race of men, with long hair of a reddish hue, which they rendered still more red by artificial means. The women were almost as tall and courageous as the men. The Roman historians give strange accounts of this people.

What was the date of the conquest of Northern Italy by the Gauls?—How was their territory bounded and divided?—What is said of them by the Roman historians?

BRITAIN.

The Phœnicians traded at this time with the inhabitants of England and Ireland. At a very early period they had visited the coasts of the Mediterranean, and settled in Spain; thence, coasting along the north of that country, they had found their way to the western coast of France, and finally to Britain. That they had extended themselves in this direction at this early period, at least as far as the Straits of Gibraltar, is evident from the inscription (mentioned by Procopius, *Vandal*, b. ii., ch. x.), legible for many ages on the two pillars near the fount of the Magi at Tangiers: "We fly from the face of Joshua, the robber."

There are reasons for believing that Ireland was known earlier, or at least more intimately, than Britain was, to the Phœnicians. The grounds for this belief are set forth in Moore's *History of Ireland* (vol. i., pp. 10, 11). The waters and harbors of Ireland were better known, through the resort of commerce and navigation, than those of Britain (Tacitus, *Agricol.*, ch. xxiv.): so that Ireland was in possession of channels of intercourse distinct from Britain. Combining the proofs of this early intercourse between Ireland and the Phœnician Spaniards, with the title of "Sacred" bestowed upon Ireland in far distant ages, Mr. Moore thinks that her pre-eminence in religion was the chief source of the distinction to which she attained, and that she was chosen for the depository of the Phœnician worship in that portion of the world. The rites of sun-worship were practised by the people, that luminary being worshipped under the sacred name of "Re." The moon ("Mis") was likewise adored. The worship of fire also constituted a part of the old Irish superstitions. Annually, at the time of the vernal equinox, the great festival of La Baal-tinne (or, "the day of the Baal-fire,") was celebrated; and through every district in Ireland it was strictly ordered that, on that night, all fires should be extinguished; nor were any, under pain of death, to be again lighted till the pile of sacrifices in the palace of Tara was kindled. The famous Round Towers of Ireland owe their origin to this fire-worship. They are round edifices, being about 40 feet in diameter, and 120 feet high. Towers exactly resembling them have been found at Bhaugulpore, in Hindostan.

What is said of the trade of Ireland at this early period?—Of the religion of the country?—Of the worship of fire?—And of the Round Towers?

B.C. 1400—1300.

FRANCE.

The characteristics of the ancient Gauls were, personal bravery, unrivalled in their time by other nations; an open, impetuous, and eminently susceptible disposition; and great intelligence, combined with extraordinary fickleness, inconstancy, repugnance to order and discipline, much ostentation, and excessive vanity. Hence they lived in perpetual disunion and discord.

The sovereignty of the whole of Gaul, says Mr. Ritson (*Memoirs of the Celts*, vol. i., ch. iv., and see the authorities there cited), seems to have been possessed by some particular State, and that of each State by some particular family. There were frequently two kings, at a time, of the same State. The multitude, in the most ancient times, chose a prince every year, and likewise a Captain-general of war. It was the custom among the Gauls to attend their assemblies completely armed. They preserved order there by a singular custom. If any one interrupted or disturbed the person speaking, the beadle came to him with a drawn knife, and, using threats, ordered him to be silent; and this he did a second and a third time: and if the offender still persisted in disturbing the meeting, the beadle cut off from his mantle as much as made the rest useless. On their assembly days the Celts met in great numbers in their groves. There the Druids presided over the public and private sacrifices, and taught religion. They also held tribunals for the trial of crimes and suits, and decreed rewards and punishments. They were exempt from military service and from taxes; in short, they enjoyed immunity in all things. The nobles devoted themselves entirely to war: this was their whole study and occupation. The common people were accounted little better than slaves: they dared do nothing by themselves, and were not admitted to the councils. Most of them were oppressed, either with debt, or with the magnitude of the tributes, or with the tyranny of the powerful; and in order to obtain protection, they voluntarily became serfs of the nobles, whose power and quality came to be estimated by the number of their vassals, and of those whom they kept in pay; for these were the only marks of grandeur they made any account of. The country was thus split up into factions, from States down to families.

What were the characteristics of the ancient Gauls?—The form of government?—The functions of the Druids?—The occupations of the nobles?—Condition of the people?

SPAIN.

In the fabulous history of this country, we find that the Celtic Hercules, shortly before his death, appointed Hes′perus, the brother of Atlas, one of his companions, to succeed him. This king was so renowned for his virtues that Spain was named after him, "Hespe′ria." But his merits did not preserve his throne to him. His brother, Atlas, having gained the good will of the army, deposed him, and took possession of the kingdom. Hesperus fled into Italy, where he was hospitably entertained by Co′ritus, or Co′rythus, king of Tuscany. Atlas was so enraged at this, that he invaded Italy, and made Coritus prisoner: he also planted a colony of Spaniards in Sicily. Hesperus died in the meanwhile, and Atlas remained in Italy, having confided the government of Spain to his son, Sic′ulus. Mariana cites Philis′tius Siracusa′nus as his authority for this statement, and for the subsequent exploits of Siculus in Italy, after the death of Atlas (*History of Spain*, b. i., ch. iii.): though he appears to consider these legends of the ancient kings of Spain as "little better than old women's tales." The story is that Electra, the daughter of Atlas, married Coritus, the captive king of Tuscany: and that on his death, her two sons, Ja′sius and Dar′danus, contended for their father's dominions. Their uncle, Siculus, went over to Italy to pacify them, but Dardanus murdered his brother Jasius; whereupon Siculus drove him out of Italy. Having collected a number of the aborigines, Dardanus emigrated into Asia Minor, where he founded the famous city of Troy. Siculus visited Sicily, and gave the island the name it now bears. These legends probably owe their origin to the imagination of the ancient historians, who, being desirous of accounting for the nomenclature of countries and cities, invented eponymous personages to suit the occasion. The legend of Dardanus is, however, related by several ancient writers, and it will be further referred to in the column devoted to Asia Minor.

Siculus, having seated Jasius on the throne of Tuscany, returned to Spain, and from this time we do not find an account of any other actions of his. The names of his successors are probably fabulous. From one of them, named Testa, the tribe of Contestani is said to have derived its name.

Who succeeded the Celtic Hercules?—Whence the name Hesperia?—Relate the legend of Atlas.—Of Dardanus.—The exploits of Siculus.—What is said of his successor?

GERMANY.

The number of tribes into which the Germans were subdivided was very great. We have already noticed the principal divisions: the student will find a full account of them, and of the subdivisions, in Menzel's *History of Germany*, vol. i., ch. iv., v., vi. The ancient Vendi′li appear to have inhabited the whole of the vast tract of country between the Elbe and the Vistula, and known by the general name of "Suithiod." The Peu′cini lay nearest to Asia, their native land, and took their name from an island supposed to have been held sacred, and which may possibly have had some connection with that of Samothrace, where the religions of the north and of Greece intermingled, or with the oracle of Delphi in Greece, which was founded by the Pelasgians in the earlier ages of antiquity. Zamolxis, the sage, who first taught the doctrine of the immortality of the soul, dwelt, at a very remote period, among the Getæ, the principal nation of the Peucini.

The Germans were distinguished from other nations by their blue eyes, light hair, and gigantic stature. They destroyed sickly and deformed children, and they drowned men who had been mutilated. It was a common thing for their old men, who had become useless, to deprive themselves of life. An existence devoid of strength and beauty appeared to them worthless; and, according to their religion, the joys of heaven were granted only to those who fell by the sword. They despised the refinements of civilized life: they built no cities, and destroyed those of the countries they invaded. Menzel asserts that no towns were to be found in Germany before the 10th century after Christ, except a few sacred places known by the name of Asenburgen (*History of Germany*, vol. i., p. 18). The heroism and the powers of endurance possessed by the ancient Germans, are described by all ancient historians as truly extraordinary. Cæsar says that the Gauls fled at the sight of them; and the Emperor Titus exclaimed: "Their bodies are great, but their souls are still greater!" In their peculiar attachment to a wandering life, we may trace a portion of the Divine plan, whereby a hardy race of men was preserved for so many ages in order to replace the degenerate inhabitants of the Roman Empire, when the latter had reached the last stage of corruption.

What is said of the Vendili?—Of the Peucini?—Who was Zamolxis?—What were the principal characteristics of the Germans?—What did Cæsar and Titus say of them?

ASIA MINOR.

Scattered notices of this division of the earth's surface appear from time to time in ancient history, but nothing like a connected narrative is to be found. Asia Minor was inhabited by a vast number of tribes, each ruled over by its own chief or king. It was frequently invaded by the powerful monarchs of Assyria and Egypt: and was the cradle of the great Pelasgian race which peopled Greece and Italy. We read of kings of Damascus and of Colchis; and a number of tributary princes from Asia Minor are depicted on the Egyptian and Assyrian monuments.

In this century we come to the foundation of a kingdom immortalized by Grecian poetry, though otherwise of very small importance to the world, viz., that of Troy. Mr. Grote observes (*History of Greece*, vol. i., p. 284), that it would require a large volume to convey any tolerable idea of the vast extent and expansion of this interesting fable (the legend of Troy), treated as it has been in every conceivable manner by poets, epic, lyric, and tragic, by historical inquirers and by philosophers. The Greeks, however, generally believed in its truth. The primitive ancestor of the Trojan line of kings is Dar′danus, the son of Jupiter and of Electra, the daughter of Atlas. It is said that he came from Samothrace, or from Arcadia, or from Italy. In the column devoted to the history of Spain, during this century, will be found an account of the expulsion of a chieftain of the name of Dardanus from Tuscany by one of the Spanish monarchs. Homer says nothing about the country whence Dardanus came: the authorities on the subject are Hellan′icus, Diony′sius of Halicarnas′sus, Apollodo′rus, and Varro. The first Dardanian town founded by this chieftain was on Mount Ida: there he established his kingdom. His son, Erichtho′nius, became one of the wealthiest of men. His flocks and herds multiplied; he had in his pastures three thousand mares, the offspring of some of which produced horses of preternatural swiftness. Hence the allegory that the father of them was Bo′reas, the north wind. Erichthonius was succeeded by his son Tros, the ancestor from whom the Trojans derived their name. Tros had three sons: Ilus, Assar′acus, and Ganyme′de. The beauty of the latter induced Jupiter to steal him to become his cup-bearer.

What is said of the earliest history of Asia Minor?—Of the legend of Troy?—Who was Dardanus?—What city did he found?—What is said of Tros?—And Ganymede?

THE 13TH CENTURY

EGYPT.

The preceding series of kings has been deduced from various testimonies beside the authority of the ancient historians. Among them may be mentioned the Tablet of Aby′dus, made thirteen generations after the death of Rame′ses III.; the inscriptions of Medinet Aboo (already referred to), made four generations after him by a king who claimed to have descended through this series; the inscription on the Memnonium at Thebes, where Rameses II. claims these kings as his ancestors. The Tablet of Abydus is broken: one king's name is gone wholly, and one partially, and we have only the Theban list to depend upon. After the interval of these two reigns the Tablet no longer agrees with the Theban list, or with the names on the Theban buildings, and we are led to conjecture that Thebes and Abydus were no longer under the same king. Rameses III. possibly did not reign over the whole of Egypt. So much uncertainty prevails about the 19th dynasty, that we pass on to the 20th, which commences with the reign of Rameses IV. (B. C. 1251). This prince, in the 4th and 5th years of his reign, reduced to submission various nations of Asia, and conquered Cyprus. In the 11th and 12th years he again carried on war in Asia, and probably in Syria; but these foreign wars were productive of no permanent result, and were undertaken mainly for the purpose of obtaining tribute, plunder, and captives. The Egyptians made use of the latter in their public works, the natives acting as "task-masters," or foremen, over them. Rameses IV. was succeeded (B. C. 1235) by his brothers Rameses V. and Rameses VI., the duration of whose reigns is not known. The inscriptions do not disclose any historical facts respecting them worthy of notice. Egypt began to decline during the reigns of these princes, and in the succeeding century, in which this family of Rameses lived, it retrograded considerably. Of Rameses VII. there is no memorial left but his tomb.

We may here notice the Egyptian mode of computing time. The student will find repeated mention made in history of the Sothic, or Sothiac Cycle. This was a period of 1460 years of 365 days each, at the expiration of which the months returned to the same day of the year. The name Sothiac is derived from *Sothis*, the dog-star (Sirius), at whose heliacal rising the year was supposed to commence. One of these cycles ended on the 20th of July, in the year 1322 B. C. The Egyptian priests asserted that 341 generations, or 11,340 years had elapsed between the creation of man and the reign of Sethos (B. C. 1050), which would carry back the era of the first man to 12,390 years B. C.; but in this period is included a period of 9000 years, ascribed by Manetho to the reign of Vulcan, prior to the race of mortal kings. These 9000 years are probably lunar months of 29 days and 15 hours each (see Nolan's *Egyptian Chronology*), in which case they would constitute a period of 730 years, or half a Sothiac cycle, and the length of time between the mythical reign of Vulcan and that of Sethos would thus be reduced to 3070 years. Herodotus states (book ii., 3, 4), that the Egyptians first defined the measure of the year, which they divided into twelve months of thirty days, adding five days to the end of each year; that they invented the names of the twelve gods; and that Hercules was one of the twelve who were produced from the eight gods before Amosis: that in the course of the 11,340 years (before mentioned), no divinity had appeared in human form; but it was not so previously nor afterwards: that during this period the sun had four times deviated from his ordinary course, having twice risen where he is wont to set, and twice set where he is wont to rise. Previous to this period, gods reigned in Egypt under one superior. Pan was the most ancient of the gods, and one of the eight accounted first in order of time. From these eight proceeded twelve gods of the second order, of whom Hercules was one; and from these twelve proceeded the gods of the third order. Of these, Horus, the Apollo of the Greeks, and the son of Osiris (Bacchus), was the last. By him Typhon was expelled. The demigods, Hercules and the eleven others, reigned 2000 years. From Bacchus to Amosis a period of 15,000 years elapsed: but the Greeks computed only 1600 years; and from Bacchus to Hercules, 900 years; from Hercules to Pan, 800 years. From this statement an idea of the value of Egyptian Chronology may be formed. The people themselves had no chronology except what their priests manufactured for them, and that was mystified in a variety of ways.

Name the principal sources of information as to the ancient kings.—Who was the first of the 20th dynasty?—Who were his successors?—What was the condition of Egypt under them?—What was the Sothiac Cycle?—What is said of the Egyptian computation of time?—Of the great period?—And of the three orders of gods?

SYRIA.

After the death of Gideon, his son, Abimelech, endeavored to obtain the crown which his father had refused. Having formed a conspiracy with his mother's kindred at Shechem, he fell unexpectedly upon Ophrah, seized his seventy brothers, and slew them all; and, in a convention of the neighboring people, was elected king. But his authority did not extend beyond Shechem and its vicinity: the other tribes neither assisted nor opposed him. After three years the Shechemites attempted to throw off the yoke, whereupon the usurper destroyed their city; but in following up his victory he was wounded by a woman during an attack on Thebes, and, disdaining to die thus, he commanded his armor-bearer to pierce him with his sword. After Abimelech, Tola, of the tribe of Issachar, administered the public affairs for 23 years. Next came Jair, a Gileadite, who was judge for 22 years.

We now come to an interesting episode in ancient Hebrew history, which illustrates the piety as well as the ferocity of the age. The Philistines and the Ammonites, combining their forces, attacked the Israelites on the south and the east. The tribes beyond Jordan were speedily subdued, and the remainder were overcome during the year 1263 B. C. For eighteen years did these oppressors " vex Israel." At length the people turned their eyes to Jephthah, a natural son of Gilead, who, having been wrongfully expelled from his father's house, had taken refuge in a wild region, and became the captain of a band of freebooters, a profession which was not then held in particular disrepute. They sent for him, and made him chief of the city of Gilead, and empowered him to treat with the king of Ammon. He accordingly sent an embassy to that prince, remonstrating on his aggression. The king, in reply, demanded the surrender of the provinces beyond Jordan, as the patrimony of his own ancestors. Jephthah then prepared for war: but before setting forth, he made the memorable vow that, if he returned victorious, he would sacrifice as a burnt-offering "whatsoever should come forth of the doors of his house to meet him." He prevailed over the enemies of his country, and, having expelled the Ammonites, he returned home, and was met by his only daughter, at the head of her attendants, who came forth out of his house to greet him. The unhappy father, perceiving too late the consequences of his rash vow, rent his clothes in agony. His heroic daughter, however, insisted on his fulfilling it, and only requested permission to retire for a while to bewail upon the mountains the frustration of the hope which appears to have been the ruling one among Hebrew women, viz., that of becoming a wife and a mother in Israel. At the expiration of this period (two months) she returned and submitted to her fate. This event was commemorated by the custom of the Jewish maidens to lament four days in every year the sacrifice of the heroic girl (Judges xi. 40).

Jephthah was at this time at deadly war with the Ephraimites, who haughtily resented their not being summoned to take the lead in the Ammonitish war. Having threatened to wreak their vengeance on him and his adherents, Jephthah marched against them, and defeated them. Here, again, we meet with an illustration of the ferocity of the times. The Ephraimites had a peculiarity in their pronunciation, being, apparently, unaccustomed or unable to pronounce the letter *h*. In driving them across the Jordan they were tested by being made to pronounce the word *Shibboleth* (*i. e.*, "water streams"): those who pronounced it *Sibboleth* were put to the sword, and in this manner 42,000 of them perished. The word *Shibboleth* is now frequently used figuratively to signify "a test." After this sanguinary affair, Jephthah remained undisputed head of Israel for six years. Of the remainder of his life no incidents are recorded. He was buried in Mizpah, one of the cities of his native district, Gilead, B. C. 1239. St. Paul (Heb. xi. 32) classes Jephthah among those who, through faith, subdued kingdoms, and did other great works, receiving, through their trials, the greater reward of their endurance. The story of Iphigeni′a, the daughter of Agamemnon, seems to have been borrowed from that of Jephthah and his daughter. Some learned commentators have endeavored to show that Jephthah did not sacrifice his daughter, but dedicated her to the Lord, *i. e.*, to seclusion and celibacy. As to this, see Calmet's *Dictionary of the Bible*, tit. "Jephthah."

The succeeding judges were Ibzan (B. C. 1239–1232), Elon (B. C. 1232–1222), Abdon (B. C. 1222–1214). (Judges xii.)

What was the career of Abimelech?—Who became judges after him?—Who was Jephthah?—Narrate his principal actions; his vow; his cruelty to the Ephraimites.—What is the origin and the meaning of Shibboleth?—What does St. Paul say of Jephthah?—What was the supposed fate of his daughter?—Who succeeded Jephthah?

INDIA.

Siva is described as sometimes wandering about drunk and naked, covered with ashes, ornamented with human skulls and bones, and surrounded by ghosts and goblins. He has three eyes, carries a trident, and is sometimes seated in an attitude of profound thought. Bloody sacrifices were offered to him, and his votaries inflicted the most horrible wounds and tortures on themselves (Ward's *Hindoos*, vol. iii., p. 15; Heber's *Journal*, vol. i., p. 77). He does not pay much attention to the affairs of mankind. His heaven is in the midst of the eternal snows and glaciers of Keilas, one of the highest and deepest groups of the stupendous summits of the Himalaya Mountains. His consort, De′vi, or Bhava′ni, is as much worshipped as Siva, but is represented in still more terrible colors than he is. At her temple, near Calcutta, 1000 goats are sacrificed to her every month. Secret orgies are also held in her honor; in these, both sexes meet to feast on flesh and spirituous liquors, and to indulge in the grossest debauchery.

Vishnu is represented as a comely and placid young man, of a dark azure color, and dressed like a king of ancient days. He is also painted in the forms of his ten principal incarnations, which we may mention to illustrate the genius of Hindoo fiction. These incarnations were: — 1. A fish, to recover the Vedas which had been carried away by a demon in a deluge. 2. A boar, who raised on his tusks the world, which had sunk to the bottom of the ocean. 3. A tortoise, that supported a mountain, on which rested the world. 4. A man, with the head and paws of a lion, who tore to pieces an infidel king. 5. A dwarf, who obtained from a tyrannical king as much ground as he could step over in three steps. On this occasion, Vishnu took the first step over the earth, the second over the ocean; and no space being left for the third, he released the king from his promise, on condition of his descending to hell. 6. A Paris Ram, a Brahmin hero, who exterminated the Cshatriyas. 7. The hero Rama. 8. Balla Rama, who delivered the earth from giants. 9. Buddha, the teacher of a false religion. 10. Crishna, whom we have previously mentioned as one of the two great heroes of India.

Give an account of the form of Siva.—Of Devi.—What is said of them?—How is Vishnu described?—Which were his ten incarnations?

ASSYRIA.

The remainder of the kings who reigned prior to the revival of the Empire under Ninus, are:

	B. C.
Lampa′res	1296
Pany′as	1266
Sosar′mus, or Derce′to	1250

This last is the conjectural reading, according to Layard, of the name found on the inscriptions at Nineveh.

About the year B. C. 1230, the second Ninus, surnamed Mithræ′us (from *Mith′ras*, the sun, on account of the brilliancy of his exploits; and called Belus II. by the Greeks), became monarch, and revived the ambition and military renown of the ancient Empire. His predecessors, for a thousand years, had remained comparatively inactive. Probably the Empire had been divided into a number of small sovereignties; but now they became united under Ninus, who in a few years made himself master of Upper Asia, from India to the Greek colonies in Asia Minor. The empire that he established is called "the Second Empire."

Historians are not agreed as to the dates of the accession of Ninus and his successors, nor as to the right reading of their names. For instance, the king who succeeded Ninus is called by the Greeks Teut′amus, and by Mr. Layard Divanuk′ha, or Divanu′rish (see Layard's *Nineveh and Babylon*, p. 502). The latter dates the accession of Divanukha at B. C. 1200, whilst Usher places it in 1207, and Clinton in 1186.

We must be content with the mere names of these kings, until the researches of antiquaries shall have thrown more light on this portion of ancient history. We may, however, assume that it consisted of very nearly the same incidents as in preceding and subsequent ages. On the inscriptions we find successive Assyrian kings fighting with exactly the same nations and tribes, some of which were scarcely more than four or five days' march from the gates of Nineveh.

The Jewish tribes, as has long been suspected by biblical scholars, can now be proved to have held their dependent position upon the Assyrian king from a very early period, long, indeed, before the time to be inferred from any passage in Scripture. Whenever an expedition is mentioned in Assyrian records, it is stated to have been because these tribes had not paid their customary tribute.

Give the names of the Assyrian kings during this century.—Who founded the second Empire?—What is said of the Jewish tribes?—And the Assyrian domination?

PERSIA.

Persia abounds with the ruins of forgotten splendor. The poet Ferdusi alludes to this fact in the Shah Nameh, when he says: "The curtains of the palace of Cæsar are woven by the spider! and the owl replaces the nobut (drum) on the watch-tower of Afrasiab!" The ruins of Persepolis are the grandest that yet remain, and (according to Malcolm, *History of Persia*, vol. i., p. 251), from what is left of this, the most famous of Persian cities, we may infer that it once contained edifices which rivalled in magnificence those of Greece and Rome. The foundation of this city is, as we have already stated, attributed to Giamschid, who built a fortified palace on the fine plain of Murdasht, at the foot of a hill. It was of hard black granite, each stone being from 9 to 12 feet long, and broad in proportion. It was 90 feet high, with two great flights of stairs, so easy of ascent that a man could ride up on horseback. There were 40 pillars, each 60 feet high, of stone carved as delicately as the softest wood. It is not known whence this granite was brought, for there is none like it now to be found in Persia. There are several figures of Giamschid in the sculpture. In one he has an urn in his hand, in which he burns benzoin, while he stands adoring the sun. In another he is represented as seizing the mane of a lion with one hand, while he stabs him with the other. This famous palace, which was styled the Tukht, or throne, of Giamschid, is said to have been destroyed by Alexander the Great in the 4th century B. C. The city of Istakhar, near which it stood, long survived its destruction.

The ruins of Susa are still to be seen, extending a distance of twelve miles between the town of Desful and the river Karasoo. They consist of mounds of bricks and colored tiles, resembling those found in the ruins of Babylon. At the foot of one of them stands the tomb of the prophet Daniel. It is a small building, used as a dwelling for the holy men who watch the remains of that illustrious man. The ruins of Ker′manshah′, however, are the finest in Persia. At Ecbat′ana may still be seen the tombs of Mordecai and Esther, to which Jewish pilgrims have for centuries resorted, and which are still objects of veneration.

What is said of the ruins of Persepolis?—Of the palace of Giamschid?—Of the ruins of Susa?—The tomb of Daniel?—Of Kermanshah?—The tombs of Mordecai and Esther?

CHINA.

Woo-ting reigned in peace, and died B. C. 1265, and was succeeded by his son, Tsoo-kang, an idle and vicious prince. Tsoo-kang's younger brother, Tsoo-kea, who began to reign in 1258, was a still more vicious man. In consequence of this, the Shang dynasty declined more and more in political importance. During the reign of the latter-named prince was born the celebrated Wan-wang, father of the founder of the Chow dynasty, and grandson of Koo-kung. The State which Woo-wang governed having, through his energy, increased continually in prosperity whilst the rest of the Empire declined, the people inclined more and more to the Chow family, and looked to them for deliverance. Two other worthless princes, Lin-sin (B. C. 1223), and Kang-ting (B. C. 1219), the successors of Tsoo-kea, rendered the Shang dynasty still more despicable.

The foregoing is all that is worth extracting from the Chinese annals of this period. We may devote the space that remains to noticing some peculiarities of this extraordinary people. Their principal characteristic is sameness. Not only in outward appearance, in the features, the color of the eye, and the shade of the hair, but in their mental qualities, do the inhabitants of the various provinces closely resemble each other. Despotism is undoubtedly the primary cause of this phenomenon; for the multitude, reduced to nearly the same level, and actuated by the same wants and passions through long ages, naturally assimilate. The Chinese are very deficient in personal beauty. They are industrious, polite, and affable, and frequently kind and generous. They honor their parents, and are fond of their children. Their women make good wives and mothers. On the other hand, they are cowardly, cunning, and deceitful; cruel to their wives, blunt in their sensibilities, and gross in their enjoyments. Their wishes tend toward this world, and their hopes do not extend beyond the grave. Their principal desires are, to possess riches enough to enable them to lead an easy life, to have male children, and to exercise some public employment. In these attributes they have undergone but little change for very many centuries; they were probably, in the 13th century B. C., very nearly the same people that they are now.

Who were the successors of Woo-ting?—Who was Wan-wang?—Mention some of the peculiarities of the Chinese; their merits; and their defects.

GREECE.

This century is the heroic age of Greece. Pe′lops, Beller′ophon, Her′cules, Castor, Pollux, The′seus, Ja′son, and the Argonauts, Œ′dipus, Nestor, Agamem′non, Ulys′ses, Adme′tus, Melea′ger, Pe′leus, Tel′amon, and others, flourished at this epoch. Their adventures form the staple of Grecian legendary lore.

Attica.—Pandion died in exile, leaving a son named Æge′us. The latter was the father of the famous Theseus, who expelled the Metion′ides from Athens, and replaced him on the throne. Theseus went to Crete, and destroyed the Minotaur, thereby releasing his country from the hard conditions imposed upon it by Minos. On his return he neglected to hoist the white sail, which was to have been the signal of his success; and Ægeus, thinking that he had perished, threw himself into the sea, which, it is said, was thence called the Æge′an Sea. Theseus thus became king of Athens (B.C. 1235). He abolished the separate governments of Attica, and erected Athens into the capital of a single commonwealth, and thus laid the foundation of its greatness. Among other exploits recorded of him are his destroying many monsters, robbers, and ferocious beasts that infested the country. One of the famous robbers slain by him was Procrus′tes, who used to tie upon a bed all travellers who fell into his hands: if they were shorter than the bed, he stretched their limbs till they were of the same length; if they were longer than the bed, he made them of the same size by cutting off some of their limbs. Hence, "the bed of Procrustes" became proverbial. Theseus also overcame the A′mazons, a race of female warriors from Asia, who invaded Attica. He is said to have taken part in the Argonautic expedition, the Calydonian hunt, the battle of the Lapithæ with the Centaurs, and the carrying off of Hel′en and Proser′pine. The history of this great Athenian hero is so mixed up with fables, that it is impossible to say how much of it is worthy of credence. His exploits have doubtless been greatly magnified and added to in the course of ages, but that they have some foundation in reality, we can scarcely doubt (see Plutarch's *Lives, Theseus;* Thucydides, book ii., 15).

The Argonautic expedition was so called from the name of the ship "Argo," in which the adventurers sailed. It was under the command of Jason, the son of Æson, king of Thessaly. His uncle, Pe′lias, dreading his abilities, sent him to fetch the golden fleece belonging to the speaking ram that had carried away Phryxos and Helle, which was in the possession of Æe′tes, king of Colchis, and was guarded by a dragon. The principal heroes of Greece accompanied Jason in the Argo, on this expedition: among them was the celebrated musician, Orpheus, who enlivened them with his harp. Hercules also was one of the Argonauts, but there is great discrepancy about his connection with the expedition. He left it when it reached the coast of Mysia; for there his favorite youthful companion, Hylas, was stolen by the nymphs of a fountain, and Hercules, wandering sorrowfully about in search of him, neglected to return. The inhabitants of Prusa, for many centuries, commemorated this search for Hylas, by running around Lake Ascanias, and clamoring for him. The Argonauts, having visited Lemnos, Thrace, and Mysia, reached the conntry of the Beb′ryces, where occurred the famous pugilistic contest between their king, A′mycus, and Pollux, so graphically described by Theo′critus and Apollodo′rus. In Bithynia they delivered the blind prophet, Phin′eus, from the Harpies, a set of winged monsters, who came down from the clouds whenever his table was laid, and defiled his food. In gratitude for this service, Phineus instructed them how to pass through the Symple′gades, two rocks which alternately opened and shut with violent collision, so that a bird had hardly time to fly through. Passing Mount Cau′casus, they saw the eagle which gnawed the liver of Prometheus, and heard the groans of the sufferer. Arrived in Colchis, they demanded the golden fleece; but Æetes refused to grant it, unless Jason could harness to a plough the two fire-breathing bulls, with brazen feet, which had been given to the king by Hephœstus, and plough a large field, and sow it with dragon's teeth. By the aid of Mede′a, the daughter of Æetes, who was famed for her skill in medicaments, Jason accomplished the task, and slew the men who sprang up out of the furrows after he had cast in the dragon's teeth. Medea having given a magic potion to the dragon that guarded the fleece, Jason obtained possession of it, and fled from the fury of Æetes, taking with him Medea and her brother Apsyrtus. To distract Æetes in the pursuit after them, Medea cut her brother into pieces, and threw the latter into the sea; and while Æetes was collecting the fragments, the Argonauts escaped. They visited many countries (among others, Libya in Africa,) on their return home, and met with a number of adventures (see Grote's *History of Greece*, vol. i., ch. xiii.). Medea accompanied Jason to Greece, where he deserted her for the daughter of Creon, king of Corinth. She revenged herself by murdering Jason's young wife. Various stories are told as to her death: but she is said to have become immortal, and was honored with divine worship.

The Calydonian hunt took place near Cal′ydon, an ancient town of Ætolia, and was instituted to destroy a ferocious boar that caused great havoc. Theseus, Admetus, Castor, Pollux, and other heroes, took part in this famous hunt.

The Centaurs (or bull-killers, as the name implies,) were natives of Thessaly, fabled to have been half horses and half men, on account of their expertness on horseback. The Lapithæ were a Pelasgian people, and, at the time of the battle, were governed by Pirith′ous. It was at his wedding that the Centaurs endeavored to carry off the bride, Hippodami′a; a bloody struggle ensued, in which the Centaurs were defeated; and in this conflict, Theseus, Castor, Pollux, and other heroes took part.

Castor and Pollux were twin brothers, called also the Dioscu′ri (or sons of Jupiter). They were the sons of Leda and Tyndareus, king of Lacedæmon; hence they are called Tyndar′idæ. They were the brothers of the beautiful Helen, who was the wife of Menela′us, and the cause of the famous Trojan war. Castor was famed for his skill in taming horses, and Pollux for his skill in boxing. They took part in all the heroic expeditions and exploits of their time. On the Argonautic expedition, Pollux killed A′mycus, king of the Beb′ryces, in a pugilistic contest. They recovered their sister Helen from Theseus, who had carried her off. Castor was killed in a contest with the sons of Apha′reus, in Messe′ne, and Pollux prayed to be allowed to die with him. According to the fable, Castor was mortal, but Pollux was immortal; and, on the death of the former, the twins were translated to the heavens, where they shine as stars in the constellation *Gemini*. They were worshipped as the protectors and helpers of men.

Pelops was another Grecian hero, said to have been cut to pieces, boiled, and brought to life again. He was king of Pisa in Elis, and restored the Olympian games with great splendor. He was the father of A′treus, and the grandfather of the celebrated Agamemnon and Menelaus.

Beller′ophon, the son of Glaucus, and grandson of Sisyphus, king of Corinth, was the hero of many adventures. He killed the Chimæ′ra, a fire-breathing monster, said to have been compounded of a lion, a dragon, and a goat, which caused great havoc in Lycia. He accomplished this by means of the winged horse, Peg′asus, given to him by Minerva. Upon this horse he attempted to soar to heaven, but fell down to earth. Bellerophon distinguished himself in the war with the Amazons in Asia Minor, and married the daughter of the king of Syria. His fate is doubtful. All that is related of it is that he became insane, and wandered in the Ale′ian field.

Hercules, the greatest of all the heroes of Greece and of antiquity, was the son of Amphytrion of Tyrins, and Alcmene. He was born at Thebes about the year 1263 B. C. It is difficult to distinguish the real from the ideal in the history of this famous personage, so much have his exploits been embellished by poets and historians. Many of them are inventions of a later age. Fables say that he began them when an infant, by destroying two serpents in his cradle. As he grew up his prodigious strength was developed. He also learned music from Linus, whom he killed in a passion. When eighteen years old he killed a great lion in Mount Cithæ′ron. Soon afterward he delivered Thebes from the annual payment of 100 oxen to the king of Orchome′nus, by defeating the troops of the latter. He then became insane, and in that state killed his children. When he recovered his reason, he, by order of the oracle of Delphi, bound himself to serve Eurys′theus, king of Tyrins. That prince ordered him to perform twelve labors, all of which he accomplished, and were as follows: 1. To kill the Neme′an lion. Hercules strangled this monster, and brought its dead body on his shoulders to Eurystheus, who was so frightened at the gigantic

Name the kings of Attica during this century.—What is said of Theseus?—Of the bed of Procrustes?—The Amazons?—Of the Argonauts?—Who was Jason?—Who were his companions?—Who was Hylas?—What were the Harpies?—The Symplegades?—Relate the adventures of the Argonauts.

What became of Jason and Medea?—What was the Calydonian hunt?—Who were the Centaurs and the Lapithæ?—Castor and Pollux?—What became of them?—Who was Pelops?—Bellerophon?—What of the Chimæra?—And Pegasus?—Who was Hercules?—When and where was he born?

strength of the hero that he ordered him in future to deliver outside of the town the account of his exploits. 2. To kill the Lernæ′an Hy′dra, a monster with nine heads, the middle one of which was immortal. Hercules struck off the heads with his club, but two grew in the place of every one. Whereupon, with the aid of his servant Iola′us, he burned off the eight, and buried the immortal one. As he had not accomplished the task unaided, he was not allowed to reckon it among the twelve. He dipped his arrows in the hydra's blood, which made them poisonous. 3. To capture the Arcadian stag, with golden antlers and brazen feet. This was done after pursuing it for a whole year. 4. To destroy the Eryman′thian boar. In executing this exploit, Hercules had a fight with the Centaurs, and accidentally wounded his friend, Chiron, with one of his poisoned arrows, of which wound Chiron died. 5. To cleanse the stables of Au′geas, king of Elis, which contained 3000 oxen, and had not been cleansed for thirty years. This was done by diverting the water from the rivers Alphe′us and Pene′us into the stables, whereby they were cleansed in a single day. 6. To destroy the Stymphalian birds, which ate human flesh. Hercules killed them with his arrows. 7. To capture the Cretan bull. This bull was mad, and did great havoc. Minos, king of Crete, therefore, gladly allowed Hercules to carry it off to Greece. When it arrived there it escaped, but was killed at Marathon by Theseus. 8. To capture the mares of Diome′des, king of Thrace, which fed on human flesh. In this enterprise Hercules lost his friend Abde′rus. 9. To obtain the girdle of Hippol′yta, the Queen of the Amazons. Hercules accomplished this by the aid of a band of volunteers. He killed Hippolyta, and the two sons of Boreas, Cal′ais and Zetes. On his way home he landed in Troas, where he rescued Hesi′one, the daughter of King Laom′edon, from the monster sent against her by Neptune. 10. To capture the oxen of Ge′ryon, in Erythi′a (or the Balear′ic Isles). In search of these oxen, Hercules visited Spain and the Straits of Gibraltar, where he erected two pillars, one on each side of the strait. He met with many adventures on his way home through France, Italy, and Thrace. 11. To bring away the golden apples of the Hesper′ides. The Hesperides were the guardians of the apples given by Terra to Juno on her marriage with Jupiter. As Hercules did not know where the gardens of the Hesperides were, he had to find them. After various adventures in Europe, Asia, and Africa, he found them near Mount Atlas, and brought away the apples. 12. To bring from the lower world Cerberus, the dog that guarded the entrance to Hades. This was the most difficult of all his labors, but he accomplished it with the permission of Pluto; and, having shown the dog to Eurystheus, he carried him back again. Besides these feats, Hercules performed several others, which were called "Parerga" (superfluous labors) by the ancients.

Hercules, among his other exploits, also took part in the Calydonian boar hunt, the Argonautic expedition, and a variety of other adventures. He was married several times. His last wife was Dejani′ra, who was unwittingly the cause of his death. She having been assaulted by Nessus, the Centaur, Hercules slew the latter. Dejanira staunched the blood of the dying centaur with a garment, which she afterwards gave to Hercules to put on. The blood was poisonous, and caused Hercules the greatest agony. In his delirium he raised a pile of wood on Mount Œta, on which he burnt himself (B. C. 1209). He was most extensively worshipped, not only in Greece, but all over the ancient world: but many other nations had their own Hercules. On his death, his sons were expelled from Tyrins. They fled to Attica, and did not regain their inheritance until more than a century afterwards, though they invaded Peloponnesus, and remained there one year, until driven out by a plague.

To this age may also be referred the poets and musicians: Or′pheus, Li′nus, Amphi′on, Olen, Pamphos, and Musæ′us. Orpheus is the most celebrated of the early Greek poets, and there are numerous legends respecting him. He was said to be so skilful in playing on the harp, that he enchanted wild beasts, trees, and stones, and made them follow him. He accompanied the Argonauts to Colchis, and, by his music, saved the ship from being crushed by the Sympleg′ades. His wife, Euryd′ice, having died from the bite of a serpent, he followed her to Hades, where his music induced Pluto to restore her to earth, on condition that he should not look back upon her until they had reached the upper world. But his love and anxiety were so great that he could not refrain from turning round to see whether she was following him, and he beheld her caught back to the infernal regions. His grief led him to treat the women of Thrace, where he lived, with contempt, and in revenge they tore him to pieces in one of their Bacchanalian orgies. Amphion, like Orpheus, moved stones and trees with the music of his lyre.

Linus was the instructor of Hercules in music, and was killed by him in a fit of passion. But there was another Linus who flourished at an earlier period, and composed dirges and lamentations, which were sung by women at the public sacrifices, and were called, after him, *linoi*.

Musæus was the author of various poetical compositions, the most celebrated of which were his Oracles. Olen was the earliest Greek lyric poet, and the author of several sacred hymns. Pamphos was another poet of this age.

Æscula′pius, the famous physician, also flourished. He was so skilful in restoring people to health, that Jupiter killed him by a flash of lightning, lest men might escape death altogether. He was most extensively worshipped in after ages as the god of medicine. His sons, Macha′on and Podalir′ius, were physicians in the Greek army at the siege of Troy. His daughters, Hyge′ia (health) and Panace′ia (all-healing) were worshipped as goddesses. His descendants were called *Asclepi′adæ*. They were priests who practised medicine, which they looked upon as a sacred secret, transmitted from father to son in their families.

Œd′ipus was another hero of this age. His adventures have furnished materials for two of the finest tragedies of Soph′ocles. He was the son of La′ius and Jocas′ta, king and queen of Thebes; and, while he was a child, was exposed on Mount Cithæron, because an oracle had foretold that he should slay his father. He was found by a shepherd, who named him, from his swollen feet, *Œdipus*. He was adopted by Pol′ybus, king of Corinth, with whom he remained until he grew up to manhood. When of age, he quitted Corinth and went to Delphi. On his way he met Laius driving a chariot: Laius insultingly bade him make way for it; whereupon a scuffle ensued, and Laius was slain. Near Thebes, Œdipus encountered the Sphinx, a female monster, with the winged body of a lion, the head and upper part of the figure being that of a woman. She was seated on a rock, and put a riddle to every Theban that passed by, killing all who were unable to solve it. The riddle was as follows: "What being is that, which, having four feet, has two and three feet, and only one voice; but its feet vary, and when it has most it is weakest?" Œdipus solved the riddle by saying that it was man, who in infancy crawls upon all fours, in manhood stands erect upon two feet, and in old age supports his tottering legs with a staff. The Sphinx, enraged at the solution of the riddle, threw herself down from the rock. Œdipus, having thus delivered Thebes from the monster, obtained the kingdom, and married Jocasta, neither he nor she being aware of the close relationship existing between them. When they discovered it, Jocasta hung herself, and Œdipus put out his own eyes. His subsequent fate is a matter of doubt. He is said by some to have wandered to Colo′nus, in Attica, where he was honorably entertained by Theseus, and there he died. Others say he was expelled from Thebes by his sons, whom he cursed. Others, again, say he continued to reign at Thebes, and afterwards fell in battle. His sons, Ete′ocles and Polyni′ces, succeeded him. The former expelled the latter, who fled to Adras′tus, king of Argos. Adrastus undertook to reinstate Polynices, and induced six other heroes to join him in the expedition. This war is celebrated in Grecian story as that of "the Seven against Thebes." They all fell, except Adrastus and Polynices. Eteocles and Polynices then resolved to decide the contest by single combat, and fell by each other's sword.

The adventures and exploits of the principal mythical personages of Greece during this, the heroic period, have here been briefly sketched. The student must refer to the detailed history and the poetry of Greece for further particulars. The history of the different States, during this century, offers nothing worthy of notice beyond what has already been mentioned. At the close of the century, Agamemnon was king of Myce′næ; Menela′us, of Lacedæmon; Nestor, of Pylos; Ulysses, of Ithaca. All of them became chief actors in the Trojan war at the beginning of the next century.

Enumerate the twelve labors of Hercules.—What other labors did he perform?—What were the Hesperides?—How and when did Hercules die?—What became of his sons?—Who was Orpheus?—Relate the legend of his wife, Eurydice.—What was the fate of Orpheus?

Who was Amphion?—Linus?—Musæus?—Olen?—Pamphos?—Æsculapius?—What became of him?—Name his sons and daughters.—Relate the legend of Œdipus and Laius, the Sphinx, and Jocasta.—What was the war of the Seven against Thebes?—Name the kings at the close of this century.

ITALY.

About the middle of this century a colony of Rasena, or Tyrrhenians, originally from the great city of Rezen, in Mesopotamia, under the command of Tarchun, landed at Gravisca, in Umbria, where, being favorably received, they settled. Tarchun is supposed to be the same person as the Evander of Roman tradition. This great man, Tarchun (or Evander), founded the State of Etruria, which, under his auspices, became the most polished and civilized of all the Italian States. The Rasena, or Tyrrhenians, spoke a language partly Phœnician and partly Egyptian. It is only known from inscriptions found upon sarcophagi (stone coffins) and bronzes in their tombs, upon statues, and liturgical tables and marbles, which have from time to time, within the last two centuries, been dug up in Italy, and are now preserved in various museums. Etruscan words are also found in many of the Greek and Latin historians. The Rasena introduced Egyptian arts and sciences into Italy. The origin of the laws of Etruria, called the "Tagetic" laws, is narrated by Cicero (*De Divinitate*, ii., ch. xxiii., 38), as follows: "Tarchun was one day ploughing, when a child, with a man's head, appeared to him out of the ground. It sang to him the unalterable, eternal, and divinely-inspired laws of his future government, and then sank down and expired. The name of this child was Tages." He is the same personage as the Phœnician Tana'tes, or Taua'tes, and the Egyptian Thoth (a Coptic word signifying "hand"). These laws were propounded by Tarchun to the chiefs and the people, and adopted by them. They were written down in three books, called the Books of Tages. Tages was to the Italians what Menu was to the Hindoos, and Moses to the Jews—their inspired lawgiver. It is said by some that a nymph received him before he disappeared; but this is only a continuation of the allegory, and refers to the priestess Byg'oë, who, after the death of Tarchun, wrote a commentary on the laws of Tages, and is therefore said to have received, nourished, and sung to him. The three books of Tages were translated into Latin in the days of Lucretius: they were styled the *Libri Fatales*, the *Libri Tagetici*, and the *Sacra Acherontica*. They became the foundation of the laws of Rome.

The Etruscans acknowledged one Supreme God, but they had images to represent his three great attributes: strength, riches, and wisdom. The first of these was named Tina, the second Talna, and the third Menerfa (or Minerva, a name evidently of Egyptian origin, and derived from Menef-ra). The national divinity was always worshipped as a triad. Every city might have as many more gods, and gates, and temples, as the inhabitants pleased; but three sacred gates, and one temple to the three divine attributes, was obligatory wherever the laws of Tages were received. The only gate that remains in Italy of this olden time undestroyed is the beautiful "Porta del Arco," at Volterra, and it has upon it the three heads of the three national divinities, one on the keystone of the arch, and one on each of the side pillars. This gate is the pride of Italy. "It is as old as the walls, and the walls are as old as the foundation, and the foundation is coëval with Etruscan domination, which, according to Virgil, was firm and established when Æneas landed B. C. 1180." (Mrs. Hamilton Gray's *History of Etruria*, vol. i., p. 148.)

Tarchun built the great national temple at the city of Tarquinii, which he founded. He dedicated this temple to the gods Tina and Talna, and the goddess Minerva. He also established twelve States in Etruria, viz., Lucca, Volterra, Vetulonia, Arretium, Cortona, Perugia, Clusium, Rusella, Felania, Vulci, Tarquinii, and Falerii (or Faliscii). He constructed a variety of public works of great size and beauty. He also taught the use of auguries (or divination), and established Augurs and Vestal Virgins, whose special duty it was to guard the sacred fire. Omens were obtained by the Augur himself, who drew lightning from a cloud, and pronounced the prayer of consecration, when it was required to make ground holy for the building of a temple. The form of this prayer is given by Müller (*On Etruscan Antiquities*, vol. iii.), who proves that the Etruscan Augurs had complete power over the electric fluid, thus anticipating Franklin's discovery three thousand years. The Augurs also drew two lines, intersecting each other at right angles: one named "cardo," the other "decumanus." The four regions thus marked out were called "cardines;" whence our word "cardinal," as applied to the four points of the compass. By this means the answer of the gods was obtained.

Who were the Rasena?—What Italian State did they found?—Who was Tarchun?—And Tages?—What is said of the Tagetic laws?—Of the Etruscan language?—And religion?—What cities did Tarchun found?—What is said of the Volterra gate?—And of the practice of augury?—Whence is the word "cardinal" derived?

BRITAIN.

The identity of the religion of the ancient Irish with that of the Phœnicians may be seen in their rites and ceremonies. They used the sacred grove and well; the circle of erect stones surrounding either the altar or the judgment-seat; the unhewn pillars, adored as symbols of the sun; the sacred heaps, or Cairns, dedicated to the same worship; the tomb altars, called Cromlech, supposed to have been places of sepulture as well as of sacrifice; and lastly, those horrible rites, in which children were the "burnt-offerings," which the Jewish idolaters perpetrated in a place called, from their so doing, "the Valley of Shrieking," and "Tophet," from the practice of beating drums during the ceremony, to drown the cries of the children sacrificed in the fire to Moloch. In Ireland these frightful scenes were styled *Magh-Sleacth* (or, "the place of slaughter"). The worship of the sun may still be traced in the names of places in Ireland, such as *Cairn Grainey* ("the sun's heap"), *Grian Beacht* ("the sun's circle"), *Knoc-greine*, *Tuam-greine* ("hills of the sun"). The Celtic word *grian* ("the sun") is the root of the epithet *Grynæus*, applied to Apollo by the Romans.

It appears that water was also worshipped among the ancient Celts. It was customary to visit fountains, or wells, especially those in the neighborhood of a blasted oak, or an upright unhewn stone, and to hang rags, or pieces torn from garments, upon the branches of particular trees. There is scarcely a nation in Asia among whom this primitive practice has not been found to prevail. The Irish professed to do it as a preventive against the sorceries of the Druids. They also observed the great festival of Samhin (or Heaven), the great Cabiric divinity (worshipped under the same name in Samothrace), in April every year. On this occasion they offered up their first-born children to their chief idol, Crom-Cruach, a frightfully-deformed image, whose head was of gold, and who was surrounded by twelve lesser idols, representing, probably, the twelve signs of the zodiac. The chief scene of these dreadful crimes was a place in the county of Leitrim, called the Field of Slaughter. The great circle of stones, at Stonehenge, in England, which is still to be seen, was a temple to the sun, and used for the like practices, as is proved by the black altar-stone, which was a peculiar feature in these temples of Moloch. It is composed of immense blocks of stone, with an opening to the east, and there is a tradition in England that these blocks were brought from Ireland, having been previously brought to that country by giants from the extremities of Africa.

The ancient Celtic inhabitants, both of England and Ireland, reverenced particular stones and rocks, such as the *Lia Fail* (or Stone of Destiny), used in the election of Irish monarchs, and the rocking-stones (worshipped also by the Phœnicians under the name of Bæ'tyli, or animated stones), found in some parts of Cornwall and Wales. Sacred hills and tumuli (sepulchral mounds,) were also used by the Irish for a variety of purposes. From the summit of them the legislator promulgated his decrees, and there the king was presented with the wand of power. Of these consecrated places, the Hill of Usneach, in Westmeath, was the most famous, because upon its summit the limits of the five provinces of Ireland met, and the Druids held their solemn meetings; there also the National Convention frequently met, and peculiar sacredness attached to the spot. Groves and particular trees were also worshipped. In Irish history we meet with mention of "the Plain of Oaks", "the Tree of the Field of Adoration", and "the Sacred Oak of Kildare". Under the Tree of the Field of Adoration the Dalcassian chiefs were inaugurated. The four great Dalcassian families were the O'Briens, the MacMahons, the O'Kennedys, and the Macnamaras.

There is an entire absence of history as regards England and Scotland during this century. We meet with accounts among the Irish bards of a great exploit of the Nemedian colonists of Ireland: this was the storming of the Tower of Conan, the stronghold of the African or Fomorian pirates or traders. This fortress stood upon an island on the sea-coast of Ulster, named, after it, Tor-Inis, or "the Island of the Tower". The Nemedians entirely destroyed this edifice; but the Fomorians, having been joined by fresh forces, gained a general battle by land and sea, and the Nemedians were all dispersed and destroyed. After this event the country lay desolate for two hundred years.

How is the identity of the ancient Irish religion with that of the Phœnicians proved?—What did they worship beside fire and the sun?—What is said of the Crom-Cruach?—Of Stonehenge?—Of the Lia Fail?—Of the hill of Usneach?—Of tree-worship?—Of the Dalcassians?—Of the Tower of Conan, and the Nemedians?

B.C. 1300—1200.

FRANCE.

In this century, according to Thierry (*Histoire des Gaulois*, vol. i., part i., ch. i.), some Oriental navigators visited Gaul for the first time, and having been struck by the natural richness of the country, they returned and built trading depôts. The French historian asserts that gold and silver mines abounded: that iron, precious stones, and coral, were equally plentiful in those days. These Phœnician visitors at once opened a lucrative trade, importing, in exchange for these valuable productions, glass, woollen cloth, wrought metals, tools, and weapons of war. As they traded at an earlier period with England and Ireland, we may well believe that they did the same with France. The same historian notices (vol. i., p. 19) the ancient tradition, prevalent among the Celts, that the Tyrian god, Hercules, had visited Gaul, and done great works there. This deity was probably the same personage already noticed in the history of Spain (see 14th century B. C.) but must not be confounded with the Greek demigod of that name, although he also is said to have visited Gaul. There are several heroes or deities named Hercules. There were: 1. The Egyptian Hercules, whose Egyptian name was Som or Chon, and who was the son of Amun. 2. The Cretan Hercules, one of the Idæan Dactyls, who also came from Egypt. 3. The Indian Hercules, called, by the later Greeks, Dor′sanes, and supposed by them to be their own Hercules, who had visited India, and become the ancestral hero of the Indian kings. 4. The Phœnician or Tyrian Hercules, whom the Egyptians considered to be more ancient than their own, and who was worshipped at Carthage and at Cadis, and to whom children were sacrificed. He is evidently the same as, 5. The Celtic Hercules, who founded the cities of Alesia (now Arles) and Nemausus (now Nismes), in France. 6. The Greek Hercules, particulars of whose exploits and career are given on pp. 40, 41. The Tyrian Hercules arrived at the mouth of the Rhone, where he was attacked by the inhabitants, whom he dispersed. He penetrated into the interior of France, still subduing his opponents, and founded the two cities above named. He thence introduced many arts and sciences till then unknown among the Gauls. By marriages and other alliances he laid the foundation of a powerful kingdom.

What particular event happened during this century?—What did the Phœnicians trade in?—What is said of the Tyrian Hercules?—The Egyptian?—Cretan?—Indian?

SPAIN.

Soon after the time of Siculus, a Greek colony from Zante landed on the eastern coast of Spain, and founded the town of Saguntum (now Monviedro). They also erected a great temple to Diana on the promontory now called Deni′a. The next visitors were Dionysus, or Bacchus, and his followers, who went about, like knight-errants, delivering the people from their oppressors. In this way, it is said, they rendered good service to Spain. They founded the city of Nebrixa, at the mouth of the Guadalquiver. If there be any truth whatever in this story, which is gravely related as a fact by Mariana (*History of Spain*, ch. iv.), it must mean that a second Greek colony arrived in Spain, and that they introduced the use of the grape for making wine.

About the same time a native chief, named Mil′ico, became very powerful, and his successors built the city of Cas′tulo (now Gazlana), formerly one of the large cities of Spain. The Spanish historian above cited claims for his country the honor of a visit from the Argonauts, among whom was Hercules, but this is evidently a fable: it may, however, have some foundation in the visit of a body of Phœnician colonists, under some eminent leader. The arrival of the Tyrian Hercules in Spain has already been noticed; but we cannot too often caution the student to avoid being misled by receiving for authentic history what is for the most part mythical. It is tolerably certain that some colonies of Phœnicians had long been settled on the coasts of Spain, and that they had established trading-depôts on the north shore in Gallicia, even at this early period. The traditionary history of Ireland gives an account of an ancient Pharos, or lighthouse, erected in the neighborhood of the port now called Corunna, for the use of navigators on their passage between that coast and Ireland. They carried on an extensive commerce with that country, and with Britain, especially with that portion of it known in ancient times as the Œstrum′nides, or Tin Islands (the Scilly Islands). Both Spaniards and Irish had similar customs; one in particular, of worshipping a certain god by dancing in the night of the full moon, with their whole families before their doors, and feasting all night (Ritson's *Memoirs of the Celts*, p. 201).

When did a Greek colony arrive in Spain?—Where settle?—What is said of Bacchus?—Of Milico, and his successors?—Of Hercules?—Of trade with Ireland and Britain?

GERMANY.

The civil institutions of the ancient Germans, their customs and superstitions, arose from the peculiar and warlike form of government necessary for a nation of free warriors who owned no laws save those of chivalry and honor. But in these they rose far above the robber-hordes, who for ages wandered over the vast plains of Asia; which confirms the opinion that the pure Germans descended at a very remote period from some warrior caste of Northern India, from which they inherited a spirit of equality and fraternization, which, strengthened by the lapse of centuries, became at length indelibly stamped on the national character (Menzel's *History of Germany*, vol. i., p. 20). The customs of war were preserved even during peace. The land was considered lawful booty, and equally partitioned among the people, who, nevertheless, generally preferred the chase to agriculture. At stated times they assembled in the open air, armed, to deliberate on public affairs. The place of assembly was called *Malstatt*, or *Dingstatt* (council-place), and was generally distinguished by a great tree, either a sacred oak, ash, or lime, or by enormous stones, which were sometimes used as sacrificial altars, and sometimes as seats for the audience, and as places for the orators. In this custom we trace the Druidical system, which prevailed more or less among all the Celtic nations of antiquity. The different tribes appear to have been held together by a very frail federative system. The chief authority was never vested in one individual, but was delegated to three or four; sometimes even to twelve: these numbers being supposed to have mystical power. The largest tribes were divided into communities of a hundred men each, which were subdivided into tens: this regulation remained in force in many parts of Germany down to late times. The ancient Germans had no public, but only a private law. All their oldest laws refer merely to the mutual rights of the free-born, and to those of the free over the slaves or serfs. The State assembly took cognizance of, and decided, all public and private affairs; and beyond these decisions there was no law. Every free man was entitled to life, liberty, honor, and property; but there were only two modes of punishing injuries to either, viz., single combat and fines.

What is said of the civil institutions of the Germans?—Of their assemblies?—Their chief authorities?—Divisions of their tribes?—Public and private law?—Modes of redress?

ASIA MINOR.

This century offers no marked features in the history of this country. The famous Argonautic expedition from Greece to Colchis, if it has any historical reality, must be referred to this period. An account of it is given in the portion devoted to Greece (p. 40). The Greeks and Phœnicians traded along the shores, though many of their voyages were purely piratical; the carrying off of the inhabitants for slaves being one of the principal objects.

We will continue the legendary history of that little portion of Asia Minor situate on the shores of the Bosphorus and Dardanelles, and called the Troad. We have already stated that Tros, the king of this country, had three sons: Ilus, Assar′acus, and Ganymede. From Ilus and Assaracus the Trojan and Dardanian lines diverge; the former passing from Ilus to Laom′edon, Pri′am, and Hector; the latter from Assaracus to Capys, Anchi′ses, and Æne′as. Ilus founded the city of Ilium on the plain of Troy, which was styled holy, because Jupiter cast down upon the plain a "Palladium" (or image of Minerva), while the city was in process of erection. The god also compelled Neptune to aid in building the walls, and Apollo to tend the flocks and herds. Ilus was succeeded by Laomedon, a perfidious and cruel tyrant. According to the legend, when Apollo and Neptune claimed the reward, he refused to give it, and threatened to cut off their ears, bind them hand and foot, and sell them as slaves. For this treachery, Neptune sent a sea monster to ravage the country. To rid himself of this, the king offered the immortal horses given by Jupiter to his grandfather Tros, as a reward to any one who would destroy the monster. But an oracle declared that a noble maiden must be sacrificed to it, and the lot fell on Hesi′one, the daughter of Laomedon. Hercules, returning from the Argonautic expedition at the critical moment, slew the monster, and rescued the maiden. In return for this service, the king gave him six mortal, instead of the six immortal, horses. Hercules then raised a strong force, attacked and captured Troy, and slew Laomedon, giving Hesione to his friend and auxiliary, Telamon. He also placed Priam, one of the sons of Laomedon, on the throne. Of this famous king, and of his family, we shall say more when treating of the Siege of Troy.

What is said of Asia Minor?—What was the Troad?—Who built Troy?—Why was it called the holy city?—Relate the legend of Laomedon and his daughter Hesione.

EGYPT.

The reign of Rameses VIII., the last of the four brothers reigning in succession, is supposed to have been short. Nothing is known of him.

Rameses IX. was the son of Rameses VII. He began a temple to Chons, on the Nile, near Karnak, but left it unfinished.

Of Rameses X., nothing is known.

Rameses XI. is known to have reigned 17 years, from inscriptions found in Egypt.

Of Rameses XII., XIII., and XIV., nothing beyond their names is known, a fact which is the more indicative of the inactivity which characterized the last years of this dynasty, inasmuch as Rameses XIV. is known to have reigned at least 33 years. It is conjectured that there was a Rameses XV., by whom a hall was added to the temple of Chons, at Karnak. Under this dynasty, not only the power of the country, but its taste and skill in the arts and sciences, declined.

History has preserved no account of the manner in which the sceptre passed from the preceding dynasty to the 20th, or Tanite. The city of Tanis, or Zoan, had long been the most important city on the coast of Egypt, and was at this period of sufficient influence to send forth the sovereigns of the new dynasty, seven in number, who governed Egypt during 130 years. Reckoning back from the first year of Shishak, the founder of the next (21st) dynasty, which is well ascertained to have been the year 978 B. C., we get the date 1108 B. C., as that of the commencement of the reign of Smendes, the first monarch of the 20th dynasty.

In the absence of more information as to the events of this century, we may devote the remaining space to noticing the mythology of Egypt.

Seb, or Thore, was the father of the gods Osiris, Isis, Typhon, Horus, and Athur. He is the same as the Saturn of the Greeks. Neith is the mother of the gods, and may be identified with the Grecian Rhea. Osiris was worshipped all over Egypt, though he was only an inferior god. He has been identified as the bearded Bacchus, who invaded India, and subdued the country beyond the Ganges. He is the god of Amenti, the regions of the dead; whence he is styled Petemp-Amentes, and he presides at the trial of the dead. Isis, his sister and queen, generally accompanies him: she is considered to be the same as the Grecian Ceres. The city of Bubastis was her especial property. She is styled by Ovid (*Metamorphoses*, ix., 686,) Inachis; and the Greek name Io (or Ioh, which is the Coptic for the moon,) is borrowed from her. Horus, the son of Isis and Osiris, reigned on earth after his father. He is represented as the god of beauty and of silence, and is considered to be the same as the Greek Apollo: he is sometimes called Aroeris. Anubis, the dog, or deity with a greyhound's head, is sometimes identified with the Greek Hermes, or Mercury. Athur was the Aphrodite, or Venus, of the Greeks. Thoth, the inventor of letters, was the Hermes Trismegistus (or thrice great) of the Greeks. Nephthis is probably the same as Diana, and is sometimes called Bubastis. Typhon, the successor of Horus on the throne, is frequently mentioned by the Greek historians as an evil genius.

The Egyptians had a variety of other deities. They also worshipped certain animals, viz., the cow, ram, greyhound, hawk, vulture, ibis, crocodile, frog, asp, crayfish, scarabœus (or beetle), and some nondescript animals, such as the Sphinx. Wings also were employed as emblems of divinity: thus there are winged goddesses, winged crowns, winged asps, and winged suns. In after ages other divinities were introduced. Thus we read of Cano′pus, the pilot of Menelaus, deified in the time of the Ptolemies; Sera′pis, whose origin and attributes are imperfectly known, but who subsequently became identified with Osiris; the River Nile, represented as a man with a lotus on his head, and a vase in his hand. The Egyptians believed in the immortality of the soul, and in the rewards and punishments of a future state. In their pictures they represent Osiris and the assessors presiding, while the actions of the deceased are weighed in the scales. From the care they took of the body after death it is evident that they believed in its resurrection; and there is further evidence of their belief in an overruling Providence. The priests, however, mystified the people by a system of ceremonies and emblematical processions, so absurd that Cicero wondered "how priest could meet priest without laughing."

What is said of Rameses VIII.?—Rameses IX.?—Rameses X.?—Rameses XI.?—And other kings of the same name?—Of the transition from the 19th to the 20th dynasty?—Of the city of Tanis?—Of the date of the accession of Smendes?—Of the Egyptian mythology?—Name the principal gods.—What else was worshipped?

SYRIA.

After the death of Abdon, Eli, the high-priest, judged Israel for nearly forty years. At length those implacable enemies of the Hebrew nation, the Philistines, again ravaged Palestine, and remained masters of it for forty years. (Judges xiii. 1.) They dispersed, and almost annihilated, the tribe of Simeon. Gaza and Ascalon fell into their hands; and they were preparing to march northward, when their progress was checked by the most extraordinary hero we meet with in the Jewish annals — Samson, the son of Manoah, of the tribe of Dan. He is to the Jews what Hercules was to the Greeks, viz., the embodiment of prodigious personal strength, combined with the most romantic love of adventure. His parents dedicated him in his infancy to the Lord: his hair was never cut, nor was he allowed to drink wine. All Scripture readers are familiar with the story of his slaying the lion with his hands, and of his propounding a riddle respecting the bees which settled in the carcase. The Philistines on several occasions experienced his prowess; this made them anxious to get him into their power, and they endeavored to induce his wife (a Philistine woman) to betray him. Samson, however, repudiated her; and, by the expedient of sending foxes with firebrands tied to their tails into their cornfields, burnt their corn, and avenged himself on them. Upon this they raised a large force, destroyed his father and his wife by fire, and demanded him of the men of Judah. Samson took refuge in the rock Etam, whither 3000 of the men of Judah pursued him, calling upon him to give himself up. He did so on their promise not to harm him. Whereupon they bound him with cords to deliver him to the Philistines, but he snapped the cords asunder, and, seizing the jawbone of an ass, slew therewith a thousand of the enemy. This bold and extraordinary action appears to have intimidated them, for we find that after this Samson became judge or leader in Israel, and ruled the land for 20 years. The close of his career was disgraceful and melancholy. At Gaza, the capital city of the Philistines, he visited a woman of bad character, and escaped being caught by his enemies only through his prodigious strength, which enabled him to burst open, and carry away the gates of the city (Judges xvi. 3). He then became enamored of Delilah, a woman of Sorek, by whose blandishments he was induced to give up the secret wherein lay his strength. This woman then betrayed him to the Philistines, who put out his eyes, and set him to grind at a mill. He was made the subject of their derision, and publicly exhibited; but at length, his strength returning, he seized an opportunity of signalizing his strength for the last time. Having been brought out of prison to be made sport of at a public exhibition, in a kind of rude amphitheatre, the main portion whereof, crowded with spectators, was supported by two pillars, he contrived to grasp these pillars, and pull them down, whereby the whole building was thrown down, the crowd were crushed, and Samson perished along with them.

About this time was born the illustrious prophet Samuel, the son of Elkanah, a Levite, and Hannah, his wife. He was born at Rama-Zophim, a city in Mount Ephraim, and from his infancy was devoted to the service of the Lord, and was educated in the service of Eli, the high-priest. During his early youth the child displayed great piety, and even ministered in the temple (1 Sam. ii. 18). For twenty years the Ark of the Lord rested in Kirjath-Jearim, under the ministration of the venerable Eli. But his sons, Hophni and Phineas, were dissolute men, and brought disorder and licentiousness into the sacred ceremonies. In fact, they attempted to introduce the impure rites of the neighboring nations, and are on this account styled "sons of Belial" (1 Sam. ii. 12). Samuel warned Eli of the fate which awaited his family, which prediction was soon after realized. The Philistines again invaded the land: a bloody battle was fought at Aphek, in the northern part of Judah, in which the Israelites were totally defeated. In their desperation they sent for the Ark, and, placing it in the centre of their ranks, they again faced their enemies. Another battle ensued, but the Israelites were again routed: 30,000 of them were slain, and the Ark fell into the hands of the Philistines. Hophni and Phineas were slain. The aged Eli sat by the wayside awaiting the result of the battle; and when a messenger arrived with the news, the blind old man, then ninety-eight years of age, fell from his seat, broke his neck, and died. Thus was the denunciation uttered by Samuel verified. The wife of Phineas gave premature birth to a male child, whom she named "Ichabod", because the glory had departed from Israel (1 Sam. iv. 21, 22).

Who judged Israel after Abdon?—Who was the next deliverer?—Relate the exploits of Samson.—And the manner of his death.—What is said of the youth of Samuel?—Of the sons of Eli?—Of the battle of Aphek, and the death of Eli?—Of the power of Samuel?—What name did the wife of Phineas give her child?—Why?

INDIA.

Indra was a god formerly worshipped as the ruler of heaven, and as king of the gods. He has been supposed to be the same as the Jupiter of the Greeks. His mansion was of immense extent and unrivalled splendor, illuminated with light more brilliant than that of the sun, and thronged with Apsa′ras (heavenly nymphs) and Gandar′vas (choristers). Music, dancing, and feasting were the occupations of the inhabitants. But Indra is now nearly forgotten: so is Cama, the once popular god of love. The Hindoos also believed in good and evil genii, who are spread throughout creation. The Asu′ras are the kindred of the gods, but have been disinherited, and cast into darkness. The Deit′yas are another species of demon, strong enough to have mustered armies, and carried on war with the gods. The Rak′shasas are also gigantic and malignant beings, and the Pisa′chas are of the same nature, though, perhaps, inferior in power. Bhutas are evil spirits of the lowest order, corresponding to the ghosts and goblins of modern times. Lastly, the Hindoos worshipped village gods, a most extensive body of deities; for each village adores two or three as its especial guardians, but sometimes looks upon them as its persecutors and tormentors. Many of them are regarded in the present day as the spirits of deceased persons (mostly those who had died violent deaths), who have attracted the notice of the neighborhood.

The Hindoo gods have always something monstrous in their appearance, and are represented as wild and capricious. They are of various colors, red, yellow, and blue; some have twelve heads, and most of them have four hands. The powers of the three great gods are coëqual and unlimited, and there is no regular subordination of the other gods to them or to each other. The mythology of the Hindoos is full of legends, relating to the personal adventures, amours, quarrels, sufferings, and punishment of the gods. One of the most extravagant of them is that of the churning of the ocean by all the gods and the Asuras, to procure the nectar of immortality; after obtaining which, the gods cheated the Asuras out of their share of it. Another is the descent of the River Ganges from heaven, at the invocation of a saint; on which occasion it fell with violence on the head of Siva.

What is said of the god Indra?—What were the Apsaras?—Gandarvas?—Asuras?—Deityas?—Rakshasas?—Pisachas?—The village gods?—What of the Hindoo mythology?

ASSYRIA.

Of the first monarchs who ruled the second Empire during this century, we know something more than their mere names. The successor of Ninus was, according to the Greeks, Teut′amus; according to the inscriptions, as interpreted by Mr. Layard, and as already mentioned (p. 39), it was Divanukha, Divanubar, or Divanurish. The dates B. C. 1207, 1200, and 1186, have been respectively assigned for the commencement of his reign (see also p. 39). There are full historical annals of the thirty-one years of this monarch's reign. They are engraved upon the black obelisk, and upon the backs of the bulls in the centre of the mound of Nimroud. Divanubar was a great conqueror, and waged war in Syria, Armenia, Babylonia, Chaldæa, Media, and Persia. An interesting account of the discovery of the palace built by Divanubar, and which was subsequently rebuilt by Pul, or Tiglath-Pileser, is given by Mr. Layard (*Nineveh and Babylon*, p. 534). This palace was situated in the centre of the platform of Nimroud. The before-mentioned great inscribed bulls were found in it, as was also the black obelisk. Several chambers were excavated by Layard's exploring party, and numerous fragments of sculptures were found. The edifice, however, was so pulled to pieces by Esarhaddon for materials for his own palaces, that the place of it cannot now be traced.

The next monarch is Teutæ′us, who began to reign, according to Hales, B. C. 1183; according to Clinton, 1154; according to Usher, 1156. The name of the successor of Divanubar, according to the inscriptions, is supposed to be Shamas-Adar, or Shamsiyar — Teutæus being the Greek name given to him by Ctesias.

After Teutæus follows Thine′us, the date of whose accession is also a matter of dispute. Hales places it in B. C. 1139; Usher, in 1135; Clinton, in 1114. Then follows a king whose name is not in the list given by Ctesias. The name found by Mr. Layard on the slabs taken from temples in the northern portion of the mound of Nimroud (Nemrood), on the Bavian tablets, and on other monuments and remains, is Anakbar-bethhira, according to Rawlinson; or Shimishbal-bithkira, according to Dr. Hincks. The accession of this monarch is placed by Mr. Layard in 1130 B. C.; by Hales, in B. C. 1109. The Greeks name him Der′cylus.

Who was the successor of Ninus?—What is known of Divanubar?—Of his successors?—Where was his palace?—What was found there?—Who was the last king in this century?

PERSIA.

We find from the inscriptions discovered at Nimroud that one of the monarchs of the second Assyrian Empire during this century, Divanubar, extended his conquests into Persia. It is tolerably certain that the western provinces had long owned the sway of the Assyrian and Babylonian princes. The eastern may have had independent rulers of their own: while the north was subject to the Turanian or Tartar chiefs, who dwelt in Bucharia. A long period of darkness hangs over Persian annals, and no researches have as yet enabled us to penetrate it. One thing alone is clear, viz., that, as a nation, Persia had no existence for many centuries. It is not until the 8th century B. C. that she reappears upon the stage of history as an independent monarchy.

The ancient Persians had singular customs with respect to the burial of their dead. The followers of Zoroaster exposed the body of the deceased on the tops of cemeteries, built "where neither man nor water passeth;" and when the flesh was eaten off by birds, or wasted by exposure, the bones, instead of being separately interred, were thrown into a great cavity in the centre of the common sepulchre. According to Herodotus, the Persians did not inter their dead until the flesh had been eaten by dogs and birds. When they buried the body they first enclosed it in wax, and afterwards placed it in the ground. Zoroaster professed to derive his authority for establishing such a practice from Espendermad, one of the guardian angels of animals and of the elements. These angels appear to have had the names and functions following:

Bah′man,	guardian of	cattle.
Ar′dibehesht′,	"	" fire.
Shah′erawar′,	"	" weapons.
Esp′endermad′	"	" the soil.
Awa′,	"	" water.
Amardad′,	"	" plants, fruits.
Khurshid,	"	" the sun.
Mohor,	"	" the moon.
Gowad,	"	" the air.
Teshtar Tir,	"	" rain.

These angelic beings are styled Iz′-ads (angels) and Amshas′pands (archangels), who are invisible to men, but cannot behold the Lord, because he is greatly superior to them, and is without shadow and form. (Wilson's *Parsi Religion*, ch. ii.)

What is said of the state of Persia during this century?—Of the burial of the dead by the ancient Persians?—The guardian angels?—What were their names, functions, and titles?

CHINA.

Woo-yik, who ascended the throne B. C. 1198, "feared neither Heaven nor man." He removed the capital to Ho-pih, in Ho-nan, but his cruelty and impiety drove the people into rebellion, and many emigrated to Japan and the neighboring isles. He is said to have been struck dead by lightning.

Tae-ting, his successor (B. C. 1194), employed the Chow family in the highest stations to reform abuses; but he was a weak prince, and his reign was short. His son, Te-yik (B. C. 1191), was also a weak prince, but was fortunate in having an upright minister in Wan-wang. To him was confided the government, and he proved faithful.

Chow-sin, the last Emperor of this family, ascended the throne in the year B. C. 1154. He was a monster of iniquity, and given up to the most abominable debauchery, in which he was encouraged by his wife, the beautiful but infamous Tan-ke. The stories told of these imperial libertines are almost incredible. The most disgraceful scenes of debauchery were publicly exhibited. Those who remonstrated against these frightful excesses, were punished by being made to hold a red hot iron vessel in their hands. Tan-ke also invented a novel punishment: this was a pole of brass, which, being well oiled, was laid over a fire; the victim was then made to walk along this slippery pole until he fell into the flames, which afforded the greatest delight to this imperial tyrant. The Emperor was not less ferocious. With his own hands he ripped open several persons who had offended him; and on one occasion, seeing several persons walking over the ice, he ordered their legs to be cut off, in order that he might inspect the marrow of their bones. The people at length took up arms, but Wan-wang succeeded in pacifying them. After the death of this able minister they rose again, and Woo-wang, his son, put himself at their head, and routed the imperial forces. Chow-sin fled to his palace, set it on fire, and perished in the flames. Tan-ke was put to death. Woo-wang became the founder of the Chow dynasty, B. C. 1122, and removed the Court to Haou, in Shen-se. He re-established the five orders of nobility, and allotted them lands, thereby creating a feudal system which afterwards caused much misery. He died, B. C. 1115, and was succeeded by his son, Ching-wang.

What is said of Woo-yik?—Of Tae-ting?—Te-yik?—Wan-wang?—Chow-sin and Tan-ke?—Their lust and cruelty?—Who founded Chow dynasty?—Who succeeded Woo-wang?

GREECE.

The great event of this century was the Siege of Troy (or Ilium, its real name). The genius of Homer has forever consecrated the memory of this famous war between the Greeks and the Trojans, in his great epic poem, "the Iliad," which relates some of the exploits of the chiefs on both sides who took part in the contest. There is, however, great doubt whether the city of Ilium, spoken of by Homer, ever had any real existence: but there is evidence that the district in Asia Minor called the Troas, wherein Troy was situated, was the scene of a great conflict at a very early period, between the Thracian princes in the northwest of Asia Minor and the rising power of the Greeks; and that the victory of the latter was fruitless, owing to their imperfect civilization. The date usually assigned to the taking of Troy is B. C. 1184, and should be carefully remembered, because it is the starting-point of various computations, but it is of no historical authority.

The origin of this war is given in the page devoted to Asia Minor (p. 49): so are the leading incidents of it. Helen, the wife of Menelaus, king of Sparta, having been carried off by Paris, the son of Priam, king of Troy, the injured husband aroused the princes of Greece to fit out an expedition to avenge him. After a considerable time a force of 1186 ships and 100,000 men, was assembled at Aulis, in Bœotia, under the chief command of Agamemnon, king of Mycenæ, and brother of Menelaus. The other leaders were Nestor, of Pylus; Idom′eneus, of Crete; Diome′des, of Argos; Ulysses, of Ithaca; Ajax, of Salamis; Elephe′nor, of Eubœa; Pene′leus, of Bœotia; Ajax Oi′leus, of Locris; Menes′theus, of Athens; Achilles, of Phthi′a; Protesila′us, of Phyl′ace; Euryp′ylus, of Armenium; Macha′on and Podalir′ius (sons of Æscula′pius), of Tricca; Adme′tus, of Pheræ; Philocte′tes, of Melibœa; Polypœ′tes (son of Pirith′ous), Gu′nous, and Proth′ous, of Thessaly; Tlepol′emus (son of Hercules), of Rhodes; Phidippus and An′tiphus (grandsons of Hercules), from Cos; and Ni′reus, of Syme. Ulysses attempted to evade joining the expedition by feigning insanity, but he was detected by Palame′des, of Ithaca, and forced to go. Thetis, the mother of Achilles, also endeavored to dissuade that young hero from embarking in the enterprize, but, with his friend Patroclus, he eagerly obeyed the call.

The Greeks proceeded to Ten′edos (B. C. 1194), whence they sent Menelaus and Ulysses to Troy to demand Helen. The Trojans having rejected the demand, the attack was resolved upon. It having been foretold that the first Greek who landed should perish, Protesilaus devoted himself as the sacrifice, leaped on shore, and was slain by Hector, the son of Priam. The Trojans were aided by the Dardanians under Æne′as, the Lycians under Sarpe′don, and by the other nations of Asia Minor: but they could not prevent the Greeks landing. Achilles drove them within the walls of Troy, and took twelve towns on the sea-coast, and eleven in the interior. He had previously taken Scyros, where he married Deidami′a, the daughter of Lycome′des. He also killed Tro′ilus, the son of Priam, and captured several other sons of the aged and unfortunate king, selling them as slaves. In these expeditions nine years were consumed. The murder of Palamedes, by Ulysses and Diomedes, occurred about this time; and, soon afterward, the quarrel between Achilles and Agamemnon, with which the poem of "the Iliad" opens. The remaining incidents of the war are briefly sketched in the page devoted to Asia Minor. There remains now to notice the fate of the leading heroes.

Protesilaus was the first slain. Achilles fell by the hand of Paris. Ulysses, after ten years of wandering, returned to Ithaca, where he was welcomed by his faithful wife, Penel′ope (see Asia Minor). Menelaus, having recovered Helen, returned to Sparta, and lived happily with her. Nestor, Diomedes, Neoptolemus, Idomeneus, and Philoctetes, reached home in safety, according to some authors, but, according to others, they were doomed to long wanderings, and founded cities and colonies in Italy and elsewhere. Ajax Telamon, on the death of Achilles, claimed the honor of being the greatest among the Greeks, but the decision having been given against him, he fell upon his own sword. Teucer, the son of Telamon and Hesione, founded Sal′amis in Cyprus, and some settlements in the Iberian Peninsula. Agape′nor founded Pa′phos, in Cyprus. The other chieftains settled with their followers in different parts of the countries bordering the Mediterranean; at all events, the Greeks asserted this. We shall notice the adventures of Ulysses and Æneas on page 49. With regard to the latter hero, different legends prevail. Some say he abandoned Troy during the conflagration, taking with him his wife, Creusa, his father, Anchises, and his son Iulus, or Asca′nius, and settled in Mount Ida, where he remained on friendly terms with the Greeks. Others say he was carried off prisoner by Neoptol′emus, the son of Achilles, who also took away Androm′ache, the wife of Hector, and Hel′enus, the son of Priam. The popular legend is, however, that which ascribed to Æneas the foundation of the Trojan kingdom in Italy. Ante′nor, the friend of Æneas, settled with a colony of Hene′ti, or Vene′ti, in Italy, where he founded the city of Pad′ua.

Agamemnon, who had been the commander-in-chief of the Greek forces, returned to his kingdom at Mycenæ, with Cassandra, the daughter of Priam. There he found his faithless wife, Clytemnes′tra, with her lover, Ægisthus. The two invited him and his companions to a banquet, where the unfortunate king was killed, along with Cassandra and his followers. His son, Orestes, was saved by his nurse. For seven years Ægisthus and Clytemnestra reigned in tranquillity at Mycenæ; but in the eighth year, Orestes, grown to manhood, returned to Mycenæ, and slew them both. He recovered his father's kingdom, and succeeded Menelaus in that of Sparta. He was aided in his undertakings by Pyl′ades, with whom he contracted a friendship that became proverbial. The adventures of Orestes and Pylades, in their pilgrimage of atonement for the murder of Clytemnestra, are favorite topics with the ancient authors.

The other incidents of Grecian story, during this century, worth mentioning, are: 1. The Second Theban War. 2. The return of the Heracli′dæ (or descendants of Hercules). 3. The Æolian emigration.

The second Theban war was undertaken by the sons of the seven who had been slain in the former war. These youthful warriors (called the Epig′oni, or descendants,) were Ægi′aleus, the son of Adrastus; Thersan′der, the son of Polynices; Alcmæ′on and Amphil′ochus, the sons of Amphiaraüs; Diomedes, the son of Tydeus; Sthen′olus, the son of Capane′us; Prom′achus, the son of Parthenopœ′us; and Eury′alus, the son of Mecis′theus. In this celebrated war Alcmæon plays the principal part. Thebes was taken, the prophet Tire′sias having advised the inhabitants to abandon the city, and Thersander was made king (B. C. 1198).

The Heraclidæ, under their leader, Cleodæ′us, made an attempt (B. C. 1154) to recover the Peloponnesus. In this effort they failed. Their fourth attempt, under the guidance of Aristom′achus, also failed (B. C. 1124). But their fifth, under Ox′ylus, was successful (B. C. 1104). They subdued the greater part of the Peloponnesus, gave Argos to Tem′enus, and Messenia to Cresphon′tes; while Pro′cles and Eurys′thenes, the twin sons of Aristode′mus, the grandson of Hercules, were made joint kings of Sparta.

The Æolian emigration to the islands and coasts of Asia Minor took place about the year B. C. 1124. The emigrants were the majority of the Peloponnesians vanquished by the Heraclidæ, and fled from the subjection forced upon them. Popular tradition connects Orestes with this great movement of the people. He or his sons are supposed to have conducted the Achæans and Æolians to Asia Minor, to escape from their Dorian conquerors.

We may here notice the legend of Tan′talus, and his daughter Ni′obe, which, however, properly belongs to the preceding century. Tantalus, residing near Mount Sipylus, in Lydia, had two children, Pelops and Niobe. He was blessed with happiness and immense wealth, and enjoyed free intercourse with the gods. Intoxicated with prosperity, he became impious. He stole nectar and ambrosia from the table of the gods, and revealed their secrets to mankind. He also killed, and served up to them at a feast, his own son, Pelops. The gods were horror-struck; but Jupiter restored Pelops to life, supplying the piece of his shoulder, which had been eaten by Ceres, with an ivory shoulder. Tantalus was then placed in the under world, with fruit and water seemingly close to him, yet eluding his touch as often as he tried to grasp them, and leaving his hunger and thirst incessant and unappeased. His daughter, Niobe, was married to Amphion, the musician, and had many children; but setting herself up above Latona, the mother of Apollo and Diana, the latter avenged their mother by killing her children. Niobe wept herself to death, and was turned to a rock.

What is said of the historical merit of the legend of Troy?—Relate the origin of the war.—Who were the principal leaders of the Greeks?—Of the Trojans?—What were the principal incidents of the war?—What was the fate of Achilles?—Of Ajax?—And of the other leaders?

What became of Æneas?—Of Agamemnon?—Who was Orestes?—What friendship became proverbial?—Which are the other three leading incidents of Grecian history during this century?—Relate the particulars of each of them.—Also the legend of Tantalus and Niobe.

ITALY.

It appears that Tarchun was a conqueror as well as a colonizer and a lawgiver. He took the Pelasgic towns of Agylla, Alsium, Pisa, Fale′ria, Fescen′nium, Perugia, and Cortona. The whole of Etruria proper was conquered from the Umbrians, and three hundred of their villages were taken and destroyed. The Umbrians sued for peace, and were offered such equitable terms that the treaty was never afterwards broken. They gradually adopted the religion, laws, and customs of the Rasena, and joined them annually in the ceremony of worshipping in common. It appears to have been the practice of the Rasena to offer to those whom they conquered such terms as gave them an interest in the prosperity of the State, whereby they were converted from bitter enemies into firm friends. To this hour the Tuscans dwell side by side with the Umbrians, and the small tribes of the Sarsinati and the Camerti inhabit their ancient soil. (Mrs. Gray's *History of Etruria*, vol. i., p. 70.) The Etrurians also planted colonies between the Po and the Alps.

Tarchun, having conquered a sufficient extent of territory for his purposes, established the Feciales, a body of men appointed to watch over the public peace, whose duty it was to mediate between contending parties, and, in case of war, to endeavor to bring about a reconciliation before the commencement of hostilities. He also dedicated a temple to Voltumna, the goddess of national union and concord; whither, once a year, in the spring, the sovereigns or heads of the twelve States were bound to repair in order to celebrate their common origin and union. Their first act was to elect a dictator, styled, variously, "Embratur" (whence *Imperator*), or Meddix Tu′ticus (whence *magistratus*). He was elected either for life, or until the purpose for which he was chosen was accomplished. He was the Lar of the Lares, or protector of the family of States; the word "Lar" signifying prince, or chief. At this meeting all public questions were discussed; and the Augurs, Feciales, and Arus′pices (priests), were bound to attend. The ceremony of binding together twelve rods, one for each State, was gone through: this was the origin of the Roman custom of the twelve *fasces* of the lictors' rod. A similar ceremony appears to have been ordained for the Israelites (see Numbers xvii. 2). A great fair was held at the same time, to which merchants from all countries resorted.

The Etruscans had an order of nobility styled "Lucumo". The dignity was hereditary, and from this class the Augurs and other chief officers of the State were chosen. The Lucumoes were the chief landholders: their eldest sons succeeded them in their dignity and estates; the younger sons were styled "Aruns." The Senate was composed of Lucumoes, and it elected the king: the ten principal nobles had a right to the "curule chair" (literally, "a chariot seat," but here meaning the seat of magisterial dignity). They appear to have lived in clans, like the Highland chieftains of ancient Scotland; and the word "clan" is actually found in the Etruscan sepulchres (Mrs. Gray's *History of Etruria*, vol. i., p. 196, and the authorities there cited). We read also that women were held in high esteem among them, and had places of honor allotted to them at the public games — a conclusive proof of advanced civilization.

The Rasena were divided into tribes, probably twelve in number. The Senate of each State consisted of Lucumoes, ten of whom, called "the Decurions," represented each nation — Etruscan, Umbrian, and Latin. The Decurions, again, were captains of the "curia," or ten peers, whose votes they represented; for the Senators voted in curias, and therefore ten votes counted only for one. For further particulars as to the Constitution of Ancient Etruria (from which that of Rome was mainly derived), the student is referred to the histories of Rome by Müller, Niebuhr, Arnold, and Livy, and the works of Dionysius of Halicarnassus, Cicero, Plutarch, and Varro. The States were further subdivided into "centuries," or divisions of one hundred families, to whom certain land (called "Fundus") was allotted, and the care of the boundaries was given to officers styled "Arvales". Every year they walked round them in procession, to see that they were uninjured; so that the custom of "beating the bounds", which prevails in England at the present day, is one of remote antiquity. They offered sacrifices to Terminus, the god of boundaries; at which ceremonies, a pig, a sheep, and a bull were slaughtered, and the Arvales were crowned with oak.

Beside the nobles, with their clans, and the "Plebs" (or people), there were three classes who paid taxes to the State, and served in the army. These were Æra′rii, the Isopol′ites, and the Municip′ia. The Ærarii were not landholders, and therefore were not members of centuries or tribes. They were merchants, peasants, strangers, all who had protection from the State, but were not members of it. The Isopolites were foreign neighbors or allies, admitted by treaty to an equality with the Rasena. The Municipia were communities having their own laws, but allied to the Etrurians, and dwelling among them. The Etrurians had slaves, who consisted either of prisoners taken in war, or of men sold for debt among themselves or from neighboring States. These slaves became domestic servants, and were degraded as a caste, but might be emancipated, and thus enabled to act as freemen.

The Etrurian calendar was instituted by Tages. It consisted of one great year, called a secle, which comprised 110 minor years, divided into 22 Lustrums, or periods of five solar years. The minor years were either civil or sacred. The civil year began in March, and consisted of 365 days, divided into 10 months, and two intercalary months. The sacred year began in September, and consisted of 10 months, and no intercalaries. These 10 months were divided into 34 weeks, each week consisting of 8 days, which were probably named after the Jewish fashion: the Jewish days were styled "One of the Sabbath", "Two of the Sabbath", "Three of the Sabbath", and so on; the Tuscan were styled "One of the Feast", "Two of the Feast", and so on. The month was also divided into "Ides", "Kalends", and "Nones". The Ides (from the Etruscan word *iduo*, "to divide") were the epoch of the full moon, and divided the month into half: they occurred on the 13th of the month, except in March, May, July, and October, in which the Nones occurred on the 7th day, and the Ides on the 15th. The Kalends were always the first day of the month. The Nones were the fifth day, except in the months before mentioned; they meant each ninth day, counting from the Ides.

Tarchun introduced a copper coinage, of which the bronze Æs, or As, was the measure. It had on it the double head of Janus, who some say was an Italian king, others an Egyptian, others an Assyrian. He established a system of weights and measures, of roads and fairs (or markets), of drains, tunnels, and channels for irrigation for the cities as well as the fields and marshes; and he is said to have introduced the vine. He foretold for his people "one day of rule" in Etruria, to consist of 1100 years; and he died "old and full of days". His body was embalmed after the manner of the Egyptians, but the exact spot of his grave is not known. Some historians suppose that Tarchun and Janus were the same person (Mrs. Gray's *History of Etruria*, vol. i., p. 306). After his death, we meet with no person of great eminence among the Etruscans for several centuries.

The legend of Æneas and his Trojan followers settling in Italy after the siege of Troy, about 1180 B. C., and of his founding the city of Alba, was an invention of later times. Virgil, in his Æneid, has but embodied the traditions which were current in his time (1st century A. C.). According to them, not only Æneas, but Nestor, Philoctetes, Idomeneus, and Diomed, found their way from Troy into Italy. Æneas landed in La′tium, then ruled by a prince, or chief, named Lati′nus, who at first received him kindly, but afterwards quarrelled with him, and sought the aid of Turnus, king of the Ru′tuli, to expel him. A war ensued, in which Latinus was killed. His daughter, Lavin′ia, married Æneas, who then became king of the country, his own people amalgamating with the natives, and calling themselves Latins. Turnus then applied to the Etrurian prince, Mezen′tius, for aid. A battle was fought on the banks of the Numi′cius, in which Turnus was killed. Æneas disappeared in the river, and was succeeded by his son, Ascanius, who continued the war. Lausus, the son of Mezentius, was slain in a night surprise; whereupon Mezentius concluded a peace, fixing the Tiber as the boundary of Latium. Thirty years afterwards, Ascanius led the Latins from the low marshy grounds near Alba, to Lavinium Alba, which he founded. But there is another tradition that Lavinium was founded by 600 Alban and Latin families combined (Niebuhr, *History of Rome*, ch. xv.). The leader of this movement was Sylvius, who subsequently became king of the Albans and Latins. Mezentius, having been expelled from his capital, Agylla (which name he changed into Cære), by Astur of Tarquinii, retired to Ardea, where he died: according to Virgil, he killed himself. There seems good reason to believe that he was a real personage, and a bold and wicked man.

What is said of the exploits of Tarchun?—What were the Feciales?—What was Voltumna?—What officers were elected?—What were the Lucumoes?—The Decurions?—The Curiæ?—The Arvales?

What were the Ærarii?—The Isopolites?—The Municipia?—What is said of the slaves?—Of the calendar?—The works and death of Tarchun?—The legend of Æneas?—Of Sylvius?—And Mezentius?

BRITAIN.

The early history of Britain is lost in the obscurest tradition. Some of the earliest Saxon historians pretend that Brutus, the great grandson of Æneas, the son of Priam, king of Troy, having collected a number of followers, set forth in search of adventures, and at length found his way to Britain: that he landed at Totness, in Devonshire, in the year B. C. 1109, and finally settled on the banks of the Thames, where he founded a city which he named "New Troy", after the celebrated capital of his ancestors. This was the foundation of the present city of London. There he was buried, after a reign of 24 years.

This legend is found in Geoffrey of Monmouth's *British History*. He professed to have derived it from a very ancient work in the British language. We insert it here, because having given the legendary history of other nations, there is no reason why that of England should not be given also.

The illustrious poet, Milton, adopts the fables of Geoffrey of Monmouth, in his own *History of England*. His apology for so doing may be found in the second page of that work. He appears to have thought that the long line of quasi-historical kings and exploits could not be altogether unworthy of belief; the more so as they were "defended by many, denied by few." In the times immediately following the age of Geoffrey of Monmouth (the middle of the 12th century A. C.), the history of these ancient kings was implicitly believed. In the dispute which took place during the reign of Edward I. (A. D. 1301), between England and Scotland, the descent of the kings of England from Brutus, the Trojan, was solemnly embodied in a document put forth to sustain the rights of the Crown of England, and it was not impugned by the opposing party. The modern student, however, must take care not to be misled by it. The historians of Greece and Italy make no mention of Brutus and his adventures.

In Ireland, a Celtic tribe, the Bholgs, Fir-Bholgs, or Belgians, under the leadership of the five sons of Dela, established themselves, and acquired regal authority. They divided the island into five portions, and each became king of a separate part. This arrangement lasted for nearly 2400 years!

Of Scotland, we have no accounts at this early period.

What are the traditions respecting the foundation of the kingdom of Britain?—Of that of London?—What historians narrate them?—Who were the Bholgs?—The sons of Dela?

FRANCE.

The kingdom founded by the Tyrian Hercules (or the chieftain who appears under that name), did not long flourish. The city of Alesia (Arles) was a great and magnificent city; and became the "hearth and metropolis of all Gaul." But when Hercules quitted it to go into Italy, it declined rapidly; for the uncivilized people of the neighborhood mingled with its inhabitants, and all returned gradually to barbarism. A lapse of three centuries occurs, however, before the supplanting of these Phœnician settlements in the south of France by the Greeks: but though Alesia may have lapsed into barbarism, it still remained an important city, and in the history of after ages is frequently mentioned.

Of the population of France at this early period we have no certain account: but there is reason to believe that it was comparatively dense, more so, perhaps, than that of any other nation in Europe. In Cæsar's time (1st century B. C.) it numbered several millions. Cæsar tells us that in ten years he defeated four millions of men; of which, one million were taken prisoners, and as many slain! and that he reduced under his obedience four hundred nations (or tribes), and eight hundred cities! They had the reputation of affluence, but their wealth consisted mainly in gold and cattle. It is difficult to believe that gold could have been so plentiful among them, although we are told that there were gold mines in some parts of France. We are inclined to suspect both the Roman and the native historians of exaggeration with regard to it.

The northern portion of France, extending from the river Seq′uana (Seine) to the Scaldis (Scheldt), was inhabited by a division of the Celtic race called Belgians. This name is a corruption of the word Bolgæ, or Bholgs, given to the Tectos′ages in early times; and the people here mentioned are the same as those spoken of in Irish history under the title of Fir-Bholgs, who sailed from the mouth of the Rhine to Ireland about this period. They came from the north of Germany. Thierry (*Histoire des Gaulois*, introduction, vol. i., p. 57) computes that the settlement of the Belgians in France took place about the beginning of the 4th century, B. C. But if a colony strong enough to conquer Ireland could go forth in the 12th cent., B. C., it is very probable they extended over the north of France at a much earlier period.

What is said of Alesia?—Of the population of France?—Of the wealth of the people?—Who inhabited the north of France?—What is said of the Belgians?

SPAIN.

Spain, as well as Italy, has her legends respecting the heroes of the Trojan war. Thus, Teucer, the step-brother of Ajax Telamon, is said to have founded a city called Teu′cria, where Carthage′na now stands. According to Mariana (*History of Spain*, p. 9, and the authorities there quoted), there is little doubt that he sailed through the Straits of Gibraltar, and coasted Spain until he reached Galicia, where he founded the city of Hele′ne (now Ponteve′dra), and that of Amphilo′chia, subsequently called Aquæ Calidæ by the Romans, Auria by the Suevi, and Orense in modern times. Tydeus is said to have visited several places on the coast, but meeting with opposition, he sailed on to Portugal, where he founded the city of Troy, or Tyde, between the rivers Minho and Lima. Menestheus landed at the mouth of the river Belon (now the Gua′dale′te), where he built a city of his own name, which is now known as Port Santa Maria; also a temple between the two branches of the Gua′dalquiv′er, which was called by the Romans "Orac′ulum Mnesthe′um." It is also asserted that Ulysses came into Spain, and made his way round the coast to the mouth of the Tagus, where he built the city of Ulys′ipo (or Olysipo), now Lisbon. But it is tolerably certain that these legends, although confidently put forward as truth, have no historical reality.

The only personage, beside the Grecian heroes above mentioned, whose name appears in the annals of Spain at this epoch, is Gar′garis, king of the Cure′tes, who held his residence in the forest of the Tarresii. He was called "Mellic′ola," from having discovered a mode of taking honey from the beehive. The Trojan war occurred in his time, and he is said to have been endowed with many virtues, but stained his reputation by his cruelty to his grandson, Ab′ides, whom, on account of the misconduct of the child's mother, he caused to be exposed to wild beasts. The infant was left untouched by these animals, and also escaped being torn to pieces by the king's dogs. He was then thrown into the sea, whence he was also miraculously drawn, and preserved to become one of the greatest of the ancient kings of Spain. This legend is in keeping with the practice of antiquity—the heralding of great men by miraculous signs and deliverances.

What cities were founded by Teucer?—Tydeus?—Menestheus?—Ulysses?—Who was Gargaris?—What war occurred in his time?—What is the legend of Abides?

GERMANY.

The mythology of ancient Germany is peculiar, partaking of the vigor of the northern mind, as well as of the gloomy aspect of nature in cold regions. According to this system, the most ancient god is Allfa′dur, or Allfa′ter (or the Father of all), the Creator and Preserver of the universe, and of the inferior gods, whom he will one day destroy. He will also destroy the present world, and erect a new one in its stead. The three Nornen (or fates), the past, the present, and the future, continually proceed from him, and the whole of nature's creations, both gods and men, are regarded as merely temporary emanations from him.

Allfater reigned over boundless void, which, by his will, split into two halves: Muspelheim (light) and Nilfheim (darkness). The Spirit of Light was Surtur; that of Night, Hela. Then Allfater commanded them to mingle, and accordingly a shower of sparks fell from Muspelheim upon Nilfheim; fire and water battled together until there sprang forth from the ferment the divine cow, Audhum′la, the symbol of nutrition, and the giant Ymer, the symbol of brute force. Ymer assumed the rulership of the world: from his right and left foot issued a six-headed son, the father of the Hrymthursen, or wicked ice-giants. The cow licked the good deity, Buri, out of a rock of salt; from him came Bör, from whom descended the three brothers, Odin, Wile, and We (see page 29). These good gods slew the wicked Ymer, tore his body into pieces, and created the earth out of it. Of his skull they formed the sky; of his brains, the clouds; of his hair, the forests; of his bones, the mountains; and of his blood, the sea. They then made man out of the oak, and woman out of the alder, and ruled over the human race and over the universe; but they foolishly allowed Loki, one of the race of Ymer, to take his seat among them as the god of evil, who was one day destined to allure them to destruction. This spirit of evil is perpetually struggling against the spirit of good. This system of cosmogony is confused: for though nature is supposed to have been created out of the body of Ymer, yet it is also supposed to have proceeded from the primary worlds of light and darkness existing beyond its limits.

What is said of the mythology of Germany?—What were the Nornen?—Muspelheim?—Nilfheim?—Surtur?—Hela?—Ymer?—Buri?—The sons of Bör?—How was nature formed?

ASIA MINOR.

The origin of the Trojan war is traced back to a dispute between three of the goddesses. The legend runs thus: At the celebration of the nuptials of Pe′leus, king of the Myrmidons in Thessaly, with the sea-goddess, Thetis, all the gods were invited to the marriage, except Eris (strife). Enraged at her exclusion, the goddess threw a golden apple among the guests, with the inscription, "To the fairest." The apple was claimed by Juno, Minerva, and Venus. The dispute was referred to the arbitration of Par′is, the beautiful son of Priam, the king of Troy, who was tending his flocks on Mount Ida. The goddesses appeared before him accordingly. Juno promised him power and riches, if he would decide in her favor; Minerva promised him glory; Venus promised him the fairest of women for his wife. Paris decided in favor of Venus, and gave her the golden apple. She then directed him to visit Greece, and go to the court of Menela′us, the king of Lacedæmon, whose wife, Helen, was the most beautiful woman in the world. He did so, and, though hospitably entertained by Menelaus, he carried Helen off with him to Troy. Menelaus, accompanied by Ulysses, king of Ith′aca, went to Troy to demand her restitution, but the journey was of no avail. Thereupon, Menelaus and his brother, Agamem′non, king of Argos, resolved to muster all the forces of Greece, and attack Troy. Among the princes who obeyed the summons were Ulysses, king of Ithaca; the venerable Nestor, king of Py′los, renowned for his wisdom; Achilles, the son of Peleus and Thetis, and the most famous hero among the Greeks (said, also, to have been dipped by his mother in the river Styx, and to have been thereby made invulnerable, except in his heels); Ajax, the son of Tel′amon, king of Sal′amis, the next in renown to Achilles; Ajax, the son of Oil′eus, king of the Locrians; Diome′des, king of the city of Argos; and Patro′clus, the friend of Achilles. Machaon and Podalirius, sons of Æsculapius, also accompanied the expedition as physicians. After two years of preparation, the expedition sailed from Aulis, in Bœotia. There, Agamemnon having offended the goddess Diana, the sailing was delayed by a calm. The king offered up his daughter, Iphigeni′a, as a sacrifice, but the goddess carried her off to Tauris, and another victim was substituted. The Greeks arrived in the Troas in the year B.C. 1194. The war was not confined merely to the siege of the city of Troy, but extended over the country. Achilles destroyed twelve towns on the coast, and eleven in the interior. In the tenth year of the war a dispute arose between Achilles and Agamemnon, because the latter had taken away from the former his favorite slave, Brise′is. Achilles thereupon refused to take any further part in the war, and shut himself up in his tent. It is at this point in the contest that the poem of the Iliad opens. The reverses which befell the Greeks are attributed to the wrath of Achilles, who remains inexorable, and deaf to all entreaties. The Greeks at last are driven to their ships by the Trojans, and reduced to the direst extremity. At this juncture, Patroclus borrows the armor of his friend Achilles, and, heading the troops of the latter, repulses the Trojans; but he is slain by Euphorbus and Hector, two of the bravest chiefs of the Trojans, by whom he is stripped of his armor. Achilles gives way to the deepest grief; but his mother, Thetis, exhorts him to rescue the body of his friend, and rouse himself to exertion. He rushes into the fight, and routs the Trojans, seeking everywhere for Hector. Euphorbus having been killed by Menelaus, Hector, after taking an affectionate leave of his wife, Andromache, issues forth to meet Achilles, and is slain by him. Achilles, in triumph, fastens Hector's body to his own chariot, and drags it three times around the walls of Troy, and thence to his tent. The aged Priam, the father of Hector, repairs to the Grecian hero's tent, and begs the dead body of his son. His petition is granted. Achilles, after slaying Penthesile′a, queen of the Amazons, and Memnon, prince of Æthiopia, allies of the Trojans, is subsequently killed at the battle of the Scæan gate by Paris, who shoots him in the heel with an arrow. Ulysses then devises the stratagem of the wooden horse; a large hollow image of that animal is constructed, and filled inside with armed men. It is then sent to the city as an offering to the goddess Minerva-Pallas, whose image (or Palladium) was preserved in Troy. The Trojans permit the horse to be brought inside the gate, in spite of the distrust of Laoc′oön, the priest of Neptune, who, striking the side of the horse with his spear, found it to be hollow; for which act, two serpents were sent by the gods to destroy him. In the night, the heroes concealed inside it come out and open the gate, admitting their companions. The city is then set on fire, and sacked. A great slaughter ensues. Priam and his sons, Deiph′obus and Poli′tes, are slain. Helen is carried back to Greece, and thus the war is ended.

The poem, however, does not comprise the scene of the final destruction of Troy. It concludes with the burial of Hector, whose body has been ransomed by his disconsolate father, Priam. The remaining events of the war are taken from a poem called the Æthiopis, by Arctinus, and from another named Ilias Minor, by Lesches. The subsequent career of the renowned Grecian heroes who took part in the Trojan war, is sketched on the page devoted to Greece (p. 46). The historical character of the legend of Troy has been doubted by some, and denied by others. It seems improbable that so sanguinary a contest should have originated in the abduction of one woman, and that it should have lasted so long when she might have been restored. Many conjectures have been made to account for the war, assuming it to have historical reality. Herodotus asserts that he was told by the Egyptian priests that Helen never was carried to Troy, for that Paris, after leaving Sparta, was driven by storms to Egypt, and the Egyptian king, Pro′teus, detained her until her husband should come for her, at the same time sending Paris out of the country. When the Greeks reached Troy, and demanded her, the Trojans solemnly assured them that she was not in their power, but the latter were unable to convince their foes of the truth of this statement, and so the war was prosecuted to the last. The historian adds: "It was the Divine will that the Trojans should be destroyed, root and branch, in order to make it plain to mankind that the gods inflict great punishments upon great crimes." Menelaus, visiting Egypt on his return from Troy, recovered Helen, who returned with him to Sparta, where she lived happily, and, after her death, became immortal. She was worshipped, with her brothers, Castor and Pollux.

Such is "the tale of Troy divine." It is the basis of two other great epic poems, the Od′yssey and the Œne′id, with which the student ought to make himself acquainted. The Odyssey was also composed by Homer, and narrates the adventures of Ulysses (or "Odysseus", whence the name "Odyssey"), on his return home from Troy. By a series of calamities he is forced to wander for ten years, so that he is absent from Ithaca twenty years altogether. His faithful wife, Penel′ope, has rejected numberless suitors, and his son, Telem′achus, has wandered into various lands in search of him. The principal adventures of Ulysses are laid in a variety of places, viz., in the country of the lotus eaters in Lybia; in Sicily, where he kills the giant, Polyphe′mus, and escapes from the cannibals called Læs′trigons; in the island of Œœ′a, where the sorceress Cir′ce turns his men into swine, and detains him prisoner; in the land of the Cimmerians; in the island of the Sirens, whose sweet voices enchanted all who heard them, and lured them to destruction; on the rock Scylla and the whirlpool Charyb′dis, between which he narrowly escaped shipwreck; in the island of Ogyg′ia, where Calyp′so, the queen, detains him for a long period; and finally, in Ith′aca, where he makes himself known, and puts to death the suitors of Penelope.

The Œneid is an epic poem, written by the Roman poet, Virgil, who lived in the first century of the Christian Era. It relates the adventures of Æne′as, the son of Anchises, and a relative of Priam, king of Troy. On the taking of that city, Æneas and his friends made their escape, and sailed to many places on the shores of the Mediterranean. Among others, Virgil conducts him to Carthage, where the queen, Dido, falls in love with him, and destroys herself because he deserts her (the poet forgetting that more than 300 years elapsed between the supposed era of Æneas and that of Dido). Æneas finally makes his way to Latium, in Italy, after seven years' wandering; there he marries Lavin′ia, the daughter of the king, Lati′nus, who is slain in a war with Turnus, king of the Ru′tuli. Æneas was killed in battle also, but his descendants ruled over the kingdom he founded, and from them the Romans claimed descent. But the whole story of Æneas is mythical, and probably without foundation. Notice has been taken of it in the page devoted to Italy (p. 47), and fuller details have there been given of the fate of this hero and his successors.

What was the fabled origin of the Trojan war?—The actual origin?—Name the principal heroes among the Greeks.—What is said of Achilles?—Of Iphigenia?—With what does the Iliad commence?—Relate the story of Patroclus.—The death of Hector.—Of Achilles.—By what stratagem was Troy taken?

What was the fate of Priam?—With what does the Iliad conclude?—Whence is the remaining account of the siege drawn?—What is said of the entire legend?—What is the Odyssey?—Relate the principal adventures of Ulysses.—What is the Œneid?—Relate the chief adventures of Æneas.—Who was Dido?

THE 11TH CENTURY

EGYPT.

The reign of Smendes may be computed to have ended B. C. 1082. His successors appear to have been:

	B. C.	B. C.
Psousen'nes I. . .	1082 to	1041
Neperche'res . .	1041 "	1037
Amenoph'this . .	1037 "	1028
Osochor'	1028 "	1022
Psin'aches . . .	1022 "	1013
Psousennes II. . .	1013 "	978

Of these kings we know nothing more than their names; but occasional notices of them occur in the Old Testament.

It is related in the first book of Kings (xi. 14–22), that when Joab, in the reign of David, king of Israel, slew all the males in Edom, Ha'dad, one of the royal family, made his escape into Egypt, where he was hospitably entertained by Pharaoh (or, the king), who gave him in marriage "the sister of Tah'penes, the queen." The name of this queen has not been found on any monument, and we cannot decide which of the above kings was her husband.

During the reign of Solomon, king of Israel, an active commerce in horses, chariots, and linen-yarn, was carried on with Judea. Solomon not only furnished his own armies with horses and chariots from Egypt, but sold them again to the Hittites and the kings of Syria. The Pharaoh whose daughter married Solomon (1 Kings iii. 1), was one of the kings of this dynasty; and the town of Gezer, in Palestine, was given with her as her dowry. It is not until the next century that the history of Egypt assumes a definite and connected shape. There is a mysterious grandeur connected with the earliest centuries of the existence of this once mighty land that forcibly strikes us. The colossal proportions of the architectural remains which survive, enable us to form some conception of the power and splendor of a nation which was already ancient in the days of Abraham, and was beginning to decay in the days of Solomon. Yet the people who raised these magnificent edifices appear to have been pigmies in stature. From the measurement of a number of mummies, it appears that the average height of Egyptian men was only five feet three inches — and of the women, five feet. Ancient writers place the dwellings of the Pigmies (a fabulous race of dwarfs, always at war with the Cranes,) near the sources of the Nile.

When did the reign of Smendes end?—Who were his successors?—What is said of them?—Of the Scriptural allusions to them?—Of the ancient Egyptians?—Who were the Pigmies?

SYRIA.

The sons of Samuel were corrupt men. The people, foreseeing the difficulties likely to arise on his death, therefore demanded that their republican government should be changed into a monarchical one. Samuel endeavored to dissuade them from taking this step, but in vain. He therefore selected Saul, the son of Kish, of the tribe of Benjamin, to be king of all Israel, apparently on account of his personal strength and beauty (1 Sam. viii., ix., x.). Moses had made provision in the Law for such a contingency (Deut. xvii. 14–20), but Saul and his successors lamentably departed from his injunctions. Saul was elected king by the assembly of the people at Gilgal; and Samuel, at the same time, surrendered his judicial authority (B. C. 1095). Thus ended the second period of Jewish history. The first, from the call of Abraham to the death of Moses (a period of about 470 years), relates to the origin and formation of the nation. The second (a period of 356 years,) comprises the settlement of the Israelites in Canaan, and the duration of their republican form of government, ending with the establishment of a monarchy. During this last-mentioned period the people enjoyed greater happiness than at any other time in their history: they suffered occasionally from foreign invasion and their disobedience to the laws of Moses, but by far the greater part of the time was passed in a state of pastoral happiness and simplicity. The rule of the kings, though for a short time it elevated the nation to great power and splendor, ultimately proved the cause of its downfall, as we shall see in the sequel.

The first act of Saul was to repel an invasion of Nahash, king of the Ammonites. He then formed a regular army, and sent it forth, under the command of his son Jonathan, against the Philistines, who were sweeping the country with fire and sword. The heroism of Jonathan at Gibeah (1 Sam. xiv.) saved the nation, although he came near losing his life through ignorantly violating a vow made by his father (1 Sam. xiv. 38–46). Soon after this, Saul was afflicted with insanity, and his attendants introduced to him a musician to beguile the time. This person was David, the son of Jesse, of the city of Bethlehem, whose skill in music restored Saul to reason (1 Sam. xvi. 23). The king was now able to take the field once more against the Philistines, who were encamped at Ephes-dammim, in Judea. Here one of their noted warriors, a man of gigantic stature and strength, named Goli'ath, challenged the Hebrew warriors to single combat. All of them, however, shrank from the contest; but David accepted the challenge, and slew the giant with a slung stone. This heroic exploit intimidated the Philistines: they fled in disorder, and were pursued with great slaughter. It also gained for David the love of Jonathan (1 Sam. xviii. 1–4), whose friendship became proverbial, like that of Orestes and Pylades, and of Damon and Pythias, among the Greeks. David married Michal, the daughter of Saul; but his high reputation aroused the jealousy of his father-in-law, who sought to take his life. He fled to the mountains, and took up his abode in the cave of Adullam, where he became the captain of a band of adventurers. Saul wreaked his vengeance on the priesthood, because they had assisted David in his distress; he hotly pursued the latter. But accident having thrown the king into David's power, and the latter having nobly disdained to take advantage of it, Saul became reconciled to him for a time. The reconciliation was not of long duration, however. Saul again sought to take David's life, and the latter fled to Achish, king of the Philistines. There he married Abigail, the widow of Nabal, and defeated the Amalekites. The Philistines, in great force, marched against Saul, and totally defeated him at Gilboa. Jonathan and other of his sons were slain, and Saul in despair killed himself (B. C. 1055). David escaped to Hebron, in Judea, where he was, by common acclamation of the tribe of Judah, made king. But Abner, the commander-in-chief of the army, set up Saul's only surviving son, Ishbosheth, and a civil war ensued. Ishbosheth was wholly incompetent for the office, and Abner deserted him. The young prince was assassinated, and Abner fell by the hand of Joab, whose brother he had slain. The other tribes now concurred in the election of David, who became king of all Israel (B. C. 1053).

After residing seven years and a half at Hebron, David founded the city of Jerusalem, where he established the seat of religion and of government (B. C. 1048). Thither he removed the Ark, and he built a royal palace, being aided with timber and artisans by Hiram, king of Tyre. He defeated the Philistines, and subdued Edom: Hadad, the king, fled to Egypt. He conquered the Moabites, the Syrians of Nisibis and Damascus, and extended his dominions to the Euphrates. He raised the Jewish kingdom to a high pitch of greatness, and adorned the land with noble buildings. He also excelled as a poet and musician, and composed many of the sublimest of the Psalms. Commerce flourished, and the national religion revived. But in the midst of his greatness he fell by his own sins. The particulars of his dreadful transgression will be found in 2 Sam. xi. His love for Bathshe'ba, and the murder of Uri'ah, drew down upon him the denunciation of the prophet Nathan. The Ammonites ravaged the country, but were repulsed by Joab, and treated by David with merciless cruelty. The sons of the king were guilty of the most dreadful crimes. Ab'salom put to death his brother Amnon, and, under the guidance of Achit'ophel, a man of great intelligence, revolted against his father, and drove him out of Jerusalem. There Absalom, contrary to the advice of Achitophel, abandoned himself to pleasure, and David was enabled to retrieve his fallen fortunes. His general, Joab, collected an army, and defeated Am'asa, the commander of Absalom's forces. The young prince was slain by Joab's own hand, and Amasa was subsequently put to death. Three years' famine, followed by a desolating pestilence, added to the misery of the nation. Factions divided the army, the royal family, and the priesthood. Adoni'jah, the brother of Absalom, set up a claim to the succession; but David thwarted him by anointing and proclaiming Solomon (his own son by Bathsheba) his successor. Soon afterwards David died (B. C. 1015), having reigned forty years. He was the most illustrious man of the age in which he lived, but his glory was eclipsed by that of his successor.

Solomon was but twenty years of age at his accession to the throne as ruler of Israel. He at once put to death Adonijah, Joab, and Shim'ei, and banished Abi'athar the priest; and, having thus secured his throne, he commenced his peaceful reign, during which the people enjoyed the greatest degree of prosperity and happiness. (See 1 Kings iv. 20–25.)

Why did the Israelites demand a king?—Who was appointed?—What did Samuel do?—What is said of the first period of Jewish history?—Of the second period?—What was the first act of Saul?—What was Jonathan famed for?—Who was David?—How came he to be known to the king?—Relate the story of Goliath.—What is said of the friendship between David and Jonathan?—Of Saul's subsequent conduct and death?—Of Ishbosheth?—Of the reign and acts of David?—Of his crimes?—Misfortunes?—Character?—Who succeeded him?

INDIA.

We have already noticed the fact that great doubts exist as to the age in which Menu, or the author of the code bearing that name, lived. Sir William Jones fixes it at about B. C. 1280, and Mr. Elphinstone computes it at about B. C. 900, a difference of nearly 400 years. That the code is very ancient is proved by its obsolete style, and by the difference of religion and manners from those of present times.

The Institutes of Menu proclaim the knowledge of one true God, and that the substance and the form of all created beings were derived from the substance of the self-existing cause. He first, with a thought, created the waters, and placed in them a productive seed. From this seed sprung the egg in which he was born in the form of Brahma. He then produced the heavens, the earth, and the human soul, and gave names and occupations to all creatures. He also created inferior deities. But this creation is only to endure for a certain period; and when that shall expire, the divine energy will be withdrawn, Brahma will be absorbed in the supreme essence, and the whole system will fade away. These extinctions of creation, with corresponding revivals, occur periodically, at terms of prodigious length. According to Menu, the inferior deities represent the elements: his list varies somewhat from the ordinary Brahminical list (see Elphinstone's *History of India*, vol. i., ch. iv.). He never alludes to Rama or Crishna, nor to Siva and Vishnu. Brahma is sometimes named, but his mystical union with Vishnu and Siva is never hinted at.

Distinct from the gods are the genii, giants, nymphs, demons, and Pitris (or progenitors of mankind). Man is endowed with two souls, the vital and the rational. The first gives motion to the body, the second is the seat of the passions and the good or bad qualities: they are independent of each other, but are connected with the divine essence. The vital soul expiates the sins of man by suffering torments and transmigration into inferior beings, animals, and even plants, until it is purified, when it recommences a career which may lead to eternal bliss. God endowed man with conscience as an internal monitor, and "made a total difference between right and wrong," as well as between pleasure and pain, joy and sorrow, and so on.

What was the era of Menu?—What do his Institutes teach?—Wherein consists the difference between him and the Brahminical code?—What is his doctrine as to the soul?

ASSYRIA.

Another century of nothing but the names of kings is presented to us. They are as follows:

	Hales.	Clinton.
Dercylus	B. C. 1109	or 1084
Mardokempad, or Mesess′imordacus, according to Layard, but the name is not found in Ctesias' list. It has been discovered on a cylinder from Shereef Khan.		
Eupa′les	1069	or 1044
Laos′thenes	1031	or 1006
Adram′melech I. (Layard) began to reign B. C. 1000, but his name is not found in Ctesias. It has been discovered on bricks from the northwest palace at Nimroud.		

Mr. Layard comments upon the entire absence of columns and of stone pedestals for them to rest upon, which is remarked in the Assyrian ruins. We cannot, therefore, form an idea as to the height of their great edifices, as we can of those of Egypt, Persia, and Greece. He supposes, however, that there must have been something in the shape of columns to support the roof, or that portion of it through which light was admitted. But it is very probable that the inner chambers remained in almost entire darkness, the absence of light being considered essential to secure a cool temperature. The sculptures and decorations in them could then only be seen by torchlight. The great halls were probably open to the air, like the court-yards of the modern houses of Assyria, the walls being adorned with sculptured alabaster. It is also supposed that the roof was sustained by pillars of wood or of brick-work, and rose so far above the surrounding part of the building that light was admitted by columns and buttresses immediately beneath the ceiling. It is probable there were two or three stories of chambers opening into them, either by columns or windows, as is the case in modern houses in some parts of Persia. In these a great central hall, called an Iwan, rises to the top of the building, and has small rooms in two or three separate stories, opening by windows into it, while the inner chambers, having no windows at all, have no more light than that which reaches them through the door. Sometimes they open into a centre court, and a projecting wooden roof protects the carved and painted walls from the weather. Awnings are also used for the same purpose.

What monarchs are mentioned during this century?—In what mode is it supposed that the Assyrian palaces were constructed?—How do they resemble modern edifices in Persia?

PERSIA.

The ancient and pure religion of Zoroaster deteriorated in the lapse of ages. The modern Ghebers, or Parsees, have added a variety of absurd doctrines to it, so that the fire-worshippers of Bombay at the present day bear very little resemblance to those of ancient Persia. The standard of faith among the Parsees is a book called the Vandidad, which professes to report the result of an interview of Zoroaster with Hormuzd, the principle of good. This book is considered by them to be the real production of Zoroaster himself, but there is little doubt that it is the production of a much later age. It is divided into 22 *fargards*, or sections, which contain doctrines and ceremonial institutions, most of them of a very puerile kind. We may here notice the principal features of this work. According to it, Hormuzd created 16 holy localities upon earth, Persia, Hindostan, Khorassan, Bokhara, and China, being among them; but Ahriman destroyed their bliss by creating various evils. Jemsheed, the son of Vivanghao, promoted agriculture, and removed all disease and wickedness, and during his reign all was happiness. A variety of punishments for sin are ordained, which are strikingly absurd. For instance, breaking a verbal promise is to be punished by 300 years' torment in hell; breaking an engagement to sell small cattle, by 700 years' torment; and one to sell large cattle, by 800 years: while cutting off a limb may be expiated by 90 stripes: lights are to be kept burning for a month near the place where a man has expired, and a series of purifications from defilement by touching the corpse must be performed: dogs are especially to be venerated, and severe punishments are ordained for striking them, or giving them bad food. Of such trivialities as these is the Vandidad, the Bible of the modern fire-worshippers, composed. Professor Stuhr (*Religions-Systeme des Orients*,) appears to think that it was composed during the period which elapsed between the death of King Darius Codoma′nus and the accession of the Sassanide dynasty of Persian monarchs (B. C. 331 to A. C. 226).—The student will find a full and interesting account of the system of Fire-worship, both ancient and modern, in Wilson's *Parsi Religion*, as propounded and practised by the modern Zoroastrians.

What change has the religion of Zoroaster undergone?—What is the Vandidad?—When was it written?—What does it contain?—Mention some of its peculiarities.

CHINA.

Ching-wang was very young when he ascended the throne (B. C. 1115), but the greatest attention was paid to his education by his preceptor, Chow-kung, the brother of Woo-kung. Woo-kang, the son of the lately-dethroned Emperor, Chow-sin, whose life had been spared on a previous occasion, rose in open rebellion, and was aided by the three uncles of Ching-wang; but though the rebels were joined by large numbers, the Emperor speedily put down the rebellion, and pardoned all the offenders except Woo-kang, who was put to death. This Emperor instituted new tribunals, and everywhere superintended the strict administration of justice. He built the city of Lo-yang for the adherents of the expelled Shang dynasty, and he also brought into circulation the metal money which is in use at the present day. The fame of so great a prince spread far and wide, and ambassadors came to him from Tun-kin (Cochin China). His reign was long and happy; and, when near his death, he called his ministers around him, and recommended to their special care his son, Kang-wang. He died B. C. 1078, leaving the Empire to Kang-wang, whose reign was also peaceful and happy.

Chaou-wang, the son of Kang-wang, succeeded him (B. C. 1052). The first act of this Emperor was to celebrate the obsequies of the deceased monarch in the most splendid manner. The most gorgeous pomp was displayed before the nobles of the Empire, in order to show profound grief and boundless esteem for the departed Emperor. But Chaou-wang gave himself up entirely to hunting, and not only neglected the affairs of State, but oppressed the nation. The consequences soon became apparent: the tributary princes began to wage war against each other, but Chaou-wang did not interfere. The people south of the Yellow River, rising in rebellion, Chaou marched against them. He was suddenly seized by his passion for hunting, during which he laid waste the country around, destroying the harvests of the farmers for his pastime; but having to cross a bridge built by the reluctant peasants at his command, the bridge gave way while he was on the middle of it, and he and his whole train were drowned, to the great joy of his subjects (B. C. 1001).

Muh-wang, his son, succeeded him on the throne.

What is said of Ching-wang?—What great city did he build?—What else is recorded of him?—Who was his successor?—What did Chaou-wang do?—What was his end?

GREECE.

Sparta.—The conquest of the Peloponnesus by the descendants of Hercules is not a pure myth, but is, in the main, genuine history. In the story we perceive that the ancient Achæan population was subdued by bands of Dorian invaders, and that the Achæans became partly the slaves (Helots), and partly the subjects (Periœci), of their conquerors. The country was divided among the three Dorian chiefs—Tem′enus, Aristode′mus, and Cresphon′tes. Temenus ruled at Argos. His descendants were subsequently expelled: they fled to the north of Greece, and founded the kingdom of Macedon. Cresphontes was slain in an insurrection at Messenia. The two twin sons of Aristodemus, Procles and Eurys′thenes, established the Heraclidan kingdom of Sparta, both being joint kings. From them descended the two royal families of Sparta, hence called the Procli′dæ and the Eurysthen′idæ. Agis, the son and successor of Eurysthenes (B. C. 1059), gave the name also of Ag′idæ to that branch of the family: and Eu′rypon (B. C. 1028), the grandson of Procles, gave the name of Eurypon′tidæ to the other. There is nothing worth recording of these kings.

Corinth.—In the year B. C. 1068, Ale′tes, a descendant of Hercules, expelled the descendants of Sisyphus from Corinth, and established his own dynasty there. The family of Aletes ruled Corinth 140 years.

Attica.—In the preceding century the descendants of Theseus had filled the throne. The reigns of Demoph′oön, Oxyntâs, Aphi′das, and Thymœtes, occupied 60 years; at the expiration of this period, the Dorians from Corinth drove Melanthus and the Neleid family from Pylus. The expelled princes took refuge in Athens: and soon afterwards Melanthus distinguished himself in a dispute between the Athenians and the Bœotians, by slaying Xanthus, king of the latter, in single combat. For this service he was raised to the throne. Melanthus and his son, Codrus, reigned for nearly 60 years: the kingdom was terminated by the death of Codrus. The Dorians from Peloponnesus, under Aletes of Corinth, had invaded the country, assured, by an oracle, of victory if they abstained from injuring the person of the king. This oracle was secretly communicated to the Athenians by a Delphian citizen named Cleomantis. Codrus thereupon resolved to sacrifice himself for his country. He entered the enemy's camp in disguise, quarrelled with the soldiers, and was slain. As soon as the Dorians discovered what had happened, they were struck with despair, and retired; but retained possession of Meg′ara, where they established permanent settlers. As no one was thought by the Athenians worthy to succeed so patriotic a ruler, the kingly dignity was abolished, the people declaring that Jupiter alone should be king of Athens. Archons (magistrates) were elected to administer the government, and were appointed for life. The first Archon was Medon, the son of Codrus (B. C. 1045); after him, Acastus (B. C. 1025).

To this epoch may be referred the settlement of the Ionians in Asia Minor (B. C. 1043).

What is said of the conquest of Peloponnesus by the Heraclidæ?—Who founded the kingdom of Macedon?—Sparta?—Corinth?—What became of the descendants of Theseus?—Why was Melanthus made king?—What of Codrus?—Archons?

ITALY.

In this century a vast horde of the Pelasgi, supposed to have emigrated from Lydia, passed through Thrace and Illyria, and entered the north-east of Italy. Pouring into the plains of Lombardy and Liguria, they made themselves masters of Umbria, and subdued the Umbrian Gauls. The Etrurians also felt their power, but this new influx of people soon settled peaceably in the land, and, blending with the conquered, communicated to them many of their arts.

But little is known of the history of Etruria. It continued for several ages to be governed by the twelve States; and, as Rome grew in importance and ambition, it became by degrees mixed up in wars with the Imperial City, to whose power it ultimately succumbed. In this century it is believed that the Etrurian chief, Janus (probably of the tribe of the Faliscii), flourished. He had a palace on the Janic′ulum. He introduced the cultivation of the vine, and the games of the Saturna′lia; and was killed in a drunken fray by his subjects, because when the wine mounted into their heads, they fancied he had poisoned them. Of his wife, Veni′lia, and his sister, Camese, but little is known. The latter reigned jointly with him. He had a son named Fontus, in honor of whom yearly feasts were kept among the Romans, called Fontina′lia. He had also four daughters. Some say he was the father of Tiburi′nus, king of Veii, who was succeeded by Vertum′nus, or Vadimon, and then by Aunus. But there is little doubt that his sister Camese succeeded him on the throne. Janus was subsequently deified. Mention of this personage has already been made (p. 17): the student will notice the discrepancy between the eras assigned to him.

Queen Camese was chief of the Vestal virgins, and seems to have been the same as Camæna of the Latins, or Carmenta, or Car′mina, the muse of song, the undying Sybil, the oracle of justice, called also Tethys, whose shrine was afterwards so often visited by the Romans, the Sabines, and the Tuscans. Feasts, called Carmentalia, were held in her honor. She uttered oracles in verse, and became the goddess of married women. Next to her in renown was the Sybil, Bygoë, who wrote a treatise on lightning, and whose verses and maxims were taught in all the Etruscan schools. They were collected in "the Sybilline books." These books were made either of the leaves of palm trees, or of linen, or of tablets of wood, covered with a thin coating of wax, and they were written upon with a small pointed style of bronze or iron.

The other Etrurian heroes of this early period were Malœo′tus, king of Tarquinia and Cere, who resided at Gravisca, carried on trade with the Greeks, and visited Athens; and Meleus of Pisa, a general who ruled over all Turrhenia, and is said to have invented the trumpet.

The cities of Fiesole and Veii were founded in B. C. 1090, and Lavinia in B. C. 1083. The first Greek colony in Southern Italy was planted in B. C. 1060.

What is said of the history of Etruria?—Who was Janus?—What did he do?—How did he die?—Who was Camese?—For what is she celebrated, and under what names?—Who was Bygoë?—Malœotus?—Meleus?—What cities were founded?

BRITAIN.

To continue the legendary history of Britain. Brutus had three sons, Locrine, Albanact, and Camber, between whom the island was divided: Locrine taking England; Albanact, Scotland; and Camber, Wales. The country was invaded in his time by the Scythians, under a chief named Humber, who took possession of Yorkshire. Albanact fell in battle with him. Locrine and Camber avenged their brother's death, defeated the Scythian king, and drove him into the channel, which was named "the Humber," after him. In this contest, Estrildis, the beautiful daughter of Humber, was captured by Locrine, who became enamored of her, and sought to break off his engagement with Guen′dolen, daughter of Corine′us, duke of Cornwall. Being forced to marry Guendolen, he deserted her for Estrildis: whereupon she assembled an army in Cornwall, and defeated her husband in a battle near the river Sture, wherein he was killed. His daughter, Sabra, was thrown into the river, named after her Sabri′na, or Severn. Milton alludes to this legend in the *Masque of Comus*. After governing fifteen years, Guendolen resigned the kingdom to her son, Madan, who ruled well and peacefully for forty years, and left the throne to his sons, Mempricius and Malim, the latter of whom was murdered by the former.

In Ireland, the sons of Dela had not reigned more than 30 or 40 years, when the Tuatha-de-Danaan, a people famed for necromancy, coming from Norway to Scotland, crossed thence into Ireland under their chief, "Nuad of the Silver Hand," and defeating the Belgians in a celebrated and most sanguinary battle at Moytura (long remembered as "the battle of the field of the tower"), made themselves masters of the country. The Belgians fled to the Isle of Man, North Arran, and the Hebrides.

Not long after this invasion, a colony of Spanish Phœnicians, under the command of the sons of Mile′sius, the great chief, set sail from Gallicia in Spain for Ireland in thirty ships. They landed at Bantry Bay, on Thursday, the first of May, A. M. 2934 (B. C. 1070), encountered the Tuatha-de-Danaan at Sliabh-Mis, and achieved the great victory which secured to them and their descendants the supreme dominion over all Ireland for more than 2000 years. This legend, or fable, has been fondly adhered to by the Irish; they pride themselves on their Milesian origin, and trace back the descent of some of their most illustrious families to this mythical Milesius. The most impartial of their own historians have denied the historical reality of this Spanish colonization. Moore, in his *History of Ireland* (vol. i., p. 91), says that there are no grounds for believing that this Spanish (Scythian, or Scotic,) colony settled in Ireland at a remoter period than two centuries before the Christian Era, at the very earliest. The Scots (Scuits, or Scythians,) landed in England and Ireland at a very remote period. The Picts were also a Scythian race, from Thrace, who, roaming in search of a settlement, landed in Ireland, but subsequently settled in England. They were the original inhabitants of Scotland (according to Moore).

Who were the three sons of Brutus?—What is said of them?—Relate the legend of Locrine and Estrildis.—Of Guendolen and Sabra.—Who were the Tuatha-de-Danaan?—Relate the legend of Milesius and his sons.

B.C. 1100—1000.

FRANCE.

It would seem that the Belgians of this early period were an emanation from the great Scythian stock, whence came the Nemedians and the Tuatha-de-Danaans, as well as the Fir-Bholgs of Ireland. Some antiquarians say that the Nemedians were the same as the Nemetes who inhabited the region where now are Worms, Spires, and Mayence (Mentz); and that the Danaans were the Danes and Norwegians. They assert that these Belgians were a Teutonic people, to whom the Scots were akin both in origin and language. The conflicting opinions of historians on these points demand more investigation than can here be bestowed upon them. But the student will find a full discussion of the subject in Thierry's *Histoire des Gaulois*, introduction; Moore's *History of Ireland*, ch. vi.; and Ritson's *Memoirs of the Celts*, and the authorities there cited. The name "Belgian" is a corruption of the word "Volk," which became transformed into "Volg," then "Bolg" (or Bholg), and "Belg." It is not applied as a generic term, but solely to denote the inhabitants of the north of France, and of some portions of the British Isles. There is little doubt that they extended themselves into Bretagne or Armor′ica, whence they are sometimes called Armoricans. In subsequent ages Bretagne, or Brittany, figures as a country apart from France, and the tribes inhabiting it formed a confederation distinct from that of the Gallic nations, and which, indeed, drew into it the neighboring Celtic tribes, but nevertheless entertained much more intimate relations with Belgium. Thierry concludes that the word "Belgian" signified nothing more than the title of confederation, and that the Armoricans allied themselves with the confederates, but that their settlement in Gaul was much more ancient than that of the Belgians. M. de Roches, in his *Mémoire sur la religion des peuples de l'ancienne Belgique*, treats them as a people wholly distinct from the Gauls; but the modern Belgians entertain diversity of opinion as to their origin, some claiming it to be Teutonic, others Celtic. The colony which settled in Ireland spoke a different language from that of the Celtic natives: the particular form of speech used by them was styled by the Irish "the Belgaid;" whence it is fair to infer that they were not the same people as the Celts of France.

What is said of the early Belgians?—Of the Nemedians?—Of the origin of the word "Belgian"?—To whom is it applied?—Were they Celts, Teutons, or the same as the Gauls?

SPAIN.

According to the Spanish historians, Abides was the greatest of the ancient mythological kings of Spain. He was contemporary with David, king of Israel. Among the many useful acts recorded of him, the following are specially enumerated. He persuaded his subjects, who previously had lived dispersed, to gather themselves into towns and cities, whereby they became more civilized. He restored the use of wine, and the best mode of tilling the ground. He instituted laws, erected tribunals, and appointed judges and magistrates. By these means he gained great renown both at home and abroad, and, having lived to a very great age, he died full of honors, and universally regretted. It is said that his descendants reigned after him, but none of their actions, nor even their names, have come down to us. No remarkable event occurs in the history of Spain for a considerable period, except a most extraordinary dearth which lasted twenty-six years, so that many rivers were dried up, and a severe famine drove thousands of the people into other countries. But Mariana doubts the truth of this account (*History of Spain*, ch. iv.) upon very reasonable grounds.

According to Irish tradition, a colony of Phœnicians settled in the north of Spain under the leadership of Milesius. But a prophecy having foretold that their ultimate place of rest was to be an island in the Western Sea, Heber and Heremon, the two sons of Milesius, fitted out a grand expedition, and set sail with thirty ships from Gallicia for Ireland. There they gained a great victory over the Tuatha-de-Danaan, and divided the country among themselves. They appointed their brother, Amergin, Arch-Bard, or presiding minister over Law, Poetry, Philosophy, and Religion. But these Spanish colonists did not long live in harmony. The wife of Heber coveting a portion of the possessions of Heremon, a quarrel ensued between the two brothers, and a battle was fought on the plains of Geisiol, wherein Heber lost his life, leaving Heremon sole possessor of the kingdom. The other brother, Amergin, soon afterwards became embroiled with the conqueror, and, in a subsequent battle, fell a victim to Heremon's sword. The latter transmitted his crown to his descendants. Such was the (fabulous) career of the sons of Milesius.

For what was Abides celebrated?—What event occurred after his death?—Who was Milesius?—Where did his colony settle?—What became of his sons?—Is it real history?

GERMANY.

Muspelheim, the empire of Surtur, was far above the heavens, and the sun, moon, and stars, were merely streams of light flowing down from it. Beneath the earth was Nilfheim, the abode of Hela, whose palace was Misery; whose table was Hunger; whose servant was Delay; whose threshold, Ruin; whose bed, Sorrow; and whose color, Decay. All mortals who died like cowards on their beds had to ride nine nights through dark valleys, until they reached Giöll, the river of hell, and crossed the bridge into Nilfheim. Those who had been liars and thieves were cast into the deepest pit, called Huergelmir, completely built of snakes' heads, unceasingly spitting poison on the damned.

Between the middle world and Muspelheim, lay another world called Liosalfarheim, or Lichtalfheim. Here dwelt the elves of light, the genii of the elements, the Fylgien, or guardian spirits, and the Walkyren, the messengers of Odin. The fairies, the wood nymphs, the sylphs, water Nixen and Undines, the river and tree elves, also came from Lichtalfheim.

Between the middle world and Nilfheim lay another world, called Schwartalfheim. Here dwelt the black elves who infest the mountains, and the Kobolds, who watch over mines, and endeavor to corrupt mankind. These evil beings delighted in subterraneous dwellings. The story of Tannhaüser, who entered the Venusberg, and took up his abode underneath with the mountain-queen, who assumed extraordinary beauty, and allured him thither; and the legend of Rubezahl, the mountain-king, who assumed the form of a man, and tempted maidens to enter the interior of the Priesen gebirge, are popular illustrations of this very ancient belief in Kobolds. The water-spirits were sometimes wicked, though generally only sportive.

The middle world, or earth, placed between these double worlds of light and darkness, was called Mannheim (or, "the home of man"). It was divided into an upper and a lower part. The first was named Asgard, the heaven of the gods, with its beautiful palace, Walhalla, from whose windows was seen the paradise of pious women and children. The access from the lower part, the earth, to Walhalla, was by means of the rainbow, Rifrost; on this the gods descended to the earth, and the souls of men mounted to Walhalla.

Where was Muspelheim?—Nilfheim?—Describe the abode of Hela.—The receptacle of sinners.—What was between the earth and Muspelheim?—The earth and Nilfheim?

ASIA MINOR.

This is the era of Greek colonization. After the destruction of Troy a period of obscurity elapsed, during which we meet with but slight notices of Asia Minor. The Assyrians extended their Empire over the eastern portion of it. The Lydians, the Carians, and other nations, had their own kings, but make no figure in the history of the period. But after the death of Codrus, king of Athens, the Greeks turned their eyes toward the western shores of this beautiful country. Medon and Nileus, the sons of Codrus, having quarrelled about the archonship, referred to the oracle at Delphi for advice. The oracle decided in favor of Medon, whereupon Nileus resolved to seek a new home. It happened, too, that Attica abounded with a surplus population of Greeks and foreigners, who were ready to embark in any enterprise. He, therefore, with other members of the family of Codrus, planned and carried out the memorable Ionic Emigration, as it is termed, although the Ionians expelled from the Peloponnesus formed but a small proportion of the colonists. The tribes that joined in it were the Cadmians of Thebes, the Minyæ of Orchomenus, the Abantes of Eubœ′a, the Dry′opes, the Moloss′i, the Phocians, the Bœotians, the Arcadian Pelasgians, and the Dorians of Epidaurus. They settled in the islands of the Cyc′lades in the Ægean Sea, in the isles of Samos and Chios, and on the coast of Asia Minor, from Phocæa on the north to Mile′tus on the south. The cities of Smyrna, Cyme, Lesbos, Eph′esus, and others, were founded: twelve States were formed, and they adopted the Ionic name.

The Doric Emigration was also a consequence of the return of the Heraclidæ. The leader of this movement was Theras, a descendant of Cadmus, and uncle of Eurysthenes and Procles, kings of Sparta. A number of Minyæ, of Laconia, joined this expedition. They first landed on the island of Thera, which took its name from Theras. Some settled in Crete and Melos, but the larger number reached the southwest corner of Asia Minor, where they founded the cities of Cos, Cnidus, Halicarnassus, and Rhodes. Another Dorian emigration, under Althæ′menes, sailed to Rhodes, expelled the Carians, and founded the cities of Lindus, Ial′ysus, and Camirus.

Thus were extended the language and institutions of Greece to Asia Minor.

What was the condition of the country after the Trojan war?—Who originated the Ionic emigration?—What cities did they found?—What ones did the Dorians found?

THE 10TH CENTURY

EGYPT.

The 21st dynasty ended with Psousennes II., but we are not informed why. The 22d commences B. C. 978, with Shishak I. (or Sesonk). This monarch is called Shishak in the Old Testament. He is styled Sesonchis by Manetho, and Sesostris by Herodotus. He is the first Egyptian king who is mentioned by name in Scripture. From this circumstance the epoch of his reign can be determined with certainty, and hence Egyptian history assumes a more authentic shape. Jeroboam, to save his life from the jealousy of Solomon, fled to Egypt, and took refuge with this monarch. Afterwards, when Rehoboam was placed on the throne of Israel, Shishak marched with an army into Judea, took Jerusalem, and speedily reduced the country to subjection, making Rehoboam his tributary. The rule of the Egyptian king over the Jews does not appear to have been oppressive. He reigned 21 years, and was succeeded (B. C. 957) by Osorkon I. This monarch is supposed to be the Cushite king who invaded Judea, but was defeated by Asa, and pursued to the southern boundary of Palestine (B. C. 941). Of his successors, Pehor, Osorkon II., and Shishak II., we have no particulars, except that their reigns occupied 25 years altogether.

Takello′this I. (B. C. 917) is the next name we meet with, but the notices of him are very meagre. According to Manetho he reigned 13 years, but inscriptions have been found which bear date the 25th year of his reign. It is said of him that he reigned at Thebes; and there is reason to believe that a new dynasty had arisen at Tanis; that Memphis, Sais, and Ethiopia, were independent; and that there was a Cushite sovereign in the north of Arabia. Thus shorn of its dominions the ruling dynasty held its court in Upper Egypt, but the wealth and power of the country was never again displayed in architecture or sculpture. Yet the later kings preserved the monuments and buildings of their ancestors, though they did not add to them.

This portion of Egyptian history is so confused that nothing more than an approximation to fact can be attempted. The names of the kings, and the order and dates of their accession, are disputed by the best authority. See Bunsen's *Egyptens Stellung in der Weltgeschichte*, and Kenrick's *Ancient Egypt under the Pharaohs*.

With whom did the 21st dynasty end?—The 22d commence?—What is said of Shishak?—Of Osorkon I., and his successors?—Of Takellothis I.?—Of the state of Egypt?

SYRIA.

The reign of Solomon is the most brilliant one in the history of the Jews. The nation attained to its greatest prosperity under his administration, and commerce was carried on with all the known world. Solomon was renowned for his wisdom, and he was visited by persons of distinction from all parts of the earth, who came to hear his wise sayings. Among the most frequently mentioned of these visitors was Balkis, queen of Sheba, who was magnificently entertained by the king. The sayings of Solomon were collected, and have been handed down to us in the Book of Proverbs: they far surpass in beauty, wisdom, and number, those of all the other sages of antiquity. Solomon founded Tadmor (Palmyra) in the wilderness, to serve as a place of resort and reunion for the traders of various nations who travelled in that direction. But his greatest work was the Temple at Jerusalem, which was a building of extraordinary magnificence. A full description of it is given in 2 Chron. ii. 7. Solomon also built and beautified other cities (2 Chron. viii.), and died full of honors (B. C. 976), after reigning 40 years. The power and magnificence of Solomon was a favorite theme with the poets and writers of the East: by them his seal was said to have power over evil spirits.

On his death, his son Rehobo′am ascended the throne. The splendor of Solomon had been maintained by heavy taxes. The people now clamored for a reduction of their burdens, but Rehoboam refused to listen to their prayer. Whereupon ten of the tribes revolted, and set up Jerobo′am, the son of Nebat, as king (B. C. 975). Henceforth there were two kingdoms, viz., Israel and Judah: for Rehoboam remained king over the tribes of Judah and Benjamin, and held his court at Jerusalem. There was continual war between him and Jeroboam.

In the year B. C. 972, Shishak, king of Egypt, invaded Judea, and plundered Jerusalem, carrying off all the ornaments of the temple, but he did not dethrone Rehoboam, contenting himself with exacting tribute from him. The reign of Rehoboam came to an end in the year 959. He was succeeded by his son, Abi′jah, whose brief reign of three years is distinguished by a great victory which he gained over Jeroboam, whereby the revolted tribes were for a time "brought under" (2 Chron. xiii. 18). But after the death of Abijah (B. C. 956), and in the reign of his son, Asa the righteous, it appears that the rival kingdom of Israel raised its head once more.

The reign of Asa is distinguished as an era of revival of piety. The young king did his utmost to extirpate idolatry among the Jews, and great success attended his efforts. In B. C. 941, Judea was invaded by the Egyptians, under Zerah the Ethiopian, but Asa defeated them at Mare′shah, with great slaughter, and delivered the country from them. Continual troubles arose between the rival kingdoms of Israel and Judah; in fact, their normal state was one of warfare. Jeroboam had died B. C. 955. His successor, Nadab, died two years afterwards (953), and was succeeded by Ba′asha, who formed the design of blockading Judah. To thwart this, Asa made a league with Benha′dad, king of Syria, and forced Baasha to discontinue building the fortresses he had begun (B. C. 940). The remainder of the reign of Asa was unmarked by extraordinary events. He died in the 41st year of his reign (B. C. 915), and was succeeded by his son, Jehosh′aphat, a pious prince, who walked in the footsteps of his father. It was in the reign of Asa that Hana′ni, the prophet, and Jehu, his son, flourished.

In Israel, Baasha, who had slain Nadab, his predecessor, ruled in as wicked a manner. He put to death all the family of Jeroboam, and carried on perpetual war with the king of Judah. He died B. C. 931, and was succeeded by his son Elah, who, after a reign of two years, was slain by Zimri, captain of half his chariots, "as he was in Tirzah, drinking himself drunk" (1 Kings xvi. 9). Zimri completed the tragedy by slaughtering all the family of Baasha: then finding that the people were exasperated with him, he set fire to the king's house, and perished in the flames. Omri, commander-in-chief of the army, was then set up as king by one faction, and Tibni, the son of Ginath, by another. Omri's party prevailed, and he ascended the throne of Israel. He reigned twelve years, and is remembered as being the founder of the city of Sama′ria (1 Kings xvi. 24). That city was built B. C. 926.

Omri died B. C. 919, and was succeeded by his son Ahab, one of the most depraved of the Hebrew kings. He revived all the idolatrous rites of Jeroboam, and married Jezebel, the daughter of Ithobal, king of Sidon. His sins were reproved by the prophets Elijah and Elisha, whose extraordinary powers were manifested in various ways (see 1 Kings xvii.–xxii., 2 Kings i.–ix.), during this and the following reign.

Phœnice, or Phœnicia, was divided into several small kingdoms. Tyre, Sidon, Arad, Damascus, Hamath, and Zobak, had their separate governors. The Greeks say that Age′nor, the son of an Egyptian monarch, leaving Egypt (in the 13th century B. C.), settled in Syria, and became king, and the father of Cadmus, Europa, and other children. His son, Phœnix, from whom the country was named Phœnicia, succeeded him in the kingdom of Sidon. We meet with mention of Phalis, king of Sidon, in connection with the Trojan war. He was an ally of the Greeks, and tried to induce Sarpe′don, king of Lycia, to abandon the cause of the Trojans. Homer styles him "most illustrious" (*Odyssey*, b. iv., 627). According to Josephus (*Antiquities*, b. i., ch. vii.), Sidon, the eldest son of Canaan (Gen. x. 15), was the founder of the city of that name. The Sidonians are mentioned frequently in Scripture, but no express notice is taken of their kings until the time of the prophet Jeremiah (Jeremiah xxvii. 3). Of the kings of Tyre, the first mentioned is Abi′bal, who was contemporary with David. He was succeeded by his son, Hiram, the friend of David and Solomon.

The principal deities of the Phœnicians were: Beel-samen (the lord of heaven); Baal-berith (Saturn); Baal (the sun); Baal-Zeus (Jupiter); Apollo; Astarte, or Ashtaroth (Venus); Melicarthus, Melcartus, or Melcander (Hercules); Baal of Sidon (Neptune); Thammuz (Adonis); the Cabiri, and the Patœci (small statues carried in ships for the protection of seafaring men). The practice of annually mourning for the death of Thammuz was universal among the Phœnician women, who, at the ceremony, shaved their heads, and uttered loud lamentations. The story of Thammuz is the same as that of Adonis (see p. 17): though Maimonides says that the ancient Sabians held Thammuz to have been an idolatrous prophet, who, preaching to a certain king the doctrine of worshipping the seven planets and the twelve signs of the zodiac, was by him put to death: whereupon all the gods assembled in the temple of the Sun, and mourned his fate.

What is recorded of Solomon?—Of Rehoboam?—Jeroboam?—Abijah?—Asa?—Nadab?—Baasha?—Jehoshaphat?—Elah?—Zimri?—Omri?—Who founded Samaria?—What is said of Ahab?—Who was Jezebel?—What great prophets lived then?—What is said of Phœnicia?—Of Agenor?—Phœnix?—Sidon?—Hiram?—Of the Phœnician deities?—With what Greek personage is Thammuz identical?—What is said of him?

INDIA.

As regards the belief of the Hindoos in a future state, the main feature of it is transmigration. According to their theory, man will either enjoy thousands of years of happiness in some of the heavens, or suffer torments of similar duration in some of the hells. Hope is denied to none: the most wicked man, after being purged of his crimes by ages of suffering, and by repeated transmigrations, may ascend in the scale of being until he enters heaven, and even attains the highest reward of all the good, which is incorporation in the essence of God.

Among the Brahmins there are several sects. The three principal are the Saivas, or followers of Siva; the Vaishnavas, or followers of Vishnu; and the Saktas, or followers of some one of the Saktis; that is to say, the female associates or active powers of the members of the triad. Each of these sects has subordinate branches, and beside them there are sects which worship Surya (the sun) and Ganesa (the remover of difficulties): these two approach very near to pure deism. But the orthodox Hindoos profess a comprehensive system, opposed to the exclusive worship of particular divinities, and draw their ritual from the Vedas and the Puranas.

There are two other religions which belong to the same stock as that of the Hindoos, although differing from it. These are the religions of the Baudhas, or worshippers of Buddha, and the Jains. The most ancient of the Buddhist sects entirely deny the being of God, and some of those which admit His existence, refuse to acknowledge Him as the creator or ruler of the universe. The former, or atheistical sect, held that nothing existed but matter, which is eternal; that the power of organization is inherent in matter, and although the universe perishes from time to time, this power restores it after a period, and carries it on towards new decay and regeneration, without the guidance of any external agent. The chief good in existence is a state of perfect apathy and inactivity, and those who attained to this are the highest in the scale of being. This attainment is effected by the actions and austerities of men who have undergone a long series of transmigrations in this and former worlds. The beings thus exalted lose all activity, but retain consciousness, their qualities operating on matter without any exertion or volition.

What is the belief of the Hindoos in a future state?—Which sects are there among the Brahmins?—Which are the principal?—What is said of the Baudhas or Buddhists?

ASSYRIA.

In this century we find the names of the following kings:

	B. C.	B. C.
Adram'melech I. . .	1000	to 961
Pyriti'ades	961	" 960
An'aku-Mer'odak, or Shimish-Bar (according to Layard),	960	" 931
Ophratæ'us	931	" 930
Ash'urakhbal', or Sardanapa'lus I. (Layard)	930	" 910
Ophrate'nes, or Ephech-e'res, ...	910	" 900
Divanubar (Layard) .	900	

Mr. Layard has found inscriptions recording expeditions of king Ash'urakhbal' to Car'chemish, to the country of the Khabour, to the Euphrates, and thence to the Orontes and Syria. The last-mentioned king, Divanubar (or Temenbar, as Col. Rawlinson reads the name on the inscriptions), was the son of Ashurakhbal. The warlike exploits of a former monarch of this name are also attributed to him, leaving it uncertain whether the two are confounded, or whether they achieved similar deeds. But, as has been observed before, these military expeditions of the Assyrian kings were confined to the neighboring nations, and almost always related to the levying of tribute and the procuring of slaves. It is not at all surprising, therefore, to meet with the constant repetition of the same campaigns.

We may here notice the etymology of the name "Assyria." It is commonly believed to be derived from Ashur: but some antiquaries contend that it was deduced from the Hebrew words *ash* (fire), and *aurim* (lights); *i. e.*, "lights of fire," either from the temples of the fire-worshippers, or from the mineral fires with which the country abounded. Others derive it from *Ai Shur*, or *Ai Tur*, which, in Chaldee, signifies "the land of the bull," referring to the extensive use of the figure of that animal, which was among the ancients an emblem of strength, and also of radiating light. Others again derive it from the Hebrew *ash* (fire), and *shurim* (regulators); *i. e.*, "regulators of fire." Some place Assyria much farther east than the Tigris, even between Persia and India. The Persians were once called "Cephe'nes," from Cephe'ne, a branch of the Indus. —(Calmet's *Dictionary of the Bible*, title "Assyria.")

Mention the names of the monarchs of this century.—What is the etymology of the name "Assyria"?—What is said of its locality?—What were the Persians once called?

PERSIA.

This country during the preceding, the present, and the next century, formed part of the second Assyrian Empire. It has no annals of its own. In the absence, therefore, of history, the space allotted to it may be devoted to the consideration of some remarkable points connected with Oriental chronology. No reliance can be placed upon any of the ancient systems, Chinese, Hindoo, Persian, or Egyptian. The main reason of this is that they have been artificially constructed on a mystical system of numbers. The rules of this system may be thus briefly stated. There were two principal objects in view: 1, the production of coincidences of equality or proportion between periods; and 2, the reduction of numbers to certain favored scales or cycles. The motions of the moon formed the basis of the two most favored scales. From the month of 28 days was derived the septenary (*i. e.*, consisting of seven), and from the month of 30 days that of the sexenary (*i. e.*, consisting of six). This is illustrated in a variety of ways; as, for instance, in the labor-day week of six days, and the sacred week of seven. Multiples of six and seven were frequently used. The motions of the sun furnished another series of mystical numbers. The number of revolutions of the moon determined in reference to them, furnished the numbers 336, 348, 354, 355, 360, 365, and their multiples; as, for instance, the Sothic period, 1460 years = 365 × 4. From the year of 52 weeks was derived a series running 13, 26, 52, 104, 208, and so on.

Then there was the sacerdotal scale formed of combinations of the numbers 7 and 24, to which peculiar sanctity was attached. The numbers 7 and 12, with their multiples, occupy a very prominent place. Preferential numbers were also used; as, 50 times 168 days = 23 years; hence the series, 23, 46, 92, and so on. The series, 101, 202, 303, 404, also frequently occurs, and is expanded into 1001, 2002, 3003, 4004 (this last the commonly-received era of the creation of man). Also, 111, 1111; 222, 2222; 333, 3333. There was a variety of combinations beside these, in which the priests, who were the mathematicians and historians of the ancient world, particularly delighted, and there is good reason to believe that they adapted their history to their chronology.

What is said of Persia?—Of the Oriental chronologies?—On what rules were they based?—Mention some of the principal combinations of numbers employed.

CHINA.

Muh-wang gave himself up to personal gratification. The Tartars of Lesser Bucharia (who are now mentioned for the first time in Chinese history), observing his indolence, invaded China. Muh-wang marched against them with a powerful army, but they retreated into the deserts, devastating the country as they went, and leaving the emperor to contend with nothing but wild beasts. The emperor appears to have reformed his conduct after this inauspicious expedition. Just before his death he uttered a number of wise maxims relating to government, which have been preserved in the *Shoo-king*.

Kung-wang, who succeeded Muh-wang B. C. 946, was an old man when he began to reign. He governed the country well, but was guilty of one act of ferocity, which we relate, because it is illustrative of Oriental despotism. Having, in his old age, had the folly to fall in love with *three* beautiful young ladies at the same time, he forgot his station as emperor, and behaved so rudely that their father removed them from his sight; but the emperor could not rest, and, having sought for them in vain, he vented his anger by burning the town of Meih (the birthplace of the young ladies), and razed it to the ground.

E-wang, who ascended the throne in B. C. 934, was a truly indolent prince.

Heaou-wang, his brother, who succeeded him B. C. 909, was just as bad; so that the unfortunate empire gradually sank into decay and confusion.

The histories of Oriental nations amount to scarcely anything more than a narrative of the actions and caprices of the monarchs who ruled over them; hence the unimproving and uninteresting character of such histories. That of China is peculiarly so, and is consequently unusually monotonous. It would be difficult to invent, and still more so to find, a narrative of a nation's career combining so much childishness, superstition, wanton ferocity, obscenity, practical atheism, and utter absence of manliness and self-respect, as is to be met with in the annals of this country. In abridging them for the purposes of the present work, the author has frequently been compelled to lay them down for a time, from sheer disgust at the atrocities recorded, and fatigue produced by the monotony of the history.

What is recorded of Muh-wang?—Of Kung-wang?—Of E-wang?—Of Heaou-wang?—Of the character of Oriental history generally, and of Chinese in particular?

GREECE.

This century possesses very meagre interest. Of the different States there is but little worthy of note.

Attica.—The Archons who succeeded Acastus were Archippus (B. C. 980), Thersip′pus (B. C. 970), Phor′bas (B. C. 947), Meg′acles (B. C. 916).

Corinth.—The successors of Ale′thes and Ixi′on were Ag′elas (B. C. 996), and Prymnis (B. C. 959). A tribe of the Heraclidæ, under Bacchis (B. C. 924), got possession of the supreme authority, abolished the monarchy, and established an oligarchy, (*i. e.*, the rule of a few). The family of the Bacchi′adæ elected out of their own number an annual Pryt′anis, or president, and they kept possession of Corinth for nearly three centuries.

Sparta.—The descendants of Eurys′thenes and Procles reigned jointly. We give their names, but there is nothing worthy of note to be said of them.

Eurysthe'nidæ, or Ag'idæ.		Procli'dæ, or Eurypon'ti'dæ.	
Eches′tratus	1028	Eu′rypon	1028
Labo′tas	989	Pryt′anis	975
Doryss′us	952	Eu′nomus	926
Agesila′us	923	(supposed by some to be the same person as Polydec′tes).	

The Thracians are said to have acquired maritime ascendancy in the Mediterranean during the early part of this century. They were deprived of it by the Rhodians in the latter part, and it was probably disputed throughout the whole period by the Phœnicians.

It is generally believed that Homer, the great epic poet of Greece, flourished in this century. But his era and his birthplace are alike matters of dispute. Seven cities, viz., Smyrna, Rhodes, Colophon, Sal′amis, Chios, Argos, and Athens, claimed the honor of having given birth to him. The probability is that he was born at Smyrna, and that he fled to Chios (or Scio) when the Ionians were driven out of the former place. He was universally regarded by the ancients as the author of the two grand poems, the "Iliad" and the "Odyssey." But some modern critics have maintained that he was merely the collector of poems that were current in his time; and some have supposed that he was no real individual, but only the embodiment or personification of the persons who composed the various Homeric poems. This subject is fully discussed in Grote's *History of Greece*, vol. ii., ch. xxi. Other poems were attributed to Homer. His compositions were preserved and handed down to posterity by the Rhapsodists, or Minstrels, who sung at the banquets of the great, and at public festivals. They were first collected in a written form by Pisis′tratus, king of Athens, about the year B. C. 535. Homer was the greatest poet of antiquity. Tradition says that in his old age he was blind and poor, and that he begged his bread in the cities which afterwards claimed the honor of having given him birth. Byron alludes to him as "the blind old man of Scio's rocky isle."

What is said of Attica?—Of Corinth?—Of Sparta?—Of the Thracians?—The Rhodians?—Who was Homer?—Where was he born?—What poems did he compose?—Did such a person really exist?—What is the tradition respecting him?

ITALY.

The city of Veii is said to have been founded by Hale′sus, who established the dynasty of the Faliscii. In fragments of popular songs, and in stray quotations, mention is made of several of the kings of Veii. Morrio was the founder of the Salii, a band of priestly warriors, all noble, who danced a kind of sword-dance in procession in honor of Mars. There were twelve of these Salii, one to represent each Etruscan State. Some authors derived both the name and the institution of "Morris (or Morrice) dancers," once so popular in England, from King Morrio: a more probable derivation, however, is from the Morisco or Moorish dancers. In the days of Morrio, the men of Veii made what was termed "the vow of a sacred spring," and sent out a colony to build Cape′na, which became an independent city, but was ever attached to the fortunes of the parent State. Of King Vejo and King Mer′alus but little is said. Deheb′eris (latinized into Tiberis,) is said to have been drowned in the river Rumon, which was named after him the Tiber, an appellation which it has retained to the present day. He ruled over Alba, whence it would appear that he had conquered the Latins. He is called the son of Janus. The city of Fide′næ was founded in the time of Tiberis. His son, Bia′nor, founded a city which he named Man′tua, in honor of his mother, Manto, the daughter of Tire′sias; but this legend has been treated as a myth by some historians, and interpreted to mean that Bianor was styled the son of Tiberis, because he came from the Tiber, and he was called, after his death, the son of Mantu, the Tiresian god of death, or of disembodied spirits. He appears to have been one of the greatest of the Etruscan princes, and his tomb was visible in Virgil's time (*Eclogue* ix.). Aule′tes was another powerful king of Mantua (*Œneid*, b. x., 207).

At this period the Etruscans had colonized a great portion of the northeast of Italy. The Rhœtian colonies there founded were very prosperous. The valley of the Erid′anus (the river Po,) was drained as well as irrigated by a series of dikes; the river was carried through lake Comma′chio, and thence by seven canals, known as the "Fossæ Filistinæ," into the sea, at the point now called Bron′dolo. The district of the Milanese was converted from a swamp into a well-watered land. A harbor was formed at A′dria and at Spina (the mouth of the Po), and trade was carried on with Greece, and with the remote tribes on the Elbe, the Vis′tula, and the Danube. We have thus reason to form a very exalted opinion of the Etruscans, or ancient Tuscans, who appear to have ever retained their Phœnician habits and ideas of commerce, and to have conducted their dealings with strangers in a spirit of equity and peace which made them welcome wherever they went. If they conquered by the sword, they at once admitted the vanquished to equal privileges with themselves. It was this same policy which in after ages added so greatly to the power of the Romans; but the latter did not adopt it so readily as the Etruscans appear to have done.

What is said of Veii?—Of the early Etruscan kings?—Who instituted the Salii?—What was the ancient name of the Tiber?—Who founded Mantua?—What great works did the Etruscans carry out?—What is said of their commerce, etc.?

BRITAIN.

Britain.—Mempricius is said to have been devoured by wolves, after a reign of 19 years. His son and successor, Ebrank, reigned 48 years. He was a man of vast strength and stature, and is said to have crossed over with an army into Gaul and Germany, which countries he ravaged. Some of his sons settled there. He also founded the city of Caer-branke, near York, and built a castle on the site of Edinburgh. Holinshed, quoting from Geoffrey of Monmouth, gravely relates all this as authentic history (*Chronicles*, vol. i., p. 445), and adds other marvellous things; as, that Ebrank had 21 wives, 20 sons, and 30 daughters, and that the latter were sent to Alba Sylvius, king of the Latins in Italy, to be married to his nobles. His son, Brutus (surnamed "Greenshield," from the color of the shield which he carried), invaded France, and conquered the greater part of it, but suffered a severe defeat in Hainault. He was cotemporary with Asa, king of Judah. He reigned 12 years, and was buried at Caer-branke (York). After him came Leil, who founded the city of Caer-Leil (now Carlisle). We are told that this prince was at first upright and just, but as he grew old he became vicious, and abandoned himself to excesses of every kind, so that he was detested by his subjects.

Ireland.—We have seen that the Tuatha-de-Danaan, or Danaanians, were dispossessed of the sovereignty by Heber and Heremon, the sons of the Spanish chief, Milesius. The fate of these two mythical heroes is mentioned in the history of Spain in the preceding century. Heremon, having slain his brothers, Heber and Amergin, became master of all Ireland. Of his immediate successors little is recorded worthy of note, except the death of the idolatrous king, Tighernmas (pronounced Tierna), who, while offering sacrifice to the monstrous idol, Crom-Cruadh, at the Magh-Sleachta, was miraculously destroyed, together with the vast multitude around him. He was the first king who erected Pagan altars in the island. During his reign gold was first worked in Ireland, a mine having been discovered near the river Liffey. It is recorded of Tighernmas that he established a law throughout his dominions that the quality of every person should be known by his garb. The clothes of a slave were to be of one color; a soldier was to wear two colors; an officer, three; a gentleman, four; a nobleman, five; the royal family, and persons of great learning, six. By this last clause the king showed that he appreciated learning more than war, a very unusual thing at that barbarous period of the world's history. A similar fancy for parti-colored dresses existed among the Celts of Gaul: their trowsers were plaided, and they derived their name *braccæ* (or breeches) from the Celtic word *brac*, signifying anything speckled or parti-colored. Joseph wore a coat of many colors as a sign of rank (Gen. xxxvii. 3). Tamar and the king's daughters wore similar dresses (2 Sam. xiii. 18): "And she had a garment of divers colors upon her; for with such robes were the king's daughters that were virgins apparelled."

What is said of Mempricius?—Ebrank?—Brutus?—Leil?—Heber and Heremon?—Tighernmas?—What law as to dress did he make?—What is said of this custom among the Celts and the Jews?

B.C. 1000—900.

FRANCE.

That interesting portion of France called Bretagne, or Brittany, was, as has been already stated, peopled by the Cimbri, and subsequently by the Belgians. Allusion has been made (p. 29) to Hu Gadarn, who, at a very remote period, led the Cimbri, or Cimmerians, from the shores of the Black Sea to the west. According to Breton tradition, this chief planted colonies in Brittany; but whether he is to be considered as a historical reality, or as a mythical personage, is a matter of doubt. He became deified, or reverenced as the representative of God upon earth. Many fables are related of him, of his wife, Koridwen, and of his three children, which point to the story of Noah and of Moses for their origin. Hu Gadarn (*i. e.*, Hu, the powerful,) figures in all the traditions of Wales, Denmark, and Brittany; we, therefore, give the principal myth relating to him.

Hu dwelt near an immense lake, whose waters, being above the level of the surrounding land, threatened it with inundation. Vast dikes were raised to prevent this catastrophe; but a beaver worked his way through one of them, and the world was drowned, all except one man and one woman, who saved themselves by means of a ship with sails, which they had had the foresight to build. These two persons were Hu and Koridwen. They took with them a male and female of each kind of animal. But the earth was kept under water by the beaver. Hu therefore harnessed his bulls to the earth, and made them drag it up to the surface of the water. The bulls died after making the effort. Hu having thus saved the earth and the races of men and animals, founded the institutions of mankind. He formed the primitive race into families, and taught them justice and agriculture. His chariot is eternally surrounded by the rays of the sun; the rainbow is his girdle; his oxen are led in heaven by five genii, and are covered with golden harness and flowers, and coupled by a chain of gold. Hu is the god of war, the conqueror of the giants, the protector in darkness, the defender of the sanctuary. He gives strength to heroes, inspires patience under suffering, and constancy in toil. He is the father of the Druids, the king of the bards, and presides in the Cromlech (circle of stones), representing the world.

What is said of the Cimbri in Bretagne?—Who was Hu Gadarn?—What is the meaning of his name?—What is the tradition connected with him?—What are his attributes?

SPAIN.

The Celts from France helped to repair the desolation caused by the immigration of the natives mentioned in the last century, and a large number of them settled in that part of Spain north of the Ebro, and east of the river Idube′da. They spread southward, and founded the cities of Segob′riga, Belsi′no, Urce′sia, Osma, and Agre′da. Among these Celtic tribes figure the Dura′ci, Neri′tæ, Pelen′dones, Presamar′ci, and Cile′ni.

It is said that the Rhodians, who were among the earliest maritime nations of the world, visited Spain, and built the city of Rhod′ope, or Rhoda (now Rosas), upon a large bay near the foot of the Pyrenees. In the time of the Goths (A. C. 600), Rhodope was a large city, and the seat of a bishopric, but is now an inconsiderable town. The Rhodians are said to have been the first who taught the Spaniards to make cables, and to weave rushes for many uses, and also to make horse-mills for grinding corn. They also introduced the use of copper coin, and built temples to Diana and Hercules.

Mariana relates a marvellous legend respecting the Pyrenees. The event, if it really occurred, must be referred to this century. "About twelve miles from Rosas, is Empu′rias, at the foot of the Pyrenees; at which place, about this same time, the mountain was fired, whether accidentally or by design, is not known; but certain it is, these hills by the Greeks (Rhodians) were called *Pyr*, that is, "fire," either by reason of this accident, or for the great lightning that is often on the tops of them. This great fire melted the veins of gold and silver which were very plentiful there, and in many other parts of Spain, in such manner that these metals ran down the sides of the mountain, to the great surprise of the inhabitants, who admired the beauty, but understood not the value of them. But the fame hereof being spread abroad, induced foreigners to flock thither, in hopes to gather that neglected treasure, or to purchase it of the natives for things of small value." But as we are told that the Celts of France had settled in this locality in great numbers, and that gold had been very common among them for a long period, we can hardly reconcile the legend related by the Spanish historian, and derived from the Greek writers, with that fact.

What cities did the Celts found?—Who built Rhodope?—What did the Rhodians teach the Spaniards?—Relate the legend of the Pyrenees, and the discovery of gold there.

GERMANY.

To proceed with the ancient German, or rather Scandinavian, mythology. The earth was believed to be round, and to be surrounded by Ymer's blood (the ocean), or by the great Mitgard snake, Jormungardur. In the ocean dwelt the god Œgir, and innumerable sea-nymphs. The giant race of Ymer inhabited the mountains and the seas. The extreme north was full of Hrymthursen, or ice-giants. Niord was the god of the cold air and of the north; Uller was the god of winter; Kari, the god of the wind; and his sons, the gods of frost, ice, and snow. In the Saga (or legends and war-songs of the Scandinavian bards,) we meet with many poetical illustrations of the manner in which these giants are mixed up with the operations of nature. "When Gerdha, the daughter of the giants, closed her house-door, heaven and earth were illumined by the reflection of her beautiful white arms;" *i. e.*, the northern lights. "As Hvenilda, the daughter of the giants, carrying earth in her apron, was wading through the ocean, the apron tore open, and the earth, falling into the water, formed the isle of Hven." "Uller (the god of winter) challenged Freyr (the sun) to single combat, and threw down upon the ground a gauntlet (a glacier), in token of defiance, but Freyr was not able to take up the glove, although he strove, and still strives day after day to do so, with the point of his bright lance." There is great poetical beauty in this imagery. The student who desires to familiarize himself with the Scandinavian mythology, is referred to the ancient book styled the "Edda" (an Icelandic word, signifying "mother of poetry"). There are, properly, two Eddas; one was reduced to writing from ancient oral tradition, in Iceland, between the years 1056 and 1133; the other is an abridgment of the first, with a new arrangement of the parts. He may also consult Bishop Tegner's beautiful poem, *Frithiof's Saga*, and Snorre Sturleson's *Heimskringla*.

As in all other mythologies, so in this, the primary notions became debased in process of time. The great God of the universe, and his wonderful attributes, became divided and subdivided, and blended with the human. Guodan, or Wodan (God), was first imaged as a burning sun, but afterwards as standing before this sun under the form of a human hero, Odin-Sigge.

What of the earth?—Of Œgir?—Niord?—Uller?—Kari?—Repeat the specimens given of northern allegory.—What is the "Edda"?—What changes in the mythology?

ASIA MINOR.

At the period of the Greek immigration, Asia Minor was divided into a number of States. On the western coast were Mys′ia (which also included the Troas), Lyd′ia (including Mæo′nia, and Ca′ria). On the northern shores were Bithyn′ia, Paphlago′nia, and Pontus. In the centre, Phryg′ia (including Lycao′nia), Gala′tia, and Cappado′cia; and on the southern coast, Lycia, Pisid′ia (including Pamphyl′ia and Isau′ria), and the two Cilic′ias (Trache′a and Campestris). The large and beautiful island of Cyprus must also be treated as a portion of Asia Minor.

Mysia was divided into five parts: Mysia Major, Mysia Minor, the Troas (where the kings of Troy reigned), Æ′olis (where the chief cities of the Æolian confederacy were planted), and Teuthra′nia, so called from Teuth′ras, who, in the 13th century B. C., founded a kingdom there. It is said that he gave his daughters to Hercules, and was succeeded on the throne by Tel′ephus, the son of that famous hero.

Lydia was at first called Mæo′nia. We find traces of an ancient kingdom here as far back as the beginning of the 13th century B. C. Manes was the name (real or mythical) of the first king. His son, Atys, succeeded him. After him came his son Lydus, from whom the country took the name of Lydia.

Caria was celebrated for its figs, and carried on an extensive commerce with Greece in corn, wine, and oil. The people were nearly allied in kindred to the Mysians and the Lydians, but were considered mean and stupid.

Bithynia was inhabited in the earliest times by the Beb′ryces, Cauco′nes, and Myg′dones; the northern part was occupied by the Mariandy′ni. Mention has been made of Am′ycus, king of the Beb′ryces, who was killed by Pollux in a pugilistic contest, during the expedition of the Argonauts (p. 40). The country was subsequently subdued by the Lydians.

Paphlagonia was visited by the Argonauts. We read of Paph′lagon, the son of Phin′eus, as being the eponymous (or name-giving) hero of the country. Pylæ′menes, king of the Paphlagonians, was an ally of the Trojans. The Heneti and the Caucones inhabited the land at a very remote period. It was sometimes called Pylæme′nia, from the king, Pylæmenes.

Into what countries was Asia Minor divided?—What is said of Mysia?—Lydia?—Caria?—Bithynia?—Paphlagonia?—Who was Teuthras?—Lydus?—Amycus?

THE 9TH CENTURY

EGYPT.

We have placed the reign of King Takello′this in the last century, following the table of the 22d dynasty, according to Manetho. Bunsen places it at the beginning of this century, B. C. 880, and the received chronology fixes it in the year 838.

There is a gap in the history of Egypt at this period, which modern researches have not yet enabled us to fill up. We therefore pass on to the first monarch of the 23d, or Tanite dynasty, Petuba′tis, or Petubastes. Of him, Eusebius says that he reigned 25 years. Manetho says that he reigned 40 years, and that "in his reign was the first Olympiad," which is undoubtedly a mistake, since the first Olympiad began B. C. 776. The balance of authorities leads us to place the commencement of his reign in the year B. C. 825, and that of his successor, Osorchon, or Osorthon II. (Chon, in Egyptian, means Hercules), in the year B. C. 800.

No particulars are recorded of this dynasty, the people being all the time of little or no account, as is the case with all Oriental history. In fact, as we have elsewhere remarked, the history of the nations of the East is little more than the personal record of sultan, emperor, or king. The names of the four kings of the 23d dynasty are given by Africanus. For a long time no monuments of them had been discovered; but recently Lepsius found the escutcheons of the first two, Petubastes and Osorchon, whose names in the Egyptian idiom were Pet-Pacht and Osorkna. The empire continued to decay under their rule, and in the next century fell under the sway of the kings of Ethiopia; thus completing the third period of the history of the new empire, according to Bunsen. That learned writer divides the history of Egypt into the following parts:

- I. The Old Empire, in three periods.
  1. Menes to end of 4th dynasty.
  2. End of 4th to end of 11th dynasty.
  3. End of 11th dynasty to Shepherd kings.
- II. The Middle Empire, which is the period of the Shepherd kings.
- III. The New Empire in three periods.
  1. End of 17th to end of 21st dynasty.
  2. End of 21st to end of 26th dynasty.
  3. End of 26th to end of 30th dynasty, or conquest by Alexander the Great.

What is the era of Takellothis?—Of Petubastes?—What is said of the 23d dynasty?—Into what periods does Bunsen divide the history of Egypt?

SYRIA.

Israel.—Ahab and his wicked sons and successors, Ahaziah and Jehoram, brought Divine wrath on themselves by their conduct, and heeded not the warnings of the prophet Elijah. The first was slain in battle against the Syrians (B. C. 897); the second died from an accident (B. C. 895); the third was slain by Jehu, who exterminated the family of Ahab, and suppressed idolatry (B. C. 884). Elijah was the greatest of the prophets. His second coming was foretold by Malachi (iv. 5), and affirmed by Matthew (xi. 14; xvii. 10). Jehu, when king, fell from the right path, and was involved in ruinous war with Haz′ael, king of Syria, who, in the time of his son and successor, Jehoahaz (B. C. 855–39), almost destroyed Israel. Joash, the son of Jehoahaz, however, influenced by the prophet Elisha, retrieved these disasters, thrice defeated the Syrians, and discomfited and killed Amaziah, king of Judah. Joash was succeeded by his son, Jeroboam II. (B. C. 823), who recovered Damascus and Hamath. In his time the prophet Jonah began to prophesy at Nineveh.

Judah.—Jehoshaphat governed the country well, and encouraged commerce. His son and successor, Jehoram (B. C. 891), ruled badly, and was unable to suppress entirely a revolt of the Edomites. Ahazi′ah, the son of Jehoram, who began to reign B. C. 885, was slain by Jehu, as being of the family of Ahab (B. C. 884). Ahaziah's cruel and infamous mother, Athali′ah, then murdered all the royal family, excepting Jeho′ash, who was secreted, and thus escaped. Athaliah reigned over Judah seven years. But Jehoi′ada, the priest, having accomplished the destruction of Athaliah, placed Jehoash on the throne (B. C. 877). The reign of the latter was troubled by war with the Syrians, whom he was obliged to bribe to leave the country, and he was ultimately slain by his own servants (B. C. 837). His son and successor, Amazi′ah, reigned well, and was a good king; but becoming elated by his victory over the Edomites, he challenged Joash, king of Israel, to meet him in battle. This challenge was accepted, and Amaziah was defeated by Joash, who then plundered Jerusalem. Amaziah was slain by conspirators; and the people placed his son, Azari′ah, or Uzzi′ah, on the throne (B. C. 808).

Mention the kings who reigned in Israel and Judah during this century.—What prophets lived?—What were the principal occurrences?—When and where did Jonah preach?

INDIA.

Another class of Budhists hold that there is a Supreme Being, eternal, immaterial, and intelligent, with free will and moral qualities, but remaining in a state of perpetual repose. He is the sole eternal and self-existing principle. But there is another class of Budhists who believe that matter is a separate deity, and that from the union of the eternal principle with matter sprang a third deity who created the world. From the Supreme Being have emanated five (or seven, according to some,) Budhas, and, from these Budhas, five (or seven) other beings, called Bhodisatwas, each of whom is appointed to create a world. These Bhodisatwas having perfected their creations, return to a state of repose, leaving inferior agents to maintain them in order. As regards this world, the Bhodisatwa who created it also created Brahma, Vishnu, and Siva to operate upon it.

As regards those who have risen through transmigration to the rank of Budhas, some think them the productions of nature, as men are, and that when they arrive at the state of repose they retain an independent existence. Some think them emanations from the Supreme Being, through some of the Budhas, or Bhodisatwas, and that they are ultimately absorbed into the divine essence. There have been a number of these human Budhas in this and in former worlds. Some authors enumerate 130 of the first order; but the last, Gota′ma, or Sakya, revealed the present religion, and established the rules of worship and morality. Although he has passed into a higher state of existence, he is still the religious head of the world, and will continue to be so until he has completed his allotted period of 5000 years. We shall notice the evidence relating to the historical era of Gotama (Budha,) when we come to the history of India in the 6th century B. C.

Beneath the Budhas of the first order there is an infinite number of Budhas of different orders, mostly consisting of human beings who have exalted themselves by their superior sanctity during their life upon earth. There are also innumerable celestial and terrestrial beings in the theology of Budha. But there is much diversity of opinion among the disciples of Gotama; those of Southern India inclining to atheism, those of Northern to theism.

Give further particulars as to the tenets of the Budhists.—What are the Bhodisatwas?—What is said of Gotama?—What other Budhas are there in the system?

ASSYRIA.

Divanubar began his reign about this time (B. C. 900). There are inscriptions on the ancient Assyrian monuments recording the conquest of Armenia, Syria, Persia, and the adjacent countries by this monarch. Probably these nations had been in their usual chronic state of revolt. We have seen that they had previously formed part of the empire, had revolted, and been as often subdued. The inscriptions also inform us that he received tribute from Jehu, king of Israel (B. C. 883). In all probability the Hebrew kings were always tributary to the Assyrian kings.

Shamas-Adur, or Shamsiyav, is the name of the next king (according to Layard), and began his reign B. C. 870. The successor of Shamas-Adur was Acrazanes (B. C. 860). Then Adrammelech II. succeeded to the throne. During the reign of this last-named prince, the prophet Jonah preached to the inhabitants of Nineveh, who, in obedience to his exhortations, "believed God, and proclaimed a fast, and put on sackcloth, from the greatest of them even to the least of them;" and the king, Adrammelech, is said to have followed their example. On this point Mr. Layard says: "It was not necessary to the effect of his preaching that Jonah should be of the religion of the people of Nineveh. I have known a Christian priest frighten a whole Mussulman town to tents and repentance, by publicly proclaiming that he had received a divine mission to announce a coming earthquake or plague." (*Nineveh and Babylon*, p. 507, note.) Near Mosul, on the supposed site of Nineveh, is still shown the tomb of Jonah, now surrounded by a mosque, which the Mahommedans have erected. The memory of the prophet is held in great veneration by them, and pilgrims visit this tomb. (*Ibid*, p. 482.)

The prophet describes Nineveh at this time to have been "an exceeding great city of three days' journey," and to have contained "six-score thousand persons that could not discern between their right hand and their left hand."

Ton′osema′chus, or Sar′danapa′lus, is the king who succeeded Adrammelech (B. C. 818). And after him (according to Layard), Baldasi (B. C. 800). About this time the canal and tunnel of Negoub were constructed for the purpose of conveying the waters of the river Zab to Nineveh.

What is recorded of the kings during this century?—Of the prophet Jonah?—Of his preaching?—Of his tomb?—Of the state of the inhabitants of Nineveh?

PERSIA.

The following numbers were used mystically. The number 3 is mystic with almost every nation. There were 3 wise men of the East; 3 celestial emperors in China; 3 chief deities in India; 3 fates; 3 furies; 3 gorgons; 3 graces; 3 horæ; $3 \times 3 = 9$ muses: the use of the triad, indeed, is so common as to need no further notice here. The number 4 is that of an Olympiad, of the authentic gospels, of the Evangelists, of the great prophets, of the cardinal points, the elements, the seasons, the weeks in a lunar month. It was frequently used by the Jews in combination with 10, the perfecting number: hence 40, or 4×10, signifies, generally, the fulness of the time required. 5 is the number of the senses; the years of a *lustrum*, or Roman period for purification of the people; the intercalated days of the year, $360 + 5$. The number 7 relates to the days of the week; $7 \times 10 = 70$, the years of man's life; 70 "weeks" for the coming of the Messiah; also $62 \times 7 = 434$ (Daniel ix. 25). The number of angels who made the world (according to ancient belief), was 7 (see also Amos v. 8). There were the 7 hills of Rome; the 7 wonders of the world; the 7 wise men of Greece. 10 was "the number of perfection," *i. e.*, the number which multiplied others to the full time. The Jewish Sanhedrim had 10 removals. 12 is the number of the signs of the zodiac, of the months, of the sons of Jacob, of the tribes of Israel, of the Apostles, of the Cæsars, of the great gods of Olympus, of the Asen of the Scandinavians. 14 was the number of the family of Jacob (Gen. xxxvii. 9), and Mary bore Jesus when she was 14 (*Gospel of Mary*, v. 3). 15 was the number of the years of "the cycle of Indiction" (or proclamation); also of the stairs of the temple at Jerusalem, and of the Psalms of degrees. 19 years is the cycle of the moon, or Metonic cycle = 235 lunations. 24, the number of hours in the day. 28 (4×7), the years of "the cycle of the sun," the number of days in a lunar month. 39 is the number of stripes allowed, and of purification days. 72, the number of generations between Adam and Christ; the rate of the precession of the equinoxes (1 degree in 72 years). 84 (7×12), and 112 (7×16), were cycles used in the western church. 223, the years of the Chaldæan Saros, or cycle of lunar eclipses.

What is said of the number 3?—4?—5?—7?—10?—12?—14?—15?—19?—24?—28?—39?—40?—72?—84?—112?—223?—What was the Metonic cycle?—The Saros?

CHINA.

Heaou-wang died B. C. 894, leaving the empire to his nephew, E-wang, who inherited the faults of his father. The tributary States rose to great importance. Among the most powerful of them were Loo, which comprised a part of Shan-tung, the present Yen-choo-foo, the native country of the celebrated Kwong-fu-tsze (or Confucius); Tse, the other half of Shan-tung; Chin, in Honan; Tsoo, in Hoo-kwang; Tsaou, likewise in Shan-tung; Han, in Shen-se; Yen, in Pih-chih-le; Woo, in Ke-ang-soo; Sung, now Kwei-tih-foo, in Honan; and Tsin, in Shan-se. The rulers of these States became independent; their quarrels were incessant, and were the curse of China.

Under the reign of Le-wang, who ascended the throne B. C. 878, these evils increased. This prince was solely engaged in amassing riches, and resorted to the greatest cruelties to extort money from the people. His order to his treasurer, Yung-e-kung, has been recorded: "The only thing I want is money; fill my treasuries, and I am satisfied." The infamous minister obeyed the command, and became indefatigable in his oppression. The people at length became infuriated, and broke into the imperial palace, but the emperor escaped. Highly exasperated, the populace demanded from the minister, Chaou-kung, that the emperor's son should be given up to them; but this faithful minister, instead of doing so, delivered up to them his own son, who was immediately torn to pieces by the crowd. Thus the emperor's son was saved, but Le-wang himself fled, and ended his life in exile. The maxims of Chaou-kung on government are excellent; one saying in particular is worthy of remembrance: "It is more perilous to stop the mouths of the people than to arrest the rapids of a torrent."

When Le-wang's death was known, his son, Souen-wang (B. C. 827), ascended the throne. The reign of this prince was disturbed by the constant invasions of the Tartars, who were repeatedly repulsed by the celebrated Chinese general, Tsin-chung; but at last, in a great battle, the emperor was defeated, and Tsin-chung slain. However, the people raised another army, and drove back the Tartars. These troubles, together with those occasioned by the tributary princes, broke the heart of the emperor.

What occurred during the reign of E-wang?—What is recorded of his successor?—What is said of Chaou-kung?—What occurred during the reign of Souen-wang?

GREECE.

Attica.—In tracing the succession of the Archons, we find the names of Diogne'tus (B. C. 888), Pher'ecles (B. C. 860), A'riphron (B. C. 841), Thes'picus (B. C. 821).

Corinth.—Kings, Ag'elas (B. C. 889), Eude'mus (B. C. 839), Aristode'mus (B. C. 834).

Sparta.—Soon after the death of Polydectes (B. C. 873), his widow bore a son, who was named Charila'us. She proposed to Lycurgus, the brother of the deceased king, to murder the child, and then to share the throne. He seemingly consented, but, when he had got possession of the child, he openly proclaimed him king, and acted as his guardian for a time. The clamors of faction induced Lycurgus to quit Sparta. He visited many foreign countries, and, after a long absence, returned to find his own country in a state of anarchy. He was hailed by the people as a deliverer, and, at their solicitation, undertook the task of reforming the State. He was the great lawgiver who founded the celebrated institutions of Sparta, which raised that State to the eminence it afterwards acquired. He framed a government, consisting of two kings, who fulfilled the duties of high priests, judges, and leaders in war; of an elective Senate, composed of old men, who for 60 years had performed the duties of citizens; and of a popular assembly, consisting of every Spartan above 30 years of age, of good character, and able to contribute to the common table. The Senate had the sole right of originating measures; the Assembly could only affirm or reject them. The latter, in a subsequent age, delegated their authority to deputies, called "Ephors," who, in the end, engrossed the whole power of the State. The Periœ'ci (part of the ancient Achæan population,) were deprived of all civil rights, but allowed their liberty. The Helots (the remaining part) were reduced to abject slavery. They were sold with the land on which they lived, and their masters had power of life and death over them. The Spartan citizen existed only for the State. He had no property but what belonged to the State, but all citizens were entitled to an equal share of the common property. The Spartans gave their whole attention to war and martial exercises; agriculture was neglected; mechanical labor was despised; commerce was obstructed by restrictive laws, and by the use of heavy iron money, the only coin allowed. The citizens dined at common tables, the old men apart from the young. These meals were called "syssit'ia," or "phidit'ia." Arts, science, and literature, were henceforth completely extinguished in Sparta; and while the institutions of Lycurgus remained in force, her history is simply that of a band of warriors.

Lycurgus having exacted from the people an oath that they would keep his statutes inviolate until his return, quitted the country forever (B. C. 825). There are no traces of his fate. He was subsequently worshipped as a god. Charila'us was succeeded by his son, Nicander (B. C. 821). Agesilaus was succeeded by Archela'us (B. C. 879), and Tele'clus (B. C. 823).

He'siod, one of the earliest Greek poets, was born at Ascra, in Bœotia, in this century. He was the author of several poems, the principal of them being the *Theogony*, or an account of the origin of the gods; *Works and Days*, a homely poem, containing moral and social precepts, and the fable of Prometheus and Pandora; the *Shield of Hercules* and the *Catalogue of Women*. The latter is lost. The Theogony reduced the obscure mythology of the Greeks into a systematic form, although it differs in many respects from the myths which were current in Hesiod's time, and in after ages, concerning the parentage, adventures, and acts of the gods and the demigods. In this work the order of nature, physical and moral, is explained in the personification of principles. Very little is known of the life of Hesiod.

Iph'itus, king of Elis, restored the Olympic games, and decreed the cessation of all war during their celebration. The epoch of this decree has been fixed at B. C. 884. The Olympic games were celebrated from the earliest times in Greece. They were solemnly dedicated to Jupiter, and were performed once in every four years. They consisted of horse, chariot, and foot races, athletic sports, and friendly contentions in music, poetry, and oratory; and were held on the plain of Olympia, in Elis, at the confluence of the rivers Alphe'us and Cla'deus, where was the sacred grove of Jupiter, called Altis. In process of time numerous public buildings and statues were erected there.

Who was the great lawgiver of Sparta?—Relate his history.—What was the peculiar features of his system of government?—What was its effect?—Who was Hesiod?—Which were his principal works?—Who re-established the Olympic games?—What were they?—Where were they held?

ITALY.

Great obscurity hangs over the history of Italy during this period. The country was divided into several States, the most important of which was Etruria, in the centre. Occasional notices of the kings of these kingdoms are found in the ancient histories. Livy gives the names of several Latin and Alban kings (*History of Rome*, b. 1, sec. 3), but no great reliance is to be placed on this portion of his history. According to him, the genealogy of the kings from Æne′as to Rom′ulus was as follows: Æneas (whom Livy assumes to have been the veritable founder of the race of Latin kings,) was succeeded by his son, Asca′nius; but whether this Ascanius was the Ascanius (otherwise called Iülus) who escaped with Æneas from the Trojan war, the historian cannot decide. Ascanius' son, called Sylvius (from having been born in the woods by some accident), succeeded him in the kingdom. Sylvius' son, Æneas Sylvius, was the next king; and he, in like manner, transmitted the crown to his son, Lati′nus Sylvius, and the surname "Sylvius" was thenceforth given to all the kings of Alba. From Latinus was born Alba; of Alba came Atys, and of Atys, Capys. Nothing but the names of these kings is recorded. But of Cape′tus, the son of Capys, we are told that he reigned twenty-six years, and was the father of Tib′eris (Tiberi′nus, or Deheb′eris), who has been already mentioned. The latter was drowned in the river Rumon, thence named, after him, the Tiber (see page 56). His son Agrippa reigned next; and after Agrippa, Romulus. Sylvius, the son of Romulus, received the kingdom from his father; but having been struck by lightning, demised it to Aventi′nus, who being buried on that hill which was afterwards part of the city of Rome, gave it his name. After Aventinus came Procas, who had two sons, Nu′mitor and Amu′lius, of whom more will be said in the next century. Thus we have seventeen monarchs reigning during the period which elapsed between the supposed arrival of Æneas in Italy, B. C. 1180, and the foundation of Rome, B. C. 753, being an average of 25 years to each reign. Beside these, the names of Tarche′tius and Cluill′ius have come down to us. Plutarch represents Tarchetius, king of the Albans, as having been one of the most wicked and cruel of men (*Lives*, Romulus). His name is not in the list given by Livy, nor is that of Cluillius, who is represented to have been as great a benefactor to his country as Tarchetius was a curse. Cluillius was the constructor of the immense drain called the "Fossæ Cluilliæ," which, after the foundation of Rome, formed the boundary of the territories of Alba toward the west, and made arable the marshy swamp through which it was conducted. It is also probable that he caused other works, of which the vestiges still remain, to be executed in the immediate neighborhood of Alba. Of Tarchetius it is said that he was dethroned and punished by certain men, who, in their infancy, had been thrown into the Tiber by his orders, but were miraculously saved.

The south of Italy, comprising Campa′nia, Magna Græ′cia, and Sicily, appears to have been early brought under the influence of the Etrurians. After founding the Rhœtian colonies, the Lares and Lucumones met at Voltumna, and sent colonists to settle in the half-occupied lands of the Ausonian Siculi. These colonists, in the 10th century B. C., founded twelve new States upon the exact model of the mother country, but independent of her. The towns which they founded on the coast, directly south from Circe, were Pute′oli, Hercula′neum, Pompe′ii, Sta′biæ, Saler′num, Phlis′tu, and Ve′lia. Inland they built the towns of Nola, Vultur′num, Casili′no, Cala′zia, Suessa, Acerra, Trebella, Cale′no, Abella, Vena′fro, Atella, Nuce′ria, Alfaterna, Compulte′ria, Liturnus, Blera, Acherontia, An′xia, and Heracle′a; also (according to Müller), Marci′na Sarras′te. Salernum was probably the capital; it was famed for its Etruscan temple, dedicated to Kupra (Juno). Cuma had been founded in the eleventh century, B. C. 1060. It is said that Homer visited this city. Vulturnum became a great city, rivalling Carthage and Corinth in wealth. It afterwards took the name of Cap′ua (an Etruscan word, signifying "a hawk"). In the year B. C. 800, the cities of Croto′na and Syb′aris were founded by Achaians, who carried on commerce with Greece. These cities were at first only fortresses, but by degrees, as the Greek colonists established friendly relations with the Etrurians of the interior, they became extensive marts of commerce. The Sybarites (or Achaian Greeks,) conquered from the Siculi the localities where subsequently arose Tem′esa, Taran′to, Messa′pi, Brundi′si, and Metapon′tus.

What does Livy say of the Alban kings from Æneas to Romulus?—What is said of Tarchetius?—And Cluillius?—What great works did the latter execute?—What seaport towns did the Etrurians found in the south of Italy?—What inland towns?—Who founded Crotona and Sybaris?—Who were the Sybarites?

BRITAIN.

England.—In Leil's time there broke out civil discord, which was not appeased until his son Lud, or Lud Hudibras, became king. This prince founded the cities of Caer-kin (now Canterbury), Caer-guant (now Winchester), and Mount Paladour (now Shaftesbury). He reigned 29 years, and died, leaving the throne to his son, Bladud, who was skilled in astronomy and magic. Having met with medicinal waters at a romantic spot in Somersetshire, he founded there a city, since called Caer-bad, or Bath. Bladud dedicated the waters to Minerva, in whose temple he kept fire continually burning. He met with a fate similar to that of Icarus; having made wings, he was killed in the attempt to fly, at Troynovant (or London), after having reigned 20 years. His son, Leir, succeeded him. Leir was a wealthy and prosperous man, and lived to a good old age. He had three daughters, named Gonorilla, Regan, and Cordeilla, and in his dotage resolved to give his kingdom to the one who loved him most. The apparently-indifferent conduct of Cordeilla so angered him that he divided his kingdom between the other two. These daughters, with their husbands, Maglan, duke of Albany, and Hennin, duke of Cornwall, so ill treated the old king that he fled to Cordeilla, who had married Aganippus, one of the princes of Gaul. By the aid of the latter he was re-instated on the throne, Maglan and Hennin being slain. He died two years afterwards, and was buried at Caer-Leir (or Leicester), which city he had built.

Ireland.—The reign of the celebrated Ollamh Fodhla (pronounced Ollav Folla,) may be referred to this period, though some historians place it in the 14th, some in the 10th, and some in the 7th century before Christ! He was the great legislator of the ancient Irish, and instituted the great "Fes," or triennial convention at Tara, where the three orders of the community, viz., the king, the priests, and the people, were convened to make laws, and to record the history of the country in a register called the "Psalter of Tara" (which was extant in the time of Henry II.). In Ollamh Fodhla's time offices and employments were made hereditary in families, a custom adhered to by the Irish down to recent times. He instituted the "Mur-ollamh-am," or college of the learned, at Tara.

What is said of Lud Hudibras?—Of Bladud?—Leir?—Relate the story of his three daughters.—Who was Ollamh Fodhla?—For what was he celebrated?

FRANCE.

The following myth is a specimen of the Breton mode of allegorizing. Hu and his wife, Koridwen, dwelt in Pen-Lenn. They had three children, viz., Mor-Vran, their eldest son (the chief of navigators); Creiz-Viou, a daughter (the symbol of life); and another son, Avank-du (the black beaver), a hideous being. To bestow intelligence on the latter, Koridwen resorted to the temple of the Just One, in the Land of Repose, and instructed the dwarf Gwion (the spirit) to prepare the water of divination. A blind man, named Morda, was placed in charge of the fire, and of the vase in which the water was to boil for a year and a day. But three drops of the hot liquid having fallen upon the finger of Gwion, he hastily put the scalded member into his mouth, whereby he unthinkingly tasted the water. Immediately the future was revealed to him, and he perceived that Koridwen would seek to destroy him. The water, excepting the three drops, was poisoned; he therefore broke the vase, and fled. At the expiration of the year and the day, Koridwen came to the temple, and finding her labor frustrated, she set out in pursuit of Gwion. The three drops enabled the dwarf to transform himself into various shapes to escape from her, but she transformed herself in like manner in order to catch him. Thus when he became a hare, she became a dog, and so on. He ultimately assumed the form of a grain of wheat, in which shape he was swallowed by her, she having assumed the form of a hen. In consequence of this, Koridwen brought forth a son, whom Hu condemned to death. The unhappy mother thereupon concealed him in a cradle covered with leather, and threw him into the sea. This happened near the palace of King Gouydno, whose son, Elfin, an unhappy being, was allowed to wander about by way of occupation. Elfin saw the cradle floating, and drew it out of the water. On opening it he found the child, whom he named Taliesin (radiant forehead), and he took him to Gouydno. To the king's amazement the infant began to prophesy, and informed him that he (Taliesin) had been born thrice; that he held within his bosom the source of all knowledge, and that he knew all that was to be. This myth typifies the origin of man and the development of his faculties.

Relate the legend of Hu and Koridwen.—Of Gwion, Elfin, and Taliesin.—What does the name Taliesin mean?—Of what is the myth typical?

B.C. 900—800.

SPAIN.

The Spanish historians assert that Sichæ'us, of Tyre, the husband of the famous queen, Dido, gained all his wealth by trading with the inhabitants of the eastern coast of Spain. After having murdered Sichæus, Pygma'lion set out from Tyre with a fleet, and landed in Andalusi'a, at a spot where he built the town of Axis (now Almunecar). He also proceeded as far as Cadiz, then called Gadi'ra (or "bulwark"). These Tyrians, or Phœnicians, are said to have built Mal'aga and Abde'ra. Those who settled at Char'taca, in Africa, and founded Carthage, in process of time emulated their Tyrian brethren in their ambitious attempts to extend their commerce and acquire new territories. They attempted to subdue Sicily, Sardinia, and Corsica, but were unsuccessful at first. It was not until their own power had been consolidated at home, that the Carthaginians were able to get possession of these rich islands. They then directed their course towards Spain, and possessed themselves of Iviça, one of the Balea'ric islands. We find that Majorca and Minorca were also attacked, but apparently without success. The name "Baleares" was given by the Greeks to the inhabitants of these islands, on account of their skill in slinging stones. The name of Clumba was given by the same people to Majorca, and that of Nura to Minorca. It we may believe the Spanish historians, the inhabitants of these islands were so fierce that the Carthaginians dared not land, but returned home, and for a long period did not molest Spain or her islands.

The Tyrians and the Greeks introduced into Spain forms of idolatry unknown to the original inhabitants. If the worship of the one God ever prevailed in ancient Spain, it must have been confined to the Iberians. The remains of a variety of ancient deities are found in various parts of the country; also the circles of stones and altars peculiar to the Druids. The names and attributes of these gods are very imperfectly understood. Endobelion was much worshipped. Salambo (Venus) was adored at Seville. Ipsistos (probably "the unknown God") was introduced by the Greeks. Rauvea'na, Bandua, Bariccus, Navi, Eiduo'rius, Sutu'nius, Viscus, the Lugoves, Togo'tis (or Toxotis), Netoz (or Netuce), were some of the deities worshipped in Spain.

What did Sichæus do?—The Tyrians?—What part of Spain did the Carthaginians attack?—Whence the name Balearic?—What deities were worshipped in ancient Spain?

GERMANY.

While we are on the subject of the ancient German mythology, we may mention the mythological Odin and his sons, though the historical personage of that name founded a kingdom in Sweden in the 1st century B. C. The name "Odin" is, perhaps, a corruption of the word Wodan, or Guodan (God), and thus the supreme deity became represented as a demigod. Of this divinity, Odin, many Saga, or legends, are related. He is represented as riding on the eight-legged horse, Sleipnir; and as presiding over the feasting that was carried on in the Walhalla, where the souls of departed heroes were regaled with mead from golden goblets held by beauteous Walkyren, and with steaks cut from the bear, Sährimnir, which always remained whole, no matter how many steaks were cut from him. They also ate the apples of Iduna, which conferred perpetual youth, and they daily rode with the gods on the plains of Ida, and battled with each other in martial sport. Odin personified the brightness of heaven; his wife, Frigga, represented the earth, and is described as riding in a chariot drawn by cows. The twelve Asen (or chief deities subordinate to Odin), were: 1. Thor, or Dunar, the god of thunder, represented as drawn by black goats through the air, carrying in his hand the hammer, Miölner, and a great drinking-horn, with which he causes the ebb and flow of the tides. He was worshipped by the Gauls under the name of Tar'anes, and by the Finns and Lapps under that of Tiermes. 2. Balldr, or Balder, the god of beauty. 3. Niord, the god of cold air and the north. 4. Freyr, the son of Odin, the god of the sun, and guardian of white elves. 5. Tyr, the god of war (supposed by some to be identical with Thor). 6. Braga, the god of poetry. 7. Heimdall, the god of the three classes of men—the nobles, the free-born, and the slaves. 8. Widar, the god of locomotion, who walked through and crushed everything with his iron shoes. 9. Wali, the god of the spring. 10. Uller, the god of winter. 11. Forsete, the god of peace and justice. 12. Loki, the god of evil. These gods assist Odin in governing the world. They are considered by some to signify the twelve months of the year, Odin being the sun; but it is difficult to trace the resemblance.

Mention the attributes of Odin.—Of Frigga.—Name the twelve Asen.—What were their respective attributes?—What do they?—What do they represent?

ASIA MINOR.

Pontus was the north-easternmost district of Asia Minor. It was originally part of Cappadocia, and is mentioned in the legends of the Argonauts. On the east of the river Iris, and on the banks of the Thermo'don, dwelt the Am'azons, a mythical race of female warriors who came from the Cau'casus into Pontus, where they founded the city of Themiscy'ra. They were governed by a queen, and they permitted no males to live among them. But to preserve the race they visited the Gargare'ans, in Mount Caucasus, once a year. Their male children were sent away, or put to death, and their females were brought up as Amazons. Each female had her right breast cut off, to enable her to fight more freely. Many warlike exploits are recorded of them. They invaded Lydia, in the days of Iob'ates, and were defeated by Beller'ophon. They fought the Trojans in the early days of Priam. Their queen, Hippol'yte, was slain by Hercules, who carried away her girdle. In the reign of Theseus they invaded Attica, where they were routed by that hero. During the Trojan war they aided the Trojans, and their queen, Penthesile'a, was killed by Achilles. It is said that they founded the cities of Eph'esus, Smyrna, Cyme, Myri'na, and Paphos. The Greeks appear to have believed in the existence of this nation of savage women, but it is difficult to say upon what grounds.

Phry'gia.—The early inhabitants of this district were an entirely distinct people from those of the rest of Asia Minor. They claimed for themselves very great antiquity. There was a tradition that they formerly dwelt in Macedonia, under the name of Briges; and it is probable that they were part of the great Thracian family that once occupied the north-western portion of Asia Minor; indeed the Roman poets often use the word "Phrygian" as equivalent to "Trojan."

Gala'tia was so named after the Gauls, who settled there in the 3d century B. C.

Cappado'cia is a name of Persian origin. Its inhabitants came from Syria, and were called, from their complexion, White Syrians. It anciently included Pontus, and was divided into Cappadocia Major and Cappadocia Minor. In the earliest ages it formed part of the Persian and the Assyrian empires.

What is said of Pontus?—What were the Amazons?—What is said of them?—Who was Hippolyte?—Penthesilea?—What of Phrygia?—Galatia?—Cappadocia?

CARTHAGE.

The foundation of Carthage has been attributed to Elissa, or Elisa, a Tyrian princess, better known by the name of Dido. The exact era is a matter of dispute. The Roman historian, Livy, states that, at the time of its destruction (B. C. 146), it had existed 700 years, which would carry the era back to the year B. C. 846. Petavius asserts that Carthage was founded 137 years before Rome, which would, therefore, fix the date at B. C. 890. Dido was the daughter of Agenor (or Mutgo), king of Tyre, and grand-daughter of Ith'obal (or Ethba'al), the father of the infamous Jez'ebel, the wife of Ahab, king of Israel. She was married to her uncle, Acer'bas (or Sichæ'us), a priest of Hercules, and a man of immense wealth. Her brother, Pygmalion, having murdered Acerbas in order to obtain the treasures, Dido, with a few friends, escaped from Tyre with her husband's wealth. She fled to Cyprus, whence she subsequently departed with eighty Cyprian girls for the coast of Africa. Arrived there, at a place called Chartaca, she purchased as much land as could be included in a bull's hide; but cutting the hide into the thinnest possible strips, she inclosed a piece of land whereon she built a citadel, which became the nucleus of a city. Its original name was Betz'ura, or Bosra, and it stood upon a peninsula surrounded by the sea on all sides, except the west. There were other Phœnician colonies already in the neighborhood when Dido settled there. Utica had been founded nearly three centuries previously, 27 miles north-west of Carthage. Tunis was 10 miles southwest.

Hiar'bas, a neighboring king, being jealous of the rising State, insisted that Dido should marry him, and threatened to destroy the city in case she refused. The queen, having vowed fidelity to her late husband, and finding that her people wished her to marry Hiarbas, erected a funeral pile, on which she stabbed herself in the presence of her subjects. After her death she was worshipped as a divinity. Such is the story of this mythical personage. Whatever historical truth there may be in it, Carthage was certainly founded by a Phœnician colony. They were peaceful traders, and remained friendly with the natives, to whom they paid tribute for the ground on which the city was built. This relation between them existed until the Carthaginians subdued them.

Who was Dido?—Relate the story of the foundation of Carthage.—What was its ancient name?—What other cities were near it?—What was the fate of Dido?

EGYPT.

Osorchon reigned eight years. According to the Greeks, he was called by the Egyptians Chon, or Hercules. Psammus (B. C. 791), comes next on the list, and, after him, Zet, with whom ended the 23d dynasty. There are no private monuments which throw light on the condition of Egypt during this period. That it was one of decline and decay, we may infer from the ascendancy which the Ethiopians acquired in the next dynasty, apparently without an effort.

Boc′choris, of Sais (called, by the Egyptians, Pehor, and by Herodotus, An′ysis), was the first and only king of the 24th dynasty (B. C. 787). He is said to have been mean, and feeble in body, but to have surpassed his predecessors in ingenuity and wisdom. He enacted laws which regulated commercial contracts, and the prerogatives and duties of the sovereign. He is celebrated, also, for the wisdom of his judicial decisions, many of which were handed down to very late times. He practised strict justice and economy; but all was of no avail to raise the Egyptian character, which had sadly deteriorated; and when the Ethiopians, under Sab′aco, invaded Egypt (B. C. 740), the nation succumbed almost without a struggle. Bocchoris is said to have been taken, and burnt alive by order of Sabaco; but this is contradicted by Herodotus. The Ethiopians of this period were little inferior to the Egyptians in civilization. They are mentioned in Scripture in equality with Egypt and Babylon.

Sabaco, or Shabek, the founder of the 25th, or Ethiopian dynasty, surpassed in piety and clemency all his predecessors. He abolished the punishment of death, and substituted for it compulsory labor on public works, the chief of which were embankments that prevented the Nile from inundating the towns of Lower Egypt. Sabaco has left inscriptions at Thebes and at Abydus; and a Greek inscription at Aboo Simbel, by the Ionian and Carian auxiliaries of Psammetichus, proves that this king attempted to recover possession of that country. Sabaco retired from Egypt to Ethiopia (B. C. 725), leaving the government of the former to Sev′echus (Seb′ichus, Seva, or So; 2 Kings xvii. 4), whose first act was to enter into an alliance with Hoshe′a, king of Israel (B. C. 722), against Shalmane′ser, king of Assyria. Many Israelites fled from the threatened invasion into Egypt, and settled there. But little more is known of Sevechus. He was succeeded (B. C. 713) by Tirha′kah (Tara′cus, or Tear′co). This monarch was king of Ethiopia and Upper Egypt during the invasion of Judea by Sennacherib, and sent assistance to King Hezekiah. We are told that after the retirement of the Ethiopian (Sabaco) from Egypt, and the resumption of power by the king who had fled into the marshes, Sethos (Bocchoris?), a priest of the sun, made himself king, probably of Lower Egypt. In this state of confusion was Egypt when Sennacherib invaded it, but he did not advance so far even as Pelu′sium; for, according to the Egyptians, it happened one night that an immense multitude of field-mice covered the encampment of the Assyrians, and gnawed the strings of their bows and the straps of their shields. The Assyrians, finding themselves thus defenceless, fled, and many were slain by the Egyptians.

It would seem as if the confusion in Egypt, foretold in the 19th chapter of Isaiah, came to pass at this time. Mr. Sharpe, in his *History of Egypt* (pp. 158–162), makes use of the Egyptian chronology to determine the date of the Trojan war, which, according to him, should be placed between the years 925 and 900 B. C., on the following grounds. Herodotus says that Proteus, the king of Egypt who received Paris and Helen, was contemporary with the Trojan war; that there was only one reign between him and Sesostris (Shishak), who conquered Jerusalem B. C. 960; and that there were twelve reigns between him and the Persian invasion of Egypt, B. C. 525. Allowing the computation of Herodotus as to the length of these reigns, this period would amount to 390 years, which would give the year B. C. 915 as that of the capture of Troy. Again, Manetho says that Thuoris, who reigned seven years, lived in the time of the Trojan war, and that he was succeeded by the 20th dynasty, which reigned together 135 or 172 years. Assuming that the 21st, 22d, 23d, and 24th dynasties reigned contemporaneously with it, computing from the reign of So (B. C. 730), we have the year B. C. 900 as the date. Ahab, king of Israel, married (B. C. 918) Jezebel, daughter of Ithobal, king of Tyre; Dido fled to Carthage on the death of Ithobal; and Æneas, according to Roman tradition, visited her on his flight from Troy: thus fixing the fall of that city at about B. C. 886.

What was the state of Egypt during the reigns of Osorchon, Psammus, and Zet?—What is said of Bocchoris?—Of Sabaco?—Of the Ethiopians of this period?—What remarkable events occurred during the reigns of Sevechus and Tirhakah?—State some of the arguments from Egyptian history for fixing the date of the Trojan war at about the year B. C. 900.

SYRIA.

This century was a fatal one to the Hebrews. It saw the destruction of the kingdom of Israel, and the reduction of that of Judah to a tributary State by the Assyrians. Of this impending visitation, a series of bold and eloquent men, Joel, Amos, Hose′a, Isa′iah, and Micah, inspired with prophetic vision, had warned the corrupt and idolatrous Jews, but in vain. Their sublime prophecies and denunciations will be found in the books of Scripture bearing their respective names.

Israel.—Jerobo′am II. was on the throne at the opening of the century, but the kingdom fell into confusion on his death. On that occurrence his son, Zachari′ah, the last of Jehu's race, was placed on the throne (B. C. 772); but he had hardly occupied it six months, during which he committed all sorts of wickedness, when he was assassinated by Shallum, the son of Jabesh, who usurped the throne, but, after a reign of one month, was in his turn murdered by Men′ahem. This last-named chieftain contrived to maintain himself by the most ruthless ferocity (2 Kings xv. 16) on the throne for ten years. He averted an invasion of the country by Pul, king of Assyria, by paying him a heavy tribute. He left the kingdom to his son, Pekahi′ah (B. C. 759), who, after an evil reign of two years, was slain by Pekah, one of his captains, who "reigned in his stead." This king also "did evil in the sight of the Lord," and conspired with Rezin, king of Syria, to crush Ahaz, king of Judah; but Tiglath-Pileser, king of Assyria, came to the assistance of the latter, and, marching against the city of Damascus, took it, slew Rezin, and carried off the inhabitants.

Hoshe′a, the son of Elah, conspired against Pekah, caused him to be assassinated, and became king (B. C. 730). His reign was of short duration. Shalmane′ser, king of Assyria, forced him to pay tribute; but having found out that Hoshea had secretly formed an alliance with So (or Sethos), king of Egypt, the Assyrian king besieged and took Samaria, and carried away Hoshea and the ten tribes of Israel into captivity (B. C. 719). Thus terminated forever the independent kingdom of Israel. The captives were settled in Assyria and Media.

In Judea the first half of the century witnessed the comparatively peaceful reigns of Uzziah (B. C. 808–756), and of his son Jotham (B. C. 756–741). During their reigns were delivered most of the prophecies of Joel, Amos, Hosea, Isaiah, and Micah. Ahaz, the son of Jotham, succeeded to the throne of Judah in the 17th year of Pekah, king of Israel (B. C. 742). Pekah entered into a confederacy against him with Rezin, king of Syria, and invaded Judea. This first expedition was not successful; but on the retreat of the Syrians, Ahaz ventured on a battle, which resulted in the most frightful disaster. 120,000 Jews were slain, and 200,000 were carried into captivity. The king's son, Maa′seiah, was slain, and his principal officers also fell. But the victorious Israelites, moved with compassion for their suffering kinsmen, treated the captives kindly, and sent them home. Meanwhile the king of Damascus seized Elath; the Edomites and the Philistines revolted; and Ahaz, in desperation, solicited protection from Tiglath-Pileser, king of Assyria, who had already subdued the trans-Jordanic tribes. That monarch, as we have seen, took Damascus, and carried off the inhabitants; but he also exacted a very heavy tribute from the king of Judah. Ahaz renounced the national faith, and fell into the grossest idolatry. He established in his kingdom the worship of the gods of Syria, defaced the temple at Jerusalem, and made his children pass through fire to Moloch. In the year B. C. 726 this guilty monarch died, and was succeeded by the best and wisest of the kings of Judah, Hezeki′ah. This upright man at once extirpated idolatry, and restored the ancient religion and priesthood, destroying the last vestiges of superstition, even to the brazen serpent made by Moses in the wilderness. He endeavored to re-unite all the Israelites who remained in Syria under one government, but he was unsuccessful. He, however, threw off the yoke of Assyria, and gained some important advantages over the Philistines: and he fortified Jerusalem. After the fall of Samaria (B. C. 719), Shalmaneser laid siege to Tyre, but the inhabitants of that city resisted him for five years, and his death (B. C. 713) put an end to the siege. His successor, Sennacherib, invaded Judea, levied tribute, and marched on towards Egypt, leaving a large force to act against Jerusalem. The destruction of the army of Sennacherib (2 Chron. xxxii. 21) by a simoom, saved Judea, for the division left there speedily retreated. The remainder of the reign of Hezekiah passed in peace.

What prophets prophesied during this century?—What is recorded of the kings of Israel during this century?—What became of the ten tribes?—What of the kings of Judah?—What did Ahaz do?—And Hezekiah?—What of the siege of Tyre?—And the destruction of the army of Sennacherib?

INDIA.

The Budhists deny the authority of the Vedas and the Puranas. They differ very greatly from the Brahmins in many respects, especially in their having no castes among them. Their priests are taken from all classes of the community, and greatly resemble European monks. They live in monasteries, wear a uniform yellow dress, go with their feet bare, and their heads and beards shaved, and perform in a body a constant succession of services at their places of worship. They have processions, chanting, incense, and candles, as the Roman Catholics have. But they differ widely from the Hindoo priests in other matters also. They are strictly bound to celibacy, and to renounce the pleasures of the flesh; they eat together in one hall; they sleep *sitting* in a prescribed posture; and leave their monastery once a week, when they march in a body to bathe, and once a day when they go out to receive alms for the community, but they are not allowed to beg. They do not eat after noon, nor drink after dark for fear of swallowing minute insects; and they carry a brush with which to sweep every place before they sit down, lest they should inadvertently crush any living creature, so great is their respect for animal life. Some even tie a thin cloth over their mouths to prevent their drawing in small insects with their breath. They venerate the relics of holy men, and often erect over them solid cupolas, or bell-shaped monuments, which are often of a stupendous size. In India there are many of these, also some magnificent remains of the former splendor of the Budhist temples. The most curious are the cave temples, which consist of excavations from the solid rock, in the form of colonnades, like aisles, with vaulted and ribbed roofs, like Gothic temples. Those at Ellora and at Carla are the finest specimens. The Budhists also had nunneries for the seclusion of women. They have an extensive literature, both in India, China, and other countries where their religion prevails. It is all on the Brahmin model, and all originally from India (Hodgson, *Asiatic Researches*, vol. xvi., p. 433). The Pali, or local dialect of Magadha, where Gotama lived, seems to be the language generally used in the religious writings of the Budhists (see Elphinstone, *History of India*, vol. i., ch. iv.).

* What are the principal points of difference between the Budhists and Brahmins?—What remains of their temples are there?—What is said of their literature?—Sacred language?

ASSYRIA.

According to Mr. Layard, Ashurkish reigned after Baldasi. After him came Pul, supposed by some to be the Belus II. of the Greeks, the date of whose accession is placed by Hales and Newton in B. C. 790, by Usher in B. C. 769.

Pul invaded Israel, and compelled Menahem to pay him 1000 talents of silver by way of ransom (2 Kings xv. 19). He built the temple of Belus at Babylon. On his death this king's dominions were divided between his two sons, Tiglath-Pileser, who became sovereign of Assyria, and Nabonassar, who ruled in Babylon. At the commencement of the reign of the latter (B. C. 747), began the "Era of Nabonassar." The history of the two kingdoms here diverges.

Assyria. — Tiglath-Pileser, having been invited by Ahaz, king of Judah, to assist him against Pekah, king of Israel, and Rezin, king of Damascus, went to the assistance of Ahaz, slew Rezin, and took Damascus. He then carried away captive the inhabitants of the land, and the tribes of Reuben, Gad, and Manasseh, and planted them in Media (B. C. 740). He was succeeded by Shalmanasar (or Sargon), B. C. 730, who, in the fourth year of Hezekiah, invaded Israel, took Samaria (B. C. 719), and carried away the seven remaining tribes to Media, filling their places with a mixed colony of strangers. He also endeavored to conquer Syria and Phœnicia, and besieged Tyre (B. C. 717), but in vain. He was succeeded by his son, Sennach′erib (B. C. 714), who invaded Judea with an immense army, which was destroyed in one night by a pestilential blast; after which he returned to Assyria, where he was assassinated by his two eldest sons (B. C. 711). Esarhaddon, on his ascending the throne, had to contend with a revolt of the Medes and Babylonians, who for a time subdued Assyria. This prince is also called Sardanapa′lus, but is not the monarch who perished in the final overthrow of Nineveh.

Babylon.—After the accession of Nabonassar, this city became one of the most famous in the world; the king's mother, or wife, Semir′amis (see Hales' *New System of Chronology*, vol. iii., p. 61), erected the most splendid buildings there. Of the successors of Nabonassar, we have but little more than the names. The separation of Babylon from Assyria was fully accomplished about B. C. 710.

What is said of Pul?—Of Tiglath-Pileser?—Of Nabonassar?—Of the division of the empire?—Of Shalmanasar?—Sennacherib?—Esarhaddon?—Of Semiramis?

PERSIA.

The student has already been informed that great discrepancy exists as to the dates of the accession of the ancient Persian monarchs. The reign of Zohak (conjectured to mean the duration of the Assyrian conquest,) is said to have lasted 1000 years, and that of Feridoon 1000 years (according to Ferdusi). During the period of the Assyrian rule the finest edifices in Persia were erected. They are attributed to the Assyrian queen, Semir′amis, of whom so many marvels are related, but respecting the date of whose reign historians are not agreed; Helvieus placing it B. C. 2248; Syncellus, B. C. 2177; Eusebius, B. C. 1984; Usher, B. C. 1215; Herodotus, B. C. 713: a difference of more than 1500 years!

The probability is that Feridoon is the Arba′ces of the Greeks (see Malcolm's *History of Persia*, vol. i., ch. 7), who, according to Ctesias, reigned from B. C. 748 to 730. If this conjecture be correct, the exploits of Zal and Roostum must also be referred to this period. Arbaces, the Mede, was induced by the contemptible character of Esarhaddon to attack Nineveh, which he took, and for a time overthrew the Assyrian monarchy. In this great national movement, Kawah, the blacksmith (already mentioned, p. 19), took a leading part. (Persian history here repeats itself, owing to confusion in the chronology.)

Arbaces was a just and pious king. His death took place B. C. 730. He was succeeded by his son, Manda′ces (or Manuchehr); but Persia appears to have been involved in troubles, owing to the disputes between the descendants of Arbaces. During this period the Scythians conquered Persia, and remained masters of it for twelve years. Mandaces was succeeded by his son, Sosarmus (Nouzer). During this period of anarchy, two princes, named Artia (Zoo), and Arbianes (Kershasp), occupied the throne for a short time. At length the people called a public assembly to deliberate on the affairs of the nation. At this meeting, Kai-Kobad (better known by the name of Dei′oces, or Dej′oces, given to him by the Greeks), one of the hereditary chiefs or princes of Seistan, or Nimroz, and connected with the ancient royal family of Persia, a man renowned for his wisdom and justice, was unanimously elected king. The date of this event is placed by some historians in the year B. C. 709, by others in B. C. 696.

What is said of the period of Zohak?—Of Semiramis?—Of Arbaces?—And of the Scythian conquest?—Who was Dejoces?—When was he elected king of Persia?

CHINA.

On the death of Souen-wang (B. C. 781), Yew-wang mounted the throne. He was a prince very like his ancestors, indolent, and addicted to low pleasures. But the indulgence of his desires led him to the commission of great wickedness. Being enamored of a beautiful woman, named Paou-sze, he, at her request, divorced his wife, and set aside the heir to the crown, thus indulging her whims at no matter what cost. The following extraordinary story is told of her. Being unable to make her smile and be cheerful, Yew-wang made the signal of general alarm by lighting fires upon the mountains. The tributary princes and great officers consequently repaired hastily to the palace, where they were greeted by the laughter of Paou-sze, and sent back in disgrace. The Tartars renewed their incursions, and the people groaned under the burden of their oppressors, who had now grown very numerous. Yew-wang marched against the State of Shin, where his disinherited son had taken refuge, and the prince of that State, unable to resist the imperial forces, called in the aid of the Tartars. The emperor's troops then deserted him, and, despised by all, he was slain by the Tartars (B. C. 770), and his much-beloved Paou-sze shared the same fate.

Ping-wang, the son of the last emperor, ascended the throne by the aid of the prince of Tsin. His first business was to get rid of the Tartars, against whom he had to fight a very bloody battle. These barbarians were the scourge of China. To free himself from them the emperor gave the greater part of the imperial domain of Chaou to the prince of Tsin, under pretence of rewarding him for his services, but in reality that he might fight his (the emperor's) battles against these ferocious savages. That valiant prince soon cleared the country of them. His son took advantage of this to extend his authority and establish his independence, an example which was followed by many other of the emperor's vassals, who, in the year B. C. 758, declared their independence, and formed no less than 21 independent kingdoms. The miseries entailed upon the country by these numerous masters were very great, but Ping-wang did not live to see the worst of them. He died B. C. 720, having previously removed the capital to Lo-yang. His grandson, Hwan-wang, succeeded him peaceably.

What is said of Yew-wang?—And of his favorite, Paou-sze?—What great event took place in the reign of Ping-wang?—What of Hwan-wang?

GREECE.

Attica.—In this century we pass from the domain of legend to that of history. The events recorded, however, are unimportant. In Attica, we have a mere list of names of Archons (chosen for life), in the following order:—Thes′picus, B. C. 801–794; Agamestor, B. C. 794–777; Æs′chylus, B. C. 777–754. After this, the Archons were elected for ten years; and Charops was the first who was chosen (B. C. 752) under the new system. The Archons above-named were of the family of Codrus, and the office was held by members of the same family down to the year B. C. 714, when Hippom′enes was deposed for cruelty to his own daughter. The office was then thrown open to all the nobility.

Argos.—The system of computing time by Olympiads, or the interval which elapsed between the celebration of the Olympic games (four years), dates from the year B. C. 776, when the people of Elis inscribed the name of their fellow-citizen, Corœ′bus, as the winner of the foot-race; and thus began the practice of inscribing, in like manner, in each recurring fifth year, the name of the victor in the same race. It appears either that the Eleians were excellent runners, or that the Olympic games were for a long time purely local, for the prize was carried off at the first twelve Olympiads by a native of Elis, or of its neighborhood. During the celebration of these games pacific communion prevailed among the Grecian States. Sacred legations were sent from each State to offer sacrifices in common on these occasions, and the city where the ceremonies took place enjoyed inviolability of territory during the month of their occurrence. Heavy fines were imposed by Elis upon other cities for violation of the truce.

About the year B. C. 770, Phi′don, a descendant of Temenus, made himself despot of Argos, and re-established the ascendancy of that city over all the others of her confederacy. He endeavored to acquire dominion over Corinth, and to extend his sway over the greater part of the Peloponnesus, but it does not appear that he succeeded. He further claimed the right of presiding at the celebration of the Agones, or religious games instituted by Hercules, and especially the Olympic Agon; and at the celebration of the 8th Olympiad (B. C. 748), he marched to Olympia with an armed force, and dispossessed the Eleians of their privilege. But the latter having received aid from the Spartans, Phidon was defeated, and forced to resign his pretensions.

This king coined both silver and copper money in Ægi′na, and first established a system of weights and measures, which, through his influence, became adopted throughout Peloponnesus, and ultimately acquired footing in all the Dorian States, Bœotia, Thessaly, and Macedonia, under the name of the Æginæan scale. Of this system Mr. Grote observes (*History of Greece*, vol. ii., p. 319), that it was probably borrowed immediately from the Phœnicians, and by them from the Babylonians. The Euboic scale arose subsequently in Greece, at an uncertain period, and prevailed in Attica and the Ionic cities generally. The Æginæan and Euboic scales had cotemporaneous currency in different parts of the Persian Empire, the divisions of the money scale being the same in both, viz., 100 drachmæ to a mina, and 60 minæ to a talent. [The drachma equalled 14½ cents of United States currency; consequently the mina was equal to $14.50, and the talent to $871.20.] The Babylonian, Hebrew, Phœnician, Egyptian, and Greek scales of weight were so nearly conformable as to warrant the belief that they were all derived from a common origin, and that origin the Chaldæan priesthood of Babylon. The Hebrew shekel, which was both a weight and a coin, was nearly equal to half an ounce avoirdupois, or 9 dwts., 2.4 gr., Troy, and its value was about 60 cents. Of Phidon's fall we have no information. But no leader of eminence appeared after him. The line of Argive kings continued to the last Persian war, but the government became democratic.

Sparta.—Tele′clus and his son, Alcam′enes, had, at the beginning of this century, extended their dominions. The system established by Lycurgus was in full force. In the year B. C. 760, the king, Theopom′pus, instituted the Eph′ori—magistrates, whose duty it was to call all public functionaries to account for their actions. They, by degrees, usurped the duties of the officers over whom they watched, and became possessed of the power in the State.

The most remarkable event in the history of Sparta during this century is the first Messenian War. According to the historian, Pausa′nias, it began in the year B. C. 743, and ended B. C. 723, thus lasting 20 years. The remote cause of it was the killing of the Spartan king, Teleclus, at the border temple of Diana, where the Messenians and Spartans were both offering sacrifices. This event happened during a fray between the two parties. But the war did not break out until some time after, when Alcamenes and Theopompus were kings of Sparta, and Anti′ochus and An′drocles, kings of Messenia. The immediate cause of it was a private altercation between the Messenian Polych′ares and the Spartan Euæph′nus. The latter demanded redress of the Messenians, but they refused to give up Polychares, though their king, Androcles, strongly insisted on their doing so, and was slain in the tumult which his opposition occasioned. The Spartans then began the war, without formal notice, by surprising the town of Ampheia, and putting its defenders to the sword. The Messenians, under their king, Euph′aes, heroically resisted the Spartans with success for four years. In the fifth year of the war, the Spartans, under their kings, Theopompus and Polydo′rus, made a more vigorous effort, and drove the Messenians into the recesses of Mount Itho′me. In their distress, the latter consulted the oracle of Delphi, and were told that a virgin of the royal race of Æp′ytus must be sacrificed for their salvation. Aristode′mus, one of that family, thereupon put to death his own daughter; but the war still continued many years. In the 13th year of it an indecisive battle was fought, in which Euphaes was slain, and Aristodemus was then elected king in his stead. Five years afterwards Aristodemus gained a great victory over the Spartans, but the tide soon turned against the Messenians. Aristodemus, agonized with the reflection that he had sacrificed his daughter in vain, put an end to his existence. In the 20th year of the war, the Messenians abandoned Ithome, and fled the country. The few who remained behind were reduced to submission, and Messenia was annexed to Sparta.

Corinth.—The Bacchi′adæ, as we have seen, formed the governing caste of this State, intermarrying usually among themselves, and choosing their own *prytanis* (or president). Of their internal government we have no account, except the tale relative to one of them, named Ar′chias, whose brutality to a youth, named Actæ′on, made him so detested that he was forced to flee from Corinth. He took refuge in Sicily, where a number of Greek colonists were settled, and there he founded the city of Syracuse, which afterwards became so famous (B. C. 735). Telestes, one of the last of the Bacchiadæ, was put to death. His successor, Autom′enes, reigned one year; and the people then adopted the system of electing their own chief magistrate annually. At the close of this century (B. C. 703), Amin′ocles, of Corinth, first built triremes (ships with three tiers of benches for rowers) for the Samians, and he was appointed commander-in-chief of the Athenian navy.

Macedonia.—The foundation of the kingdom of Macedon was laid by Perdiccas and his brothers, Gaua′nes and Aër′opus, who were of the race of Tem′enus of Argos. They settled at Mount Ber′mius, and thence subsequently extended their dominions (Herodotus, b. viii., 137). This may be referred to the year B. C. 729. But others say that Car′anus of Argos, a descendant of Hercules, settled at Edessa, in Macedonia, with an Argive colony (B. C. 750), was the founder of the kingdom, and that Perdiccas was the fourth king. Be that as it may, Perdiccas was one of the earliest monarchs of Macedonia, and was succeeded by his son Argæ′us.

Little worthy of notice is recorded of the other States of Greece at this period. Colonization set in strongly, and the coasts of the Mediterranean were settled by Greeks, who carried with them everywhere their skill in the arts and sciences, their genius and taste, their laws, and their noble aspiration for free institutions and self-government. They founded Pando′sia, Metapon′tum, Rhe′gium, Nax′os, Leon′tium, Cat′ana, Meg′ara-Hybla, Thas′os, Aby′dos, Nicome′dia, Croto′na, Taren′tum, Syr′acuse, and Corcy′ra.

Arcti′nus of Mile′tus, and Cinæ′thon of Lacedæmon, two of the poets of "the Epic Cycle," flourished during this century. The Epic Cycle comprises the authors who continued the narrative of the Iliad, and the heroes who figure therein. Of these poets there were several. Arctinus wrote the *Æthi′opis*, a continuation of the Iliad, and the *Destruction of Il′ion*, comprising the subsequent events until the departure of the Greeks. A very valuable account of the Homeric poems generally will be found in Grote's *History of Greece*, vol. ii., ch. xxi.

What is said of the history of Attica?—In what year was the first Olympiad?—What solemnities attended the Olympic games?—Who was Phidon?—What were his principal acts? Whence was the Greek coinage derived?—What was the value of the drachma?—The mina? —Talent?—Shekel?—What became of Phidon?—Who instituted the Ephori?—And when?

How long did the first Messenian war last?—What was its cause?—Who were the chief actors in it?—What was done by Aristodemus?—What occurred at Corinth?—Who was Aminocles?—Who founded the kingdom of Macedon?—What colonies were planted by the Greeks?—What is the Epic Cycle?—Who were Arctinus and Cinæthon?

ITALY.

The great event in the history of Italy during this century is the founding of the city of Rome. This is, indeed, an epoch in the history of the world, as well as of Italy. According to the received chronology, the date of this event is fixed in the year B. C. 753. This is founded on the statement of the great Roman antiquary, Varro, who says that the building of Rome took place in the 4th year of the 6th Olympiad, which would be the year above mentioned. According to Cato, it took place in B. C. 751; according to Polyb′ius, in B. C. 750; according to Fa′bius Pictor, in B. C. 747; according to Cin′cius, in B. C. 728. But universal testimony confirms the supposition that Rome was founded about the middle of the 8th century B. C. The year B. C. 753 is reckoned by most of the Roman writers as the year of the building of the city, (*Anno Urbis Conditæ*, whence the initials A. U. C., which distinguish the Roman Era).

The origin of Rome is involved in obscurity. It probably was due to a colony from Alba Longa. The word "Rome" is of Greek derivation, and signifies "strength." The account of the foundation of the city given by the Roman historian, Titus Liv′ius, commonly called Livy (*History of Rome*, book 1), was that generally received, until the critical researches of Niebuhr, in the beginning of the present century (19th A. C.) proved that the early Roman legends were mythical, and that but a small amount of historical truth could be detected in them. The student is referred to Niebuhr's great work, the *History of Rome*, for fuller information on this subject; also to Arnold's *History of Rome*, where it is very ably treated. Having premised thus much, we give the legend of Rom′ulus, as related by Livy.

It has already been mentioned that Livy gives a list of Alban kings, from Æne′as down to Nu′mitor and Amu′lius, the sons of Procas. This monarch at his death bequeathed his kingdom to Numitor, as the eldest son. But Amulius dethroned his brother, and put to death the male offspring of Numitor, making the latter's daughter, Rhea Sylvia, a vestal virgin, so as to preclude the possibility of issue. But the vestal had twins by the god Mars: whereupon Amulius loaded her with chains, and cast her into prison, and ordered the children to be thrown into the Tiber. It happened at this time that the river had overflowed its banks, and the trough in which the children were was floated into a pool, which became dry when the tide retired. A thirsty she-wolf from the neighboring mountains directed her course to the spot, and, being attracted by the cries of the children, went to the trough, and licked the babes with her tongue. In this attitude she was found by the king's shepherd, Faust′ulus, who took the children home to his wife, Acca Lauren′tia, to be nursed. They were named Romulus and Remus, and were brought up as shepherds. They subsequently became very hardy and daring, and were famed for attacking wild beasts and robbers. They gradually formed a band of youths, of whom they were the leaders, and carried on their exploits and their sports. Among these sports were those of the Luper′cal, which were celebrated on the Palatine Hill, and had been instituted by Evander in honor of the Arcadian Pan, whom the Romans afterwards called In′uus. [This same god, however, was an ancient Italian deity, named Luper′cus, who was worshipped by the shepherds as the protector of their flocks against wolves. On the north side of the Palatine Hill was a cave surrounded by a grove, wherein was worshipped the image of Lupercus by his priests, the Luperci. He is represented as having a wife, Luper′ca, or Lupa, who, in the shape of a she-wolf, suckled Romulus and Remus, whence she is sometimes identified with Acca Laurentia.] While the youths were celebrating the Luperca′lia (sports of the Lupercal), they were surprised by a band of robbers, who carried off Remus, and delivered him up to the king, Amulius, on a charge of plundering the lands of Numitor. Remus was given up to Numitor to be punished. Upon this, Faustulus, who had all along suspected the youths of being the twins of Rhea Sylvia, which had been exposed by order of Amulius, imparted the affair to Romulus. It was also communicated to Numitor, and a conspiracy was organized against the king. Romulus and Remus, with their adherents, forced their way into the palace of Amulius, and slew him. Whereupon Numitor called an assembly of the people, and related the case to them. The youths hailed their grandfather as king, and the multitude ratified the act. Thus Numitor was reinstated in the kingdom of Alba.

State what dates are assigned to the foundation of Rome.—Which is the usually-received date?—What do the initials A. U. C. mean?—What is said of the origin of the city of Rome?—Relate the legend of the birth of Romulus.—What was the Lupernal?—What happened there?

Romulus and Remus now resolved to build a city on the spot where they had been exposed, and they assembled a number of their followers to carry out the project. But a quarrel arose between the brothers as to the right to name and govern the new city. They thereupon agreed to decide the dispute by augury. Romulus chose the Palatine Hill; Remus, the Av′entine, on which to await their auguries. The first omen, consisting of six vultures, appeared to Remus; after which, double that number appeared to Romulus. Each was proclaimed king by his respective followers; an altercation ensued, and on their meeting they came to blows. Remus was slain, and Romulus assumed the leadership. He selected the Palatine Hill as the locality for the first buildings, and gave to them the name of Rome. There is another account of the death of Remus, which is more generally received. It is that Remus, in derision of his brother, leaped over the new wall which Romulus was building, and that Romulus killed him in a passion, exclaiming: "So perish every one that shall hereafter leap over my wall."

Romulus now assumed kingly dignity—caused himself to be attended by twelve lictors—established a sanctuary—created a hundred senators—and sent out ambassadors into the neighboring States, to form alliances, and to procure wives for his subjects. These ambassadors were everywhere treated with contempt. Romulus then planned the famous stratagem known as "the rape of the Sabine women." He ordered solemn games, called Consualia, to be celebrated in honor of the equestrian Neptune (called by him Consus), and he invited the neighboring tribes to join in them. The people of Cæni′ne, Crustu′mium, and Antem′næ, attended with their families; but in the middle of the festivities, at a given signal, the maidens were carried off by the Romans. The outraged visitors appealed to Titus Ta′tius, king of the Sabines, for revenge. An army was hastily assembled by the three cities, and sent against Rome, but was defeated by Romulus, who also pillaged Cænine. He gained a victory also over the Antemnatians, and at the request of Hersilia (the only married woman among the Sabines carried off), who had become his wife, he admitted the vanquished into citizenship. He did the same with the Crustuminians, but the war with the Sabines was more serious. The latter gained possession of the citadel by bribing Tarpe′ia, the daughter of the governor, Spu′rius Tarpe′ius, to admit them. As soon as they entered they threw their shields upon her, and killed her. The memory of this event was preserved by the name "Tarpeian Rock," given to a part of the hill (the Saturnian) on which the capitol stood. The contest between the Romans and the Sabines was brought to a conclusion by the mediation of the Sabine women. A treaty was concluded (B. C. 745), whereby the two nations were combined into one, and the united people were called Quiri′tes, from the town of Cures. The two kings, Romulus and Tatius, reigned together thenceforward in concord until the death of the latter, who was slain some years afterwards in a tumult at Lavin′ium.

The remaining exploits of Romulus consisted of successful wars against Fide′næ and Ve′ii. He had consolidated the kingdom which he had founded, and for nearly forty years presided over its destinies. At length, one day, while reviewing his army on the plain, near lake Capra, a sudden storm arose, and he was enveloped in a thick cloud which hid him from sight, and he was never more beheld upon earth. Such is the legend of Romulus. He is not a historical personage, though the Romans believed in his existence, and deified him. The historian (Livy) adds that on his death the Sabines claimed the right to elect a king, but the Romans resisted this pretension. The Senators, to prevent anarchy, divided the government among themselves, forming out of their number ten decades, each decade having a president, and each, in rotation, governing the State for five days. In this manner a year passed, but the people then clamored for a king. The Senate, thereupon, advised the people to elect whom they pleased. The choice having been left with the Senate, Nu′ma Pompil′ius, a native of Cures, and a person renowned for his wisdom, was elected (B. C. 713).

This century is further remarkable for the foundation in Italy of several important cities by the Greeks. Sicily and Southern Italy had the benefit of colonization by them; and the cities of Syracuse, Naples, Naxos, Leontium, Catana, Sybaris, Crotona, Locri, and Tarentum, sprang into existence, and became flourishing commercial emporiums.

What was the dispute between Romulus and Remus?—What were the first acts of Romulus when he became king?—Relate the legend of the rape of the Sabines.—What ensued?—Who was Tarpeia?—Whence the name Quirites?—What was the end of Romulus?—How was Rome governed after his death?—Who was Numa Pompilius?

BRITAIN.

England.— Cordeilla succeeded her father, and reigned five years in peace, until her sons, Morgan and Cunedag, deposed her. The legend adds that this drove her to despair, and she destroyed herself. On this story of Leir and Cordeilla, Shakspeare has founded his magnificent tragedy of King Lear, but varied the fate of the heroine. Her sons divided the country between them, but quarrelled soon afterwards, and Morgan was slain. Cunedag ruled ably for 33 years; according to Holinshed (*Chronicles*, vol. i., p. 449), the date of the accession of this king is 45 years before the building of Rome. As the era of this last event is usually fixed at B. C. 753, the era of Cunedag, the son of Hennin and Regan is B. C. 798. These fabulous Chronicles make up in pretended accuracy what they want in reality. Rivall, the son of Cunedag, is the next king on the list. He reigned 46 years "in great wealth and prosperity," and was buried at York (B. C. 719). During his reign flourished two famous prophets and astrologers, named Perdix and Heren. After Rivall came his son, Gurgustius, who ruled Britain 37 years.

Ireland.— Nothing worthy of record occurs between the reign of Ollamh Fodhla and that of King Kimboath, in the 5th century B. C., when the dawn of authentic history appears. If the Bardic historians, says Moore (*History of Ireland*, vol. i., p. 113), in describing the glory and magnificence of some of these reigns, have shown no ordinary powers of flourish and exaggeration, it is to be hoped, for the credit of human nature, that they have also far outstripped the truth in their accounts of the discord, treachery, and bloodshed, by which almost every one of these brief paroxysms of sovereignty was disgraced. Of 32 kings who are said to have reigned in this interval, only three died a natural death, and the great majority of the remainder fell each by the hand of his successor. The events which are recorded of their reigns consist chiefly of plagues and desolating pestilences, of civil strife, and battles with pirates. It is recorded of King Eadna Dearg, that he erected a mint, and caused money to be coined at Airgiod Ross; and of King Siorlamh, it is said that nature had furnished him with hands so long, that when he stood upright his fingers would touch the ground.

What became of Cordeilla?—What is said of her successors?—What of the period between the reign of Ollamh Fodhla and that of Kimboath?—Of Eadna Dearg?—Siorlamh?

FRANCE.

In addition to what has been already said respecting the Druids, we may, in default of historical accounts of this and the succeeding century of the history of France, extract some interesting particulars from Chevalier's admirable work, *La Bretagne, ancienne et moderne* (ch. i.).

The sacerdotal hierarchy of the Druids consisted of three degrees — the bards, the diviners, the druids. The bards were the sacred poets and singers of ancient Gaul (France). At public festivals they sang the national traditions and the exploits of the chieftains; they encouraged victims on the sacrificial stone, and warriors on the field of battle. In their songs they accompanied themselves on an instrument with three rows of strings. They wore short vestments and trowsers that descended to the heel; they carried a tunic to use in the cromlech, a cuirass when following the army, their musical instrument slung on the shoulder, and a battle-axe in the hand.

The diviners, or augurs, had charge of the material part of the public worship and sacrifices, the druids taking charge of the spiritual. They studied the natural sciences, astronomy, medicine, divination by the flight of birds and the entrails of victims. No public or private act, civil or religious, could be accomplished without their intervention. They wore the priestly robe, but without ornaments.

The druids were the superior and learned class. They were the arbiters of peace and war, and senators by right; and they had the exclusive control of theology, legislation, and education. Their teaching was oral, and reduced into verse that it might be fixed in the memory. They trusted nothing to paper, stone, or cloth; thus all that remains of them is obscure traditions, and some rude monuments which we have much difficulty in deciphering. The order of druids was elective, and was recruited by adepts formed by a long novitiate. This novitiate was very severe; it was passed in caves and forests, and sometimes lasted 20 years. An arch-druid, vested with power of life and death, presided over the order. The druids held tribunals for the trial of causes and the discussion of public affairs. Their most solemn assemblies were held once a year near Chartres, or on the plains of Carnac.

How many degrees of druids were there?—What were the bards?—The augurs?—The superior druids?—How was the latter class recruited?—And the order governed?

SPAIN.

The population of Spain was divided in these early times into two races, viz., the Iberian in the most remote ages, and the Celtic at a more recent period. Added to these were the Greek and Phœnician settlers on the sea-coasts.

The Celtic race consisted of five powerful tribes: 1. The Astu′rians, who inhabited Asturias, Leon, and Old Castile. They have been in all ages the hardiest and most industrious and virtuous of the people of Spain. 2. The Can′tabres, who dwelt in Biscay, Guipusco′a, and Ala′va. They were a very ferocious and quarrelsome race, and in many of their customs resembled the Irish; in their dress and manners they resembled the Tartars. 3. The Vas′cones (or Basques), who inhabited Navarre and Aragon. We have elsewhere noticed this very ancient people, who, however, claim to be a primitive race, much more ancient than the Celts. They are here classed among the Celtic tribes, in accordance with the views of modern historians (see Dunham's *History of Spain*, vol. i., introduction). The student who desires information, may consult Masdeu's *History of Ancient Spain*, Aspiros on the *Primitive Language of Spain*, and the works of Larramendi and of Astartoa on the Basque language. 4. The Calla′ici, or Gallicians, who inhabited the northern coast of Spain, a very pugnacious race, who worshipped the sun and moon. 5. The Lusitanians, who inhabited Portugal, Estremadu′ra, and part of Leon. They were subdivided into the Turdeta′ni, Tur′duli, and Lusita′ni.

The Iberian race occupied the southern and eastern parts of Spain. It comprised the following tribes: The Be′tures, in Granada; the Bas′tuli, in Granada also; the Turduli, in Cordova (these three became mixed up with Celts, Phœnicians, and Carthaginians); the Bastita′ni, in Murcia; the Edeta′ni, in Valencia and Aragon; the Ilerca′vones, in Valencia; the Coseta′ni, in Catalonia; the Laleta′ni, near Barcelona; the Indige′tes, near the eastern Pyrenees; the Ilerge′tes, whose capital was Ilerda (now Lerida); and the Ausetani, who were a portion of the last-mentioned tribe. The Iberians were remarkably slender and active. They worshipped the sun and moon.

The Celtiberians were divided into four great tribes, of which the Arevari were the most powerful.

Into how many tribes was the Celtic race in Spain divided?—Name them, and their respective localities.—Name the various tribes of Iberian origin.—What of the Celtiberians?

GERMANY.

The following is the mythological system of the government and process of the universe which prevailed among the ancient Scandinavians and Germans (Menzel's *History of Germany*, vol. i., sec. 26).

As the outward frame of the earth was supposed to have been created out of the body of the giant Ymer, the ash tree, Ygdrasill, was supposed to represent its external growth and internal life. This tree reached from the bottom of Nilfheim far beyond all the heavens. It had three roots, by each of which there was a source: Urdarborn, the source of time; Mimer's well, the source of wisdom; and Huergelmir, the source of poison. Nidhöggur, the dragon, the father of all the snakes in Huergelmir, unceasingly gnawed the roots. The three Nornen, or fates — the past, the present, and the future— sat around the source of time. Far above, at the top of the tree, perched the fire-eagle, the self-animating phœnix, the symbol of perfection, whilst a squirrel ran busily up and down, making mischief between the dragon below and the eagle above. As soon as the dragon gnawed through the roots, the noble tree was to fall, and time and all earthly things were to cease. This beautiful world was not to endure forever. The gods, like men, mere creatures of Allfater, were subject to evil and destruction. All that was earthly would pass away, but Allfater would renovate earth and heaven. Both gods and men would be destroyed in expiation of their crimes, but they would perish courageously, fighting to the last, and falling on the battle-field. The first song of the Edda, called the Voluspa, is an illustration of the mode in which the gods carry on their wars. It runs as follows:

A Wale advances into the circle of the gods, and announces their fall and the destruction of Asgard at the general conflagration of the world. This event will be caused by the gods, who will sin in common with the wicked of Ymer's race, and be abandoned by the inward light which they derived from Muspelheim. However, the golden age is still of long duration; vengeance is not immediate. The gods gamble in heaven, and, heated by play, do not perceive the approach of the three daughters of the giants, who steal their golden Runic tablets upon which Allfater has inscribed the laws of the universe.

Give an outline of the Scandinavian mythology of the universe.—What is contained in the Voluspa?—Are the gods immortal?—What is Ygdrasill?—And Nidhöggur?

B.C. 800—700.

ASIA MINOR.

Lyc′ia was a small district on the southwest of Asia Minor, in which are found the mountain Climax and the river Xanthus. The most ancient name of the country was My′lias, and the earliest inhabitants were called Mil′yæ, and afterward Sol′ymi. Then the Ter′milæ from Crete settled among them; and Lycus, the son of Pandi′on, king of Athens, fled from his brother Ǽge′us to this country, and gave it the name of Lycia. It was the scene of the exploits of Bellerophon (see page 40), and of the famous legend of the Harpies and the daughters of Pan′dareus of Ephesus, which is as follows: Aëdon, the eldest daughter, was married to Zethus, king of Thebes, the brother of the musician Amphion. As she had but one son, It′ylus, she became envious of Niobe, the wife of Amphion, who had six sons and six daughters. She therefore determined to murder one of them, Amale′us, in the night; but by mistake she killed her own child. The other daughters, Mer′ope and Cleodo′ra, being deprived of their parents by the gods, remained helpless orphans in their father's palace. Venus fed them with milk, honey, and wine; Juno gave them beauty and understanding; Diana gave them dignity; and Minerva, skill in the arts: but when Venus went up to Olympus to arrange the nuptials for her maidens, the sisters were carried off by the Harpies (*harpuiai*, robbers, or spoilers). The Greek poets differ among themselves as to the nature of these beings. Homer introduces them as the impersonation of storm-winds; Hesiod describes them as fair-haired and winged maidens; Æschylus represents them as ugly creatures with wings; and later writers represent them as disgusting monsters, in the form of birds, with the heads of girls (see p. 40). Their number also varies, some enumerating two, others eight.

Pisid′ia was an inland district, inhabited by savage tribes. Pamphy′lia was a narrow strip on the southern coast, inhabited by a mixture of races, called by the Greeks *pamphuloi* (of all races), whence the name of the country. The first Greek settlements were made by Mopsus, after the Trojan war, whence the land was sometimes called Mopsopia. Isau′ria was an island district, north of the Taurus, inhabited by robbers. Cilic′ia bordered on Syria, and is said to have derived its name from the mythical Cilix, the son of Agenor, and brother of Cadmus. Cyprus was colonized by the Phœnicians at a very early period. The Greeks settled there soon after the Trojan war. It was anciently divided into nine kingdoms, each governed by an independent king. The names of these States were Am′athus, Ceryn′ia, Cit′ium, Cu′rium, Lape′thus, Ma′rium, Paphos, Sal′amis, and Soli. There were two cities named Paphos, styled respectively Old Paphos (*Palaipaphos*), and New Paphos (*Neapaphos*). The first was founded by the Syrian king, Cinyras, at the beginning of the 12th century B. C. The other was founded by Agapenor, king of Arcadia, on his return from Troy. Old Paphos was the chief seat of the worship of Venus, who, it is said, landed at this place after birth among the waves, and is hence frequently called "the Paphian goddess." She is also styled Cypris, or Cypria, because she was the deity principally worshipped on the island; her votaries were thence called "Cyprians."

Lydia.—The descendants of Hercules ruled this country until the year B. C. 716, when Candaules, or Myrsilus, the last of them, was murdered at the instigation of his wife. The latter immediately afterwards espoused the assassin, Gyges, one of the Lydian family named Merm′nadæ, and he ascended the throne.

Bithynia.—In the year B. C. 712, a colony from Megara, in Greece, founded the city of Ast′acus, which afterwards received fresh colonists from Athens, who named it Olbia. In subsequent times it received the name of Nicomedia.

Aby′dos, on the Hellespont, was founded B. C. 715, by a colony from Miletus. It was the birthplace of Leander, who, being in love with Hero, the priestess of Venus, in Sestos, on the opposite shore, swam across the Hellespont at night to visit her, and returned before daybreak. But one stormy night he was drowned, and his body was washed ashore at Sestos: whereupon Hero threw herself into the sea.

We may here observe that, by the ancients, Asia was divided into Upper and Lower Asia, the river Halys, east of Lydia, being the boundary at first, but subsequently the Euphrates being chosen. It was also divided into Asia within the Taurus, and Asia beyond the Taurus. The modern division into Asia Major and Asia Minor was adopted in the 4th century of the Christian Era.

What is said of Lycia? — Relate the legend of the three daughters of Pandareus.—What were the Harpies?—What is said of Pisidia?—Pamphylia?—Isauria?—Cilicia?—Cyprus?—What is said of the worship of Venus?—Who was Gyges?—What cities were founded?—Relate the legend of Hero and Leander.—How was Asia divided?

CARTHAGE.

Of the history of Carthage during this century but little is known. The Carthaginians and the Phœnicians gradually extended their settlements in Sicily, but met with a check to their progress from the Greeks, who, during the latter part of this century, poured into that island in great numbers. The first body of these colonists who landed there was composed of Chalcidians from Eubœa, and of Mægarians, led by The′ocles, the Athenian. They built the town of Naxos (B. C. 735), and were followed by others who founded the cities of Syracuse (B. C. 734), Leonti′ni and Cat′ana (B. C. 730), and Meg′ara-Hybla (B. C. 726).

The Constitution of Carthage was peculiar. It was partly republican, partly oligarchical. There was a Senate, partly hereditary and partly elective, consisting sometimes of as many as 600 members. Within the Senate, and selected out of it by the body at large, was the Gerusia, or Centumvirate, composed of 100 or 104 members, whose duty it was to control the chief magistrates, and to watch over the liberties of the commonwealth. The Gerusia, however, was not established until about the year B. C. 400, and therefore does not appear in the earliest history of Carthage. Of the mode of electing its members we have no certain information. It would seem that the Senate appointed committees of five, entrusted respectively with the control of certain departments of State affairs, and that they nominated the Gerusia. The latter appointed the military officers. The executive power was intrusted to two chief magistrates, called Suffe′tes (from the Hebrew *Shoph′etim, i. e.*, judges). They were elected for life by the people in general convocation, but whether they were nominated by the latter or by the Senate is uncertain. Sometimes the two offices were blended in one person. The general assembly also decided questions upon which the Senate and the Suffetes disagreed, and their approval was necessary to the appointment of the Generals of the army. The Suffetes were not paid for their services, and they were bound to abstain from wine while they held office. The Gerusia exercised a censorship over public morality. That during the earlier period of Carthaginian history the people enjoyed a large share of influence in the government, is certain; but in after ages they lost much of their power, and the management of public affairs fell into the hands of a few of the leading families.

The manners of the Carthaginians were marked by ferocity. Their punishments were very severe, and the usual mode of inflicting death was by crucifixion. They offered up human sacrifices to their deities, which were the same as those of their mother country, Tyre. Ashtaroth and Æsculapius were especially worshipped; the tutelar deity was styled Melcarth (*i. e.*, king of the city), and was probably the same as the Tyrian Moloch. The Carthaginians excelled in architecture as well as in commerce, and the neighborhood of Carthage was one of the best cultivated pieces of land in the ancient world. The army of the State was formed of mercenaries from the adjoining countries.

Of the rest of Africa during this early period our knowledge is very slight. The history of Egypt will be found in the column devoted to that country. So will the occasional notices which occur respecting Ethiopia and Nubia. The northern portion of Africa was divided into Numid′ia and Maureta′nia. Numidia was inhabited by wild tribes whose occupation was that of herdsmen They were styled *Nom′ades* (wanderers) by the Greeks, whence the name Numidians. Their country extended from Carthage to Mauretania (the modern Morocco), and from the Mediterranean to the Atlas mountains and the territory of the Gætuli. Mauretania extended along the northern and north-western coast of Africa. Its earliest known inhabitants were the Gætulians, a widely-extended nomad race, composed of several tribes, the principal of which were the Autol′oles and Pharu′sii on the west coast; the Daræ, or Gæ′tuli-Daræ, in the Steppes of the great Atlas region; and the Mel′ano-Gætuli, a colored race resulting from the intermixture of the southern tribes with the negro races of Central Africa. The pure Gætulians are supposed to have been of Asiatic origin, and are believed to be the ancestors of the Berbers.

Tradition tells of a mighty king of the Gætulians, named Atlas, who possessed great knowledge of astronomy, and taught that heaven had the form of a globe. This personage has been converted by mythology into a mountain bearing heaven on its shoulders. The conversion was effected by Perseus, by means of the head of Medusa, because Atlas refused him shelter. Atlas is represented as the father of the Plei′ades, Hy′ades, Hesper′ides, Œnom′aus, Calypso, etc.

What cities did the Greeks found in Sicily during this century? — Give an account of the Carthaginian form of government.—What deities were worshipped at Carthage?—What is said of the manners of the people?—What of Numidia?—And of Mauretania? — Of the Gætuli? — Of Atlas?

EGYPT.

At the commencement of this century the Ethiopian power still maintained itself at Thebes, while Sethos called himself king at Memphis; and another power, seated at Saïs, claimed to be the depository of legitimate authority. Following the list of the Saite kings we have: Stephinates, B. C. 691–684; Nechepsos, B. C. 684–678; Nechao (or Necho) I.; of all of whom very little is known.

When the government of Sethos, the priest, came to an end, a revolution took place. The Egyptians divided Egypt into twelve parts, and set up a king over each part. These kings bound themselves by oath, respectively, that neither of them would attempt to become master of all Egypt. One of their number, however, Psamme′tichus, whose father, Necho I., of Saïs, had been put to death by the Ethiopians, and whose dominions lay nearest to the sea, had cultivated the friendship of the Greeks, the Phœnicians, and the Western Arabians, and from them he obtained an auxiliary force which enabled him to project the conquest of Egypt, and to attack the eleven kings. They combined against him, and met him at Momemphis, on the shore of lake Mareotis, where a decisive battle was fought; some of the kings were slain, the rest escaped into Lybia, and Psammetichus established himself as monarch of all Egypt (B. C. 670).

Having done this by means of his foreign auxiliaries, he allotted them, by way of reward, a district on the Pelusiac branch of the Nile, near the city of Bubastis. To his Phœnician allies he gave a location for a settlement at Memphis. He likewise caused a number of Egyptian children to be instructed in the Greek language, so as to form a class of interpreters between that people and his own.

Psammetichus encouraged works of art, and undertook sundry military enterprises, one of which was the siege of Ashdod, or Azotus, which is said to have lasted 29 years. A serious revolt of his troops took place at Elephantine, which he was unable to suppress; but fortunately the mutineers, instead of turning their weapons against him, betook themselves to Ethiopia. After this he applied himself to ameliorating the condition of his country, and to the cultivation of the friendship of the Greeks, especially of the Athenians. Towards the end of his reign (B. C. 630), Egypt was threatened with invasion from the Scythians, but Psammetichus, by presents and entreaties, prevailed on them to withdraw from the frontiers, and carry their depredations elsewhere. He reigned 54 years, and was succeeded (B. C. 616) by his son, Necho (or Nechao) II. (the Pharaoh-Necho of Scripture).

The first undertaking of this monarch was to cut a canal to join the Nile with the Red Sea, but he did not complete it, although he sacrificed 120,000 men in the attempt. Herodotus says that Necho desisted from completing it because he had been warned by an oracle that he was only constructing it for the use of barbarian invaders. He appears to have cared little for the lives of his subjects. He invaded Syria, and marched against the Babylonians, but was intercepted at Magdolus, or Megiddo, by Josiah, king of Judah, who was a vassal of Babylon, but endeavoring to stop Necho's progress, was defeated, and mortally wounded (B. C. 609). Necho took Jerusalem, dethroned Josiah's successor, Jehoahaz, and placed Jehoiakim on the throne of Judah. Necho advanced to the Euphrates, where he conquered the Babylonians, took Carchemish, or Circesium, and established a garrison there. Four years afterwards (B. C. 605) he marched once more to the Euphrates, but at Carchemish he was totally defeated by Nebuchadnezzar, then viceroy of Babylon for his father, Nabopolassar. The effect of this battle was to strip him of all his Asiatic dominions. It is said that he was taken prisoner. Nebuchadnezzar appears to have invaded Egypt after his victory, but he did not retain possession of the country, and Necho was permitted to return to his kingdom, where he died (B. C. 600), after a reign of 16 years, and was succeeded by his son, Psammetichus (or Psammis) II. One of the last acts of Necho was to send a Phœnician fleet from the Red Sea, with orders to circumnavigate Africa. This celebrated expedition set sail from the Arabian Gulf, and accomplished the voyage in rather more than two years, returning through the Straits of Gibraltar to Egypt. It is strange that this exploit, a great one for those ancient times, should have proved so barren of results. The passage to India round the Cape of Good Hope by Vasco di Gama in the 15th century A. C., had the effect of an entirely new discovery on the commerce of the world.

What revolution took place in Egypt after Sethos?—Who was Psammetichus?—What is recorded of him?—Of Necho II.?—What great enterprises did he undertake?—Why did he not finish his great canal?—What was the result of the Phœnician voyage of discovery round Africa?—Who succeeded Psammetichus?

SYRIA.

Hezekiah was succeeded (B. C. 697) by Manas′seh, to whose crimes the Jews attribute their ruin and slavery. Manasseh restored idolatry and superstition of every kind, and revelled in bloodshed. By his orders the prophet Isaiah was sawn in half (Milman's *History of the Jews*, vol. i., p. 309). The state of the country seems to have induced Esarhaddon, king of Assyria, to invade it. He took Jerusalem, which offered no resistance, and carried Manasseh away captive. The ravaged and desolated country of Palestine was then peopled by colonists sent thither by the Assyrian monarch. After some time passed in prison, Manasseh was released. He returned to his kingdom an altered man, and passed the remainder of his long reign in the observance of law and religion.

His son, Amon, who succeeded him (B. C. 642), fell a victim to a conspiracy after a reign of two years.

At the age of eight years, Josiah came to the throne (B. C. 640). He surpassed his predecessors in zeal for the reformation of the national religion. In his reign, Hilki′ah, the high-priest, discovered a copy of "the Law" (2 Kings xxii. 8), which had been lost during the troubled times of David, and had not been seen for 400 years; but so little were its contents known, that, on its first reading, the king, struck with terror at its denunciations, sent to consult with the prophetess, Huldah, respecting them. The book was read in public, and Josiah and all the nation renewed the solemn covenant with their God (B. C. 623). The king extirpated idolatry throughout the land; but, having ventured to oppose the march of Necho, the king of Egypt, against the Assyrians, he was defeated at Megiddo, where he received a mortal wound (B. C. 609).

Jeho′ahaz, a younger son of Josiah, had been raised to the throne; but Necho, returning from his expedition against the Assyrians, took Jerusalem, deposed Jehoahaz, and placed Eli′akim (or Jehoi′akim) on the throne, B. C. 609.

Jeremiah and Uriah, the prophets, had in vain warned the king to submit to Nebuchadnezzar. In the year B. C. 604, that monarch took Jerusalem, and carried Jehoiakim away to Babylon. Here commenced the seventy years of captivity. Jehoiakim was restored to his kingdom; but he, three years after, revolted against the Assyrians.

What were the acts of Manasseh?—What was the fate of Isaiah?—Of Amon?—Josiah?—Jehoahaz?—Jehoiakim?—In what year did the 70 years of captivity commence?

INDIA.

Beside the Brahmins and Budhists there is a third sect of religionists, called Jains, who occupy an intermediate position between these two sects. They originated about the 6th century A. C., but are mentioned here for the sake of convenience. They deny the existence, or rather the activity of God; they believe in the eternity of matter; they worship saints; revere animal life; have no hereditary priesthood; disclaim the divine authority of the Vedas; use no sacrifices, and do not worship fire. They also hold that a state of impassive abstraction is the supreme felicity to which mortals can attain. So far they agree with the Budhists. But they have castes among them, which are as strictly observed as those of the Hindoos. They admit the whole of the Hindoo gods, and worship some of them, though considering them as entirely subordinate to their own saints. To this extent they agree with the Brahmins. But they have changed the rank and circumstances of the Hindoo gods, increased the number of them, and at the same time lowered the position of the superior deities. But the chief objects of worship among the Jains are a limited number of saints, who have raised themselves by austerities to a superiority over the gods. These saints are called Tirtankaras. They are 72 in number: there being 24 for the past, 24 for the present, and 24 for the future. Of these, the most worshipped are Rishoba, Parasnath′, and Maha′vira, who are respectively the 1st, the 23d, and the 24th of the Tirtankaras of the present age. It has been conjectured that the last two, Parasnath and Mahavira, were the founders of the sect of the Jains. They are supposed to have attained to the supreme state of apathetic beatitude, and to take no share in the government of the world.

The Jains have no monastic establishments, and do not venerate relics. The priests are called Jatis, and are selected from all castes. They wear loose mantles, do not cover their heads, but cut their hair and beard; they subsist upon alms, and they never bathe. Their temples and caves are celebrated for magnificence, and some of the finest ruins in Hindoostan are remains of these Jain structures. This sect has a literature of its own, but it is far more extravagant than that of the Brahmins. The sacred language of the Jains is the Magadi or Pali.

When did the sect of the Jains originate?—What are their tenets?—What are the Tirtankaras?—How many are there?—Which are the principal?—What else is said of the Jains?

ASSYRIA.

There were several kings of Babylon in this century, but we are entirely unacquainted with their history, excepting that of the four last. Their names, which have come down to us, are:

	B. C.	B. C.
Bel′ibus	702 to	699
Asorda′nes	699 "	693
Regiba′lus	693 "	692
Mesessimordachus	692 "	688
(*Interregnum*)	688 "	680
Asaridi′nus	680 "	667
Saosduchi′nus, or Nabu′chodonosor	667 "	647
Chin′alada′nus, or Sar′acus	647 "	625
Nab′opolas′sar	625 "	604
Neb′uchadnez′zar	606 "	562
Those of Assyria were:		
Esarhaddon, or Sardanapa′lus I.	711 "	693
Asorda′nes, or Nergilus	693 "	691
Adram′melech, or Sammu′ghes	691 "	670
Axer′dis	670 "	650
Nab′uchodono′sor, or Sardanapa′lus II.	650 "	630
Saracus, or Ninus, or Sardanapa′lus III.	630 "	606

It appears that some of these kings ruled over both Nineveh and Babylon, and it is difficult sometimes to distinguish between the two histories.

Esarhaddon reigned over both empires 13 years. He re-annexed Syria and Palestine to the empire, carried off a vast number of the people of Israel, and took prisoner Manasseh, king of Judah, whom he afterwards released.

Saosduchinus (or Nabu′chodono′sor) was the monarch who defeated Phraortes, king of the Medes, at Ragau, and put him to death. He appears to have ruled both Babylon and Nineveh. In his time, Tobit foretold the destruction of the latter city; and in the 18th year of his reign, his general, Holofernes, sent against the Jews, was slain by the Jewess, Judith, the beautiful widow of Manasseh, of the tribe of Simeon (see *Book of Judith*, in the Apocrypha of the Old Testament).

Saracus, better known as Sardanapalus, or Chinaladanus, was a feeble and effeminate prince. He passed his time in his palace, unseen by his subjects, dressed in female apparel, and surrounded by women. His effeminacy induced Nabopolassar, king of Babylon, to form a league with Cyaxares, king of the Medes, for the subversion of the Assyrian empire. They advanced at the head of a formidable army against Nineveh. But all of a sudden Sardanapalus threw off his luxurious habits, and appeared as an undaunted warrior. He twice defeated his enemies, but was at length driven into Nineveh, where he sustained a siege of two years. Finding it impossible to hold out any longer, he collected all his treasures and wives, and placing them on an immense pile of wood, he set the latter on fire, and perished with the women in the flames (B. C. 606). This celebrated king was the founder of the cities of Anchialus and Tarsus, according to an inscription on a monument found near the former of those cities by the Greeks, and described by Arrian the historian. The inscription, descriptive also of the character of the monarch, ran thus: "Sardanapalus, the son of Anacyndaraxes, in one day founded Anchialus and Tarsus. Eat, drink, play: all other human joys are not worth a fillip." The inconsistencies in the accounts of the last Assyrian king are very great. The student will find them discussed in Mitford's *History of Greece*, vol. ix., p. 311. On the story of Sardanapalus Byron has founded a magnificent drama. From this time Babylon became the capital of the empire. Nabopolassar associated his son, Nabuchodonosor, or Nebuchadnezzar, with him in the government, and died B. C. 604.

Nebuchadnezzar was one of the most celebrated princes of the East. But his celebrity rests more upon the record of him which we find in Scripture, than upon his exploits as a monarch. He is there represented as a medium chosen for the display of the power of the Almighty on several remarkable occasions. As his father's lieutenant, he marched against the Egyptian king, Necho, who was preparing to invade Assyria, and totally defeated him at Carchemish, on the Euphrates, B. C. 604. He took Jerusalem, and carried many Jews into captivity.

What kings reigned in Babylon and Assyria during this century?—What is said of Esarhaddon?—Of Saosduchinus?—Of Sardanapalus?—What was the fate of the latter?—What cities did he build?—What inscription was found?—What of Nabopolassar?—And of Nebuchadnezzar?

PERSIA.

The reign of the Median king, Kai-Kobad, or Dejoces, was very long: the Persian historians say it lasted 120 years, but if we include the reign of Phraortes (whom they do not recognize), it could not have lasted more than 75 years; and if we exclude the latter, it lasted only 53 years. This last is the usual mode of reckoning. Dejoces was celebrated for his justice. He was succeeded by his son, Phraortes, B. C. 656. Of Phraortes, or Aphra, little is known. He is said to have conquered all Persia, and to have been involved in war with the Assyrians, by whom, at the battle of Ragau, he was defeated, taken prisoner, and put to death (B. C. 634).

Kai-Kaoos, or Cyax′ares, said by some to have been the son, and by others the grandson, of Dejoces, succeeded to the throne of the Medes. After the overthrow of Phraortes by the Assyrians, Cyaxares occupied himself at first with consolidating his power at home. He then turned his arms against Mazenderan and other provinces of Upper Asia, whilst the Scythians were ravaging Cappadocia, Armenia, Pontus, and Colchis. He next joined the Babylonian king, Nabopolassar, and laid siege to Nineveh, but was called away to oppose the Scythians, who, after ravaging Upper Asia, were now moving southward. Cyaxares collected all his forces, and met them, but was totally defeated (B. C. 630), and the Scythians remained masters of Upper Asia for 23 years. At last the king got rid of them by stratagem. Having invited their chiefs to a banquet, he caused them to be slain while they were intoxicated, and the Scythians, thus taken by surprise, were massacred by the Medes, who then repossessed themselves of the provinces they had lost, and extended their empire to the Halys. Cyaxares, now at liberty, returned to aid Nabopolassar in the siege of Nineveh, took that city, and utterly destroyed it; and, prosecuting his victories, made himself master of all the other cities of Assyria, except Babylon. A war ensued between him and Alyattes, king of Lydia, which lasted six years. In the last battle occurred the eclipse of the sun, foretold by Thales, the Greek philosopher, which put an end to the fight. During this period the Persians inhabited only one province. Their king, Achæ′menes, was the grandfather of Cyrus.

What is said of Dejoces?—Phraortes?—Cyaxares?—Of the Scythian invasion?—Of the war with the Lydians?—Of the state of the Persians at this period?

CHINA. JAPAN.

On the death of Hwan-wang (B. C. 696), Chang-wang ascended the throne, and became nominal emperor of China; but of his reign, and of those of his successors, Le-wang (B. C. 681–676), and Hwuy-wang (B. C. 676–651), little need be said.

Seang-wang became emperor in the year B. C. 651. Towards the close of his reign the empire was disturbed by the efforts of the powerful State of Tsin (which afterwards became supreme over the whole empire), to subdue a smaller State of the same name.

King-wang, who began to reign in the year B. C. 618, was very much beloved on account of his good qualities; but the affection of his people by no means proved an effectual barrier against the encroachments of his vassals. His reign was short.

His son, Kwang-wang, who ascended the throne in B. C. 612, was not unlike him. This prince possessed talents to rule over the whole empire, but he was without a shadow of power. His brief reign of five years came to an end B. C. 607.

During the reign of Ting-wang, his successor, the vassals grew tired of continual wars, and resolved finally to enter into a confederation, in order to punish those refractory rebels who disturbed the public peace. Eleven States embraced this opportunity of pacifying the country, but even this league could not stem the torrent of dissension, and new wars and quarrels arose to harass the unhappy land.

Japan.—The Japanese, like other ancient oriental nations, have three eras: the first era is that of their seven chief gods, and comprises an almost infinite number of ages; the second is that of their demigods, or five heroes, and is said to have lasted 2,342,467 years; the third is that of the present race of mortal men, or ecclesiastical hereditary emperors, successors of Avase-dsuno, the last of the heroic race. The original mortal emperors of Japan are styled "Mikaddos." The first of them was Sin-mu, who began his reign B. C. 660. He civilized his subjects, made a thorough reformation of the pre-existing laws and government, and introduced chronology, dividing the time into years and months. The grand Japanese Era of Nin-o begins with his reign. In the year B. C. 601, the worship of foreign idols was brought from China and India.

What are the principal events in the history of China during this century?—What are the eras of Japan?—Who was the first Mikaddo?—When did the era of Nin-o begin?

GREECE.

Sparta.—The Messenians, after a state of thraldom, which lasted 38 years, made another effort to regain their independence; and, having formed an alliance with the Argives and the Arcadians, they raised the standard of revolt under their gallant leader, Aristom′enes (styled by the oracle "the best of the Greeks"), B. C. 685. The struggle lasted fifteen years, and was signalized by the most determined bravery on the part of the Messenians, and by the extraordinary adventures and escapes of Aristomenes. Three great battles were fought during this war: the first with indecisive result at Deræ; the second, a signal victory on the part of the Messenians at the Boar's grave; the third, a decisive defeat by the Spartans, who gained the victory through bribing Aristoc′rates, king of Orchom′enus, the ally of the Messenians, to desert. Aristomenes carried his incursions into the very heart of Sparta, even into the city itself, and hung up his shield in the temple of Minerva, in token of defiance. He was thrice taken prisoner, but escaped twice. The third time he was thrown down a steep cavity of Mount Taygetus, but escaped unhurt, and groped his way out of the cave by following a fox which he had caught. But at length the Messenians were overcome, and their territory became finally annexed to Sparta. Aristomenes and his heroic followers forced their way through their assailants, and quitted the country. Some retired to Arcadia, and emigrated to Rhegium, on the southern coast of Italy, where the sons of Aristomenes founded a flourishing community. Aristomenes passed the remainder of his days in Rhodes, where he dwelt along with his son-in-law, Damage′tus, the ancestor of the noble Rhodian family called the Diagor′idæ, celebrated for its numerous Olympic victories. Another remarkable personage who figured during the second Messenian war was the poet Tyrtæus, a native of Aphidne, in Attica, whose strains greatly animated the Spartan youth, and remained for a long time popular with that people. The establishment of the Carneian festival at Sparta, for musical competition, also took place during this war, and the Lesbian harpist, Terpander, gained the first prize. The Spartans continued the war with the Arcadians and the Argives without any important results.

Attica.—The office of Archon underwent another change, and was made annual (B. C. 683); but instead of one Archon, there were appointed nine, to each of whom different functions were allotted. Three of them bore special titles. There was the Archon Eponymus, from whose names the designation of the year was derived; he determined all disputes relative to the family, and the relations between the *gens*, the *phratry*, and the tribe. (There were, in theory, 30 gentes to one phratry, and 30 phratries to one tribe.) He was also the legal protector of orphans and widows. The Archon Basileus, or king Archon, had jurisdiction in cases of religious disputes and of homicide. The Polemarch was leader of the military forces, and the judge of disputes between citizens and non-citizens. The six other Archons were styled Thesmothetæ, or framers of ordinances, and had jurisdiction in disputes and complaints generally. These new officers abused their authority, perverting the Constitution into an aristocracy oppressive to the working-classes. The trade of Athens flourished, nevertheless, and increased considerably. But the want of fixed laws being much felt, Draco, one of the Archons, was appointed to frame a code for the State (B. C. 624). That which he prepared decreed the penalty of death for the most trivial offences, and was otherwise so unreasonably severe as to defeat its own ends. Nevertheless it contained some good provisions, but it soon fell into disuse. Draco met with a singular death: he was smothered by the number of hats and cloaks showered upon him as a mark of honor in the theatre at Ægi′na.

In the year B. C. 612, one of the nobles, named Cylon, seized on the Acropolis, or citadel of Athens, and attempted to make himself master of the city. But the people rallied around the Archons, and blockaded the conspirators. Cylon escaped by stealth; several of his companions died of hunger; the remainder surrendered on the promise of having their lives spared, but this promise was violated, and they were all put to death. This period, and that immediately succeeding, is called "the age of the tyrants." The first tyrant of whom we read is Orthag′oras, of Sicyon (B. C. 676). He is said to have been originally a cook.

Corinth.—The Heraclidan family of the Bacchiadæ had usurped all power in the State. In the year B. C. 655, Cypselus, one of the family, contrived to gain the favor of the people, and eject the ruling dynasty. He became "tyrant," or ruler, but his rule was mild and just. After a peaceful reign of 30 years he left his power to his son, Periander (B. C. 625), a tyrannical prince, yet elegant in his tastes, a patron of literature, and so wise as to be counted one of the seven sages of Greece. His life was embittered from his having killed his wife in a fit of jealousy, and incurred the deadly hatred of his son, Lyc′ophron, who attempted to take his life. After vainly trying, both by rigor and conciliation, to conquer this feeling on the part of his son, Perian′der sent him to reside at Corcy′ra, which was then dependent upon his rule; but when he found himself growing old and disabled, he recalled him to Corinth. Lycophron refused to come; whereupon Periander threatened to go over to Corcyra, which so alarmed the people of that colony that they put Lycophron to death. In revenge for this, Periander seized 300 noble Corcyran youths, and sent them as slaves to King Alyattes, at Sardis. Periander lived to a very advanced age, and was succeeded, after reigning 40 years, by a relative, named Psammet′ichus.

Macedonia.—Perdiccas I. was succeeded by Argæus (B. C. 678), Philip I. (B. C. 640), Ær′opus (B. C. 602), of whom little need be said.

Besides Draco, Periander, Aristomenes, and Tyrtæus, whom we have already mentioned, this century produced many eminent persons. We may mention: Simon′ides, of Amergos, author of Iambic poems, principally satirical. Terpander, of Lesbos, already mentioned; he is called the father of lyric poetry, and was the improver of the lyre. Thale′tas, of Crete, a famous musician and poet. Alcman, the lyric poet. Lesches, author of a poem called "the Little Iliad," relating the destruction of Troy, and all that happened after the death of Hector. Pisander, of Rhodes, who wrote a poem on the exploits of Hercules. Mimnermus, of Smyrna, a much-admired elegiac poet. Ari′on, a celebrated musician, and the inventor of dithyrambic poetry. The story of his escape from being murdered by the sailors on his voyage home from Sicily to Corinth, is very famous. He had won great treasure at a musical contest in Sicily, and on his voyage home the sailors determined to kill him for the sake of plunder. After pleading in vain for his life, he obtained permission to play once more on his harp. Placing himself in the prow of the ship, and invoking the gods, he plunged into the sea, but was rescued by the song-loving dolphins, one of whom carried him to Tænarus, whence he returned in safety to Corinth. Alcæ′us, of Mitylene, the earliest of the Æolian lyric poets, and the inventor of the Aleaic metre. Sappho, also of Mitylene, the lyric poetess, and the head of a female literary society in her native city, whence she fled to escape some unknown danger, between the years B. C. 604 and 592. She is said to have fallen in love with a youth named Phaon, but finding her love unrequited, she leaped from the Leucadian rock into the sea. This story is probably an invention of later times. The name of Phaon does not occur in her poems: and the leap from the Leucadian rock is a metaphor borrowed from an expiatory rite connected with the worship of Apollo. The ancients professed the most unbounded admiration for her poetry; it was contained in nine books, but of these only fragments have come down to us. Pit′tacus, of Mitylene, distinguished as a warrior, statesman, philosopher, and poet, was one of "the seven wise men of Greece." Zaleucus, the lawgiver of the Locrians. His laws were very severe, and he fell a victim to them. One was that no citizen, under penalty of death, should enter the Senate-house armed. Zaleucus inadvertently transgressed this law; whereupon he fell on his sword, thus vindicating his own enactment. Stesich′orus, the Dorian choral poet, author of numerous short heroic poems, hymns, and songs. Epimen′ides, of Crete, a celebrated poet and prophet, said to have fallen into a deep sleep which lasted 57 years. He is quoted by the Apostle Paul in his epistle to Titus (ch. i., v. 12), and has been, by some, reckoned one of the seven wise men. Thales, of Miletus, a famous philosopher, and one of the seven wise men. He founded the study of philosophy and mathematics in Greece, and accurately predicted an eclipse of the sun. He maintained that water was the origin of all things. He left no works behind, and died at ninety.

The seven wise men of Greece were: Thales, of Miletus; Bias, of Priene; Pittacus, of Mitylene; Solon, of Athens; Periander, of Corinth; Chilon, of Sparta; and Cleobulus, of Lindus.

When did the second Messenian war break out?—What were the exploits of Aristomenes?—Who were Tyrtæus and Terpander?—What was the Carneian festival?—What change was made in the office of Archon?—What is said of the laws of Draco?—How did he die?—What is said of Cylon?—Orthagoras?—Cypselus?

What is said of Periander?—Lycophron?—Of the kings of Macedonia?—Who was Simonides?—Thaletas?—Alcman?—Lesches?—Pisander?—Mimnermus?—Relate the legend of Arion.—Who was Alcæus?—What is known of Sappho?—Of her poetry?—Pittacus?—Zaleucus?—Stesichorus?—Epimenides?—Thales?—Who were the seven wise men of Greece?

ITALY.

The legend of Numa Pompilius is as follows. He was very pious, and consulted the gods before doing anything. He asserted that he did everything by direction of the nymph Ege′ria, who made him her husband, and taught him, in her sacred grove, by the spring that gushed forth from the rock, what he was to do. She made him ensnare the gods Picus and Faunus, in the grove on the Aventine Hill, and force them to tell him how to ascertain the will of Jupiter. When he invited friends to supper, and set before them earthen dishes and cups, Egeria would change them into precious stones; the couches became covered with costly trappings; and the meats and drinks most delicious. No wonder the Romans chose him for their king. When he was installed in his kingdom he divided among the people the lands which Romulus had won in war: landmarks were set out, and placed in the keeping of the god Terminus. He divided the craftsmen of the city into nine companies. All was peace in his time, and the gates of the temple of Janus were never opened. He built a temple to Faith, and appointed a solemn worship for her. He died at the age of 80, having reigned more than 40 years (B. C. 681), and he was buried under the hill Janiculum. The books of his sacred laws were buried near him in a separate tomb. It is said that they were discovered by accident 500 years afterwards (B. C. 181), on the farm of a notary named Lucius Petillius, which was situated at the foot of the Janiculum, by some workmen who were digging there. These men dug up two stone chests, one of which was empty, but bore an inscription stating that it contained the body of Numa Pompilius; the other contained two bundles tied round with waxed cords. They consisted of seven books, in Latin, on ecclesiastical law, and seven in Greek, on philosophy; the latter were burned by command of the Senate, the former were preserved. But the story of their discovery is evidently a forgery.

When Numa was dead the Senators again shared the kingly power among themselves. But they soon chose for their king Tullus Hostilius, the grandson of Hostus Hostilius, who had fought with Romulus against the Sabines. Tullus was a warlike monarch, yet kind to the poor, among whom he divided the lands which fell to him as king, and he encouraged those who had no houses to settle on the Cælian Hill. He soon found an opportunity for indulging his warlike propensities, for the people of Alba were perpetually quarrelling with those on the Roman borders. The Alban dictator, Caius Cluilius, marched an army against Rome, and encamped within five miles of the city. There he died, and Mettius Fufetius was chosen dictator in his room. Tullus marched against the Albans; but when the two armies were in face of each other, Mettius proposed that champions should be chosen on both sides to decide the contest. So three twin brothers, named the Horatii, were chosen out of the Roman army, and three twin brothers, named the Curiatii, were chosen out of the Alban. The combat took place in sight of both armies, and was long undecided. Two of the Horatii were slain, and all of the Curiatii were wounded. Seeing this, the surviving Horatius pretended to flee: the wounded Curiatii followed him as well as they were able, when he encountered them severally, and slew them all. Thus the supremacy over Alba was adjudged to Rome. On his return to the city, the surviving Horatius was met at the Capenian gate by his sister, who was betrothed to one of the Curiatii. She recognized the spoils of her lover, and burst into tears. At this Horatius drew his sword, and stabbed her to the heart, exclaiming: "So perish every Roman maiden who shall weep for her country's foe." For his crime Horatius was condemned to death, but was let off on account of the public service he had rendered, being merely made to pass under a gibbet, with his head veiled, and led by his father. The Albans being now subject to the Romans, were called upon by Tullus to aid him against the people of Veii and Fidenæ. But during the battle, their leader, Mettius Fufetius, stood aloof; whereupon Tullus caused him to be seized, bound to two chariots, and torn asunder. Alba was then destroyed, and the Albans were made to take up their abode in Rome. Tullus next made war upon the Sabines; but a plague broke out, and he was seized with it. His death, however, is ascribed to lightning (B. C. 640).

The Romans then elected for their king Ancus Martius, the son of the daughter of Tullus Hostilius. It is related of Ancus Martius that he caused the laws of Numa to be published on whited boards, and hung up round the forum. He conquered the Latins, and brought them to Rome, assigning them the hill Aventinus for their dwelling-place. He divided their lands among the Romans, and gave up the forests near the sea to be public property. He founded a colony at Ostia; and built a fortress on the Janiculum, joining the hill to the city by a wooden bridge over the Tiber. He constructed a great dyke, called "the dyke of the Quirites;" and he built a prison under the hill Saturnius. He died B. C. 616, after a reign of 23 years.

At this period the people of Rome were divided into the three tribes of the Ramnenses, the Titienses, and the Luceres. The Titienses were Sabines; the Luceres, Etrurians; the Ramnenses were probably Latins. Each tribe was divided into ten smaller bodies, called "Curiæ," so that the whole population was divided into thirty tribes. Each curia was made up of "gentes," or houses, which "gens," or house, was a union of several families, bound together by the performance of certain religious rites. These families had their dependents, who were called clients. These latter held a political (not a domestic) relation to the houses. They could not intermarry with them, nor share in the government or the property of the State; but they might possess property, and regulate their own municipal and domestic affairs. These were the original Plebs, plebeians, or commons of Rome; the mass of them were conquered Latins. The assembly of the curiæ was the assembly of the people. The Senate consisted of 200 members chosen in equal numbers from the two higher tribes, the Ramnenses and the Titienses. The power of the king was ill-defined. He was absolute over the commons, but he was absolute over the houses only in war, and outside the city. Within its walls every citizen could appeal from him to the great council of the curiæ. The king had his own royal lands, and received his share of the spoils in war.

Rome, at this period, occupied seven elevated spots, known by the names of the hills of Palatium, Velia, Cermalus, Cælius, Fagutal, Oppius, and Cispius. The Aventine Hill was a suburb; and the city was distinct from the Sabine city on the Capitoline, Quirinal, and Viminal Hills. The two cities had a separate existence, and were not blended together until the next century. The hills first mentioned were not the famous seven hills of imperial Rome: they belonged to, or formed part of three of them, viz., the Palatine, the Cælian, and the Esquiline. These three, with the Capitoline, Quirinal, Viminal, and Aventine, constituted the famous seven.

The legends respecting the four earliest kings of Rome are not to be accepted as history. How much of the historical element there is in them, is a question not easy to answer. The student will find the subject elaborately discussed in Niebuhr's *History of Rome*. The stories of the three later kings undoubtedly contain much that is historical, mixed up with much that is fabulous, but it is difficult to sift the chaff from the wheat. The legend of Tarquinius Priscus, the successor of Ancus Martius, is as follows. In the days of Ancus Martius there came to Rome, from Tarquinii, a city of Etruria, a wealthy Etruscan and his wife. The father of this stranger was a Greek, a citizen of Corinth, who left his native land because it was oppressed by a tyrant, and found a home at Tarquinii. There he married a noble Etruscan lady, and by her he had two sons. But his son found that, for his father's sake, he was still looked upon as a stranger: so he left Tarquinii, and went with his wife, Tanaquil, to Rome; for there, it was said, strangers were held in more honor. Now, as he came near to the gates of Rome, riding in his chariot with Tanaquil, an eagle plucked the cap from his head, and bore it aloft into the air — then flew down, and replaced it on his head. Tanaquil understanding augury, was delighted, and interpreted the omen to indicate that her husband would rise to greatness. When he arrived in Rome, they called him Lucius Tarquinius. He was brave in war, wise in council, and his riches won the good will of the multitude. He soon became known to the king, who employed him in his service. He served Ancus Martius faithfully, and was held in great honor by him — so much so, indeed, that when he died, he named him by his will guardian of his children. On the death of Ancus Martius the people set aside the sons of that ruler, and elected Tarquinius king (B. C. 616). An account of the exploits of this monarch, who was celebrated more for his peaceful than for his warlike labors, will be given in the next century.

Relate the legend of Numa Pompilius.—Who was Egeria?—How long did Numa reign?—What became of his sacred books?—Who succeeded him?—What were the chief exploits of Tullus Hostilius?—Describe the fight between the Horatii and the Curatii.—What crime did Horatius commit, and how was it punished?—What were the acts of Ancus Martius?

What were the divisions into which the people of Rome were divided?—What hills did the city stand upon?—Name the seven hills.—What is said of the history of the seven kings?—Relate the legend of Tarquinius Priscus.—Who was Tanaquil?—In what year was Tarquinius elected king?

BRITAIN.

The history of this country during this century offers nothing worthy of notice, supposing the accounts we have of it to be anything more than the merest fables or legends, to which it is impossible to say what credit is to be attached. The narrative of Geoffrey of Monmouth runs as follows:

"After him (Gurgustius), Sisillius; after him, Jago, the nephew of Gurgustius; after him, Kinmarcus, the son of Sisillius; after him, Gorbogudo, who had two sons, Ferrex and Porrex." The Latin form of these names adds materially to the suspicion that they are mere inventions of the old chroniclers.

The student will find the principal works of these ancient authors in a small book edited by J. A. Giles, entitled "Six Old English Chronicles." These consist of: 1. Ethelwerd's *Chronicle*, written in the middle of the 10th century A. C. 2. Asser's *Life of Alfred*, written during the reign of that monarch. 3. The works of Gildas the wise, supposed to have lived in the 6th century A. C. 4. Nennius' *History of the Britons*, written some time between the years 796 and 994. 5. Geoffrey of Monmouth's *British History*, written in the early part of the 12th century. 6. Richard of Cirencester's *Ancient State of Britain.* Henry of Huntingdon, Alfred of Beverley, Giraldus Cambrensis, Holinshed, Matthew Paris, and other antiquaries, have drawn largely from these old chronicles. Geoffrey of Monmouth was a learned monk, and was made bishop of St. Asaph, A. D. 1152. His great work was written in Latin, and first translated into English by Aaron Thompson, of Oxford, in 1718, who gives us the following account of the origin of this very remarkable collection of fables and traditions:

"Walter Mapes, Archdeacon of Oxford, in the reign of Henry I., a zealous antiquary, happened, while in Brittany, to meet with an ancient history of Britain, written in the British tongue. He brought it over to England, and induced Geoffrey of Monmouth to translate it into Latin." This ancient British work is said to have been preserved in the Cottonian library at Oxford, and several copies of it are extant in the Welsh language. It is mentioned by Archbishop Usher, in his work on the early Christian Church of Britain.

What particulars are extracted from Geoffrey of Monmouth?—Who and what was he?—What account have we of his great work? Name the ancient chroniclers of Britain.

FRANCE.

This century is remarkable for the introduction of an additional element into the population of Gaul. The Celtic tribe of the Cimmerii (Cimbri, or Cymri,) had dwelt for ages in the north of Europe. They were of kindred race with the Gauls, but long separation had made them strangers. The Cimmerii roamed through the vast plains of Central Europe and Southern Russia, and occasionally carried terror into Asia Minor and Greece. Driven, in their turn, by the Scythians, or Teutons, from the Crimea and the plains of the north, they pressed upon Asia Minor and the east of Europe; and a vast multitude of them, crossing the lower Rhine, entered Gaul in the year B. C. 631. According to national traditions, this host was under the leadership of Hu, or Hesus the powerful, a great warrior, legislator, and priest (Thierry, *Histoire des Gaulois*, vol. i., page 33). Mention has already been made of a great Cimmerian leader, named Hu Gadarn (pp. 29, 57), whose era has been carried back to a more remote period by the Breton traditions. It may be that there were two chieftains of the name of Hu, the word Gadarn being merely a descriptive term; but it is very difficult to peer through the mist of obscurity which envelops the earliest history of such unlettered and unsettled tribes.

History does not furnish us with the details of the conquest of Gaul by the Cimmerians, but the relative position of the conquerors and the conquered, after it had been accomplished, enables us to form an idea of the course of the struggle. The Cimmerians, marching along the shores of the Northern Ocean, crossed the Rhine, and the first scene of the war was on the northern shores of France, in Armorica, or Brittany. The Gauls driven thence, maintained themselves behind the mountains of the Vosges and Auvergne. The tribe of the Bitu′riges held their ground behind the middle Loire; the Aquita′ni, behind the Garonne, at the mouth of which river, nevertheless, the Cimmerian Boii established themselves. The struggle lasted considerably beyond the close of the century, and France was a scene of bloodshed and confusion.

The Phœnician empire of the sea had been gradually giving way to that of the Greeks. The Rhodians succeeded the Phœnicians, and were in their turn supplanted by the Phocæans.

What great race poured into France?—What is known of the Cimmerii?—What of Hu Gadarn?—The Bituriges?—Aquitani?—Duration of war?—Rhodians and Phocæans?

SPAIN.

The first half of this century presents us with nothing of historical note; and, but for occasional notices of Spain in the history of other nations, we might almost forget her existence. This epoch was that of colonization. We have seen that in the century preceding, and in fact for a long time previously, the Phœnicians had planted colonies on the coasts, and the Greeks had recently settled in Catalonia. The aggressions of the former at length roused the hostility of the Spaniards. Towards the close of the century, that is, about the year B. C. 620, flourished Arganto′nius, king of the Tartessi, who was famed for his skill in war. The Spaniards elected him their generalissimo against the Phœnicians, who were now openly aiming at the sovereignty of Spain. Using policy as well as strength, they sowed dissension among the natives, and by that means possessed themselves of several places. The natives, under Argantonius, not only checked them, but drove them out of the province of Bœtica, or Andalusia, and even out of the island of Cadiz. It is alleged that numbers of the Phœnicians were called away to assist in the defence of Tyre, then besieged by Nebuchadnezzar, and so they were forced to abandon all their possessions in Spain. The relief thus afforded to the Tyrians enabled them to hold out for four years. Nebuchadnezzar being called away into Egypt, raised the siege. Having subdued the greatest part of Northern Africa, he passed over into Spain. Mariana quotes Josephus as authority for the conquest of Spain by Nebuchadnezzar; but that author merely cites Megasthenes' assertion, that "he conquered a great part of Libya and Iberia" (if by the latter we are to understand Spain). See *Antiq. of Jews*, b. x., § 1; *Apion*, b. i., § 20. The Jews say that many towns in Andalusia and the kingdom of Toledo have hence derived Hebrew names: such as Toledo, from Toledoth, signifying "families"; Escalona, from Ascalon; Noves, from Nobe; Maqueda, from Mageddo; Yopes, from Joppa; etc. But though the Spanish historians assert these and other things in regard to the alleged visit of Nebuchadnezzar to Spain, but little reliance is to be placed on their statements. After the return of the Babylonians the Dorians of Rhodes visited the eastern coast of Spain, and supplanted the Phœnicians.

What is said of the first half of this century?—Who was Argantonius?—What Asiatic monarch invaded Spain?—What does Josephus say?—What of the Hebrew names of cities?

GERMANY.

The Golden Age is at an end. Care and anxiety take possession of the gods, who, forgetful of their given word, kill Angurbode, one of the three giantesses. Loki finds her torn-out heart, and falls in love with her; and as until now he was accounted one of the Asen, he goes over to the wicked giants in order to plot the destruction of his former companions. At the same time a young wolf, Fenrix, which was brought up in Asgard, grows to such an enormous size, that the Asen begin to feel uneasy. In vain they bind him; he breaks every chain. At length they try to bind him with a charm, but he does not allow the chain to be placed upon him until they swear that it is not a charm. They forswear themselves, and Tyr has the courage to lay his hand, as security, in the wolf's mouth, who instantly bites it off on discovering the deception. The gods are no longer worthy of life. Iduna, or immortality, is tempted from them by a giant; however, they still possess Balder, or enchanting beauty: but the ugly quarrel with him, and his only brother, the blind Hödur, is unwittingly incited to kill him by Loki; and his wife, Nana, burns herself upon his funeral pile. Then the Asen take foul revenge on Loki, and, sinning against nature, they bind him with the bowels of his only son to three pointed rocks, and suspend over his head a snake distilling poison. His convulsions produce earthquakes. The end of all things is now at hand. The rage of the gods and the wickedness of men increase. Enmity and hate have universal rule; then come fear and woe, the hatchet and sword age, the storm and wolf era. For three years there is unbroken icy winter, the frightful Fimbul weather, during which everything is buried in frozen sleep before the awful end. The earth begins to shake; the dragon has gnawed through the roots; and the ash tree, Ygdrasill, will fall, and crush the whole world. The wolf, Fenrix, madly struggles with his bonds, and bursts them. Loki also breaks away from the rocks. Across the sea come the giants, the Hrymthursen, in the ship Nagelfar, entirely built of the nails of dead men fastened together, a proof of the antiquity of the world: the Mitgard snake rises from the ocean like a gigantic ghost, and they besiege Asgard.

What is said of Angurbode?—Loki?—Fenrix?—Tyr?—The Asen?—Iduna?—Balder?—Hödur?—The tortures of Loki?—The ash tree, Ygdrasill?—The Hrymthursen?

B.C. 700—600.

ASIA MINOR.

Before commencing the authentic history of Asia Minor, we ought not to omit noticing two famous personages whose names will be frequently met with in classic literature, viz., Gor′dius and Mi′das. Gordius was a poor Phrygian peasant, who, by an extraordinary incident, became king of Phrygia. Civil dissensions having broken out, the people consulted an oracle, and were told that a wagon would bring them a king who would heal their differences. While they were deliberating upon this, Gordius happened to pass in his wagon, and he was at once hailed as king. Out of gratitude he dedicated his chariot to Jupiter. The pole of it was fastened to the body by a knot of bark, and an oracle foretold that whoever should untie the knot should reign over all Asia. Alexander the Great, on his arrival at Gordium, solved the prophecy by cutting the knot with his sword. Midas was the son of Gordius. As he is said to have been the pupil of Orpheus, the era in which he lived must have been the 13th century B. C. He was very wealthy and very effeminate. Several stories are related of him. Having hospitably entertained Sile′us, the companion of Bacchus, the god allowed him to ask any favor—whereupon Midas requested that whatever he touched should be changed into gold. The request was granted; but as all the food he touched was turned into gold, he begged the god to take back the favor. Midas was ordered to bathe in the river Pacto′lus: this cured him, but thenceforward the river had gold in its sand. Midas was once visited by a satyr, who mocked him. The king thereupon mixed wine in a well, and when the satyr drank of it, he fell asleep, and was caught. Midas decided a musical contest between Pan and Apollo, in favor of the former—whereupon Apollo changed his ears into those of an ass! Midas tried to conceal them under his cap, but the servant who cut his hair discovered them. The secret so troubled the man that, as he dared not divulge it, he dug a hole, and whispered it into the ground. But a reed grew up on the spot, which uttered it to the world, and Midas destroyed himself by drinking bullock's blood.

The Lydians have a list of 22 kings (beginning with Hercules), who reigned over them for 505 years, down to the time of Candaules, who was murdered in the year B. C. 716, by his wife, in conjunction with Gyges, captain of the guards. Candaules was the last of the Heraclidan dynasty, and Gyges founded that of the Mermnadæ. He reigned 38 years, and died B. C. 678, being succeeded by his son Ardys, who reigned 49 years (B. C. 678–629). This long reign was signalized by two events of considerable importance to the Asiatic Greeks, viz., an invasion by the Cimmerians, and the first collision between the Lydians and the Medes, who were pushing their empire westward.

The Cimmerians were at this period the chief occupants of the Crimea. They were a nomadic people, like the Scythians who inhabited Southern Russia and the regions of the Caucasus. The latter having attacked the Cimmerians, they divided themselves into two parties; the majority agreeing to flee from the land, while the chiefs, or kings, of the different tribes resolved to perish at home. The latter fell by each other's hands near the river Tyras, where their sepulchres were still shown in the days of Herodotus. The mass of the Cimmerians abandoned their country to the Scythians, and passing to the west of Mount Cau′casus, made their way into Colchis, and established themselves on the north coast of Asia Minor. They ravaged Paphlagonia, Phrygia, Lydia, and Ionia, and, in the year B. C. 635, occupied the town of Sardis, the capital of Lydia, sacked Magnesia, and threatened Ephesus. They ravaged Asia Minor during the reign of Ardys, and that of his son Sadyattes (B. C. 629–617). But Alyattes, the son and successor of Sadyattes, finally expelled them from Asia, excepting those who had settled in the neighborhood of Sin′ope. By some, their occupation of Asia Minor is estimated at 260 years (B. C. 876–617).

The Scythians invaded Upper Asia, and nearly ruined the countries they passed through. The Median king, Cyax′ares, called away from the siege of Nineveh to oppose them, was totally defeated. They advanced to the borders of Egypt, where the Egyptian king met them, and by costly presents redeemed his kingdom from invasion. Their oppression lasted 28 years. At length, Cyaxares, having invited the Scythian chiefs to a banquet, slew them when intoxicated (B. C. 608). The barbarians were then expelled, and the Medes regained their empire. A war ensued with the Lydians, which was terminated by the marriage of Alyattes' daughter to the son of Cyaxares.

What is said of Gordius?—Of Midas?—Who was Candaules?—What dynasty did Gyges found?—What two important events occurred during the reign of Ardys?—Who were the Cimmerians?—What befell them?—What did the Scythians do?—What took place between the Medes and the Lydians?

CARTHAGE.

In Sicily, the Greeks continued to arrive in great numbers. The city of Gela was founded B. C. 691, by Antiphemus of Rhodes. Selinus was founded B. C. 626.

Of the history of Carthage and Northern Africa, during this century, we have no particular accounts. There is a chasm of nearly three hundred years after the death of Dido. We are vaguely informed that Carthage was much agitated by civil dissensions, and harassed with the plague, during part of this period; and that the people had got a strong footing in Sicily, Sardinia, Spain, and elsewhere. But the Carthaginians' archives were destroyed by the Romans, and no accounts have come down to us except what it pleased the conquerors to furnish us with. Throughout the history of Carthage we must bear in mind that it was the practice of the Romans to vilify their enemies; they had little or no magnanimity towards the conquered: therefore we are not to believe that the Carthaginians were so bad as they are described to have been.

The traditions (or, rather, mythological fables) relative to the children of the ancient Gætulian king, Atlas, are as follows:—His son, Hyas, was killed in Libya by a wild beast. Hyas is also a mystic surname of Diony′sus, or Bacchus. His daughters were numerous, and are classed as the Hyades, Pleiades, and the Hesperides. The mythological accounts of these personages vary greatly as to the number of them. According to some statements there were seven Hyades—according to others, twelve or fifteen. The common number is seven, and their names were Ambro′sia, Eudo′ra, Pedi′le, Coro′nis, Polya′o, Phy′to, and Thye′ne, or Dio′ne. Jupiter confided to them the care of the infant Bacchus, and afterwards placed them among the stars. Dione is, in some of the fables, represented as the mother of Venus. The name of the constellation Hyades is derived from the Greek word ὕειν, signifying "to rain". The Pleiades were sisters of the Hyades, and were seven in number. Their names were Electra, Maia, Tay′gete, Alcyone, Celæno, Ster′ope, and Mer′ope. They died of grief at the fate of their father, and were placed among the stars, where they formed one of the most beautiful constellations in the heavens. Maia, the eldest and most beautiful of them, was the mother of Mercury. One of them, Sterope, became the wife of Œnomaus, king of Pisa, in the Peloponnesus, and was thus lost to the heavenly choir: six of the sisters remaining visible, the other becoming invisible. This fable of "the lost Pleiad" has furnished a theme for much beautiful poetical imagery.

The Hesperides were the guardians of the golden apples (another name for oranges), which Terra (the earth) gave to Juno (the air), on her marriage with Jupiter. They were assisted in watching them by the dragon, Ladon, which was slain by Hercules, when he carried away the apples. They were sisters of the Hyades and the Pleiades. Their number is variously stated at three, four, and seven; and the names of Ægle, Arethusa, Hestia, Orytheia, and Hesperia, have been assigned to them. They were celebrated for their sweet singing, and dwelt in the extreme west of Libya.

Calypso, the daughter of Atlas (according to Homer), inhabited the island of Ogygia, on which Ulysses was shipwrecked. The hero remained seven years with her, and she promised him immortality if he would remain with her; but the gods compelled her to allow him to depart. Hesperus, the son of Atlas, was devoted to astronomy, and disappeared after ascending Mount Atlas to observe the stars.

There is another famous personage who figures in what may be called the African portion of Grecian mythology, viz., Antæ′us, of whom we have the following account. He was the son of Neptune and Terra (the sea and the earth: in other words, he was born near the sea-side), and became a mighty wrestler and giant in Libya, whose strength was invincible so long as he remained in contact with his mother earth (*i. e.*, could stand on his legs). The strangers who visited his country were compelled to wrestle with him: the conquered were slain, and with their skulls Antæus built a temple to his father, Neptune. But Hercules discovered the secret of his strength, lifted him from the earth, and crushed him in the air. The tomb of Antæus, which formed a moderate-sized hill in the shape of a man stretched out at full length, was shown near the town of Tingis, in Mauretania, down to a late period; but the tradition is about as authentic as that which at this day points out the tombs of Achilles, Ajax, and Protesilaus, on the Trojan shore.

What took place in Sicily during this century?—What is said of the history of Carthage?—Of the mode in which the Romans treated their enemies?—What is the legend of Hyas?—The Hyades?—Dione?—The Pleiades?—Maia?—The lost Pleiad?—The Hesperides?—Calypso?—Antæus?—The tomb of the latter?

THE 6TH CENTURY

EGYPT.

Of Psammetichus II. no public building remains, nor is any large work of art extant. He made an expedition into Ethiopia, died on his return, and was succeeded (B. C. 594) by his son, Uaph′ris (the A′pries of the Greeks, and the Hoph′ra of Scripture). The first object of this prince was to recover in Palestine the ascendancy which Egypt formerly possessed. He accordingly fitted out an expedition, took Sidon by storm, reduced all the coast of Phœnicia, and defeated the Cyprians (who were allies of the Phœnicians) at sea. After this he sent an army into Judea to assist king Zedekiah against Nebuchadnezzar, but this army returned to Egypt without a contest (B. C. 587). On the taking of Jerusalem by the Assyrians many of the Jewish chiefs fled into Egypt, carrying with them the prophet Jeremiah, who died at Daphne, near Pelu′sium. Some say he was stoned to death by the people, others that he was put to death by Uaphris, foretelling in his last prophecy the fate of that monarch (Jer. xliv. 30).

Nebuchadnezzar having, after a siege of 13 years, taken Tyre (B. C. 591), is believed to have marched into Egypt, and ravaged it, but he did not permanently occupy it.

Adicran, king of the Libyans, having implored aid from Uaphris against the Greek colony of Cyrene, the king sent an army to his assistance, which was routed and destroyed by the Greeks (B. C. 570). The news of this defeat produced a revolt in Egypt, and Uaphris sent Ama′sis, one of his officers, to appease the mutineers; but they offering the crown to Amasis, he accepted it, and marched with them against Uaphris, who had only his Greek auxiliaries to rely upon. These were defeated, and the king was taken prisoner. Amasis delivered him into the hands of the people, by whom he was strangled (B. C. 569). Amasis established a strict administration throughout Egypt, and raised it to a high degree of prosperity. His frank and jovial qualities made him a universal favorite. He cultivated the friendship of the Greeks, and it is said that Solon and Pythag′oras visited Egypt in his time. He enlarged the temple of Minerva at Sais, and erected an immense colossus at Memphis. His reign lasted 44 years, and he died just as his kingdom was on the point of being invaded by the Persians under Camby′ses (B. C. 525). His son, Psammeni′tus, assembled his Greek and Egyptian forces, and met the invaders at Pelusium, where, after a long struggle, the Persians were victorious. Cambyses besieged and took Memphis, and speedily became master of all Egypt, but failed in his attempt to conquer the Ethiopians. During his absence on this expedition, Psammenitus raised a revolt: this was suppressed by Cambyses with great cruelty, and Psammenitus was put to death. Cambyses committed great outrages on the unhappy Egyptians: fortunately for them he died on his return to Persia (B. C. 520). His successor, Dari′us Hystas′pes, gained great popularity by his wise administration. He left the government of Egypt to his satrap, Aryan′des, under whom the country was peaceful during the remainder of the century.

What is said of Psammetichus II.?—Of Uaphris?—Who was Amasis?—Name his principal acts.—Who succeeded him?—What Persian monarch conquered Egypt?—What became of Psammenitus?—Who succeeded Cambyses?

SYRIA.

Nebuchadnezzar left the suppression of the revolt in Judea to the neighboring tribes. These, for three years, ravaged the country, and shut up Jehoiachim in Jerusalem. The latter was killed in a sally, and his remains were buried (as the prophet foretold), "with the burial of an ass." Jehoia′chin (Jeconi′ah, or Coni′ah), his son, had scarcely mounted the throne when Nebuchadnezzar appeared at the gates of Jerusalem, and the city surrendered. The king, the royal family, army, nobility, and treasures were carried away to Babylon. Over this wreck of a kingdom, Zedeki′ah (or Mattani′ah), the younger son of Josiah, was allowed to reign for eleven years. In the ninth year of his reign he endeavored to assert his independence, in connection with Uaphris, king of Egypt; but the Assyrians defeated the Egyptians, and laid siege to Jerusalem, which was starved into surrender. Zedekiah was seized, his children were slain before his face, and his eyes were put out; and the last king of the royal house of David was led away to a foreign prison (B. C. 587). The Assyrians destroyed the city and temple: the chief priests were put to death, the others led into captivity. The remnant of the people were placed under the command of Gedali′ah, and the seat of government was fixed at Mizpeh. Here Gedaliah was assassinated by Ishmael, a man of the royal blood, who was driven out by Joha′nan and the rest of the Jews. These fled into Egypt, carrying with them the prophet Jeremiah, whom, it is said, they afterwards put to death, though there is a tradition that this was done by order of Uaphris, king of Egypt.

The Samaritans remained in the land of their fathers. It is said, by the Hebrews, that they were descendants of the Cuthæan colonists introduced by Esarhaddon. They preserved the book of the Mosaic law, written in the ruder and more ancient character; the Jews, after their return from Babylon, adopted the more elegant Chaldean letters.

At one of the settlements of the Jews on the river Chebar, north of Babylon, dwelt the prophet Ezekiel, who, during their captivity, kept up the drooping spirits of his countrymen by his encouraging prophecies. At length the prophet Daniel, who had become one of the principal ministers of Cyrus, king of Persia, prevailed with that monarch to issue his edict for the return of the Jews to their native country, and for the rebuilding of the temple (B. C. 536).

Under Joshua and Zerub′babel the Jews returned to the land of their fathers, and commenced the rebuilding of their temple (B. C. 535). From this period there was an entire alteration in their national character. From being idolatrous, and prone to form alliances with the neighboring nations, they now became exclusive, and devoted to the observance of "the Law." They became most passionately attached to their country and religion, hating foreigners, and cherishing the idea of the coming of a Messiah to be their king. The building of the temple was completed in the reign of Darius Hystaspes (B. C. 515), through the exertions of Zerubbabel, and the prophets Haggai and Zechariah.

What befel Jehoiachim?—Jehoiachin?—The last king of Judea?—The remnant of the people?—Jeremiah?—What is said of the Samaritans?—Ezekiel?—Daniel?—Rebuilding the temple?—The change in the national character?

INDIA.

The best authenticated accounts fix this century as the era of Gotama, or Guatama, the founder of Budhism. This is the epoch given by the Hindoos and the people of Ava, Siam, and Ceylon; but the Cashmerians place his advent 1332 years before Christ; the Chinese, Mongols, and Japanese, about 1000; of thirteen Tibetian authors, four give an average of 2959 years B. C., and other authorities differ in like manner (see Elphinstone's *History of India*, vol. i., pp. 209–211). Gotama was of the race of Sakya. He was a native of Capila, to the north of Gorakpoor; some say he was a Cshatriya, others that he was the son of the king of Magadha. At an early age this sage retired into solitude, where, after six years' meditation, he framed his system of religion. He then made his appearance in the city of Benares, where he taught his doctrines, and made thousands of proselytes. He attained to eminent piety and sanctity, and died (about the year B. C. 550, in the reign of Ajata Satru,) in his 80th year, revered by all. He was styled Budha, or "the sage" (literally, "intelligence"), by the Hindoos. In China he was called Fo-ta and Fo. In Siam, Mongolia, and other countries, he received different appellations. The religion of Budha became the dominant religion in India in the 3d century B. C., but did not remain so for more than ten centuries. We shall find that after that time it was gradually superseded by the ancient faith of Brahma, and ultimately extinguished by the Mohammedan conquerors. In the 3d century B. C. it was introduced into Ceylon, which became the head-quarters of this faith. It spread into Nepaul and Tibet. It did not reach China until A. D. 65, and did not make much progress there until the 5th century of the Christian era. It was carried into Corea A. D. 528, and Japan A. D. 552.

It has been already stated that the principal tenets of Budha were that there were three distinct Gods, each having his own attributes, and never interfering with the other two; and that he taught the eternity of matter, and the immortality of the soul, but not its perpetual individuality—for he held that after an indefinite number of existences it would be absorbed into divinity. It is on this account that, in the present day, the Grand Lama of Tibet is said to refrain from accepting the highest grade of mortal existence, in order that he may continue to be born again and again for the benefit of mankind: were he once absorbed into the divine spirit he could return no more to earth. The disciples of Budha at the present day number over three hundred millions.

Towards the close of the century, Darius, king of Persia, sent Scylax, a native of Caryanda, in Caria, with a flotilla to explore the Indus. That officer set out from the city of Caspatyrus, reached the sea, and then sailed west through the Indian Ocean to the Red Sea, performing the whole voyage in 30 months. Darius then invaded India with a large force, defeated the armies sent against him, and extended his dominion over the western provinces, but it is not known how far he pushed his conquests.

Who was the founder of Budhism?—What eras are assigned to him?—What was his origin?—Where did he teach?—Into what countries did his system spread?—What were its principal doctrines?—What expedition did Darius send out?

ASSYRIA.

The revolt of the Jews continuing under their king, Jehoiachim, and his successor, Jechoniah, Nebuchadnezzar went in person, and took Jerusalem (B. C. 598), plundering the temple, and carrying away the Jewish king. In the place of the latter he set up Mattaniah, or Zedekiah, the uncle of Jechoniah. Zedekiah, however, leagued himself with the king of Egypt, and revolted; whereupon Nebuchadnezzar laid siege to Jerusalem a second time, and, after a twelvemonth, took it by storm, put out the eyes of Zedekiah, carried him to Babylon, and destroyed the city and temple (B. C. 587). On his return to Babylon he set up a golden statue, which he commanded his subjects to worship. It was on this occasion that the three Hebrew youths, Anani′as, Misa′el, and Azari′as (better known by their Persian names — Shadrach, Meshach, and Abednego), displayed their heroism in testifying to the faith of their fathers (see Daniel iii.).

The next exploit of Nebuchadnezzar was the siege and destruction of Tyre (B. C. 585), which cost him incredible efforts for 13 years, and had no permanent result; for the Tyrians removed to a neighboring isle, one mile from the shore, where they built the modern city of Tyre, which soon eclipsed the glories of the ancient city. Nebuchadnezzar spent the remainder of his days in the rebuilding or embellishing of Babylon, but was afflicted with mental derangement for seven years. He died in the year B. C. 561, and was succeeded by his son, Evil-Merodach (or Ilvaroda′mus), who soon rendered himself so odious by his vices that his own relations put him to death. His wife, Nitocris, is the queen who raised so many noble edifices in Babylon, and is, by some historians, supposed to be the Queen Semiramis, of whom such marvellous traditions are preserved.

Neriglissor (or Nericosolassar), the brother-in-law of the late king, made war on the Medes, and was defeated and slain by the Persian king, Cyrus (B. C. 556). His successor, Laborosoarchod, was a monster of iniquity, and was slain by his own subjects, after a reign of nine months (B. C. 555).

Nabonadius, or Belshazzar, is supposed to have been the son of Evil-Merodach and Nitocris. He appears to have been a prince given up to debauchery and impiety: in him were fulfilled the prophetic denunciations against the guilty city of Babylon. Cyrus, king of Persia, turned his arms against the king, defeated the Babylonians, and laid siege to the city. He took it, after a long time, by diverting the course of the Euphrates, which flowed through the midst of it, entering it by the dry channel of the river, while Belshazzar and his court were feasting. The prophet Daniel had warned him in vain of his approaching end. The words, *Mene, Tekel, Upharsin*, written in luminous characters on the wall, were explained to him (Daniel v. 25–28); but the impious king heeded not the warning, and was slain that same night. The prophet was spared, and promoted to high office by Cyrus.

Such was the end of the famous empire of the Assyrians and Babylonians.

What were the exploits of Nebuchadnezzar?—Who succeeded him?—With whom is Nitocris identified?—What is said of the succeeding kings?—Of Belshazzar?—What was fulfilled in him?—What became of Daniel?

PERSIA.

On the death of Cyaxares (B. C. 594), his son, Asty′ages, succeeded, and reigned 35 years, but we have no particulars of his reign. This prince is called Ahasue′rus in Scripture. He had a son, Cyaxares, who succeeded him; and a daughter, Manda′ne, married to Camby′ses, king of Persia, from whom came Cyrus. Cyaxares (called, in Scripture, Dari′us the Mede,) became king of Media, and Cyrus (or Kai-Khosroo) became king of Persia (B. C. 559). Many interesting tales are told of the latter, which will be found in the works of Herodotus, Xenophon, and Ferdusi, the Persian poet.

Cyrus's first exploit was to subdue the revolted king of Armenia (B. C. 557). He then compelled the Chaldeans to sue for peace. His next expedition was, in conjunction with Cyaxares, against the Babylonians (B. C. 556), whom he defeated; their king, Nericosolassar, being killed in the battle: but he did not follow up his success. He made war on Crœsus, king of Lydia, who had assisted the Babylonians. Cyrus fought a battle with him at Thymbra (B. C. 546), in which the former was victorious. Crœsus retreated to Sardis, which city Cyrus besieged and took. He afterwards (B. C. 544–539) subdued the Greek colonies, thus uniting all Asia Minor to the Persian Empire. His next grand exploit was the siege and capture of Babylon (B. C. 538). He made his uncle, Cyaxares, governor of that city; and he framed a scheme of government for the whole empire, which he divided into 120 provinces, each governed by a satrap. He appointed three superintendents over these satraps — Daniel, the venerable Hebrew prophet, being one. Cyaxares died B. C. 536, and Cyrus then became sole king of the Medes and Persians. In this year he decreed the rebuilding of the temple at Jerusalem, and the restoration of the Jews to their own country. Cyrus died universally lamented in the year B. C. 529. He was one of the greatest men recorded in ancient history. There are conflicting accounts of his death: the most probable one is that he was killed in an expedition against the Massagetæ.

He was succeeded by his son, Camby′ses (B. C. 529). This prince invaded and subdued Egypt (B. C. 526), where he was guilty of very great cruelties. On his way home to Persia he heard that his throne had been usurped by Smerdis, the Magian, who pretended to be Smerdis, the king's brother. While mounting his horse to proceed against this impostor, Cambyses received a wound from his own sword, which proved fatal (B. C. 522). As he died without heirs, the Kaianian dynasty became extinct. Smerdis was slain by Gushtasp, or Hystaspes, governor of Persia (B. C. 521); who, being elected king, assumed the title of Darawesh (or Darius, by which name he is generally known). Darius confirmed the edict of Cyrus as to the rebuilding of the temple at Jerusalem. He then (B. C. 514) led a vast army into Thrace, and pursued the Scythians beyond the Danube, where he narrowly escaped destruction. His next attempt was on India, in which he was successful (B. C. 508); but failed in his attack on the isle of Naxos (B. C. 501).

Who was Astyages?—Cyaxares?—Cyrus?—What is said of the latter?—State his exploits, character, and death.—How did he frame the administration of the empire?—What is said of Cambyses?—Smerdis, the Magian?—Darius?

CHINA. JAPAN.

Kien-wang (B. C. 583) was not more fortunate than his predecessors. Under Ling-wang, his successor (B. C. 571), the empire became a little more peaceable. In the year B. C. 552, in the city of Tsow-yih, in Chang-ping-keang, was born the most famous of Chinese philosophers, Kong-fu-tsze (or Confu′cius, as he is generally called, the name having been Latinized), a man who has greatly influenced the destinies of China through all succeeding generations. His system of religion and philosophy has been adopted by the leading classes of China for more than 2300 years. According to M. Gutztaff (*History of China*), he was the author of the only Chinese work wherein the doctrine of a Supreme Being is taught! The Chinese never define their religious ideas; and when talking of God, they confound Him with a material heaven, and ridicule the idea of a spiritual being. The principal works of Confucius were: 1. The *Chun-tsew*, a chronological history of his native State, the kingdom of Loo, for 241 years. 2. The *She-king*, or Book of Odes, a collection of popular songs. 3. The *Yih-king*, a symbolical representation of nature and its changes, attributed to Fo-hi, and revised by Confucius. 4. The *Le-ke*, a general code of rites. 5. The *Shoo-king* (his best work), a collection of traditions, inculcating morality. This work is the text-book of the Chinese in all that relates to science, moral and political philosophy, political economy, astronomy, music, etc. These are the five books, or *Woo-king*, held in highest estimation. The morality taught by Confucius is not of a high order; much of it consists in external decorum, and obedience to parents and rulers. He assigned an inferior position to women, whereby he put a barrier against the improvement of society. His words and actions are contained in the *Lun-yu;* his scientific teachings in the *Ta-keo;* his destiny of man in the *Chung-yung;* his treatise on filial piety in the *Heaou-king*. These are the four classical books put into the hands of children as they enter school. More will be said of the doctrines of Confucius in the history of the next century.

At the same time flourished Laou-keun, or Laou-tsze, who also promulgated religious doctrines, which have been largely adopted by the Chinese, but his followers are now idolaters. He taught the perfectibility of human nature, and passed his life in search of the Elixir of Immortality.

Ling-wang died B. C. 544, and was succeeded by King-wang, who, in turn, was followed by another emperor of the same name, in the year B. C. 519. During their reigns there was nothing but war and bloodshed, which tore the empire to pieces.

Japan. — Sin-mu died B. C. 580. Having secured the succession to his posterity, he was succeeded by his third son, Sui-sei, who reigned 38 years, and left the crown to his second son, I-to-ku (B. C. 548). This prince fixed his court at Keitz, and died B. C. 511. He was succeeded by his son, Ko-si-o, in the fifth year of whose reign (B. C. 506), a war arose between the provinces of Yo and Jetz. This is the first war recorded in Japanese history.

What emperors ruled China during this century?—What great philosopher flourished?—What effect had his teaching?—What are his principal works?—The "five books"?—The "classics"?—Who was Laou-tsze?—What occurred in Japan?

GREECE.

Athens.—Solon, a descendant of Codrus, persuaded his countrymen to attack Salamis, then belonging to Megara. He was appointed to conduct the war, which was settled by the arbitration of Sparta in favor of Athens (B. C. 596). The State being rent by civil commotions, Solon was chosen Archon, and invested with full power to remedy the evils complained of (B. C. 594). One of his measures was to depreciate the currency, whereby he relieved debtors of one-fourth of their liabilities. He repealed the laws of Draco, and remodelled the constitution. He made property the basis of the citizen's rights, dividing the people into four classes, graduated and taxed according to their wealth. Each class sent a hundred representatives to the Boule (or deliberative assembly). The Ecclesia (or assembly of magnates) had the power of vetoing the measures of the Boule, but could not originate any itself. Solon enacted many good laws, and having exacted from the Athenians an oath to observe them for ten years, he visited foreign lands. He had an interview with Crœsus, king of Lydia, and in reply to the question, "Who was the happiest man he had ever seen?" said, "No man could be deemed happy till he had finished his life in a happy way."

During Solon's absence, the factions in Athens (styled respectively the parties of the Plain, of the Highlands, and of the Coast,) broke out into open feud. Pisis′tratus, a cousin of Solon, distinguished for his beauty and ability, headed the party of the Highlands, and gained great influence. He seized the supreme power (B. C. 560), and became tyrant (ruler) of Athens, in spite of Solon, who died soon after (B. C. 558). Pisistratus administered the government ably; but the other factions, headed by Meg′acles and Lycurgus, drove him out of Athens (B. C. 556), and he remained in exile six years. Then Megacles offered to reinstate him, on condition of his marrying his (Megacles') daughter. The restoration was accomplished (B. C. 548) by a stratagem, and Pisistratus married the lady, but treated her so badly that her father again drove the tyrant out. He then retired to Ere′tria, in Eubœa, where he remained ten years; when, having collected an army, he retook Athens (B. C. 537), surrounded himself with mercenaries, and seized the children of the principal citizens as hostages for their submission. He, nevertheless, faithfully administered the laws, and encouraged literature and the arts. He collected the compositions of Homer, and he formed a public library. Under his auspices, Thespis, the actor, introduced his form of tragedy at Athens (B. C. 535), and dramatic contests were made a regular part of the Dionysia (or festivals of Bacchus). Pisistratus built the famous temples to Apollo and Jupiter, the Lyceum, and the fountain of the nine springs at Athens. He died B. C. 527, and was succeeded by his sons, Hippias and Hipparchus. They governed with great virtue and ability, and patronized literature and the arts. About the year B. C. 514, Hipparchus endeavored to break up the romantic friendship existing between Harmo′dius and Aristogi′ton, two beautiful Athenian youths. The latter attempted to assassinate him and Hippias. They killed Hipparchus, but were both slain before they could reach Hippias. For this attempt they were honored as patriots. Hippias became morose, and put to death great numbers of the citizens. The Alcmæon′idæ conspired to dethrone him, and having obtained aid from Cleom′enes, of Sparta, they drove him and his family into perpetual exile (B. C. 510). He fled to Persia, and instigated Darius to send an expedition against Greece. It is said he was present at the battle of Marathon, and that he fell there; but other accounts say that he died at Lemnos. He was the last of the Pisistrat′idæ. After his fall, the oligarchs, headed by Isag′oras, and the democrats, headed by Clis′thenes, struggled for power. The latter were successful, and, from this period, democracy became triumphant. The four classes were abolished, and ten new ones were substituted. Other changes were made in the laws of Solon, and the system of ostracism, or banishment by the people, was instituted. It took its name from the Greek word οστρακον, a shell, or piece of pottery, on which the vote of acquittal or condemnation was written by each voter. The sentence of the law ran thus: "If any one aim at obtaining superiority over his fellow-citizens, let him go and excel elsewhere." The period of exile was ten years.

Corinth.—Periander was succeeded (B. C. 585) by his son, Psammetichus, who died B. C. 581, and the "tyranny" expired with him. The government then became an aristocracy.

Who was Solon?—What institutions did he frame?—What of his interview with Crœsus?—Who was Pisistratus?—Relate his career.—What famous edifices did he build?—Who was Thespis?—Who were Hippias and Hipparchus?—Harmodius and Aristogiton?—What became of Hippias?—What changes were made in Athens?—What is said of Corinth?

Macedonia.—Ær′opus was succeeded by Al′cetas (B. C. 576), and Amyn′tas I. (B. C. 540).

Sparta.—The military institutions of Lycurgus had made the Spartans the most warlike people in Greece. They gradually deprived the Argives of the sea-coast of Peloponnesus. For many years they contended for the district of Cynuria. The contest was decided by 300 champions on each side (B. C. 548): in this battle the Spartans were triumphant. Cleomenes, who became king B. C. 520, at last subdued the Argives. He also assisted the Athenians to dethrone Hippias; and he dethroned his own colleague, Demara′tus, who fled to Persia, and afterwards accompanied Xerxes in his expedition against Greece.

Beside the eminent men already mentioned, there flourished in this century: Æsop, a writer of fables, who was originally a slave, but received his freedom: he was thrown from a precipice by the people of Delphi for refusing to contribute to the expenses of the oracle. Anac′reon of Teos, a poet and voluptuary, wrote many songs, but few of them have come down to us. Simon′ides of Cos, one of the most famous lyric poets of Greece. Telesilla of Argos, a poetess and heroine, who fought against the Spartans. Pythag′oras of Samos, one of the most celebrated philosophers of antiquity. He discovered that every triangle inscribed in a semicircle is right-angled, and that the square of the hypothenuse of a right-angled triangle is equal to the sum of the squares of the other two sides. He travelled in Asia and Egypt, whence it is supposed he derived many of his ideas. He settled at Croto′na, in Italy, where he founded a sect of religious freemasons, 300 of whom were formed into a select brotherhood, sworn to mutual aid and secresy. They held festivals peculiarly connected with the worship of Apollo, and recognized each other by secret signs. Pythagoras taught that all things originated in number, and that music, or harmony, was the regulating principle of the universe. Hence arose the celebrated doctrine of the harmony of the spheres, which we have now lost the power of hearing. He taught that happiness consisted in the perfection of virtue, and that after death the souls of men transmigrated into animals to undergo purification: if incurable, they were sent into Tartarus; if purified, they attained to incorporeal existence. His disciples became famous for their uprightness, but their exclusiveness excited great animosity. While they were assembled in the house of Milo, the people of Crotona set the building on fire, and killed a large number of them. It is not known with certainty what became of Pythagoras; the tradition is that he fled to Metapontum, and starved himself to death. His tomb was shown there in the time of Cicero (1st century B. C.). Milo, his friend and disciple, was possessed of extraordinary strength, and could eat an enormous quantity of animal food. When he was old, seeing a tree partly split open by woodcutters, he attempted to rend it further, but the wood closed upon his hands, and held him fast; and being unable to extricate himself, he was devoured by wolves. Anachar′sis, a Scythian prince, visited Athens B. C. 594, and became famous for his observations; some reckon him among the seven wise men. He was slain by his brother on his return to his native country. Anaxim′enes of Miletus taught that air was the primary form of matter, into which all things could be resolved. Chilon of Lacedæmon was one of the seven wise men. He died (B. C. 590) of joy, when his son gained the prize for boxing at the Olympic games. Cleob′ulus of Lindus was another of the seven wise men (B. C. 580), and the author of several lyric poems. His daughter, Cleob′uline, invented the famous riddle on the year: "A father has twelve children, and each of these has thirty daughters, on one side white, on the other black, and, though immortal, they all die." Anaximan′der of Miletus (born B. C. 610, died B. C. 547,) was distinguished for his knowledge of astronomy, mathematics, and geography. He introduced the use of the Gnomon, or dial. Pherecy′des of Scyros, the tutor of Pythagoras, taught the doctrine of metempsychosis, or the transmigration and immortality of the soul. Eu′gamon of Cyre′ne wrote a poem, "Telegonia," a continuation of the Odyssey, concluding with the death of Ulysses. Chæ′rilus exhibited tragedies at Athens for forty years (B. C. 523–482). Susa′rion of Meg′ara improved upon the coarse buffoonery used in comedy. Hecatæ′us of Miletus was an eminent geographer and historian. Phry′nichus introduced, into tragedy, choruses with music and the use of masks representing females. The poets Onomac′ritus, Lasus, and Ib′ycus.

What is said of Macedonia?—Sparta?—The 300 champions?—Cleomenes and Demaratus?—What is said of Æsop?—Anacreon?—Simonides?—Telesilla?—Pythagoras and his disciples?—Milo?—Anacharsis?—Anaximenes?—Chilon?—Cleobulus and Cleobuline?—Anaximander?—Pherecydes?—Eugamon?—Chærilus?—Susarion?—Hecatæus?—Phrynichus?

ITALY.

The reign of Tarquinius Priscus was a prosperous one. Successful in his wars with the turbulent neighbors of Rome, the Latins and the Sabines, he conferred far greater benefits on the city than extending her dominions. He constructed the Cloaca Maxima, a vast drain, to carry off the water round the Palatine Hill: he built a forum or market, a circus for horse and chariot races, a great temple on the Capitoline Hill, and a wall of stone round the city. He added 100 new members to the Senate: to each of the former centuries he added another, and he increased the number of the Vestal Virgins from four to six. The king had in his service a young man, named Servius Tullius, the son of a slave. This youth was much beloved by the people, and did the king good service, which excited the anger of the sons of Ancus Martius, so that they resolved to kill Tarquinius, lest he should make Servius his heir. They employed two shepherds to do the deed, who went to the king's palace, and pretended to be quarrelling. The king came forward to hear their story, when one of them struck him on the head with an axe. Tanaquil, his wife, however, concealed his death for a time, and appointed Servius to rule in his name. But after a time, when the truth was known, the people elected Servius Tullius their king (B. C. 576), and the sons of Ancus Martius were deprived of the expected result of their villany. They fled from Rome, and never returned.

Servius Tullius gave a new Constitution to the Roman State, making a twofold division of the people — one territorial, the other according to property — whereby he gave to the *plebs* (people) political independence, and to the wealthy political influence. He made a law that there should be no king after him, but that the State should be ruled by two men chosen by the people to govern them year by year. One reason for this may have been that he had no son to succeed him, his family consisting only of two daughters. He also instituted the festivals called Pagana'lia and Compita'lia. The former were celebrated in the *pagi*, or strongholds upon high ground, which were places of refuge in case of invasion. In these the people met once a year to keep festival, and every man, woman, and child, paid a certain sum to the priests. In the city every person paid a certain sum at the temple of Juno Lucina for every birth in his family, another sum at the temple of Venus Libitina for every death, and a third at the temple of Youth for every son who came of age. The Compitalia were a yearly festival in honor of the Lares, or guardian spirits, celebrated at all the *compita*, or places where several streets met. Servius incorporated the Quirinal, Viminal, and Esquiline Hills, with the city; and he formed an alliance with the Latins, by which Rome and the cities of Latium became members of one great league. A census of the population taken by him shows that Rome, in his time, contained 85,000 inhabitants. He erected a temple to Diana on the Aventine Mount, and made other additions to the public buildings. But he was hated by the patricians because he had thrown so much power into the hands of the plebeians. They therefore conspired with Lucius Tarquinius, a descendant of Tarquinius Priscus, to deprive him of life. Lucius had married one of the two daughters of Servius; his brother, Aruns, had married the other. Tullia, the wife of Aruns, a cruel and ambitious woman, aided her brother-in-law, Lucius, in his bloody schemes. She persuaded him to murder his wife, while she murdered her husband. The guilty couple then married, and proceeded to murder Servius. Lucius, arrayed in the royal robes, entered the Senate, and summoned the Senators to attend him as their king. Servius hastened thither, and ordered Lucius to descend from the throne; but the latter, seizing him, flung his aged father-in-law down the steps, and, as the old man was hastening home, the servants of Lucius killed him in the road, near the Esquiline Hill. His unnatural daughter, Tullia, is said to have driven over his dead body in her chariot (B. C. 534). Her equally wicked paramour was then proclaimed king.

Lucius Tarquinius, surnamed Superbus (or, the proud), began his reign without going through the form of being elected. His first act was to set aside the privileges granted by Servius Tullius to the plebeians. He then exiled all whom he mistrusted, and surrounded himself with a body-guard. His tyranny was so great toward the people, whom he compelled to labor at his public works, that many put themselves to death to avoid it. But, though cruel at home, he raised the power of Rome abroad. He became the head of the Latin confederacy, defeated the Volscians, and took Suessa, with the spoils of which town he began building the capitol of Rome. In the vaults of that temple he deposited the Sibylline books, which he had bought from a sibyl. He took the city of Gabii by stratagem, but allowed the people to become Roman citizens. While at the height of his power, one of his sons, Sextus, outraged Lucretia, the wife of his cousin, Lucius Tarquinius Collatinus. The lady, having revealed the fact to her husband, killed herself. Thereupon the enraged husband, with Lucius Junius Brutus (the nephew of the king), and Publius Valerius Publicola, or Poplicola (*i. e.*, the people's friend), aroused the people to avenge the deed. Tarquinius and his family were banished (B. C. 510); the regal power was abolished, and an aristocratic republic was established, with two annually-elected consuls at its head. The first two consuls elected were Brutus and Collatinus. King Tarquinius and his wife, Tullia, with his sons, Titus and Aruns, went to live at Cære. His other son, Sextus, went to Gabii, where the people slew him. Lucius Tarquinius Collatinus was requested to leave Rome, and he settled at Lavinium; after which, the Senate and the people decreed that all the house of the Tarquinii should be banished, even though they were not of the king's family. A plot to procure the reinstatement of the king was soon afterward discovered. Among the conspirators were Titus and Tiberius, the sons of Brutus. These unfortunate youths were brought before their father, who was sitting on his judgment-seat in the Forum. Brutus ordered the lictors to bind them, and scourge them with rods according to law; and, after they had been scourged, their heads were struck off in the presence of their father, who neither stirred from his seat, nor turned away his eyes. The fortitude of this old Roman hero, and his not sparing his children, who had been guilty of treason to their country, have been much admired.

The people of Tarquinii and Veii espoused the cause of the exiled tyrant, and marched against Rome. A bloody battle was fought, in which the two cousins, Brutus and Aruns, the son of Tarquin, slew each other, but the Romans were victorious. The matrons of Rome mourned a whole year for Brutus, because he had well avenged Lucretia's death. His colleague, Publius, called the people together in their centuries, and they chose Spurius Lucretius, the father of Lucretia, to be consul in the room of Brutus; but Spurius dying in a few days, they chose in his stead Marcus Horatius. Tarquin then applied to Lars Por'sena, king of Clusium, for aid. Porsena marched against Rome at the head of a powerful army, and took possession of the hill Janiculum. He would have entered the city by the Sublician bridge, but for the extraordinary valor of Horatius Cocles, who, with his comrades, Spurius Lartius and Titus Herminius, defended the bridge against the whole Etruscan army, while the Romans broke it down behind them; which done, Horatius plunged into the river and swam ashore in safety. Porsena, thus baffled, laid siege to the city, which soon began to suffer from famine. A young Roman noble, named Mucius Scæ'vola, then resolved to assassinate Porsena, and entering the camp, by mistake killed his secretary. Being seized, and threatened with torments, he thrust his hand into the fire to show how little he feared pain. Porsena, admiring his courage, released him. Scævola then tried to intimidate the Etruscan king by telling him that three hundred others beside himself had sworn to kill him. But Porsena reduced the Romans to terms. Another heroic act was that of the noble maiden, Clælia, who had been sent as one of the hostages to Porsena for preserving the peace. She escaped from the Etruscan camp, and, persuading her maidens to follow her, swam across the Tiber, and reached her home. Porsena completely conquered the Romans, but their historians endeavor to conceal the fact. He prohibited them from using iron for any other purpose than agriculture, but he did not reinstate Tarquinius. However, the Romans did not long remain subject to Porsena; for his son, Aruns, having been defeated by the combined Latin forces, the Etruscans were confined to their own territory, and the Romans took advantage of this to recover their independence.

The only other events worthy of notice in the history of Italy during this century are the concluding of a treaty of commerce between Rome and Carthage (B. C. 509), whereby the former was bound not to navigate beyond Cape Bon — and of a treaty of alliance with the Sabines.

What were the principal works of Tarquinius Priscus?—Who was Servius Tullius?—What was the end of Tarquinius?—What laws were made by Servius?—What were his great works?—What were the Paganalia and the Compitalia?—What was the population of Rome in his time?—What was his end?—What is said of Tullia and Tarquinius Superbus?

What is said of Lucretia?—Lucius Junius Brutus?—Publicola?—What became of the Tarquin family?—Of the kingly power?—What form of government was established?—What of Brutus and his sons?—Lars Porsena?—Horatius Cocles?—Mucius Scævola?—The fate of Rome?—What other events are recorded?

BRITAIN.

Continuing the extracts from Holinshed and Geoffrey of Monmouth, we come to Gorbogudo, or Gorboduc, the successor of Kinmarcus. He had two sons, one named Ferrex, the other Porrex. The legend of these brothers is related by Geoffrey as follows: "When their father grew old they began to quarrel about the succession, but Porrex, who was the most ambitious of the two, formed a design of killing his brother by treachery, which the other discovering, escaped and passed over into Gaul. There he procured aid from Suard, king of the Franks, with which he returned, and made war upon his brother. Coming to an engagement, Ferrex was killed, and all his forces cut to pieces. When their mother, whose name was Widen, came to be informed of her son's death, she fell into a great rage, and conceived a mortal hatred against the survivor; for she had a greater affection for the deceased than for him, so that nothing less would appease her indignation for his death than her revenging it upon her surviving son. She took, therefore, her opportunity when he was asleep, fell upon him, and, with the assistance of her women, tore him to pieces. From that time a long civil war oppressed the people, and the island became divided under the power of five kings, who mutually harassed one another." The death of Porrex put an end to the ancient dynasty of the Trojano-British kings, descended from the first Brutus. The five kingdoms into which Britain now became divided were Cornwall, Albany, Loegria, Cambria, and Northumberland. All tradition concurs in regard to the fact of there having been in very ancient times a kingdom in Cornwall, sometimes called the Lionesse in the romances of the Middle Ages: a considerable portion of it extending more than thirty miles beyond the Land's End, has been submerged by the encroachments of the sea. It is possible that we have here the dawn of authentic history in Britain; and that the convulsions which are said to have distracted the country in this century were occasioned by an invasion of the Cimmerii, or Cymri, who, in the year B. C. 631, poured forth from the Crimea and the Steppes of Russia into Asia and Europe, and, in B. C. 587, reached Gaul. The foundation of such a kingdom as Cambria (*Cumraig*, or, home of the Cymri), confirms this idea.

Relate the legend of Ferrex and Porrex.—What befel Britain after the death of Porrex?—What is said of Cornwall?—And of an invasion by the Cimmerii?

FRANCE.

In the year 600 the first Phocæan vessel, commanded by Eux′enes, cast anchor on the southern coast of France. The crew were hospitably received by Nann, king of the Segob′riges, who gave his daughter, Gyptis, in marriage to Euxenes, and allotted him the bay, where he had landed. Here Euxenes founded Massilia (Marseilles), and was joined by a number of his countrymen. The colony prospered greatly, extending itself along the coast. The Greeks founded Nice, Mon′aco, and other cities on the Genoese coast. An attempt was made by Coman, the son of Nann, to surprise the city of Massilia, but he perished in the attempt.

During the greater part of this century the contest between the people and their Cimmerian invaders raged furiously, but the country was gradually conquered. A portion of the Gallic population amalgamated with the conquerors; but while the first movement of the invasion drove the greater number of the Gauls from the west to the east upon the tribes of the Bitu′riges, the Ædui and the Arver′ni, one tribe of the Bituriges crossed from the east to the west, and established itself between the Gironde and the ocean. The driving of the native population back upon the centre and the west necessitated emigrations of great magnitude.

In the year 587 two grand and simultaneous migrations of Gauls took place; one under the command of Sigove′sus, the other under that of Bellove′sus. The emigrants numbered 300,000 souls. Descending the Rhine, and traversing the Hercynian forest, they encamped at the foot of the Alps. Here deputies from Marseilles arrived to implore their assistance against the Lig′ures, then besieging that city. Bellovesus acceded to the request, and drove away the Ligures from Marseilles. He then turned his steps toward Italy. The Roman historians attribute this act to one Ambigat, king of the Bituriges, who thus got rid of his superfluous population. They also say that an Etrurian citizen, named Aruns, having been outraged by a Lu′cumo of Clusium, persuaded the Gauls to march into Italy. Bellovesus subdued the northern portion of that country, where he founded the city of Mediola′num (Milan). A second army, under Elito′vius, subdued another portion of Northern Italy, and founded Brixia (Brescia) and Vero′na.

Who founded Marseilles?—Relate the story of Euxenes.—What was the result of the contest with the Cimmerii?—What two grand migrations took place?—And when?

SPAIN.

The Dorians were, in their turn, dispossessed by the Phocæans, who had founded a prosperous colony at Marseilles, and were settling in the south of France. But the Phœnicians returning, tried to re-establish themselves in the south of Spain. For a time they were successful, their great adversary, Argantonius, being dead. At length, Bau′cius Cape′tus, prince of the Turdetani (an Andalusian tribe), roused his countrymen to arms. Having collected a numerous army, he attacked the Phœnicians, and reduced them to such straits that they were forced to apply to the Carthaginians for assistance. The latter, glad of an excuse to get a footing in this fertile and beautiful country, sent an expedition, under the command of Meherbal, to their aid about the year 516 B. C. According to the Spanish historians, Baucius was successful against the Carthaginians, who were nearly all cut to pieces, Meherbal escaping with great difficulty. They contrived, however, to retain their hold on the coast. The death of Baucius soon afterwards deprived them of their most formidable antagonist. They next attempted to expel the Phœnicians. According to Mariana, the latter fell unexpectedly upon them in the island of Cadiz, and reduced them to extremities. The contest ended in a treaty, whereby both parties were placed on an equal footing, and trade was re-established. Great uncertainty hangs over the history of this period. It is, in fact, too conjectural to deserve the name of history, though some few facts glimmer through the darkness which surrounds them. But that the Phœnicians located themselves in the interior of the country, is evident from the fact that they left traces of their existence in the medals, coins, monuments, inscriptions, religion, language, and manners of the people.

The year 501, according to some, was remarkable for a great drought and famine, and for violent earthquakes, which did immense damage in Spain.

We may here mention the tradition among the Jews of that country, that a Spanish king, named Pyrrhus, went to Nebuchadnezzar's assistance with an army, brought back with him many Jewish captives, some of whom were of royal blood, and located them at Seville. Thence they spread over Spain and Portugal. The illustrious Rabbi, Isaac Abar′banel, was descended from them.

Who supplanted the Dorians?—Who was Baucius Capetus?—What is said of the Phœnicians and Carthaginians?—What is the tradition respecting the Jews in Spain?

GERMANY.

The Asen and all the Einheriar are armed, and fight their last glorious battle, nor do they despair of success, until Muspelheim opens from above, and Surtur issues in flames at the head of his fiery squadrons, beneath whom the rainbow bridge, the symbol of union, breaks asunder, and everything is lost. Heimdall and Loki kill themselves; Thor slays the Mitgard snake, but dies of his poisoned wounds; Freyr is burnt by Surtur; Odin is swallowed alive by the wolf, Fenrix, whose open jaws reach from beneath the earth to heaven. Finally the whole world is destroyed by the flames of Surtur, and becomes Ragna-rok, or the incense of the gods. After this Allfater will create a new world devoid of evil.

This is an outline of the ancient mythology of the Germans, which was essentially the same as that of the Scandinavians. All the German nations, before their conversion to Christianity, called their superior gods by the same names, and had the same idea of nature, and consequently the same superstitions, fables, and legends. The student who desires further information on the subject is referred to Jacob Grimm's work on German mythology.

The gods were worshipped in groves and forests, where human sacrifices were offered, and whoever entered the groves wore chains in token of submission to the deity. Public worship was also solemnized beneath gigantic and solitary trees, on whose branches trophies and the heads of sacrificed horses were hung. The gods were worshipped on lofty mountains, in circles of enormous stones, which may still be seen. There were three high festivals in the year which were held peculiarly sacred, and the whole nation then assembled to offer sacrifice. They were all called sacrifices to the sun, the holiest being the Yule feast, held during the twelve darkest nights of the whole year, in the winter solstice. During this period the gods and spirits were supposed to descend upon the earth.

The irruption of the Gauls into Italy, through Germany and Switzerland (noticed in the column devoted to France), under Sigovesus and Bellovesus, caused horrible devastation. But numbers of Germans and Swiss (Helvetii) joined the invaders, and went with them into Italy. The other historical notices of Germany during this century are very scanty.

Relate the legend of the destruction of the world.—Where were the gods worshipped, and how?—How many high festivals were there?—Name the principal.—What else happens?

B.C. 600—500.

ASIA MINOR.

Alyattes carried on various operations against the Ionian Greeks. He took Smyrna, but was defeated in the territory of Clazom′enæ. He reigned fifty-seven years, and, on the whole, peacefully. During this long reign he accumulated those treasures which afterwards contributed to render the wealth of his son and successor, Crœsus, proverbial. An enormous pyramidal mound, on a stone base, was erected to his memory near Sardis, by the joint efforts of the whole Sardian population. It was situated north of the city, near Lake Gyges, and was a mile in circumference. It was considered inferior only to the gigantic edifices of Egypt and Babylon, and may still be seen. Alyattes died in the year B. C. 560.

When Crœsus ascended the throne, a strong party favored the pretensions of his brother, Panta′leon, but the king crushed it with great cruelty, torturing one of the richest chiefs on a spiked carding-machine. His reign lasted fourteen years only (B. C. 560–546), but it was occupied in aggressive wars. He attacked and conquered the nations of the Asiatic Greeks, one after the other, and made himself king of all Asia, west of the river Halys. Under him the Lydian empire reached its height, and the treasures which he amassed exceeded anything ever before known. These treasures were derived from his numerous tributaries, and from mines and the auriferous sands of the Pacto′lus, and the comparison, "rich as Crœsus," became a proverb. Herodotus observes (i. 141) that before the reign of Crœsus all the Greeks were free; it was by him first that they were subdued into tribute, and that this event was the first of a series out of which arose their hostile relations with the Persians. The latter, however, became the enemies of Crœsus; for that monarch extended his dominions to the boundaries of those of Cyrus, and this dangerous proximity soon brought on a war between two such ambitious men as they were. Crœsus commenced it by ravaging the country beyond the Halys. Cyrus met him on the Pterian plain, south of Sinope, where a battle was fought, but neither party proved victorious. Crœsus, however, returned to Sardis, and disbanded his army. On hearing of this, Cyrus suddenly marched against that city, and besieged and took it. Crœsus was forced to surrender, and thus Lydia became a portion of the Persian Empire (B. C. 546). There is a curious legend connected with the fate of Crœsus. The famous Grecian sage, Solon, being on a visit to Sardis, whither the munificence of Crœsus had drawn many illustrious men, the king asked him "who was the happiest man he had ever seen?" the sage replied that "no man could be considered happy until he had ended his life happily." When Crœsus was taken by Cyrus, he was condemned to be burned. As he stood by the fire he remembered the remark of Solon, and uttered his name aloud thrice. Cyrus inquired whom he was invoking, and, on hearing the story, not only spared the life of Crœsus, but made him his friend. We find Crœsus subsequently accompanying Cambyses in his expedition into Egypt (B. C. 525). He was the last of the dynasty of the Merm′nadæ, under whose sway Lydia had attained to a high degree of prosperity and power.

Cyrus then subdued the Grecian colonies in Asia Minor, and extended his empire from the Indus to the Mediterranean, and from Scythia to Ethiopia (B. C. 544–539). Of this celebrated man an account is given in the history of Persia. He was long regarded, in the East, as the greatest hero of antiquity. His name is derived from the Persian word *Kohr*, signifying "the sun". After the conquest of Lydia, the history of Asia Minor merges into that of Persia. It has ever been the fate of this beautiful portion of the earth to be subject to foreigners: it has very little proper history of its own. Persian, Greek, Roman, Saracen, and Turk, have each in turn possessed it. Strictly speaking, it should have no distinct column in this work; but so many important events have taken place on the soil, that the division has been made for the sake of convenience. Moreover, several minor kingdoms flourished thereon at different epochs, but they were all ephemeral. One of these was founded at this period, viz., that of Pontus, which acquired considerable notoriety in after ages. It was created by Darius, king of Persia, in the year B. C. 514, in favor of Artaba′zus, a Persian nobleman. From Artabazus descended a long line of monarchs who filled the throne of Pontus after him.

The island of Samos acquired considerable celebrity during this century, owing to the exploits and abilities of its tyrant (or ruler), Polyc′rates. In the 13th century B. C. it was the chief seat of the Carians and the Leleges, and became a kingdom under the rule of Ancæ′us, one of the heroes of the Argonautic expedition. The well-known proverb, "There is many a slip 'twixt the cup and the lip," was uttered in reference to Ancæus. He had been told that he would not live to taste the wine of his own vineyard; and some time afterward, when he was on the point of tasting it, he turned to the person who had uttered the foreboding, and laughed at him. The seer replied to this sarcasm in the words of the proverb. At the same instant Ancæus was told that a wild boar was near; whereupon he put down the cup without tasting the wine, went out to attack the animal, and was killed by it.

Polycrates was enabled, by the aid of his brothers, Pantagno′tus and Syloson, to make himself master of Samos (B. C. 532). At first he and they ruled jointly; but he soon put Pantagnotus to death, and banished Syloson. By this perfidy he became sole despot, and in a very short time he made his court one of the most celebrated in Greece. He lived in the most extravagant pomp and luxury, and invited to the island the most illustrious philosophers, poets, and artists. To them he was very bountiful. His friendship for Anacreon is celebrated; so was the respect he testified for Pythagoras, who, however, did not stay very long in Samos. Polycrates also erected many great public works; and he raised a powerful fleet, with which he subdued the neighboring islands and several towns on the main land. He formed an intimate alliance with Amasis, king of Egypt, respecting which the Greek historian, Herodotus, tells a curious story (book i. 77). Amasis thought that the extraordinary good fortune of Polycrates would be followed by some signal calamity. He therefore wrote to him, and advised him to throw away one of his most valuable possessions, in order that he might, by injuring himself, obviate the anger of the gods. Polycrates accordingly threw a very beautiful and costly signet-ring into the sea; but a few days afterwards it was found in the stomach of a fish which had been presented to him by a fisherman. His predicted fate was realized by the treachery of Orætes, the Persian satrap of Sardis, who allured him to the main land, where he was seized and crucified (B. C. 522).

How long did Alyattes reign?—What was erected to his memory?—What is said of Crœsus?—By whom was he dethroned?—What is the legend connected with his fate?—What dynasty ended with him?—What becomes of the history of Asia Minor?—What kingdom was founded by Darius?—What was the early history of Samos?—Relate the legend of Ancæus.—What was Polycrates?—For what is he celebrated?—What anecdote does Herodotus relate of him?—What was his fate?

CARTHAGE.

It is alleged that about the year 600 B. C. a Phœnician fleet was sent by the Egyptian king, Necho, from the Red Sea, to sail around Africa into the Mediterranean. The authenticity of this statement is, however, disputed. In the year B. C. 510 the Carthaginians sent a similar expedition under Hanno, which reached a point in latitude 10° north, on the western coast. A similar "Periplus", or voyage, around Africa, is noticed as having occurred in the next century. That the Carthaginians had commerce with the interior of the continent, south of the desert of Sahara, has been inferred from the number of elephants they kept.

During this century Carthage was also extending her enterprise in the Mediterranean. At the solicitation of the Phœnicians in Spain, a Carthaginian army was sent to their assistance (B. C. 516). The command of this force was given to Meherbal, who was unsuccessful: he lost his army, and narrowly escaped death. But the Carthaginians retained their hold on the coast of Spain, and, by a treaty with the Phœnicians, obtained an equal footing with them as regarded trade with that country. They possessed a formidable navy in the time of Cyrus and Cambyses. In conjunction with the Etruscans, they attacked the Phocæan colonists in Corsica. A naval battle ensued; the Carthaginians were defeated, but the Phocæans suffered so much that they left the island to the enemy, who then took quiet possession of it. The Carthaginians then extended their conquests in Libya and Sicily. But their general, Machæ′us, having been defeated, they banished him. In revenge, he returned with his army to Africa, and laid siege to Carthage. His son, Car′talo, a priest of Hercules, having offended him, he caused him to be crucified in his robes, in the presence of the city, which soon afterwards surrendered. Machæus put to death ten of the Senators, and endeavored to subvert the Constitution: for this offence he suffered condign punishment. Mago, a man of great ability, was installed in the high posts which Machæus had filled. In the year B. C. 503, the Carthaginians made their first treaty with the Romans. It related to commerce, but excluded the Romans from all territories subject to Carthage, and prohibited the Carthaginians from erecting forts in Latium.

What were the chief maritime exploits of the Carthaginians during this century?—Who was Machæus?—What did he do to Carthage?—Who succeeded him?—What of B. C. 503?

EGYPT.

After the defeat of Darius at Marathon, the Egyptians, hoping to recover their liberty, revolted. Darius died at this juncture, and left the suppression of the revolt to his son Xerxes, a task which he accomplished without much difficulty (B. C. 484). Xerxes appointed his brother, Achæ′menes, satrap of Egypt, who governed the country 24 years. The Egyptians furnished ships and men to assist Xerxes in his grand expedition against Greece, and fought for him at Artemisium and Platæa.

In the reign of Artaxerxes Longimanus, In′aros, a descendant of the ancient Saïtic kings, organized a revolt against the Persians. The Athenians aided him with a large fleet, and he expelled Achæmenes, and gained possession of the country for a time. The Persians were defeated, and Achæmenes killed, at Papremis; but Artaxerxes having sent a powerful force into Egypt, the revolt was crushed, the Athenian fleet burnt, and Inaros carried prisoner to Susa, where, after five years, he was crucified. This revolt lasted from B. C. 462 to 456. Amyrtæ′us, another descendant of the Saïtic kings, maintained his independence in the marsh lands for some years, but ultimately submitted; and his son, Pausi′ris, was allowed to rule over the districts he had governed. Sarsames was appointed satrap of Egypt in the place of Achæmenes. About this time the celebrated Greek historian and traveller, Herod′otus, visited Egypt. He has given a vivid description of the state of the country.

Artaxerxes governed his vast empire with great moderation and ability. He died in the year B. C. 425. Xerxes II., Sogdianus, and Darius Nothus, successively occupied the throne of Persia. The Egyptians revolted (B. C. 421), but unsuccessfully. In the year B. C. 414 another revolt took place, and Amyrtæ′us, the Saïte, was called to the throne. He was the founder of the 28th dynasty, but is not the Amyrtæus before mentioned. He died B. C. 408, and was buried with splendor, and the Saïte dynasty expired with him. He was succeeded by Nepheri′tes, the first of the 29th, or Mendesian dynasty. The Persians were too much occupied with the Greeks and their own satraps to attempt to regain their dominion. Nepherites was succeeded (B. C. 402) by Achoris, according to some; by Psammet′ichus (B. C. 400), according to others.

What happened in the time of Xerxes?—What of Achæmenes?—Inaros?—Amyrtæus?—Pausiris?—Herodotus?—Artaxerxes Longimanus?—Amyrtæus?—Nepherites?

SYRIA.

The history of the Jews during this and the first half of the next century is comparatively uneventful. While Greece and Persia filled the world with their renown and their rivalry, the Jews lay hid in peaceful obscurity in their native valleys. Syria and Palestine were provinces of the Persian Empire, but they were mildly governed, and the Persian satraps did no more than exercise a general superintendence over the affairs of these provinces. Thus the internal government of Jerusalem fell into the hands of the high-priests.

The principal events in Jewish history, during the first half of this century, were the completion of the temple, which was accomplished in the reign of Darius Hystaspes; and the deliverance of the people from a wanton decree for their extermination, issued by Xerxes, the successor of Darius. The latter, on his return from his unfortunate expedition against the Greeks, maddened by the defeat of his army, gave himself up to cruelty and debauchery, and issued the decree above mentioned. The influence of the beautiful Esther (or Amestris), who had become the wife of the Persian monarch, prevented its being put in execution. The elevation of her cousin, Mordecai, to the high rank of vizier, and the execution of his rival, Haman, are events familiar to every reader of the Bible. In the reign of the mild and humane Artaxerxes Longimanus, a new migration took place from Babylon to Judea, headed by Ezra, the high-priest, who was invested by the Persian monarch with full powers to raise money for the adornment of the temple, and for establishing magistrates in every part of the holy land.

The Persians were compelled by the Greeks to make peace on certain conditions, one of which was that they should not approach within three days' journey of the sea. To nullify this, they determined to restore the Jews, and enable them to fortify Jerusalem. For this purpose Artaxerxes sent his cup-bearer, Nehemi′ah, to rebuild the city with all possible expedition, stealth, and secrecy. This was accomplished by Nehemiah, in spite of domestic treachery and the opposition of the Samaritans, Ammonites, and Arabians, under Sanballat, Tobi′ah, and Geshem. After solemnly dedicating the wall, Nehemiah returned to Persia for a short time, leaving his brother, Hana′ni, and Hanani′ah, governors. On his return he caused the genealogies of all the congregation to be made out, and a census of the nation to be taken, when it was found that Israel numbered no more than 42,000 persons! Meanwhile, Ezra compiled the sacred books of the Jews, but a considerable portion of them had been lost, viz., the Book of Jasher, the Book of the Wars of the Lord, the writings of Gad and Iddo (the seers), and those of Solomon on natural history. Ezra divided the sacred books into three parts: 1st. The Law, containing the five books of Moses. 2d. The Prophets, containing the historical and prophetical books, excepting Malachi. 3d. The Hagiog′rapha, containing the Psalms of David and others, Proverbs, Ecclesiastes, and the Song of Solomon. The books of Malachi, Ezra, Nehemiah, and Esther, were added 150 years afterwards, in the time of Simon the Just. The Law, thus revised and corrected, was publicly read by Ezra, and solemnly ratified by covenant, and the Jewish Constitution was finally re-established. Ezra, it is said, died at the age of 120, in Persia; and his tomb is shown at Zamuza, though Josephus says he was buried at Jerusalem. There are four books attributed to him, but only one is certainly his.

Joshua, the high-priest, died B. C. 480, and his successor, Joi′achim, B. C. 462. Eliashib was the next. During the absence of Nehemiah in Persia, affairs fell into disorder, and the solemn covenant was forgotten, notwithstanding the remonstrances of Mal′achi, the last of the prophets. So little is known of this personage that it is doubtful whether his name is a proper name, or merely a generic one: it signifies "an angel". Many commentators, and most of the ancient Jews, believed that he and Ezra were the same person. But on Nehemiah's return (B. C. 408), invested with the authority of a Persian satrap, all the disorders that had taken place were reformed, and the observance of the Sabbath was enforced. Manasseh, the son of the high-priest, Joiada (who succeeded Eliashib, B. C. 441), was expelled from the priesthood on account of his unlawful marriage with the daughter of Sanballat. In revenge, Sanballat built a rival temple on Mount Gerizim, and appointed Manasseh high-priest, and thus the schism between the Jews and the Samaritans was perpetuated. Nehemiah governed the people in peace for about 30 years, and died at Jerusalem.

What was the state of the nation at this period?—What were the principal events?—What did Ezra do?—Nehemiah?—What was the number of the people?—What sacred books were lost?—How did Ezra divide the Scriptures?—What books were added?—What else occurred?—What is said of Malachi?—Manasseh?—The temple on Mt. Gerizim?

INDIA.

The kings of Magadha always possessed extensive authority. For many centuries they were Cshatriyas: but the last of these, Nanda, was born of a Sudra mother; and Chandragupta, who murdered and succeeded him, was also of a low class. From this time the Sudras held the ascendancy.

During this century the kingdom of Pandya, in the Deccan, was probably founded by a person of the agricultural class, who gave it his name. It appears to have been of small extent, only occupying what are now the districts of Madura and Tinivelly. Yet it survived until the last of its royal race (the Nayacs) was conquered by the Nabob of Arcot, in the year 1736. Pandya was a State of considerable consequence in the 9th century. Strabo, the geographer, makes mention of an ambassador from the Pandyan king to Augustus Cæsar. Such a potentate is also mentioned in the "Periplus of the Erythræan Sea", apparently the work of an experienced sailor (Elphinstone, *History of India*, vol. i., p. 317).

The kingdom of Chola, adjoining that of Pandya, was also founded about this time. This State attained to greater importance than Pandya did, and at one time (about the Christian era), ruled over the Carnatic, Telingana, and the country up the river Godavery as far as Nandidrug. In the 12th century the Cholans were driven back within their ancient frontiers, where they continued until the end of the 17th century, when a brother of the founder of the Mahratta kingdom, who was at that time an officer under the Mussulman king of Beejapore, having been detached to aid the last Rajah, supplanted him in his government, and was the first of the present Tanjore family. The capital of Chola was at Conjeveram, west of Madras.

The history of the other States of the Deccan is very obscure. The Concan was a thinly-peopled forest region. Kerala, which included Malabar and Canara, was gained from the sea by Paris Ram, the conqueror of the Cshatriyas, and as miraculously peopled by him with Bramins: such, at least, is the Hindoo myth. Chera was a small State, between Pandya and the Western Sea, and comprehended Travancore, part of Malabar, and Coimbetore. It was subverted in the 10th century A. C., and its territory partitioned among the neighboring States.

What was the origin of the kingdom of Pandya?—Its extent and fate?—What else is said of it?—Of Chola?—The Concan?—Kerala?—Chera?

PERSIA.

Aristagoras having raised the standard of revolt in the Ionian cities (B. C. 500), a struggle took place, which lasted six years, but ended in the subjugation of the revolted cities by the Persians. Having severely punished them, Darius sent a large army and fleet against the Greeks, who had aided the rebels, under the command of his son-in-law, Mardo′nius (B. C. 493). That general crossed the Hellespont into Thrace and Macedonia. Both of those, and all the neighboring countries, submitted to him; but his fleet having been shattered in a storm near Mount Athos, he returned to Asia. A second expedition was then fitted out (B. C. 490), under the command of Datis and Artaphernes, who forced a passage into Greece, stormed Eretria, and had advanced to Marathon, within 30 miles of Athens, when they were encountered by the Athenians, and totally defeated. The disheartened Persians returned home, and the expedition failed. But though unsuccessful in the West, Darius extended his empire in the East beyond the confines of India. He was meditating an invasion of Greece in person, when a formidable revolt broke out in Egypt, and arrested his movements: he died before this revolt could be suppressed (B. C. 486).

It was during the reign of Darius Hystaspes that Zoroas′ter introduced, or rather revived, the worship of fire. We have seen that a person of the same name lived and taught the same doctrines many centuries previously. It is a proof of the confusion and obscurity which hang over the annals of Persia, that we cannot decide whether there were really two Zoroasters, or, if not, which of the two spoken of was the founder of the Magian religion. In like manner, the exploits of Zal and Roostum are referred to the age of Cyrus.

The first care of Darius' son, Xerxes (called Esfendiar, or Isfundiar, by the Persians), was to suppress the Egyptian revolt, which he accomplished (B. C. 484). He then made immense preparations to invade Greece, and spent three years in collecting for this purpose the largest army ever assembled; and, neglecting no means in his power, he engaged the Carthaginians to attack the Greek colonies in Sicily and Southern Italy. The Persian army amounted, it is said, to nearly 2,000,000 men; but if this were really the case, a very large proportion of them must have been mere servants, attendants, and hangers-on. It is difficult to conceive how provisions and stores for so vast a number could have been procured. The troops crossed the Hellespont on a bridge of boats, and entered Greece. They were met at Thermopylæ by a small army under Leonidas, king of Sparta, who fell with his gallant band in a heroic attempt to cut his way through the Persian host to the tent of Xerxes. The Persian monarch then marched on to Athens, which city he burnt, but he was compelled to witness the destruction of his fleet at the battle of Salamis, and he returned in dismay to Persia, leaving Mardonius to prosecute the war with 300,000 men (B. C. 480). Mardonius was defeated and slain at Platæa (B. C. 479), and the remains of the Persian fleet and army were destroyed at Mycale. The Greeks in a few years destroyed the power of the Persians in the Mediterranean, and made them tremble for their provinces in Asia Minor.

Meanwhile, Xerxes, maddened by his ill success, returned to Susa, where he gave himself up to debauchery and cruelty. There is but little doubt that this prince is the same as the Ahasuerus (Achash Zwerosh, or brave hero) of Scripture (see the *Book of Esther*); but the Persian historians say that Gushtasp (Darius Hystaspes) was not succeeded by his son, Isfundiar (Xerxes), but by his grandson, Ardisheer Dirazdust (Artaxerxes Longimanus). The student will find the subject investigated in Malcolm's *History of Persia*, vol. i., ch. 7). It is recorded of Xerxes that he yielded to the demands of favorites, and exposed his queen to great public indignity by summoning her to display her beauty at a grand imperial banquet. Vashti refused to comply with his command, whereupon she was degraded from her royal station. The king then caused a number of beautiful maidens to be brought before him, and out of them he selected a Jewish maiden, named Amestris (Hadassah, or Esther,) for his wife. Her cousin, Mordecai, by her means acquired great influence, which excited the jealousy of Haman, another eminent Jew (a descendant of one of the ancient Amalekite kings), who thereupon represented to the king that the Jews were a dangerous race. The tyrant, to please Haman, ordered a massacre of that unhappy people. From this cruel decree they were delivered through the influence of Esther, who procured the death of Haman and his children, but whose subsequent cruelties have stained her name.

Xerxes was murdered by a captain of his guards, named Artabanus (B. C. 465), who conferred the crown on Ardeschir Bahman (Artaxerxes Longima′nus, or, the long-handed), the third son of Xerxes, who, on his accession, put to death the murderer and his accomplices. Artaxerxes is celebrated for his just and beneficent administration. He commissioned the Jewish priest, Ezra (B. C. 458), to rebuild the temple of Jerusalem. The war with the Greeks proved disastrous to Persia, and Artaxerxes was at last forced to sign a dishonorable peace, by which he recognized the independence of the Ionian Asiatic colonies (B. C. 449). He then sent Nehemiah to organize a government for the Jews, and to fortify Jerusalem. In′aros and Amyrtæ′us raised a revolt in Egypt, which was suppressed with great difficulty (B. C. 463), as was another revolt by Megaby′zus, satrap of Syria (B. C. 447).

On the death of Artaxerxes (B. C. 425), his son, Xerxes II., ascended the throne, but within 45 days was murdered by his natural brother, Sogdia′nus, who, in his turn, was deposed by Ochus. This prince, on his accession (B. C. 424), took the name of Darius II., also surnamed Nothus. Under his administration the empire declined rapidly, owing to the power and turbulence of the satraps. Amyrtæus, a descendant of the Saite kings of Egypt, succeeded in establishing himself on the throne of that country (B. C. 414), though he owned the nominal supremacy of the Persian monarchs. The Persians, however, acquired a paramount influence in the affairs of Greece; and Cyrus, the second son of Darius, whom his father had intrusted with the government of Western Asia, allied himself with the Spartans, and helped to overthrow the power of the Athenians. On the death of Darius, his son Artaxerxes (surnamed Mnemon, from the strength of his memory), ascended the throne (B. C. 405), but was opposed by his brother Cyrus, who was instigated by Parysatis, the queen-mother, and aided by Greek auxiliaries under the command of Xenophon. A civil war ensued, and Cyrus was slain at the battle of Cunaxa (B. C. 401). The Greeks, who survived to the number of 10,000, made their escape out of the Persian dominions under the guidance of Xenophon, who wrote an account of this famous "Anab′asis", or retreat.

Who commanded, and what befel, the first expedition against the Greeks?—And the second?—What is said of the remainder of the reign of Darius?—The invasion of Greece by Xerxes?—His subsequent career?—His identity with Ahasuerus?—Of Esther and Mordecai?—The death of Xerxes?—Of Artaxerxes Longimanus?—Ezra?—Inaros and Amyrtæus?—Xerxes II.?—Sogdianus?—Ochus?—Darius Nothus?—Artaxerxes Mnemon?—Cyrus the younger?—The battle of Cunaxa?—The retreat of the 10,000 Greeks?—Xenophon?

CHINA. JAPAN.

The history of China during this century is one of confusion, bloodshed, and decay. The nominal sovereigns were:

	B. C.	B. C.
King-wang	519 to	475
Yuen-wang	475 "	468
Ching-ting-wang . .	468 "	440
Kaou-wang . . .	440 "	425
Wei-lee-wang . . .	425 "	401
Gang-wang . . .	401 "	375

The empire existed only in name: the powerful vassals of the crown being, in reality, independent kings of their respective provinces.

The doctrines taught by Confucius took root in China. His belief that man was originally happy and pure, that he fell by his own act from his pristine state, and that he can in like manner regain his happy condition, became generally received. He taught the worship of the spirits of ancestors and of natural objects, as mountains, rivers, etc. Also that the universe was generated by the two material principles, Yang (heavenly) and Yu (earthly). From the continued opposition of these two arose motion and the human race: but there is no *Supreme Creator* in the system of Confucius. The philosopher is described as tall in person, and imposing in appearance. His descendants have ever enjoyed the highest honors and privileges, and are the only hereditary nobility in the country. In every city in the empire there must be one temple dedicated to him, and all rulers are bound to worship there.

Japan.—The sovereigns of this country were very long lived. Ko-si-o reigned 83 years, and died (B. C. 476) in the 115th year of his age. His second son, Ko-an, who succeeded him (B. C. 392), lived to the age of 136, and reigned 101 years. He removed the imperial residence to Mu-ro, in the province of Farima, and, some years afterwards, to Khuroda.

Siam.—The history of this ancient empire dates from the death of Sommona Kodom (B. C. 544), the founder of the Siamese religion. It is very meagre. What little is known of it will be found in the *Modern Universal History*, vol. 7, to which work the student is referred for such particulars as are known relative to the history of Cochin China, Siam, Pegu, and other kingdoms of the Malayan Peninsula.

What emperors reigned?—What is said of the history of China in this century?—The doctrines of Confucius?—His appearance?—Descendants?—What of Japan?—Of Siam?

GREECE.

We come now to the most brilliant period of the history of Greece. In this century the great contest took place between the intelligence and courage of Eastern Europe on the one side, and the barbaric hosts and the luxury of Western Asia on the other, and resulted in the supremacy of the former. It was, like the Trojan War, a struggle in which the whole strength of the two parties was brought to bear, but in a more extended field of action.

When Darius, king of Persia, returned from his Scythian expedition, he was enabled to make good his retreat, through the fidelity of Histiæus of Miletus, and other Ionians, who had been left to guard his bridge of boats across the Danube. Milti'ades, the Athenian, endeavored to persuade Histiæus to destroy this bridge, but was unsuccessful; and Darius rewarded Histiæus by making him ruler of Mityle'ne and part of Thrace. The Persian monarch, however, grew suspicious of Histiæus, and sent for him to Susa. There he was kept prisoner, though treated kindly. Histiæus then instigated his brother-in-law, Aristag'oras of Miletus, to excite the Ionian colonies to revolt. Aristagoras went to Athens and Sparta to solicit assistance: the latter State refused to grant it; the former sent a fleet and troops. With the aid of these, Aristagoras took and burnt Sardis (B. C. 499); but he was defeated at Ephesus, and driven to the coast. He fled to Thrace, where he was murdered, and the revolt was suppressed (B. C. 494). Histiæus, who had been sent back with orders to quell the revolt, participated in it, but was captured and put to death by Artapher'nes, the Persian satrap (or governor) of Ionia. Darius, exasperated with the Athenians for the part they had taken in the contest, and instigated by Hippias, who was an exile at his court, now resolved to invade Greece. He sent an embassy to Athens, requiring that city to receive back Hippias. The Athenians refused to do this; whereupon Darius sent a vast army under his son-in-law, Mardonius (B. C. 492), to ravage Greece. But the fleet which conveyed it was wrecked off Mount Athos, and the Thracians destroyed the greater part of the army, so that the expedition was a failure. Darius then sent another army under Datis and Artaphernes against Athens, having been further instigated thereto by the conduct of Miltiades, governor of the Chersonese, who had taken possession of the islands of Lemnos and Imbros, which formed part of the Persian dominions. The army crossed the Archipelago, and, by the advice of Hippias, who accompanied it, landed on the coast of Attica, near Mar'athon, about 30 miles from Athens (B. C. 490). The Athenians mustered all their forces (about 30,000 men), and placed them under the command of ten generals, who took the chief command by turns, the principal of them being Miltiades, Callim'achus, Aristi'des, and Themis'tocles. The Persian troops were four times as numerous. The ever-memorable battle took place on the plains of Marathon, on the 28th September, B. C. 490, Miltiades having the chief command of the Greeks on that day. The Persians were completely routed and driven to their ships, and they thereupon returned to Persia. It is said that Hippias was slain on the field of battle. From this time forth the superiority of the Greeks over the Persians was established. Miltiades then persuaded the Athenians to intrust him with a secret expedition. This he conducted against the island of Paros, but he failed in his plans, and returned home wounded. His ungrateful countrymen accused him of having accepted bribes from the enemy, and sentenced him to death; but the punishment was commuted to a heavy fine, and he was thrown into prison, where he died of his wounds.

After the death of Miltiades the glory of Athens was maintained by Aristides and Themistocles. Aristides, surnamed "the Just", became Archon (B. C. 489), but his extreme probity excited the envy of his compeers, especially of Themistocles (who said he was weary of hearing him praised), and he was ostracised (B. C. 482). It was to him that Themistocles, on one occasion during the Persian war, confided his plan for treacherously destroying the ships of all the Greek allies of Athens, so that the latter might be mistress of the sea, but he nobly refused to countenance it. Meanwhile, Xerxes, the successor of Darius, anxious to avenge the defeat at Marathon, fitted out an enormous army (said to have numbered 2,000,000 persons), with which he crossed the Hellespont (Dardanelles) on a bridge of boats. It is related of him that the waves having roughly interfered with the construction of this bridge, he ordered them to be scourged with rods. He marched through Thrace and Macedonia, his fleet following him, and sailing through a canal cut purposely through the isthmus of Athos. The Greeks were in the utmost consternation. Themistocles was appointed to the command of the Athenian fleet, and, by his advice, the Athenians deserted their city, and took refuge in the island of Salamis. He also induced the other States to send forces to aid them. Leon'idas, king of Sparta, with 6000 men, marched to the pass of Thermop'ylæ, in Thessaly, between Mount Œta and an inaccessible morass. By this route Xerxes advanced with all his host; and there he was encountered by Leonidas and his troops, and kept at bay for some time, for it was the only road by which the Persians could enter Southern Greece. At length, Ephialtes, a Thessalian, whose name deserves to be handed down to eternal infamy, pointed out to the Persians a narrow pathway across the mountain. When Leonidas found that the Persians were passing to the rear of him, he dismissed all his troops except 300 of his Spartan warriors, and then rushed upon the enemy. In the desperate encounter which ensued, Leonidas fell, but his body was rescued by the Greeks. His Spartans were all cut off to a man (B. C. 480). On the hillock, in the pass where they fell, a lion of stone was set up in after times, with this inscription, written by Simon'ides: "O stranger, tell it at Lacedæmon that we died here in obedience to her sacred laws".

The Persians now poured down upon Attica. They pillaged and burnt Athens, but the inhabitants had fled to Salamis and Ægina. The Grecian fleet, consisting of 380 ships, surrounded those islands. The Persian fleet, consisting of 1200 sail, was sent to attack it. On this occasion Themistocles saved his country by a stratagem. Perceiving that Eurybi'ades, the Spartan commander, intended to withdraw with his ships, he sent a slave to the Persian commanders, informing them that if they would cut off the retreat of the Greeks the victory would be certain. The Persians accordingly did so, and thus the whole Greek force was compelled to fight. Xerxes, from an eminence, was a witness of the battle, which ended in the destruction of the greater portion of the Persian fleet. He hastily returned to Persia, leaving Mardonius with 300,000 men to prosecute the war. That general was soon afterward totally defeated at Platæa by the Athenians and Spartans, under Pausa'nias, the nephew of Leonidas (B. C. 479); and, on the same day, the allies under Leotych'ides and Xanthip'pus, annihilated the remains of the Persian fleet at Myc'ale. From this day the independence of Greece was assured. Athens was rebuilt and fortified, notwithstanding the opposition of the Spartans (B. C. 477), and its supremacy over the other States commenced. Pausanias followed up his success by taking Cyprus and Byzantium, but afterward entered into treasonable correspondence with the Persians, which ended in his disgrace and death. Themistocles, being implicated in it, fled to Persia, where he was handsomely provided for, and where he died (B. C. 449). He was a man of extraordinary abilities and eloquence, but of no morality, and so he died an exile and a traitor. Of him is recorded the memorable expression—"Strike, if you will, but hear!"—which he made use of during a dispute with Eurybiades, who was angry with him.

Aristides was recalled to Athens after the disgrace of Pausanias, and, in conjunction with Cimon, the son of Miltiades, was appointed to the command of the Athenian fleet. Aristides revised the laws of Athens, and reduced the taxes. This great and good man died B. C. 471, so poor that he did not leave enough to pay for his funeral. Cimon succeeded him in influence and popularity. This enterprising commander expelled the Persians from Thrace, and destroyed a large Persian fleet and army on the river Eurym'edon, in Pamphilia (B. C. 466). But he lost his popularity through the arts of Pericles, the leader of the democratical party, and was exiled for a short time. On his return he negotiated a five years' truce with Sparta (B. C. 450). Next year (B. C. 449), the war with Persia was renewed, and Cimon was appointed to the chief command. He sailed with a large force to Cyprus, and laid siege to Cit'ium, where he died. Pericles had for some years previously assumed the leading part in public affairs. By procuring the passage of laws for the more immediate benefit of the poorer citizens, he gained complete control over them, and by his wonderful eloquence swayed the entire people. He concluded peace with Persia, stipulating for the freedom of all the Grecian cities of Asia. He lavished immense sums on public buildings, festivals, and games, and patronized genius of every

What was the cause of the animosity of Darius against the Athenians?—What is said of Histiæus?—Aristagoras?—And Hippias?—Give the particulars of the first expedition, under Mardonius.—Of the second, under Datis and Artaphernes.—Of the battle of Marathon, and the fate of Miltiades.—What is said of Aristides?—Of Themistocles?

Give the particulars of the third expedition under Xerxes.—What is said of Leonidas and the pass of Thermopylæ?—Of the battle of Salamis?—Platæa?—And Mycale?—What became of Pausanias and Themistocles?—What is said of Cimon?—Of Pericles?—Of the acts of Cimon on his return from exile?

description. Athens was now at the meridian of her glory, and aspired to the domination of all Greece. Pericles commanded the Athenians in their campaigns against the Sicyonians and Acarnanians (B. C. 454); in the Phocian Sacred War (B. C. 448); in recovering the island of Eubœa (B. C. 445); and the conquest of Samos (B. C. 440). He fostered the commerce and the navy of Athens, but did not escape the virulent attacks of envious factions. The Spartans, jealous of the greatness of the Athenians, made demands upon the latter which they knew would not be acceded to. Accordingly, when they were refused, the Spartans formed a combination with the other States to humble Athens, and the result was "the first Peloponnesian War," which began B. C. 431, and lasted 28 years. All the eminent men in Greece were engaged in it. The Thebans, being allies of the Spartans, began it by attacking Platæa. This was followed by the invasion of Attica, on which occasion the Athenians, by the advice of Pericles, removed their flocks to Eubœa, and shut themselves up in Athens, leaving the country to be ravaged by the Spartans. The same policy was resorted to next year, but it drew down upon Pericles the reproaches of the people. A plague broke out, and carried off his sons, and he himself sank under the effects of grief (B. C. 429). His fame rests upon many solid bases, but he introduced an incurable taste for luxury and prodigality, though, in his own case personally, combining with it genius and taste. On his death, Cleon, a popular demagogue, became the favorite of the people, and for six years enjoyed the principal share of power. He was a strenuous advocate for war, and took an active part in the great struggle. Many actions were fought by land and sea, and Attica was subjected for some years to an annual invasion. Soc′rates, Xen′ophon, Thucy′dides, Alcibi′ades, Nic′ias, and others, distinguished themselves in this great war. The leading events in it may be thus summed up. The Thebans, Corinthians, Spartans, and some of the minor States, were leagued against Athens — Sparta taking the lead. A war had previously broken out between Corinth and Corcy′ra, the latter being supported by the Athenians and their allies, the Thracians. The first two years of the Peloponnesian war were occupied by invasions of Attica, and the siege of Platæa by the allies; also by the siege of Potidæa by the Athenians. It was before the latter place that Socrates saved the life of Alcibiades. The Athenians took Lesbos, Mitylene, and Potidæa, but lost Platæa. In the seventh year of the war they took Pylos, and captured a Spartan force in Sphacteria. Their general, Nicias, next year ravaged the coast of Laconia, and captured Cythera, but lost the battle of Delium, wherein both Socrates and Xenophon fought (B. C. 424). Thucydides, the historian of the war, also took part against the Spartans at Amphipolis, and was exiled in consequence of the loss of that city (B. C. 423). He remained in exile 20 years. A truce for a year was followed by a battle at Amphipolis, wherein Cleon, the Athenian general, and Bras′idas, king of the Spartans, were slain, B. C. 422. Then came a truce for 50 years, which was broken as soon as made. Alcibiades carried the war into Peloponnesus, and effected a league between the Athenians and the Argives. Varied success attended the combatants. In the year B. C. 415 the Athenians sent an expedition against Sicily, under the command of Nicias, Alcibiades, and Lam′achus; but Alcibiades was recalled to take his trial for mutilating the busts of Hermes at Athens, which mysterious transaction had excited great fears in the minds of the Athenians. He fled to Sparta, and was sentenced to death by the Athenians; he was, however, soon driven out of Sparta, and then fled to Tissapher′nes, Persian satrap (or governor) of Lower Asia, who had espoused the cause of the Spartans. By his arts he persuaded Tissaphernes to join the Athenians. For this service he was forgiven, and recalled home (B. C. 411). The expedition to Sicily, under Nicias, was at first successful: the famous siege of Syracuse was undertaken, and the city almost taken, when a Spartan army, under Gylippus, relieved the place. Nicias was compelled to surrender, and was, with his colleague Demosthenes, put to death by the Syracusans (B. C. 413). The general dissatisfaction caused by the reverses paved the way for the downfall of the Democracy of Athens. The oligarchical party, headed by An′tiphon, the orator, succeeded in establishing the Council of the Four Hundred (B. C. 411), by whom the affairs of the State were soon brought to confusion. They were driven out of office, and Antiphon was put to death. Alcibiades was recalled to Athens, but he paid little heed to the call, and remained abroad for the next four years, at the head of the Athenian forces. He gained the battles of Cynesse′ma, Cyz′icus, and Aby′dos, and took Byzantium and Chalce′don. In B. C. 407 he returned to Athens, and was appointed commander-in-chief; but the defeat of his lieutenant, Antiochus, at Natium, by Lysander and the Spartans, caused him to be superseded (B. C. 406), and he went into exile in the Thracian Chersonesus. His successors, Callicrat′idas and Conon were defeated by the Spartans in the fatal battles of Arginusæ (B. C. 406), and Ægos Potamos (B. C. 405). The former was put to death, and the latter fled to Cyprus. Lysander now besieged and took Athens (B. C. 404), and that humiliated city was compelled to demolish its port, and bind itself to limit its fleet to twelve ships, and not to undertake any military enterprise, unless under the command of the Spartans. Thus the first Peloponnesian war ended. Democracy was abolished in Athens, and the government was entrusted to thirty citizens, since remembered by the name of "the thirty tyrants."

These thirty tyrants held their power for eight months, during which time they indulged in such cruelty that most of the citizens fled, and Athens was almost deserted. Their career was cut short by Thrasybu′lus, a leading Democrat, who organized a successful revolt against them, and ultimately restored the Democratic government (B. C. 403). The year previously, Alcibiades, who had fled to Asia Minor, was assassinated by a band of armed men, supposed to have been employed by the Spartans. On the restoration of the Democracy at Athens, a general amnesty was published, and Thucydides, Lysias, Andoc′ides, and other illustrious exiles, returned to Athens. The year B. C. 401 is memorable as that in which "the ten thousand" Greeks, in the service of Cyrus of Persia, after the unfortunate battle of Cunaxa, made good their retreat from that country, under Xenophon, who has left an interesting account of it.

Sparta. — The history of this State offers fewer events than that of Athens. The kingly republic took an active part in the struggle with the Persians when they invaded Greece, as we have already seen. At the commencement of the century, Cleom′enes I. and Demaratus were the joint kings of Sparta. Demaratus was forced to flee from the country, owing to the intrigues of Cleomenes, and he took refuge in Persia. Cleomenes committed suicide (B. C. 491). He was succeeded by his half-brother, the heroic Leon′idas, whose gallant conduct and death at Thermopylæ (B. C. 480) have already been noticed. His colleague, Leotych′ides, commanded the Greek fleet at Myc′ale, but was afterwards dethroned for accepting bribes. The leading man in Sparta at this time was Pausanias, the nephew of Leonidas, and guardian of the young king, Pleistarchus. During the Persian war he marched at the head of a strong force to the assistance of the Athenians, and assumed the command of the Grecian army at Platæa, where he defeated the Persians under Mardonius. He then led a fleet against Cyprus, which island he subdued. He next sailed to Byzantium, and having mastered the city, he formed the idea of making himself king of all Greece, with the assistance of the Persian king. His treachery being suspected, he was recalled to Sparta, and tried for treason, but acquitted. Accident, however, revealed his treasonable correspondence with Xerxes, and he was stoned to death (B. C. 467) in the temple of Minerva, his aged mother having been one of the first to lay a stone for the purpose of blocking up the door. In the year B. C. 464, Sparta was reduced to ruins by an earthquake, and a revolt of the Helots and Messenians broke out, which lasted ten years. Archid′amus II., the successor of Leotychides, commanded the Spartan forces throughout this war, and also throughout the Peloponnesian war, until his death in B. C. 427. His son, Agis II., succeeded him, and also held the chief command during the great war. The most eminent Spartan of this period was Lysander, who destroyed the Athenian fleet at Ægospot′amos (B. C. 405), and terminated the Peloponnesian war. At the close of the century he was the most powerful man in Greece.

Corinth. — During the Peloponnesian war this State was one of the bitterest enemies of Athens. Thebes was also very hostile to Athens. During the war the citizens abolished their oligarchical government, and established a democracy.

What is said of Cleon?—Give a sketch of the first Peloponnesian war.—Who distinguished themselves in it?—What is said of Nicias, and the siege of Syracuse?—Of the fall of the Democracy of Athens?—Of Alcibiades?—Lysander?—The thirty tyrants?—Thrasybulus, and the restoration of the Democracy?

What is said of the retreat of the ten thousand Greeks under Xenophon?—What was the fate of Cleomenes and Demaratus?—Leotychides?—Pausanias?—What calamities happened to Sparta, B. C. 464?—What is said of Agis and Lysander?—What is said of Corinth?—Of Thebes?

GREECE.

Macedonia.—Alexander I. succeeded his father, Amyntas, and was forced to take part with the Persians against the Greeks. He died about B. C. 454, and was succeeded by his son, Perdiccas II. It was during the reign of this monarch that the Spartan general, Brasidas, made his celebrated expedition into the country to drive out the Athenians. But a misunderstanding arising between Perdiccas and Brasidas, the former joined the Athenians. His natural son, Archela′us, on his death in B. C. 413, obtained the throne by murdering his half-brother. But though he began his career with this horrid crime, he proved an able monarch, and greatly improved the internal condition of his kingdom. He was also a munificent patron of literature and art.

The century was as fertile in great literary men and artists as in warriors, statesmen, and orators. Athens has the immortal honor of having either produced or patronized the noblest intellects of Greece. Foremost among some sixty names of eminence are those of Pindar, Æs′chylus, Soph′ocles, Eurip′ides, Herod′otus, Thucyd′ides, Soc′rates, Phid′ias, Zeuxis, Aristoph′anes, Crati′nus, Hippoc′rates, and Xen′ophon.

Pindar was born at Thebes, B. C. 522, and was the greatest lyric poet of Greece. He was the pupil of Lasus of Hermione, the founder of the Athenian school of dithyrambic (or wild and enthusiastic) poetry; and he was also instructed by the celebrated poetesses, Myrtis and Corinna, of Tan′agra. He composed poems for many of the then reigning sovereigns of Greece and of Syracuse, but only his "Epinicia," or triumphal odes, have come down to us entire. He wrote hymns, dirges, drinking-songs, and a variety of other small poems, fragments of which are still extant. He died in his 80th year, B. C. 442, respected by all classes.

Æschylus was born at Eleusis, in Attica, B. C. 525. He is styled the father of Greek Tragedy, from having introduced so many improvements into the drama. He is said to have written seventy tragedies, but seven only are extant, namely: "The Persians," "The Seven against Thebes," "The Suppliants," the "Prometheus," the "Agamemnon," "The Choeph′ori," and "The Eumen′ides." Æschylus was present at the battles of Mar′athon, Sal′amis, and Platæa. He died at Gela, in Sicily, B. C. 456.

Sophocles, born at Colo′nus, near Athens, B. C. 495, was the greatest dramatist of Greece. He wrote 113 dramas, but only seven are extant, namely: "Antigone," "Electra," "Trachin′iæ," "Œd′ipus Tyran′nus," "Ajax," "Philocte′tes," and "Œdipus Colo′nus." He was the successful rival of Æschylus, Euripides, Chœ′rilus, Arist′ias, Ag′athon, and other poets, and carried off the first prize twenty-four times. In a lawsuit with his son, Iophon, respecting the disposal of his property, he was represented as being insane; on this occasion he uttered his famous reply: "If I am Sophocles, I am not beside myself; if I am beside myself, I am not Sophocles." He then read an extract from his unpublished play, Œdipus Colonus, and gained the suit. He died in his 90th year, B. C. 406.

Euripides, born at Salamis, B. C. 480, on the day of the battle, was one of the greatest tragic poets of Greece. He studied physics under Anaxag′oras, and rhetoric under Prod′icus, and was on intimate terms with Socrates. He wrote 75 plays, of which 18 are extant: the principal being "Iphigenia in Aulis," "Iphigenia in Tauris," "Orestes," "Helena," "Andromache," "Elecra," "Medea," and "Alcestis." He was torn to pieces by the dogs of the king of Macedonia, B. C. 406.

Aristophanes, a celebrated comic poet, born at Athens B. C. 444, was a great patriot as well as poet, and opposed Cleon and the demagogues. In his plays he satirized the vices of the age. He was a poet of the highest order, and the author of 54 plays, but not more than 13 of them have come down to our times. The principal are "The Clouds," "The Wasps," "The Frogs," "The Horsemen," "Lysistrata," and "Plutus." He died B. C. 480.

Cratinus, the rival of Aristophanes, was born B. C. 519. He wrote 21 plays, and gained many prizes. He was the first who made use of comedy for personal attacks. We have only fragments of his works. He died B. C. 422.

Herodotus, the famous historian, was born at Halicarnas′sus, in Asia Minor, B. C. 484. He was of a noble family, and spent many years in travelling in Europe, Asia, and Africa. He settled at Thurii, in Italy, where he died. He wrote an account of his travels, which is most valuable from its truthfulness, and the mass of information which it contains. He also wrote the history of Crœsus, of Lydia, of Persia, of Egypt, and the expedition of Cambyses, and of the war between the Greeks and Persians.

Thucydides was an Athenian, born B. C. 471. He studied philosophy under Anaxagoras, and oratory under Antiphon. He commanded a squadron of ships at Thasus, but was exiled for failing to save that place. He lived in exile 20 years, and met with a violent death about B. C. 401. He wrote a history of the Peloponnesian war, in which he displayed great accuracy and elevation of mind.

Socrates, born near Athens, B. C. 469, was the greatest of all the Greek philosophers. He was the son of a statuary, and followed his father's profession. He served in several campaigns. At the battle of Potidæa he saved the life of Alcibiades; and, at that of Delium, his own life was saved by Alcibiades. In middle age he went about lecturing, publicly and privately, on the advantages of morality and self-knowledge. He was hated and ridiculed by the poets and orators, and persecuted by the ruling party, the Thirty Tyrants, and their successors. He was impeached on a charge of corrupting youth, and of despising the popular deities, and was condemned to die by poison. During the 30 days which intervened between his sentence and his execution, he reiterated his views on the immortality of the soul, on religion, and on nature, which are distinguished for their exalted character. He professed to be attended by a familiar spirit, whom he spake of as a divine sign, or supernatural voice. His friend, Crito, in vain urged him to escape, but he refused to make the attempt. He drank the poison with the utmost heroism, and died with calmness equal to that of a Christian (B. C. 399). His wife, Xanthippe, is renowned for having been a quarrelsome shrew to her philosophic husband. The sentence pronounced by the court of the Areop′agus against Socrates was formally reversed by the modern court at Athens in the year 1859, exactly 2258 years after his death!

Phidias, the greatest sculptor and statuary of Greece, was born at Athens, B. C. 490. His great works were the Propylæa of the Acropolis, the Parthenon at Athens, and the colossal statues of Jupiter Olympus and Minerva. As a sculptor he has not been surpassed. He was thrown into prison on a charge of impiety, and he died from disease there, B. C. 432.

Zeuxis, the great painter, was born at Heraclea, on the Euxine, and flourished at the close of the 5th century (B. C. 424–400). His famous rival, Parrhasius, lived at the same epoch, and was a native of Ephesus, though he practised his profession of painter at Athens.

Hippocrates, the most celebrated physician of antiquity, was a native of the island of Cos, and born about B. C. 460. He wrote several works on medicine, and was the author of many moral reflections: the famous aphorism, "Life is short, and Art is long," is one of them.

Xenophon, the celebrated soldier and historian, was born at Athens, B. C. 444. His life was saved by Socrates at the battle of Delium. He commanded the 10,000 Greeks who had been in the service of Cyrus the younger, the son of Darius Nothus, king of Persia, and were left alone after the fatal battle of Cunaxa. Xenophon commanded them in their famous retreat along the course of the Tigris through Armenia to Trebizond. He wrote a history of this retreat of the 10,000 Greeks; and also a history of Greece, from the time when the history of Thucydides ends to the battle of Mantinæ′a, B. C. 362. These works are styled "The Anab′asis, and "The Hellen′ica." He likewise wrote "The Cyropædia," or youth of Cyrus, a political romance; "The Memorabilia," or conversations of Socrates; "The Apology," or defence of Socrates; "The Symposium," or banquet of philosophers; and other works on statistics, horses, dogs, domestic economy, etc. The place and manner of his death are uncertain, but it took place subsequently to the year B. C. 362.

Beside those, there were many other eminent persons, namely: the poetess Telesilla; the poets, Epichar′mus, Pherecy′des, Emped′ocles, Bacchyl′ides; the historians and geographers, Hellan′icus and Hecatæ′us; the philosophers, Anaxag′oras, Parmen′ides, Democ′ritus, Archela′us, Protag′oras; the orators, Andoc′ides, Gor′gias, Ly′sias, Isoc′rates; the architects, Icti′nus, Callic′rates, and Mnes′icles; the painters, Polygno′tus and Panænus; the sculptor, Polycle′tus; and the astronomer, Meton.

What is said of Macedonia?—Of Perdiccas and Brasidas?—Of Archelaus?—Mention the names of the most illustrious writers and artists of this century.—What is said of Pindar?—What works of his remain?—Who were Myrtis and Corinna?—Who was Æschylus?—Name his extant works.—What is said of Sophocles?—What occurred between him and his son?

What is said of Euripides?—Who was Aristophanes?—What is said of Cratinus?—Herodotus?—Thucydides?—Socrates?—What doctrines did he teach?—What was the manner of his death?—When was the sentence reversed?—What is said of his wife, Xanthippe?—Name the other eminent persons of this century.

ITALY.

Tarquin, neglected by Porsena, took refuge with his son-in-law, Mamilius otavius, of Tusculum. The latter induced the Latin States to espouse Tar- uin's cause, and march against Rome. A battle was fought near Lake Regil- us, B. C. 496, in which the Romans were completely victorious. Tarquin was ounded, and fled to Cumæ, where he died, a wretched old man. Lake Re- illus is now a small pool; but the chronology of this period of Roman history so confused that there is no saying to a certainty when the battle was fought, or, indeed, that it was fought at all.

The tyranny of the patricians drove the plebeians to arms, but the strife nded in the concession of all the demands of the latter, and the restoration of ıe Valerian laws. The family of the Valerii, after whom these laws were amed, enjoyed great privileges, and always advocated the rights of the ple- eians: the laws which they proposed were the charters of Roman liberty. In ıe year B. C. 491 there was a severe famine in Rome. On this occasion, a aughty patrician, Caius Marcius, surnamed Coriola′nus, from the heroism e had displayed in the capture of the Volscian town of Corioli, proposed that ıe corn sent from Sicily should not be distributed among the people, unless ıey gave up their Tribunes (magistrates chosen annually by the people to 'atch over their rights). For this he was impeached and exiled. He fled to ıe Volscians, then at war with the Romans; and Attius Tullius, the Volscian ing, gave him command of the army. With this he marched against Rome, ut was induced, by the tears and prayers of his mother and his wife, to desist. e led his army back, and it is said that he was put to death on his return, by ttius Tullius, B. C. 488.

Spurius Cassius, who had negotiated the league with the Latins, and that ith the Hernicans, introduced the first Agrarian Law that was ever proposed t Rome. It enacted that the portion of the patricians in the public lands ıould be strictly defined, and the remainder divided among the plebeians. his law was passed B. C. 486. But next year the patricians accused Spurius f aiming at regal power, and put him to death. He was thrown from the arpeian rock, a mode of punishment adopted towards State criminals. The arpeian rock, so often mentioned in Roman history, was a portion of the Capi- line Hill, and, as has been already mentioned, derived its name from Tarpeia, ıe daughter of Spurius Tarpeius, governor of the Roman citadel on that hill ı the time of Romulus, which was surrendered to the Sabines through her 'eachery. She had been induced to open the gates by the offer of all the gold n the Sabine bracelets and collars, but, as the Sabines entered, they threw ıeir shields upon her, and thus crushed her to death. The Agrarian Law ıused furious disputes between the patricians and the plebeians, and the 'oubles of the commonwealth were still further increased by the continued ar with the Veientes and Volscians. The illustrious patrician family of the a′bii seceded from the patrician party, and joined the plebeians. As this rew down upon them the animosity of the Senate, they withdrew from the ty, taking up a position near the Creme′ra, with their clients and dependents. here they were surprised and slaughtered by the Veientes (B. C. 477), 306 ıembers of the family perishing in the fatal encounter. The Romans suffered reat losses in this war. The city itself was endangered, but at length a forty ears' truce was concluded (B. C. 474).

The domestic strife became more furious than ever. The tribune, Cneius Ge- ucius, having impeached the consuls, Fabius and Manlius, was assassinated y their orders. The consuls sought to divert public attention by levying 'oops for a war, but the levy was stopped by a centurion (captain of a hun- red), named Publil′ius Vole′ro, who raised a fierce commotion, and compelled ıe patricians to make further concessions. He effected an important change ı the Constitution, by causing the election of the tribunes to be transferred rom the centuries to the tribes, to whom was also given the power of delibe- ating upon, and determining, all matters affecting the whole nation, and not uch as only concerned the plebs, as had previously been the case. By this aw (styled, after him, the *Publilia Lex*,) he struck a fatal blow at the supremacy f the patricians. The consul, Appius Claudius, was so enraged at the passing f this law, that he vented his fury by decimating the troops who refused to erve under him. For this he was impeached, but escaped punishment by com-

What was the result of the battle of Lake Regillus?—What of the chronology of this pe- od?—What is said of Coriolanus?—Spurius Cassius, and the first Agrarian Law?—The 'arpeian rock?—The Fabii?—Domestic strife?—The Publilian Law?—Appius Claudius?— ppius Herdonius?—The war with the Æqui?

mitting suicide (B. C. 470). After his death the internal dissensions of Rome ceased for awhile, and the nation devoted its energy to external conquests. But the results were not very encouraging. The Æqui and Volsci drove the Latin peasantry to take refuge in the city, where the general distress was aggravated by pestilence. In the year B. C. 460, Appius Herdo′nius, a Sabine chieftain, with a band of outlaws and slaves, made himself master of the capitol, but it was retaken four days afterwards by the consul, Valerius Public′ola, who was killed in the action. The consul, Minucius, having been blockaded by the Æqui in the defiles of Mount Æ′gidus, the Senate, in the emergency, resolved to appoint a dictator, with supreme powers, to rescue the State from its danger. They selected for that office Lucius Quintius Cincinna′tus, an old hero, who cultivated his farm with his own hands. He was working at the plough when the deputation arrived to offer him the dictatorship. He accepted it, raised troops, defeated the enemy, extricated the Roman army from its dan- gerous position (B. C. 458), and, within sixteen days, returned to his farm and resigned his high office. Peace was shortly after concluded with the Volscians.

The population of Rome at this time was upwards of 130,000. Internal dis- sensions broke out afresh. The people got ten tribunes appointed instead of five. One of them, Sicin′ius Denta′tus (styled "the Roman Achilles," from having fought 120 battles, and received 45 wounds), obtained the assent of the Senate to the framing of a new code of laws. Ten persons (*decem viri*), called "the Decemvirs," were appointed with consular powers for this purpose. No appeal from their decision was allowed. By them the laws, known as "the Twelve Tables," were promulgated (B. C. 449). These laws were favorable to the plebeians. But the Decemvirs abused their office; and because Dentatus endeavored to persuade the people to assemble at the Sacred Mount to oppose them, they caused him to be assassinated. One of their number, Appius Clau- dius, having attempted violence against Virginia, the daughter of a brave officer named Virginius, the father slew her in public to save her from dishonor. He then roused the people to action. The Decemvirs were deposed. Appius Claudius died, or was put to death in prison, and the rest were banished; and consuls and tribunes were again elected (B. C. 449). The dismayed patricians yielded still farther to the demands of the people, and the tribune, Canuleius, obtained a law permitting marriage between patricians and plebeians. This law was called the "Canuleian Law." Three military tribunes were appointed instead of consuls, but this arrangement lasted only three months, and consuls were again elected. A censorship was also established (B. C. 443). War was also carried on successfully with the Æqui and Sabines, the former being com- pletely routed near Rome.

In the year B. C. 439 a severe famine caused great distress. Spurius Mælius, a wealthy plebeian, bought vast quantities of corn in Etruria, and distributed it among the citizens of Rome. For this he was accused by the patricians of designs upon the State. They appointed the venerable Cincinnatus dictator once more, and Servilius Aha′la master of the horse. Mælius was summoned to appear before the tribunal of the dictator, but refusing to do so, Ahala killed him. For this crime Ahala was brought to trial, but escaped condemation by voluntary exile (B. C. 438). The next event of importance was the revolt of the city of Fide′næ. Having placed itself under the protection of Lar Tolum- nius, king of the Veientes, its inhabitants, at his instigation, murdered the four Roman envoys sent to inquire into their conduct. The Romans marched against the rebels, and gained a complete victory over Tolumnius, who was killed in the battle (B. C. 437). Fidenæ was destroyed, and Veii compelled to sue for a truce. A few years afterwards the war was renewed; the Romans were rapidly growing powerful, and subjecting their neighbors. Towards the close of the century (B. C. 405), they undertook the destruction of their ancient enemy, the Veientes. The city of Veii was besieged, and, after a siege of ten years, was taken by storm, and destroyed (see next century). It was during this war that the Romans first established a standing army.

Domestic agitation continued; but the plebeians gained ground, and, in the year B. C. 408, were first admitted to the quæstorship (treasurership and re- ceivership of taxes).

What is said of Cincinnatus?—The population of Rome?—The appointment of tribunes?— Sicinius Dentatus?—The Decemvirs?—The twelve tables?—Virginius and his daughter?— Appius Claudius and the Decemvirs?—The Canuleian Law?—Spurius Mælius and Servilius Ahala?—The revolt of Fidenæ?—The war with Veii?—The progress of the plebeians?

BRITAIN.

After half a century of desolating warfare, Dunwallo Molmutius, the son and successor of Cloten, king of Cornwall, a man of great valor and gracefulness of person, found means to reduce the whole island into one monarchy. Having defeated and killed the other kings, he established the code of laws traditionally known as "the Molmutine laws," which became the common law of the land, and are said to have been translated into Saxon by King Alfred the Great, 1300 years afterwards. Molmutius reigned 40 years and was buried at London, B. C. 442, near the temple of Concord, which he had built in that city when he first established his laws. On his death his two sons, Belinus and Brennius, quarrelled as to the succession, but ultimately divided the country between them. Belinus took Loegria, Cambria, and Cornwall; Brennius the rest. The ambitious Brennius having entered into a league with the king of the Northmen, whose daughter he had married, was dispossessed of his portion by his brother. Landing in England with an army, he was defeated, but escaped to France. There his cause was espoused by the chief of the Allobroges, who sent him with an army to Britain; but through the mediation of their mother peace was made between the two brothers, who then joined their forces in a predatory excursion on the continent of Europe. The historian says they conquered the Franks in Gaul and marched to Rome, which city they besieged, took, and plundered, taking prisoner the Roman consul Porsenna!! This legend is evidently founded by Geoffrey of Monmouth on the fact that Rome was taken by the Gauls under Brennus.

Brennius died in Italy; but Belinus returned to Britain, which he governed during the remainder of his life in peace. This prince built several cities, amongst others Caer-leon; and he added a gate, a haven, and a tower to London, on the top of which tower his ashes are said to have been deposited in a golden urn. He was a wise and able prince, as were his successors, Gurgund, or Gurgiunt Brabtruc, and Guitheline, in whose reign was framed that code of laws known in after ages as the "Marchen-lage," or the Mercian law, which was incorporated by King Alfred the Great with the West Saxon laws.

What is said of Dunwallo Molmutius?—Of the Molmutine laws?—Belinus and Brennius?—Their history?—What did Belinus erect?—What of Gurgiunt and Guitheline?

FRANCE.

The Gauls and Cimbri fusing into one people by degrees, joined their forces in those predatory excursions wherein they ravaged Italy during this century. But the history of France at this period is little known; the classical historians being chiefly occupied with the miseries inflicted on Italy by the barbarous Gauls, who are described as living in towns without walls, and houses without furniture, sleeping on grass or straw, eating nothing but meat, occupying themselves with nothing but war, and a little agriculture, and caring for nothing but their flocks and gold (*Polybius*, b. 2, p. 106). They ravaged all Italy, avoiding, however, the mountaineers of the Apennines, and the Romans and Latins. They did not destroy the cities of Mantua, Ravenna, and Rimini, for these were the markets where they disposed of their plunder. Nevertheless they caused these cities horrible suffering, and rendered their existence precarious and uncertain. For instance, the city of Melpum having displeased its new masters, was suddenly assailed by them, pillaged, and utterly destroyed.

Every spring bands of adventurers set out from their villages to plunder some rich city in Etruria, Campania, or Græcia Magna, and on their return they threw the spoils into a common stock, which became the treasure of the community. Græcia Magna was the favorite scene of the excursions of the Gauls, for there they found an inexhaustible booty, and the republics of Sybaris, Tarentum, Crotona, Locris, and Metapontum, so famous for their luxury and effeminacy, fell an easy prey to their audacity. All this portion of Italy was horribly ravaged. The entire population of Colon fled from these savages and crossed over into Sicily. In these distant expeditions the Cisalpine Gauls generally marched along the coast to the extremity of the peninsula. As we have already observed, they avoided the Romans and Latins, who were very poor but very warlike. Thierry observes (*Histoire des Gaulois*, introduction, p. 15) that by a remarkable chance, it was always under the sword of the Romans that the power of the Gaulish nations fell: as the Roman domination extended, the Gaulish domination receded and declined. After two centuries of warfare the Cisalpine Gauls were subdued.

What description does Polybius give of the Gauls?—Which cities in Italy did they spare?—Which ravage and destroy?—What does Thierry remark as to their domination?

SPAIN.

In the year B. C. 482, the Carthaginians sent out fresh troops to Cadiz, and planted a colony at the mouths of the Guadalquiver. Sappho, the son of Asdrubal, was appointed governor of their possessions in Spain. He was of great service to Carthage by making a diversion in Mauritania, when the city was hard pressed by the army of that nation, B. C. 470. He was recalled in B. C. 463, and his cousins Himilco, Hanno, and Gisgo, were sent in his place. On their way they visited Minorca, where, it is said, they founded Jama, Magon, and Labon. Hanno explored the southern coast of Spain, and suggested to the Carthaginian Senate the advantages that might result from an exploration of the western and northern shores of Spain and France, and of the western and southern coasts of Africa. In compliance with this suggestion, the Senate commissioned Himilco and Hanno to undertake these voyages of discovery. Himilco sailed round the west coast of Spain, thence northwardly to Britain and the Baltic, whence he returned after an absence of two years. Hanno, with a fleet of 60 galleys and 30,000 colonists, sailed from Cadiz round the African coast, planting colonies where he thought proper. It is said that he sailed round the Cape of Good Hope and along the eastern coast of Africa into the Red Sea. He returned to Carthage B. C. 441, after an absence of five years. An account of this famous voyage has been handed down to us. (See 'Αννωνος Καρχηδονιων Βασιλεως Περιπλους, or "the Voyage round of Hanno, prince of the Carthaginians," translated by Falconer.) Hannibal and Mago succeeded Gisgo in the government of the Carthaginian colonies in Spain. The former built a town (now called Albor) near Cape St. Vincent, A bloody war broke out (B. C. 438) between the inhabitants of Betica and the Lusitani; in which Hannibal, taking part with the latter, was slain.

The year B. C. 426 is remarkable for a dreadful plague which devastated the whole world, and created such distress in Spain, that thousands of Spaniards were glad to enlist in the service of Carthage, and fight her battles in Sicily. Dionysius, the tyrant of Syracuse, endeavored to induce them to desert, but they remained faithful to the Carthaginians, despite the evils they had inflicted on their country.

What is said of Sappho and other Carthaginian chiefs? — What was the "Periplus" of Hanno?—What other voyages were made in this century?—What cities founded?

GERMANY.

The Getæ (called by the Romans Daci) and the Pannones, German tribes dwelling near the mouths of the Danube, now appear in history. Zamolxis, the sage, taught them the immortality of the soul; and their king, Dice'neus, employed him to frame laws for them. Zamolxis (or Zalmoxis) is said to have derived his name from the bear's skin in which he was wrapped up as soon as he was born. According to Greek tradition, he was a Getan, who had been a slave of the celebrated philosopher, Pythagoras, in the island of Samos, but had received his freedom. He acquired great wealth, and travelled very extensively. He gained large stores of knowledge from the Egyptians and from Pythagoras. He then returned among his countrymen, the Getæ, and introduced among them the civilization and the religious doctrines which he had acquired, especially the doctrine of the immortality of the soul. It is said that he retired into a subterraneous cave for three years, and after that period he again made his appearance among the Getæ. The Greek historian, Herodotus, however, says that Zamolxis lived long before Pythagoras, and expresses a doubt not only about the story itself, but as to whether Zamolxis were a man or an indigenous Getan deity. The latter is supposed by many to have been the real state of the case. The Getæ believed that the souls of the departed went to him.

Darius, king of Persia, invading Thrace, crossed the Danube amongst the Pannones, who sought his alliance. They sent him, as ambassador, a tall and beautiful girl, bearing on her head a vessel filled with water, and spinning whilst she led a horse by a bridle on her arm. On observing the king's surprise, they informed him that they were descended from the Trojans, and that their women were all as industrious as the maiden he beheld. On his penetrating deeper into the steppe, the Scythians sent him a bird, a mouse, a frog, and five arrows, thereby intimating that unless he could fly away like a bird, hide in the earth like a mouse, or in the water like a frog, their arrows would slay him before he could reach their frontiers, — a threat they very nearly fulfilled, for having enticed the Persian army up the country, they surrounded it, and it was rescued from destruction only by a stratagem.

Who were the Getæ and Pannones?—Who was Zamolxis?—What is related of him?—What does Herodotus say? — What befel Darius among the Scythians?

B.C. 500—400.

ASIA MINOR.

This part of the world formed a portion of the Persian empire at the beginning of this century, but was for many years filled with commotions by the immense Persian armies which traversed it on their road to Greece. A revolt of the Ionian colonies, instigated by Histiæ′us, governor of Miletus, and Aristag′oras, his brother-in-law, caused great misery and bloodshed. It lasted six years, and though the Athenians sent aid to the insurgents, the attempt to throw off the Persian yoke was unsuccessful. Histiæus was defeated, and taken prisoner (B. C. 494). He was impaled by order of Artaphernes, satrap of Ionia, and his head was sent to the Persian monarch, Darius. Aristagoras fled to Thrace, where he was slain by the Edonians. Sardis was burnt, and Ephesus, Miletus, and Cyprus, were taken. On the suppression of the revolt, Darius, and, after him, Xerxes, occupied themselves with their expeditions against Greece, until the year B. C. 479, when, after the battles of Platæa and Mycale, the Persians returned home in disgrace; and the Greeks, making themselves masters of Thrace, entered into a confederacy with the cities of Ionia, which again revolted from the Persians, and this time successfully. The Athenians, under Cimon, following up their victories, drove the Persians out of Asia Minor, and finally triumphing at Eurym′edon (B. C. 466), compelled them to make a humiliating peace. The independence of the Ionian colonies was fully established, and it endured for nearly a century. The Greeks who dwelt in these rich and fertile provinces became celebrated for their refinement, arts, and literature. Their restless and free spirit fully developed itself, and their commerce became extended over the neighboring countries and the Mediterranean. But they gave way to luxury, and subsequently degenerated in force of character. They produced some of the most brilliant men of genius of antiquity: such as Anacreon, Thales, Anaxagoras, Hecatæus, Zeuxis, Apelles, and Parrhasius.

A kingdom was founded on the Bosphorus (B. C. 480), which existed 200 years, until merged in that of the successors of Alexander the Great. The dynasty of the Archæanactidæ, its first kings, reigned 42 years. To them succeeded Spartacus I. (B. C. 438), his son Seleucus (431), and Satyrus I. (407).

What was the state of the country at this period?—What were the principal events in its history?—What kingdom was founded?—What eminent men flourished?

CARTHAGE.

The history of Sicily now becomes so mixed up with that of Carthage that it is necessary to give some particulars of it. At the commencement of the century, Hippocrates, king of Gela, was the most powerful personage in the island. Gelon, a native of Gela, having rendered great military service to him (B. C. 483), acquired such influence that he was enabled, on the death of that monarch, to seize upon his dominions. He next made himself master of Syracuse, giving to his brother, Hiero, the government of Gela. He became so powerful that his alliance was courted by neighboring nations, and he made one with the Athenians and Spartans against the Persians. The Persian king at the same time entered into one with the Carthaginians, against the Greeks and their allies. In pursuance of this treaty the Carthaginians invaded Sicily. They sent thither Hamilcar, the son of Hanno, with, it is said, an army of 300,000 men. Hamilcar invested the town of Himera, where he was surprised and slain by Gelon, and his whole army was cut to pieces. This battle was fought on the same day as the battle of Salamis. The Carthaginians immediately sued for peace, and obtained it on very generous terms. Gelon appears to have been a good as well as a great man. He was adored by the Syracusans, whose happiness he studied; and, on his death, which happened B. C. 471, they raised a magnificent mausoleum in honor of him. He was succeeded by his brother, Hiero, a man of a different character, who was actuated by jealousy of his own brother, Polyzelus. The latter fled to Theron, king of Agrigentum, and this led to a war between Hiero and Theron, which was ended by a general reconciliation. Hiero expelled the inhabitants of Catana and Naxos, and transplanted them to Leontini. In their stead he established a colony of Syracusans and Greeks. He died among these new colonists (B. C. 460), and left behind him two characters: one, that of a cruel tyrant—the other, that of a just and generous prince. He was skilled in music, and patronised literary men. He invited Simonides, Pindar, Æschylus, Bacchylides, and Epicharmus, to his court, who in return sang his praises.

Hiero was succeeded by his brother, Thrasybulus, a blood-thirsty tyrant, who was speedily driven out of Syracuse (B. C. 459). The city was then declared free, and a popular government was established, which lasted fifty-five years. But the republic was torn by the dissensions of those who aimed at power, and a system like that of the Athenian ostracism was introduced to remedy the evil, and expel the disturbers of the public peace. It was styled "petalism" (from the Greek word πεταλον, a leaf), because the citizens wrote on a leaf the name of the person whom they desired to banish. Meanwhile, Ducetius, prince of the Siculi, having taken Enna, and overcome the Agrigentines, threatened Syracuse. He defeated the forces of the latter, but was himself soon afterwards reduced to the necessity of suing for peace. The next important event in the history of Sicily is the war between the Syracusans and the Leontines, the cause of which is unknown, but it led to the interference of the Athenians in the affairs of the island. The Leontines, having been hard pressed by the Syracusans, applied to the Athenians for aid. The latter sent a fleet, under Lachetes and Chabrias, to their assistance, and committed great devastation. But the Leontines, fearing that the object of the Athenians was the conquest of the island, made peace with the Syracusans (B. C. 426).

Ten years afterwards a dispute arose between the inhabitants of the towns of Egesta and Selinus, concerning their boundary. They, of course, went to war; but the Egestines, getting the worst of it, applied to the Athenians for aid. The latter eagerly seized the pretext for invading Sicily, and sent Alcibiades, Nicias, and Lamachus, with a powerful force, and a commission to regulate affairs in Sicily. They reduced Catana, Naxos, and Hyccara, and advanced against Syracuse. The siege was undertaken, and it lasted three years. During this time the Spartans and Corinthians sent aid to the Syracusans. A number of battles were fought, generally to the disadvantage of the Athenians. In one of them their admiral, Eurymedon, was killed. Their generals, Nicias and Demosthenes, were several times defeated. They were both forced to surrender, together with all their troops and stores; and were whipped, and put to death (B. C. 413). The other prisoners were treated with the greatest barbarity during eight months, by which time nearly all of them perished.

The Egestines now called upon the Carthaginians to assist them. The latter agreed to do so, and sent Hannibal, the son of Gisco, and grandson of Hamilcar, to their aid with an immense army. The towns of Selinus and Himera were taken and destroyed, and the inhabitants were massacred. Hannibal then returned to Carthage, where he was received in great triumph. Meanwhile, great disturbances took place in Syracuse. Hermocrates, one of the popular leaders, having been expelled, raised an army, and attempted to surprise the city. But he was killed in the attempt, and all who had aided him were sentenced to perpetual banishment (B. C. 406). His son-in-law, Dionysius, who had been a clerk in a public office, procured the deposition of the successful party, and his own nomination to the chief command of the forces. Having thus raised himself, he secured the fidelity of his soldiers by paying them very liberally. He then deposed his colleagues, and usurped the whole power of the State.

The Carthaginians sent a second expedition into Sicily, under Hannibal (B. C. 406), and laid siege to Agrigentum. They lost numbers of men, among them Hannibal, by the plague. Hannibal's colleague, Imilco, the son of Hanno, assumed the command, and prosecuted the siege. Dionysius sent an army to the relief of the Agrigentines, and defeated the Carthaginians, reducing them to great straits; but Imilco intercepted the convoy of provisions to the besieged city, whereupon the inhabitants abandoned it, and retired to Gela, having held out eight months. Dionysius then concluded peace with the Carthaginians, they being allowed to retain the western part of the island as far as the river Halicus, while he took possession of Naxos, Catana, and Leontini.

In the year B. C. 470, Carthage was seriously endangered by an attack from the Mauretanians. Disputes with the Cyreneans took place respecting boundaries, but were settled by negotiation in a remarkable way. Two commissioners on each side met to decide the question; but the Cyrenean, having taken offence, proposed to the Carthaginian that the latter should either give up the boundary, or suffer themselves to be buried alive. To their surprise, the Carthaginian commissioners assented to this, were buried alive, and thus secured to their country a large extent of territory.

What is related of Hippocrates and Gelon?—What great victory did the latter achieve?—Who succeeded him?—What is said of Hiero?—Thrasybulus?—How long did the republic of Syracuse last?—What was petalism?—Who was Ducetius?—What was the next important event?—What occasioned the siege of Syracuse?—Relate the incidents of the war.—What did the Egestines do?—What resulted?—Who was Dionysius?—What was the result of Imilco's invasion?—What other events occurred?—What of the Carthaginian commissioners?

EGYPT.

Achoris assisted Evag′oras of Cyprus, with a fleet and money, against the Persians, and took Cha′brias, the Athenian, into his pay, with an army of Greek mercenaries. Psam′muthis succeeded Achoris (B. C. 376), but nothing is known of him, or of his successor, Nepherites.

Nectan′ebus I. established himself on the throne (B. C. 375), with the assistance of Chabrias, and founded the 30th, or Sebennytic, dynasty. He was immediately called upon to defend the country against the Persians, and their Greek auxiliaries under Iphic′rates, who, at the head of 200,000 men, marched into Egypt. Nectanebus made a gallant defence, but would have succumbed, had it not been for the dissensions between the enemy's commanders, and also the overflowing of the Nile, which opportunely took place. These two disasters broke up the enemy's plans, and caused them to retire. Egypt enjoyed peace during the remainder of this reign.

Teos, or Tachos, was the successor of Nectanebus (B. C. 363). He fitted out an expedition against the Persians, and appointed his brother-in-law, Nectanebus, to the chief command. But the heavy taxes which Teos imposed on the Egyptians caused them to revolt, and offer the crown to Nectanebus, who deposed his brother-in-law, and established himself on the throne. Teos fled to Persia, where he died.

Nectanebus II., with the aid of the Greeks, suppressed a revolt which broke out on his assuming the crown (B. C. 361), and remained at peace several years. At length (B. C. 350) the king of Persia, Dari′us Ochus, invaded Egypt with an immense army, and, principally through his Greek troops, subdued the country. Nectanebus fled into Ethiopia, and Egypt again formed part of the Persian empire. Thus ended the 30th dynasty of Egyptian kings.

Darius Ochus returned in triumph to Persia (B. C. 350), having first razed the walls of the principal towns of Egypt, and plundered the temples. Of the affairs of the country during the rest of his reign, and that of his successor, Darius Codoma′nus, but little is known. Meanwhile, Alexander the Great, having become master of Greece, turned his arms against Persia. A series of victories made him master of Asia Minor and Syria, and when he reached Pelu′sium, on the frontiers of Egypt, Maza′ces, the Persian satrap, did not attempt to oppose his progress. The Egyptians welcomed Alexander as a deliverer from the Persians, and that politic monarch did his utmost to conciliate them. Having visited Memphis (B. C. 332), he returned and founded Alexandria, at the mouth of the Nile. About the same time he visited the temple of Jupiter Ammon, in the desert of Libya, and was saluted by the priests as the son of that god. He appointed Doloaspis, an Egyptian, governor of all Egypt, and, leaving a small body of troops behind, rejoined his fleet at Tyre. Alexander never again visited Egypt, but his corpse was brought thither from Babylon, and deposited at Alexandria in a sarcophagus (B. C. 322).

On his death (B. C. 323), a contest took place amongst his principal generals for his vast empire. Ptolemy (surnamed Soter, or the saver, the son of Lagus,) secured Egypt for himself, and fixed his dynasty firmly there. Perdiccas, regent of the empire for Alexander's half-brother, Philip Aridæus, attempted to reduce Ptolemy to submission, but his army, wearied by the long siege of Pelusium, conspired against him, and murdered him in his tent (B. C. 321).

Antig′onus having established himself in Asia Minor, sent his celebrated son, Demetrius Poliorcetes, against Ptolemy, but the latter defeated him at Gaza, and made himself master of Palestine and Phœnicia (B. C. 312). He took Jerusalem by attacking it on the Sabbath. From Palestine he transplanted many thousand Jews to Alexandria and Cyrene, where they settled, encouraged in their industry, and protected in the exercise of their religion, by the enlightened ruler of Egypt. Next year, however, Antigonus retrieved his disasters, and Ptolemy was forced to resign Phœnicia to him. A short peace followed. Three years afterwards (B. C. 308), Antigonus renewed the war, and sent his son Demetrius with a fleet to Cyprus, where he completely defeated the Egyptian fleet, and wrested the island from Ptolemy, who, in revenge, sent aid to Rhodes, then (B. C. 305) besieged by Demetrius, and forced the latter to raise the siege. For this service the Rhodians gave him the title of Soter (saver). Ptolemy joined the grand confederacy against Antigonus; and, after the latter's death (B. C. 301), he was fully recognized as monarch of Egypt, Syria, and Palestine.

What were the acts of Achoris?—Psammuthis?—Nepherites?—Nectanebus I.?—Teos?—Nectanebus II.?—Darius Ochus?—What did Alexander the Great do in Egypt?—What title was conferred on him?—Which of his generals obtained Egypt for his share?—What wars did Ptolemy wage?—Why was he called "Soter"?

SYRIA.

From the administration of Nehemiah to the time of Alexander the Great, there is scarcely any memorable transaction in the annals of Judea. Joi′ada (or Judas) was succeeded in the high-priesthood by Jonathan I. (B. C. 397). The latter, jealous of the influence of his brother, Jesus, with Bagoses, the Persian governor, murdered him within the precincts of the sanctuary (B. C. 366), for which the whole people were heavily fined by Bagoses. Jonathan was succeeded (B. C. 350) by Jad′dua, who held the high-priesthood for 26 years.

The peace of Syria was at length interrupted by Alexander the Great (B. C. 333), king of Macedon, who, following up his victories over the Persians, laid siege to Damascus and Tyre. Damascus was soon taken, but Tyre offered an obstinate resistance of seven months. It was at length captured and sacked; and, after this, it never regained its former consequence. Its commerce was, for the most part, transferred to Alexandria. But it recovered sufficiently to be a strong fortress and flourishing port under the early Roman emperors. It was one of the last places held by the Christians during the crusades. The Saracens and Turks completed its ruin, and it is now a poor village. Such was the fate of one of the proudest cities of antiquity. Its destruction was foretold by Isaiah (ch. xxiii.), but the period named by him (70 years), for the occurrence of the event, must not be understood in a literal sense.

After the destruction of Tyre, Alexander marched against Gaza, which he also destroyed. On his way he sent to demand the surrender of Jerusalem. The Jews at first refused, but, on his advancing against the city, Jaddua went forth in his robes, with the priests in their ceremonial attire, and the people in white garments, to meet him and make submission. It is related that, on seeing them, Alexander fell prostrate, and adored the Holy Name, saying that he had previously seen the figure of the high-priest in a vision. But this story is of doubtful authenticity.

Alexander appointed Andromachus commander in Samaria; but some of the inhabitants of that district having rebelled, he ordered the whole people to be expelled, and he planted a Macedonian colony in their room. The Samaritans retreated to Shechem, whence they are called, in Ecclesiasticus, "the foolish people that dwell in Shechem."

Alexander is said to have transplanted 100,000 Jews to his new colony in Egypt (B. C. 331), and to have bestowed on them equal privileges and immunities with the Macedonians. On his death (B. C. 333), Judea came into the possession of Laom′edon, one of his generals. Antig′onus, who had made himself master of Asia Minor, coveted possession of Syria, Palestine, and Egypt, in which latter country, Ptolemy Soter, king of Egypt, had previously established himself. But after the death of Perdiccas (the regent of the Macedonian empire), Antigonus sent his son, Demetrius Poliorcetes, to subdue these countries. Demetrius partly succeeded at first, but was at length defeated by Ptolemy at Gaza (B. C. 312), and his career was stopped.

Ptolemy attempted to seize the whole of Syria. He advanced against Jerusalem, where Onias I. was high-priest (he having succeeded Jaddua, B. C. 324), and assaulted it on the Sabbath, knowing that the Jews would not violate the holy day, even in self-defence. The city fell without resistance (B. C. 320), and Ptolemy carried away a vast number of captives, whom he settled chiefly in Alexandria and Cyrene; but he also endeavored, by kindness and liberality, to attach the Jews to his cause. He enrolled an army of 30,000 of them, and entrusted the chief garrisons of the country to their care. Jerusalem, after its capture by Ptolemy Lagus, in B. C. 320, remained subject to the Greek kings of Egypt until the conquest of Palestine by Antiochus the Great (B. C. 198).

Syria and Judea did not escape the anarchy which ensued in the destructive warfare waged by the generals and successors of Alexander. Twice these provinces fell into the power of Antigonus, and twice were regained by Ptolemy, to whose share Cœle-Syria and Judea were allotted, on the partition of the empire, after the decisive defeat of Antigonus at Ipsus (B. C. 301). The rest of Syria fell to the share of Seleucus. The maritime towns, Tyre, Joppa, and Gaza, were the chief points of contention between the rival generals, but Jerusalem seems to have escaped the horrors of war. During this troubled period, Onias, the high-priest, administered public affairs. After presiding 21 years, he was succeeded (B. C. 300) by Simon the Just, whom Jewish tradition has endeared to that people.

What events occurred between the time of Nehemiah and that of Alexander the Great?—What was the fate of Damascus?—Tyre?—Jerusalem?—Samaria?—The Jews?—Which of the generals obtained Judea?—How did Ptolemy get possession of Jerusalem?—How did he treat the Jews?—What befell Syria?—What is said of Onias?—Simon the Just?

INDIA.

In this century Hindoo civilization had reached an advanced stage. The country was traversed by excellent roads, furnished with mile-stones and houses of refreshment. It was divided into three large kingdoms, besides a great number of petty States. The chief kingdom was that of the Prasii, whose capital was Palibo′thra (now Patna), and extended over the vast plain of the Ganges. The other two occupied the Punjab. In the Deccan, there were a variety of kingdoms. Such was the state of India when Alexander the Great, of Macedon, invaded it. Having previously subdued the adjoining countries, Persia and Bactria, Alexander advanced with his victorious Greeks to the Indus (B. C. 327), and invaded the Hindoo kingdom of the Punjab then governed by a monarch named Porus. He also threatened the neighboring kingdom, ruled by a prince whom the Greeks call Tax′iles. Porus encountered Alexander on the banks of the Hydaspes, where he was defeated, wounded, and taken prisoner. He conducted himself with so much dignity as to win the esteem of Alexander, who restored to him his liberty and kingdom, and aided him to conquer some smaller states and annex them to his dominions. Alexander made no permanent conquests in India, but built a fort at Pattala, or Tatta, which became a great trading mart. He went as far as the river Hyph′asis, where his soldiers murmured at the distance to which he was leading them. There he erected twelve massy altars as a memorial of his expedition, and then returned to Candahar. He sailed down the Indus to the ocean, and sent his admiral, Near′chus, back with the ships up the Persian Gulf. Nearchus set out on the 21st of September, B. C. 326, and arrived at Susa in safety in February, B. C. 325. He wrote an account of his voyage, the substance of which has been preserved by Arrian, the historian, in his work on India. Nearchus was a native of Crete, and an intimate friend of Alexander. For his services in conducting the fleet in safety to Persia, he was rewarded with a crown of gold, and, after Alexander's death, received the government of Lycia and Pamphylia, under Antigonus. He also sent Onesic′ritus of Egina, who had been chief pilot of his fleet, to explore India. Onesicritus visited a large portion of it, and is supposed to have reached Ceylon: he wrote an account of his travels, but so mixed up fiction with facts, as to destroy the credibility of his narrative. On the death of Alexander (B. C. 323) one of his generals, Seleucus Nicator, possessed himself of Bactria, and is believed to have extended his rule over the kingdom of Cabul, and what are now the Sikh States. He sent Megasthenes as ambassador to Sandracottus (or Chandragupta), the descendant of Nanda, who reigned about the close of the 5th century, and the successor of Porus, at Patna. From this time to the invasion of the Arabs, little is known of the history of India. Buddhism supplanted the religion of the Brahmins in many parts, and extended itself all over the Peninsula. We also find that trade was carried on with Egypt and Rome.

What was the state of India at this period? — What did Alexander the Great do? — Who was Porus? — Taxiles? — Nearchus? — Onesicritus? — What occurred on Alexander's death? — Who was Sandracottus? — What else is said of India?

PERSIA.

The weak-minded Artaxerxes was a mere puppet in the hands of his mother Parysa′tis, whose inveterate hatred of Queen Stati′ra, and of all whom she suspected of contributing to the downfall of her favorite son, Cyrus, filled the palace with murders and treason. The Spartans, taking advantage of this state of things, sent Dercyl′lidas to attack the Persians in Asia Minor (B. C. 399). Under him and Agesila′us of Sparta, they carried their victorious arms into Caria, Phrygia, and Paphlagonia. The satrap Tissaphernes, who had unsuccessfully opposed them, was put to death; and his successor, Tithraustes, then resorted to the expedient of bribing the other States of Greece to combine against Sparta, — a combination which compelled Agesilaus to return to Greece (B. C. 394). The Persians under Pharnaba′zus, co-operating with Conon, the Athenian, reduced the power of Sparta at sea. The last-named State at length sent Antal′cidas to make peace with Artaxerxes. By the treaty which he made, the Grecian States in Asia Minor, and Cyprus, were abandoned to the Persian monarch (B. C. 387). The Greek cities also submitted to him; but Evag′oras, king of Cyprus, was not subdued until after a very gallant resistance (B. C. 376). He was allowed to remain ruler of the town of Salamis, in that island, on payment of tribute.

Artaxerxes next endeavored (B. C. 384) to subdue the Cadusians, who, under their heroic prince, Dat′ames, successfully resisted him; which so enraged the king that he caused Datames to be murdered.

In Egypt, Nectan′ebis I. having, with the aid of Cha′brias the Athenian, established himself on the throne, Artaxerxes sent a powerful army of Persians and Greek mercenaries against him (B. C. 375); but owing to a sudden overflow of the Nile, and to the dissensions of the Grecian and Persian commanders, the expedition returned without accomplishing the subjection of Egypt.

The domestic calamities of Artaxerxes were more afflicting than his misfortunes abroad. He was obliged to put his eldest son, Dari′us, to death for conspiring against him. His youngest son, Ochus, murdered the second son in order to secure the succession to the crown. After losing two sons in this dreadful manner, Artaxerxes died of a broken heart. Ochus then usurped the crown (B. C. 359), and took the name of Artaxerxes III. To secure himself on the throne, he put to death 80 of the royal family. Although a cruel tyrant, he was conspicuous for his military talents. Artaba′zus, satrap of Asia Minor, aided by the Athenians and the Thebans, sought to dethrone him; but Ochus succeeded in suppressing the revolt (B. C. 355–353), and also a revolt in Cyprus (B. C. 351). He then marched into Egypt, which speedily submitted to him, and was reunited to the Persian empire (B. C. 350). Ochus, at the solicitation of the Athenians, sent them assistance against Philip, king of Macedon (B. C. 340). His cruelties at length induced his chief minister, Bago′as, to poison him (B. C. 338), and place Arses, Ochus's youngest son, on the throne.

The Greek States now declared war against Persia (B. C. 337), and appointed Philip of Macedon their general; but Philip having been assassinated, the meditated expedition against Persia was deferred. Arses was murdered by Bagoas (B. C. 336), who transferred the crown of Persia to Darius Codom′anus, a descendant of Darius Nothus. The new king speedily put Bagoas to death. But the hour for the destruction of the Persian empire was at hand. Alexander the Great, crossing the Hellespont (B. C. 334) marched into Asia Minor, subdued Caria, and took the city of Halicarnassus. Darius mustered all his forces to oppose him, but was totally routed on the banks of the Grani′cus. Alexander then subdued Lycia and Syria, took Damascus, besieged Tyre, and defeated Darius at the battle of Issus, taking prisoners that monarch's family (B. C. 333). After the fall of Tyre (B. C. 332), Phœnicia, Palestine, and Egypt submitted to Alexander almost without a struggle. Leaving Egypt, Alexander crossed the Euphrates (B. C. 331), entered Persia, routed Darius's army at Gaugame′la, and pursued him 50 miles, as far as Arbela, took Babylon, Susa, and Persep′olis, and thus extinguished the second ancient Persian empire.

Darius sought refuge in a remote part of Bactriana, where he was perfidiously murdered by the governor, Bessus (B. C. 330), who was afterwards punished by Alexander for the crime. Darius was a gentle prince, and merited a better fate. Alexander speedily subdued the eastern provinces of the empire, and carried his arms into India (B. C. 330–324). He married Roxa′na, the daughter of Oxyartes, prince of Bactria, and returned to Babylon, where he died (B. C. 323).

On his death his vast empire was divided amongst his generals. Syria and Phœnicia were given to Laom′edon; one of the Medias was allotted to Atrop′ates; and the other to Perdiccas; Persia was assigned to Peucestes; Babylonia to Archon; Mesopotamia to Arces′ilas; Parthia and Hyrcania to Phrataphernes; Bactria and Sogdiana to Philip; Lycia, Pamphylia, and the greater Phrygia to Antig′onus; Caria to Cassander; Lydia to Menan′der; the lesser Phrygia to Leona′tus; Armenia to Neoptol′emus; and Cappadocia and Paphlagonia to Eu′menes. In this manner was the Persian empire partitioned. Seleucus, the son of Antiochus, was placed at the head of the cavalry of the allies, and Cassander, the son of Antip′ater, commanded the guards.

Philip Arrhidæus (or Aridæus), the imbecile half-brother of Alexander, was placed on the throne of Macedon, and Perdiccas was appointed regent. But the generals aimed at forming independent sovereignties of the several provinces thus allotted to them, and a series of conspiracies and wars ensued between them, which soon ended in the breaking up of the empire. Antigonus expelled Peucestes and Seleucus. The latter fled into Egypt, but soon returned to Babylon, where he was welcomed. In the year 312 he totally routed Antigonus, and re-established his own empire. From this year dates the Era of the Seleu′cidæ. After the battle of Ipsus (B. C. 301) Seleucus was acknowledged monarch of Upper Asia.

What effect had the influence of Parysatis? — What was the fate of Tissaphernes? — And of the Spartan expedition? — What was the treaty of Antalcidas? — What is said of Evagoras? — What other wars did Artaxerxes undertake? — What were his domestic troubles? — What were the acts of Ochus (Artaxerxes III.)? — What was his end and that of Arses? — What were the principal events of the reign of Darius Codomanus? — What befel Persia after the death of Alexander?

CHINA. JAPAN.

Gan-wang reigned from B. C. 401 to 375. Under Lee-wang, his successor, the celebrated philosopher, Meng-tsze (Mencius), was born,—a man who, in the estimation of the Chinese, ranks next to Confucius. He was a disciple of Tsze-sze, the grandson of Confucius, and taught the doctrine of the original and still subsisting goodness of human nature, and that self-interest was the root of all evil. His works form part of the four classics of China, and are held in high esteem for beauty of diction and strength of sentiment, according to the Chinese standard of excellence. Heen-wang ascended the throne B. C. 368, with the mere title of sovereign, and if the vassals had not been constantly engaged in mutual wars, he might have lost even this. Chin-tsing-wang, who came next (B. C. 320), saw with despair the growing power of the State of Tsin, which had rendered the other States tributary, but he was too indolent to attempt to remedy the evil. Nan-wang succeeded his father B. C. 314, and looked around for help against the overpowering influence of Tsin, but saw himself forsaken by almost all the princes. Chaou-seang, king of Tsin, an able warrior, then announced to the world that he was about to claim the imperial crown for himself. The prince of Tse alone disputed with him the palm of victory, but was speedily subdued. The emperor now invoked the aid of the other princes, who, however, could scarcely help themselves, and were therefore unable to assist him. As soon as the prince of Tsin was informed of the emperor's proceedings, he invaded the imperial territories. Nothing then remained for Nan-wang but to sue for an ignominious peace, at the same time offering his cities and soldiers to the conqueror, and engaging to pay tribute to him. Chaou-seang accepted the offer, and sent the emperor back to his own country, where he died unregretted and unknown, leaving no heirs. Chaou-seang immediately took possession of the imperial domains, and thus became the founder of the Tsin dynasty. He at once proceeded to compel obedience from the rest of the States.

Japan.—Koan, whom we have before mentioned, reigned from the year B. C. 392 to B. C. 290, upwards of 100 years. But the Japanese annals are singularly barren of events, and but little more is recorded of this emperor.

What were the principal events of this century?—What is said of Meng-tsze?—Who was the founder of the Tsin dynasty?—What is said of Japan?

GREECE.

At the commencement of this century Sparta was the predominating State in Greece. The glory of Athens was rapidly declining, through the increasing luxury and corruption of the people. One of the most disgraceful acts of the popular party was (as we have seen in the previous century) the persecution and death of Socrates (B. C. 399) on account of his religious teachings, which were opposed to the idolatry and superstition of the Greeks. Henceforth the commonwealth of Athens plays but a subordinate part in the history of Greece; but the city was the seat of learning and the arts, and continued to be so for many centuries, even throughout the most glorious days of Rome. We therefore turn to Sparta, as the State on which the thread of Grecian history now hangs.

The kings of Sparta, Pausa′nias and Agis II., vigorously followed up the war in Asia Minor against the Persians. At the same time they attacked the State of Elis and reduced it to subjection (B. C. 399). Their generals, Thymbron and Dercyllidas, attacked Pharnaba′zus and Tissaphernes, the Persian satraps, but without much success. But on the death of Agis, Lysander induced the people to elect as king Agesila′us II., the half-brother of the deceased king, in the place of the rightful heir, his nephew Leotych′ides; and under the auspices of this celebrated man, the war in Asia was pushed vigorously for three years (B. C. 396–5–4). Agesilaus was meditating an advance into the heart of Persia, when he was recalled to defend his country against a confederation of the Grecian States, which had been organized through the influence of the gold of Artaxerxes, king of Persia. In the first battle (that of Haliartus, B. C. 395), Lysander was slain. Agesilaus was victorious at Corone′a, in which battle Xen′ophon, the famous soldier and historian, fought against Athens, his native State. In revenge, Conon, the Athenian admiral, defeated the Spartan fleet under Pisan′der, at Cnidos (B. C. 394). The war was carried on for some years with varied success. In 390 the Persians changed sides, and for a time espoused the cause of the Spartans. The Athenians then sent aid to Evag′oras of Cyprus, and succeeded in humbling the foes of both. The Spartans sued for peace; and their envoy, Antalcidas, concluded a treaty whereby all the Grecian colonies in Asia were ceded to Artaxerxes, who allowed the Athenians to retain Scyros, Lemnos, and Imbros (B. C. 387). This disgraceful treaty enabled the Spartans to hold their supremacy in Greece. Agesilaus drove the Thebans out of Platæa, while his colleague, Agesip′olis, who had succeeded Pausanias, gained possession of Mantinea after a severe battle (B. C. 385), in which the two famous Thebans, Pelop′idas and Epaminon′das, were wounded.

In B. C. 382 commenced what is called "The Olynthian War," from Olynthus, a town in Macedonia, of which the Spartans tried to gain possession. It lasted four years, and ended by the submission of the city to the Spartan general, Polybi′ades. But the chief interest in Grecian history now centres in Thebes, whose citadel had been perfidiously seized by the Spartans (B. C. 382), and was recovered by the Theban exiles (B. C. 379). This led to a war between Thebes and Sparta, in which the former not only regained its independence, but forever destroyed the supremacy of the latter. Thebes became for a few years the leading power in Greece, owing mainly to the abilities of Epaminondas and Pelopidas. The Spartan kings, Cleom′brotus and Agesila′us II., invaded Bœo′tia: they also made an attack upon Attica. The Thebans and Athenians united against them. The former organized their famous "Sacred Band" of heroes while the Athenians improved their fleet. This famous war was distinguished by a series of battles both by sea and land, in which the leading actors were the Spartan kings Cleombrotus and Agesilaus, the Theban chiefs Pelopidas and Epaminondas, and the Athenian commanders Cha′brias, Pho′cion, Iphic′rates, Timo′theus, and Callis′tratus. The Spartan fleet was totally destroyed off Naxos by Chabrias (B. C. 376); and at Corcyra by Timotheus (B. C. 374). Their army was defeated by the Thebans at Teg′yra (B. C. 375), and Cleombrotus was killed at the battle of Leuctra (B. C. 371). Jealous of Thebes, the Athenians made peace with Sparta (B. C. 369), but the Thebans carried the war into the Peloponnesus, which was the scene of intestine strife. Archid′amus the Spartan defeated the Arcadians and Argives in a battle called "the tearless", because he won it without losing a man (B. C. 367). Arcadia and Elis were fighting each other; and in this manner all the States of Greece were hastening to decay. For the next few years after the fatal battle of Leuctra, Sparta had to struggle for her existence amid dangers without and within, and it was chiefly owing to the skill, courage, and presence of mind of Agesilaus, that she survived the many shocks she received. In the year B. C. 361, he crossed over into Egypt with a body of Spartan mercenaries: there he displayed his ancient skill and valor, although 80 years of age. He died B. C. 360, and his body was embalmed in wax, and sent over to Sparta, where it was interred with great splendor. The Thebans were ravaging the north of the Peloponnesus, while the Spartans were warring in the centre and south. The former also attacked Alexander of Pheræ, the tyrant of Thessaly, who had treacherously imprisoned Pelopidas. Released by Epaminondas, Pelopidas marched against Alexander, but was defeated and slain at Cynosceph′alæ (B. C. 364). Epaminondas fell at the battle of Mantinea soon after (B. C. 362), and after his death the power of Thebes rapidly declined. A general peace now ensued, probably on account of the exhaustion of all parties.

At this period the power of Macedon rapidly rose, soon to overshadow and absorb all Greece and great part of Asia. In the year B. C. 359, Philip ascended the throne, and began a vigorous system of government. His career was rapid. In the first year of his reign he made peace with the Athenians, and defeated the Pœonians and Illyrians. In the next he took Amphip′olis. Meanwhile the Athenian colonies of Eubœa, Chios, Rhodes, and Byzantium revolted, and what is termed "The Social War" commenced. At the same time the Phocians seized Delphi, and this brought on the before-mentioned "Sacred War" with the Thebans. Thus the discord among the States paved the way for their conquest by Philip. In 356 he took Potidæa; in 353 he seized Peg′asa and laid siege to Metho′ne. Next year he overcame the tyrant of Pheræ, and marched towards Southern Greece. His progress was for a time stopped by the Athenians at Thermopylæ, where, 128 years before, Leonidas had resisted the Persians. Roused by the eloquence of Demos′thenes, the Athenians sent aid to the Olynthians, who were attacked by Philip; but the star of the latter was in the ascendant. Olynthus fell; Eubœa was conquered by Philip, who at the same time put an end to "The Sacred War" by the conquest

What was the relative position of Athens and Sparta at the beginning of this century?—What were the principal events of the Persian war?—What is said of Agesilaus II.?—Antalcidas's treaty?—The Olynthian war?—The Theban war?—Pelopidas and Epaminondas?—The "Sacred Band"?—What heroes took part in the war?—Which were the principal events?—What was the fate of Pelopidas?—Of Epaminondas?—Relate the career of Philip of Macedon.

of Phocis. Having made peace with Athens, Philip was placed at the head of the Amphyctionic Council. By intrigues he sought to subvert Sparta and Athens. He succeeded as regards the former, but the latter was roused to action by the orations of Demosthenes. Aided by the Persians, the Athenians for a time resisted him; but at the fatal battle of Cheronæ'a (B. C. 338), wherein Demosthenes shamefully ran away, their strength was entirely broken. Philip was now virtually master of Greece. The States, in an assembly at Corinth, declared war against Persia, and appointed Philip their general; but at this juncture his career was cut short by a noble Macedonian youth named Pausanias, who, out of private resentment, assassinated him at a festival at Ægæ (B. C. 336), in honor of the nuptials of his (Philip's) daughter with Alexander of Epirus. Pausanias stabbed him as he was walking in the procession. The assassin was pursued and slain by the royal guards. Philip's wife, Olympias, and his son, Alexander, were, however, suspected of being concerned in the plot. Philip was succeeded by his son, ALEXANDER, afterwards surnamed "the Great".

The career of this extraordinary man is one of the most remarkable in history. In early youth he gave evidence of his daring and powerful spirit. On one occasion Philomius, the Thessalian, offered a very vicious horse named Buceph'alus (or Bucephalas) to King Philip for 13 talents (equal to about $14,300); but the king was unwilling to purchase it. Alexander, though quite a youth, undertook, for the wager of the price of the horse, to manage it, and succeeded in doing so, in the presence of the Court. When he had done it, Philip kissed him, saying: "Seek a greater empire; Macedonia is too small for thee." These were prophetic words. He ascended the throne at the age of 20, surrounded by enemies. But he put down rebellion in his own kingdom, and then completed the conquest of Greece. He was elected to the command of the expedition against Persia, by the assembled States. He first marched against the barbarians north of Mount Hæmus, defeated and subdued them as far north as the Danube, and returned by rapid marches to suppress a revolt in Thebes. He destroyed all the buildings in that city, with the exception of the house of the poet Pindar, and killed or sold into slavery all the inhabitants (B. C. 335).

Alexander then (B. C. 334) crossed the Hellespont with 35,000 men. He encountered the Persians at the river Grani'cus, and routed them. The cities on the western coast of Asia Minor surrendered to him, one after another, with the exception of Halicarnassus, which was taken by assault. He then marched through Lycia and Pamphylia, and thence into Phrygia. At Gordium, the capital of that country, he cut the celebrated Gordian knot; the legend whereof is given at page 73, in the column devoted to Asia Minor.. No one had been able to untie this knot, but when Alexander saw it, he drew his sword and cut it, and thus solved the prophecy in his own way. In B. C. 333 he marched into Cilicia. The Persian king, Darius, who was at the head of a vast army, met him on the plain of Issus. In this memorable battle Darius was utterly routed. Alexander then subdued Syria, and laid siege to Tyre. That memorable siege occupied him seven months; and that of Gaza, which followed, two. He next marched into Egypt, where, in the beginning of the year B. C. 331, he founded the famous city of Alexandria. He then set out to meet Darius, who had assembled another enormous army. Marching through Mesopotamia, he reached the plains of Gaugame'la, where, in October, B. C. 331, he completely routed the Persians. The whole of the family of Darius fell into his hands, but he treated them with the greatest kindness. He pursued the enemy to Arbe'la, a distance of 50 miles, and thence to Susa, Babylon, and Persep'olis, all of which cities surrendered to him. At the latter he set fire to the palace, at the instigation of Thaïs, an Athenian courtesan. Thence he marched into Media in pursuit of Darius, who fled into Bactria, where he was treacherously murdered by Bessus, the satrap of that country. Alexander sent the body of Darius for honorable interment at Persepolis, and pursued Bessus into Sogdiana, where the rebel was put to death. From the Oxus, Alexander marched to the Iaxartes (Sir), and subdued several Scythian tribes north of that river. In the year B. C. 328, he undertook the conquest of Sogdiana, which he completed in two years. There he married Roxa'na, the daughter of Oxyar'tes, the Bactrian prince. In the spring of B. C. 327 he marched into India, defeated the Indian king Porus, and founded the cities of Buceph'ala and Nicæ'a. He advanced as far as the Garra, when his soldiers refused to go further, and he was obliged to return. On his way back he was severely wounded in a battle with the Malli. He founded a city at Patt'ala on the Indus, and there established vast numbers of his Macedonian followers as colonists. He made the Euphrates and Tigris navigable, and fixed his Court at Babylon. There he died of fever brought on by drinking wine, B. C. 323, at the age of 32. This celebrated man by his conquests contributed greatly to the spread of knowledge and civilization; but he was guilty of great excesses and occasional cruelty when under the influence of wine, as, for instance, in putting to death his friend Parme'nio, with his son Philo'tas; and in killing with his own hand Clitus, another of his friends, at a banquet. He left a son, Alexander Ægus, by his wife Roxana; but his half-brother, Philip Aridæ'us, was elected king of Macedonia, Alexander being associated with him. PERDICCAS, one of the deceased monarch's principal generals, was appointed regent; and as Philip was imbecile and Alexander an infant, he assumed the supreme power. MELE'AGER, another of Alexander's generals, resisted the claims of Perdiccas, and was for a time associated with him in the regency; but was shortly after assassinated by his orders. The other generals of Alexander, viz., ANTIP'ATER, governor of Macedon, CRAT'ERUS, governor of Greece, PTOLEMY, governor of Egypt, and ANTIG'ONUS, governor of Western Asia, also combined against Perdiccas. EU'MENES, who had been private secretary to Philip and Alexander, and was now governor of Cappadocia, Paphlagonia, and Pontus, espoused the cause of Perdiccas; and while the latter marched against Ptolemy, he attacked Antipater and Craterus. Craterus was defeated and slain (B. C. 321), but Perdiccas was routed at Pelusium, whereupon his troops rose in mutiny and slew him in his tent.

The Greeks, excited by the eloquence of Demosthenes, attempted to regain their liberty about this time. Har'palus, the treasurer of Alexander the Great, had fled from Babylon with the money intrusted to him, and the gold was freely distributed among the Athenians. On Alexander's death they rose in arms, and besieged Antipater in La'mia, whence it was called "The Lamian War"; but they were vanquished by him at the battle of Cranon, in B. C. 322. Demosthenes fled to Calauria, where he put an end to his life by poison. Thus ended the struggle. On the death of Perdiccas, Antipater became supreme regent. The remainder of his regency was occupied in an unsuccessful attempt to subdue Eumenes. He died B. C. 318, bequeathing the regency to Polysperchon, one of Alexander's generals. His own son, CASSAN'DER, rebelled at this arrangement, and a war ensued, in which Polysperchon was ultimately overcome (B. C. 316), and Cassander became master of Macedonia. The latter put to death OLYM'PIAS, the mother of Alexander the Great, and the instigator of the murder of Philip Aridæus. He also formed a league with Ptolemy, governor of Egypt, LYSIM'ACHUS, governor of Thrace, and SELEUCUS, governor of Babylonia, against Antigonus, governor of Western Asia. The war which followed was signalized by a variety of reverses. Eumenes had previously been taken and put to death (B. C. 316) by Antigonus. Seleucus fled into Egypt, but with the aid of Ptolemy regained Babylon (B. C. 312).

In Athens, Polysperchon had surrendered PHO'CION to the people, who cruelly put him to death (B. C. 318). This distinguished man deserves more than a passing notice. He was a pupil of Plato and Xenoc'rates, and distinguished himself at Naxos under Chabrias, and in the war between Philip and the Athenians. He recommended peace with the Macedonian king, and rebuked Demosthenes for his invectives against Alexander. The latter cultivated Phocion's friendship, who, however, refused to receive the king's presents, begging him "to leave him no less honest than he found him." He perished at the age of 85, and a brazen statue was erected to his memory by the Athenians. Cassander, having taken Athens, appointed DEMETRIUS PHALEREUS, a celebrated orator and statesman, its governor (B. C. 318). Demetrius governed with great popularity for about ten years, when he gave himself up to dissipation, and was driven out by DEMETRIUS (surnamed Poliorcetes, or "the besieger of cities"), the son of Antigonus. Cassander, still claiming Athens as his own, endeavored to wrest it from Demetrius, but was repulsed (B. C. 303). The political aspect of

What is said of Demosthenes?—The fall of Greece?—The death of Philip?—The youth of Alexander the Great?—Of Bucephalus?—The revolt of Thebes?—The battle of the Granicus?—The Gordian knot?—The battles of Issus and Arbela?—The fate of Darius?—The marriage of Alexander?

What is said of Alexander's exploits, death, and character?—Who succeeded him?—What is said of Perdiccas?—Meleager?—Antipater?—Craterus?—Ptolemy?—The Lamian war?—The battle of Cranon?—Demosthenes?—Polysperchon?—Olympias?—Philip Aridæus?—Eumenes?—Phocion?—Demetrius Phalereus?—Demetrius Poliorcetes?—The battle of Ipsus?

the Macedonian empire was, however, materially changed by the celebrated battle of Ipsus, in Phrygia, where the decisive contest took place between Alexander's generals for the succession to his empire (B. C. 301). In this battle Lysimachus and Seleucus defeated Antigonus and his son Demetrius. Antigonus was slain, and the victorious allies then agreed to partition the great emperor's dominions among themselves in independent kingdoms. Cassander became king of Macedon, Greece, and Cilicia; Lysimachus, king of Thrace and the north of Asia Minor; Ptolemy, king of Egypt; and Seleucus, the rest of Asia Minor, the whole of Syria, Persia, Bactria, and Sogdiana. This last was the largest and most powerful kingdom. Demetrius obtained Cilicia by marrying his daughter Stratoni′ce to Seleucus (B. C. 300); and thus the great Alexander's empire fell to pieces in little more than 20 years after his death.

This century, though it produced some of the greatest minds of ancient Greece, shows a falling off from the previous one. In the world of philosophy, the names of PLATO, ARISTOT′LE, and EPICU′RUS stand forth pre-eminent; as do those of DEMOSTHENES and ÆS′CHINES in oratory; APELLES in painting; CTE′SIAS in history; and EUCLID in mathematics.

PLATO was born at Athens in B. C. 428. He received the best education of the times, and when 20 years old became a pupil of Socrates. He then travelled extensively. In B. C. 389 he visited Sicily. On his return to Athens he taught and gave lectures at the Academy and its avenues. He received private pupils at his house, over the door of which was the inscription: "Let no one ignorant of geometry enter." In 360 Plato went to Sicily to try to reconcile the disputes between Dionysius and Dion. He was unsuccessful in this attempt, and returned to Athens, where he resumed his teaching and writing. He died in the 82d year of his age, B. C. 347. His writings have come down to us complete. They are models of elegance and acuteness, and are composed mostly in the form of dialogue. They embrace a variety of subjects, such as politics, morals, religion, and philosophy. His views were very elevated and pure. He believed in the immortality of the soul, and in the power of the Love of Wisdom to bring the human soul into communion with the Divine Being. He was the worthy pupil of his great master, Socrates.

ARISTOTELES (commonly called ARISTOTLE) was born at Stagira in Macedonia, B. C. 384. His father was physician to King Amyntas II.; hence Aristotle derived his knowledge of medicine. In B. C. 367 he went to Athens and became a pupil of Plato, who highly esteemed him, and named him "the intellect of the school". On the death of Plato, Aristotle left Athens. In 342 he was appointed by Philip of Macedon tutor to the young prince Alexander (afterwards "the Great"). He filled this situation for four years, and to him Alexander was indebted for many grand ideas. In 335 he returned to Athens, and gave lectures in theology, physics, and philosophy, while *walking up and down*, whence his school was called *The Peripatetic.* It became the most celebrated school in Athens; and he presided over it for 13 years, during which time he composed the greater part of his works. On the death of Alexander, he was looked upon with suspicion by the Athenians, and he was accused of impiety. He fled to Chalcis in Eubœa, where he died B. C. 322. He was buried with great honors at Stagira, his native city. His works are very numerous, and for nearly 2000 years were regarded as the standard of philosophy. He wrote on dialectics and logic, on theoretical philosophy, physics, metaphysics, mathematics, meteorology, and natural history; on politics and ethics; on art and poetry; and on rhetoric.

EPICURUS was born at Samos B. C. 342. He studied under Xenocrates at Athens; taught philosophy for five years at Mitylene; but finally settled at Athens B.C. 306, surrounded by numerous friends and pupils. He died B. C. 270, aged 72. He taught that true pleasure was not momentary, but pure and lasting, consisting of mental enjoyments and freedom from pain and disturbance of the mind; and that it was the highest good. That our knowledge of things was obtained by means of images of them reflected through our senses into our minds, and that we obtained our knowledge of the gods in like manner. Also, that as the gods were perfectly happy, they did not trouble themselves much about the world. Hence he was accused of atheism. His sect flourished long.

PYRRHO, the founder of the skeptical school of philosophy, also flourished at the time of Alexander the Great, but we know not the year of his birth or of his death. He asserted that *certain* knowledge on any subject was unattainable, and that the great object ought to be to lead a virtuous life. His philosophical system was reduced to writing by his disciple, TIMON of Athens, the satirist.

DEMOSTHENES, the most celebrated orator of antiquity, has been already noticed. He was a native of Attica, and was born B. C. 385. He received instruction from the orator Isæ′us; some say he was taught by Plato and Isocrates. He labored under great physical disadvantages. His voice was weak and his utterance was defective; he could not pronounce the letter R, and constantly stammered. It was only by unwearied efforts that he overcame these defects. It is said that he spoke with pebbles in his mouth, to cure himself of stammering; that he repeated verses of the poets as he ran up hill, to strengthen his voice; that he declaimed to the sea-shore to accustom himself to the noise and confusion of the popular assembly; and that he lived for months in a cave under ground, engaged in copying Thucydides's History of the Peloponnesian War, to form a standard for his own style. But much reliance is not to be placed on these tales. His first effort at public speaking was unsuccessful, but he was induced by the actor Satyrus to persevere, and he finally overcame all obstacles. Of his orations, 61 have come down to us, some of them probably spurious.

ÆSCHINES, the rival of Demosthenes, was born at Athens B. C. 389, and became one of the principal orators of that city. He ultimately founded a school at Rhodes, where he died B. C. 314.

CTE′SIAS of Cnidus was private physician to Artaxerxes Mnemon. He wrote a history of Persia, in 17 books, but portions of it only have come down to us.

APELLES, the most eminent painter of Greece, was the friend of Alexander the Great. He was born at Colophon in Ionia, but we have not the particulars of his birth nor of his death. He was the only artist permitted to take a portrait of Alexander. His greatest work was his picture of Venus rising out of the Sea. PRAXIT′ELES, of Athens, was the greatest sculptor of the age.

MENAN′DER, the most distinguished poet of the New Comedy, was born at Athens B. C. 342. He was the pupil of Theophrastus, and the friend of Epicurus. He wrote upwards of 100 comedies, but only fragments of them have come down to us. He enjoyed the friendship of Demetrius Phalereus, and of Ptolemy Lagus, who invited him to settle at Alexandria, but Menander declined the honor. He is said to have been drowned in the harbor of the Piræus (B. C. 291).

DIOG′ENES the Cynic was born at Sinope in Pontus, B. C. 412. His father was a banker; he himself was very dissolute in his youth. He went to Athens and became the pupil of Antisthenes. He made himself notorious by his eccentricities and his bold speaking. It is said that he took up his abode in a tub belonging to the Metroum, or temple of Cybele (Rhea), the mother of the gods. On one occasion he walked about the streets in the day time with a lantern, pretending to look for an honest man. On a voyage to Ægina he was captured by pirates and sold in Crete as a slave. When asked what business he understood, he replied: "How to command men." He was purchased by Xeni′ades of Corinth, who took him to that city. At Corinth his celebrated interview with Alexander the Great took place. The latter said: "I am Alexander the Great." Diogenes replied: "I am Diogenes the Cynic." Alexander then asked if he could do anything for him;—to which Diogenes replied: "Yes, you can stand out of the sunshine." We are told that Alexander admired him so much as to say: "If I were not Alexander, I should wish to be Diogenes." He died at Corinth B. C. 323, at the age of 90.

EUCLI′DES (Euclid), the celebrated mathematician, lived at Alexandria in the time of the first Ptolemy, and was the founder of the mathematical school of that city. He it was who uttered the famous aphorism: "There is no royal road to learning." The place and date of his birth are uncertain. He left numerous works, many of which have come down to us, and are of inestimable value.

These were the principal men of renown in this century. There were many others of inferior note; as, the philosopher Xenoc′rates; the tragic poet Astyd′-amas; the comic poets Antiph′anes, Anaxan′drides, Eubu′lus, Philip′pides, Steph′anus, Arched′icus; the historians Theopom′pus and Philis′tus; the orators Andoc′ides, Dinar′chus, Isoc′rates; and the astronomer Eudox′us; but it is sufficient here to mention their names only.

How were the dominions of Alexander partitioned, B. C. 300?—Who were the most eminent men of the age?—What is said of Plato?—Aristotle?—The Peripatetic School?—What influence did its doctrines exercise?—Who was Epicurus?—What were the leading doctrines of the Epicureans?—What is said of Pyrrho?

Who was Demosthenes?—How did he overcome the defects under which he labored?—What is said of Æschines?—Ctesias?—Apelles?—Menander, and his works?—Diogenes?—Relate his conversation with Alexander the Great.—What is said of Euclid?—Name the other eminent persons who flourished during this century.

ITALY.

The destruction of Veii was one of the exploits of the celebrated Fu′rius Camill′us. Appointed dictator (B. C. 396), he gained a great victory over the Falisci, and took Veii. For this he was honored with a triumphal reception at Rome. But being accused of unfairness in the distribution of the booty, he went into exile (B. C. 391). The story of the fall of Veii is one of the most interesting in the Roman annals, but it must be received as a poetical legend; it is in fact the last of the poetical legends of old Rome. Had it been fortunate enough to meet with a poet like Homer or Virgil to have celebrated it, the siege of Veii would have taken its place by the side of that of Troy. The student will find it related in full in Arnold's *History of Rome*, vol. i., ch. xviii.

It was not long before Furius Camillus was recalled from exile, for, in the year B. C. 389, Brennus (or, more properly, the Brenn, or chief, of the Senonian Gauls), at the head of a vast horde, issued from the North-eastern Alps, and, pouring into Italy, laid waste Etruria, and besieged Clusium. The Romans sent to Etruria three of their citizens to observe the movements of the enemy. These deputies arrived at Clusium just as the Gauls were beginning to besiege that city, and they aided the citizens in a sally, in which one of them slew a Gaulish chief. The Gauls then discovered that these strangers were Romans; and they immediately sent deputies to Rome, to demand that the man who had slain the chief should be delivered up to them. The Senate was in favor of delivering him up; but his father, who was one of the military tribunes for the year, appealed to the people against the decision of the Senate, and persuaded them to annul it. The Gauls then broke up their camp before Clusium, and marched upon Rome. The greatest consternation prevailed in the city. An army of 40,000 men was assembled in the greatest haste, and sent out to encounter the invaders as far as possible from the city. They found the Gauls at the little stream of the Allia, about twelve miles from Rome, and there they awaited the attack. It was not long in coming. The Gauls showed consummate ability and bravery, and in a very short time decided this memorable battle. The Romans were utterly routed at the Allia, and pursued to the very gates of Rome. The citizens fled to Veii, Agylla, and Cœre, and the patricians shut themselves up in the capitol. The Gauls sacked and burnt Rome, and laid siege to the capitol. It is said that they found eighty of the most aged and venerable patricians seated immovably in their chairs in the forum, and at first thought they were statues—but, having pulled the beard of one of them, Marcus Papirius, the insult was fiercely resented, whereupon they massacred them all. The consul, Marcus Manlius, bravely defended the capitol. One night, when the Gauls attempted to surprise it, he was awakened by the cackling of his geese, and, hastily collecting his men, repulsed the enemy. For this exploit he was surnamed Capitolinus. For many months did the Gauls blockade the capitol. At length they reduced the garrison to extremity. The Romans offered a thousand pounds weight of gold as a ransom. The Brenn accepted this sum, although he had them wholly in his power; but in weighing it, he cast his heavy sword into the scale, and thus compelled the Romans to pay a greater weight. When the tribune asked him what he meant by it, he replied "*Væ victis*" (woe to the conquered), a memorable expression. The Romans implored Camillus to return, which he did; but, when he arrived, Brennus had already agreed to depart on payment of one thousand pounds of gold. The Romans afterwards tried to make the world believe that Camillus had killed Brennus, and cut his army to pieces.

Camillus, again appointed dictator, persuaded his countrymen to leave Veii, and return to Rome. The States formerly in subjection had revolted, but he again subdued them. Under his influence the patricians recovered the greater part of their original power, and resumed their harsh treatment of the plebeians. Manlius Capitolinus defended the cause of the latter; for this he was thrown into prison by the dictator, Cornelius Cossus, the successor of Camillus. Upon this the plebeians threatened to resort to arms; whereupon Manlius was released. But next year (B. C. 383), having openly exhorted them to resort to force, he was condemned to death, and thrown from the Tarpeian rock. After this tragedy the patricians continued their arbitrary career, until the election of Caius Licin′ius Stolo and Lucius Sextus Latera′nus as tribunes of the people, for the year B. C. 375. These eminent men brought the disputes between the patricians and the plebeians to a happy termination, and may be said to have changed the destiny of Rome. They procured the enactment of four laws, or "rogations," which were: 1. That in future there should be no consular tribunes, but only consuls, one of whom should be a plebeian. 2. That no one should possess more than 500 acres of public land, with a certain number of cattle on it. 3. A debtor and creditor law. 4. That the Sybilline books should be entrusted to ten persons, five of whom should be plebeians. The patricians offered the most vehement opposition to these rogations. They even reappointed the venerable Camillus, then 80 years old, dictator. But the latter persuaded them to yield to the demands of the plebeians; while he, having accepted the office, took the field once more against the Senonian Gauls. The Licinian laws were passed (B. C. 367), Lateranus being the first plebeian consul elected under them. The offices of Prætor and Curule Ædile were also created. The prætor was a magistrate, answering to the modern mayor. At first there was only one, but in after times there were two. Of these, the one administered justice between the Roman citizens, and was thence styled "Prætor Urbanus"; the other administered justice between the citizens and foreigners, and was thence styled "Prætor Peregrinus". The former held the higher rank; his edicts were named "Jus honorarium". The days on which the prætors held their court were called "Dies fasti" (or days for uttering the three words, Do, Dico, Addico (*I give* the writ; *I pronounce* sentence; *I award* damages): the days on which they did not officiate were termed "Dies nefasti". The Ædiles Curules were officers appointed to take care of the public buildings, sewers, and roads; to inspect markets, provisions, weights, and measures; and to enforce decent behaviour among the people. They also had to exhibit public games. When these appointments had been assented to, and Lateranus was installed, Rome tasted domestic repose for the first time after long years of discord.

In the year B. C. 362 the earth in the forum at Rome gave way, and a great chasm appeared, which the soothsayers declared could only be filled by throwing into it Rome's greatest treasure. The legend says that thereupon a noble youth, named Mettius Curtius, mounted his steed in full armor, and, declaring that Rome possessed no greater treasure than a brave and gallant citizen, leaped into the abyss, upon which the earth closed over him. That part of the forum was named after him, the Lacus Curtius.

Camillus died B. C. 365. After his death the Senones once more attacked Rome, and, for more than three years, established themselves on the Alban Mount. They were at length dislodged (B. C. 358), and external peace was apparently secured. But in the next year the town of Privernum was attacked and taken by Marcius Rutilus, who was subsequently appointed dictator, being the first plebeian who held that office. In his dictatorship he defeated the Etruscans with great slaughter. This war with the Etruscans lasted eight years, from B. C. 357 to 349. Its cause is not known, but it is remarkable for several incidents. In the year B. C. 356, the people of Tarquinii having defeated the Roman consul, Fabius, sacrificed to their gods 307 Roman prisoners. In a battle fought two years afterwards, the priests of the Faliscans and Tarquinians, with long ribbons of various colors in their hair, and burning torches in their hands, fought in front of the army, and so terrified the Romans that the latter were driven back in confusion. This disgrace was signally avenged by Rutilus in the battle first mentioned; 358 of the noblest prisoners were sent to Rome, and there scourged and beheaded. Three years afterwards peace was concluded for forty years. In B. C. 349 the consul, Camillus Crassus, defeated the Senones. Marcus Vale′rius, who served under him, here gained his surname, "Corvus". The legend is that he had accepted the challenge of a gigantic Gaul to single combat, and, while fighting him, a raven (*corvus*) settled on his helmet, and then flew in the face of the barbarian, who, being thus confounded, was easily slain. In the war with the Samnites, M. Valerius Corvus was one of the most successful generals of the Romans. This war was occasioned by the encroachments of the Samnites into the valley of the Liris, and by the war between Rome and the Auruncans in the year B. C. 343. The Romans having advanced as far as Campania, found the Samnites pressing upon Capua; the people of that city implored assistance from the Romans and the Latins, and this having been granted, war immediately ensued. The consuls, Valerius Corvus and

Which was the principal exploit of Camillus?—What befell him?—What was the cause of the war with the Gauls?—What great battle was fought?—What remarkable scene occurred at Rome?—Who was Marcus Manlius?—What saved the capitol?—How was the war terminated?—What did Camillus then do?—What was the end of Manlius?

What were the Licinian rogations?—What offices were created?—What was the prætor?—What the Ædile Curule?—Relate the legend of Curtius.—When did Camillus die?—What happened next?—What of Marcius Rutilus?—The war with Tarquinii?—How did Valerius acquire the name of Corvus?—What occasioned the Samnite war?

Cornelius Cossus, advanced against the Samnites at the head of two armies of the allies: Valerius undertaking to defend Campania, while Cossus attacked Samnium. The former defeated the Samnites at Mount Gaurus and at Suess′ula (B. C. 343), and extended the sway of Rome to the river Liris. He was next instrumental in appeasing the tumults at Rome (B. C. 341), occasioned by the expenses of the war and the distress of the people. He also figures in the disreputable law which was passed at the demand of the commons for the relief of their debts. This was an act prohibiting creditors from recovering their debts. All debtors who had pledged their personal liberty for the payment of their liabilities were released from their bond. Thus all existing debts were abolished, and the patricians were robbed of the money they had lent. Moreover, a law was passed making even the lowest rate of interest illegal, and enacting that the man who exacted more than the actual sum loaned should restore the excess fourfold. This is a specimen of the public morality of the Romans.

Peace was then made with the Samnites (B. C. 340), without the consent of the Latins, who were thus left to continue the war single-handed. The latter then made proposals to the Romans for a more intimate union between Rome and Latium. They suggested that the two nations should be completely united, each furnishing an equal number of senators and public officers, Rome being considered the capital. The Romans indignantly refused to accede to these proposals, insulted the Latin deputies, and determined to annex Latium by force. They appointed Manlius Torquatus and Decius Mus to take command of their army, and marched to encounter the Latins near Mount Vesuvius. The famous battle which ensued was fought near the little stream Ves′eris (B. C. 340). It is remarkable for two events. The son of Manlius having been challenged by Gem′inus Metius, one of the Latin chiefs, went out of the camp, fought, and slew him; but, on returning to the camp, was beheaded in the presence of the whole army by order of his father. During the battle the left wing of the Romans, under Decius, being hard pressed, that heroic officer sent for the Pontifex Maximus (or chief of the Augurs), to instruct him how to devote himself and the enemy to the gods of death. The augur bade him wrap his cloak round his head, set his feet upon a javelin, and utter certain words. Having done this, Decius plunged into the enemy's ranks, and was slain. But the battle was only won by the skill of Manlius; in it three-fourths of the Latins perished, and Campania submitted to the Romans. Next year (B. C. 339), the consuls, Publilius Philo and Æmilius Mamerci′nus, defeated the Latins at Trifanum, and the Latin confederacy was broken up forever. Æmilius then appointed Publilius dictator, who in that capacity proposed the celebrated Publilian laws, which abolished the power of the patrician assembly of the Curiæ, and elevated the plebeians to an equality with the patricians for all practical purposes. In the year B. C. 338 the Latins were entirely subdued by, and incorporated with, the Romans.

The prætorship having been thrown open to the plebeians, Publilius was elected to fill that office. In the year B. C. 329 a war broke out with the people of Privernum, but the cause is not known. It was excited mainly by Vitruvius Vaccus, a citizen of Fundi, who had been disappointed in obtaining the consulship. He raised an army, but being defeated, fled to Privernum. The Romans, under Æmilius Mamercinus and Plautius Decianus, besieged and took that city, but it cost them much trouble to take it. Æmilius received the surname of "Privernas", in honor of his exploit. The people of the conquered city sent deputies to Rome to sue for mercy. On this occasion, one of them having been asked, "What penalty they deserved?" replied, "The penalty due to those who assert their liberty." Having been again asked, "If spared, what peace might be expected from them?" the same deputy replied: "Peace, true and lasting, if the terms be good; if otherwise, peace that will soon be broken." The Senators, struck with these noble answers, admitted the people of Privernum to the rights of Roman citizenship.

Two years afterwards, some disputes between the Roman settlers in Campania and the Greeks of Southern Italy brought on a second war with the Samnites. The Romans had encroached on the territory of the latter, who refused all offers to settle the matter by arbitration. This war with the Samnites was begun in the year B. C. 327. It lasted more than twenty years, but its events are so complicated that we can give but the merest outline of them. Their cities, Palæo′polis and Nea′polis, were betrayed into the hands of Publilius (B. C. 326); and next year, Quintus Fabius (afterwards styled "Maximus", or greatest), gained a great victory over the Samnites, contrary to the order of the dictator, Papir′ius Cursor, for which he was threatened with capital punishment. It was at this time that the fame of Alexander the Great, of Macedon, filled the world; and Rome, and many other Italian States, thought it politic to send embassies to conciliate the great conqueror of the East.

The victories of Fabius reduced the Samnites to great straits; nevertheless, they rejected the terms offered by the Romans. Their despair made them fight all the more valiantly; and in B. C. 321 they succeeded in surrounding the Roman army, in the pass of Caudium (now the valley of Arpaia). The Romans sued for mercy, and the Samnites generously released them on their swearing to restore the towns they had taken; but the Senate refused to ratify the treaty. A truce was agreed to, but the war was renewed in B. C. 316. The Romans laid siege to Satic′ula, while the Samnites captured Sora. But in B. C. 315, Fabius was completely routed at Laut′ulæ. This disgrace was retrieved by a decisive victory gained at Cinna in the following year, after which several Samnite towns were taken.

In the year B. C. 312, Appius Claudius, the blind, was elected censor without having previously been consul, as was the rule. During his censorship, which he held for four years, contrary to law, he constructed the Appian aqueduct, and commenced the Appian road from Rome to Capua. He also made a canal through the Pontine marshes. In the south, the consul, Junius Bubulcus, penetrated into Samnium, where he was surrounded by the enemy, but cut his way through with great courage. The Etruscans now took up arms on behalf of the Samnites, but were forced by Fabius Maximus to make peace. The same general defeated the Samnites at Allifæ (B. C. 308). Three years afterwards they were so badly beaten at Bovianum by the consul, Postumius Megellus, that they were completely at the mercy of the Romans Peace was then concluded, and a large territory was ceded to the great republic (B. C. 304). Next year the Romans annexed the territory of the Hernicans, Æqui, and Marsi to their own, and they then became the leading power in Italy.

In the year B. C. 306, Cneius Flavius, the son of a freed man, and secretary to Appius Claudius, published his "Calendar of Court Days", divulging certain technicalities of law procedure, which had previously been kept secret, as being the exclusive privilege of the patricians and the pontifex. The publication of this work gained for him such popularity that he was elected Curule Ædile; and, having conciliated all the orders of the State, he erected a temple of concord in commemoration of the fact.

This century was a brilliant one in the history of Rome, although the people went through great trials before they attained the high position they occupied at the close of it. At one time, indeed, Rome was literally subdued by the Gauls. But having purchased an ignominious peace, the State resumed its wonderful vitality; and immediately the ancient contest between the patricians and plebeians, the aristocratic and democratic elements of the nation, broke out afresh. The result was the triumph of the plebeians — that is, they obtained their share in the government. This was, perhaps, the era of the republic in which it attained to its greatest strength. There was unity of councils, and a systematically-resolute national spirit, which, combined with the central position of their capital, and the natural military genius of the people, gave to the Romans a preponderance over all the nations of Italy. The Latin and Samnite wars not only extended but consolidated their power. The exploits of their generals and leaders raised the renown of the Romans to a very high point, and, at the close of the century, there was not a power in the civilized world, except Carthage, which was capable of contending with them single-handed. It is to be regretted that the accounts we have of this period of Roman history are so poorly supplied by contemporary native writers, for during it Rome did not produce a single historian, poet, orator, or philosopher; there being, therefore, a total want of materials whence to obtain a picture of Roman character and manners.

What disgraceful law was passed?—What was the cause of the Latin war?—What befell the son of Manlius?—What great battle was fought?—What did Decius do?—What was the result of the war?—Give the particulars of the war with Privernum, and the replies of the deputies.

Mention the cause of the second Samnite war.—What happened at Caudium? — What were the principal events of the war?—Who were the chief actors in it?—Who was Appius Claudius? —What is said of Cneius Flavius? — Sum up the retrospect of the history of the century.

BRITAIN.

England.—Upon Guitheline's death, the kingdom passed to his son, Sisilius, under the guardianship of his widow, Martia, to whom was mainly ascribed the Marchen-lage (or, as Geoffrey of Monmouth styles it, *Pa Marchitle Lage*). The legendary history gives us the names of a series of kings, but very few incidents concerning them. If there be any truth in this history, the country must have fallen into a very disturbed state about this time, since the historian gives us the names of no fewer than 39 kings in the course of three centuries. Of Morvid it is related that he repelled an invasion of the Northmen. Gerbonian was celebrated for his justice. Arthgallo was a cruel tyrant, who was dethroned by his people, but reinstated by his brother Elidure, who ultimately succeeded him. It is asserted that Elidure was imprisoned in the Tower of London by his nephews, who divided the kingdom between them. Coillius fell in battle against Fergus, an Irish chieftain, who, landing in Scotland with an army of Scots from Ireland (B. C. 330), founded the kingdom of Scotland: —the Picts retaining the south-western portion of that country; the Scots keeping the northern and mountainous portion. Britain itself was now divided into tribes, of whom the Brigantes came in time to be the most powerful. They had their separate chiefs or kings. The names of some of them have been handed down to us, together with some of their exploits; but there is so little worth recording of them, that it will not be necessary to do more than mention a few of the leading incidents.

Scotland.—Of Scottish history, some of the historians of that country profess to furnish authentic records from the time of Fergus I. downwards. The authenticity of these accounts has been disputed; they are said to have been concocted by Buchanan and others to gratify the vanity of James I., by tracing his descent back to this remote antiquity.

According to Buchanan, Fergus I. was drowned near Carrick-Fergus, after reigning 24 years. He left two infant sons, Ferleg and Main. The chiefs of the Scottish clans appointed Fergus's brother, Feritha′ris, king; who governed wisely for 15 years. But his domains must have been very circumscribed, as the Picts were the principal inhabitants of the country, and were governed by their own kings.

What state was the country in after the death of Guitheline?—What is related of Morvid?—And of his successors?—Of Fergus I.?—And the history written by Buchanan?

FRANCE.

Increasing rapidly in numbers, the Gauls in Italy resolved to extend their territories. About the same time, 30,000 of the warriors of the German tribes, the Senones and the Baii, crossing the Alps, suddenly appeared before the city of Clusium, and proposed to the inhabitants a fraternal partition of their lands. The people of Clusium set them at defiance, and sent to Rome for assistance. The latter State deputed three of the family of the Fabii to mediate between the combatants; but these envoys violated their instructions, and incited the Clusians to resistance. They suddenly attacked a detachment of the Gauls, who were far from suspecting such a breach of the truce. Quintus Ambus′tus Fa′bius led on the Clusians, and was recognized by the Gauls as the Roman ambassador. Their leader at once ordered the fight to be stopped, and called a council of the chiefs of the army. It was resolved to despatch a messenger to Rome to demand the surrender of the guilty parties. The demand was rejected, owing to the powerful influence of the Fabian family. Exasperated at this, the Gauls turned their arms against Rome, and by forced marches arrived at the Allia, about half a day's journey from the city. There they met and completely routed the Roman army, on July 16th, B. C. 390. Soon afterwards they marched to Rome, which they found deserted by all except the garrison of the citadel. In the vestibule of the Senate, they saw the Senators sitting in silence in their seats. These venerable men remained immovable until one of the astonished Gauls touched the beard of one of them, who instantly struck the man violently with his ivory staff. Furious at this, the Gaul killed his assailant. A general massacre ensued, and the city was burnt. The inhabitants fled to Veii, but the patricians shut themselves up in the Capitol. After a siege of seven months, a peace was purchased by the Romans. The war, however, continued nearly 40 years with varying success, until at length a peace was concluded (B. C. 349), and these Cisalpine Gauls were quiet in Italy for half a century.

In the first half of this century, the Bolgs, or Belgians, crossing the Rhine, invaded the south of France. Two of their tribes, the Arecomici and Tectosages, acquired a permanent settlement in Aquitaine, making Toulouse their capital.

What occurred at Clusium?—What was the result?—What occurred after the battle of the Allia?—What of the Senate?—What befell the Gauls?—What tribes settled in France?

SPAIN.

This century is noted for the remarkable earthquakes, floods, and storms which desolated Spain, especially during the years B. C. 355 and 348.

Hanno, the Carthaginian governor, being a very avaricious man, was guilty of great extortion, whereby he drove the Spaniards into revolt, so that it was found necessary to recall him (B. C. 355). Of the actions of the governor who succeeded Hanno, we have no account. The names of Boodes and Meherbal are mentioned as those of governors of Spain, but nothing worth recording of them occurred.

About the year B. C. 334, the people of Marseilles sent a colony into Spain. These colonists settled at Empurias, at the foot of the Pyrenees. At the same time the Spaniards appear to have first become acquainted with the Romans, their future masters. The renown of Alexander the Great also reached the Peninsula; and the Spaniards on the coast of the Mediterranean sent an embassy to him to solicit his protection against the Carthaginians. The ambassadors were kindly received at Babylon by Alexander the Great, and obtained the promise of his assistance. They returned home laden with presents, but the illustrious Macedonian did not furnish the promised aid.

About the same time a Carthaginian ship, either designedly or forced by stress of weather, crossed the Atlantic, and discovered a very large and beautiful island. It being uninhabited, several of the crew settled there; the rest returned and gave an account of what they had seen. Some are of opinion that this island was one of the Canary islands; others that it was one of the West India islands, or part of the continent of America. The jealous and cruel policy of the Senate of Carthage is shown in their decreeing that the discovery of this great island be kept a secret. By their orders the discoverers were put to death, lest their glowing reports should induce the Carthaginians to seek their fortune in the unknown land. What became of those who settled there is unknown. It is probable that ships were occasionally driven across the ocean by strong winds, in these ancient times; and thus the peopling of South and Central America may be easily accounted for; as may also the resemblance found between the antiquities of Mexico and Peru and those of Phœnicia and Egypt.

What is this century remarkable for?—What is said of Hanno and his successors?—Of the Marseillese?—Alexander the Great?—And the discovery of a transatlantic island?

GERMANY.

In the beginning of this century, Hel′ico, a carpenter, came to the Senones, who then inhabited what is now modern Swabia, and to the Boii, who dwelt in what is now modern Bavaria, and brought with him specimens of the fruits of Italy. Eagerly desiring to possess a land which produced such delicious fruit, and incited by the description of it given by Helico, they resolved to emigrate thither. A vast horde, under a leader named Brennus, crossed the Alps and descended into the plains of Lombardy. There is a discrepancy here between the French and the German historians. Thierry asserts that the name "Brennus" is but the Latin form of the Senonian word "Brenn", which signified "king" or "leader": and that the Romans mistook this title for a proper name (*Histoire des Gaulois*, vol. i. p. 52). The German historian Menzel (*History of Germany*, sect. xxviii) says that it was the chieftain's name. He also attributes to him and the Senones the entire glory of the defeat of the Romans and the destruction of Rome (B. C. 389). The French historian asserts that the Gauls took a very important share in the war, especially at the battle of the Allia. We incline to the statement made by Thierry. However, it is clear that Brennus, or the Brenn, had the chief command at the taking of Rome. His departure was purchased by 1000 pounds' weight of gold, but at the time of weighing it, Brennus threw his sword into the scale, and bade the Romans add its weight to the ransom. The Senones and Boii afterwards settled in the north of Italy, but did not long remain at peace with the Romans. There arose continual disputes and wars, but they terminated in the supremacy of the Romans.

In the year B. C. 340, Alexander the Great, of Macedonia, undertook an expedition against the Getæ and the Triballi, at the mouth of the Danube, to punish them for having ravaged Thrace. On this occasion some of their chiefs visited his camp. Alexander received them courteously, and invited them to a banquet. Having asked them what they feared most in the world, he received for answer: "We fear nothing but the fall of the sky; nevertheless, we prize the friendship of such a man as thou art." Surprised and mortified, Alexander thought it prudent to make peace with them.

Who was Helico?—What emigration took place?—What is said of Brennus?—What became of the Senones and Boii in Italy?—What is related of Alexander the Great?

ASIA MINOR

Though the principal portion of this country (in which we include the Caucasian States, the Crimea, the Bosphorus, and Armenia,) was under the dominion of Persia, there were independent kingdoms in it. That of Caria threw off the Athenian yoke (B. C. 380), and chose Mauso′lus for its king. This personage is remembered on account of the magnificent monument raised to his memory by his widow, Artemis′ia (B. C. 354), whence similar structures have received the name of "mausole′um".

In Cyprus, Evagoras, a descendant of Teucer, established a kingdom (B. C. 410), which he governed with great virtue and ability for many years. He was, after a stubborn resistance, compelled to submit to the Persians (B C. 386), but was allowed to retain possession of Salamis, with the title of king. He was assassinated (B. C. 374), together with his son, Pnytag′oras, and was succeeded by his son Nic′ocles, of whose reign very few particulars are known. It is related of Nicocles that he rewarded Isocrates, the celebrated Attic orator, with twenty talents (about $22,000), for an oration in praise of Evagoras; also that he died a violent death, but neither the period nor the circumstances of this event are recorded. Cyprus and the shores of Asia Minor were the scene of the incessant struggles between the Greeks and Persians for dominion. The Spartans, under Agesila′us, had nearly made themselves masters of the country, and Tissaphernes, the satrap, had been put to death (B. C. 394), when his successor, Tithraustes, by bribing the other Greek States to combine against Sparta, raised a force sufficient to compel Agesilaus to return home. Sparta, occupied with her domestic enemies, sent Antal′cidas (B. C. 387), to conclude a peace with Artaxerxes Mnemon, king of Persia, whereby the Greek cities of Asia Minor and Cyprus were given up to him; the Athenians were allowed to retain only Lemnos, Imbros, and Scyros, and the independence of the other Greek cities was guaranteed.

In the year B. C. 362, a rebellion of the satraps of Asia Minor gave considerable trouble to the Persian king, Artaxerxes, and this spirit of revolt spread throughout the empire. On the night in which Alexander the Great was born (Oct. 13th, B. C. 356), the great temple of Diana, at Ephesus, was set on fire and burnt, by a madman named Eros′tratus, who was actuated to do the deed by the idea of immortalizing his name in connection with this event.

The cruelties of Ochus, the successor of Artaxerxes, induced Artabazus, the satrap of Asia Minor, to revolt (B. C. 356), and in this he was assisted by the Athenians and Thebans; but although victorious in several encounters, he was ultimately forced to take refuge with Philip, king of Macedonia. He was afterwards pardoned by Artaxerxes, and became a faithful adherent of Darius Codomanus, who raised him to great honors. So good an opinion of him had Alexander the Great that the latter appointed him satrap of Bactria, and married his daughter Barsi′ne. Ptolemy Lagus married his second daughter, Artocama; and Eumenes married his third daughter, Artonis.

In Bosphorus, Sat′yrus I. was succeeded by Leucon (B. C. 392–353); Spar′tacus II. (B. C. 353–348); Parys′ades (B. C. 348–311); Satyrus II., who reigned only nine months. Pryt′anis, who had attempted to seize the throne, was slain by Eu′melus, who became king (B. C. 310), and was succeeded by his son, Spartacus III. (B. C. 304).

The year B. C. 334 is memorable for the commencement of the career of Alexander the Great in Asia. Crossing the Hellespont at the head of 35,000 men, he conquered Caria, and took Halicarnassus. He totally defeated the Persians under Memnon, at the river Grani′cus, in Mysia (May, B. C. 334). This battle was followed by the capture or submission of the chief towns on the west coast of Asia Minor. Halicarnassus was taken in the autumn of B. C. 334, after a gallant defence by Memnon of Rhodes, the Persian monarch's ablest general, and brother-in-law of Artabazus. Memnon planned the carrying of the war into Greece, but his untimely death (B. C. 333) put an end to the scheme, and relieved Alexander of his most formidable opponent. The Macedonian king then conquered Lycia and Pamphylia, and marched north into Phrygia, where he cut the famous Gordian knot (see page 91). In B. C. 333 he marched into Cilicia, where he nearly lost his life from bathing, when heated, in the river Cydnus. Darius, king of Persia, collected an immense army of more than half a million of men, with 30,000 Greek mercenaries, to oppose Alexander, and encountered him in a narrow valley near the town of Issus, in the south-eastern extremity of Cilicia; but notwithstanding the enormous disparity between the two armies, Darius was completely defeated, and his army was destroyed. He fled across the Euphrates, but his family fell into the hands of Alexander, by whom they were treated with the greatest respect. The conqueror then marched into Syria, having annexed all Asia Minor to his empire.

On the death of Alexander (B. C. 323), his empire, which extended from the Adriatic to the Indus, was partitioned into provinces, over each of which one of his generals was appointed satrap. Lycia, Pamphylia, and greater Phrygia, were given to Antig′onus; Caria to Cassander; Lydia to Menander; the lesser Phrygia to Leona′tus; Armenia to Neoptolemus; Cappadocia and Paphlagonia to Eu′menes. Cappadocia and Paphlagonia had formed a kingdom, ruled over by Ariara′thes, and had not been subjected by the Macedonians. Pontus was also a kingdom, founded by Darius Hystaspes in favor of Artabazus (B. C. 514), and several princes had reigned there after him. The sixth king was Mithrida′tes I. (B. C. 404–363); his son, Ariobarza′nes, succeeded him (B. C. 363–337). Mithridates II. (B. C. 337–302) fled from the fury of Antigonus. He was succeeded (B. C. 302) by his son, Mithridates III.

The history of Asia Minor, from the death of Alexander the Great to the battle of Ipsus (B. C. 323–301), is that of the struggles amongst his generals and successors for supremacy. The first pretext for quarrelling was the refusal of Ariarathes, king of Cappadocia, to acknowledge the supremacy of Macedon. Perdiccas, regent of the empire, sent an army against him under Eumenes, and ordered Antigonus and Leonatus to join the expedition. This they refused to do, and Perdiccas then marched in person against the Cappadocian monarch, defeated and took him prisoner, and crucified him (B. C. 322). Having crushed the Cappadocians, he summoned the disobedient generals before his tribunal. Antigonus, seeing his danger, entered into a league with Ptolemy, Antip′ater, Crat′erus, Neoptolemus, and other generals, against Perdiccas and Eumenes. A civil war ensued. Perdiccas, in order to strengthen his power, assassinated Meleager, who had been associated with him in the regency. Eumenes defeated and killed Craterus and Neoptolemus on the plains of Troy (B. C. 321). The latter was slain by Eumenes with his own hand. Perdiccas, marching against Ptolemy, was defeated in Egypt, and murdered by his own soldiers in his tent at Pelusium.

Antipater, succeeding Perdiccas as regent, resolved to employ the whole force of the empire to crush Eumenes. He entrusted the conduct of the campaign to Antigonus. The struggle was carried on for several years. It was conducted by Eumenes with consummate skill, and, notwithstanding the numerical inferiority of his forces, he maintained his ground against his enemies until he was betrayed; he thereupon fled to Mithridates, king of Pontus.

On the death of Antipater (B. C. 318), Antigonus, by the aid of a fleet sent by Cassander, made his authority paramount in Asia Minor. Eumenes, supported by Mithridates, still held out for the royal cause; but this brave and good man was ultimately delivered up by his mutinous soldiers to Antigonus, who put him to death (B. C. 315). Eumenes was but 45 years old at this time: he was the ablest general and statesman among the successors of Alexander. The reason why he did not occupy a more prominent position under the conqueror was that he was a native of Cardia, in the Thracian Chersonese; and was not, therefore, looked upon with favor by the Macedonians.

Antigonus now openly aimed at the sovereignty of the empire. He banished Peucestes from Persia, and Seleucus from Babylon; put Python of Media to death, declared war against Cassander, Ptolemy, and Lysimachus. He overran Syria and Asia Minor, and took Tyre, carrying on the war with varying success (B. C. 315–312). But Ptolemy and Seleucus defeated Antigonus's son, Demetrius Poliorce′tes, at Gaza, and Seleucus became monarch of Persia, while Ptolemy established himself in Egypt.

Alarmed at their success, Antigonus concluded a temporary peace (B. C. 311), whereby he was allowed to have the government of all Asia. But the peace did not last more than a year. In B. C. 307, Antigonus sent his son, the famous Demetrius Poliorcetes, into Greece against Cassander. Demetrius met with great success. At Athens he was received with enthusiasm by the people as

What is said of Asia Minor generally?—Mausolus?—Artemisia?—Evagoras?—Nicocles?—Continue the history until the peace of Antalcidas.—What was the effect of that peace?—When and by whom was the temple of Diana at Ephesus burnt?—What is said of Artabazus?—Of his daughters?—Give an outline of the career of Alexander the Great.

What two great battles did Alexander win?—How was his empire partitioned after his death?—Who were kings of Pontus?—Give an outline of the contest between the successors of Alexander.—What of Perdiccas?—Eumenes?—Antipater?—Antigonus?—Cassander?—Demetrius Poliorcetes?

B.C. 400—300.

ASIA MINOR.

their liberator. Demetrius Phalereus, who had been appointed Governor of the city by Cassander, was driven out, the fort at Munychia was taken, and divine honors were paid to Poliorcetes. He was then sent by his father against Cyprus, where he annihilated the fleet of Ptolemy (B. C. 306). Next year he laid siege to Rhodes, because the Rhodians had refused to assist him against Ptolemy. He employed the most gigantic machines to take the city, but after making prodigious efforts for more than a year, he was obliged to give up the siege, and conclude peace with the Rhodians. He then crossed over into Greece (B. C. 304), compelled Cassander to evacuate all the country south of Thermopylæ, and for two years prosecuted the war with the greatest success. But in B. C. 302 he was recalled by Antigonus to Asia to support him against the new confederation, for, in spite of the victories of Demetrius obtained in Greece and Cyprus over Cassander and Ptolemy, those confederated generals now united in greater force. Cassander attacked Southern Greece, Ptolemy entered Syria, Lysimachus invaded Thrace, and Seleucus marched into Asia Minor with a powerful army from Persia. The junction of the armies of Seleucus and Lysimachus in Phrygia brought on a great battle at Ipsus, a small town in that country, which decided the fate of the empire (B. C. 301). Antigonus was aided by his gallant son, Demetrius, but owing to the impetuosity of the latter, was defeated and killed. Demetrius fled to Greece, where he went through many vicissitudes of fortune. The Athenians who had previously paid him divine honors now refused to receive him. But Seleucus married his daughter, Stratoni′ce, and granted to that prince the province of Cilicia, which, with Cyprus, Tyre, and Sidon, made him a respectable potentate. On the partition of the Macedonian empire, Seleucus became monarch of Upper Asia, Ptolemy of Syria and Palestine, and Lysimachus of the northern provinces of Asia Minor.

During this century the historian Cte′sias of Cnidus, the poet Anaxan′drides of Rhodes, the astronomer Eudoxus of Cnidus, the poet Heracli′des of Pontus, the philosopher Epicurus of Samos, and the painter Protog′enes of Caria, flourished—all being natives of Asia Minor.

What is said of Demetrius Phalereus?—Of Poliorcetes?—Of the siege of Rhodes?—Of Ptolemy Lagus?—What eminent men flourished?

CARTHAGE.

The peace concluded between Dionysius and the Carthaginians was a hollow one. Dionysius having induced the Greek States to join him, suddenly captured several of the Carthaginian fortresses, and massacred their merchants, at the same time declaring war against them (B. C. 397). The Carthaginians, roused to fury, sent Imilco with a large army into Sicily. Having captured several small towns, that general laid siege to Syracuse, and would probably have taken it, but a dreadful plague broke out in his camp, and Dionysius, sallying out, slaughtered the enfeebled troops. Imilco surrendered, and, on his return to Carthage, committed suicide. The African tribes, who had furnished the greatest number of soldiers to assist the Carthaginians, furious at the sacrifice of their brethren, flew to arms, and laid siege to Carthage, but being without any leader of eminence, they finally dispersed.

The Carthaginians sent another armament, under Mago, to retrieve their losses in Sicily, but this army was routed, and its leader slain (B. C. 390). The younger Mago, having been reinforced, again attacked the Syracusans, and defeated them (B. C. 389), which induced Dionysius to conclude a peace with Carthage. This peace was followed by a disastrous plague, which desolated Carthage and its provinces, causing great distress and fierce insurrections; but the Carthaginian Senate, by its firm and temperate policy, restored the State to its former vigor and prosperity.

Dionysius now turned his arms against the Greek colonies in Southern Italy. He subdued Caulonia and Hipponium, and besieged Rhegium, which he took after a long siege, showing great barbarity to the conquered. He was twice again engaged in war with the Carthaginians, once in B. C. 383, and the other time in 368, in the midst of which he died (B. C. 367). He was a great patron of learned men, and of the arts and sciences, but he was extremely tyrannical, avaricious, and cruel. He took extraordinary precautions to secure himself from assassination, of which he was constantly in dread. Of him it is related that one of his courtiers, Dam′ocles, having expressed a strong desire to enjoy the splendor of the palace for one day, was allowed to do so, but at the feast was compelled to sit with a drawn sword suspended over his head by a single horse-hair, which sight destroyed all his happiness. The well-known incidents illustrative of the friendship between Damon and Phintias (or Pythias, as he is usually called), occurred in the reign of Dionysius. The tyrant had condemned Phintias to death; and the latter had obtained permission to go home for the purpose of settling his private affairs, on condition of finding a friend who would be security for his return. Damon unhesitatingly offered himself, and was accepted as security; but Phintias returned in time to redeem him, and Dionysius was so struck with the magnanimity of both that he released them. He was succeeded by his son Dionysius (usually styled "the younger"), a dissolute tyrant, whose conduct filled the State with tumult and distraction. He disregarded the counsels of his brother-in-law, Dion, as well as that of the celebrated philosopher, Plato, and banished the former, while he sold the latter as a slave. Plato was redeemed from slavery by Archytas, the philosopher of Tarentum. Dion, however, returned to Sicily with a small Greek fleet and army, and made himself master of the city while Dionysius was absent in Italy (B. C. 356). His reign was short-lived, for he was assassinated by his pretended friend, Callippus (B. C. 353), who got possession of the chief power, but was expelled thirteen months afterwards. Dion was one of the distinguished men of that age. He was of a proud and stern character, an ardent disciple of Plato, and a despiser of dissolute pleasures; nevertheless, he contrived to amass great wealth by his connection with Dionysius. Great confusion ensued on the expulsion of Callippus; taking advantage of which, Dionysius returned and reinstated himself (B. C. 347). But he became more cruel and brutal than before, and the people of Syracuse applied to Icetes, king of Leontium, for help. Meanwhile the Carthaginians sent an expedition into Sicily to subjugate the island, upon which the Syracusans applied to the Corinthians for aid, and the latter sent Timo′leon with forces to help them (B. C. 343). The career of this celebrated man was an extraordinary one. He belonged to one of the noblest families in Corinth. His youth was stained by the murder of his own brother, Timophanes. The latter having endeavored to subvert the liberties of his country, Timoleon slew him. The Corinthians were debating how to punish him, when the embassy of the Syracusans arrived. They thereupon decided to send him in command of the Greek forces—premising that if he conducted himself badly, they would punish him as a fratricide; but if he behaved justly, they would honor him as a regicide. Timoleon met with rapid success. With 700 men he forced Dionysius to surrender Syracuse, and sent him to Corinth. He then destroyed the citadel, and established a democracy. Next he proceeded to expel the tyrants from the other Greek cities of Sicily, but was interrupted by a formidable invasion of the Carthaginians, who sent 70,000 foot and 10,000 horse, under Asdrubal and Hamilcar to Lilybæum (B. C. 339). Timoleon, with 12,000 men, gained a complete victory over them at the river Crimi′sus, obtaining immense booty, the greater part of which he sent to Corinth. By treaty the river Haly′cus was fixed as the boundary between the Greek and Carthaginian possessions in Sicily. Timoleon also crushed Icetes of Leontium, Mamercus of Catana, and the other Sicilian tyrants—and then, resigning his power, retired into private life, and died greatly honored (B. C. 337).

In the interval, Hanno tried to make himself master of Carthage by poisoning the Senate, but failed, and was put to death. After many years of dissensions, Agatho′cles, a potter, contrived to raise himself to power, and became master of Syracuse (B. C. 317). His first attempt was to expel the Carthaginians from Sicily, but he was totally defeated by the Carthaginian general, Hamilcar, at Himera. The latter shut him up in Syracuse, and besieged the city (B. C. 309). Agathocles, however, contrived to escape, and levy an army. Leaving Syracuse to its fate, he conceived the daring idea of invading Africa, before Hamilcar could know anything of his movements. The Carthaginians, taken by surprise, sent Hanno and Bomilcar to oppose him, but they were defeated. Agathocles, leaving the command of the African army to his son, returned to Sicily, where Hamilcar had been defeated and slain; but his Greek and African troops deserted, and went over to the Carthaginians. He then returned to Africa, but, unable to retrieve his affairs, he fled back to Sicily, abandoning his sons and his army. The latter slew their leaders, and surrendered themselves to the Carthaginians; and Agathocles died soon after, from grief, or poison (B. C. 307).

What provoked war between Syracuse and Carthage?—What was the result of it?—Of Mago's expedition?—What was the character of Dionysius?—The legend of Damocles?—Of Damon and Pythias?—What of Dionysius the younger?—Dion?—Callippus?—What was the early history of Timoleon?—What was the result of his enterprise in Sicily?—What attempt did Hanno make?—What is said of Agathocles?—His fate, and that of his sons?

THE 3D CENTURY

EGYPT.

Ptolemy Soter, the son of Ptolemy Lagus, was the wisest statesman among the successors of Alexander the Great. His first care, after he had become firmly established on the throne of Egypt, was to regenerate the entire social system of the nation. He revived its ancient religious and political constitution, and restored the priesthood. Memphis was made the capital, and a museum, university, and library were founded in Alexandria. Thither the most celebrated men resorted for study and society. Euclid, the geometer, Stilpo, Theodo′rus, and Diodo′rus, the philosophers, Phile′tas, the poet, and Zenod′otus, the grammarian, resided there. The painters Antiphilus and Apelles also practised their art in Alexandria; Menander and Theophrastus were likewise invited, but declined the invitation. The illustrious Demetrius Phale′reus was one of the chief ornaments of the Court of Ptolemy Soter. Deprived of the governorship of Athens, he fled to Egypt, where he was welcomed by the monarch; and he rendered great assistance to him in his measures for the encouragement of literature. Trade and navigation were encouraged; the harbor of Alexandria and a lighthouse on the island of Pharos were constructed; to reach the latter a causeway a mile in length was made. The Jews were allowed to have a temple in the city, and the Septuagint version of the Old Testament from Hebrew into Greek was subsequently made for their use. Papyrus for the leaves of books was brought into general use, instead of linen, wax, or the bark of trees, stone, brass, or lead, as had been previously the case. Alexandria became the centre of civilization and of literature. The conquest of the Syrian frontiers, the ancient kingdom of Cyrene, great part of Ethiopia, and the island of Cyprus, added to the external security of Egypt. Towards the end of Ptolemy Soter's reign, the worship of Sera′pis was introduced into Egypt. It is said that the king was induced by a vision to send to Pontus for an image of the god. (See Tacitus, *Annals*, IV. 83.) Be that as it may, a Grecian idol was brought to Alexandria, and set up in a very extensive and splendid temple, named (after the god) Serapium, built purposely for its reception. It has been supposed that this idol was called in the Coptic language Rhacotis, which word has the same signification as Pluto, in Greek. (Whyte's *Egyptiaca*, Part I. p. 103.) The worship of Serapis appears to have introduced a change into the religious ceremonies of Egypt. Hitherto animals had been held sacred, but with Serapis sacrifices were introduced, and the ancient veneration for animal life died out. Ptolemy was the greatest monarch of his age. In the year B. C. 285 he abdicated in favor of his youngest son, Ptolemy Philadelphus, the child of his beloved wife Berenice. He died two years afterwards (B. C. 283), greatly regretted.

The reign of Ptolemy Philadelphus was as prosperous as that of Ptolemy Lagus. The epithet Philadelphus (signifying "one who loves his brother") was bestowed upon him in irony, because he put to death two of his brothers. Great public works were undertaken. Ports for the Indian and Arabian trade were made on the Red Sea at Arsin′oë (now Suez), Myos-Hormos (now Cosseir), and Bereni′ce. From the two latter stations, caravan roads were made to the Upper Nile, and the lower river was united to the Red Sea by a canal which was continued to the harbor of Alexandria. The character of Ptolemy Philadelphus was stained with vice. He put to death his two brothers; divorced his first wife, Arsinoë, and banished her on a charge of treason; and he married his own sister Arsinoë, the widow of Lysimachus. For this second wife he evinced the greatest affection, erecting monuments to her memory, and naming cities by her name. But he had some redeeming qualities. He was fond of literature, and under his patronage Alexandria became the resort of learned men. He went to great trouble and expense in collecting books of value; and he purchased from Eleazar, the high-priest of the Jews, an authentic copy of the Hebrew Scriptures. This copy was by his orders translated into Greek, seventy-two learned men being employed in the work. This version has been styled the Septuagint, from the Latin word *Septuaginta*, signifying seventy, and in reference to the number of translators, though, in strictness, there were seventy-two. It became extensively used, and is frequently alluded to and quoted by the writers of the New Testament.

In the year B. C. 264, the peace of the country was disturbed by Magas, the brother of Ptolemy, who endeavored to re-establish the kingdom of Cyrene, and was assisted in his rebellion by Antiochus, king of Syria. The war was brought to a close by a treaty by which Magas acquired undisputed possession of the Cyrenaïca, and his infant daughter Berenice was betrothed to Ptolemy's son. The king was engaged in frequent wars with Antiochus, but he terminated them at last by giving his daughter Berenice in marriage to that monarch. During the remainder of Ptolemy's reign, Egypt enjoyed a large share of prosperity. Ptolemy was wise enough to cultivate the friendship of the Romans, then rapidly rising in power. He sent ambassadors to them, and received those whom they sent in return with extraordinary splendor, loading them with presents. He was one of the greatest potentates of that age. At the close of his reign, it is said that he possessed a standing army of 200,000 infantry and 40,000 cavalry, a fleet of 1500 ships, and an amount of treasure estimated at 740,000 talents ($811,000,000) (B. C. 247). He was succeeded by his son, Ptolemy Euer′getes (the benefactor), a warlike and enterprising prince, whose first exploit was to avenge the murder of his sister, Bereni′ce, by Laod′ice, the wife of Antiochus, king of Syria. With a powerful army he invaded the dominions of that monarch (B. C. 245), overran Syria, Babylonia, Persia, and Upper Asia, and returned to Egypt with immense booty, bringing back with him the idols which Cambyses had carried away from Memphis and Thebes 280 years before. The restoration of these idols to their respective temples gained him very great popularity, and the appellation of Euergetes. His queen, Berenice, had made a vow that if he should return in safety she would devote her hair to Venus. Accordingly, when he returned she cut it off and sent it to the temple of Venus at Zephyrum in Cyprus, where it was lost. To soothe the anger of Euergetes at this negligence, the astronomer Conon of Samos pretended that the hair had been carried up to heaven and converted into a constellation of seven stars near that of Leo. The king and queen were much pleased with this gross flattery, and the constellation was named "Berenice's hair" (*Coma Berenices*). He also subdued a great part of Abyssinia and Arabia (B. C. 225), and opened new roads for trade through these countries.

With the death of Euergetes (B. C. 222) ended the glory of the Ptolemies. His son Ptolemy, surnamed Philop′ator (lover of his father), was a weak and dissolute prince, who was always under the evil influence of favorites. At the instigation of his prime minister, Sosibius, he put to death his brother, Magas, and Cleom′enes, the exiled king of Sparta. Antiochus the Great, king of Syria, took advantage of Ptolemy's incapacity, and made war upon Egypt (B. C. 218), but he was defeated at Raphia (B. C. 217). Ptolemy, after this victory, visited Jerusalem, and made an attempt to enter the sanctuary of the Temple, but being prevented by the priests, became so enraged, that on his return to Egypt he determined to exterminate all the Jews that had settled in his kingdom. For this purpose they were brought from the most distant parts of the country to Alexandria, and cast into the Hippodrome (or Circus), where 500 elephants were prepared to destroy them. These animals were made drunk to increase their fury, but instead of attacking the Jews they rushed upon the spectators, and committed frightful havoc. Ptolemy, struck with remorse, restored to the Jews their privileges. He did not carry out his wicked design, but soon afterwards he murdered his wife and sister, and transferred his affections to Agathocle′a, whose brother, the infamous Agatho′cles, had succeeded to the position and influence of Sosib′ius. At length Ptolemy's dissipation broke down his constitution, and he died (B. C. 205) of premature infirmity, though in the very prime of life. He was a monster of infamy. He left behind him an only son, a child about 5 years old, who succeeded him.

Ptolemy Epiph′anes (or the illustrious) was placed under the care of regents, who proved unworthy of their trust. The kingdom was menaced by Antiochus the Great, king of Syria, who had combined with Philip of Macedon to wrest Egypt from the Ptolemies, and had made himself master of Cœle-Syria and Palestine. The regency of the country was therefore offered to and undertaken by the Roman Senate, which saved Egypt from being involved in the Syrian war.

Amongst the eminent men of Egypt in this century were Euclid, the mathematician; Callim′achus, grammarian, poet, and librarian; Eratos′thenes of Cyrene, geographer; Sosib′ius, grammarian; and Mane′tho, an Egyptian priest, the first who gave in the Greek language an account of the religion and history of his country, derived from the sacred books of the Egyptians.

What was the character of Ptolemy Soter?—Which were his chief works?—What eminent men did he patronize?—What dominions did he acquire?—Who succeeded him?—What was the character of Ptolemy Philadelphus?—What is the Septuagint version of the Old Testament?—What new god was worshipped?—What is said of Magas and his rebellion?

What was the condition of Egypt during the reign of Ptolemy Soter?—How did the king act towards the Romans?—What were the exploits of Ptolemy Euergetes?—Relate the legend of Berenice's hair.—What is said of Ptolemy Philopator?—Ptolemy Epiphanes?—What eminent men flourished?

SYRIA.

Seleucus Nica'tor being now (B. C. 300) master of Upper Asia (*i. e.* the countries between the rivers Oxus, Indus, and Euphrates), as well as of Syria, built Antioch for his capital, and consolidated his Syrian kingdom. He also founded two cities, one on the Tigris, the other on the Oron'tes, both of which he named Seleu'cia. He married the daughter of Demetrius Poliorcetes (B. C. 299), whom he established as governor of Cilicia. He also gave Upper Asia (B. C. 294) to his own son, Anti'ochus. Seleucus was the most powerful of all the successors of Alexander. The ambitious designs of Demetrius Poliorcetes, who had now become king of Macedonia, once more embroiled the East. Seleucus combined with Ptolemy and Lysimachus against him, and after a two years' contest he was driven into Asia Minor, taken prisoner, and kept in captivity for the rest of his life by Seleucus; who, however, otherwise treated him kindly. Demetrius being disposed of, peace was restored. The next event of importance was a war between Seleucus and Lysimachus, king of Thrace; which was occasioned by the former espousing the cause of the widow of Lysimachus' step-son Agathocles, whom the latter had murdered. The two monarchs met on the plain of Corus, where Lysimachus was killed (B. C. 281). Seleucus was soon after assassinated by Ptolemy Ceraunus, the son of his old friend Lysimachus, whom he had protected and benefited. Seleucus founded a number of Macedonian colonies in Asia, which became centres of civilization. Sixteen of these were named Antiochia, after his father Antiochus; five were named Laodice'a, after his mother Laod'ice; seven were named Seleucia, after himself; three were named Apame'a, after his first wife; and one, Stratonicea, after his second wife. He also founded Bere'a, Edessa, and Pella. His son, Antiochus Soter, reunited Syria to Upper Asia (B. C. 280). He gave up his claims over Macedon to Antigonus Gona'tas, but pursued his father's plans of conquest in Asia Minor. He was defeated by Nicome'des, king of Bithynia (B. C. 278), and was equally unsuccessful against Eu'menes, king of Pergamus (B. C. 263). Bero'sus, a Babylonian priest, the historian of Chaldæa, flourished about this time. He wrote in Greek a history of Babylonia, comprising the earliest traditions about the human race, a description of Babylonia and its inhabitants, and a chronological list of its kings down to the time of Cyrus. Berosus says that he derived the materials for his work from the archives in the temple of Belus. The work is lost, but fragments of it have been preserved. Ill luck pursued Antiochus in all his enterprises. Aiding Magas, the brother of Ptolemy, to set up a new kingdom at Cyrene, his forces were defeated in every engagement, and his coasts ravaged by the Egyptian fleet (B. C. 264). He then marched against the Gauls (or Galatians), who had advanced to Ephesus, and by them he was defeated and slain (B. C. 261).

His son and successor, Antiochus (surnamed by the Milesians Theos, or the God, because he delivered them from their tyrant Timarchus), defeated the Gauls, but was unable to resist the progress of the Parthians, who, under Arsa'ces, were now establishing their kingdom in Upper Asia. He made peace with Ptolemy and married his daughter Berenice (B. C. 249), divorcing his own wife, Laod'ice, who in revenge poisoned both him and Berenice (B. C. 246). His son, Seleucus II. (surnamed Callin'icus, or illustrious conqueror) succeeded to the throne, and immediately found himself engaged in a war with Ptolemy Euer'getes, who was eager to avenge the murder of his sister Berenice, put to death by Seleucus. Ptolemy overran Syria, Babylonia, Persia, and Upper Asia (B. C. 245), defeated Seleucus, and forced him to take refuge in Antioch. Eumenes, king of Pergamus, also added a portion of Seleucus's dominions to his own; and Antiochus Hierax, the brother of Seleucus, attempted to usurp the throne of Syria. He was at first successful (B. C. 242), but the ravages of the Gauls (Galatians) had the effect of reuniting all the subjects of Seleucus; and thus strengthened, the Syrian monarch crushed the rebellion, and totally routed the Gauls. He then (B. C. 238) turned his arms against the Parthians, but was defeated by their king Arsaces; and in a second campaign (B. C. 236) was taken prisoner by them, and kept so until his death, which occurred B. C. 226, and was occasioned by a fall from his horse. Seleucus III. (surnamed in derision Ceraunus, or the thunderbolt) succeeded his father, but being feeble both in mind and body, he was assassinated by two of his officers. His cousin, Achæus, secured the throne for Antiochus, satrap of Babylon, the younger brother of the deceased monarch (B. C. 224). Antiochus III. (surnamed "the Great") was led by the intrigues of his minister, Hermeias, into a quarrel with Achæus, whom he drove into rebellion. The brothers of Hermeias, having been made satraps of Media and Persia, likewise revolted, but were subdued and executed (B. C. 220). Meanwhile Achæus, having leagued himself with Ptolemy king of Egypt, ravaged Asia Minor; while Ptolemy attacked Antiochus, and defeated him at Raphia near Gaza (B. C. 217). Achæus, besieged in Sardis by the joint forces of Antiochus, and Attalus, king of Pergamus, was there betrayed and put to death (B. C. 216). Antiochus then attacked the Parthians and Bactrians (B. C. 212), but though he gained some victories over them, he was forced to acknowledge their independence. He gave his daughter in marriage to Demetrius, son of the king of Bactria, and joined that prince in an expedition against Northern India (B. C. 206). He also made some efforts to revive the commercial system founded by Alexander the Great, and encouraged the trade of the Persian Gulf. On the death of Ptolemy Philopator, and the accession of his infant son to the throne of Egypt (B. C. 205), Antiochus entered into an alliance with Philip, king of Macedon, to wrest Egypt from the family of the Ptolemies. He conquered Cœle-Syria and Palestine, but was prevented from pursuing his success by the interference of Attalus and the Romans.

Judea. — This portion of Syria suffered much during the complicated wars of the kings of Syria and Egypt, but the high-priests appear to have had the management of the affairs of the Jewish people. The history of this period is unimportant. Simon the Just, the high-priest, completed the canon of the old Testament by adding to it the books of Ezra, Nehemiah, Esther, and Malachi. His successors were Eleazar (B. C. 292–260), Manasseh (B. C. 260–233), Oni'as II. (B. C. 233–219), Simon II. (B. C. 219–195). Of these priests there is not much to record. The neglect of Onias to pay the tribute due to the king of Egypt, caused that prince to threaten an invasion of Judea; but the country was saved from this danger by the adroitness of Joseph, the nephew of Onias, whose singular conduct and success are detailed in Milman's *History of the Jews* (vol. ii., page 33).

What cities did Seleucus Nicator found? — What was the end of Demetrius Poliorcetes? — And of Seleucus? — Who succeeded him? — What is said of Antiochus Soter? — Berosus? — Seleucus Callinicus? — Antiochus Hierax? — Seleucus Ceraunus? — Antiochus the Great? — Who was Achæus, and what befell him? — What treaty and conquests did Antiochus make? — What is said of Judea? — Simon the Just? — For what was he celebrated? — Who succeeded him? — What did the misconduct of Onias occasion?

INDIA.

The Bactrian kingdom founded by Seleucus, king of Syria, flourished during the reigns of several of his descendants, until their own civil wars and the impending revolt of the Parthians induced the governor of the province to assert his independence. Theod'otus was the first king (B. C. 250). There were three different dynasties, who had much intercourse with Northern India. They are mentioned in the Purans as the Yâwân, or Ionian kings. Eight of them reigned in the north of India.

In other parts of the Peninsula, the Maga'di sovereigns were the most powerful. Of these, Chandragupta (the Sandracottus of the Greeks), already noticed, was the most celebrated. He was a man of mean origin, and was the leader of a band of robbers before he obtained the supreme power. In the troubles which followed the death of Alexander, he extended his dominions over the greater part of Northern India, and conquered the Macedonians who had been left by Alexander in the Punjaub. The history of Chandragupta forms the subject of a Hindoo drama, called the *Mudra Rahshasa*. He died about 300 years before Christ, and was succeeded by his son, Mitragupta, who appears to have paid tribute to the Bactrian princes. The state of India under the Magadi dynasty is described as prosperous and happy. Arts, commerce, literature, and husbandry, all flourished. A royal road is said to have extended from the capital, Palibothra, to the Indus, and another to Broach, in Gujerat. Mitragupta and his successors patronized learned men, and supported a brilliant Court. In his reign the Sancrit language attained its highest state of polish and refinement. His dynasty continued to rule for more than eight centuries, or until about the year 450 of the Christian era. This century is the epoch of the reign of Aso'ca (the third of the line of Chandragupta), whose influence appears to have extended from north to south of the Indian peninsula. He was the great champion of Buddhism, which made great progress throughout the land, and was introduced into Ceylon by his missionaries. His edicts inscribed on rocks have been deciphered. They relate to the establishment of hospitals and other charitable institutions, and to the triumph of the new religion, and they prove that this monarch held intercourse with Egypt.

What is said of the Greek kingdom of Bactria? — Of Chandragupta? — Mitragupta? — And the state of India? — How long did his dynasty endure? — What is said of Asoca?

PERSIA.

This country now formed part of the dominions of the Seleucidæ, or successors of Seleucus, whose capital was Antioch. The history of them is, for a time, blended with that of Syria.

Bactria and Sogdiana, situated at the extreme eastern verge of the ancient Persian empire, was, on the first division of the empire of Alexander the Great (B. C. 323), allotted to Philip, one of his generals. On the second division (B. C. 301), after the battle of Ipsus, it became part of the dominions of Seleucus Nicator, king of Syria. The government of the province was administered by governors appointed by the Syrian monarchs. One of these, named Theod′otus, whilst Antiochus Theos was engaged in war with Egypt, revolted, and made himself independent (B. C. 250). He then assumed the regal dignity, subjected the cities which remained loyal to Antiochus, and strengthened himself so effectually in his new position that it became impossible to reduce him to obedience. His example was followed by the neighboring provinces, which were thus lost to Antiochus. About the same time (B. C. 250), Agatho′cles, the Greek governor of Parthia, having incensed the people by his tyranny, Arsa′ces, a man of humble origin, killed him; and having roused the people, expelled the Macedonians. He caused himself to be elected king of the Parthians, and he established an independent government which was feudal in its form, the monarchy being elective, with a proviso that the king should always be chosen from the members of his family. Arsaces reigned only two years, and was succeeded by his brother, Tirida′tes, called also Arsaces II.

In the year B. C. 245, Ptolemy Euergetes, king of Egypt, then at war with Seleucus, king of Syria, overran Babylonia, Persia, and the provinces of Upper Asia, and plundered them, taking back to Egypt an immense booty, and some of the spoils which Cambyses had carried off from Egypt 280 years before. In the year B. C. 243 a treaty of alliance was formed between Parthia and Bactria. Seleucus tried to reduce the Parthians to subjection, but was defeated by their king, Tiridates (B. C. 238). In a second campaign (B. C. 236), Tiridates took him prisoner, and kept him in captivity until he died (B. C. 226). In the year B. C. 220, Media and Persia were the scene of a revolt, instigated by Molon, satrap of Media, and his brother, Alexander, satrap of Persia, the brothers of Hermeias, the prime minister of Antiochus the Great. But on the appearance of the young king, Antiochus, the troops threw down their arms and submitted. The conspirators were taken prisoners, and executed. Antiochus then made an attempt to reduce the Parthians and Bactrians to submission. He marched into Media, which the Parthians had taken from him, and repossessed himself of that province. He also entered Parthia, and obliged Tiridates to retire into Hyrcania. Here his success ended, for Tiridates collected an army of 120,000 men, and re-entered Parthia. The war was renewed with great fury, but Antiochus, though successful in several battles, found it impossible to subject his adversaries, and at length recognised their independence (B. C. 210). He made a treaty with Arsaces, by which he resigned Parthia and Hyrcania to the latter, upon condition that he would assist him in reconquering the other revolted provinces. Antiochus then marched against Euthyde′mus, king of Bactria, who had succeeded Theodotus in the year B. C. 221, but he was not more successful against him than he had been against Arsaces, and was obliged to make terms with him. We know nothing of the circumstances attending the elevation of Euthydemus to the sovereignty of Bactria. On his death, Menander became king; and Antiochus made a league with the new monarch, giving his own daughter in marriage to Menander's son, Demetrius. Antiochus joined that prince in an expedition against Northern India. Menander was one of the most powerful of all the Greek rulers of Bactria, and made extensive conquests.

Tiridates, king of Parthia, was succeeded by his son, Artabanes I. (B. C. 211). Malcolm says (*History of Persia*, vol. i., p. 250): "It is impossible to reconcile the Persian dates with those of either Grecian or Roman historians, which arises from the simple fact of Asiatic writers having no account of this period that merits the name of history. They give us a mere catalogue of kings; and their calculation of the years the monarchs they mention reigned, is less, by some centuries, than the actual time which this epoch includes." The Parthian empire became one of the most considerable and powerful that ever existed in the East. It extended over all Upper Asia, and made even the Romans tremble.

To whom were Bactria and Sogdiana allotted?—To whom, after the battle of Ipsus?—Who was Theodotus?—Arsaces?—What monarchy did he found?—What did Ptolemy Euergetes do?—What befell Seleucus?—What was the result of the contest between Antiochus and Tiridates?—And Arsaces?—What is said of Menander?

CHINA. JAPAN.

The people of Chow ranged themselves round the standard of Chow-keun, a descendant of the Chow princes, whose heroic efforts to retrieve the fallen fortunes of his race deserved a better fate. Chow-keun was forced to submit to the ferocious Chaou-seang, the Tsin general, who had founded the Tsin dynasty. On Chaou-seang's death (B. C. 249), his son, Heaou-wan-wang, ascended the throne, but died a few days after his accession. E-jin succeeded him. He subdued the provinces of Han, Tsoo, and Chaou; but five of the States formed an alliance against him, and defeated him. He died of vexation (B. C. 246). His successor was the famous Che-hwang-te, the reputed child of E-jin, but in reality the son of a merchant, and foisted upon the emperor as his own son, by the artifices of his real father and mother. Che-hwang-te was guilty of great cruelty to his mother, and, as filial piety has been always accounted in China the first of virtues, he became very much disliked. Many of the "philosophers" of his court remonstrated with him, but in vain; he put twenty-seven of them to death, and caused their limbs to be suspended outside the palace, in order to strike terror into the others. One of them, however, named Maou-tseaou, ventured to upbraid the emperor with his cruelty, and, struck with his intrepidity, Che-hwang-te pardoned him, retaining him at court as a faithful adviser. This emperor formed the design of subjecting all China to himself. By dint of bribery and artful machinations he contrived to sow such dissensions amongst the petty princes as prevented their uniting against him. He was thus enabled to overcome them one by one.

The northern provinces of the empire having been repeatedly ravaged by the Heung-noo (or Huns), whose empire then extended to the west of Shen-se, Che-hwang-te resolved to attack them. This he did suddenly (B. C. 215), took them by surprise, and slaughtered great numbers of them. To put a stop to their inroads, he resolved to erect a monument which should be a lasting memorial of his greatness. This was the Great Wall of China, commencing in Lin-teaou, in the western part of Shen-se, and terminating in the sea, at the foot of the mountains of Leaou-tung, a distance of more than 1500 miles. It was strengthened with fortresses, and was so broad that six horsemen could ride abreast upon it. Five years were required to build it, and every third man in the empire was forced to work on it, under the direction of the architect, Mung-tëen. It was completed B. C. 210.

When Che-hwang-te became sole master of the empire he assumed the title of Emperor, changed the imperial color from yellow to black, and introduced a regular system of despotism. But he encouraged astronomy, and published a calendar; embellished his chief city, Hëew-yang, and visited all parts of his empire, introducing innovations and improvements everywhere. This drew down on him the reproaches of the learned, which so enraged the despot that he ordered 460 of them to be buried alive, and all the ancient books to be burned. This measure introduced the greatest confusion into the annals of China, on which account the memory of Che-hwang-te is detested by the Chinese.

His son, Hoo-hae, succeeded him (B. C. 210), but was a worthless prince, living only for his own pleasures, and never quitting the palace. He put to death Mung-tëen, the architect of the great wall, and also his own brother. A universal rebellion took place, headed by a robber named Lew-pang. The emperor finding himself deserted by all, put an end to his life. Tsze-ying, the emperor's nephew, endeavored to repel the army of Lew-pang, but without success; so he submitted to the conqueror, and thus ended the Tsin dynasty (B. C. 206).

Lew-pang marched boldly to the capital. The prince of Tsoo also endeavored to get possession of it, but the people proclaimed the king of Choo, Hwae-wang, emperor, and allotted to Lew-pang the provinces of Pa, Choo, and Han-chang. China was desolated by intestine wars until B. C. 202, when Lew-pang, master of the empire, and adopting the name of Kaou-tsoo, founded the dynasty of Han.

Japan.—Ko-re-i succeeded Ko-an (B. C. 290). In the year 285 the lake and river of Oomi were formed in one night by a sudden convulsion of the earth. In the year 244 Japan was divided into thirty-six provinces. Korei died at the age of 128 (B. C. 214). His son, Kow-kin, removed his court to Karutz. In his time the Chinese emperor, Che-hwang-te, sent 300 youths and 300 maids into Japan, in search of the Elixir of Immortality.

For what was Chow-keun famous?—Who founded the Tsin dynasty?—Mention the acts of Che-hwang-te.—Describe the great wall, the name, and the fate of the architect.—Why is the memory of Che-hwang-te detested?—Who founded the Han dynasty?—What occurred in Japan?

GREECE.

After the battle of Ipsus (B. C. 301) Demetrius Poliorcetes fled to Greece, established himself in the Peloponnesus, and commenced a naval war against Lysim'achus, king of Thrace; while Seleucus, king of Syria, supplied him with the means of getting possession of Athens (B. C. 299). On the death of Cassander (B. C. 296), Macedonia was left to the three sons of that general;—one of whom, Philip IV., died; another, Antip'ater, having murdered his mother, fled to Thrace, where he died. The survivor, Alexander, sought aid against Lysimachus, from Pyrrhus, king of Epirus, and Demetrius Poliorcetes, the latter of whom, taking advantage of the necessities of the young prince, got possession of the throne, and Alexander was slain. Demetrius was now (B. C. 294) master of Macedon, Thessaly, Bœotia, and Attica; but a combination between Pyrrhus and Lysimachus drove him from Macedon into the Peloponnesus, then governed by his son, Antig'onus (B. C. 287). Pyrrhus seized the throne of Macedon, but in his turn was expelled by Lysimachus, who remained master of it (B. C. 286). Demetrius, driven into Cilicia, was taken prisoner by Seleucus, and kept in prison till he died (B. C. 284); but his son Antigonus maintained himself in the Peloponnesus. Lysimachus, having put to death his own son, Agathocles, Lysandra, the widow of the young prince, fled with her brother, Ptolemy Ceraunus, to Seleucus, who forthwith (B. C. 282) espoused their cause, and invaded the dominions of Lysimachus. The latter, then in his 80th year, was defeated and slain (B. C. 281). Ptolemy, with the basest ingratitude, murdered Seleucus, who had thus assisted him, and made himself king of Macedon. In the same year, a horde of Gauls (or Celts from Pannonia), poured into Macedon and Thrace, and plundered Delphi. Ptolemy was defeated by them, taken prisoner, and put to death. He was succeeded by Sos'thenes, a Macedonian officer of high birth.

The Gauls soon after were cut to pieces by the Ætolians, and the Achæan league was revived in Southern Greece. Meanwhile (B. C. 280–275) Pyrrhus, king of Epirus, having been invited into Italy by the Tarentines, defeated the Romans at Heracle'a and As'culum, but sustained severe losses himself. On this occasion he uttered the memorable exclamation: "Another such victory, and I am ruined!" Unable to overcome the Roman general, Fabricius, he crossed into Sicily, where he attacked the Carthaginians and besieged Lilybæ'um. Being forced to raise the siege of that city, he returned to Italy, and was totally defeated by the Romans at Beneven'tum. Meanwhile, Sos'thenes, having been slain in battle against the Gauls (B. C. 277), was succeeded in Macedon by Antigonus Gona'tas, the son of Demetrius Poliorcetes. Pyrrhus, on his return from Italy, excited a revolution in Macedon, and seized the throne (B. C. 273); whereupon Antigonus fled into Southern Greece, pursued by Pyrrhus, who was also aiding Cleon'ymus to dethrone his nephew, A'reus, king of Sparta. The career of this ambitious prince was here cut short (B. C. 272). From Sparta he marched to Argos to support Aris'teas, the leader of one of the factions in that city. In the night time Aristeas admitted Pyrrhus into the city; but the alarm having been given, the citizens flew to arms, and Pyrrhus found it advisable to retreat; but as he was fighting his way out, an Argive woman hurled down a heavy tile from a house top upon his head. He fell from his horse, and was immediately dispatched. He was the greatest warrior and one of the best princes of his time. In subsequent times, he was regarded as one of the greatest generals that had ever lived. Hannibal said that of all generals Pyrrhus was the first, Scipio the second, and himself the third; or, according to some, that Alexander was the first, Pyrrhus the second, and himself the third. He was succeeded in his kingdom of Epirus by his son, Alexander II. On the death of Pyrrhus, Antigonus regained Macedon, and retained it until his death (B. C. 239).

In the year B. C. 251, the city of Sic'yon, misruled by tyrants, was freed by the courage of the patriotic citizen Ara'tus. The Sicyonians then joined the other cities which formed the Achæan league. Aratus also by a bold attempt drove the Macedonian garrison out of Corinth (B. C. 243); and this city, with Træze'ne and Epidaurus, likewise joined the league. In B. C. 229 Athens did the same, and the confederacy became formidable.

On the death of Antigonus Gona'tas (B. C. 239), his son, Demetrius II., became king of Macedon. The ten years of his reign were spent in war with the Ætolians. On his death, Antigonus Doson, his cousin, succeeded, nominally as regent for Philip V., the son of Demetrius II.

In Sparta, Agis IV. endeavored to revive the laws of Lycurgus (B. C. 244), but the opposition of Leon'idas, the other king of Sparta, brought about a counter revolution (B. C. 240), and Agis was strangled by order of the Ephori. Cleomenes succeeded Leonidas (B. C. 236), and endeavored to carry out the reforms proposed by Agis. Turning his arms against the Achæans (B. C. 227), he compelled Corinth and Argos to secede from the league; he also reduced Aratus to such extremities that the latter was forced to solicit aid from the king of Macedon (B. C. 222). Antigonus, who came to the assistance of Aratus, routed Cleomenes at Sella'sia, made himself master of Sparta, and restored the ancient constitution. Cleomenes fled to Egypt, where he died. Antigonus died soon after (B. C. 220), and was succeeded by Philip V. This prince became involved in a contest with the warlike Ætolians, who attacked him and his allies, the leagued cities, and defeated their general, Aratus, at Caphyæ; but the increasing power of the Romans now became so threatening, that the States of Greece were induced to make peace amongst themselves (B. C. 217), and unite for the common defence.

Philip being recognized as the head of the Greeks (B. C. 215), entered into a league with Hannibal, the famous Carthaginian general, against the Romans; but excited the indignation of all Greece by causing Aratus, who was an obstacle to his designs, to be poisoned (B. C. 213). That illustrious man has left us a history of his own times, down to the year 220. The Romans, to distract Philip's attention, formed a league with the Ætolians, Sparta, Pergamus, and Elis (B. C. 211). With the aid of their ally, Att'alus, king of Pergamus, they soon became masters of the sea; but were too hotly pressed at that time by Hannibal to continue their assistance to the Ætolians. Meanwhile Philopœ'men had succeeded Aratus as the prætor of the Achæan league, and he, marching against the Spartans, defeated and slew with his own hand Machan'idas, the usurper of Lacedæmon (B. C. 210). The Ætolians, after this, made peace, and withdrew from the Roman alliance. Philip then (B. C. 208) allied himself with Pru'sias, king of Bithynia, against Attalus, king of Pergamus; and with Anti'ochus, king of Syria, against Ptolemy, king of Egypt. He invaded Asia Minor, but though successful by land, he was defeated at sea by the Rhodians and Attalus. He next attacked Athens (B. C. 201), which city applied to Rome for assistance. The Romans sent a fleet and army just in time to save the still illustrious, though fallen, city. Egypt saved herself also by placing the regency of the country in the hands of the Roman Senate.

The degeneracy of the Greeks at this period is shown not merely in their naval and military undertakings, but in the inferiority of the men of letters who flourished in this century, as compared with those of the age of Pericles. At the beginning of the century there were four schools in Athens, presided over respectively by Zeno, Arcesila'us, Epicu'rus, and Strato. The other men of eminence were the philosophers Cra'tes, Chrysip'pus (who left 705 works), Po'lemo, and Evander; the poets Posidip'pus and Bion; the historians Timæ'us, Nean'thes, and Phylar'chus; Zenod'otus of Ephesus, the celebrated grammarian; Erasis'tratus, the physician; and others of less note.

Zeno was a native of Cyprus: the date of his birth is not known. He settled at Athens, and studied philosophy under Stilpo, Philo, and Xenocrates. He subsequently started a system of his own, which he taught in the famous porch (Stoa) of Polygnotus; hence his school was called "the Stoic". He was a man of great probity, and was highly esteemed. The date of his death is unknown.

Strato taught that there is no God out of the material universe; that every particle of matter can mould itself, but is without sensation or intelligence; that life, sensation, and intellect are but the forms and accidents of matter.

Theoc'ritus, a native of Syracuse, was the creator of Greek pastoral poetry. He studied at Alexandria, but returned to Sicily, where he passed his life.

Eratos'thenes of Cyrene was born B. C. 276, and studied at Athens. He died of voluntary starvation at the age of 80, being tired of life. He was extensively learned in astronomy, mathematics, and geography, and was the first who attempted to measure the size of the earth. In doing this he invented and employed the method which is used at the present day.

Who obtained the Peloponnesus?—Macedonia?—Relate the changes which took place in the affairs of Greece.—What befell Demetrius Poliorcetes?—Lysimachus?—Ptolemy Ceraunus?—What is said of the Gaulish invasion?—Of the exploits, death, and character of Pyrrhus?—Aratus?—The Achæan league?—Who succeeded Antigonus Gonatas in Macedon?

What is said of Agis IV. of Sparta?—Leonidas?—And Cleomenes?—Philip V.?—The fate of Aratus?—The war with the Romans?—The fate of Athens?—And Egypt?—Philopœmen?—The literary character of the age?—Zeno?—Strato?—Theocritus?—Eratosthenes?—What other eminent men flourished?

ITALY.

The reduction of the Samnites was one of the first things that occupied the Romans at the beginning of the century. That heroic people showed a bravery equal to that of the Romans themselves; and, assisted by the Umbrians, Etrurians, and Gauls, they withstood for eight years (B. C. 300–292) the efforts of the consuls, Fa′bius Maximus, De′cius, and Cu′rius Denta′tus. The veteran Fabius obtained a decisive victory at Senti′num (B. C. 295), where, it is said, 25,000 Samnites were killed, and 8000 taken prisoners; the Roman loss amounted to upwards of 8000 men killed, and a large number (not stated) wounded. In this famous battle the Gauls took a conspicuous part, but were almost exterminated. The Samnites would neither surrender nor disperse, but retreated from the field in a body. The consul, Decius, was slain, and his body was found under a heap of slaughtered Gauls. Fabius pronounced a funeral oration over him, and buried him with military honors. But the Samnites did not give up the contest, notwithstanding their severe losses. They raised another army, and bound the soldiers by the most solemn oaths to conquer or die. It required several more campaigns to terminate the war. The consuls, Papir′ius Cursor and Spurius Carvilius, ravaged Samnium; the former gained a great battle near Bovianum, but did not follow up his success. Quintus Fabius Gurges, son of the great Fabius, was then sent against the enemy, who, under their veteran hero, Pontius Herennius, had invaded Campania. In this campaign the old Fabius served under his own son as lieutenant. In the first battle Fabius was defeated, but in the second the Samnites left 20,000 men dead on the field, and their commander, Pontius, and 4000 men, were taken prisoners (B. C. 293). Even after this blow the Samnites held out for another year, when they were finally overcome, and a Roman colony of 20,000 persons was planted at their stronghold, Venusia, on the frontiers of Lucania and Apulia. For the successful termination of the war, a triumph was decreed to Fabius at Rome. But the glory of the achievement was, however, stained by the wantonly putting to death of the brave Samnite general, Pontius (B. C. 292). Such was the end of the third Samnite war. The subjection of the Sabines (B. C. 290) completed the extension of the domination of Rome over Central Italy. The aspiring republic now turned its arms against the south of the Peninsula, notwithstanding the distress occasioned by the Samnite war, to relieve which, and to appease the people, the "Hortensian Laws" were passed. These decreed a general reduction in the amount of debts, an apportionment of seven acres of land to every citizen, and the depriving of the Senate of its veto. They were named after their proposer, Quintus Hortensius. Another law, styled the Mænian, from its originator, Caius Mæ′nius, was passed about the same time. It took away the veto from the curiæ in the election of magistrates. By these enactments the people gained great power.

The Tarentines, jealous of the growing power of Rome, secretly instigated other Italian States to hostilities, while they placed themselves under the protection of Pyrrhus, king of Epirus. The Senones suddenly invaded the Roman territories, and defeated and killed the consul, Cæcil′ius Metel′lus, at Arretium (B. C. 284). This victory cost them dear; for, next year, the consul, Corne′lius Dolabella, defeated and almost exterminated them, and followed up his success by routing their allies, the Etruscans and the Gauls, near the Vadimonian Lake (B. C. 283). The military superiority of the Romans was fully established in these battles. But the people of Southern Italy had yet to be convinced of this. The Tarentines and Lucanians commenced hostilities by attacking the Roman fleet, and insulting their ambassadors (B. C. 282). The Lucanians took Thurium, in despite of the efforts of the consul, Fabricius Lusci′nus (B. C. 281) The consul, Æmilius Bar′bula, invaded Tarentum without success. After him, the consul, Valerius Lævi′nus, entered that territory to meet Pyrrhus, who had come to the assistance of the Tarentines. Valerius was defeated at Heraclæa, and Pyrrhus offered to mediate between Rome and Tarentum (B. C. 280). This offer was peremptorily rejected, and Pyrrhus then marched upon Rome. He, however, thought it better to turn back, and he was followed by the Romans, who encountered him at Asculum (B. C. 279). A desperate battle ensued, and Pyrrhus nominally remained master of the field, but he exclaimed, at the close of the day, "Another such victory, and I am ruined!" Disheartened by his small success, he crossed into Sicily (B. C. 278) to deliver the Greek States from the Carthaginians. The small States in the south of Italy speedily fell victims to the Romans, but the Tarentines held out, and implored Pyrrhus to return. This he did, but only to be totally defeated (B. C. 275) at Beneventum, by the consuls, Curius Dentatus and Cornelius Lentulus. The elephants captured in this battle were sent to Rome to be exhibited. They were the first animals of the kind ever seen there. Pyrrhus fled to Greece, and the Romans finally established their supremacy over Southern Italy. The city of Rome at this time contained about 280,000 citizens.

The ambitious republic now coveted Sicily, and soon found a pretext for attacking it. The Mamertine mercenaries, who had deserted from the Carthaginians, and were besieged in Messina, solicited the protection of Rome. This was gladly accorded, and thus began The First Punic (Phœnician) War. The consul, Appius Claudius, was sent into Sicily with an army, in the year B. C. 264, a year which is memorable for the introduction of the brutal exhibition of gladiators (combatants with swords) at Rome. The Romans were successful in Sicily. Claudius defeated Hiero and the Carthaginians. The consul, Valerius, took Messina and Agrigentum (B. C. 263), whereupon Hiero made peace with the Romans, and became their faithful ally. The Romans then turned their attention to naval affairs. They built a fleet, which they sent out under the consul Duilius, who gained a complete victory over the Carthaginians, off Mylæ, on the north coast of Sicily (B. C. 260). The consul Scipio attacked Sardinia and Corsica, while Malta surrendered without much resistance. The consul, Marcus Atil′ius Reg′ulus, surrounded by the Carthaginians in Sicily, had a narrow escape (B. C. 258), but the Romans were progressing fast at sea. An indecisive naval battle took place off Tyn′daris (B. C. 257), but a complete victory was gained near Ecno′mus (B. C. 256); after which, the victorious consuls, Atilius Regulus and Manlius Vulso, carried the war into Africa. The Carthaginians now engaged the Spartan general, Xanthippus, to conduct the war. By him Regulus was defeated and taken prisoner, in a sanguinary battle, wherein only 2000 Romans escaped. A series of disasters befell the Roman fleets at sea, which discouraged them from naval warfare. But in B. C. 250, the proconsul, Cæcilius Metellus, gained a great victory over the Carthaginian general, Asdrubal, at Palermo, and laid siege to Lilybæum. On this occasion, it is said (but on very doubtful authority) that the Carthaginians took Regulus out of prison, and sent him *on parole* to Rome, to make peace; but, instead of doing so, he exhorted his countrymen to continue the war, returned to Carthage, and was there put to a most cruel death. The war continued with varying success for some years, Hamilcar Barca sustaining the falling fortunes of the Carthaginians in Sicily; but at last the proconsul, Luta′tius Cat′ulus, completely annihilated their fleet near the Æga′tes (B. C. 241), and deprived them forever of the command of the sea. Hamilcar surrendered his army, and the Carthaginians evacuated Sicily, paying a tribute of 3200 talents ($3,575,000). Such was the first Punic War, whereby the Romans obtained Sicily (allowing the eastern portion of the island to remain under the government of Hiero), and acquired supremacy over all the world at sea. Sardinia and Corsica were given up to them in the year B. C. 238.

A period of tranquillity followed, and the temple of Janus was closed for the first time since the days of Numa Pompilius, as a sign of peace with all the world. Some troubles occasioned by the Gauls on the northern frontier, and a revolt in Sardinia, were all that disturbed the external peace of the republic for several years. But considerable dissension was occasioned at Rome by the tribune, Caius Flamin′ius, who obtained the passing of an agrarian law (B. C. 232), for dividing among the people the lands taken from the Gauls in Pice′num.

The next affair of consequence was the Illyrian war. The piracies of the Illyrians had provoked the Senate to remonstrate with Teuta, the widow of king Agron, and queen of Illyria. She not only refused redress, but caused one of the Roman ambassadors to be assassinated. War immediately followed, and the Romans forced queen Teuta to surrender the coast of Dalmatia and the island of Corcyra to the republic (B. C. 229). A new treaty with the Carthaginians bound the latter not to extend their dominion in Spain to the north of the Ebro (B. C. 226).

Who were the leaders in the third Samnite war?—What great battle was fought?—What was the result of the war?—How did the Romans stain their triumph?—What tribe did they next subdue?—What were the Hortensian laws?—What did the Tarentines do?—The Senones?

What is related of Pyrrhus?—What was the population of Rome?—What was the next great war?—Relate the principal incidents of it.—What is said of Regulus?—What celebrated battles were fought?—What was the result of the war?—What was the cause of the Illyrian war?

ITALY.

In the year B. C. 225 the republic was exposed to great danger from an invasion by the Celtic tribes from the Alps and the Po. They advanced in immense numbers, and were met at Clusium by the consuls, Atilius Regulus (son of the famous Regulus) and Æmilius Papus, whom they defeated. In a second battle, at Telamon, the Romans gained a bloody victory, but Regulus was slain. The Celts then quitted Italy. The subjection of the Boii followed (B. C. 224), and the consul, FLAMINIUS NEPOS, overcame the Insubres (B. C. 223). In the next year, the consul, CLAUDIUS MARCELLUS, gained the *Spolia Opima*, by killing with his own hand the Insubrian chief, Virid′omar, at Clastidium. The *Spolia Opima* were the richest booty, consisting of the armor and property of the enemy's commander. Marcellus dedicated them to Jupiter Feretrius — the third and last instance in Roman history of such an offering being made. The Veneti and Istrians now submitted to Rome. Placen′tia (Piacenza) and Cremo′na were founded, and Mutinum (Modena) was fortified (B. C. 221). All Northern Italy became subject to the Romans. The censor, Flaminius, availed himself of this brief interval of peace to construct the "Via Flaminia", or Flaminian road, from Rome to Arim′inum, and to build the "Circus Flaminius".

The most celebrated war in which the Romans were ever engaged now broke out. This was THE SECOND PUNIC WAR. It is related that HANNIBAL, the son of Gisco, and grandson of Hamilcar Barca, had, when only nine years old, sworn on the altar of Baal eternal enmity to the Romans. Arrived at maturity, he had displayed extraordinary military abilities, and was appointed commander-in-chief of the Carthaginian armies in Spain. There he meditated and secretly prepared the invasion of Italy and the destruction of Rome. In the year B. C. 218 he began his operations. He commenced his march from Spain at the head of 100,000 men. Having previously taken Saguntum, he crossed the Alps by the pass of the little St. Bernard, and reached the valley of the Po. The consul, CORNELIUS SCIPIO, endeavoring to stop him, was defeated and wounded near the river Tici′nus (Ticino); and his colleague, Sampro′nius Longus, was routed at the Trebbia. Next year (B. C. 217), Hannibal passed through the marshes of the Arno, being joined by all the Gaulish tribes, but losing the sight of one eye from ophthalmia contracted there. The consul, Flaminius Nepos, hastened to meet him, but was defeated and killed at the bloody battle near the lake of Thrasyme′nus. In this dreadful conflict, 15,000 Romans were taken prisoners, and the remainder were cut to pieces. Hannibal then marched into Apulia, where he spent the summer. The Romans, undismayed, thought not for a moment of peace. They raised a fresh army, and placed it under the command of QUINTUS FABIUS MAXIMUS, whom they appointed dictator; and they sent an expedition into Spain, under PUBLIUS SCIPIO and CNEIUS SCIPIO. Hannibal wasted much time in Southern Italy; but in August, B. C. 216, the consuls, TERENTIUS VARRO and ÆMILIUS PAULUS, marched into Apulia, at the head of 90,000 men, to attack him. He encountered them at Cannæ, and annihilated their army. 50,000 men perished on the field in this dreadful battle. Æmilius Paulus was slain, and the rest of his troops were dispersed or taken prisoners. But instead of following up his success, Hannibal went into winter quarters at Capua, where he remained all the winter. The Scipios gained several victories over Asdrubal in Spain, and in Italy the Romans raised another army, but, under the guidance of Fabius, changed their tactics. Avoiding encounters in the open field, they harassed the troops of Hannibal, and cut off his supplies; and, though he traversed Italy in all directions, he could not, in consequence of this policy, gain any advantage over Fabius. The Romans regained strength and courage. The consul, MARCELLUS, was sent into Sicily to besiege Syracuse, which city he took after an obstinate defence of nearly two years, protracted by the ingenuity of the celebrated mathematician, ARCHIME′DES, who was slain in the storming of the city (B. C. 212). The Scipios, however, were defeated and killed in Spain (B. C. 212). Hannibal then marched to the gates of Rome, but returned into Apulia, defeating the consul, Fulvius, near Herdonia. PUBLIUS CORNELIUS SCIPIO (afterwards Africanus) was now sent into Spain, where his success was brilliant. He took New Carthage, and drove the enemy to the Atlantic. Fabius recovered Tarentum, and Lævinus subdued the rest of Sicily. Hannibal was now at bay, but his brilliant genius did not fail him. He drew the consul, Marcellus, into an ambuscade, and cut his troops to pieces. Marcellus was killed, and his colleague, Crispi′nus, mortally wounded. Asdrubal, advancing from Spain to the assistance of Hannibal, crossed the Alps, and descended into Italy; but was routed and slain at the Metaurus, by the consuls, Claudius Nero and Livius Salina′tor (B. C. 207) — and this put an end to the schemes of Hannibal, who remained inactive in Bruttium. The supineness of Hannibal, after going into winter-quarters at Capua, is almost inexplicable. There is but little doubt that had he rapidly followed up his victory at Cannæ, and marched upon Rome, there would have been an end to the republic. That he should have wantonly foregone the cherished object of his life — the destruction of Rome — is scarcely credible. No satisfactory explanation of his conduct has been given: the only reason that is at all plausible is, that he may have meditated a sudden return to Carthage to establish himself and family in supreme power, and for this purpose moved to the south of Italy. The intrigues of the Barca family, to which Hannibal belonged, kept the Carthaginians in constant turmoil. But even this motive would hardly have been sufficient to induce him to refrain from destroying Rome. We are constrained to believe that an overruling Power set limits to his ambition, and preserved the Romans for purposes which the Carthaginians could never have accomplished.

Scipio, having driven the Carthaginians out of Spain, went to Africa to negotiate an alliance with Syphax, king of Numidia (B. C. 206), previously to attacking Carthage. Syphax, however, did not ally himself with the Romans, but lent his aid to the Carthaginians; and Scipio, crossing into Africa with a large army, defeated him and took him prisoner, giving a large part of his territories to Masinissa. Hannibal was recalled from Italy to defend Carthage, and was totally defeated by Scipio at Zama (B. C. 202). The Carthaginians now submitted to the terms imposed by the conqueror. These were: to make amends for injuries done to the Romans; to restore all prisoners; to give up all their ships of war; not to engage in war without the consent of the Romans; to restore to Masinissa all his dominions; to feed the Roman army for three months, and pay it until it should be recalled; to pay 10,000 Euboic silver talents (about $11,750,000), and to give up all their ships. These terms having been complied with, peace was concluded (B. C. 201). Scipio was honored with a splendid triumph and the title of Africanus, and the close of the Second Punic War left the Romans the principal naval power in the world, and masters of Spain and Sicily.

During all these wars literature and art were but indifferently cultivated by the Romans. Liv′ius Andro′nicus, the earliest Roman poet, wrote several tragedies and comedies. His first drama was acted B. C. 240. Cneius Næ′vius, a dramatist and poet, wrote an epic upon the First Punic War. He died B. C. 202. Quintus Fabius Pictor was the earliest prose historian of Rome, but only a few fragments of his history have come down to us. Cin′cius Alimentus, a celebrated antiquary and jurist, wrote Annals of the Second Punic War; fragments only of his works have survived. These were the principal literary men of Rome during this century. Caius Fabius (surnamed Pictor) painted the temple of Salus. This is the earliest Roman picture on record; it probably represented a victory over the Samnites.

We may here introduce the story of the invitation given by the Romans to the god Æsculapius to come to Rome, and stay a plague which had been raging there for three years. The legend is illustrative of the manners and superstition of the times. It is as follows: An embassy was sent (B. C. 291) to Epidaurus, the peculiar seat of Æsculapius, to invite him to Rome, and to ascertain how he ought to be worshipped. In answer to their petition, one of the snakes, sacred to the god (who, it is said, assumed the form of that reptile when he visited Sicyon), made its way to the sea-shore, and climbed into the ship of the Roman ambassadors. They immediately sailed away with it to Italy; but when they stopped at Antium, the snake left the ship, went ashore, and coiled itself round a palm tree in the precincts of a temple of Æsculapius, where it remained three days. It then returned on board, and did not leave the ship until it arrived in the Tiber, when it again crawled forth, but instead of landing with the ambassadors, swam to an island in the middle of the river, where it took up its abode. Upon this spot a temple was erected to the god.

What was the Celtic war?—What was the exploit of Marcellus?—What were the *Spolia Opima?*—What is said of the second Punic war?—Of Hannibal?—When did he commence operations?—What was his first step?—What happened at the lake of Thrasymenus?—What is said of Fabius Maximus?—Of Publius and Cneius Scipio?—Of the battle of Cannæ?

What of the inaction of Hannibal?—The tactics of Fabius?—Marcellus?—The siege of Syracuse?—The death of Archimedes?—The exploits of Scipio Africanus?—Of Syphax?—What was the result of the battle of Zama?—What were the terms granted to the Carthaginians?—What eminent civilians flourished in this century?—Relate the legend of Æsculapius.

BRITAIN.

England.—The records of this century are very meagre. The Irish, the Scots, and the Picts now appear in the history of England, and their encroachments provoked a border war, in which the Britons were victorious. We recognize purely British names in those of kings Urian, Eliud, Merian, Bledun, Oen (or Owen), and Blegabred. Of the last-named prince it is recorded by Geoffrey that he excelled all the musicians that had been before him, in singing and playing upon musical instruments, "so that he seemed worthy of the title of the God of Jesters."

Ireland.—After a lapse of several centuries we come to the reign of Kimboath, who built the splendid palace of the princes of Ulster at Emania, whence they were called Kings of Emania. This is a prominent era in the Irish annals. In the neighborhood of this palace stood the mansion of the celebrated 'knights of the Red Branch', whose exploits have so often been the themes of the Irish bards.

The accession of Hugony the Great (as he was called) is the next event of importance. By his influence with the assembled States at Tara he succeeded in annulling the Pentarchy, and prevailed on the four kings to surrender their right of succession in favor of his family. He then divided the kingdom into twenty-five districts or dynasties — an arrangement which lasted nearly 300 years. After the reign of Hugony succeeds a long interval of sterile events not worth recording, except the return of king Labhra from Gaul with a colony, which he established in Wicklow and Wexford.

Scotland.—The immediate successors of Ferthar (or Ferith′aris), Main and Deamdill, were able princes, and ruled for more than half a century. Then came Rothein, who attempted to convert the limited monarchy into an absolute tyranny, but he was thwarted by Donald, a Pictish chieftain from Galloway, and slain, and a youth named Reuther placed on the throne. This caused a war between the Scots and Picts, in which Donald was killed, and Reuther deposed. The Britons, taking advantage of these feuds, invaded and subdued the valleys, driving the Scots and Picts into the mountains. After occupying the country for 12 years, a peace was concluded, and the Britons left Scotland. Reuther was then restored, and reigned 29 years.

What is said of the history of Britain during this period?—Of Blegabred?—Of Kimboath?—Of Hugony the Great?—Of the Scottish kings?—And the war with the Britons?

FRANCE.

The Gauls played a prominent part in the affairs of the world during this century. In Cisalpine Gaul they joined the league of the Italian nations against Rome, and were the principal sufferers in the disastrous battle of Senti′num (B. C. 295). They suffered a second defeat at Vadimo by Dolabella (B. C. 283), and the Romans subdued the whole of the territory of the Sen′ones.

In B. C. 281 a large number of Tectos′ages emigrated from Toulouse into Germany, where they joined the Gauls and Cimbri, who were then meditating a descent on Greece. This expedition was composed of Teutons, as well as Gauls and Cimbri, under the command of their Brenn, or chief. In the first campaign the Macedonians were routed, and their king, Ptolemy Ceraunus, was slain (B. C. 280). Next year the Gauls ravaged Thessaly, but were routed at Thermopylæ; yet they ravaged Ætolia, and burnt the temple of Delphi, but were finally overcome by the allied Greeks, and forced to make a disastrous retreat. Driven out of Greece, the Gauls entered Asia Minor, placed Nicomedes on the throne of Bithynia, and made themselves masters of the coasts of the Ægean Sea (B. C. 278–241). Dreaded everywhere, all the cities of Asia Minor paid them tribute for more than 30 years. At last the armies of Antiochus, king of Syria, and Attalus, king of Pergamus, drove them into Upper Phrygia. Antiochus pursued them night and day as far as the Adorean mountains, where he permitted them to stop and settle on the banks of the river Halys. They made the ancient city of Ancyra their capital. The portion of Asia Minor thus colonized was named after them, Galatia. On account of his victory over the Gauls, Antiochus received the title of Soter (saviour).

After this we find the Gauls sought for as mercenaries by all the Asiatic monarchs, and swarms of them left France to take service in the armies of the kings of Egypt, Syria, Cappadocia, Pontus, and Bithynia. They entered into the service of Pyrrhus, king of Epirus, and of Carthage, at which place they took part in a sanguinary but unsuccessful revolt.

In Italy the Gauls of Insubria were reduced to subjection by the Romans (B. C. 238–236). Gallic mercenaries and allies also rendered important service to Hannibal throughout the second Punic war (B. C. 218–202).

Narrate the exploits of the Gauls in Italy, Greece, and Asia Minor.—What befell them in the last-mentioned country?—What else is said of them?

SPAIN.

In the year B. C. 251 a revolt broke out with great fury, and the Carthaginians suffered severe losses. They sent Hamilcar Barca with a large army to subdue the country. He was successful to a great extent, and recovered all the territory that had been lost; but he was subsequently defeated and killed at Castrum Altum, in Betica (B. C. 229). He founded the city of Barcelona. As′drubal succeeded him as governor of Spain, and founded the city of Carthagena. The Romans had now turned their ambitious view towards Spain, and formed leagues with several of the provinces in the north of that peninsula against the Carthaginians. Asdrubal, aware of their intentions, made vast preparations for war, and sent to Carthage for Hannibal to take command of the army. Asdrubal having been assassinated (B. C. 221) in the midst of these preparations, Hannibal succeeded him. The first measures of this famous general were the subjugation of the people of Toledo, and the siege and destruction of Saguntum, which fell after a most heroic struggle during eight months (B. C. 217). On the last day of it, the Saguntines collected all their effects into a vast pile, and placed their wives and children on it. They then sallied forth, and plunged into the enemy's ranks, but were cut to pieces. Their wives then set fire to the pile, and perished in it with their children. The Carthaginians entered a deserted and desolated city. This siege will ever be memorable in the annals of mankind. The Romans, as allies of the Saguntines, then declared war against Carthage, and Hannibal, having levied an immense army, marched into Italy. Meanwhile, Cneius Scipio, with a Roman army, entered Spain, and routed the armies of Asdrubal and Hanno. The war was carried on with varied success on both sides. Cornelius Scipio having been sent with reinforcements (B. C. 215), defeated Asdrubal in several battles; but the latter, having been reinforced by Masinissa, king of Numidia, gained a complete victory (B. C. 210) at Ilorcis, in which battle both the Scipios were slain. This triumph was of short duration, for the Romans sent Lucius Marcius and Publius Scipio with another army into Spain, and these two generals ultimately expelled the Carthaginians. They substituted the dominion of Rome for that of Carthage (B. C. 215).

What is said of Hamilcar Barca?—Asdrubal?—Hannibal?—The siege of Saguntum?—What Roman generals fell in the battle of Ilorcis?—What befell the Carthaginians?

GERMANY.

In this century the Senones, Boii, Cimbri, and other nations, uniting under their Brenn (or leader), invaded Greece, and at first were successful, enriching themselves with a vast booty; but, attempting to seize the treasures of the temple of Delphi, they were repulsed, and large numbers of them slain. It is said that those who survived, after killing their wives and children, voluntarily burnt themselves alive, to the number of 20,000 men, together with their booty, in their encampment.

The Romans attempting to crush the Senones and Boii who were settled in Upper Italy, 200,000 Germans, under Britomar, marched towards Rome, their leader vowing that he would not loosen his girdle until he had taken the capitol. They twice defeated the Romans; but the whole of Italy rising up to aid the latter, Britomar was routed by Paulus Æmilius, near the river Tel′amon: 40,000 Germans were slain, and Britomar taken prisoner (B. C. 225). Another chief, and all his followers, killed themselves in despair. A third, Ariovis′tus, supported by the Cenomanni and Hene′ti, fled to the mountains, whither he was pursued and overcome (B. C. 224); and next year, Virid′omar, with 30,000 Germans from the Rhine, was defeated and slain by the hand of the consul, Marcellus. The Boii joined Hannibal in his invasion of Italy, and Ducari′us, their leader, slew the consul, Flaminius, in single combat at the battle of Thrasyme′nus (B. C. 217), where 25,000 Romans fell. But when Hannibal left Italy, the Romans attacked the Boii; and, after two desperate and bloody battles, in one of which 35,000, and in another 40,000 Germans fell, they drove them to the mountains. They long and obstinately defended their fortresses beyond Lake Como, but the strongest (Fel′sina) having been taken, they took refuge in the Alps. After some years of desultory warfare they were annihilated in a battle, in which 32,000 of them were slain (B. C. 191). This victory placed the whole of the southern side of the Alps in the hands of the Romans, who quickly opened a route to the western side, and obtained a firm footing in Gaul.

The Illyrian queen, the brave Teuta, whose ships spread desolation along the eastern coasts of Italy for a long time, defied the Romans, but was at length subdued by them. She died of grief (B. C. 229).

What is recorded of the Senones and Boii during this century?—In what great battle did they help to defeat the Romans?—What became of them?—Who was Teuta?

ASIA MINOR.

On the division of the empire of Alexander the Great amongst his generals after the battle of Ipsus (B. C. 301), Bithynia, and the provinces on the Hellespont and Bosphorus, fell to the share of Lysimachus, king of Thrace, and the southern part of Asia Minor to Seleucus, king of Syria. There were also in the north the kingdoms of Cappadocia, Pontus, Paphlagonia, and Armenia. Those of Per′gamus and Bithynia shortly afterwards sprang into existence. The history of the first mentioned portions forms part of that of Thrace and Syria. That of Alexander's successors is very complicated. It is difficult to present a connected summary of it, since it consists of wars and intrigues between the rulers of the different kingdoms which arose out of the short-lived empire of Alexander the Great. Asia Minor was the scene of much of the warfare and troubles which visited mankind at that epoch. The ambition of the kings of Syria, Egypt, and Thrace, involved the minor States in perpetual wars; and the latter are to be found ranged sometimes on one side, and sometimes on the other. A system of strengthening alliances by marriages between the members of the reigning families grew up, but was productive of more strife than any other cause. The universal licentiousness of the people aided the commission of the most flagrant crimes by their rulers, and the female members of these royal families were not a whit behind the male in immorality. Arsinoë, Berenice, and Laodice have acquired an immortality of infamy. The most important circumstance in the history of Asia Minor during this century, is the appearance of the Romans on the scene of action. The great republic of Rome was destined to become the master of these fine provinces in less than two centuries from its first interference in the affairs of the East. As the leading incidents in the history of this portion of the world will be found mentioned in the columns devoted to Egypt, Syria, and Greece respectively, a cursory view of the principal events in that of the minor States will suffice here.

Cappadocia.—After the death of Eumenes, Ariara′thes III., the native prince, having obtained aid from the Armenians, attacked Amyntas, the Macedonian general, drove him out of the country, and re-established himself on the throne. Ariam′nes, his son, succeeded him, and in B. C. 284 married his eldest son to Stratoni′ce, daughter of Antiochus Theos, king of Syria. Ariarathes IV., who came next, left the throne to his infant son, Ariarathes V. (B. C. 190). The inhabitants of this country were proverbial for their infamy.

Pontus.—Mithridates III. reigned 36 years (B. C. 302–266). Of his two immediate successors we have but little account. At the close of the century, Mithrida′tes IV. was reigning: he married a daughter of Seleucus Callinicus, king of Syria, by whom he had Laod′ice, who married Antiochus the Great.

Pergamus. — The little kingdom of Per′gamus, in Mysia, was founded (B. C. 283) by Philetæ′rus, one of the lieutenants of Lysimachus, during his wars with Seleucus. Philetæ′rus was originally a servant, but Lysimachus having discovered his capacity, appointed him his treasurer, and intrusted him with the government of the city of Pergamus, where the State treasures were kept. He served Lysimachus faithfully for many years, but at last Arsinoë, the king's wife, conspired to destroy him; whereupon he revolted, and retained possession of the city and treasure. For 20 years he conducted the government with the greatest ability, and laid the foundation of a State which under his descendants became one of the most powerful in Asia Minor. He was a great patron of literature and the fine arts, and vied with Ptolemy Philadelphus in promoting them. He founded a library at Pergamus which afterwards rivalled that of Alexandria; and the world is indebted to his nephew, Eumenes, afterwards king of this State, for the invention of parchment. The discovery originated in this literary competition with the Egyptian king, who had prohibited the export of papyrus from Egypt. Philetærus left his kingdom to his nephew, Eumenes I. (B. C. 263). This prince defeated Antiochus, king of Syria, and added Æolis to his dominions; he subsequently (B. C. 242) acquired some of the western provinces of Syria. In the reign of his son and successor, Att′alus I., Pergamus was invaded by the Gauls or Galatians, a Celtic tribe, who were then pouring down from the North into Asia Minor, Thrace, and Italy. Attalus succeeded in expelling them from Pergamus, and was also fortunate in resisting the aggressions of Seleucus Ceraunus, king of Syria (B. C. 226). He afterwards took part in the Ætolian and the Macedonian wars, as an ally of the Ætolians and of the Romans, against the Macedonians and the Achæan league (B. C. 215–197); and his fleet assisted in the victory gained over Philip V. of Macedon by the Egyptians and Rhodians off Chios (B. C. 201).

Bithynia was erected into a kingdom about the same time with Pergamus, by Nicomedes I. (B. C. 279). Antiochus, king of Syria, tried to reduce this prince to subjection; and, during the war, employed against him the descendants of the Cimmerians, who had settled in Asia Minor 360 years previously. These people were found to be of the same race as the Gauls, then ravaging Asia Minor, and who subsequently settled in Galatia. Nicomedes founded the city of Nicomedia (B. C. 264), and was finally triumphant over the Syrians. He was succeeded by Zielas (B. C. 251), who, after a reign of 23 years, left his kingdom to Pru′sias I. (B. C. 220). This monarch assisted the Rhodians against the Byzantines, in a war occasioned by the heavy tolls levied by the latter on all ships entering the Black Sea.

Rhodes. — The little island and republic of Rhodes, after the death of Alexander the Great, first became remarkable in history for its gallant resistance to Demetrius Poliorcetes, who besieged it (B. C. 304). In the splendid city of Rhodes, the most celebrated paintings of Protogenes (who was then flourishing) were preserved. Its neutrality was conceded by Demetrius, and in memory of the siege, the famous Colossus was raised. This was a brazen statue of Apollo, 105 feet high, which bestrode the entrance to the port, and ships in full sail could pass between its legs. It was the work of Chares of Lindus, and occupied him 12 years. It was erected B. C. 293, and was thrown down by an earthquake 66 years afterwards (B. C. 227). Its fragments remained on the ground 896 years; at last they were sold by the general of the Caliph Othman IV. to a Jew of Emesa (A. D. 672), who carried them away on 900 camels. The quantity of brass contained in the fragments thus carried away was valued at a sum equal to $4,030,000 of U. S. currency. The earthquake which thus devastated the island laid the city in ruins, and reduced the Rhodians to the utmost distress, forcing them to apply to the neighboring princes for relief. The ready and noble response made by them to this appeal deserves to be recorded. Hiero and Gelon of Sicily, Ptolemy of Egypt, Antigonus, Seleucus, Mithridates, Prusias, and others, sent to them immense quantities of corn, money, timber, &c. Ptolemy alone contributed $330,000 for the people and $3,300,000 for the recasting of the Colossus: he also sent a million of bushels of corn, and an immense quantity of timber for buildings and ships. Rhodes was thus re-established in a few years in greater splendor than before. But the Colossus was never re-erected. Such deeds form an agreeable episode in the dreary catalogue of crimes which stain the history of Alexander's successors. The Rhodians were a very enterprising and commercial people, and extensively patronized the fine arts. The Byzantines attempted to exclude their ships from the Black Sea, by levying heavy tolls; but the Rhodians, assisted by Prusias I., king of Bithynia, compelled them to throw the trade open (B. C. 220). They also joined with Attalus, king of Pergamus, in assisting the Egyptians against Philip V. of Macedon, whose fleet they defeated off Chios (B. C. 201).

Armenia at this time formed part of the kingdom of Syria. The early history of this country is very obscure. It was an independent kingdom at a remote period; for the Chaldæan historian, Berosus, mentions the names of two of its kings, viz., Sytha and Barzanes, and says that Sytha was the first king of Armenia, and that Barzanes was his successor; also that the latter was subdued by the Assyrian monarch, Ninus. Plutarch also mentions another king, named Araxes, who, having been guilty of great cruelty to the family of Miesalcus, one of his principal men, was pursued by him to the river Helmus, and was drowned in attempting to swim across it. We have no account of the primitive government of Armenia, but in later ages it was purely despotic. The chief deity of the Armenians was the goddess Tanais, or Anaitis, whose principal temple was in Acilesina, where she was worshipped in a very peculiar manner, and licentious customs were observed. Baris was another deity peculiar to them, but we have no account of the manner in which he was worshipped. Their ancient language was the Syriac, and a knowledge of it is still cultivated by the learned men who are styled Vertabiets by the modern Armenians.

To whose share, after the battle of Ipsus, did Bithynia fall?—And Southern Asia Minor?—What is said of the history of Alexander's successors?—And that of Asia Minor?—Give a sketch of that of Cappadocia.—Pontus.—Pergamus.—Who was Philetærus?—What of the library of Pergamus?—Papyrus?

What is said of the history of Bithynia?—Who founded Nicomedia?—What of Rhodes?—Give an account of the Colossus.—Of the Armenians, and their principal deity; also of their other deities.—Who was their first king?—What is said of Araxes?—What was the ancient language of the Armenians?

CARTHAGE.

The cruelties and crimes of Agathocles did not prevent his forming alliances with many powerful princes. Among them was Ophellas, king of Cyrene, who offered him the use of his army; but no sooner had Agathocles got this prince in his power than he caused him to be murdered. He then went to Sicily to look after his affairs there. In his absence his African subjects revolted, and, though he hastened back, he was unable to retrieve his losses: his troops deserted him, and he with difficulty made his escape to Syracuse, where he was soon after poisoned by Mænon, a creature of his grandson, Archag'athus, who planned the crime (B. C. 289). On the death of Agathocles the Syracusans were harassed by intestine commotions, and the Carthaginians took advantage of these disturbances to extend their influence in Sicily, and laid siege to Syracuse. At this time the ambitious Pyrrhus, king of Epirus, was meditating the conquest of Italy and Sicily (B. C. 277). The Romans, therefore, entered into a treaty of mutual defence with the Carthaginians, and the latter sent a fleet of 120 ships, under Mago, to aid the former, but this assistance was declined. Mago then visited Pyrrhus in order to find out his designs, but that prince had already promised aid to the Syracusans, and very soon afterward landed in Sicily, where he made so successful a campaign that, in a short time, the Carthaginians had no town left there, except Lilybæ'um. But his affairs in Italy recalled him from Sicily, and he abandoned all his conquests there; exclaiming, as he left the island, "What a fine field of battle do we leave to the Carthaginians and the Romans!"

The Syracusans were fortunate in finding a worthy successor to Agathocles. HI'ERO, a young man of great personal beauty and ability, had acquired the esteem of Pyrrhus, and distinguished himself in arms. He was, moreover, a descendant of Gelon, the former king of Syracuse. It happened (B. C. 277) that disputes arose between the Syracusans and their troops, and the latter raised Hiero to the chief command. Having found means to enter the city, he behaved with so much prudence and mildness that the citizens unanimously conferred on him the office of prætor. His difficulty now was to get rid of the unruly portion of his army. For this purpose he resorted to a very cruel expedient. He assembled his troops, and marched against the Mamertines. On arriving within sight of the enemy he divided his force into two parts, one composed entirely of Syracusans, the other of troublesome mercenaries, and placed himself at the head of the former: then giving orders to advance, he suddenly withdrew the Syracusans, leaving the mercenaries to be overpowered and cut to pieces by the Mamertines. By this stratagem he rid himself of a dangerous body of men. With his Syracusan troops he subsequently defeated the Mamertines at Mylæ (B. C. 271), and on his return to Syracuse was declared king.

THE FIRST PUNIC WAR soon afterwards broke out between Carthage and Rome, the scene of which was Sicily. After the battle of Mylæ the Mamertines were reduced to extremities, and, being divided among themselves, some of them surrendered their citadel to the Carthaginians, while others applied to the Romans for aid. The latter sent the consul, Appius Claudius, with an army to Messina, of which city he possessed himself by stratagem. The Carthaginians at once laid siege to it, and formed an alliance with Hiero, who joined them with an army. The Romans sallied forth and attacked them, and, after a severe contest, gained a complete victory. Their prowess on this occasion appears to have opened the eyes of Hiero as to the probable issue of the war; for he at once withdrew from his alliance with the Carthaginians, and made peace with the Romans. The wisdom of this course became apparent in time, for during the rest of his long reign (more than fifty years), he and his people remained in profound peace, while the two most potent States in the western world, Rome and Carthage, were carrying on fierce wars with each other. He devoted himself to the welfare of his subjects, promoted agriculture and commerce, and laid down so wise a system of laws and municipal regulations that it became the fundamental code of the country, and was kept inviolable during many succeeding ages. Even the Romans, when they annexed Syracuse to their dominions, decreed that the laws of Hiero should be observed. Hiero erected many magnificent public buildings, and was the warm friend and patron of the celebrated mathematician and mechanician, ARCHIME'DES. We may here conclude our notice of Hiero II. He lived to witness the ravaging of his dominions by the Carthaginians after their victory over the Romans at Cannæ. His son, Gelon, openly espoused the cause of the Carthaginians, and induced the Syracusans to join him, but death suddenly cut short his designs. Hiero did not long survive his son: he died (B. C. 215) at the age of ninety, deeply regretted, after having reigned fifty-four years.

The first exploit of the Romans, after the alliance with Hiero, was the siege and capture of Agrigentum, which occupied them seven months. This city was the principal Carthaginian arsenal in Sicily. But as the Carthaginians were masters of the sea, the Romans knew they could not hold the island securely. They therefore resolved to equip a fleet, and contest the empire of the ocean with their adversaries. The Carthaginians sent a fleet of 130 ships to encounter this new foe, who numbered 120 ships, under the command of the consul Duillius. The two fleets met off the coast of Sicily, near Mylæ, when the Romans, boldly grappling their adversaries' ships, boarded them, and fought hand to hand. A horrible slaughter ensued: the Carthaginians were utterly defeated, losing 80 ships (B. C. 259). This was the first naval battle between the two nations, and it put an end to the supremacy of Carthage at sea. The Romans immediately redoubled their efforts to create a navy, and during the next two years gained several small battles on the ocean. They meditated carrying the war into Africa, and the Carthaginians made great efforts to repel them. In the year B. C. 255, the latter fitted out a fleet of 350 ships, manned by 150,000 men, under the command of Hanno and Hamilcar, and sent it to the coast of Sicily, where the Romans had a fleet of 320 ships, manned by 140,000 men, under the command of Regulus and Manlius. These two fleets encountered each other off Ecno'mus, and a desperate fight ensued, which ended in the triumph of the Romans, the Carthaginians losing 60 ships.

Carthage now found herself endangered. The Romans, according to their threat, "carried the war into Africa". They took the town of Clyp'ea, and overran the adjacent country, making terrible havoc. Their commander, Regulus, took several towns, routed the Carthaginians at A'dis, captured Tunis, and advanced to Carthage, offering harsh terms to the city. At this critical juncture, a reinforcement of auxiliary Greek troops, under the command of Xanthippus, the Spartan, a very able general, arrived at Carthage. The incapacity of the Carthaginian commanders being apparent, Xanthippus was appointed commander-in-chief. He at once changed the system of tactics, and, having inspired his troops with confidence, he attacked Regulus, and cut his army to pieces, Regulus himself being taken prisoner (B. C. 254). The Roman general was thrown into prison, and kept there several years. As to his subsequent fate, see the history of Italy. The blow sustained by the enemy did not discourage them. They fitted out a fleet of 360 ships, and attacked the Carthaginians off the coast of Sicily, capturing 114 of their ships, but they did little more; and next year a storm destroyed nearly all their vessels. In Sicily, Asdrubal met with a severe defeat, and the Romans laid siege to Lilybæum, the strongest of all the Carthaginian towns in Sicily (B. C. 248). Strenuous efforts were made to save this place, and Hamilcar Barca and Adher'bal, who commanded at Drep'anum, greatly distinguished themselves in its defence. The Romans sustained a severe repulse before Lilybæum, and Adherbal completely destroyed their fleet at Drepanum. These victories paralyzed the operations of the Romans for five years. But at the expiration of that time the desire to terminate the war became very strong, and they fitted out a fleet under Lutatius, and sent it to Lilybæum. There the consul overtook and surprised the Carthaginian fleet under Hanno, and entirely destroyed it (B. C. 241). On receipt of this news at Carthage the Senate saw that the war could no longer be carried on, and instructed Hamilcar Barca to make terms with the Romans. The terms agreed on were: that Carthage should evacuate Sicily, abstain from war on Hiero, restore without ransom all prisoners, and pay within twenty years 3200 Euboic talents of silver ($3,575,000). The twenty years' delay was subsequently reduced to ten, and 1000 talents additional ($1,170,000) were paid down. Also all the islands between Italy and Sicily, except Sardinia, were given up. Thus ended, disastrously for Carthage, the First Punic War.

The next memorable event was the Lybian War, or, more properly, the war against the mercenaries who had been employed by the republic in the contest

What befell Agathocles?—What occurred after his death?—What is said of Pyrrhus?—Hiero?—The rebellious mercenaries?—The Mamertine War?—What was the origin of the first Punic War?—What part did Hiero take?—What did the Romans decree as to his laws?—What great man did he patronize?

How long did Hiero reign?—What was the first exploit of the Romans?—What is said of the battle of Mylæ?—Of Ecnomus?—Xanthippus?—Regulus?—What occurred in Sicily?—What was the result of the victory of Lilybæum?—On what terms was the first Punic War concluded?

CARTHAGE.

with the Romans. These troops were composed of men of all nations, and numbered many thousands. Long arrears of pay were due to them, but, owing to the exhaustion of the public finances, these could not be paid off immediately. In consequence of this the troops became mutinous, and finally broke out into revolt. The Carthaginians, who had mainly relied upon mercenaries in their wars, were at first taken at a disadvantage. They tried negotiation, but failed in that. Their ablest general, Gisco, having been recalled from Sicily, was sent to remonstrate with them, but was seized by the ringleaders, Spendius (a Capuan) and Matho (an African), and subsequently put to death. The republic was in the greatest danger, but the citizens showed a spirit worthy of the greatest honor. All who could bear arms were mustered, ships were refitted, and mercenaries invited from all parts. Hanno was appointed commander-in-chief; but, having suffered himself to be surprised by the enemy, he was superseded, and Hamilcar Barca took his place. This general at once assumed the offensive, and defeated the rebels near Utica. He followed up his success by a series of manœuvres, by which he ultimately hemmed the enemy in, forced them to fight at a disadvantage, and completely destroyed their army. It is said that 40,000 of them perished in this battle. The cities which had taken part with them were reduced one after another, until the rebellion was crushed, and Carthage was once more safe. But the revolt of the mercenaries had spread to Sardinia, where the soldiers rose and massacred all the Carthaginians on the island. The natives, however, drove out the mercenaries: the latter took refuge in Italy, and persuaded the Romans to take possession of the island. The Carthaginians remonstrated, whereupon the Romans declared war against them, but the former were content to avert the storm by ceding Sardinia and paying 1200 talents (B. C. 237).

The indignation of the Carthaginians at this gross injustice, and at the constant aggressions of the Romans in Spain, brought on THE SECOND PUNIC WAR. Hamilcar Barca, their most able general, was appointed to the chief command in Spain. Thither he went, taking with him his son, HANNIBAL (afterwards so celebrated, but then only nine years old), who, before starting, took upon the altar an oath of enmity to the Romans. Hamilcar subdued the greatest part of Spain, and, after holding the chief command for nine years, was killed in battle. His son-in-law, Asdrubal, was appointed his successor. Asdrubal's first act was to build the city of New Carthage, now Carthagena (B. C. 228), and fortify it as a basis of operations. The Romans, perceiving his designs, entered into negotiations and made a treaty with him, by which the Carthaginians were bound not to make any conquests beyond the Iberus. But Asdrubal consolidated his conquests within the limits, and, during the eight years he was governor of Spain, he furthered the interests of Gaul. Unfortunately he was murdered by a Gaul, because of a private grudge (B. C. 220). The Senate then sent Hannibal, not without considerable opposition, however, for that body was distracted by the two factions of Hanno and of the Barca family, but in this instance the Barcinians triumphed. Hannibal at once set to work to reduce all the strongholds in Spain which still held out on the Carthaginian side of the Iberus, and finally laid siege to Saguntum (now Murviedro). That city made a most heroic defence, but was taken, and all its inhabitants were cut to pieces. The Romans were struck with anger and consternation, but they resolved to stop the progress of the Carthaginians, and at once declared war. Hannibal thereupon began his famous march into Italy (B. C. 217). He started from Carthagena early in the spring at the head of 100,000 men; but having to encounter several enemies before he reached the Pyrenees, he lost a large portion of his army, and was forced to leave another portion to maintain open communication with his rear. He reached the Rhone with 55,000 men, highly disciplined, and commanded by the ablest general of antiquity — himself: thence he marched to the Durance, and crossed the Alps into Italy. This famous achievement occupied a fortnight, and cost him a large number of men, elephants, and horses, besides loss of time: it being five months and a half from his setting out from Carthagena before he entered Piedmont. On the banks of the Ticino he encountered the Roman army, under Publius Scipio, and defeated it, following up his success by defeating them again at the Trebia. He then went into winter-quarters. Meanwhile Cneius Scipio defeated Hanno in Spain, and extended his conquests to the Iberus, and through the northern parts. In the spring of B. C. 216, Hannibal marched into Tuscany, and defeated the Romans at Thrasyme′nus with great slaughter. But instead of marching upon Rome, he ravaged Adria and Campania, where he got immense booty: he then took up quarters in Apulia. The Roman general, Fabius, adopted a new system of tactics, avoiding general engagements, but harassing the enemy by continually skirmishing and cutting off their supplies. At one time he very nearly destroyed Hannibal's army by inclosing it in the pass of Cæsili′num, but the genius of the Carthaginian general enabled him to save it by a stratagem. The student is referred to Polybius and Livy for the details of these remarkable campaigns in Italy: they are highly interesting; but while they were in progress, Cneius Scipio was gaining victories in Spain. Hannibal remained inactive till the spring of B. C. 215, when the Roman general, Varro, spurning the tactics of Fabius, advanced to attack him. The battle of Cannæ is one of the most memorable of contests; for Hannibal, with 50,000 men, completely routed the Roman army, numbering 86,000. Polybius says that more than 70,000 Romans fell in this battle, but Livy reduces the number to 43,000. Hannibal lost about 6000 men. Cannæ was a little town in Apulia, on the banks of the Au′fidus. Why Hannibal did not follow up his brilliant success by marching upon Rome, is a much-vexed question. He did not do so, but took up his quarters at Capua, a luxurious city, where his soldiers gave themselves up to enjoyment, and lost their aptitude for war. He sent to Carthage for supplies and reinforcements; but though the Senate voted them, they were never forwarded: on the contrary, they were sent into Spain. He once advanced to Rome, and threatened the city, but returned without accomplishing anything. He remained in the south of Italy thirteen years after the battle of Cannæ, and was then recalled to Africa.

Meanwhile the Romans were regaining ground in Spain. The two Scipios defeated Asdrubal, and drove him out of the Peninsula. But the Carthaginians raised three fresh armies, and sent them there, and by these the Scipios were vanquished and killed. Asdrubal, the brother of Hannibal, set out to cross the Alps into Italy with one of these armies, but was encountered by the consul Nero on the banks of the Metaurus, defeated and killed (B. C. 206). It is said that the Carthaginians lost 55,000 men in this battle. In Spain the younger Scipio took Carthagena, and gained several victories. He then crossed into Africa, routed the armies of Syphax and Asdrubal, laid siege to Utica, and threatened Carthage. The latter now sued for peace: a truce was granted, and Hannibal was recalled from Italy (B. C. 202). But while negotiations were pending, the Carthaginians violated the truce by seizing some Roman ships that had been dispersed from their fleet in a storm, and the Senate ordered Hannibal to attack Scipio. An interview took place between these celebrated men, but they could not agree upon the terms of peace. Recourse was again had to the sword, and Hannibal was finally vanquished by Scipio on the plains of Zama (B. C. 201), where the Carthaginians lost 20,000 men and 20,000 taken prisoners. After this the Senate accepted the terms of peace offered by Scipio, namely: to deliver up all prisoners, and all the ships of the State, and all captured vessels; not to make war out of Africa without leave of the Romans; to restore to Masinissa, king of the Numidians, all they had taken from him; to send corn to Rome; and to pay 10,000 Euboic talents of silver ($11,750,000) within fifty years. 500 ships were delivered up, and burnt by Scipio in sight of the city: he also hanged all the Roman deserters. Thus ended the Second Punic War (B. C. 200), having lasted seventeen years, and cost Italy 300,000 men, and the plunder of 400 towns.

In Syracuse, after the death of Hiero, the kingdom fell into the hands of his grandson, Hieron′ymus, a youth of an odious disposition. He intrigued with Hannibal against the Romans, but was assassinated before he could carry out his plans (B. C. 214). Great troubles followed his death, and ultimately drew upon the city the wrath of the Romans. Marcellus laid siege to it, but the extraordinary genius of Archimedes, the famous philosopher, who invented various machines to baffle the Romans, enabled the Syracusans to hold out for three years. The city was at length taken, but unfortunately Archimedes was killed by a brutal soldier who had been sent to conduct him to Marcellus.

What was the next memorable war?—Give a sketch of it.—Who ended it?—What occurred in Sardinia?—What caused the second Punic War?—What did Hannibal do?—What were the acts of Hamilcar?—Asdrubal?—Hannibal?—What of Saguntum?—Of Hannibal's march into Italy?—His victories there?

What great victories did Hannibal gain?—How many fell at Cannæ?—What of the tactics of Fabius?—Of Hannibal's subsequent inactivity?—Of the exploits of the Scipios?—The recall of Hannibal?—The battle of Zama?—On what terms was the second Punic War ended?—What of Syracuse?—Archimedes?

THE 2D CENTURY

EGYPT.

This century opened with a struggle on the part of Antiochus the Great, king of Syria, to get possession of Cœle-Syria and Palestine; in which he was for a time successful. Ptolemy Epiph′anes had married Cleopatra, the daughter of Antiochus; and by this arrangement the revenues of these two provinces became partly his, as his wife's dower. It is said that Antiochus designed by this marriage to get possession of Egypt, but Cleopatra was faithful to her husband's interests, and thwarted the schemes of her father. Ptolemy cultivated the friendship of the Romans and of the Achæan league, sending magnificent presents to both. But he was a weak and dissolute prince, and gave loose to dissipation. His courtiers suspected him of intending to seize their estates in order to raise money for making war on the king of Syria, which project he then entertained. To avert this danger, they caused him to be poisoned (B. C. 181). He left two sons, both under age, named Ptolemy Philome′ter and Ptolemy Physcon, and one daughter, Cleopatra. The claims of Egypt on Cœle-Syria led to a war with Syria (B. C. 171); in the course of which Antiochus Epiphanes took Philometer prisoner, and placed Ptolemy Physcon on the throne of Egypt (B. C. 168). The Romans, having been applied to by Philometer for protection, interfered on his behalf. Upon this Antiochus gave up Egypt, and the kingdom was then divided between the two brothers — Philometer taking Egypt proper; Physcon taking Cyrene, Libya, and Cyprus (B. C. 164). The latter visited Rome on this occasion, and while there fell in love with Cornelia, the mother of the Gracchi. He made her an offer of marriage, but she declined accepting it, deeming it more honorable to be one of the first matrons of Rome than to reign with Ptolemy Physcon in Lybia and Cyrene. (Plutarch, *Life of Tiberius Gracchus.*)

The conflicting claims of the temples of Jerusalem and Mount Gerizim having been referred to Philometer, he decided in favor of the former (B. C. 150). He also permitted the Jews in Egypt to build a temple like that of Jerusalem. Having been induced to support Demetrius, king of Syria, against Bala, the usurper, who was the son-in-law of Philometer, the Egyptian monarch advanced with an army to his support; but though victorious at Antioch over his opponent, he died of the wounds he received in the battle, and Physcon then became king of all Egypt. The horrible state of immorality which prevailed at this time, may be inferred from the fact that Philometer had married his own sister, Cleopatra; and that on his death, his brother Physcon married her. She had borne a son to Philometer; but on the very day of her marriage with his brother, the latter murdered the child in his mother's arms. He caused all those who showed any concern for the murdered prince to be put to death; and some time afterwards, when rejoicing that a son was born to him, he caused several of the chief men of Cyrene to be murdered, because they had cast some reflections upon one of his courtesans. He subsequently divorced his sister, and married his niece, Cleopatra, by whom he had two sons, Ptolemy, surnamed Lath′yrus (or wart), and Alexander. But the vices and cruelties of this prince drove his subjects into rebellion (B. C. 130), and he was compelled to abandon his kingdom for a time. The crown was given to his sister, Cleopatra, but he recovered it by the aid of a mercenary army, and retained it till his death (B. C. 117). He left the kingdom of Cyrene to his illegitimate son, Apion, and Egypt to his widow and to whichever of her two sons she might choose. She named Alexander, but the people of Alexandria compelled her to admit Lathyrus to reign with her. This was the occasion of more crime on the part of this incestuous family. Lathyrus had married his favorite sister Cleopatra; but his mother forced him to divorce her and marry his youngest sister, Sele′ne, whom he disliked. He was then nominated king of Egypt. The new king, Lath′yrus, is also called Soter II. His reign was troubled by the intrigues of his mother, Cleopatra, to secure the throne for her son Alexander, to whom Cyprus was given. In the midst of these disorders, Ptolemy A′pion, a natural son of Physcon, acquired the kingdom of Cyrene. Cleopatra at length by her artifices gained such an ascendency over the people, that she compelled Lathyrus to divorce his sister, Sele′ne, and abandon Egypt and content himself with Cyprus. She then brought thence her youngest son, Alexander, to reign under her in Egypt (B. C. 107). The name Ptolemy was by the custom of the royal family given to all the males, and that of Cleopatra to all the females.

What were the acts of Ptolemy Epiphanes?—What was his fate?—What events occurred in the reign of Ptolemy Philometer?—What is related of Ptolemy Physcon?—Cornelia?—Of the immorality of the royal family?—Of Ptolemy Lathyrus, and Alexander?—Of their mother Cleopatra?—Of Ptolemy Apion?—Alexander?—The royal names?

SYRIA.

Antiochus, designing to wrest Egypt from the Ptolemies, invaded Cœle-Syria and Palestine (B. C. 198); but was prevented by the Romans from following up his success. He then made preparations for the invasion of Greece (B. C. 196). The Romans again interfered. He was defeated at Magnesia (B. C. 190), and lost his dominions. He was murdered by his servants (B. C. 187), and was succeeded by his son, Seleu′cus IV. (Philop′ator). The reign of this prince passed without any remarkable event. He was poisoned by one of his own ministers, named Heliodo′rus (B. C. 175). His brother, Anti′ochus IV. (Epiph′anes), succeeded him. This prince tried to enforce a uniformity of civil and religious customs among his subjects. A pretext for interfering with the Jews occurred during the high-priesthood of Oni′as III. (who in B. C. 195 had succeeded Simon the Just). Onias having expelled Simon, governor of the Temple, the latter fled to Antiochus, and spread a report that there were vast treasures in the Sanctuary. The cupidity of the king was excited: Onias was put in prison, and Antiochus accepted a large bribe to appoint Joshua (who took the name of Jason) in his stead. Under the rule of this Jason, a general apostasy overspread the Jews. He was supplanted (B. C. 172) by his brother, Menela′us, whose iniquitous proceedings provoked riots among the people. While these events were passing at Jerusalem, Antiochus invaded Egypt (B. C. 170). There he heard that Jason had revolted. Compelled by the Romans to abandon his conquest of Egypt, Antiochus returned to Jerusalem, which he entered after a sharp resistance. He put to the sword 40,000 of the inhabitants, and sold as many more into captivity (B. C. 168). He profaned the Temple, and was guilty of great cruelty. The Jews fled for refuge to the mountains and caves, where, headed by Mattathi′as, a priest of the Asmone′an family, they began a fierce struggle for their independence. That venerable warrior sunk under his exertions (B. C. 166); but his gallant son, Judas, unfolded the banner of the "Maccabees" (a name said to be derived from the initial letters of the Hebrew words "**M**i **K**amoka **B**'*Elohim Jehovah,*" "Who is like unto thee, O Jehovah, among the gods?" Exod. xv. 11), and gained a series of victories which re-established the former independence of the Jews. The Persians revolted (B. C. 165), and defeated Antiochus, who died on his road to Babylon (B. C. 164).

Antiochus Eu′pator, his son, was placed on the throne; but Demetrius, the son of Seleucus Philopator, dethroned and put him to death (B. C. 162). Judas Maccabæ′us, having restored the ancient worship of the Jews and fortified the country, attacked the Syrian army, under Bac′chides, and was slain, fighting against fearful odds. Bacchides took Jerusalem; but the Maccabees, under Jonathan, the brother of Judas, still held out. After several indecisive engagements, peace was concluded. Jonathan was made high-priest (B. C. 152), and under his administration Judea became a flourishing State. Demetrius was slain in battle (B. C. 150) by Alexander Bala, an impostor who had personated the unfortunate Eupator, and having been supported by the Maccabees and Romans, obtained the throne. He was, in his turn, driven away by Demetrius Nicator, the son of the late monarch (B. C. 146). Theodotus Trypho, claiming the crown for Antiochus, the son of Bala, expelled Demetrius and murdered Jonathan Maccabæus (B. C. 143). He afterwards seized the crown for himself, and Simon succeeded Jonathan as high-priest. Antiochus Side′tes, the brother of Demetrius, overthrew Trypho and obtained the crown of Syria (B. C. 137). He was a good and wise sovereign. After ably administering the priesthood for eight years, Simon and his two eldest sons were murdered by Ptolemy, his son-in-law (B. C. 135); but his younger son, John Hyrca′nus, escaped, and was recognized as head of the nation. Hyrcanus finally threw off the Syrian yoke, and incorporated the Idumeans with the Jews. Antiochus fell in a war against the Parthians (B. C. 128). His brother, Demetrius, escaped from prison and regained the throne, but was defeated and slain (B. C. 125) by Zebi′nas, a pretended son of Bala. Seleucus, the son of Demetrius, was murdered by his own mother, who, being assisted by the king of Egypt, defeated and slew Zebinas, and placed her favorite son, Antiochus Gryphus, upon the throne of Syria. His first act was to put his mother to death (B. C. 121). A few years afterwards, half of his kingdom was taken from him by his half-brother Cyzice′nus. On the death of Hyrcanus (B. C. 107), the high-priesthood of the Jews devolved on Aristobu′lus; and on his decease (B. C. 105), on Alexander Jannæ′us.

State the principal events of the reigns of Antiochus III., Seleucus IV., Antiochus IV.—What did the high-priest Onias do?—How did Antiochus act towards Jerusalem?—Who was Mattathias Maccabæus?—Whence the name "Maccabee"?—What of Judas Maccabæus?—And Jonathan?—Demetrius?—Alexander Bala?—What other events occurred?

INDIA.

From the 2d century before Christ to the 8th century after, was the period in which the principal works of merit in Hindoo science and literature were written. The philosophy of the ancient Hindoos merits a brief notice, as it was undoubtedly the source whence Pythagoras and others derived their own views. There were six ancient schools of philosophy, thus enumerated by Mr. Colebrook (*Transactions of the Royal Asiatic Society*, vol. i. p. 19):—

1. The prior Mimansa, founded by Jaimani, at a period soon after the promulgation of the Vedas. It teaches the art of reasoning as applied to the interpretation of those books.

2. The latter or Uttara Mimansa, or Vedanta, attributed to Vyasa, the supposed compiler of the Vedas, about B. C. 1400, but certainly not composed earlier than the 6th centy. B. C. It is remarkable for denying the eternity of matter, and for ascribing the existence of the universe to the energy and volition of God.

3. The Niyaya, or Logical school of Gotama, which treats of metaphysics.

4. The Atomic school of Canade, so called from its teaching that the transient world is composed of aggregations of eternal atoms.

5. The Atheistical school of Capila.

6. The Theistical school of Patanjali.

The last two are styled the Sankya school, which maintains the doctrine of the eternity of matter, and disputes the existence of God. The Vedanta school maintains the eternity of God, and denies the reality of matter. It is this last-mentioned system which the Pythagorean resembles. Its leading doctrines were that God is omnipotent and omniscient; that the creation was an effort of His will; that He is the sole existent and universal soul into whom all things are resolved at last; that each individual soul is portion of His substance, emanating from and returning to Him after sundry transmigrations; that He makes it act in conformity with resolutions produced by causes extending backwards to infinity; that it is encased in a subtile body which accompanies it in all its transmigrations, and in a gross body which perishes; that the mind is distinct from the soul; that the object of suffering is to purify and exalt the soul toward perfection, which once attained, the individual merges into the Universal Soul.

What is said of this period of Hindoo history?—Name the ancient schools of philosophy.—What are the last two styled?—What are the leading doctrines of the Vedanta?

PERSIA.

The history of the Greek kingdom of Bactria presents nothing of interest. The princes who governed it were constantly occupied in wars against their neighbors, the kings of Parthia, and the chieftains of the wild Scythian or Turanian tribes. In the year B. C. 140, Eucrat′ides, the king of Bactria, allied himself with Demetrius Nicator, king of Syria, against Parthia, and they invaded that country simultaneously. The result, however, was unfortunate for both; for the Parthians conquered a large part of Bactria, and took Demetrius prisoner (B. C. 138). Thus enfeebled, the kingdom of Bactria held out but a few years longer, and finally succumbed to the wild Tartar tribes (B. C. 127).

Parthia, however, under a series of able princes of the family of the Arsac′idæ, rose in power, and became a formidable foe to Rome. Artaba′nes I., and his successors Priapa′tius (B. C. 196–181) and Phraa′tes I. (B. C. 181–174), did not materially advance the power of the kingdom. But Mithrida′tes I. (B. C. 174–139) was an active and enterprising prince, and at the close of a long reign left his kingdom one of the most powerful in the East. He subdued (B. C. 164) a large portion of the kingdom of Syria, then governed by Lys′ias, who was regent during the minority of Antiochus Eupator. He also repelled a formidable invasion by the Syrians and the Bactrians (B. C. 140). On his death (B. C. 139) his successor, Phraates II., continued the war. A large part of Bactria was conquered. Demetrius Nicator, the Syrian king, was taken prisoner. He was detained in captivity ten years. Antiochus Sidetes made an attempt to crush the Parthians, as his predecessors had tried to do; but the expedition proved a failure, and Antiochus was killed (B. C. 128). Phraates, however, met with the same fate immediately afterwards, in repelling the Tartars, who had overrun and destroyed the kingdom of Bactria. His successor, Artaba′nes II., was fully occupied, during his brief reign, in resisting the attacks of these savage barbarians. Artabanes was slain in a battle with them (B. C. 125). His successor, Mithridates II., put an end to these wars. It will be observed, throughout Persian history, that the welfare of the country has depended entirely on the character and disposition of the reigning monarch.

What was the fate of Bactria?—What did Parthia become?—Name the principal kings of that country in this century.—What were their acts, and the results to the people?

CHINA. JAPAN.

Lew-pang, having become sole master of the empire, assumed the name of Kaou-tsoo. He endeavored to restore order, and to repair the injury the country had sustained during the long previous period of anarchy. Meanwhile the Huns had again become formidable, and retaken the districts conquered from them by the celebrated general Mung-tëen. Kaou-tsoo sent several of his best generals against them; but these officers turned traitors, and went over to the enemy. The emperor therefore marched against the Huns himself, but was drawn into an ambuscade, and forced to buy an ignominious peace. Kaou-tsoo introduced a new code of laws, and endeavored to revive the ancient literature of the country, but was arrested by death in the midst of his efforts (B. C. 195). His eldest son, Hwuy-te, succeeded him. This prince gave himself up to licentious pleasures, and left the care of the empire to his mother, the empress, Lew-che. This woman was a monster of cruelty. It is related of her that, on her son's accession, the princess of Tse having desired to place her own son on the throne, she sent for that unfortunate person, degraded her to the rank of a slave, and made her pound rice. She then poisoned the princess's son, and caused her to be beaten till she fainted; her hair was then plucked out by the roots, and her hands, feet, and ears were cut off; but as she still showed symptoms of life, a large dose of poison was given to her, and her mangled corpse was thrown into the common sewer. This narrative illustrates the ferocity of the rulers of China at this epoch of her history. The cruelty of Lew-che horrified the imbecile young emperor, who now avoided all care of his empire, gave himself up to debauchery, and soon destroyed his health. He died without issue. To prevent the crown falling to any but one of her own creatures, the empress substituted the child of a peasant as the son of the emperor, and in B. C. 188 usurped the throne, as the child's guardian. Her ambition led her to commit the most horrible actions, one of them being the murder of the child she had placed on the throne. She had great talents, and was the first woman who reigned over "the Celestial" empire.

On her death (B. C. 180), Wan-te, a descendant of Kaou-tsoo, was chosen her successor. He was an excellent prince, who aimed only at the welfare of his country, and was assiduous in the administration of a paternal government: he encouraged literature and agriculture. In his reign the Chinese invented paper. The Huns, however, repeatedly invaded China, and Wan-te was obliged to pacify them by bribes. His successor, King-te (B. C. 157) was a very lenient prince, but his reign was disturbed by an insurrection of the petty princes. The country was devastated by several earthquakes and plagues of locusts. It was a time of general calamity. Woo-te, the successor of King-te (B. C. 157), ranks very high in the estimation of the Chinese. He fully deserved the high renown he acquired. He conformed strictly to the ancient form of government, and gave the greatest encouragement to literary men; but his peace was disturbed by the disputes between the disciples of Confucius, and those of Laou-tsze; and the land was desolated by a great inundation of the Yellow River, a long-continued drought, and swarms of locusts. The Huns, also, constantly attacked the frontiers, though they were as constantly repulsed. On one occasion General Wei-sing routed a whole horde, and took 15,000 prisoners. After many campaigns, Woo-te struck such a decisive blow that the Huns were unable to return for many years.

Many excellent writers flourished in his time; the most famous of them was Ize-ma-tseen, the father of Chinese history, who was appointed by the emperor to the office of "Tae-she", or great historian. He fell into disgrace and was banished, but in his exile he composed his history of China. This work regained for him the favor of the emperor, and he was promoted to high office. The religious system of Laou-keun was now in its zenith: the priests had raised numerous temples and idols, and had made many proselytes. But the emperor persecuted them with relentless fury, and destroyed their influence. The custom of giving the reign of every emperor a "Kwo-haou" (or particular name) commenced under Woo-te.

Japan.—Kow-kiu died B. C. 157. His second son, Kay-kwo, succeeded him. In the year B. C. 154, the latter removed his Court to Isagava. He died B. C. 97. The history of this country is devoid of incident and interest, especially during this early period.

What events marked the reign of Kaou-tsoo?—What was the character of Hwuy-te?—Relate the cruelty of the empress, Lew-che, to the princess of Tse.—Who was the first woman that reigned over China?—What is said of Wan-te?—And King-te?—Woo-te?—Who was Ize-ma-tseen?—What is said of the sect of Laou-keun?—Of Japan?

GREECE.

HAVING delivered Athens, the Romans marched against Philip, but were at first unsuccessful. The Consul Quintus Flamininus, however (B. C. 198), forced the defile of Tempe, and entered Thessaly; whereupon Philip's allies deserted him, and made peace. Nevertheless, he held out until he was totally defeated at Cynosceph′alæ (B. C. 197), when he submitted to the Romans, who forced him to resign his navy, and his pretensions to supremacy over the Grecian States.

In the year B. C. 196 the Romans went through the farce of proclaiming the liberties of Greece at the Isthmian games; but their real efforts were secretly directed to the weakening of the Achæan league. Philopœmen, however, labored hard to sustain the confederacy, and the independence of his country. He attacked, defeated, and killed Nabis, the tyrant of Sparta, who was an ally of the Romans (B. C. 192). Sparta then joined the league. But a new combination of forces took place when Anti′ochus, king of Syria, having declared war against the Romans, made an alliance with the Ætolians, and invaded Greece. The Achæans then declared for the Romans, and Philip did the same; but the latter, after being defeated by Antiochus, and losing much time, returned to Asia (B. C. 191). Anti′ochus was unsuccessful against the Romans, and was driven by them out of the country: they then subdued the Ætolians, and deprived them of their independence.

Philopœmen now compelled the Spartans to adopt the laws of the league, and to abrogate those of Lycurgus (B. C. 189). This caused them to carry their complaints to Rome; and the Achæans, dreading the vengeance of that power, made an alliance with Egypt. Philip, also, learning that the Romans had become jealous of the revival of his power, sent his son Demetrius to Rome to plead his cause before the Senate. Thus all Greece began to pale before the rising star of Italy. But the greatest calamity of all was the death of Philopœmen (B. C. 183), who was taken prisoner in a skirmish between the Achæans and Messenians, and cruelly put to death by the latter. He was the last great general that maintained the glory of the Hellenic race, and has been styled "the last of the Greeks". The Achæans revenged his death by the storming of Messe′ne, and the slaughter of every person who had taken part in the murder. The remains of Philopœmen were buried with the utmost honors at Megalop′olis; the historian, Polybius, carrying the urn which held his ashes.

Demetrius, having pacified the Romans, returned to Macedon (B. C. 181); but his father and his brother Perseus, jealous of his popularity, put him to death. Philip soon after (B. C. 179) died of a broken heart. His son, Per′seus, hated by everybody, succeeded him on the throne. The first act of Perseus was to form a league against the Romans; the Achæans, on the other hand, formed an alliance with them. For some years the Romans took no measures against Perseus, who treated their ambassadors with contempt. But at last (B. C. 171) they sent Licin′ius against him with an army, which met with some reverses. This emboldened Perseus to form alliances against the Romans with Antiochus, Prusias, Eumenes, and other Asiatic monarchs. For three years the Romans made little progress. At length the celebrated ÆMILIUS PAULLUS took the chief command. That general subdued Illyria in 30 days, and forced Perseus to a decisive engagement at Pydna, in which the Macedonian tyrant was defeated and taken prisoner, and he was sent in chains to Rome (B. C. 168). Thus ended the independence of Macedon. Greece was still left nominally free; but 1000 of the most eminent Achæans having been summoned to Rome as hostages, were kept there 17 years in prison. On their return from their captivity (B. C. 148), they stimulated their countrymen at Corinth to insult the Roman ambassadors, who had been sent there to settle some disputes between the Achæans and the Spartans. This led to another struggle, which was brief but decisive. The Romans defeated the Achæans everywhere. The Consul Lucius Mum′mius, after routing the army of the league at the Isthmus of Corinth, entered that city without opposition. Corinth was abandoned to pillage, burned, and razed to the ground; the inhabitants were sold for slaves; the finest specimens of Grecian art were disposed of by the ignorant Roman generals to the king of Pergamus; the remainder were sent to Rome. Greece was formed into a province of the Roman empire under the name of Achaia, and thus disappeared from history. Greece reappears no more in history as an independent State until the beginning of the 19th century, a period of nearly 2000 years.

What was the result of the battle of Cynoscephalæ?—What did the Romans then do?—What were the acts of Philopœmen?—What was his fate?—How was his death avenged?—What was the end of Philip V.?—And his son Perseus?—Who conquered Macedon?—What provocations did the Achæans receive?—What was the fate of Corinth?—And of Greece?

Among the eminent literary and scientific men of Greece in this century, were the philosophers and geographers, Pol′emo and Artemido′rus; the historian Polyb′ius; the astronomer Hippar′chus, who made a catalogue of the stars; the poets Moschus and Nican′der; Carne′ades, the founder of the third academy at Athens; Diog′enes, the Babylonian, and Antip′ater, the Stoic, philosophers; Philo of Byzantium, the celebrated mechanician, who wrote a treatise on military engineering, and an account of "the Seven Wonders of the World," which were: 1. The hanging gardens of Nebuchadnezzar at Babylon; 2. The walls of Babylon; 3. The pyramids of Egypt; 4. The Colossus of Rhodes; 5. The temple of Diana at Ephesus; 6. The statue of Jupiter Olympius at Athens, which was the master-piece of Phidias, and was made of ivory and gold; and, 7. The tomb, or mausoleum, of Mauso′lus, king of Caria:—the critic Aristar′chus; the philosopher Clitom′achus of Carthage, who wrote 400 works; the dialectician Diodo′rus; and others of less note. But Athens remained the chief seat of learning in the Roman empire.

Before concluding our sketch of the history of this remarkable people, we may notice two or three things. Four dialects were in use among them: 1. The Attic, which was spoken in Athens and its vicinity: it was the most elegant of the four: Plato, Xenophon, Thucydides, Demosthenes, Æschylus, Sophocles, Euripides, and Aristophanes wrote in it: — 2. The Ionic, used chiefly in Asia Minor: Herodotus and Hippocrates used it: — 3. The Doric, spoken by the Spartans, Cretans, and Sicilians: Theocritus, Pindar, and Archimedes wrote in it: — 4. The Æolic, spoken by the Bœotians.

The history of Greece may be divided into four periods. First, the mythical and heroic age, extending from the fabulous Jupiter to the siege of Troy. Second, the transition period, when the different States assumed their definite shapes, and the colonies were planted. Third, the brilliant period from the war with Darius to the death of Alexander the Great. Fourth, from that period until the subjugation by Rome.

The rites of burial were held very sacred by the Greeks. In the later ages it was customary to burn the body of the deceased. When it was consumed, the nearest relative collected the ashes, and deposited them in an urn, which was then buried. Libations of wine were poured out during the funeral ceremonies, and part of the clothes of the deceased were thrown into the fire. Those citizens who neglected these duties were prohibited from attaining to any high office, however well qualified for it.

It is evident that the mission of Greece was to develop the Beautiful. To no other nation has so lively a perception of what is lovely in Nature, Art, and Philosophy, been vouchsafed. To this day the sculptures of Phidias and Praxiteles have been unsurpassed. The architecture of Greece has been the model of that of succeeding generations of civilized men. The Greeks themselves were physically the handsomest and best-developed people of antiquity; and their poetry proves that they entertained the loftiest notions of patriotism, heroism, and endurance. The teachings of Socrates and Plato approach closely to the Christian standard. The beautiful speculations of Pythagoras, the heroic poems of Homer, the dramas of Æschylus, Sophocles, and Euripides, the lyrics of Pindar and Anacreon, the many beautiful myths by which the operations of Nature were typified, the philosophy of Aristotle, the geometry of Euclid, show what a variously as well as a highly gifted race the Greeks were. That they should have arisen so mysteriously, shone out for so brief a period, done so much in so short a time, and vanished so suddenly, are among the marvels of history. The period of this brilliancy lasted but little more than 300 years, yet this sufficed to bequeath to the world an imperishable influence on its ideas, languages, and literature. The inspiration of the most gifted minds of modern times has been derived mediately or immediately from Greece. Rome would not have been what she was, but for the ideas and habits she borrowed from her province of Achaia, and the schools of Alexandria. But Greece did little to elevate the position of woman: the Greek wife was, practically, not much better than a household drudge or slave. This defect in social polity, combined with the want of a definite standard of religion and morality, were the causes of the early downfall of the race. The Greeks became thoroughly demoralized, and remained so for centuries. They are only just now emerging from their fallen state.

What eminent men flourished?—Which were "the Seven Wonders of the World"?—Name the four dialects of Greece. — Where were they spoken? — Into how many periods is the history of Greece divided? — What is said of the rites of burial?—What was the mission of Greece? — What were the causes of her downfall?

ITALY.

The dominions of Rome now embraced all Italy, Spain, Sicily, and Sardinia. Before the close of the century we shall find them extended from the Atlantic to the Euphrates and the Black Sea.

Having rescued the Athenians from the clutches of Philip of Macedon, the Romans declared war against that prince, and an army was sent into Macedonia, but nothing of consequence was effected (B. C. 200). At length Quintius Flamin′inus was entrusted with the conduct of the war, and he soon forced Philip into a battle at Cynosceph′alæ (B. C. 197), totally defeated him, and compelled him to make peace. Flamininus proceeded in the work of reducing all Greece. He caused it to be solemnly proclaimed at the Isthmian games, that all the Greeks who had been subject to king Philip and the Macedonians were free and independent (B. C. 196), and he remained nearly two years in the country to carry out this proclamation.

The next war in which the republic was engaged was with the Spaniards, who sought to regain their independence. Marcus Porcius Cato (surnamed "the censor") was sent against them, and carried on the war with such success that he was decreed a triumph on his return to Rome (B. C. 194). At the same time Antiochus, king of Syria, hoping to re-establish the empire of the Seleucidæ in Asia, and incited by Hannibal (the famous Carthaginian, who had taken refuge at his Court), crossed over into Thessaly in order to renew the war in Greece. He was met at Thermopylæ (B. C. 191) by Flamininus, and defeated in a sanguinary battle, mainly owing to the conduct of Cato. His fleet was likewise defeated in two engagements. Antiochus returned to Ephesus discomfited. Cornelius Scipio Africanus, who had been previously (B. C. 193) sent to arrange terms of peace with Antiochus, was now sent with his brother Lucius to terminate the war. They soon reduced him to great straits, defeated him at Magnesia, subdued his allies (the Galatians), and forced him to give up all his possessions in Europe and Asia, north of Mount Taurus (B. C. 190). On their return they were accused of having taken bribes of Antiochus to let him off so easily. Cato, and the two Petilii, the tribunes of the people, called upon Lucius Scipio to render an account of all the sums he had received from Antiochus. He accordingly prepared the accounts, and was in the act of delivering them up, when his brother Africanus snatched them out of his hands, and tore them up before the Senate. But Lucius was declared guilty, and sentenced to pay a heavy fine. The tribune, Mimi′cius, ordered him to be dragged to prison, whereupon Africanus rescued him from the officer's hands. The contest might have ended fatally, had not the tribune, Tibe′rius Grac′chus, released Lucius. Cato, Næ′vius, and others, then brought Africanus to trial (B. C. 185). On the day of the trial Africanus reminded the people that it was the anniversary of his victory over Hannibal at Zama, and called upon them to follow him to the capitol to return thanks to the gods. The people followed him in crowds, but he then quitted Rome, and retired to his country-seat at Liternum. Tiberius Gracchus persuaded the censors to let the prosecution drop. Scipio never returned to Rome, and died about the year B. C. 183, being one of the greatest men Rome ever produced. Lucius Scipio, however, was condemned, and all his property was confiscated. In this memorable affair Cato the censor acted with extraordinary virulence against the Scipios, and against all those patricians who had introduced Grecian and Oriental luxury. He displayed this feeling during the whole of his censorship. In the year B. C. 150 he was sent to Carthage to arbitrate between that city and Masinissa, king of the Numidians. On that occasion he was so struck with the flourishing state of Carthage that he insisted on the necessity for destroying it, in order to make Rome safe. The memorable expression, "*Delenda est Carthago*" (Carthage must be destroyed), was his. He died B. C. 149, aged 85. This remarkable man, in his capacity of censor of public morals, effected many reforms, some of which died with him, others survived him. He labored strenuously to check the growth of luxury, and laid heavy taxes on dress, equipages, slaves, houses, and land. He punished the most illustrious personages for unbecoming conduct, and fiercely attacked all abuses. He had numerous enemies, and was accused forty-four times before the people, but always came off victorious. He vigorously managed the public works, and greatly amended the drainage of the city. His abilities were of a very high order, but his self-conceit was intolerable. He acted as though he was infallible, while his determined will bore down all opposition. He wrote a work on farming, which has come down to us. He was the most remarkable man of his time, and was a true type of the domineering Roman character.

During the interval between B. C. 187–172, the Romans subdued the Celtic tribes in the north of Italy, the Ligurians and the Istrians. They also continued the conquest of Spain, and were called upon to arbitrate in the disputes of various nations. About the year B. C. 168, Perseus, king of Macedon, penetrating the ambitious designs of the Romans, organized a conspiracy of several States against them; and, entering Thessaly, he attacked and defeated a Roman army on the Peneus. For some time his successes continued; but the consul, Æmilius Paullus, stopped his career at Pydna, totally defeated him, took him and his family prisoners, and annexed his kingdom to the Roman dominions. The consul then plundered Epirus; and, on his return to Rome (Nov., B. C. 167), received the most splendid triumph that had yet been seen. A thousand of the principal Achæans were brought to Rome as hostages for the tranquillity of Greece. They were thrown into prison, and detained there seventeen years. The treasure taken in the Macedonian war paid all debts contracted in its progress; and the tribute annually exacted from Macedon, added to the revenues of other provinces, enabled the government to dispense with all direct taxes upon Roman citizens in future wars. Thus the Romans became accustomed to live by the spoliation of other nations, and we are not surprised that their taste for luxury kept pace with their rapacity for plunder, until all virtue was crushed out of them, and they sunk under the yoke of ambitious military chiefs at the close of the next century. The unhappy Perseus and his three sons were thrown into a loathsome dungeon, from which they were rescued through the intercession of Paullus. The king died soon after, and his eldest son was employed as a public clerk. Such was the destiny of the last heir to the throne of Macedon.

The long-delayed destruction of Carthage was now resolved upon. The Senate, urged on by Cato the censor, found in the disputes between the Numidians and the Carthaginians a pretext for fixing a quarrel upon the ill-fated city. That unhappy State did all that could be done to avert the designs of Rome; but finding that nothing short of the entire surrender of its liberties would satisfy the Senate, it resolved to resist to the last. The Romans fitted out an immense expedition (B. C. 148), under the consul, Calpur′nius Piso Cæsoni′nus, and invested Carthage. Piso, however, did not accomplish anything of importance. He was recalled, and the command was given to Publius Cornelius Scipio (surnamed "Africanus Minor", the younger son of Æmilius Paullus, the conqueror of Macedonia, and adopted by the son of the great Africanus), who had already distinguished himself during the siege. He prosecuted the operations against the doomed city with the greatest vigor, but the Carthaginians defended themselves with the energy of despair, and it was not until the spring of B. C. 146 that the Romans forced their way into Carthage. The work of slaughter occupied many days, but the city was finally destroyed. [A fuller account of the fall of the great rival of Rome will be found in the page devoted to Carthage.] Scipio is said to have wept over its fate. He returned to Rome, where he was decreed a triumph, and was soon after elected censor. His efforts in that capacity to repress the growth of luxury were unavailing.

During the third Punic war, an impostor, named Andriscus, who pretended to be the son of Philip of Macedon, kindled another war in Greece. But he was made prisoner, and put to death by the prætor, Q. Metellus (B. C. 146), and Macedon was regained. The disputes between the Achæans and the Spartans furnished the Romans with a pretext for further interference in the affairs of Greece. Metellus attacked the Achæans, and dispersed them; but at this juncture he was sent back to Macedonia, by the consul, Lucius Mummius, who assumed the conduct of the war. That officer laid siege to Corinth, sacked, and burnt it; and after having plundered it of its statues and paintings, some of which he sold to the king of Pergamus, and others he sent to Rome, he levelled its houses and walls with the ground. Mummius was a rude barbarian, utterly incapable of appreciating works of art, but he was also indifferent to wealth, and reserved very little of the plunder for himself. A specimen of the ignorance of this destroyer of one of the most beautiful cities of ancient Greece, is shown in his suffering his soldiers to use one of the choicest works of the painter

What of the second Macedonian war?—Name the principal battle, and the Roman general who gained it.—Which was the next war?—Why did Antiochus make war?—What was the result?—Who were the leaders?—What befell the Scipios?—Who said "Carthage must be destroyed"?—What of Cato the censor?

What is said of the third Macedonian war?—Of the triumph of Æmilius Paullus?—What befell Perseus and his sons?—And the Achæans?—How did the third Punic war originate?—What is said of the fall of Carthage?—Of Scipio?—Of the fall of Corinth and of Greece?—Of Metellus and Mummius?

Aristides as a draft-board; and when Attalus offered him a large sum for the painting, he imagined it must be a talisman, and ordered it to be sent to Rome. He told the seamen who contracted to carry the statues and pictures of Corinth to Rome, that "if they lost or damaged them they should make the loss good!" Thebes and Chalcis shared the same fate as Corinth, and thus in the same year (B. C. 146) that Carthage fell, Greece became a Roman province under the name of "Achaia".

While the wars in Africa and Greece were raging, another contest more fierce than either was going on in Spain, where the natives fiercely resisted the domination of the Romans. The Lusitanians (ancestors of the modern Portuguese) displayed extraordinary bravery in this remarkable contest, which was brought about by the cruelty of the consul, Licin′ius Lucul′lus. For three years the Romans were uniformly unsuccessful. MARCUS MARCELLUS and the prætor, Galba, were unable to make any progress against the patriots under VIRIA′THUS, a shepherd. This heroic leader, the prototype of the guerilla chiefs of Spain in modern times, drove the Romans out of the west of the peninsula. The consul, Fabius Maximus Æmilia′nus, was sent against Viriathus. He remained two years in command, but effected nothing. In the year of his departure (B. C. 143), the war assumed a more serious aspect. The Celtiberians suddenly appeared in the field in formidable force. Metellus, the conqueror of Macedonia, was sent against them; and in the course of two years he shut them up in their strongholds, Terman′tia and Numan′tia: but at this point he was superseded by the consul, Pompeius, an ignorant and unskilful man, who carried on the contest two years longer, by which time his army was so reduced that he was glad to make peace on easy terms. His successor, Popill′ius Lænas, however, repudiated the treaty and continued the war, but with as little credit as Pompeius. He was superseded by Manci′nus (B. C. 137), when fresh disaster attended the Romans, and the Numantians compelled the new commander to sue for peace. He resigned his command to Lep′idus, and proceeded to Rome to justify his acts; but the Senate rejected the treaty, and sent Mancinus back to the Numantians as a sacrifice. The latter refused to accept him in lieu of the treaty, and sent him back to Rome, where he was treated as an alien, until a law was passed restoring to him his privileges.

Meanwhile Lepidus attacked the Vaccæans, near Salamanca, without much success; and Calpurnius Piso, who succeeded him, fared no better. It would seem that the Romans were no match for the Spaniards in the field, and their continued ill-fortune caused great discontent at Rome.

The contest with Viriathus might have been prolonged indefinitely, had not the consul, Cneius Cæpio, procured the assassination of the gallant chief (B. C. 138). The Lusitanians thereupon laid down their arms. But the city of Numantia defied all the efforts of the Romans for years, until Scipio Æmilianus, the conqueror of Carthage, undertook to terminate the war. This great man had led a quiet life after the conquest of Carthage. He served as censor (B. C. 142), in conjunction with Mummius, and had been sent on an embassy to Egypt. The voice of the people called him to the Spanish war (B. C. 135), and, notwithstanding the exhausted state of the country, he raised 4000 men by his personal influence, and himself advanced the necessary funds. His first step, on assuming command, was to organize the demoralized army; the strictest discipline was enforced, but considerable time elapsed before he advanced against Numantia. It was not until the spring of B. C. 133 that he and his brother Fabius laid siege to that city. He was joined on the march by Jugurtha, the son of Micipsa, king of Numidia, with a large body of African cavalry. Numantia was reduced by famine, and the wretched inhabitants were sold into slavery. The town was then so effectually destroyed that its site cannot now be discovered. For this exploit Scipio obtained the surname of Numanti′nus.

In the west of Spain, the consul, DECIUS JUNIUS BRUTUS, effected the pacification of Lusitania. He founded the town of Valentia, and, marching northward across the Tagus, crossed the Western Pyrenees. He was the first Roman who reached the shores of the Bay of Biscay, and saw the sun set in the waters of the Atlantic. He remained five years in Spain, and was honored with the title of Callini′cus for his successes (B. C. 133).

In the same year, Attalus III., king of Pergamus, died, and bequeathed his kingdom and his wealth to the Roman people. This bequest involved them in a war with Aristoni′cus, the brother of Attalus, who disputed the bequest. The consul, Publius Crassus, was slain, and the Romans had to ask assistance of MITHRIDATES, king of Pontus, before they could subdue Aristonicus. The consul, PERPENNA, had the honor of annexing this province to the Roman dominions, and Mithridates was rewarded by the gift of Phrygia.

While the Spanish war was raging a servile war broke out in Sicily. Slavery had long been established in the Roman dominions. The slaves were captives taken in war, and sold in the public markets. The number of these unfortunate persons was not great, until after the second Punic war. But at the close of that great contest, Rome entered on a career of foreign conquest. To punish the Bruttians for aiding the Carthaginians, the whole nation were made slaves. On the conquest of Greece, 150,000 natives of Epirus were sold by Æmilius Paullus. Scipio sent 50,000 home from Carthage. Thousands were sold into slavery during the Syrian, Illyrian, Grecian, and Spanish wars, and thus slave labor became plentiful and cheap. There was also a regular slave trade in the East, the principal mart of which was "the sacred isle" of Delos. Thither were brought human beings from Thrace, Asia Minor, Armenia, Persia, etc., and sometimes as many as 10,000 were sold in one day. Those who were brought into Italy were treated with great barbarity. They were employed in the fields looking after cattle, for the safety of which they were held responsible, and they were compelled to provide themselves with the necessaries of life. When not thus employed they were shut up in large prison-like buildings. The system of brigandage, for which the south of Italy has so long been noted, had its origin in Roman slavery; for the masters would instruct the slaves to obtain clothes and other necessaries from travellers, and the practice once begun could not be crushed out. It became dangerous to travel, especially in Apulia, and the rich fled into the towns. The same system prevailed in Sicily, where the slaves were perhaps worse treated than in Italy. At the city of Enna, the domestic tyranny of Damoph′ilus, a wealthy land-owner, drove them into insurrection. Headed by a Greek slave, named Eunus, they made themselves masters of Enna. Eunus assumed the royal name, Antiochus, and became the acknowledged king of the insurgents, who assembled in vast numbers. The Roman troops were defeated, and the cities of Messana and Taurome′nium were captured. The insurrection spread into Italy, but there it was speedily crushed. The consul, Fulvius Flaccus, was sent with an army into Sicily (B. C. 133), but he did very little. His successor, Calpurnius Piso, did better: he wrested Messana from the slaves, killing 8000 of them. The extinction of the revolt was reserved for the consul, Rupil′ius, who took Enna and Tauromenium. The slaves were tortured and massacred: Achæus, their leader, died bravely fighting; but their pseudo-king, Eunus, was a coward, and ended his days in a loathsome dungeon. Thus was the first servile war terminated. The decayed state of agriculture throughout Sicily now claimed the attention of the Senate, and commissioners were appointed to aid Rupilius in framing laws to meet the evil. The principal measure was the levying of tithes on the land, which were to be paid to the Romans; and courts of appeal were established to protect the inhabitants. The burdens of land-owners were thus lightened, and agriculture again flourished.

During these wars the power of the Senate increased rapidly, and the government of Rome degenerated into a tyrannical aristocracy, whose members, though distinguished by great courage and abilities, were luxurious and corrupt. The popular family of the GRACCHI were a noble exception. Distinguished above all Roman ladies for virtue and refinement was CORNELIA, the younger daughter of Scipio Africanus (the elder), and wife of the censor, TIBERIUS SEMPRONIUS GRACCHUS. She was the mother of the two tribunes, TIBERIUS and CAIUS GRACCHUS, whom she survived. On her death the people erected a statue to her, with the inscription, "Cornelia, the mother of the Gracchi." The career of this family is important in Roman history. Tiberius, observing in the course of his military duties in Spain, Africa, and elsewhere, that the avarice of the aristocracy, combined with the expenses of the wars of the republic, had completely destroyed the middle class of small land-owners, resolved to attempt the reformation of the State. Having procured himself to be elected tribune, he proposed the revival of the agrarian law of Licinius, which had been disregarded

Who was Viriathus?—Relate the principal incidents in the Spanish war.—Name the principal Roman generals, and narrate their exploits.—What is said of Scipio Æmilianus?—Of the siege of Numantia?—Of Decius Brutus?—What did Attalus bequeath to the Romans?—What did it involve them in?

What is said of Mithridates?—Perpenna?—What occurred in Sicily?—What is said of slavery?—How were the slaves treated in Italy?—Where did the servile war break out?—What caused it?—Who headed it?—What was the result?—What of Cornelia?—Of Tiberius and Caius Gracchus?

for many years. The proposal was vehemently opposed, and one of the tribunes, Marcus Octavius, vetoed the bill. The people, at the instigation of Tiberius, deposed Octavius, and the bill was carried. Tiberius, his brother, Caius, and his father-in-law, Appius Claudius, were appointed to carry it into execution. It was at this juncture that Attalus bequeathed Pergamus to Rome. Tiberius proposed that the new territory should be divided among the people. He was again elected tribune, but the Senate declared his election illegal, on the ground that no one could hold the office for two consecutive years. Tiberius paid no attention to this objection; but while the voting was going on, a band of Senators, headed by Scipio Nasi′ca, attacked the people in the forum, and Tiberius was killed (B. C. 133). His brother, Caius, was elected tribune (B. C. 123). He carried out more extensive reforms than his brother had done. The Senate were deprived of some of their most important privileges, and every branch of the administration was modified. Caius Gracchus was elected tribune again next year, when the Senate, finding it impossible to withstand his influence, resorted to artifice. They induced Caius's colleague, Livius Drusus, to propose measures more popular than those of Caius. The people fell into the snare, and, while Caius was absent at Carthage, whither he had gone to superintend the founding of a colony, many of his friends deserted him. Several of his laws were repealed. Caius returned to Rome, and appeared in the forum to oppose these proceedings. It happened on this occasion that one of the friends of the consul, Opim′ius, was slain by the friends of Caius. Upon this the Senate authorized Opimius to resort to arms. The friends of Caius fought in his defence, but he refused to arm, and fled to the grove of the Furies, where he fell by the hands of his slave, whom he had commanded to kill him. About 3000 of the adherents of the Gracchi were killed, their property confiscated, their houses demolished, and their friends strangled (B. C. 121). With this sanguinary episode perished the freedom of the Roman republic. Henceforth the power of the State fell entirely into the hands of the profligate aristocracy.

In the year B. C. 118, Micipsa, king of Numidia, died, leaving his kingdom to Jugurtha, his illegitimate nephew, and to Hiem′psal and Adher′bal, his two sons. In the course of the year, Jugurtha assassinated Hiempsal, and defeated Adherbal, who thereupon fled to Rome to invoke the aid of the Senate. But Jugurtha, by bribes, counteracted the complaints of Adherbal; and the Senate decreed that the kingdom should be equally divided between the two. Jugurtha then bribed the Senators, intrusted with the execution of this decree, to give him the larger portion. He followed up his villany by attacking Adherbal, and shutting him up in the fortress of Cirta. The Romans commanded him to release Adherbal, but he paid no attention to the command; and at length, gaining possession of Cirta, he put Adherbal to death (B. C. 112). War was now declared against Jugurtha, and the consul, Calpurnius Bes′tia, was sent with an army to Africa (B. C. 111). Jugurtha bribed him to make peace; whereupon the indignant Romans forced the Senate to send for Jugurtha to be brought to Rome under a safe-conduct. He came, but refused to plead; and even assassinated Massi′va, the grandson of Masinissa. In consequence of this act he was forced to leave Italy. The war was then renewed, and Postu′mius Albinus, with his brother, Aulus, were sent to conduct it. The army of Aulus was cut to pieces, and he was forced to make a treaty of peace. This treaty was instantly annulled by the Senate; and the consul, Metellus, was sent into Africa with a fresh army. Metellus was inaccessible to bribes, and he repeatedly defeated Jugurtha, ultimately forcing him to take refuge among the Gætulians. In the year B. C. 107, Metellus was superseded in the command of the army by Caius Ma′rius, a man of humble origin, who had risen by his bravery in Spain, and had been popular as a tribune. He had served two years under Metellus in Africa when he was appointed to conduct the war against Jugurtha. The united forces of the latter and his father-in-law, Bocchus, king of Mauretania, were defeated in a decisive battle by Marius; and Bocchus made peace with the Romans by surrendering Jugurtha to Lucius Sylla (or Sulla), the lieutenant of Marius. Sylla thereupon claimed the honor of having terminated the war, and this laid the foundation of the deadly hatred between him and Marius. Jugurtha was brought to Rome, thrown into a dungeon, and starved to death.

Meanwhile Italy was threatened by a vast horde of barbarians from Germany, consisting of Cimbri, Teu′tones, Ambro′nes, and other tribes, numbering 300,000 fighting men. They had ravaged Thrace, Illyria, Gaul, Spain, and Northern Italy, defeating every Roman army sent against them. The terrible defeat of the consuls, Cæpio and Manilius, near the Rhone (B. C. 104), by the Cimbri, wherein 80,000 soldiers and 40,000 camp followers are said to have perished, struck terror throughout Italy. By common accord Marius was elected consul for the second time. Fortunately, the barbarians, instead of pouring at once into Italy, turned southward, and crossed the Pyrenees into Spain. Thus Italy was relieved from immediate danger, and Marius had time to put forth all his energy in organizing a fresh army. But the danger had not wholly passed away. Marius was elected consul a third and a fourth time (B. C. 103). The Cimbri, repulsed in Spain, rejoined the Teutones in the south of France. Marius hastened thither, and fortified a strong camp between Nismes and Arles, on the Rhone, to resist them; but the Cimbri made a circuit through Helvetia (Switzerland), to enter Italy on the north. Luta′tius Cat′ulus was despatched with an army to meet them. The winter passed away in inactivity, but in the spring of B. C. 102, the Teutones endeavored to entice Marius from his camp; failing in this, they attacked the camp, and were driven off with great loss. They then marched eastward, and it is said so vast was their number that they were six days in defiling past the Roman entrenchments. As soon as they had disappeared Marius followed them until they halted at Aquæ Sextiæ, where he attacked them, and drove them into their camp. Two days afterwards the entire barbarian host was drawn up in front of the Romans. The former commenced the attack, but were bravely met; and the barbarians, surprised in the rear by an ambush under Marcellus, were thrown into confusion. An immense slaughter ensued: so numerous were the slain that, in after years, the people of Marseilles used the bones from the field of battle to make fences for their vineyards, and the plain was fertilized by the putrescent bodies. 90,000 Teutones were taken prisoners, and sold as slaves; their host was annihilated, and Western Italy was saved by this great victory.

The Cimbri marched into the Tyrol, and descended the valley of the Athesis (or Adige), where Catulus concentrated his forces. In the beginning of B. C. 101 they crossed the pass of the Brenner, sliding down the frozen slopes on their shields. They attacked Catulus, and captured part of his army, driving the remainder toward Placentia (Piacenza). There Marius, with his troops, joined Catulus. The Cimbrian chief, Boi′orix, demanded land and cities enough for all: Marius sent him a defiant answer. The chief then asked him to appoint a time and a place for the battle: Marius accordingly chose the third day and the plain of Vercellæ. There the combat took place, and the Cimbrian host was literally annihilated: 60,000 prisoners were taken, and the women slew themselves and their children. Thus Italy was saved, and Marius and Catulus were honored with a magnificent triumph.

In the year B. C. 100 Marius was elected consul for the sixth time. One of his first acts was to drive into exile his old commander, Metellus. He then entered into close intimacy with the lowest demagogues. Two of the latter, Apule′ius Saturni′nus and Servil′ius Glau′cia, having caused great disturbances, Marius, by order of the Senate, crushed the insurrection by armed force.

A census of the population of Rome, taken in B. C. 189, gives a return of 258,318 citizens. Another taken in B. C. 115, shows the number of 394,336.

Rome now appears in the arena of literature. En′nius, a Greek by birth, but a Roman citizen, wrote an epic history of Rome in eighteen books, and also several tragedies and comedies; fragments only of his works have come down to us. Plautus, the most celebrated comic poet of Rome, was his contemporary. He was born B. C. 254, and died B. C. 189, having written more than 100 plays. Teren′tius Afer, commonly called Terence, the celebrated comic poet, was born at Carthage (B. C. 195), and was the slave of a Roman Senator, Terentius Lucanus, who gave him his freedom. He wrote six plays, and translated 108 of Menander's comedies. He died at the age of 36 (B. C. 159). The comic poets, Cæcil′ius Statius and Turpil′ius; the satirist, Lucil′ius; the historians, Cin′cius, Albi′nus, Fan′nius, Cassius Hem′ina, Vale′rius An′tias, Licin′ius, and Quadriga′rius; the tragic poets, Att′ius (or Acc′ius) and Pacu′vius (who was also a painter) — all flourished during this century.

What was the fate of the Gracchi?—What was its effect on the republic?—Who was Jugurtha?—Give an account of the war in Numidia.—What of Caius Marius?—Of Sylla?—What was the fate of Jugurtha?—What danger threatened Italy during this war?—From what quarter?

What befell the consuls, Cæpio and Manilius?—Give an account of the exploits of Marius, and of the battle of Aquæ Sextiæ.—Also of the battle of Vercelli.—What did Marius do afterwards?—What was the population of Rome in B. C. 189?—In B. C. 115?—Name the authors who flourished.

BRITAIN.

England.—Of the various kings who ruled there are none worthy of notice until we come to Cligueill, the son of Capoir, a man described as being "prudent and mild in all his actions, and who, above all things, made it his business to exercise true justice among his people." He was succeeded by his son, Heli (by some called Nimu'can), (B. C. 164), who reigned 40 years, and is remembered as being the father of king Lud, and of the celebrated Cassib'elan (or Cadwallo). On the death of Heli, Lud succeeded him. He built several cities, and enlarged and walled the ancient city of Trinovan'tium, where he kept his court. He was a very warlike prince, and celebrated for the magnificence of his feasts and public entertainments. Although he occasionally resided in the cities he founded, he preferred Trinovantium above them all; he surrounded it with towers, and compelled the citizens to build houses and other structures in it. He made it his chief city, and named it Caer-Lud, or Lud's-town (whence London). He was renowned for his military and jovial qualities, and was buried in London near the gate, called by the Britons after him, Parth Lud (in Latin, *Porta Lud;* and by the Saxons, Ludesgata, or Ludgate).

Scotland.—The history of this portion of Britain during this century presents nothing remarkable. Reutha, an able prince, was succeeded by There, who committed all sorts of excesses, but died after a reign of 12 years. His brother and successor, Josin, encouraged the study of medicine. Finnan passed a law that no king should engage in any affair of importance without the advice and sanction of the public council. He died revered, after a reign of 30 years, and was succeeded by his son, Dethach, who abandoned himself to every species of debauchery and cruelty, and was at length slain in battle by his refractory chieftains, who elected his cousin, Jair (or Ewen), to succeed him. The kingdom of the Picts likewise flourished during this century, but the records of these barbarians are nothing more than those of border feuds with their immediate neighbors, the Scots and Britons.

Ireland.—The history of this country presents the usual story of domestic broils and feuds between the chiefs or petty kings of the provinces into which Ireland was divided.

What is recorded of Cligueill? — Heli? — Lud? — The origin of the name London? — The Scottish kings?—Records of the Picts?— The history of Ireland during this period?

FRANCE.

The Cisalpine Gauls struggled hard, but vainly, against the increasing power of the Romans, and were subdued by Lucius Flamininus (B. C. 201-170).

The Asiatic Gauls were likewise subdued by the Romans under Cneius Manlius, after the loss of two sanguinary battles — one at Mount Olympus, the other at Mount Magaba (A. D. 167). A twenty years' peace followed, after which we find the Galatians ravaging Pergamus, Cappadocia, and Phrygia.

Transalpine Gaul (modern France) flourished during this century. The first half of it passed without any particular events. But in the year B. C. 154, the Marseillese having extended their colony all along the southern coast of France, came into collision with the Ligurians, and a war was the result. The Ligurians laid siege to Antibes and Nice; the Marseillese sent to Rome for aid, and this was the occasion for the first entry of the Romans into Gaul. The consul, Opimius, subdued a portion of Liguria beyond the Rhone, and relieved the besieged cities. But in B. C. 125, the Ligurians again attacked the Marseillese, who once more sought the assistance of Rome; and the consuls, Flaccus and Calvinus, were sent with an army to help them. Teutomal, the Ligurian king, was vanquished. The tribes of the Allobroges and the Arverni then formed a league against Rome; but the consul, Domitius, defeated them at Venasque (B. C. 122), and, with the aid of the celebrated Fabius Maximus, subdued them, making prisoner their king, Bituitus. The conquered territory was formed into a Roman province (known, in the Middle Ages, as the kingdom of Provence). A Roman colony was planted at Narbonne by the consul, Licinius Crassus.

In B. C. 113, a horde of Cimbri and Teutons poured into Helvetia, and thence into Gaul (B. C. 110). The Belgians, in the east and north of the country, made a brave resistance, but at length came to terms with them. Central Gaul was next ravaged. The Roman province was attacked, and the Romans were defeated in several battles. The Cimbri then entered Spain. Meanwhile the Roman general, Marius, was appointed consul in Gaul, and gained a great victory over the Ambro-Teutons at Aquæ Sextiæ. The Cimbri returning from Spain through Gaul, entered Italy, but were cut to pieces by Marius at Vercellæ.

What happened to the Cisalpine Gauls?— The Galatians?—Marseillese?—What was the first occasion of Roman invasion?—What did they form?—What did the Cimbri do?

SPAIN.

The history of this century consists of a series of gallant struggles for liberty, on the part of the Spaniards, with the Romans. Many bloody battles were fought, and it required all the abilities of Marcus Porcius Cato, Publius Scipio Nasica, Æmilius Lepidus, Tiberius Sempronius Gracchus, Caius Flaminius, and many other of the most eminent of the Roman generals, to preserve the authority of Rome in Spain. The Carthaginian yoke had been intolerable, owing to the avidity of the local governors, the exactions and licentiousness of a mercenary soldiery, and the rigor with which the captive tribes were made to labor in the mines. But bad as it was, it does not appear that the Spaniards relished that of the Romans more. At all events, they offered the most obstinate resistance to it. By no nation which fell under the yoke of Rome was greater heroism displayed than by the Spaniards; but they were forced to succumb to the conquerors of the world. The country was divided by the victors into two provinces, viz., Hispania Citerior and Hispania Ulterior; the latter comprised Portugal and Andalusia, the former the rest of Spain.

In the year B. C. 152 commenced the first Numantian war; so called from the heroic city of Numantia, which so long defied the power of Rome. The revolt spread amongst the Lusitanians, and was not suppressed until after a desperate struggle, in which Lucius Mummius, Claudius Marcellus, Marcus Atilius, Sergius Galba, Licinius Lucullus, and Publius Cornelius Scipio, distinguished themselves. Numantia made peace with Marcellus; but the cruelties of Galba in Lusitania incited an obstinate war, in which the natives, under Viria'thus, a man of humble parentage, but of great natural abilities and courage, resisted the utmost efforts of the Romans for 14 years, so that at last they were glad to make peace (B. C. 140). This peace was, however, perfidiously broken by the Romans. Capio, the governor of Lusitania, procured the murder of Viriathus. The last hope of Spain being thus destroyed, the Lusitanians submitted; but the Numantians still defied the Romans.

The second Numantian war began in B. C. 139. During its progress the Romans suffered a series of reverses until Scipio Africanus was sent into Spain; and he, after a long siege, took and utterly destroyed Numantia (B. C. 132).

What were the principal events of this century?—What is said of the Carthaginian yoke? —How was Spain divided?—What is said of Viriathus? — The siege of Numantia?

GERMANY.

The Romans finally annihilated the Boii in Italy, in a battle in which 32,000 were slain (B. C. 191).

The Getæ and Bastarnæ acted as mercenaries in the service of Perseus, king of Macedon, against the Romans; but he not keeping faith with them, Clon'dicus, king of the Bastarnæ, in revenge, ravaged Thrace, and then returned to his own country, leaving Perseus at the mercy of the Romans.

In the beginning of this century the Cimbri and Teutones descended from the Danube to the Styrian Alps in immense numbers. There they remained several years. At length the Cimbri poured into Gaul. Thence they turned towards Italy, and, near Marseilles, they met the Roman army guarding the frontier, and demanded of Silanus, the commander, permission to settle in Italy; which being refused, a battle took place, and the Romans were defeated. Another Roman army stationed near the lake of Geneva was attacked by the Helvetii (Swiss), under their chief, Div'ico, and so completely defeated that all the Romans who escaped the slaughter were taken prisoners, and forced to crawl ignominiously under a lance placed horizontally on two low posts. Another army, under Scaurus, was also defeated, and its general was taken prisoner. Scaurus was killed by Boi'orix, the German chief, for saying that Italy would never become the prey of the Germans. Shortly after they were joined by the Teutones. The Romans sent two armies, under Manlius and Cæpio, to oppose them. Both these armies were cut to pieces, and Rome lay at the mercy of the barbarians. They, however, suddenly marched into Spain, where they wasted time by waging a futile war of three years' duration, and then returned towards Italy. The Teutones and Cimbri separated—the latter entering the Tyrol, while the former attacked the Romans, under Marius, who was posted at Aix, on the Rhone. This celebrated general cut them to pieces with enormous slaughter (B. C. 102), taking their king, Teutobach, prisoner. The Cimbri, advancing from the Tyrol, were met by Marius on the plains of Vercelli, and exterminated in one of the bloodiest battles on record. Boiorix, their king, was slain, with 90,000 of his men; 60,000 were taken prisoners. Their women slew those that fled, and then killed themselves and their children.

What is said of the Getæ and Bastarnæ?— Give an account of the wars of the Cimbri and Teutones with the Romans.—What great battle was gained by Marius?

ASIA MINOR.

PERGAMUS.—Attalus took part in the war with Philip of Macedon. He went [t]o Thebes to secure for the Romans the alliance of the Bœotians, but while ad[d]ressing their assembly he was seized with a fit. He was carried back to Per[g]amus, where he died (B. C. 197), having reigned 54 years, in a just and hu[m]ane manner. His eldest son, EU′MENES II., succeeded him. This prince [m]aintained the alliance with the Romans, and rendered them good service on [s]everal occasions. He showed his wisdom in refusing that proposed by Antio[ch]us, king of Syria, knowing well that if the latter succeeded in his war with [th]e Romans, he would subjugate all the smaller kingdoms of Asia Minor. When [w]ar broke out (B. C. 193), Eumenes joined the Romans. Pergamus suffered [se]verely at the outset; for Seleucus Philop′ator, the son of Antiochus, besieged [th]e city, and had very nearly reduced it, when the fleets of the Rhodians and [th]e Romans arrived to succour it. Seleucus was obliged to raise the siege and [q]uit the country. At the close of the war, a large portion of the dominions of [A]ntiochus was given to Eumenes. Eumenes courted the alliance of the Achæan [le]ague, offering it an annual subsidy of 120 talents (about $105,000), the inter[e]st to be applied to the support of the members of the public council. This [o]ffer was declined.

In B. C. 184 war broke out with Pru′sias, king of Bithynia. This war is [d]istinguished from others of this period by the exploits of Hannibal, the illus[tr]ious Carthaginian, who had taken refuge with Prusias. In a naval battle, [H]annibal caused a number of serpents to be put into earthen vessels: he then [o]rdered Eumenes' galley to be attacked, and the vessels thrown aboard. These [b]eing broken by this means, the serpents escaped, and caused such confusion [th]at the galley was nearly taken, and Eumenes escaped with difficulty. Prusias [g]ained this and other battles, but they did not result in anything important. [E]umenes was next involved in war with Pharna′ces, king of Pontus (B. C. 182), [w]ho took the important town of Sino′pe. Eumenes complained to the Romans; [th]e latter mediated between the two, and after some years peace was concluded. [H]e also sent an embassy to Rome to complain of Philip of Macedon, who refused [to] deliver up certain fortresses in Thrace, pursuant to treaty. But Eumenes had [lo]st favor with the Romans, for they listened to him coldly. He went to Rome [to] point out to the Senate the insidious designs of Perseus, the son of Philip; [b]ut in this case he returned loaded with honors and presents. Perseus endeav[ou]red to poison Eumenes; but the person charged with the task disclosed the [d]esign to the king and the Roman Senate, who soon after declared war against [P]erseus. Eumenes hastened back to Pergamus, and joined the Romans in the [se]cond Macedonian war (B. C. 171). He took the field in person, with his broth[e]rs, Attalus and Athenæus. The result was the capture of Perseus by the Ro[m]ans, and the annexation of Macedonia to the Roman empire. While this war [w]as in progress, the Asiatic Gauls (Galatians) committed such terrible ravages [in] Pergamus, that Eumenes sent his brother Attalus to Rome for assistance. [A]ttalus was well received; but the Romans, who suspected Eumenes of secret [n]egotiations with Perseus, offered to deprive his brother of his kingdom and to [b]estow it upon himself. Attalus at first listened to this; but his physician, [S]tra′tius, persuaded him to adhere to the path of honor. He therefore contented [h]imself with demanding the aid required, and then left Rome. The Senate, [e]nraged, threw off the mask of friendship, and sent an embassy to the Gauls to [e]ncourage them in their acts. Eumenes then set out for Rome himself, but was [fo]rbidden to enter the city. He returned home, and sent his brothers, Attalus [a]nd Athenæus, to the Senate to defend him. They succeeded in appeasing that [a]ssembly: nevertheless, Roman commissioners were sent (B. C. 165) into Asia [M]inor to ascertain secretly whether Eumenes and Antiochus were not concoct[in]g some secret plan. These commissioners failed in their mission, but the [R]omans never trusted Eumenes again. That monarch ended his troubled reign [o]f 38 years B. C. 159. He left his kingdom to his infant son Attalus (surnamed [P]hilometer), and appointed his brother ATTALUS II. (surnamed Philadelphus) [a]cting king. Eumenes left his kingdom prosperous and powerful, and rivalled [h]is father in virtue and ability; but he is chiefly remembered as the restorer [a]nd enlarger of the famous library at Pergamus, the rival of that of Alexandria.

The enmity which Prusias had borne to Eumenes was continued against [A]ttalus. The Bithynian king invaded Pergamus, and took the capital, burning and destroying all before him. Attalus sent his brother Athenæus to Rome for aid, and by the interference of the Senate the war was stopped, Prusias being ordered to pay a sum equal to $750,000 to Attalus (B. C. 154). The latter died B. C. 138. With him expired the prosperity of Pergamus; for Attalus III., his nephew and successor, was a merciless tyrant, but fortunately died after a brief reign of five years (B. C. 133). He bequeathed his kingdom to the Romans; but this bequest was disputed by his kinsman Aristoni′cus, a member of his family. The Senate sent Licinius Crassus to take possession of the kingdom, but that officer was defeated (B. C. 130), and he thereupon destroyed himself. The consul, Perpenna, avenged his death, defeated Aristonicus, took him prisoner and sent him to Rome (B. C. 129), where he was strangled. The kingdom was reduced to a province of the empire, under the name of Asia; but Phrygia Major was given to Mithrida′tes Euer′getes, king of Pontus, as a reward for the aid he had rendered to the Romans during the war.

BITHYNIA.—Prusias I. reigned over this kingdom at the commencement of this century, as we have already seen. He was solicited by Antiochus, king of Syria, to join him against the Romans, but he declined doing so. The result showed his wisdom, for the Romans were successful. They demanded of Antiochus the surrender of Hannibal, who had taken refuge with him. Upon hearing of this, Hannibal fled to Prusias, who gladly welcomed him, the more so as he could be useful in the war which that prince was carrying on with Eumenes, king of Pergamus. Hannibal gained several victories over Eumenes, but the enmity of the Romans pursued him into Bithynia. They called upon Prusias to deliver him up, and that monarch was base enough to consent to such treachery. Hannibal, however, defeated their malice by taking poison (B. C. 183). Prusias died (B. C. 181), after reigning 48 years. Prusias II., who succeeded him, mediated with the Romans on behalf of Perseus of Macedonia. He went to Rome (B. C. 166) to propitiate the Senate; but his real object was to obtain the lands which the Gauls had taken from Antiochus: these the Senate granted to him. Meanwhile he carried on his war with Eumenes, and on the decease of the latter (B. C. 159) continued it with his son Attalus. Having gained a victory, he entered Pergamus and devastated the country. But Attalus having applied to Rome for protection, the Senate ordered Prusias to lay down his arms, and compelled him to give to Attalus twenty ships, and to pay him 500 talents ($550,000). The end of this perfidious prince was a just climax to his whole career. He sent his son Nicome′des to Rome, joining with him in the embassy an agent, who was instructed to murder him; the king designing thereby to advance the interests of his children by a second marriage. But the agent disclosed the plot to the young prince, who immediately hastened home, gained over the people to his cause, and put his father to death (B. C. 148). Prusias was universally hated for his cruelty. Nicomedes reigned over Bithynia 58 years. He managed to avoid mixing himself up with the quarrels of his neighbors, and but little is known of the transactions of his reign.

PONTUS.—Mithridates IV. closed his long reign of 50 years in B. C. 190. He was succeeded by Pharna′ces I., of whom little need be said. He reigned 34 years, and was succeeded by Mithridates V. (B. C. 156). This prince, surnamed Euer′getes (or, the benefactor), rendered the Romans good service in their wars in the East. For this they gave him Phrygia Major (B. C. 128). He was assassinated by his servants (B. C. 120), and was succeeded by his son, the celebrated MITHRIDA′TES VI., styled "Eupator" (good father) and "the Great," then but twelve years old. The young prince's mother was appointed his guardian, and authorized by the will of his father to reign jointly with him; but his first act was to put her and his brother to death. His subjects did not resent the crime, so corrupt and degenerate had become the Eastern nations which formed the dominions of the successors of Alexander. Little is said of the first years of his reign. The principal incident was his bribing the Roman general who commanded in Phrygia, which province had been resumed by the Senate on the death of his father, to surrender it to him: but the Romans retook it from him; hence his enmity to them.

CAPPADOCIA.—Ariara′thes IV. reigned peacefully during 58 years. He died B. C. 190, leaving his dominions to his son, Ariarathes V. This monarch having assisted his father-in-law, the king of Syria, against the Romans, he found

State particulars respecting Attalus.—What were the leading incidents of the reign of [E]umenes II.?—What of the naval battle with Hannibal?—Of Eumenes and the Romans?—What part did he take in the second Macedonian war?—How did the Romans act towards [h]im?—What did he do thereupon?—For what is he celebrated?

What is said of Attalus II. and Prusias?—Of Attalus III.?—Of Aristonicus?—What became of Pergamus?—Of Phrygia Major?—What is said of Prusias I.?—Of Hannibal?—Of Prusias II.?—What did the Romans do?—What is said of Nicomedes?—Of the history of Pontus prior to Mithridates VI.?—What of Mithridates the Great?—Of Cappadocia?

himself at the mercy of the latter; but pardon was granted to him on condition of paying 200 talents ($220,000), afterwards reduced one-half at the request of Eumenes, king of Pergamus, who had married his daughter. Ariarathes soon after entered into an alliance with Eumenes against Pharnaces, king of Pontus; the Romans offered their mediation, but Pharnaces refused it. The allies, however, forced him to submit to hard terms for peace. Ariarathes wished to associate his son with him in the kingdom, but the youth refused to accept the offer because it was inconsistent with the respect due to his father. Such examples of filial duty were rare in that profligate age. The son received for this the cognomen of Philop′ator (lover of his father). Ariarathes V. died B. C. 162, and was succeeded by Ariarathes VI. (Philopator), who became an excellent ruler. He renewed the alliance with the Romans, applied himself to the study of philosophy, and invited learned men to visit Cappadocia. But his reign was destined not to be a peaceful one. Demetrius, king of Syria, tried to detach him from his alliance with the Romans by a marriage with his (Demetrius') sister. But he refused to marry her, and Demetrius, in revenge, caused an impostor, named Holophernes, who many years previously had been put forward by the mother of Ariarathes as her son, to be proclaimed king of Cappadocia—supplied him with troops, and, expelling Ariarathes, established him on the throne (B. C. 157). Ariarathes fled to Rome, and urged the Senate to reinstate him. Holophernes and Demetrius both sent ambassadors to Rome to defend their conduct; and the Senate, true to their perfidious maxim, "divide and conquer," decreed that Ariarathes and Holophernes should reign jointly. Fortunately, Ariarathes found a friend in Attalus, king of Pergamus, who reinstated him in his dominions. Holophernes fled to Antioch, where he joined in a conspiracy against his benefactor, Demetrius, was detected, and imprisoned. We hear but little more of Ariarathes, except that he aided the Romans against Aristonicus (B. C. 129), who had possessed himself of Pergamus; that he died in the same year, leaving six children under the guardianship of their mother, Laod′ice; that she poisoned five of them immediately, and would have poisoned the sixth, had not his relations saved him; and that the people, in a fury, destroyed the wretched woman, and placed the child, Ariarathes VII., on the throne. The Romans, in gratitude for his father's services, added Lycao′nia and Cili′cia to his dominions.

Armenia.—On the defeat of Antiochus by Scipio at Magnesia (B. C. 190), his dominions west of Mount Taurus having been given to Eumenes, king of Pergamus, the lieutenants of Antiochus in Armenia proclaimed their independence: Artax′ias setting himself up as king of Greater Armenia, and Zari′ades of Lesser Armenia. Antiochus despatched Lysias with an army to regain the province, and Artaxias was defeated and taken prisoner, but Zariades was not disturbed in his possessions. The successors of Artaxias and Zariades held the throne until the time of Tigra′nes, who united the two kingdoms (B. C. 95).

Rhodes.—The Rhodians aided the Romans against Philip of Macedon. During the war between the Romans and Antiochus they defeated Hannibal, who commanded the Syrian fleet, and blocked him up in the port of Megis′te, near Pat′ara (B. C. 191). The Romans rewarded them with Caria and Lycia. In the second Macedonian war the Rhodians would have remained neutral; but the Romans exhorted them to send forces against Perseus, affecting to suspect their fidelity. Accordingly they prepared a fleet of forty ships, but subsequently sent ambassadors to Rome to plead on behalf of Perseus. These ambassadors adopted a very arrogant tone; whereupon the amazed Senate briefly replied that as soon as they had conquered Perseus they would know what to do with the Rhodians. They also took Caria and Lycia from them. The ambassadors then humiliated themselves before the Senate, and obtained forgiveness. But the Rhodians were ordered to evacuate Caunus and Stratoni′ce, whence they drew an annual revenue of $75,000; and the Senate exempted the island of Delos from the payment of the customs which they were bound to pay to Rhodes, whereby the income of that State was further reduced to the extent of $105,000. The Rhodians submitted to these decrees, and voted a crown of gold, valued at $30,000, to the Romans. They sent this present by their admiral, Theod′otus, and solicited their alliance, which was granted after a year's delay. Henceforth Rhodes became an appendage to the Roman empire, though nominally independent.

What is said of Ariarathes Philopator?—Of the enmity of the king of Syria?—Who was Holophernes?—What did Demetrius do?—What did Attalus do?—What of Aristonicus?—Laodice?—What occurred in Armenia?—What services did the Rhodians render to the Romans?—What was their reward?—What of the second Macedonian war?—What of Rhodes?

On the conclusion of peace, Hannibal was employed in several wars in Africa; but the Romans objecting, he was recalled. He was then appointed prætor, an office which gave him control of the city. Desirous of reforming abuses in the administration of justice, he caused a law to be passed whereby the judges were to be elected for one year only. He made important changes in the public finances, whereby he acquired the esteem of the people and the hatred of the nobles. The latter persuaded the Romans that he was intriguing against them with Antiochus, king of Syria. Scipio generously defended him, but the Roman Senate demanded that he should be delivered up to them. Hannibal saw that his enemies were aiming at his life: he accordingly made his escape from the city, and fled to Tyre (B. C. 192), and thence to Antioch and Ephesus, where Antiochus was. He advised that monarch to carry the war into Italy, and offered to command the expedition. Antiochus consented, and thereupon Hannibal sent word to his friends in Carthage of what was intended. But the Carthaginians, afraid of another contest with Rome, informed the Senate. A Roman envoy was despatched to Ephesus to watch the movements of Hannibal. Antiochus, having been overcome by the Romans, agreed to deliver him up. Hannibal fled to Crete, and thence to Prusias, king of Bithynia (B. C. 184). By that prince he was employed against Eumenes, king of Pergamus, and he gained several victories. But the enmity of the Romans still followed him. Quintus Flamininus was deputed to Prusias to remonstrate against his employing Hannibal, and that monarch agreed to betray him; but Hannibal, finding escape impossible, poisoned himself (B. C. 182). Thus died, at the age of 70, the greatest man Carthage ever produced. His character has been vilified by the Romans, but it is certain that he possessed great virtues, and that he rendered illustrious services to his country; he was one of the greatest generals the ancient world produced.

The next trouble was with Masinis′sa, king of the Numidians. By the treaty with the Romans, Carthage was bound to restore to him all that he possessed before the war. Scipio gave him also the dominions of Syphax, a Numidian prince. Syphax had married the beautiful Sophonis′ba, the daughter of Asdrubal. She was taken prisoner by Masinissa at the siege of Cirta, when that prince acquired the realm of Syphax, and her charms so infatuated him that he married her; but a few days afterward, to appease his queen, he poisoned her. This crime rendered him odious to the Carthaginians, while his continued aggressions caused them great perplexity. He seized part of Syrtis, which paid tribute to Carthage, whereupon the latter complained to Rome. The Roman Senate sent commissioners to inquire into the affair (B. C. 181), but they did nothing, and it remained dormant for ten years, when fresh commissioners were sent out, who acted as the former had done, and left the dispute undecided (B. C. 171). Masinissa, meanwhile, took from the Carthaginians upwards of seventy towns. The grievance became insupportable, and a third deputation was sent to Rome to make urgent remonstrances on the subject (B. C. 156). The Romans again played the farce of sending commissioners to the spot to investigate the circumstances. Cato was one of them. On his return to Rome he declared that Rome could never be safe while Carthage existed. His cry was, "*Delenda est Carthago*" (Carthage must be destroyed).

Meanwhile dissensions broke out in the city. The people, having acquired the ascendency, banished forty of the principal citizens. These persons fled to Masinissa, who sent his two sons, Gulus′sa and Micip′sa, to Carthage to procure their recall. But the gates of the city were shut against them. Upon this Masinissa marched against Carthage. The army of the republic was defeated in the presence of Scipio, who witnessed the battle from a neighboring hill. The Carthaginians then asked Scipio to arbitrate between them and Masinissa, with which request he complied, but could not bring the parties to terms. Meanwhile a famine and a plague broke out in the Carthaginian camp, which caused such havoc that the troops surrendered to Masinissa; of 58,000 men, very few returned to Carthage. The Senate then impeached their generals, Asdrubal and Cartha′lo, for high treason, as being the authors of the war; and they sent deputies to Rome to ascertain what the Senate wished them to do. A fierce debate ensued in that assembly: Cato advocating the destruction of Carthage — Scipio opposing it; but at length it was resolved to declare war

What were the principal acts of Hannibal?—Why did he flee?—Whither did he go?—What befell him?—What is said of the war with Masinissa?—Of Syphax?—Sophonisba?—The conduct of the Romans?—Cato?—What famous saying did he utter?—Relate the particulars of the war with Masinissa.—What of Asdrubal and Carthalo?—The debates at Rome?

B.C. 200—100.

CARTHAGE.

against that city, on pretence of its having sent an army against a prince who was in alliance with Rome. At this moment the people of Utica voluntarily surrendered themselves and their territory to the Romans. This city was but a few miles from Carthage; the Senate joyfully accepted it, and at once declared war against Carthage. Thus began the THIRD PUNIC WAR.

The Romans sent 84,000 men to Africa, under the command of the consuls, Mani′lius and Censori′nus, with secret orders not to end the war but by the destruction of Carthage (B. C. 149). The Carthaginians, ignorant of what was taking place, sent another deputation to Rome; but these envoys, finding on their arrival in that city what had been done, delivered themselves up to the Romans, together with all that the State possessed. The Senate thereupon granted to the latter its liberties and laws, provided it should comply with the orders of the consuls, and send 300 of the principal young Carthaginians to Sicily as hostages. The Carthaginians complied with these conditions, sent their sons to Sicily, and delivered up to the consuls an immense quantity of arms and warlike stores. The consul, Censorinus, then informed them that they must leave the city, for the destruction of it was resolved upon. The Carthaginians burst forth into the most dismal lamentations, and so moved the consuls as to obtain permission to send another embassy to procure the revocation of the decree. During the absence of these deputies, the citizens of Carthage strained every nerve to put the city in a posture of defence—men, women, and children worked day and night in making weapons and fortifying the chief positions. They appointed Asdrubal commander outside the walls, and another Asdrubal, the grandson of Masinissa, commander within. The population of the city at the beginning of the war amounted to 700,000. The city itself stood on a peninsula 18 leagues round, situated in the centre of a gulf, and joined to the land by a narrow neck. The Romans refused to give up their wicked project, and the Carthaginians then displayed a heroism worthy of a better fate. The Romans used every effort for three years to take the city. The consuls, Manilius and Censorinus, were superseded by Calpurnius Piso and Lucius Mancinus, and they in their turn by Scipio Æmilianus; and it required all the genius of the latter to bring the war to a successful termination. During these three years the besieged suffered all the horrors of famine. At length the Romans forced their way into the city, and were met by the inhabitants with the fury of despair. They fought from house to house, till the streets were so strewn with the dead that it was hardly possible to make way through them. After seven days and nights of slaughter, the remnant of the population, numbering 50,000, surrendered, and were sent into the fields. Asdrubal with about 900 men held out in the temple of Esculapius. Worn out with fatigue, but anxious to save his life, Asdrubal came down privately to Scipio, and threw himself at his feet. Scipio pointed him out to the besieged, who at once set fire to the temple. Asdrubal's wife, placing herself with her two children in full view of the Roman general and of her husband, upbraided the latter for his baseness, and seizing her children, cut their throats, threw their bodies into the flames, and then rushed into them herself. Scipio abandoned the city to his troops to plunder. Whatever remained of Carthage was destroyed, and orders were given that no one should ever build upon her site. The cities which had aided her were razed to the ground, and the territory of the State was reduced to a Roman province. Scipio is said to have wept over the ruins of Carthage; nevertheless, he went home to enjoy a splendid triumph, and the Romans were elated beyond measure with the success of their guilt. Thus perished ancient Carthage (B. C. 145), the rival of Rome. But the intentions of her conquerors were not fully carried out for 30 years afterwards (B. C. 116). Caius Gracchus settled a Roman colony of 6000 citizens on the site of the old city. Julius Cæsar rebuilt Carthage, and it rose to be the capital of Africa, under the Roman emperors. It flourished for 700 years, but was at length destroyed by the Saracens in the 7th century after Christ. The Romans represented the Carthaginians as a people stained with avarice, perfidy, and cruelty; but it is certain that the Romans themselves were eminently distinguished for these vices, together with the additional one of lying. Whatever may have been the faults of the Carthaginians, we know that they were an enterprising and industrious commercial people, much attached to free institutions, and considerably advanced in the arts and in civilization, although their religious ceremonies were characterized by great ferocity. They greatly extended the commerce of the world, and added to the sum of human knowledge by their voyages of discovery. Their literature, if they had any, has not come down to us: it was probably destroyed by the Romans, who at that time scarcely possessed any literature worthy of the name, and thus were on a par, if not considerably behind, their victims in this respect. But the names of DIDO, HANNO, HAMILCAR BARCA, and HANNIBAL, will live as long as any name in Roman history; and the siege of Carthage will be remembered with those of Babylon, Syracuse, Saguntum, and Jerusalem. The Romans never made so heroic a defence of their own capital, but suffered it to be taken several times. Had any Carthaginian records come down to us, the history of the Romans might have presented a different aspect in some points.

Masinissa, shortly before his death, empowered Scipio to dispose of his possessions among his children, of whom he left three legitimate, viz., Micipsa, Gulussa, and Mastanabal. He died B. C. 149, being upwards of 90 years old. Scipio divided the kingdom between the three sons, but two of them dying soon, Micipsa became sole possessor of it. Of his reign we have but few particulars. It would possess little interest but for the adventures of JUGURTHA, the son of Micipsa's nephew, Mastan′abal. This celebrated man was remarkable for his talents, courage, and beauty. Micipsa, dreading his abilities, sent him to the Romans, then besieging Numantia (B. C. 134), hoping to get rid of him; but Jugurtha returned from the war unhurt, having greatly distinguished himself. Micipsa then adopted him, and made him co-heir with his two sons, Adherbal and Hiempsal. On his death-bed the king made Jugurtha swear to defend them, and exhorted them to preserve the friendship of the Romans. But no sooner was he dead (B. C. 118), than Jugurtha murdered Hiempsal and expelled Adherbal. The latter fled to Rome for aid. Jugurtha's agents in that city resorted to the most shameless bribery, and corrupted numerous senators to his interest. Commissioners were sent to Numidia to settle the affair, by dividing the kingdom equally between Jugurtha and Adherbal; but they gave Jugurtha the largest share. No sooner had they left than he attacked Adherbal, and shut him up in Cirta, his capital, which he besieged. Adherbal again applied to Rome for aid. An embassy was sent by the Senate to Jugurtha, which, having been well bribed, returned without effecting anything. Adherbal then surrendered upon condition of having his life spared, but he was immediately murdered. This barbarous act roused the indignation of the Roman people, and the corrupt Senate was shamed into declaring war against Jugurtha (B. C. 111). Calpur′nius Bestia and Æmilius Scaurus were sent to Numidia with an army; but Jugurtha's bribes proved too tempting to them, and they agreed to a peace.

The Romans were furious at this treaty; and Mummius, the tribune, caused the prætor to bring Jugurtha to Rome under a safe-conduct, to give evidence on the subject. But the Numidian prince bribed the tribune to prolong the session, and ultimately to dissolve it. Hearing that a grandson of Masinissa, named Massiva, was in Rome applying for the kingdom, he caused him to be assassinated. Jugurtha was thereupon commanded to leave Italy. The war now recommenced. The Roman army under Aulus was led into a defile, forced to surrender, and ordered to quit Numidia in ten days (B. C. 109). The celebrated Metellus was then sent against Jugurtha, and the character of the war soon changed. Metellus defeated Jugurtha, and reduced him to great distress. But, unfortunately, Ma′rius, the lieutenant of Metellus, succeeded in supplanting the latter and obtaining the supreme command. Jugurtha had recourse to his father-in-law, Bocchus, king of Mauretania, and obtained considerable succour from him; but Marius prevailed upon Bocchus to betray Jugurtha into his hands. The Numidian was accordingly delivered up to Sylla, the lieutenant of Marius, sent to Rome, and led through the streets in chains. It is said that he went distracted during the celebration of this triumph of Marius. When the ceremony was over he was thrown into prison, the lictors being so eager to seize his robe that they rent it in pieces, and tore the jewels out of his ears. He was cast naked into a dark dungeon, where, after lingering six days in the greatest agony, he died of hunger. His crimes do not entitle him to sympathy, but certainly the Romans gained no credit by their barbarous conduct. Numidia became a province of the Roman empire.

What was the cause of the third Punic war?—What did the Romans first do?—What was imposed upon the Carthaginians?—What did they do?—What was the condition of the city?—Relate the particulars of the siege and taking of Carthage.—What of Scipio Africanus?—What became of Carthage?—What character did the Romans give the Carthaginians?

What is said of the literature of Carthage?—Of the character of the people?—What became of the kingdom of Masinissa?—Relate the story of Jugurtha.—What part did the Romans take?—What of the Jugurthan war?—Of the murder of Massiva?—Of Metellus?—Marius?—Sylla?—Bocchus?—Of the fate of Jugurtha?—What became of Numidia?

THE 1ST CENTURY

EGYPT.

The new king, Alexander, reigned for some years under the control of his mother, Cleopatra; but she being unable to tolerate a rival in the supreme authority, resolved to rid herself of him. Alexander, however, having been apprised of her design, caused her to be murdered; upon which his subjects revolted, and restored his brother, Ptolemy Lath′yrus (B. C. 89). Alexander perished soon after in attempting to return to Egypt. A rebellion broke out in Upper Egypt; and the rebels having been defeated, shut themselves up in Thebes, where they defended themselves for three years. Lath′yrus at last took the city, and reduced it to ruins. He died B. C. 81, leaving the throne to his daughter Cleopatra. The Roman dictator, Sylla, sent Alexander, the son of the dethroned Alexander, to take possession of the crown of Egypt. Alexander found Cleopatra in possession: he therefore married her, and poisoned her 19 days afterwards (B. C. 80). The people of Alexandria soon expelled him, and called in Ptolemy surnamed Aule′tes (the flute player), a natural son of Lathyrus. Alexander fled to Tyre, where he soon after died, having made the Roman people his heirs. But the Senate contented themselves for the present with taking possession of his personal effects, leaving Egypt to be dealt with at a future time.

After years of oppressive rule, Auletes was expelled by the people of Alexandria, who placed his eldest daughter, Berenice, on the throne. Auletes fled to Rome for assistance; and the proconsul, Gabin′ius, was ordered to reinstate him. This was done (B. C. 55); and Auletes then put his daughter to death, and murdered others who had been his enemies. This perfidious monarch died B. C. 51, and bequeathed his kingdom to his eldest son, Ptolemy, and his eldest daughter, Cleopatra, on condition that they should marry, as had long been the incestuous practice of the Ptolemies. He also appointed the Roman Senate their guardians. This was the celebrated Cleopatra, so remarkable for her beauty and her wickedness, who influenced the destinies of the Roman empire by her personal charms,—to which both Julius Cæsar and Mark Antony became slaves. She was the last of the guilty race of the Ptolemies, a family stained by every crime that can be named. One of her and her husband's first acts of cruelty was the putting to death of Pompey, who after the battle of Pharsalia (B. C. 48), fled to Egypt, pursued by Julius Cæsar, who also claimed payment of the 6000 talents ($6,600,000) promised to him when consul, by Auletes. On his arrival in Alexandria, he was called upon to mediate between Ptolemy and Cleopatra, who had quarrelled. The latter having secretly obtained access to Cæsar, won him by her charms. This roused the jealousy and hostility of her husband, who, assembling the Alexandrians, attacked the Romans. He was taken prisoner; but in the struggle which ensued the valuable library founded by Ptolemy Lagus 250 years before, and containing 400,000 volumes, was burned — an irreparable loss to literature! Cæsar took Pelu′sium and subdued Egypt (B. C. 47), and Ptolemy, the husband of Cleopatra, having been drowned in the Nile during the contest, Cæsar confirmed her on the throne, and married her to her younger brother, Ptolemy XII., then only 11 years of age. This youth, on his reaching the age of 15, claimed his share of the royal power,—a claim which Cleopatra speedily disposed of by poisoning him. Cæsar was completely fascinated by Cleopatra, and would have married her if he could have persuaded the Romans to pass a law enabling citizens to have more wives than one. At Cleopatra's instigation he put her sister Arsinoë to death. He was called away from Egypt to Pontus, and thus his connection with her ended: he had a son, named Cæsarion, by her. In the Roman civil war, she was suspected of assisting Brutus against Cæsar; and Mark Antony having become master of the East, summoned her to Tarsus to render an account of her conduct. There this famous pair first met, and the fatal union began "which lost a world and bade a hero fly." Antony accompanied Cleopatra back to Egypt, where he became a slave to her charms, lavishing provinces and kingdoms upon her; until at length Octavius Cæsar, finding that Antony had detached himself wholly from Rome, resolved to bring him to submission. The battle of Actium decided the fate of Egypt and of Antony (B. C. 31). He fled to Alexandria, where he destroyed himself. Cleopatra was taken prisoner by Octavius; and finding that she was destined to be exhibited in triumph in the streets of Rome, she contrived to procure poison in the shape of a venomous snake. With this she put an end to her infamous life, and Egypt became a Roman province (B. C. 30).

What of Alexander and his mother Cleopatra?—Ptolemy Lathyrus?—Alexander II.?—Ptolemy Auletes?—Berenice?—The famous Cleopatra?—Her character?—Her cruelty to Pompey?—To her first husband?—The mediation of Cæsar?—The accident to the Alexandria library?—To Ptolemy?—What of Ptolemy II.?—Of Mark Antony?—Of Cleopatra's death?

SYRIA.

Antiochus Gryphus was assassinated by one of his own vassals (B. C. 96). His brother, Antiochus the Cyzicene, claimed the throne; but being defeated by Seleucus, the eldest son of Gryphus, killed himself (B. C. 95). Syria then was torn by rival claimants. Antiochus Eu′sebes, the son of the Cyzicene, obtained the greater part of the country (B. C. 94). Seleucus was drowned in the Orontes, but his brothers continued the struggle. Philip, a son of Gryphus, for a time obtained the mastery (B. C. 85); but the Syrians, exhausted by the long strife of the rival claimants, at length (B. C. 83) invited Tigra′nes, king of Armenia, to become their king. This prince accepted the invitation, and governed them well for 14 years; but Antiochus Asiat′icus, the son of Antiochus Eusebes, having applied to the Romans for aid to regain the throne, an army was sent by them, under Lucullus (then recently victorious over Mithridates, king of Pontus), against Tigranes, who, after several defeats and a gallant resistance, was forced to flee (B. C. 69). Antiochus Asiaticus was temporarily placed on the throne; but he was subsequently (B. C. 65) expelled by the Roman general, Pompey, and Syria became a Roman province. The family of the Seleucidæ became extinct shortly afterwards in the person of Seleucus Cybiosac′tes, the husband of Bereni′ce, queen of Egypt, a sordid wretch, who had no thoughts but of amassing money. His first act in Egypt had been to transfer the remains of Alexander the Great from the golden coffin in which they reposed to one of glass, that he might get possession of the metal. This action and other similar ones so disgusted the queen, that she caused him to be strangled.

Judea.—Alexander Jannæus reigned with great cruelty. He avenged himself upon the city of Gaza, which had aided Ptolemy Lathyrus, by entirely destroying it (B. C. 97). Some time after (B. C. 95), while at the Feast of Tabernacles in the capacity of high-priest, the Jews insulted him with abuse and pelting him with lemons. For this he attacked them with his guards, and massacred 6000 persons. A civil war ensued between him and his subjects, which lasted six years, and cost the lives of more than 50,000 persons. Alexander was guilty of horrible cruelty. Debauchery at length brought him to the grave (B. C. 79). He bequeathed the kingdom to his wife Alexandra for her life, empowering her to leave it after her death to whichever of her two sons, Hyrca′nus and Aristobu′lus, she should think most worthy of it. She conferred the high-priesthood on Hyrcanus, and succeeded in completely conciliating the Pharisees. On her death (B. C. 70) she nominated Hyrcanus to the throne; but his brother Aristobulus I. deposed him, and usurped it. The latter was not allowed to reign in peace, however, for an Idumæan named Antipas (or Antipater), the father of Herod, employed his whole address to reinstate Hyrcanus. Antipas having been brought up in the Court of Alexander Jannæus, had acquired ascendency over Hyrcanus, and now persuaded him to apply for redress to Pompey, who was then in Syria. Pompey summoned the brothers before him, and heard their respective statements, but deferred his decision until his return from his campaign against Aretas and his Arabs. Aristobulus returned to Jerusalem, and prepared for defence. Pompey took Petra, and made Aretas prisoner. He then marched into Judea, and with a little management got possession of the principal forts and of Aristobulus. The partisans of Hyrcanus opened the gates of Jerusalem to Pompey, but those of Aristobulus fortified themselves in the temple, which was taken in three days by the Romans, and 12,000 Jews were massacred (B. C. 63). Pompey abstained from plundering the temple, contenting himself with restoring Hyrcanus, whose friend, Antipas, retained all the real power. During the Roman civil wars, Hyrcanus sided with Pompey; but afterwards assisted Cæsar with troops in Egypt. For this service, Antipas' son, Herod, was made governor of Galilee. In the year B. C. 40, the Parthians invaded Syria, made Hyrcanus prisoner, and set up Antigonus, the son of Aristobulus, as king of Judea; but through Antony's influence, Herod was restored and made king of Judea. He had previously married Mariamne, the granddaughter of Hyrcanus (B. C. 38), and he now began a course of the most atrocious cruelty. He put to death Hyrcanus (B. C. 37), Mariamne (B. C. 29), and two of his own sons (B. C. 6), and plundered the temple. Herod died B. C. 4, and was succeeded by his son Archelaus; but the Jews appealed to Augustus Cæsar, who divided the dominions of Herod amongst the children of the latter, giving Judea to Archela′us, with the title of Ethnarch.

What of Antiochus Gryphus?—Antiochus Eusebes?—Tigranes?—Antiochus Asiaticus?—The fate of Syria?—Seleucus Cybiosactes?—Alexander Jannæus?—His cruelty to Gaza?—What of Alexandra?—Of Hyrcanus and Aristobulus I.?—Antipas?—Herod?—Antigonus?—The siege of Jerusalem by Pompey?—Mariamne?—Archelaus I.?

INDIA.

Among the celebrated names in Indian history is that of Vik′ramadit′ya. He established the commencement of his reign *as an Era*, and began to rule in Malwa, or Awanti (the modern Oujein), B. C. 56. This monarch was renowned for his virtues and bravery. He encouraged learning, and is said to have worshipped God in secret, despising the temple service and idol worship of the Brahmins. He is described as being fond of adventures, such as were sought by the Caliph Haroun-al-Raschid, and are described in the *Arabian Nights' Entertainments;* and he is therefore the hero of many a Hindoo tale. According to some accounts, the famous Sa′livaha′na, who ruled in the Deccan, was his cotemporary. But this is open to considerable doubt; for, according to Elphinstone, the era of Salivahana commenced A. D. 78, or 134 years after that of Vikramaditya, whence it is evident the two kings were not cotemporary.

Mention is made in this century of the city of Delhi, for the first time in history. At this period it appears that there were several independent kingdoms in the north of India, for we find mention made of Magadha, Gour, Malwa, Gujerat, Canouj, Mithili, Benares, Delhi, Ajimere, Scinde, and Cashmere. The historians of the latter State claim for it an antiquity extending back to 2600 B. C.; but it is first mentioned about 1400 B. C.

Towards the end of the century, a body of Scythians, called by the Chinese "Yue-chi", by the Tartars "Jits", and by Europeans "Getes" or "Getæ", made their appearance in the country of the Indus. A division of them had conquered Khorassan (B. C. 128), and thence they emigrated into Hindostan. They are to this day called Jits, or Jats. Colonel Tod says that they were incorporated into the Cshatriya caste.

In the year B. C. 75, a numerous body of Hindoos from Calinga crossed over to Java, where they settled, and in process of time civilized the inhabitants. Those colonists fixed the date of their arrival by establishing the Era still subsisting in that island, which commences with that event, in the year aforesaid. Magnificent remains of temples built by them are still to be seen; and most of the Javanese inscriptions, and historical and poetical compositions, are written in a dialect of the Sanscrit.

Who was Vikramaditya?—When did his Era commence?—What kingdoms existed in Northern India?—What are the Jits?—What island did the Hindoos colonize?—And when?

PERSIA.

During the early part of this century the Scythian tribes gave great trouble to Western Asia. After the fall of the Bactrian kingdom, they turned their arms against the western provinces of Persia, but were successfully resisted, and their best warriors were incorporated with the Parthian army. Mithridates II. died (B. C. 91) after a reign of 35 years, generally regretted by his subjects. On his death the Parthians elected Mnaskiras (or Mnascires), of whom little is known. But the prosperity of the country was impeded by a long and sanguinary struggle between him and Sinatroces for the throne; the latter being another chieftain whom a certain party among the Parthians set up as king. Sinatroces was ultimately successful in deposing Mnasciras and acquiring the crown (B. C. 76), but did not live to enjoy it many years. He was succeeded (B. C. 68) by his son, Phraa′tes III., who caused himself to be surnamed the god. He concluded a treaty of alliance and friendship with Pompey, then commander-in-chief of the Roman armies in Asia. One of the results of this alliance was an attack on Tigranes, king of Armenia, who was then assisting his father-in-law, the celebrated Mithridates of Pontus, against the Romans. Phraates joined Tigranes the younger against his father. After Pompey's return to Rome, Phraates was killed by his own children, the eldest, Mithridates III., succeeding him (B. C. 60). Mithridates was expelled by his brother Oro′des (B. C. 54). He thereupon applied to the Romans for assistance; but failing to obtain it, he was taken prisoner and put to death. The Romans, who, under the triumvir Crassus, had plundered Jerusalem and ravaged Syria, were now advancing towards Parthia, intending to subdue that country. The impetuous Crassus, deaf to all remonstrances, advanced along the banks of the Euphrates as far as Carrhæ, in Mesopotamia. There the Parthians, aided by a strong body of Armenians under Artavasdes, encountered him, and after one of the most terrible battles on record, completely destroyed his army. Crassus then attempted to make terms with Sure′na, the Parthian commander; but having been betrayed into his power, he was treacherously killed. The loss of the battle of Carrhæ (B. C. 53) was the most terrible blow the Romans had received since the battle of Cannæ. They had 20,000 men killed in it, and 10,000 taken prisoners. The rest fled into Cilicia and Syria, and were afterwards collected by Cassius, who was thus enabled to save those provinces from the Parthians. The Romans were thoroughly humiliated by this defeat, and it was not until 30 years afterwards that the Parthians consented to restore the prisoners and standards taken in that fatal battle. But Surena, the able general of the Parthians who had won it, was put to death by Orodes from jealousy of his fame. Pac′orus, the son of Orodes, entered Syria and laid siege to Antioch, but was driven back and his army dispersed by Cassius and Cicero.

During the Roman civil wars, the Parthians supported sometimes the cause of Pompey and sometimes that of Cæsar. While Mark Antony was in Egypt, Pacorus invaded Syria (B. C. 40), made the high-priest, Hyrcanus, prisoner, and set up Antigonus as king of Judea; but Antony's lieutenant, Ventidius, sustained the honor of the Roman arms, and destroyed the Parthian army in two great battles, in the last of which Pacorus was killed (B. C. 39). Orodes was overwhelmed with this blow, and did not recover from it for some time. He resolved to abdicate, and selected his son, Phraates IV., as his successor. This miscreant had scarcely ascended the throne, when he caused all his brothers to be put to death, and subsequently murdered his father and his son (B. C. 37). In the year B. C. 36, Mark Antony invaded Media, where he was totally defeated, and forced to make a most disastrous retreat into Egypt. The Parthians followed up their victory on this occasion by conquering Media and driving the Romans out of Armenia.

Tirida′tes, having raised a rebellion in Parthia, was defeated by Phraates (B. C. 25). The rebel fled to Rome, whereupon ambassadors were sent thither by the Parthian monarch to require the Romans to give him up,—a demand with which Augustus Cæsar refused to comply; and he moreover threatened the Parthians with his vengeance, if the standards and prisoners taken from Crassus and Antony were not given up. The terror of the Roman army made the Parthians restore the spoils they had acquired, and they were glad to purchase peace on such terms. In the last year of the century, the designs of Phraates on Armenia again brought on a war with Rome.

What of the Scythian tribes?—Of Mithridates II.?—Mnasciras?—Sinatroces?—Phraates III.?—Mithridates III.?—Orodes?—The Roman invasion?—Crassus?—The battle of Carrhæ?—Surena?—Pacorus?—The Parthians and the war between Cæsar and Pompey?—What of Ventidius?—The fate of Pacorus and Orodes?—Phraates IV.?—Antony?—Tiridates?

CHINA. JAPAN.

It was during the reign of Woo-te that the religious system of Laou-keun obtained the greatest popularity; but the emperor having been imposed upon by the priests of that sect, persecuted them with relentless fury. On his death (B. C. 86), his son, Chaou-te, ascended the throne. This prince sunk into indolence and dissipation, and the land was filled with war and rapine. The Tartars on the frontiers became very turbulent, and it required the whole force of the empire to keep them in check. After the death of Chaou-te (B. C. 74), his uncle assumed the government; but being worthless and indolent, he was soon dethroned by the nobles; and Seuen-te, a very young prince, was appointed emperor (B. C. 73). About this time the Huns came to render homage to the emperor, so that nominally all the country from Shen-se to the Caspian, acknowledged the Chinese sceptre. Seuen-te amended the ancient code of laws, and re-compiled the Chinese classics from fragments found here and there; on which account he is considered one of the greatest monarchs of China. Yuen-te, his successor (B. C. 48), followed in his footsteps, so that this is considered the most glorious literary epoch in the annals of the nation. But continual wars with the Tartars and a general scarcity of grain, caused great misery throughout its duration. Ching-te, the son of Yuen-te (B. C. 32), entrusted the government of the empire to his uncles. He was a weak-minded, vicious libertine, and died suddenly (B. C. 8). His nephew and successor, Gae-te, was a man of great intelligence; but he could not stop the cabals of the Court, which had long been a scene of faction. He died in the year in which Christ was born (according to the usually received chronology); and the grandson of Yuen-te, though only nine years of age, was proclaimed emperor under the title of Ping-te (prince of peace)—a remarkable coincidence.

Japan.—On the death of Kay-kwo (B. C. 97), his son, Siun-sin, became emperor. In the year B. C. 93, he moved his Court to Siki. In the year B. C. 90, a dreadful plague ravaged the country. Siun-sin created the office of "Seo-gun", or Minister of War and commander-in-chief. In the year B. C. 78, the first ships-of-war were built in Japan. Siun-sin died B. C. 29, and his third son, Sy-nin, succeeded him on the throne.

What of the religion of Laou-keun?—The Tartars?—The Huns?—The Chinese classics?—What remarkable coincidence occurred at the end of the century?—What of Japan?

ITALY.

We come now to the most important and brilliant century in the history of Rome. At the opening of it, Marius was the most prominent man in the State, which was then the prey of a set of profligate nobles. The first ten years of the century passed with few remarkable events. Marius lived in retirement. He was rich, but had not obtained his wealth unfairly (according to the Roman standard). His character for integrity stood high, but he was incapable of using the arts of the forum — hence his popularity soon declined.

A revolt of the slaves in Sicily was quelled by the proconsul, Marcus Aquil′ius (B. C. 99). Cyrene was bequeathed to the Romans by Ptolemy Apion (B. C. 96). The people of Cappadocia, disturbed by the intrigues of Mithridates, king of Pontus, appealed to Rome, and Sylla was sent to watch the proceedings of that monarch (B. C. 92). A grave question arose at the same time as to the admission of the allies of Rome as citizens. Liv′ius Drusus, the tribune, advocating this and other reforms, was assassinated (B. C. 91), whereupon several of the Italian States began to revolt. The Marsi took up arms, and the famous "Social War" began (B. C. 90). The proconsuls, Cæpio and Frontei′us, were killed by the Picentines at As′culum; the consul, Julius Cæsar, was repulsed by the Samnites; and his colleague, Rutil′ius Lupus, was defeated and killed, at the Liris, by the Marsi. In this campaign, Marius acted as legate to Rutilius, and commanded the right wing, which was not present in the battle of the Liris. The Marsian consul, Pompædius Silo, endeavored to force Marius to fight, saying: "If you are the great general you are reported to be, come out and fight." Marius replied: "If *you* are the great general you would fain be thought, make me come out and fight." The Senate now called upon Marius to act with vigor, as that officer purposely abstained from decisive action; but they did not trust wholly to military ability. They empowered the consul, Julius Cæsar, to draw up a law (called, after him, the Julian Law), granting citizenship to those of the allies who had taken no part in the war, or should cease to take part in it. This concession pacified several of the States, and alienated them from the confederates; and the Senate devoted its utmost energies to crush the remainder. The consul, Cneius Pompei′us Strabo, was successful against the Picentines; and his colleague, Lucius Porcius Cato, defeated the Marsi, but was killed in the battle. Sylla then took the command in Campania, subdued the insurgents, and, gaining several victories, penetrated into the strongholds of the Samnites, while Pompeius was no less successful in the north. He laid siege to Asculum, the first seat of the insurrection, where its leading spirit, Judacil′ius, was intrenched. Judacilius, finding that he could not hold the place, raised a funeral pile in sight of his banqueting hall, and, after giving a sumptuous entertainment to his friends, drained a cup of poisoned wine, ascended the pile, and bade his guests set fire to it. Pompeius treated the garrison with great cruelty; but several of the allied nations submitted to him, while Metellus and Sylla pursued the others, and brought the social war to an end (B. C. 88). Most of the refractory Italian States were admitted citizens of Rome, and this removed the chief cause of complaint. In this deadly struggle not fewer than 300,000 Italians perished.

The war against Mithridates was the next great affair of interest. Marius had set his heart upon obtaining the chief command in it, but Sylla was appointed by the Senate. Marius, to thwart this arrangement, allied himself to the tribune, Sulpi′cius Rufus, who had brought forward a law for distributing the Italian allies among the Roman tribes, thus adding greatly to the number of citizens. This law was carried by violence; and the tribes, having now the majority in the government, appointed Marius to the conduct of the Pontic war. Sylla had recourse to his army at Nola, and led it to Rome. Marius took to flight, and after a series of adventures, was taken prisoner near Minturnæ. The magistrates of that place resolved to put him to death, in obedience to Sylla's orders, and a Gallic soldier undertook to do the deed, but when he entered the room where Marius lay, the latter exclaimed in a terrible voice, "Man! darest thou murder Caius Marius?" which so terrified the barbarian that he fled. Marius was then placed on board ship, and sent to Carthage. The Roman officer there ordered him away; to which Marius replied, "Tell the prætor you have seen Caius Marius, a fugitive, sitting on the ruins of Carthage." Marius and his son then took refuge in the island of Cercina.

Sylla found himself in difficulties at Rome, for the Senate and people were angry at the presence of troops in the city. He, therefore, sent his troops into Campania, and procured a decree annulling the law obtained by Sulpicius Rufus. But plots were formed against his life; and the consul, Cornelius Cinna, endeavored to procure his impeachment.

Meanwhile, Mithridates, king of Pontus, having roused all Asia Minor and Greece to arms, a general massacre of the Romans in these countries took place (B. C. 88). The king of Pontus (having gathered a strong force under Archela′us in Greece, Sylla, and the quæstor, Licin′ius Lucullus, escaping from Rome, and leaving the aristocracy to fight their own battles) marched to Athens, and laid siege to that city. During their absence from Rome, Cinna endeavored to revive the Sulpician law; whereupon a furious battle ensued in the forum between the old citizens and the Italian party. The latter were routed, and Cinna, having been driven out of Rome, appealed to the soldiery, collected an army to avenge himself, and recalled Marius. Cinna and Marius laid siege to Rome; a failure of provisions caused the Senate to yield, and the two exiles entered the city as conquerors (B. C. 87). The most frightful scenes ensued. The guards of Marius stabbed every one whom he did not salute. The noblest of the Roman aristocracy perished, and the streets ran with blood. Marius and Cinna named themselves consuls for the ensuing year; but the former died soon after (Jan. 13th, B. C. 86) of pleurisy, and Vale′rius Flaccus was elected in his stead. The latter, on his march to the East, was assassinated by contrivance of Fla′vius Fim′bria, who assumed the command of his army. Sylla took Athens, and defeated Archelaus; while Fimbria, entering Asia, encountered and defeated Mithridates. Sylla, having subdued Greece, crossed into Asia Minor; and Mithridates, thus placed between two Roman armies, agreed to a peace, and resigned all his acquisitions (B. C. 84). Fimbria, deserted by his army, destroyed himself, leaving the entire glory of the war to Sylla, who set out on his return to Rome. Cinna, who had assembled an army to intercept him, was put to death by his own troops. Sylla landed at Brundusium in the spring of B. C. 83, and many of the supporters of the Marian party deserted to his standard. A civil war ensued between his partizans and the Marians, whose chief leaders were the younger Marius, the consul Carbo, Pontius, and Lamponius; but the decisive battles of Sacriportus and the Porta Collina decided the struggle in favor of Sylla. The young Cneius Pompeius (afterwards Pompey the Great) greatly distinguished himself on the side of Sylla in this war. He defeated the consul Carbo in Sicily, put him to death, and afterwards reduced Africa to obedience. Sylla entered Rome in triumph, and took bloody revenge on his enemies. He drew up a list, which he called a *Proscriptio*, of all those who were to be put to death. To this list he constantly added names. Terror reigned throughout Italy; for the proscribed parties were outlawed, their property confiscated, and rewards were offered for their destruction. Many thousands perished, and Sylla and his friends took possession of their confiscated property. The Samnites and the inhabitants of Præneste, Nola, Norba, and other cities, were massacred, and their towns plundered. All legal authority was at an end, and there was now no executive government in existence. The consuls, Carbo and Marius, were slain. The Senate was at the mercy of Sylla. At his command, Valerius Flaccus was appointed Interrex (regent) by that body; and Flaccus thereupon proposed that the ancient office of Dictator, which had been in abeyance for 120 years, should be revived. This having been agreed to, Sylla was appointed to the office, and was in express terms authorized to make laws, put citizens to death, confiscate property, distribute public lands, destroy old colonies and found new ones, and transfer the sceptres of dependent monarchs from one claimant to another (B. C. 81). Sylla proceeded at once in the most merciless manner to re-establish the power of the aristocracy. Death was inflicted on every one who in any way opposed him. He reconstituted the Senate to the old number of 300, by filling the vacancies with his own adherents, and invested it with supreme judicial power. He increased the number of quæstors from eight to twenty, and of prætors from six to eight. Thus, though the republic existed in name and in form, it was in reality a close oligarchy. He followed up his vindictive measures against the adherents of Marius by commanding all persons connected with them by marriage to divorce their wives.

What is said of Marius?—Of the slaves in Sicily?—Cyrene?—Cappadocia?—The Social War?—Livius Drusus?—Describe the principal events.—What took place at the battle of the Liris?—Who brought the war to an end?—What of Judacilius?—Of the quarrel between Sylla and Marius?—What befell the latter?

What is said of Mithridates?—The Sulpician law?—Cinna?—The return of Marius?—The massacres in Rome?—The return of Sylla?—The civil war?—The rise of Pompey?—The Proscription?—The state of Italy?—The Interrex?—The constitution framed by Sylla?

Pompey readily divorced his wife, Antistia, and married Sylla's daughter, Æmilia. But Julius Cæsar (then nineteen years old), the nephew of Marius, who had married Cornelia, the daughter of Cinna, refused to obey the decree, and escaped with his life only through the intercession of powerful friends.

Sylla deprived the tribunes of the people of all real power, and abolished the legislative and judicial functions of the *Comitia tributa*. He established military colonies throughout Italy, and created a kind of body-guard for his protection, by giving the rights of citizenship to the slaves of those whom he had proscribed. These slaves numbered 10,000, and were called Cornelii, after their patron.

While these events were passing in Italy, Mithridates suddenly attacked and defeated Lucius Muræ′na, whom Sylla had left with an army in Asia Minor. By Sylla's orders all further operations were stayed; and this ended the second Mithridatic war (B. C. 81). In the year B. C. 79, Sylla suddenly resigned the dictatorship, and retired to his estate at Puteoli, where he died the next year of a loathsome disease. He was the author of several works, and a patron of literature, but addicted to gross sensuality. He is also said to have been very witty. On his death a contest arose between the consuls, Æmilius Lep′idus and Lutatius Cat′ulus. The former espoused the popular cause, and sought to abolish several of the laws of Sylla. Catulus, supported by Pompey, took up arms against him; and Lepidus, defeated at Rome, fled to Sardinia, where he died.

In the same year (B. C. 78), Quintus Serto′rius, an old officer under Marius, who had been appointed prætor in Spain, took up arms against the partisans of Sylla. Crossing over into Mauretania he routed Paccianus, one of Sylla's generals. On his return to Spain he was invited by the Lusitani to become their chief. He acceded to their request, and raised the standard of revolt. Metellus Pius and Pompey were both sent against him with a large force, but could not subdue him. He harassed the Romans by guerilla warfare until the year B. C. 72, when he was poisoned by Perperna and some other Roman officers.

In the year B. C. 74, the third Mithridatic war broke out. The bequest of Bithynia to the Romans by its king, Nicome′des, was the cause. The consuls, Licinius Lucullus and Aurelius Cotta, were sent against Mithridates. Cotta was defeated, but Lucullus contrived to surround the army of Mithridates near Cyzicus, and to rout and disperse it (B. C. 73). Following up his success, Lucullus besieged and took Ami′sus and Eupatoria, and compelled Mithridates to flee into Armenia (B. C. 71). But Tigranes, king of that country, espoused the cause of the defeated monarch. Whereupon Lucullus crossed the Euphrates, took Tig′ranocer′ta, and routed the army of Tigranes. He also placed Antiochus Asiat′icus on the throne of Syria (B. C. 69). He laid siege to Nis′ibis, but a mutiny among his troops compelled him to return to Pontus (B. C. 67), where Mithridates had already defeated his lieutenants in several actions. The enemies of Lucullus procured his removal. Acil′ius Gla′brio was sent out to supersede him, but, proving wholly incompetent, was replaced by Pompey (B. C. 66). This able commander soon changed the face of affairs. He defeated Mithridates, and drove him across the Cimmerian Bos′phorus. Tigranes submitted to him: so did Syria. Recalled thence to oppose Mithridates once more, he again reduced that heroic king to such straits that, to escape from his enemies, he poisoned himself (B. C. 63). Pompey returned to Syria, took Jerusalem, deposed Aristobu′lus, and made Hyrca′nus king. He then returned to Rome (B. C. 61), where he was greeted with a triumph which lasted two days.

While these events were taking place in the East, Italy was the scene of a remarkable "Servile War". Spar′tacus, a gladiator and bandit, having escaped from prison, and persuaded a vast number of slaves (some say 120,000) to join him, collected a large force on Mount Vesuvius, and ravaged Southern Italy (B. C. 73). He routed the forces sent against him, defeated the consuls, Gell′ius Public′ola and Lentulus Clodia′nus, and the prætor, Quintus Ar′rius. At length (B. C. 71), the prætor, Marcus Licinius Crassus, defeated and killed him at Petil′ia, in Lucania, and suppressed this remarkable insurrection.

In the year B. C. 70, Pompey and Crassus, the former having returned successful from the war in Spain, the latter from the Servile War, encamped with their respective armies before Rome, and demanded permission to become candidates for the consulship. According to the laws of Sylla this was illegal, but the Senate did not dare to refuse, and accordingly the two commanders were elected consuls. On the very first day of his term of office, Pompey restored the power of the tribunes, and repealed several of the obnoxious laws of Sylla. It was at this time that Marcus Tullius Cic′ero, the celebrated orator and philosopher, pronounced his famous orations against Verres, Cæcilius, and others who were concerned in the infamous extortions practised upon the Sicilians. The trial of these peculators lasted some months. They were defended by the celebrated advocate, Horten′sius, and, but for the extraordinary energy of Cicero, would have escaped punishment. Verres fled to Marseilles, boasting of having amassed more than three times enough to make an opulent man. After the conviction of Verres, the Senate was forced to withdraw its opposition to the measure proposed by Pompey and Aurelius Cotta for a reform in the judicial system, and thus the Syllan Constitution was shattered. It had favored the grossest corruption, as was shown in the case of Cneius Dolabella, who had been indicted by Cæsar for the misgovernment of Macedonia, but was acquitted by the Senate. Cat′ulus and his friends next restored the censorial office, which had been suspended for sixteen years. Four censors were appointed, and by them sixty-four senators were degraded. They also revived the high rank of Princeps, and bestowed it on Catulus.

The conquest of Cilicia by Pompey (B. C. 67), and of Crete by Metellus (B. C. 67), added to the already vast dominions of Rome. The Parthians were still untamed, a thing which rankled in the heart of the ambitious republic. But her domestic troubles were far from ended. The famous episode in her history, called Catiline's Conspiracy, took place at this time. Lucius Sergius Catili′na was a patrician of infamous character, and had participated in the crimes of Sylla. Defeated in his efforts to procure the consulship, he conspired with his unsuccessful colleague, Autro′nius Pætus, to murder the consuls, Aurelius Cotta and Manlius Torqua′tus (B. C. 65), but the plot failed, owing to Catiline's having given the signal prematurely. He then organized a more extensive conspiracy to overthrow the existing government, and seize it for himself. A number of dissolute nobles and discontented plebeians joined him; and, in the year B. C. 64, he attempted to control by force the election of the consuls. But Cicero and Caius Anto′nius were chosen by a large majority in spite of him. Catiline now became desperate. On the night of Nov. 6th, B. C. 63, he assembled the conspirators, and informed them that he should wait no longer, but strike the blow at once. Cicero, however, who had been informed of what was transpiring, took measures to thwart the scheme. In a series of brilliant orations he denounced Catiline to the Senate. That traitor was declared a public enemy, and several of the confederates, among them the prætor of the city, Lent′ulus Sura, were arrested. Lentulus, Cethe′gus, and others, were condemned to death. Catiline fled to the troops that he had collected, pursued by Metellus Celer, lieutenant of Antonius, the consul, who attacked him at Pistoria, and dispersed his men. Catiline and his friends fell fighting with desperate valor; and thus ended this affair. For the services which Cicero had rendered to the State he received the appellation of "Pater Patriæ" (father of his country). A full account of Catiline's conspiracy has been given to us by Sallust. It was asserted that Crassus and Cæsar were implicated in the affair, but the evidence in support of such an assertion is very slight.

Two great men now appear prominently on the stage of Roman history. Julius Cæsar (who has been frequently mentioned), and Marcus Cato (surnamed Uticensis, from having been born at Utica). Though a tribune of the people, Cato became one of the leaders of the aristocratical party; and, along with Cicero, vehemently opposed the measures of Cæsar, Pompey, and Crassus. These three had secretly formed a coalition for the division of power among themselves. Cæsar, to ingratiate himself with the people, had carried a law for dividing the rich Campanian plain among the poorer citizens, and one for relieving the nobles from one-third of the sum they had to pay for farming the taxes in Asia. Cicero, Cato, Metellus Celer, Lucullus, and others, penetrating the designs of Cæsar, Pompey, and Crassus, opposed their measures. Cæsar, on laying down his prætorship, obtained Spain for his province, and departed for his new government. Pompey about the same time returned to Italy from the East, and was decreed a triumph; but a law to provide land for his veterans was vehemently opposed, and withdrawn. This insult was not forgotten. Cæsar, having

What were the next acts of Sylla?—His end?—What of Æmilius Lepidus and Catulus?—Sertorius's rebellion in Spain?—The second war with Mithridates?—The third?—The exploits of Lucullus?—Of Pompey?—The fate of Mithridates?—Tigranes?—Aristobulus?—The Servile War?—Who was Spartacus?—What of his career and fate?

What did Pompey and Crassus do jointly?—What great orator arose?—What of Verres and Hortensius?—Cneius Dolabella?—What measures did Catulus introduce?—What countries were added to the empire?—Narrate the outlines of Catiline's conspiracy, and the fate of the conspirators.—What of the designs of Julius Cæsar?

acquired spoils enough in Spain to repay the greater portion of his enormous debts, returned to Rome (B. C. 60) to obtain the consulship. He there joined Pompey and Crassus in a league to grasp the whole power of the State, and formed the first Trium′virate. Cæsar was elected consul, but it was in conjunction with Calpur′nius Bib′ulus, Cato's son-in-law, his violent enemy. Cæsar having proposed an agrarian law, Cicero, Cato, Bibulus, and others of the oligarchy attempted to dissolve the assembly by force; but the triumvir ordered the arrest of Cato, whereupon the factious troop dispersed, and the bill became a law. Cæsar also propitiated the Equites, the tax-collectors, and other influential parties; and managed so adroitly that, before quitting office, he obtained the chief command in Gaul and Illyria for five years. He had cemented his alliance with Pompey by offering his young and beautiful daughter, Julia, to that illustrious man. This marriage was productive of singular happiness to the two parties immediately interested: though Pompey was old enough to be her father, she was a loving and faithful wife to him — and he was so much devoted to her that he became indifferent to public life. So much was Julia beloved that, on her death (B. C. 54), the people voted her the extraordinary honor of a public funeral in the Campus Martius. Her decease broke the last tie between Pompey and Cæsar, and the former drowned his grief by plunging into the whirl of public life.

Meanwhile, Cæsar, having assumed the chief command in Gaul, proceeded to reduce that country to subjection. This he achieved in his first three campaigns (B. C. 58–56). During the next two years he was engaged with the Germans, whom he defeated with terrible slaughter near Coblenz: 150,000 men, it is said, perished in the battle. He threw a bridge across the Rhine, between Coblenz and Andernach, in ten days—which was considered a miraculous achievement. The Heneti and Helvetii also succumbed to him, and Crassus conquered Aquitaine. Thus the whole of Gaul was made a Roman province. While these campaigns were in progress, the policy of the triumvirs was going on favorably at Rome. They got rid of Cicero by driving him into exile (B. C. 58), and they sent Cato to Cyprus to unite that island to Rome. Both of them, however, soon returned, and the dissensions were renewed. The triumvirs met at Lucca (B. C. 55), and procured the voting of their respective provinces to them for five years more. Spain was given to Pompey, Gaul to Cæsar, and Syria to Crassus. Cato was imprisoned for opposing this vote.

Cæsar now crossed the Rhine, but made only a few days' campaign in Germany. He then invaded Britain, where he met with strong resistance. He returned to Gaul the same year (B. C. 55). Next year he again invaded Britain, defeated the Britons in several engagements, and obtained their submission. He then returned, leaving no garrison in the island, which consequently remained independent for more than a century. The same year Crassus set out on his unfortunate expedition against the Parthians. On June 9th, B. C. 53, his army was totally defeated, and he was killed, at Carrhæ, in Mesopotamia, by the Parthians and Armenians. Cæsar and Pompey now became the ruling men in the State; but the former was engaged with the Suevi on the Rhine, while the latter was endeavoring to gain supreme influence in Rome. The Senate hated and feared Pompey; and the people set up their favorite, Clo′dius, a lawless ruffian, who for a time had absolute ascendency. The latter was a candidate for the consulship, and Milo, a man of dangerous character, was candidate for the prætorship. Both went about attended by gladiators, and frequent combats took place in the streets between their partisans. In one of these frays Clodius was slain; and in the confusion which followed, Pompey was appointed sole consul. Milo was banished to Marseilles. Meanwhile, Cæsar was busily engaged in subduing Vercinget′orix, the Gaulish chief. Having at length taken him prisoner, he completed the conquest of Gaul (B. C. 51). Peace was made with the Parthians. Cicero was sent out of the way as proconsul to Cilicia.

While Cæsar was thus occupied in Gaul, his enemies at Rome were busy in endeavoring to destroy his power, and supersede him in his command. But Curio and Mark Antony (the grandson of Cicero) kept him informed of all that was transpiring, and thus he was enabled to thwart their schemes. He offered himself as a candidate for the consulship; but Pompey and Cato procured a decree of outlawry against him — and the consuls, Len′tulus Crus and Caius Marcellus, were appointed dictators to act against him. Cæsar was then with one legion at Ravenna: he determined to act promptly. Leaving Ravenna at night-fall, he "crossed the Rubicon," a river which divided his province from Italy, and marched to Arim′inum. Town after town submitted to him. Corfinium was defended by Ahenobarbus, and other senators for a short period, but was taken by Cæsar, who immediately pursued the consuls and Pompey. The latter left Italy for Greece; and Cæsar, returning to Rome, was appointed dictator (B. C. 49). He at once proceeded to Spain, where he reduced the partisans of Pompey to submission. He next organized an expedition to Greece, where Pompey was concentrating his forces. Cæsar was repulsed at Dyrra′chium; but, advancing into Thessaly, he encountered his rival on the plains of Pharsa′lia (August 9th, B. C. 48), and gained a complete victory. Pompey fled to Egypt, pursued by Cæsar; but he was inhumanly murdered, on his arrival there, by Ptolemy, the husband of Cleopatra. In Egypt, Cæsar became infatuated by the beauty of Cleopatra, which excited the hostility of Ptolemy. War ensued, and Cæsar took Pelusium. Ptolemy was drowned in the Nile, and Cæsar placed another Ptolemy on the throne (B. C. 47). He then marched into Pontus, where Pharna′ces, the son of Mithridates, had revolted. Cæsar, to use his own words, "came, saw, and conquered" (*Veni, Vidi, Vici*), and put an end to the kingdom of Pontus. The Senate again appointed Cæsar dictator, and Mark Antony master of the horse. Cæsar then proceeded to Africa to disperse the adherents of Pompey. He entirely defeated them at Thapsus (April 6th, B. C. 46), where Juba, king of Numidia, Petreius, and others, were killed. Metellus Scipio and Cato destroyed themselves. Africa submitted, and Numidia and Mauritania were made into one province, of which Sallust, the historian of Catiline's conspiracy, was appointed governor. On Cæsar's return to Rome he celebrated four triumphs, but stained his name by putting to death the noble Vercingetorix. Next year (B. C. 45), he overcame the sons of Pompey at Munda, in Spain. In the battle Cneius Pompey was killed: Sextus, his brother, saved himself by flight.

Cæsar was now appointed consul for ten years, and dictator for life; and became, *de facto*, emperor of Rome. His last opponent, Cæcilius Bassus, who had revolted in Syria, was crushed by Cassius; and Cæsar reached the height of his ambition. But his career was destined to be cut short. Cassius, who had ever been Cæsar's enemy, formed a conspiracy to take his life. He drew over to his plans the prætor, MARCUS JUNIUS BRUTUS (whom Cæsar had largely benefited), and about sixty others. Cæsar had vast designs for the benefit of the Roman people; and desired the title of king, to give him greater *prestige*. Mark Antony, knowing this, offered him the crown in public, but he declined to receive it, seeing that there was general dissatisfaction on the subject. The conspirators lay in wait for him; and, on the Ides (13th) of March, B. C. 44, they assassinated him at the foot of Pompey's pillar. On seeing Brutus among the assassins, he exclaimed: "*Et tu, Brute!*" ("And thou too, Brutus!") — pulled his cloak over his face, and fell. Thus died the most illustrious man of antiquity. He had many vices, but they were those of the age. His abilities were vast, and his energies inexhaustible. He projected many schemes for the reformation of the world, but that by which he is best remembered is the reform of the Calendar. The Roman year had previously consisted of 355 days, with a month of 30 days intercalated every third year. The year was now lengthened to 365 days; and the 1st of January, 709 U. C. (*Urbis Conditæ*, the Roman Era dating from the supposed founding of Rome by Romulus, B. C. 753), was made to coincide with what we call the 1st of January, B. C. 45, by adding 67 days to the year 708 U. C., which thus consisted of 445 days, and was styled "the year of confusion." It was also directed that one day should be added to February every four years. This arrangement made the Julian year 11 minutes longer than the true solar year, and in time necessitated another reform of the Calendar, which was effected A. D. 1582, by Pope Gregory XIII.

The selfish and bloody murder of Cæsar recoiled upon the heads of the wretched conspirators, who had no real love for the State, but cared only for themselves. Mark Antony took possession of the treasures and papers of Cæsar, exhorted the people to avenge his death, and in a short time became master of Rome. In this position he ran riot, and resorted to the most unscrupulous means to

---

What of the agrarian law? — Cato, Cicero, and Bibulus? — What command did Cæsar obtain? — What of his daughter, Julia? — Of his exploits in Gaul and Germany? — Who were the first triumvirate? — How did they divide the provinces? — What of the conquest of Britain? — Of the defeat and death of Crassus? — Of Clodius and Milo? — Of Vercingetorix?

What intrigues were preparing against Cæsar? — What did he do? — What is said of Pompey? — Cleopatra? — Pontus? — Pompey's adherents? — Cato? — Cassius and Brutus? — Of Cæsar's death? — His character? — His reform of the Calendar? — Its subsequent correction? — What did Mark Antony do?

carry out his projects. For this he was vehemently denounced by Cicero; and the Senate was divided between fear and interest. Both parties prepared to resort to arms. Octavius, the nephew of Julius Cæsar, to whom the latter had bequeathed all his private property, now appeared on the scene; and, adroitly taking advantage of the panic of the Senate, obtained the command of forces to attack Mark Antony. The latter was defeated, and driven across the Alps. He fled to ÆMILIUS LEP′IDUS, governor of Spain, who united with him in opposition to the Senate. Assembling a powerful army, they marched into Italy. Octavius deserted the Senate, and joined them; and in October, B. C. 43, they formed the Second Triumvirate, dividing the Roman world between themselves.

They then led their forces to Rome, where they ruled with absolute power. Bloody proscriptions followed, and numbers were put to death, Cicero being one of the victims (Dec. 7th, B. C. 43). Octavius and Antony then marched against Brutus and Cassius, who had assembled their forces near Philip′pi, in Macedonia. Two battles were fought. In the first, Cassius was defeated, after which he was found in his tent beheaded. In the second, Brutus was defeated also, after which he put an end to his own life (B. C. 42). The remainder of the conspirators fled to Sextus Pompey, in Sicily; while Antony marched into the East, and attacked Brutus's ally, the king of Cappadocia. Antony, having disposed of this adversary, summoned Cleopatra, queen of Egypt, to appear before him, and account for her conduct in the war. On this memorable occasion he fell a slave to her charms, and became so infatuated as to give up all his influence to her. Octavius followed up his successes, but was defeated in a naval battle by Sextus Pompey. The victories of Ventid′ius over the Parthians, and of Sos′sius over the Jews (B. C. 38), consolidated the empire. Octavius and Antony concerted the prolongation of their triumvirate for five years more. The consul, M. Vipsa′nius Agrippa, totally broke up the power of Sextus Pompey; and Lepidus, deserted by his soldiers, was ejected from the triumvirate (B. C. 36), but allowed to retain the office of Pontifex Maximus. Antony was defeated in Media, and made a disastrous retreat into Egypt, where he lavished kingdoms and provinces on Cleopatra. He removed the celebrated library from Pergamus to Alexandria, and detached himself wholly from Rome. Octavius sent his sister, Octavia, the wife of Antony, to reclaim him, but Antony dismissed and divorced her (B. C. 33). Octavius now prepared for war. The grand contest between the two rivals took place at Ac′tium (Sept. 2d, B. C. 31). Octavius gained a complete victory. Antony fled to Egypt, pursued by Octavius. There he put an end to his life. Cleopatra tried to fascinate the conqueror, as she had previously done Julius Cæsar and Mark Antony; but, finding her blandishments unavailing, she destroyed herself. Egypt was then declared a Roman province (B. C. 30). Octavius was now without a rival. In the year B. C. 29 he returned to Rome, and closed the temple of Janus, in token of universal peace. With the assistance of the learned and wealthy Mæcenas, and of Agrippa, he regulated the affairs of State, and beautified Rome. The number of citizens was vastly increased: the census of this year gives it at 4,164,000, whence it has been computed that the population of the empire was 128,000,000. In the year B. C. 28 Octavius resigned his power, but it was conferred on him again by the obsequious Senate for ten years, with the titles of "Imperator" and "Augustus", by which latter name he was henceforth always called. He was now, in fact, sole ruler of the vast empire of Rome. The republic had ceased to have any vitality, though the forms of its ancient institutions were retained; for the Romans, gorged with the plunder of the world, had lost their public virtue.

The remainder of the century is not marked by events of much importance. Augustus visited Gaul and Spain, and checked some unimportant revolts. He was elected tribune for life (B. C. 23), and, on the death of Lepidus (B. C. 12), he assumed the office of Pontifex Maximus (high-priest). Thus he became absolute, by blending all the offices of State in his own person. An attempt to assassinate him was made by Cæ′pio and Mure′na (B. C. 22), which proved abortive. The death of his nephew and son-in-law, Marcellus, whom he designed for his successor, clouded his prospects (B. C. 23). His daughter, Julia, the widow of Marcellus, was afterwards (B. C. 21) married to Agrippa, who was made prefect of Rome. Augustus sent his son, TIBE′RIUS, into Armenia to settle the disputes there, and establish Tigra′nes on the throne. Tiberius accomplished the mission (B. C. 20), and brought back with him the trophies and captives which had been taken from Crassus and Mark Antony.

In the year B. C. 18 the empire was again voted to Augustus for five years, and Agrippa was appointed tribune for life. Tiberius and his brother, DRUSUS, were sent into Germany and Gaul to check the refractory tribes, which occupied them for several years. Drusus was killed by a fall from his horse (July 20th, B. C. 9); and Tiberius, appointed his successor, concluded a general peace with the German tribes. In the year B. C. 8, the imperial power was again vested in Augustus, this time for ten years; and the name of the month, Sextilis, was changed to "August", in his honor.

The prevalence of peace throughout the world, and the subjection of the greater portion of it to the mild sway of Augustus Cæsar, seem to have been designed to herald the greatest of all events in the annals of the human race, viz., THE COMING OF CHRIST. The exact date of the birth of JESUS OF NAZARETH is a matter of doubt; some authorities placing it seven years before the received era; some, three years after: a variation of ten years. Following the ablest chronologists (Hales, Clinton, and Blair), it is here placed on Dec. 25th, B. C. 5.

The reign of Augustus was the most brilliant epoch of Roman literature: hence the term, "Augustan Era". Under his patronage, and that of his friend, Mæce′nas, VIRGIL, HORACE, OVID, CATUL′LUS, TIBUL′LUS, PROPER′TIUS, LIVY, SALLUST, DIODO′RUS SIC′ULUS, CORNELIUS NEPOS, and DIONY′SIUS of Hal′icarnas′sus, flourished. VIRGIL (Publius Virgilius Maro, a native of Mantua, born Oct. 15th, B. C. 70; died Sept. 22d, B. C. 19) was the greatest of the Roman poets. His most celebrated work is the "Æneid", an epic poem in twelve books, on the adventures of Æneas after his escape from Troy. He also wrote pastoral poems, called "Bucolics", and poems on husbandry, called "Georgics". HORACE (Quintus Horatius Flaccus), the greatest lyric poet of Rome, was a native of Venusia, in Apulia; born Dec. 8th, B. C. 65; died Nov. 17th, B. C. 8. He was not a voluminous writer, but exceedingly elegant. His odes are unrivalled. His satires and epistles are masterpieces. That to the Pisos, on the art of poetry, has never been surpassed in justness of sentiment. OVID (Ovidius Naso) was born at Sulmo, March 20th, B. C. 43; died A. D. 18. Many of his poems have been lost, but the "Metamorphoses", "Epistles", and "The Art of Love", remain. CATULLUS (born at Verona, B. C. 87; died B. C. 47) wrote lyric poems, elegies, and epigrams, distinguished for elegance. TIBULLUS (born B. C. 54, died B. C. 18) was the author of many elegant lyrics. PROPERTIUS (born B. C. 51, date of death unknown) wrote many fine elegies. LIVY (Titus Livius), the great historian, was born at Padua, B. C. 59; died A. D. 17. He wrote a history of Rome from its foundation to the death of Drusus, B. C. 9, in 142 books, of which only 35 are now extant. CICERO (Marcus Tullius; born at Arpi′num, Jan. 3d, B. C. 106; and beheaded, by order of Mark Antony, Dec. 7th, B. C. 43) wrote many admirable orations, epistles, and essays. JULIUS CÆSAR was an author as well as a soldier, but most of his works have been lost. His "Commentaries", on the Gallic and the civil wars, are all that have come down to us. They are remarkable for clearness and purity of style. SALLUST (Sallustius Crispus; born at Amiternum, B. C. 86; died B. C. 34) wrote a history of Catiline's conspiracy, and of the war with Jugurtha. CORNELIUS NEPOS, of Verona, wrote several works, which have been lost, and some biographies of distinguished men, which are extant. DIODORUS SICULUS was a native of Agyrium, in Sicily. He spent 30 years in collecting materials for a Universal History, portions of which only survive. LUCRETIUS CARUS (born B. C. 95, committed suicide B. C. 52) was the author of the philosophical poem, *De rerum naturâ* (on the nature of things). DIONYSIUS of Halicarnassus wrote a history of Rome, and other historical works; also some beautiful criticisms on the classical writers of Greece. VITRU′VIUS POLLIO was the author of a celebrated treatise on architecture. VARRO, the distinguished commander, was also an eminent author and patron of literature. He wrote no less than 490 books, but only two of his works are now in existence: they are on agriculture and on antiquities. We may also mention Asin′ius Pol′lio, poet and historian; Cotta, Hortensius, Plotius Gallus, and Licinius Calvus, orators; Sisenna and Nicola′us of Damascus, historians; Varro Ataci′nus and Macer, poets; and Bavius and Mævius, two inferior poets, who have acquired celebrity by their attacks on Virgil and Horace.

Who was Octavius Cæsar?—Who constituted the second triumvirate?—What were their subsequent acts?—What befell Brutus and Cassius?—Lepidus?—The adherents of Pompey?—Mark Antony and Cleopatra?—Who were Mæcenas and Agrippa?—What was the population of Rome?—The empire?—How did Octavius obtain supreme power?—What titles did he assume?

What is said of the republic?—Of the remaining events of the century?—Tiberius and Drusus?—The birth of Christ?—What authors flourished?—What of Virgil?—Horace?—Ovid?—Catullus?—Tibullus?—Propertius?—Livy?—Cicero?—Cæsar?—Sallust?—C. Nepos?—Diodorus Siculus?—Lucretius?—Vitruvius?—Varro?—And others?

BRITAIN.

ENGLAND.—Lud was succeeded by his brother, CASSIB′ELAN, or Cassibellanus, prince of the tribe called Cassii. This monarch gained repeated victories over his neighbors, and acquired high renown for his valor; but he is far more celebrated for his heroic resistance to the Romans, who, under Julius Cæsar, having subdued Europe from the Alps to the German Ocean, now desired to add Britain to their dominions. Cæsar first landed at Deal, in Kent, B. C. 55; but after a severe battle with the Britons, in which neither party was successful, he returned to Gaul. According to the British historians, Cassibelan, anticipating a second invasion, caused the cities to be fortified, and the Thames to be defended by iron stakes under the water. Cæsar, on his second attempt, sailed up the Thames, where his ships were damaged by the iron stakes, and many thousands of his men were slain. For this victory Cassibelan offered up an immense number of cattle to the gods. At this festival one of his nephew's (Andro′geus) sons was killed, whence a civil war arose between the respective partisans of Cassibelan and Androgeus. The latter being hard pressed, implored the protection of Cæsar, who, taking advantage of the fued, at once hastened to his assistance. The allied tribes of the Britons placed themselves under the orders of Cassibelan, who met the Romans with great gallantry near Canterbury, but was defeated. After this he was deserted by his allies. Several of them made terms with Cæsar, and detesting the superiority of the Cassii, led him to the capital of Cassibelan, near Verulam, which he took by storm, and secured all the treasures of the British king. Cassibelan, having failed in an attempt to burn the Roman fleet, sued for peace, which Cæsar granted him, on condition of his paying tribute. After which the conqueror returned to Gaul, leaving the island only nominally subdued; for from this time until the reign of Claudius, a period of 97 years, the Britons retained their original independence. But the Roman invasion had the effect of extending the commerce of the island, which became very valuable,—its exports consisting of corn, cattle, gold, silver, tin, lead, iron, skins, *slaves*, and dogs. The religion of the people at this period was that of the Druids, which had in the most ancient times been introduced by the original Celtic, or Phœnician settlers. Seven years after the conclusion of the war with Cæsar, Cassibelan died, and was buried at York. Androgeus having gone to Rome, his brother, Tenuantius, duke of Cornwall, was made king. He is described as a warlike and a just monarch. His son, CYM′BELINE (or Cunob′eline), was educated at Rome, and was a personal friend of Augustus Cæsar. There he contracted so strong a liking for the Romans, that afterwards when he became king of Britain, he paid them tribute when he might very well have withheld it. He was a distinguished soldier and an accomplished man.

IRELAND.—This century is marked by the restoration of the ancient division of the country into four kingdoms, viz., Leinster, Munster, Ulster, and Connaught, by King ACHY FEDLOCH. It is also distinguished by the famous "Seven Years' War" between Connaught and Ulster, occasioned by the seizure of an immense quantity of cattle by the troops of Maud, queen of Connaught. The exploits of CUCHULLIN, CONAL-CEARNACH, and other heroes of "the Red Branch knights" in this war, are among the themes on which the old chroniclers and bards delighted most to dwell; and from their songs it is supposed that Macpherson derived the groundwork of his "poems of Ossian".

SCOTLAND.—Ewen I. reigned with great ability, and divided the kingdom into circuits for the administration of justice, appointing judges for each circuit. He assisted the Picts against the Britons, between whom so dreadful a battle is said to have been fought, that both parties, struck with terror at the carnage, returned to their respective homes, leaving the victory undecided. His son Gillus (or Oilill) having murdered his brothers and relatives, gained the throne by force, but was soon dethroned and killed, and the crown was bestowed on Ewen II. This prince turned his attention to arts and commerce, which he promoted; and his example was followed by his successor, Eder-skeol, who died after a peaceful reign of 48 years. His degenerate son, Ewen III., was a most licentious prince, and procured an ordinance authorizing polygamy and the right of the king and nobles to the wives of their vassals. He encouraged prodigality and vice, but was, after a reign of seven years, thrown into jail, and condemned to perpetual imprisonment. Some person, however, entered the jail during the night, and strangled him.

What is said of Cassibelan?—Relate his exploits.—What did the Romans do after Julius Cæsar's time?—What was the religion of the people?—For what is the reign of Achy Fedloch remarkable?—Who were the heroes of Ireland at this time?—What remarkable battle took place between the Scots, Picts, and Britons?—What other events occurred in Scotland?

FRANCE.

THIS century is one of the most important in the history of France, for it witnessed the subjugation of the country by the Romans, who implanted in it their laws and language, and settling there in great numbers, became permanently incorporated with the original inhabitants. To this influx is to be attributed the formation of the French language. During the civil wars of Marius and Sylla in Italy, the Roman province of Gaul took part in the struggle. Sertorius, who had distinguished himself in Spain by his heroic opposition to Marius, persuaded the people of Aquitaine to join his standard. Defeating the Romans there, they passed into Italy on the invitation of Lepidus, but were routed by Catulus and Pompey, who drove Sertorius back into Spain, and ravaged the south of France (B. C. 77). The cruelties and oppression of which the Roman governor, Fronteius, was guilty, drove the tribe of the Allob′roges into revolt. The deputies which this tribe sent to Rome to complain of the conduct of Fronteius, entered into the conspiracy framed by Catiline, but they subsequently revealed it to the government; and the prætor, Pomptinus, having crushed the conspirators, the Allobroges laid down their arms.

In Central Gaul, the Seq′uani and the Arver′ni, enraged at the encroachments of the Ædui, engaged A′RIOVIS′TUS, king of the Suevi, to assist them in a war against that nation. The Ædui were overcome, in spite of the heroism of their Druid chief, DIVITI′ACUS, who escaped to Rome. But Ariovistus, after having delivered the Sequani from their enemies, helped himself to their lands. The Sequani thereupon made peace with the Ædui, and formed an alliance against him. He, however, annihilated their league at the great battle of Am′agito′bria (B. C. 63), and remained master of a large portion of Gaul. Meanwhile the Helvetians, under the leadership of ORGET′ORIX, the Seq′uani, under that of CAS′TIC, and the Ædui, under that of DUM′NORIX, organized an expedition into Gaul; and collecting followers to the number of 368,000, attempted to enter the country by the valley of the Rhone. There Julius Cæsar stopped their passage. He also formed a league against them with the Gauls and Ariovistus. The result was their complete defeat (B. C. 58). Cæsar's next exploit was the expulsion of Ariovistus and his Suevi from Gaul. But the Gauls discerning clearly the ambitious designs of the Romans, formed a league against them, and thus began the memorable GAULISH WAR OF INDEPENDENCE. This heroic struggle cost the Romans seven campaigns, and very severe losses. The Gauls were beaten in detail by Cæsar and Crassus, but the latter sustained some heavy reverses. The Romans were guilty of great cruelty and excesses toward the conquered people. Their military skill, however, proved too much for the Gauls. The great Gallic leader, VERCINGET′ORIX, whose nobleness of soul, military talents, and eloquence, made him the worthy rival of Julius Cæsar, and who was one of the greatest men ever produced by the Gaulish nation, made himself famous by his heroism. The defence of Carnutum, Gergovia, and Alesia, will bear comparison with that of Numantia, or of Saragossa, or of any other city mentioned in history. The details of the war, though very interesting, cannot be given here. Suffice it to say that it lasted seven years (B. C. 57–50). In the course of it, Cæsar is said to have taken 800 cities, subdued 300 tribes, and fought against 3,000,000 of men, of whom 1,000,000 perished in battle, and 1,000,000 were reduced to captivity!! Dumnorix, attempting to escape from Cæsar's spies, was killed by the Roman soldiers. After the heroic but unsuccessful defence of Alesia, Vercingetorix surrendered himself to Cæsar, who, instead of honoring his gallantry, treated him with indignity. The noble Gaul was sent to Rome, and thrown into a loathsome dungeon, where he was detained six years, at the expiration of which time he was brought forth to be exhibited in Cæsar's triumphal procession, and then consigned to the executioner. This cruel act is a great blot on the fair fame of the Romans. Cæsar labored assiduously to conciliate the conquered Gauls, and met with considerable success. Many years after his death, his successor, the first emperor, Augustus Cæsar, framed a grand plan for the administration of Gaul. He divided the country into three provinces, Aquitania, Belgium, and Lugdunum (Lyons), the latter comprising Central France from the Rhone to Brittany. He also introduced a fiscal and a military system analogous to that of the Romans, and introduced other innovations which met at first with great opposition from the natives, but the Gauls were finally induced to adopt them by the abilities of Drusus.

For what is this century remarkable?—What of Sertorius?—Of the Allobroges?—Ariovistus?—Divitiacus?—The battle of Amagitobria?—Orgetorix?—Castic?—Dumnorix?—The exploits of Julius Cæsar?—What of the War of Independence?—Its results?—The heroism and fate of Vercingetorix?—What policy was pursued by Cæsar, Augustus, and Drusus?

SPAIN.

The country was now nominally subject to Rome, but, in reality, it required incessant vigilance and exertion on the part of the Roman governors to maintain their authority., The civil wars in Italy afforded the Spaniards an opportunity for regaining their independence which was not lost sight of by them. Quintus Serto'rius, an Italian, who had distinguished himself in the former Spanish wars, having been proscribed by Sylla for siding with Marius, fled into Spain, where he contrived to gain the esteem and confidence of the people. Having induced the Lusitanians and Spaniards to join his standard, he organized a war of independence (B. C. 81). He was at first not successful. The Romans, under Sylla, routed his troops, and forced him to seek safety on the deep. He remained for some time in Iviça, when the Lusitanians offered him the chief command of their forces. He accordingly went to Lusitania, where he routed the prætors Didius and Domitius. In a short time he became master of the country, and succeeded in forming the Celtiberians and the Lusitanians into one great State, dependent on himself. He granted to them a government exactly like that of Rome: he created 300 senators, Romans by birth, and appointed numerous magistrates. He organized an army after the Roman style; founded a university at Asca; and beautified his capital, Evora, with the noblest works of art. His success alarmed the Romans. Metellus Pius and Perpenna were sent with a large army to crush him, but he made head against them. The famous Pompey was then sent against him. Sertorius was victorious on the banks of the Xucar (B. C. 76). Several other obstinate battles were fought, and victory alternated; but at length the skill of Pompey and Metellus prevailed, and Sertorius was overcome. A conspiracy was formed against him by Perpenna, who had joined him against Pompey, and he was murdered while at a feast (B. C. 72). His memory was cherished by the Spaniards, who named him "the Roman Hannibal". After his death, the war was carried on for a short time by Perpenna, who had succeeded to the chief command; but Pompey defeated him in the very first battle, took him prisoner, and put him to death. All Spain now submitted to Pompey. In the year B. C. 60, Julius Cæsar was sent into Spain as prætor. His principal exploit there was the subjugation of the Herminii, a revolted Lusitanian tribe. Quintus Cæcil'ius, the next governor, was overthrown by the Vacci, near Clunia. The Roman Senate then appointed Pompey governor for five years. That great man sent three legates to govern in his name, viz., Petreius, Afra'nius, and Varro: these officers reduced the revolted tribes to submission (B. C. 52).

Spain next became involved in the civil war between Cæsar and Pompey. It was Pompey's stronghold; accordingly his lieutenants there made great efforts to resist the victorious Cæsar, but the latter was triumphant, and drove Pompey's forces out of Spain, at the same time conciliating the natives by his judicious measures and conduct. He appointed Cassius Longi'nus governor of one portion of Spain, and Marcus Lepidus of another. The avarice of Longinus provoked a mutiny, and he was forced to leave the country. Spain then became distracted by two factions, one siding with Cæsar, the other with Pompey's sons, Cneius and Sextus. A civil war broke out, which was terminated at last by the return of Cæsar into Spain, and by the celebrated battle of Munda, near Malaga, where Cneius Pompey was totally defeated, and mortally wounded. Cordova and Seville were taken, and Spain was regained by Cæsar (B. C. 45), who appointed Asin'ius Pollio governor.

On the death of Cæsar (B. C. 44), Sextus Pompey renewed the war, and defeated and killed Pollio; but Lepidus induced him to leave Spain, and try his fortune at Rome. In the civil wars which ensued in that capital on Cæsar's death, the empire was partitioned amongst the triumvirate, Octavius, Lepidus, and Mark Antony. Spain fell to the lot of Lep'idus. In the second partition of the empire (B. C. 39), Spain was given to Octavius Cæsar, who soon after became emperor of all the Roman dominions, under the title of Augustus.

Many Roman colonies were founded in Spain, and the natives rapidly changed their manners and language for those of the Romans. But the peace of the country was once more broken by the Can'tabri, a fierce people in the north of Spain, who raised a revolt, which was deemed of such importance, that Augustus came into Spain himself, in order to subdue it. He completed the subjugation of the country.

Who was Sertorius?—What is said of him?—What great Roman general was sent against him?—What was his fate?—And that of Perpenna?—What did Pompey do?—And Julius Cæsar?—And Quintus Cæcilius?—What of Spain during the wars of Cæsar and Pompey?—Who fought the battle of Munda?—To which of the triumvirs was Spain allotted?

GERMANY.

The migration of the Cimbri and Teutones occasioned great disturbances in Germany. A new power, called the Suevic confederation, arose, and devastated every country in its vicinity. It consisted of a hundred districts, each of which annually sent forth a thousand warriors. These Suevi became a terror to the rest of the Germanic tribes, and their fame reached Rome. The Germans on the Rhine owned their inferiority to them. Unfortunately for Germany, the Suevi separated themselves from the western tribes, and instead of aiding them, attacked them and drove them into the hands of the Romans. Being thus hemmed in on every side, the Western Germans vainly attempted to defend their liberty; and the tribes on the Upper Rhine, which had united under A'riovis'tus, and those on the Lower Rhine, which had combined under Ambi'orix, were forced to yield to the victorious legions of Julius Cæsar.

In Gaul the Æ'dui and the Seq'uani having quarrelled, the latter were worsted, and they applied to the neighboring tribes on the Rhine for aid. Accordingly an army was sent under Ariovistus (B. C. 72), who, uniting his forces with those of the Sequani, completely defeated the Ædui. Instead of returning, however, he resolved to settle in Gaul, and invited his countrymen to join him there. The Gauls then applied to the Romans for help; and Julius Cæsar, who then commanded in Provence, marching against Ariovistus, ordered him instantly to quit Gaul. Ariovistus merely replied that "the Romans were not concerned in his affairs." On marching up the country, Cæsar was informed by his spies that the German women having prognosticated evil to their nation on a certain day, the Germans would, on that day, either refuse to fight, or, if forced to do so, would be spiritless. Taking advantage of this, he attacked them on the day predicted, and they were easily routed. The two wives of Ariovistus fell into the hands of the Romans, but he escaped across the Rhine (B. C. 58). The great Roman general next subdued the Helve'tii and a number of small tribes, who being at feud with each other, easily fell victims to the Romans. Soon after this (B. C. 53), the Teuc'teri and the Usip'etes, who had been driven out by the Suevi, crossed the Rhine, and demanded land of Cæsar; but he treacherously seized their leader, and massacred them. He then crossed the Rhine at Andernach, and marched against the Sicam'bri, who, laying waste their country, fled to the Wetterau. The Suevi meanwhile flew to arms. An attempt was made by the conquered Belgæ to murder every Roman in that part of Gaul inhabited by them, on a given day. This plot was organized by Induzi'omar, Ambi'orix, and Cativol'cus; but it failed. The first of these chiefs was killed; Ambiorix fled to the forest of the Ardennes, where he was surprised by the Romans, but he managed to escape; Cativolcus killed himself. After which, the Belgæ submitted to the Romans.

In the East, King Boirebis'tas, at the head of the Getæ, attacked the Boii and Tauris'ci, and laid waste their country. The Taurisci were systematically exterminated by the Romans, under Tibe'rius. When Rome was erected into an empire by Augustus Cæsar (B. C. 27), all the countries south of the Danube and westward of the Rhine were incorporated with it. Roman colonies were planted along the frontiers; German mercenaries were employed in the Roman armies; and hence new manners and customs were planted amongst the southern tribes. Augustus Cæsar, ambitious of extending his empire, sent his stepson, Drusus, with a large army to conquer the whole of Germany (B. C. 12). In three campaigns Drusus laid waste with fire and sword the country between the Rhine, the Elbe, the Weser, and the Ems, being victorious everywhere, though not without meeting with strenuous resistance. Pushing through the Cheruscian forests, he reached the Elbe, on whose bank he beheld a prophetess of gigantic stature, who with threatening gesture exclaimed, "Ah! insatiable Drusus! to what do you aspire? Fate has forbidden your advance through our unknown regions! Fly hence!" Terror-struck at the omen, Drusus retreated, but he was killed by the fall of his horse (B. C. 9). He was buried at Mayence (Mentz). After his death, his brother, Tibe'rius, invaded the country of the Usipetes and Teucteri, subdued the Sicambri, and endeavored by conciliatory measures to gain the affections of the people. In this he was not successful. Domit'ius commanded another expedition to the Elbe (B. C. 6), which was successful, and made the Roman name feared. Nevertheless, the Germans were far from being subdued.

What is said of the Suevic confederation?—Of the western tribes?—The Ædui and the Sequani?—Ariovistus?—Julius Cæsar?—The revolt of the Belgæ?—What became of their chiefs?—The Taurisci?—The countries south of the Danube and west of the Rhine?—Relate the exploits of Drusus and Tiberius.—What befell Drusus?

ASIA MINOR.

Pontus.—This kingdom was now the most important one in Asia Minor, owing to the abilities of its sovereign, Mithrida'tes the Great. That monarch having subdued the countries on the shores of the Black Sea, and married his daughter to Tigranes, king of Armenia, declared war against the Romans. In two campaigns he made himself master of Asia Minor (B. C. 88), but cruelly massacred all the Roman merchants residing there. He raised a large force in Greece under the command of Archelaus, and took Athens. At length (B. C. 86) the Romans sent Sylla against him in Greece, and his party was completely broken up; while Fim'bria, another Roman general, was equally successful in Asia. Mithridates was thus compelled to sue for peace, which was granted by Sylla (B. C. 84). Ten years afterwards, taking advantage of the civil war in Italy, he seized on Bithynia, and attacked the Roman forces there, but was defeated by Julius Cæsar (then a young lieutenant), and by Lucullus, who drove him into Armenia. Tigranes now joined him, and the war was renewed, at first with success; but when Pompey assumed the command, the war was brought to a close. Mithridates fled into Scythia, followed by Pompey, who spent two years in searching for him, and at length, believing him dead, returned to Rome. No sooner had Pompey done so, than Mithridates made his appearance in Pontus with an army (B. C. 64). He was deserted, however, by his family and by his soldiers; whereupon he tried to commit suicide, but was slain by a Roman soldier, who found him lying on the ground bleeding. Such was the end of this heroic prince. A few years afterwards (B. C. 47), his son, Pharna'ces, attempted to recover some of the provinces lost by his father, but was defeated and slain by Julius Cæsar, who put an end to the kingdom of Pontus.

Cappadocia.—The people of this State having applied to the Romans for a king, to save them from Mithridates, the Senate gave them Ariobarza'nes (B. C. 94). This country suffered greatly during the wars between the Romans and Mithridates, and afterwards became involved in the Roman civil wars. Ariobarzanes resigned the throne to his son, Ariobarzanes II. (B. C. 63), who, taking part with Brutus against Cæsar, was slain by Mark Antony (B. C. 42). He was succeeded by his son, A'riara'thes VII. This monarch was also deposed (B. C. 36) by Mark Antony, who made Archela'us king. This prince reigned 50 years.

Bithynia.—Nicome'des II., who 58 years previously had obtained the throne by parricide, was killed by his youngest son, Socrates (B. C. 91). He was succeeded by his eldest son, Nicomedes III. This prince, expelled by Mithridates, was restored by the Romans, to whom at his death he bequeathed his kingdom (B. C. 74).

Armenia.—Tigra'nes consolidated the two kingdoms of Greater and Lesser Armenia, and married the daughter of Mithridates, king of Pontus. He became involved in the wars which his father-in-law carried on with the Romans, and suffered accordingly. He was chosen by the Syrians to be their king (B. C. 83), and ruled them well until expelled by Lucullus (B. C. 69), who followed him into Armenia. He was finally compelled by Pompey to submit to the Romans (B. C. 66). He was succeeded by Artavas'des (B. C. 56). Artavasdes joined with the Parthians in repelling the invasion of the Romans under Crassus (B. C. 53), and contributed to the defeat of that general at Carrhæ. In the civil war between Cæsar and Pompey, he assisted the latter, and was forced to submit to Cæsar. He defeated Mark Antony in Media (B. C. 36), but was subsequently (B. C. 34) taken prisoner, and sent in chains to Egypt, where in Mark Antony's triumph he was exhibited in fetters of gold. His son, Artax'ias, was raised to the throne (B. C. 33). Great confusion prevailed in the kingdom for some years, until at length (B. C. 20) the Emperor Augustus sent his son Tiberius to put an end to it; which he did, and established Tigra'nes II. on the throne. On the death of Tigranes (B. C. 10), Artavasdes III. became nominally king, but the country was in fact under Roman control.

Rhodes endeavored to preserve neutrality amid the wars of her neighbors. Mithridates attacked Rhodes (B. C. 87), but was repulsed. During the war between Cæsar and Pompey, the Rhodians fought sometimes for one side, sometimes for the other. Pompey was refused admittance into the island after his defeat at Pharsalia (B. C. 48), and the murderers of Cæsar were also excluded (B. C. 44). Cassius, in revenge, besieged and pillaged the city (B. C. 43); but the Rhodians were afterwards compensated for this by Mark Antony.

State the principal incidents in the reign of Mithridates the Great.—What became of that monarch?—Of Pontus?—What events took place in Cappadocia?—Bithynia?—Armenia?—What of Tigranes?—Artavasdes?—Artaxias?—What did Augustus do?—What befell Parthia?—Rhodes?—How were Pompey and Cassius received at Rhodes?—What was the result?

AFRICA.

Numidia.—This State espoused the cause of Pompey during the civil war between that chief and Julius Cæsar. The country had been a short time previously overrun by Pompey, who had made Hiemp'sal king of it. Hiempsal having quarrelled with Masintha, a noble native chief, Julius Cæsar interfered, and grossly insulted Juba, the son of Hiempsal. The young prince thereupon warmly espoused Pompey's cause, and defeated Cu'rio, one of Cæsar's lieutenants; and having joined Publius Scipio, he reduced Cæsar to great extremities. The latter, having received reinforcements from Rome, and being aided by Bocchus, king of Mauretania, attacked Juba, Scipio, and Labienus, near Thapsus, and completely overthrew them. Juba fled into Numidia, where he caused himself to be put to death by one of his slaves. His infant son, Juba (afterwards king of Mauretania), was carried prisoner to Rome, and compelled to grace the conqueror's triumph. Cæsar then reduced Numidia to a Roman province.

Mauretania (*Morocco*).—Of the history of Mauretania we know but little until this century, when we find Bogud, king of Tingitana (the second division of Mauretania), aiding Julius Cæsar against Pompey and Juba, king of Numidia. He also contributed to the defeat of the Pompeys at Munda in Spain. He afterwards sided with Mark Antony against Octavius Cæsar, and endeavored to make a diversion in favor of the former in Spain. But while thus engaged, the Tingitanians revolted, and being supported by the troops of Octavius and those of Bocchus, king of Mauretania proper, they drove Bogud out; and Bocchus was put in possession of Tingitana. Octavius (afterwards Augustus Cæsar) confirmed Bocchus in this possession, and conferred the privileges of Roman citizens upon the inhabitants of Tingis. Bogud was at last killed by Agrippa at Metho'ne; and after the death of Bocchus the whole of Mauretania was reduced to a Roman province. Soon afterwards, Augustus conferred the two Mauretaniæ (Mauretania proper and Tingitana), with a portion of Gætu'lia, upon the younger Juba, the son of the former king of that name. This prince (Juba II.) was one of the most learned men of his time. He was well versed in history, and in several branches of science. He wrote a history of Arabia, of the antiquities of Assyria and of Rome, of theatres, painting and painters, of grammar, and of the nature and habits of animals: he also composed a treatise on the source of the Nile. He governed his kingdom in so admirable a manner, that his subjects erected a statue in honor of him, and ranked him among the gods.

Gætulia.—There are but scattered notices of this country, in the ancient authors. We read of Gætulians serving in the armies of Hannibal and Jugurtha; but they were never entirely subdued either by Masinissa or by the Romans. They worshipped the Sun and Fire; whence it has been supposed that they came originally from Persia.

Ethiopia.—Mention has been frequently made of this country in the history of Egypt. Materials for a connected narrative of its career during the early ages, do not exist. It is believed to have been the Cush of Scripture. The people have traditions respecting Moses, who they say conquered them; and respecting the queen of Sheba, who reigned over Ethiopia proper, and paid the famous visit to Solomon. The Abyssinians assert that her name was Balkis, or Make'da, and that she had a son by Solomon, who received the Jewish name of David (and the Ethiopian one of Menilehec), was educated at Jerusalem by the high-priest, and on his ascending the throne of his mother, established the Jewish religion in Ethiopia, where it flourished until Christianity was introduced. Ethiopia in ancient times included Abyssinia and Arabia Felix. After the annexation of Egypt to Rome, Can'dace, queen of Ethiopia, invaded the Thebais, but was driven back by the governor, Petro'nius (B. C. 29), who pursued her to her capital, Nepata. The Emperor Augustus granted her peace on her own terms, but the Romans considered themselves masters of Ethiopia. The student of history will find useful notices of the ancient nations of Africa in vols. xvii. and xviii. of the *Universal History*. The name of Candace was common to all the queens of Ethiopia, just as Cleopatra was to the queens of Egypt. The term "Ethiopia" anciently denoted the kingdom of Me'roë; but in its wider sense it included that of the Axom'itæ, and the tribes of the Trog-lod'ytæ, the Ichthyoph'agi of the Red Sea, the Blem'myæ, Megab'ari, and Nubæ in the interior.

What is said of Numidia?—Hiempsal?—Juba?—Of his infant son?—Bocchus?—What became of Numidia?—What is said of Juba II.?—What of Gætulia?—Of Ethiopia?—Of the queen of Sheba?—Of her son?—The establishment of the Jewish religion in Ethiopia?—What did Ethiopia include?—What of Candace?—Of the term "Ethiopia"?

SCANDINAVIA.

The historical monuments of the north of Europe go no further back than this century. We know that the Cimmerii (or Cimbri) had inhabited the land for many ages. Their invasions of Germany and Gaul, and their exploits in the south of Europe, have been already noticed; but the events which took place in Denmark and Sweden, subsequently to their settlement there, are entirely unknown. It is from the first century before the Christian Era that the history of these countries dates. An entire change in their religion and government was effected by the invasion and conquest of the North by the celebrated Odin, whose history (such as can be ascertained or conjectured from the imperfect sources we have) is as follows:—

In the reign of Grylle (about B. C. 70), Sigge, the son of Fridulph, who had distinguished himself against the Romans in his country east of the Tan′aïs (or Don), near the Black Sea, set out with his chief priests and a vast concourse of followers for the West. Leaving his brothers to rule at Asgard, the capital of his ancestors, he traversed Russia, and entered Saxland (the southern shore of the Baltic), subduing all nations as he passed. He then crossed the Baltic, and passed into the island of Funen, where he built a city, named after himself, Odensee. He next subdued Denmark and Sweden. In the latter country reigned a prince, named Gylfi, who was so struck with admiration for him, that he paid him divine honors. The Swedes came in crowds to do him homage, and, by common consent, bestowed the regal title and office upon his son, Yngve, and his posterity. Sigge fixed his abode near Lake Logur (the Mælar Sea), and erected a splendid temple at Sigtuna for the new religion which he introduced, and which rapidly spread. He either assumed the name of Odin, the supreme deity of the Scythians, probably giving himself out as the same personage as the ancient Odin; or, pretending to be the prophet or priest of that deity, the ignorance of succeeding ages confounded him with the god, thus producing, out of the attributes of the one and the history of the other, a medley, out of which nothing very certain can be extracted. He introduced new laws, also the customs of his own country, and established a supreme council or tribunal, composed of twelve pontiffs or judges, whose duties were to watch over the public weal, to distribute justice, to preside over the new worship, and to preserve the religious and magical secrets which he intrusted to them. This council held its sittings at Sigtuna (a city now destroyed, situate in the same province with Stockholm). Odin was acknowledged as a sovereign and a god by all the petty princes of Sweden and Denmark, and firmly established his empire (B. C. 50), adding Norway to it, and bestowing the crown of that country on his son, Sæming, whose descendents reigned for many generations. Odin, finding his end approaching through a lingering disease, put himself to death by giving himself nine wounds in the form of a circle with the point of a lance, in the presence of his friends, saying that he was going to join the gods in Asgard, where he would receive with honor all who should die bravely in battle. His body was solemnly burnt at Sigtuna, conformably to a custom introduced by him. He was a poet and a musician, and is said to have invented the Runic characters. This alphabet consisted of sixteen letters, arranged as follows: F, U, D (or TH), O, R, K, H, N, I, A, S, T, B, L, M, V. These Runes were distinguished at first as of four kinds, namely, bitter, favorable, victorious, and medicinal. The bitter were used to bring evil on enemies; the favorable, to avert misfortune; the victorious, to procure conquest; the medicinal, to heal, to prevent shipwreck, to counteract poison, and to win a woman's love. They were written sometimes from right to left, sometimes from top to bottom and back again. The student will find an interesting account of the Runic alphabet in Bishop Percy's translation of Mallet's *Northern Antiquities*. A summary of the religious doctrines which prevailed in the north of Europe has been already given in the columns devoted to Germany (pp. 48, 53, 57, 61).

That a great leader, bearing the name of Odin, really achieved what is related of him in Sweden and Denmark, is tolerably certain. Many marvellous exploits are said to have been accomplished by him through his skill in magic; but allowing for this belief, so natural among a barbarous people, it is clear that his superior intelligence and knowledge enabled him to overrun a vast tract of country, extending from the Don to the Northern Ocean, and to found a new religion, which endured for centuries, and prevailed among the northern German and the Scandinavian tribes so late as the 12th century A. D. Some learned men have supposed him to have been also the founder of that system of hostile aggression on the Roman empire, which burst forth with such fury in the 2d, 3d, and 4th centuries A. C. They suppose him to have been actuated mainly by hatred of the Romans, who had driven him out of his own country; and that his principal object in invading so many distant kingdoms, and there establishing his sanguinary doctrines, was to rouse the inhabitants of all nations against the Roman empire. But there is no historical evidence of his having had such a design. Whatever may have been his ruling principle, he was a man who left a deep impression on his fellow-men, and became their guiding spirit for ages, as Zoroaster, Confucius, Budha, and Mohammed have done.

On the death of Odin his authority descended to his sons. Njörd became the supreme chief; Balder became viceroy of the Angles; Heimdall, ruler of Scania; Skjöld, ruler in Zealand and Denmark; Frey (or Yngve Frey) became king of Sweden. From him sprang the dynasty of the Ynglings, the last king of which, being the 21st in descent from Frey, was Ingialld Illradi, who reigned in the beginning of the 7th century. These heroes were deified along with Odin's other children, Thor, Frigga, and Tyr. Njörd died B. C. 20, and was succeeded by his son, Freyer Yngve, during whose reigns profound peace existed. In Denmark, Skjöld greatly enlarged his dominions by subduing the Saxons, whom he subjected to an annual tribute. He was possessed of enormous strength and indomitable courage. He died B. C. 40, and was succeeded by Friedlief I., of whom we have nothing worthy of record. After a reign of 17 years he died, leaving his kingdom to Frode I., who enjoyed the reputation of unrivalled prowess as a warrior. It is said in Danish tradition that Frode carried his victorious arms into Sweden, Germany, England, and Ireland. These expeditions were probably nothing more than piratical incursions along the coasts of those countries. He compiled a civil and a military code of laws, of which he strictly enforced the observance. The descendents of Skjöld (a Danish word, signifying "a shield",) were called, after him, Skjöldungians.

What is said of the early history of the north of Europe?—Who was Odin?—Give an outline of his exploits.—In what country did he settle?—What did he introduce?—To whom did he give Sweden?—To whom Denmark?—What was the manner of his death?—What is said of the Runic alphabet?—The names of Odin's sons?—The dynasty of the Ynglings?—That of the Skjöld family?—Give the substance of the remarks upon Odin.

NETHERLANDS.

The earliest accounts we have of the Netherlands are derived from the Romans. The banks of the Rhine were peopled by a multitude of German tribes, of greater or less importance. On the Moselle dwelt the Trev′eri at Treves; farther down the Rhine, the Eburo′nes and Tungri at Tungern; the Guger′ni between the Maes and the Rhine; the Mena′pii to the south, and the Bata′vi to the north, of the mouth of the Rhine; the Caninefa′tes on the islands. Joining these to the west were the Toxan′dri and Mari′ni on the coast of the North Sea, at Dunkirk; to the south, the Atreba′tæ, the Atuat′ici, the Condru′si, the Cœre′sii, the Pœma′ni, the Nervii, the Veroman′dui at Vermandois, the Ambia′ni at Amiens, the Bellov′aci at Beauvais, the Suessio′nes at Soissons, the Valiocas′si, the Cal′eti, and other tribes. Although all these were generally denominated Belgæ, each was distinct from and independent of the other, nor were they even in alliance. They did not all belong to the Frankish nation, several of them having migrated from different parts of Germany, and some of them being Cimbri. Those tribes settled north of the Rhine were called Frisii. They subsisted chiefly on fish and wild beans. Their land was marshy and uncultivated, except in the high land in the southern parts, which now form the Walloon country. It was from the Romans that they learned the art of constructing dikes to protect themselves from the inundations of the sea. They were a very barbarous and warlike people, and were continually at feud with each other. Thus when Julius Cæsar invaded their country (B. C. 57), though he met with obstinate resistance, especially from the Menapii, who inhabited what is now the province of Flanders and the neighborhood of Antwerp, their valor was powerless against him. Fighting singly instead of in combination, they fell before him one by one, and he subdued the greater part of the Netherlands. Cæsar induced large numbers of them to enlist under his banners, and they proved the best cavalry in the Roman armies. But he behaved with perfidy and cruelty to the Teuc′teri and Usip′etes, who, driven across the Rhine by the Suevi, came to demand land of him. He arrested their leader, and killed his followers (B. C. 53). For this, Cato demanded that Cæsar should be given up to the Germans.

Whence do we derive our accounts of the early inhabitants?—Name the tribes.—What is said of them?—What did Cæsar do?—How did he act towards the Teucteri?

THE 1ST CENTURY

SYRIA.

Archela′us governed Judea with great injustice and cruelty. At the end of nine years (A. D. 6), he was summoned to Rome to answer the charges preferred against him by his brothers, as well as subjects. There he was tried and condemned, and banished to Vienne, in Gaul. Judea was then reduced to a Roman province. Thus the sceptre finally departed from Judah, and the kingdom of David, Solomon, the Asmonean princes, and Herod, became dependent on the Roman prefecture of Syria, though still remaining a subordinate district, ruled by its own governor. At this period the supreme judicial authority was exercised by the Sanhedrin, the great ecclesiastical and civil tribunal, at Jerusalem, composed of 71 persons, partly priests, partly Levites, partly elders. The high-priest usually sat as president: he was styled Nasi (prince). On his right hand sat the vice-president, styled Ab-beth-din (father of the council), and on his left "the wise man", or most learned doctor of the law. This court judged all capital offences, and inflicted punishment. It was also a court of appeal from the inferior Sanhedrins of 23 judges, in the other cities. The two prevailing religious sects were the Pharisees and the Sadducees. The name Pharisee is derived from a Hebrew word signifying *to separate:* the sect pretended to superior righteousness. The history of its origin is obscure, but it arose soon after the return from the captivity. The sect of the Sadducees was founded by Sadoc, or Tzadoc, about B. C. 260; they held that there was no resurrection, nor angel nor spirit, but the Pharisees believed in both (Acts xxiii. 8). The Essenes were a small sect, practising the strictest self-denial, having all things in common, and neither marrying nor carrying on trade. For a full account of this singular sect, see Milman's *History of the Jews*, vol. ii. book 12.

In the year 8, P. Sulpi′cius Quiri′nus was appointed to the prefecture of Syria, and Copo′nius to the subordinate one of Judea. In their time occurred the rebellion of Judas the Gaulonite, who incited the people to resist the making of the general census (or taxation, as it was called). This rebellion cost the lives of thousands of Jews, Judas himself perishing also. In A. D. 10 Coponius was succeeded by M. Ambiv′ius, and the latter by An′nius Rufus. On the removal of Rufus, the Emperor Tiberius appointed Vale′rius Gratus governor of Judea (A. D. 16), who distinguished himself by his extortions. He was succeeded (A. D. 27) by Pontius Pilate, a man of stern character. He displayed this in causing the massacre of all those who obstructed the building of an aqueduct to supply the city of Jerusalem with water. At this time the two sons of Herod reigned over their respective provinces; Herod An′tipas as tetrarch of Galilee, and Philip beyond Jordan. Herod married his niece, Hero′dias, — a marriage which was denounced by John the Baptist, who was put to death by the tyrant's order for reproving him thereupon (A. D. 29). The preaching of Jesus Christ commenced about the same time. It is not the province of this work to give the details of His mission: they will be found in the New Testament. His ministry occupied rather more than three years. His success excited the liveliest apprehensions among the Jews, and at their request He was crucified by order of Pontius Pilate (A. D. 33, according to the received chronology). On His death, His apostles and disciples dispersed themselves over the country, teaching His doctrines. Pilate was removed from his government by Vitell′ius, prefect of Syria (A. D. 36), on account of his cruelty to the people, and sent to Rome to answer the charges made against him by the Samaritan Senate. Vitellius visited Jerusalem, where he was received with great magnificence. He deposed Cai′aphas, the high-priest, and substituted Jonathan, the son of Annas, in the office. On a subsequent visit (A. D. 37), he deposed Jonathan and substituted his brother Theoph′ilus. On the death of Philip, Agrip′pa, the grandson of Herod the Great, was appointed ethnarch of the country beyond Jordan in his stead. On the deposition of Herod Antipas by the Emperor Caligula, his dominions were added to those of Agrippa. He was a mild ruler, and was the benefactor of the Jews on more than one occasion. Petronius, governor of Syria, having been commanded to place a statue of the Emperor Calig′ula in the Holy of Holies in the Temple at Jerusalem, the entire Jewish nation rose up to oppose the execution of the order, and horrible scenes would have ensued had not Agrippa, at the risk of his life, procured from the emperor a reversal of the decree. But he had the cruelty and weakness subsequently, in order to please the Jews, to put to death the Apostle James the Elder (A. D. 42), and imprison Peter (Acts xii. 2). The Jews suffered horrible persecution in Egypt, especially at Alexandria. Those settled in Mesopotamia were equally persecuted, and thousands were massacred. Judea was also a scene of bloodshed and confusion. On the assassination of Caligula (A. D. 41), Agrippa rendered great service to Claudius; in return for which the emperor conferred on him all the dominions which had belonged to the great Herod, with the title of king; and a decree was issued securing to the Jews throughout the empire the freedom of religious worship. Agrippa paid the greatest respect to the Jewish religion, and remitted many taxes. After a reign of three years over the whole of Palestine, he gave a grand banquet, at which he was seized with violent pains, and died in five days (A. D. 44). On his death Judea relapsed into a Roman province, and Cuspius Fadus was appointed governor. Fadus was succeeded by Tiberius Alexander (A. D. 46), Ventid′ius Cuma′nus (A. D. 46), and Claudius Felix (A. D. 52), the last of whom was guilty of the most flagrant crimes. The high-priest was assassinated in the Temple, with his connivance. At length Felix was recalled. Agrippa II. (son of the former Agrippa) was made king of Palestine by the Roman emperor, and the upright Por′cius Festus governor of Judea (A. D. 60), and the Jews enjoyed a brief repose. But Festus died (A. D. 62), and the tyranny of his successors, Albinus, and Gessius Florus, at length drove the Jews into rebellion; and in the year 66 the memorable war, so graphically recorded by the Jewish historian Josephus, broke out. It lasted four years, and was attended with all imaginable horrors; at the end of that time the Roman general, Titus, took and destroyed Jerusalem (A. D. 70), after a siege the horrors of which are unparallelled in history. Josephus affirms that 1,100,000 Jews perished during the war, and that 97,000 were taken captive. After the taking of Jerusalem, 11,000 voluntarily died of hunger, or were left by the Romans to starve. Only 700 persons above the age of 17 were reserved to grace the triumph of Titus; the rest were sent in chains to the Egyptian mines and quarries, or were left to fight with wild beasts. The remains of the city and the Temple were razed to the ground; the inhabitants of Judea were dispersed into other countries; the long-threatened vengeance of God was accomplished, and the Jews ceased to be a nation.

What befell Archelaus?—What was the Sanhedrin?—What were the Pharisees?—The Sadducees?—The Essenes?—What of the rebellion of Judas the Gaulonite?—What is said of Pontius Pilate?—Herod Antipas?—John the Baptist?—The ministry of Jesus Christ?—What did His apostles do?—What is related of Agrippa?—The sufferings of the Jews?—The death of Agrippa?—The governors of Judea?—Felix?—Agrippa II.?—Festus?—Florus?—The siege of Jerusalem?—The results of the war?—The end of the nationality of the Jews?

INDIA.

A flourishing trade with Rome is known to have existed in this century. About the year 47, Hip′palus, the commander of a trading vessel in the Red Sea, made his way across the ocean to Ceylon and the coast of Malabar, and returned after a most successful voyage.

The Apostle Thomas having made his way into Parthia and made many converts there, some of the latter travelled into India, where they introduced Christianity. It is supposed also that some of the Egyptian, Ethiopian, and Arabian converts came by sea to Hindostan, but their labors were not successful, and the Christian religion took no hold on the people at large. The historian Eusebius (*Eccles. Hist.*, v. 10) informs us that the Apostle Bartholomew visited India, but no trace of his labors is extant. These traditions rest upon very uncertain authority.

The principal personage in Indian history at this period (assuming that the tale of his wars with Chandragupta is fabulous) was Sa′livaha′na, prince of the Mahrattas, whose era begins from A. D. 77. He was a powerful monarch, yet scarcely one circumstance of his history has been preserved in an authentic or even credible form (Elphinstone, *Hist. of India*, vol. i. p. 423). He is said to have been the son of a potter; to have headed an insurrection, overturned a dynasty, and founded another; and to have established his capital at Paitan, on the Godavery. His empire was probably in the Deccan, where his name is still remembered, and his era in common use. After this period the history of Maharashtra (or the empire of the Mahrattas) breaks off, and we hear no more of that country until the beginning of the 12th century, when a family of Yadoos became Rajahs of Deogiri. In the year 1294 Maharashtra was invaded by the Mussulmans; in 1306 it was made tributary to them; and in 1317 it was entirely subdued.

Towards the close of this century, a prince of the northern division of the kingdom of Kerala brought from Northern India a colony of Brahmins, who, obtaining the mastery, divided the kingdom into 64 districts, and governed it by means of a general assembly of their caste, renting their lands to men of the inferior classes. The executive power was held by a Brahmin elected every three years, and assisted by a council of four.

What is said of the trade of India?—Which of the apostles visited India?—Who was Salivahana?—Where was his kingdom?—What became of it?—What happened in Kerala?

PERSIA.

Augustus Cæsar despatched his grandson, Caius, to settle matters with Phraates. The terror of the Roman arms induced the Parthian monarch to come to terms; and peace was concluded between him and Caius, in an interview which they held on a small island in the Euphrates. Phraates gave four of his sons as hostages to Augustus. He was a cruel tyrant, and was murdered by his Italian wife, Thermusa, and his son, Phraat′aces, who usurped the throne, but whose reign was of short duration, he being slain in a rebellion of his own subjects six months after his accession (A. D. 13). The Parthian nobility then elected Oro′des II. (a distant member of the royal family of Arsaces) for their king, but his outrageous barbarity caused them to put him to death (A. D. 14) very soon after. They then asked Augustus to send them one of the sons of Phraates whom he held as hostages, to rule over them. The emperor complied with their request, and sent them Vono′nes; but disgusted with his attempts to introduce refined manners amongst them, the Parthians revolted, and invited Artaba′nes, king of Media, to take his place. That prince accepted the invitation, and entered Persia with an army to enforce his authority. Vonones bravely encountered and defeated him, but losing a second battle, he fled into Armenia, and Artabanes took possession of the kingdom of the Parthians. The unhappy Vonones applied to the Emperor Tiberius for aid, and gave himself up to the Roman governor of Syria. He was kept in confinement, and was killed in trying to escape.

The reign of Artabanes II. was full of those events which constitute the staple of Oriental history, viz., revolts and intrigues, and acts of cruelty and perfidy. One of the most remarkable occurrences was the rebellion of two Jews, named Asinai and Asilai, who contrived by their valor to conciliate the king, and get themselves appointed governors of Babylon, which post they retained for 15 years. But their subsequent misconduct involved them in war with the neighboring chieftains, and was the cause not only of their own destruction, but of that of the Babylonian Jews, thousands of whom were massacred. Artabanes being guilty of great cruelty, Phraates was invited to come from Rome, and retake the kingdom. The Emperor Tiberius aided him, but he died on his arrival in Syria. Upon this the emperor set up Tirida′tes, another of the descendants of Arsaces, and he being supported by the leading Parthian chiefs, dethroned Artabanes. But these fickle and perfidious Orientals could not act loyally towards any one; and no sooner was Tiridates crowned than they recalled Artabanes; but it was through the mediation of Iza′tes, king of Adiabe′ne, that he regained his kingdom. From this time he governed with great equity, and died generally lamented, leaving seven sons, of whom he selected Barda′nes (or Vardanes) to be his successor (A. D. 43). The succession was disputed by these sons, but Bardanes, the second son, having set aside his elder brother, Gutar′zes, ascended the throne. The Roman historian, Tacitus, however, says that Gutarzes and Bardanes were the brothers of Artabanes; and that the former voluntarily resigned in favor of the latter, whom he deemed most worthy of the kingdom (*Annals*, book xi. c. viii.). Bardanes met with the common fate of Oriental sovereigns, and was assassinated (A. D. 47). Gutarzes now claimed the throne, and indeed actually took possession of it, but the Parthians applied to the Emperor Claudius to appoint them a king. He accordingly nominated Meherda′tes, the grandson of Phraates IV., then a hostage at Rome; but Meherdates, on his journey to Parthia, was betrayed into the hands of Gutarzes by Ab′garus, king of Edessa, his army was cut to pieces, and himself sent prisoner to Persia. Gutarzes died A. D. 50. His successor, Vonones II., reigned but a few months, and was succeeded by his son, Volog′eses I. (A. D. 51). This prince appointed his legitimate brothers, Pac′orus, king of Media, and Tiridates, king of Armenia. Vologeses is celebrated for the skill with which he conducted war with the Romans, and for his successful attempt to establish his brother, Tiridates, on the throne of Armenia, which he accomplished by sending him with a splendid embassy to Nero (A. D. 63), who confirmed him in his possessions. With the exception of an inroad from the Alans, one of the fiercest of the Scythian tribes, the remainder of the reign of Vologeses was peaceful. He died about the year 90, and was succeeded by his son, Artabanes III., who dying soon after, left the throne to his son, Pacorus. But little is known of this prince, except that he maintained strict friendship with the Romans during the whole of his reign.

How did Augustus interfere in the affairs of Persia?—What befell Phraates?—Orodes II.?—Vonones?—Artabanes?—What of Asinai and Asilai?—And the result of their rebellion?—Of the Emperor Tiberius?—Tiridates?—And the reign of Artabanes?—Bardanes?—Gutarzes?—What does Tacitus say?—What of the reign of Vologeses?—Pacorus?

CHINA. JAPAN.

Wang-mang was now in reality emperor. He stopped at nothing in the pursuit of money; but he was liberal of his treasures, and patronized learning. He raised the descendants of Confucius of the sixteenth generation to very high rank, which has from that time been hereditary. His ambition led him to poison the Emperor Ping-te (A. D. 5), whereby he obtained the regency of the empire, as guardian of the heir, Soo-tsze-ying, a child two years old. However, he soon threw off the mask, declared himself emperor, and degraded all the descendants of the Han family to the rank of common people. The Han princes resorted to arms, and a fierce civil war ensued, which ended in the death of Wang-mang, and the elevation of Wae-yang-wang to the throne (A. D. 23). But the country was reduced to a state of anarchy, and the brief reign of Wae-yang-wang was occupied in continual warfare with the leaders of factions. Lew-sew, his successor (A. D. 25), was forced upon the throne by the soldiers, and took the name of Kwang-woo. He was the first of the Eastern Han dynasty, and was a man of great ability. His reign was a glorious one of 32 years, during which he sustained the dignity of the empire amidst great troubles. He suppressed a formidable insurrection in Cochin China, and kept in check the barbarians on the frontiers. His son, Ming-te, who succeeded him (A. D. 58), was well versed in the learning of his country, and encouraged schools; but he caused the introduction into China from Hindostan, of the religion of Budha, an absurd system of idolatry and atheism. It is recorded that he did this in consequence of a vision which brought to his mind the saying of Confucius: "The Holy One is in the West!" He sent into Hindostan a deputation, which returned with Ho-shang, a Budhist priest, several of the Budhist classics, and a portrait of Budha. This system unfortunately took root in China, where it has maintained its ground up to the present day; an account of it will be found in pp. 55, 74. The reign of Ming-te, as well as that of his successor, Chang-te, who ascended the throne A. D. 73, was disturbed by continual wars with the Tartars. According to Syrian tradition, St. Thomas preached Christianity throughout China, and travelled as far as Pekin in this reign. Under Ho-te, the next emperor (A. D. 89), Tow-hëen, the brother of the empress, routed the Tartars with great slaughter. He penetrated a great distance into their country, and erected on a lofty mountain a monument recording the valor and victory of the Chinese troops. Tow-hëen was made a field marshal of the empire, but behaved with such arrogance that he and his family were all degraded and exiled, with the exception of Tow-kwo, at whose instigation Ho-te introduced the pernicious custom of raising worthless favorites to the highest offices of State, — a custom which subsequently caused the ruin of many an emperor. Under the reign of Ho-te, lived the celebrated lady, Pan-hwuy-pan, sister to the historian Pan-koo. She was famous for her learning, and jointly with her brother wrote a history of China, commencing with the reign of Kaou-tsoo, B. C. 206, and ending with that of Wang-mang, A. D. 23. She was the leading star of the Imperial Court, and was the author of "Instructions for females in seven rules." In this work, so famed in China, she asserts that the female is the lowest of the human species; that to her belongs the execution of inferior duties; that she ought to be the abject slave of her husband; that all she has belongs to him; that he may marry as many wives as he pleases, but that in a woman a second marriage is criminal. In one passage she says: "Formerly, when a daughter was born she was laid on the ground upon rags, where she was for three days forgotten and neglected; on the third day her father presented her to the family, whilst he laid before her some bricks, her only toys. Think on the degraded state, young ladies, which nature has assigned to you, and fulfil your duties accordingly." Such are the sentiments of China's greatest daughter upon her own sex! She died in the 70th year of her age, universally regretted, and has been ever since held up as the pattern of a wife and a mother.

Japan. — The reign of Sy-nin is full of marvels, according to the Japanese historians. In his time the people began to make fish-ponds and cultivate rice. In the year 66, Bupo, or Kobat, came from India, and brought with him, on a white horse, a book containing the mysteries of his religion. A temple, which is still standing, was erected to him. Sy-nin reigned 98 years, and was 139 years old at the time of his death (A. D. 71). His son, Key-ko, succeeded him on the throne.

What of the descendants of Confucius?—Of the Han family?—Who founded the Eastern Han dynasty?—Who introduced Budhism?—Why?—What is the tradition respecting St. Thomas?—What were the acts of Ho-te?—Who was Pan-hwuy-pan?—What were her doctrines?—What of the history of Japan?

ITALY.

At the commencement of this century the boundaries of the Roman empire were the Atlantic Ocean on the west; the Rhine, the Danube, the Black Sea, and the chain of Mount Caucasus, on the north; the River Euphrates on the east; and the Syrian deserts in Asia, and the sandy desert in Africa, on the south. Thus the empire included the fairest portions of the known world surrounding the Mediterranean Sea. At the time of the birth of Christ there was no war of any consequence raging in any part of the empire: the temple of Janus at Rome was shut, to denote the prevalence of peace; and the only troubles that clouded the emperor's prosperity were the dissolute conduct of his daughter, Julia, and the sinister character of his step-son, Tiberius, who was generally regarded as his successor. The condition of the imperial family was melancholy, and was but too faithful a reflex of the general depravity of the Roman people. The Empress Liv′ia was an artful, dissembling woman, who pandered to the vices of Augustus, and trained her sons, Tiberius and Drusus, to every species of deception. Augustus, however, was not blind to her character, nor to that of her sons, and he became anxious to settle the succession to the empire on a more worthy stock than his step-sons. Having no male heirs, he gave his daughter, Julia, to his sister Octavia's son, Marcellus, a man universally beloved. But Marcellus died soon after, and Augustus then caused Agrippa to marry Julia. All his efforts, however, to prevent Tiberius from succeeding him proved fruitless in the end: for in a few years Agrippa and his two worthless sons, Caius and Lucius, died, and then there was no competitor left. The state of public morality at Rome, under Augustus, was frightful, though the emperor was not by any means so dissolute as his nobles. He was a man of a cold, unimpressionable nature, and of a cautious and calculating temper: hence his success over the wild and reckless Mark Antony. The Roman grandees spread over all countries, carrying with them the luxuries and elegancies of life, and diffusing a knowledge of the arts. The wealth of many of them was enormous; and they covered Italy with magnificent villas, gardens, monuments, etc.; yet, with all their taste and profusion, it appears that the usurious loaning of money was a common method of increasing their wealth.

It was just at the time when the last traces of the Roman republic had disappeared that those nations which afterwards overthrew the empire first showed themselves as formidable foes. The U′bii, Vangi′ones, Trib′oci, and Nem′etes, formed settlements on the left or western bank of the Rhine, and gradually adopted Roman habits. But those who dwelt on the right bank were fierce barbarians; and even the bold Agrippa, who for some time held the chief command in Gaul, shrunk from a contest with them. They made several incursions into the Roman territories, and on one occasion (B. C. 16), they defeated and killed the consul, Lollius. Tiberius and Drusus had been sent against them, and in several successful campaigns had kept them in check, erecting a whole chain of military posts on the right bank of the Rhine. Alliances had been made with several of the northern tribes, and Roman habits and luxuries introduced. Thus a peace of several years' duration was effected, and the Romans carried their dominion into the heart of Germany, but also took with them their characteristic arrogance and cruelty, which soon produced a revulsion.

The peace of the empire was first interrupted by a sudden outbreak of the German tribes, followed by a revolt of the Dalmatians and Pannonians. Tiberius marched against the latter, and Germán′icus, the son of Drusus, and nephew of Tiberius, was sent into Germany to assist the governor, Quintil′ius Va′rus, whose extortions had provoked the revolt. Armin′ius (or Hermann), a young prince of the Cherusci, who had been educated in Italy, united his countrymen in a confederacy, and pretending friendship for Varus, led him and his army into the forest of the Teutoberg, and cut them to pieces: 24,000 Romans perished with their leader (A. D. 9). This was the greatest defeat the Romans had sustained since that of Crassus at Carrhæ, sixty-two years before. The emperor gave himself up to transports of grief, exclaiming repeatedly, "Give me back my legions, Varus!" The utmost consternation prevailed in Rome, and the severest measures were taken to fill up the ranks of the legions in Italy; but it now became apparent that the citizens and the people of Italy no longer constituted the main strength of the Roman armies. The historian, Dion Cassius, informs us that there were no vigorous young men left in Rome, so universal was the depravity of morals. Such troops as could be raised were sent to Tiberius, who, having been successful in Dalmatia, was now despatched to assist Germanicus in Germany. He advanced to the Rhine, but did not attempt to recover the posts lost in Central Germany, and he soon afterwards returned to Rome, leaving Germanicus to prosecute the war. On the death of Augustus, Tiberius was proclaimed emperor (A. D. 14). Tiberius Claudius Nero commenced his reign by procuring the murder of Marcus Agrippa, grandson of the late emperor, whom he dreaded as a rival claimant of the empire. The German and Pannonian legions mutinied, and threatened to place Germanicus on the throne; but this mutiny was quelled by Drusus, the son of the emperor, and by Germanicus himself, whose destruction was, however, resolved on by Tiberius. After several successful campaigns against the Germans, Germanicus was recalled to Rome, where he was received in triumph; but he was not suffered to remain there, for Tiberius sent him into Asia (A. D. 17). He there subdued Armenia (A. D. 18), and afterwards visited Egypt, where he died (A. D. 19), it is supposed, by poison. His ashes were brought to Rome by his widow, Agrippi′na, and the whole city went into mourning. After this, Tiberius began to indulge his natural cruelty, and put to death many nobles on the ground of high treason, but his depravity was exceeded by that of his minister, the infamous Seja′nus, whose name has passed into a proverb. This monster secretly aspired to the empire, and, to further his designs, persuaded Tiberius to retire to the isle of Ca′preæ, where he led a life of the most disgusting sensuality. Sejanus procured the murder of Drusus (A. D. 23), the son of Tiberius, and put to death the most eminent Romans on frivolous pretexts. He established a complete reign of terror, and aimed at seizing the empire; but at last the eyes of the emperor were opened, and he suddenly caused Sejanus to be put to death, together with all his relations and friends (A. D. 31). After this event, the cruelty of Tiberius increased tenfold, but his constitution was undermined by debauchery; finding himself dying, he bequeathed the empire to Caius, the surviving son of his nephew, Germanicus (A. D. 37). Believing the emperor to be dead, Caius at once assumed the throne, but had no sooner done so than he learned that Tiberius still lived. In this dilemma extreme measures were necessary, and the feeble old emperor was smothered by the advice of Macro, commander of the Prætorian guards. Caius, nicknamed Calig′ula (from "caligæ", the military boots that he wore), was then formally proclaimed emperor. The reign of Tiberius is memorable to Christians as that in which the ministry and the crucifixion of Christ took place (A. D. 29–33).

Caius began his reign by liberating all State prisoners, but had not been long on the throne before he was seized with a sickness which disordered his brain. On his recovery he was guilty of the wildest extravagances and cruelties. His first victim was Tiberius, the son of Drusus. He then ordered all the prisoners in Rome to be thrown to wild beasts, and amused himself by witnessing their sufferings. He wantonly put to death the rich for the sake of confiscating their property; and entertained the people with feasts and shows daily. He proclaimed himself a god, and erected a temple to himself. He made his favorite horse, "Incitatus", dine at the same table with himself, giving him gilt oats and costly wine, and seriously proposed to raise him to the consulship. At length the Romans became weary of his insanity, and he was slain in one of the passages of the circus by Cheræa, captain of the Prætorian guards (A. D. 41). The conspirators raised Claudius, his uncle, a man of weak intellect, to the throne. This prince became the puppet of wicked favorites, the most infamous of whom were the Empress Messali′na, and the ministers, Posi′des, Pallas, and Narcissus. Claudius Cæsar undertook a campaign into Britain, which island he subdued (A. D. 43), and was greeted with a magnificent triumph on his return. In the year A. D. 48 a census was taken, which showed that there were six millions of Roman citizens. In the same year the infamy of the Empress Messalina had reached to such a height that she was divorced by the emperor, and put to death. Soon after this he married his niece, Agrippina, the widow of Domi′tius A′henobar′bus, a woman of insatiable avarice, ambition, and cruelty. She prevailed on the emperor to adopt her son, Nero, and make him heir to the throne, in preference to his own son, Britan′nicus, whom she subsequently poisoned. The enormous crimes which these two wives of Claudius

What were the boundaries of the empire at the beginning of this century?—What of the temple of Janus?—What were the drawbacks to the emperor's happiness?—What of his family?—Of the morality of the people?—Their luxuriousness?—The barbarians on the Rhine?—Germanicus?—Arminius?—The legions of Varus?—The decay of the Romans?

Who succeeded Augustus?—What befell Marcus Agrippa?—What were the exploits of Germanicus?—What was his end?—What of Tiberius and Sejanus?—Drusus?—Caius?—The death of Tiberius?—For what is his reign memorable?—What nickname was given to Caius?—What cruelties did he commit?—What of Claudius?—Messalina?—Agrippina?

committed cannot here be specified. The imbecile emperor, to divert his mind from their intrigues, was persuaded to undertake enormously expensive public works. He completed the great Claudian aqueduct, rebuilt the theatre of Pompey, drained Lake Fuci′nus, excavated a harbor at Ostia, and erected a lighthouse there. The draining of the lake occupied 30,000 men eleven years. Agrippina is remembered as having founded Colonia Agrippina (Cologne), on the Rhine (A. D. 50), but she was possessed by all the vices of which a woman is capable. Finding that Claudius showed signs of changing the succession, she caused him to be poisoned (A. D. 54), and her son, Nero Claudius Cæsar, to be proclaimed emperor. About this time Christianity was introduced into Rome by converts from Asia Minor. It rapidly spread, notwithstanding the opposition of the priests of the old religion. Nursed in the midst of crimes, Nero cared only for the indulgence of his passions. He murdered Britannicus, and, at the suggestion of an infamous woman named Poppæa Sabina, caused his mother, Agrippina, to be put to death. He had the unblushing audacity to publish an apology for this murder; and it is melancholy to think that this work was the production of the philosopher, Sen′eca, the tutor of Nero. He then divorced and afterwards murdered his wife, Octavia, and married Poppæa. He appointed Tigelli′nus, an infamous wretch, and a panderer to his vices, his minister, and now no longer kept within the bounds of decency. He appeared as a singer on the stage at Naples. He caused Rome to be set on fire, and on the ruins of the city erected a vast palace, so profusely embellished as to be styled "The Golden House". He accused the Christians of having set fire to the city, and commenced a cruel persecution against them. Some were put to the torture; others were covered with the skins of wild beasts, and torn to pieces by dogs; or crucified; or wrapped up in combustible garments, which were set on fire. Nero lent his own gardens to the public for these frightful exhibitions (A. D. 64–66). In this persecution, the Apostles Peter and Paul, the philosopher Seneca, the poet Lucan, and other eminent men, perished. Nero, having killed the Empress Poppæa by a kick, passed over into Greece to exhibit his musical skill at the Olympic games, and took that opportunity of plundering the Grecian cities. His friends were now selected from among the lowest profligates. The banquets given by Tigellinus surpassed in luxury all that had previously been known. Petronius was made *Arbiter elegantiarum*, or master of the imperial pleasures, and the emperor gave loose to all sorts of excesses. To such a length did he push the indulgence of his wild caprices, that it seemed as though the machine of State would come to a stand-still. The discontent of the soldiery became ominous, and the emperor was so unwise as to keep them long in arrear of their pay: mutiny took place at different points on the frontier. A revolt broke out in Judea (A. D. 66), which Vespasian was sent to quell. Several conspiracies were organized in Italy, but a far more formidable and extensive one broke out in Gaul and Spain. In Gaul, the revolt, headed by Julius Vindex, was suppressed by Verginius. Sulpicius Galba, governor of Hither Spain, having been sentenced to death by Nero without a hearing, was proclaimed emperor by his soldiers, and supported by Otho, governor of Lusitania. The Prætorian guards at Rome having joined his cause, he was acknowledged emperor by the Senate. Nero fled from Rome, and killed himself (A. D. 68). During his reign Armenia was added to the empire by Domitius Cor′bulo; and the insurrection in Britain, under Boadi′cea, was quelled by Suetonius Pauli′nus; but other provinces were harassed by frequent revolts. Nero was popular amongst the lower classes, whom he bribed by large monthly distributions of corn and wine. The direct line of the Cæsars ended with Nero.

Servius Sulpicius Galba, the 7th emperor, was descended from an illustrious family, but was 63 years of age, and in failing health, and therefore unable to restrain the violent passions which animated all parties. His first step was to put to death Nymphid′ius, who commanded the guards, and had offered every soldier a heavy bribe to support Galba, but who had conducted himself as absolute master of Rome. This man and his adherents were slaughtered, and the promised bribe was never paid. Several other executions took place, and these, together with the emperor's avarice and ill health, increased the general gloom and discontent. The legions in Upper Germany demanded a younger emperor. Galba, deprived by the gout of the use of his hands and feet, resolved to elect a colleague and successor. His favorites, Vin′ius, Laco, and I′celus, advised him to choose Otho, the favorite of the guards of Nero, and the companion of his excesses; but Galba chose Piso Licinia′nus, a man of unblemished character, and presented him to the soldiery as his successor, but he did not comply with the custom of giving a donation to the troops on the occasion. Otho, taking advantage of this, by extensive bribery gained the good-will of the soldiers and the people, and formed a conspiracy to assassinate the emperor and Piso while engaged in a solemn sacrifice. It is said that Otho became irresolute when the hour for executing the plot arrived, but his comrades forced him to stand to his purpose. Both Galba and Piso were slain by them (A. D. 69), and Otho was raised to the throne. He was hailed as emperor by the legions in Syria, Palestine, and Egypt. Meanwhile the German legions proclaimed their commander, Vitellius, a man of notorious vices, emperor; and the principal towns in Gaul also declared in his favor. But he was deficient in activity and decision, and wholly given up to excesses in the pleasures of the table. One of his lieutenants, Fabius Valens, therefore, took his place at the head of the legions, and won all France; while another, A. Cæci′na, did the same in Upper Germany: the legions in England, Spain, and Upper Italy proclaimed Vitellius emperor, and Cæcina and Valens marched into Italy. Otho was incompetent to meet the emergency: he was no general, and too effeminate to be a soldier; yet his troops were heartily devoted to him, and urged him to meet his enemies. But he made not the slightest effort to aid his own cause: he took no part in the military movements, nor in the battle which decided his fate. His troops met the lieutenants of Vitellius at Bedri′acum, on the banks of the Po, where they were entirely defeated. Otho committed suicide that same night, having reigned only three months; and was subsequently extolled for having purchased with his life the blessings of peace and tranquillity for his country. Vitellius, the 9th emperor, was a slave to gluttony and debauchery, and is said to have squandered $35,000,000 on the pleasures of the table in less than four months. But fortunately his reign was destined to be a short one. Vespasian, who was carrying on the war in Judea against the revolted Jews with great success, was requested by his army to declare himself emperor, which, after some hesitation, he did; and thereupon commenced his march towards Europe. The provinces, one after the other, declared in his favor. Antoninus Primus, and Varus, at the head of the Illyrian legions, crossed the Alps, took Ravenna and Cremona, and routing the forces of Vitellius there, marched on to Rome. Antoninus Primus, wishing to spare the city, opened negotiations with Vitellius, who pusillanimously abdicated. So low had the emperor fallen in public esteem, that his own mother put an end to herself to avoid witnessing his downfall. But his depraved soldiery forced him to place himself at their head; and, attacking the adherents of Vespasian, drove them into the capitol, and set fire to the city. Sabinus, the brother of Vespasian, was killed; but Antoninus forced an entrance into the city, and cut to pieces the riotous troops of Vitellius, who also perished in the massacre. This success was followed by merciless executions and exactions, which were not stopped until the new emperor reached Rome. The civil war began in October, but the city was not completely subdued until December, A. D. 69. Immediately after that event, the Senate, by a formal decree, transferred to the new emperor all the rights which had belonged to the people and the Senate during the continuance of the republican Constitution. Tranquillity was restored by the arrival of Vespasian, whose virtues and firmness led to great reforms in the social condition of the empire. His first care was to restore order in the finances, and discipline in the army. He disbanded the mutinous soldiers of Vitellius; rebuilt the streets of Rome, which Nero had left in ruins; and collected and restored the numerous tables on which the decrees of the Senate and people had been engraved. He restored to the Senate its ancient rights, and formed it into an imperial council, augmenting the number of members, and expelling the unworthy ones. He set an example in his own person of morality and sobriety; and presented himself to the Romans as the first of the Senators only, never as an absolute ruler. But he was accused of avarice, and of driving a traffic in places, public offices, and privileges, and of participating in the profits of them. His son, Titus, concluded the Jewish war by the capture and destruction of Jerusalem, and dispersion of the Jews (A. D. 70). The victories of Cerea′lis

What is said of the acts and death of Claudius?—What of Britannicus?—Nero?—Poppæa?—Seneca?—Tigellinus?—What excesses was Nero guilty of?—What is said of Petronius Arbiter?—Galba?—Otho?—The death of Nero?—What were the acts of Galba?—What was his end?

What is said of Vitellius?—Otho's supineness?—His end?—Who was Vespasian?—What of Antoninus Primus?—Varus?—The mother of Vitellius?—The siege of Rome?—The death of Vitellius?—What were the first acts of Vespasian?—What of his private character?—What of his son Titus?

over the Batavians, and their confederates, restored peace on the German frontier. The conquest of the island of Britain was completed by Agricola (A. D. 78), who introduced many useful arts there. Vespasian restored the capitol at Rome, and began the Colosse′um; but his close attention to business brought on a mortal disease, and he died A. D. 79, being the second of the Roman emperors who had died a natural death, and the first who was succeeded by his son. Titus, the 11th emperor, was a most amiable prince, and widely celebrated for his clemency and charity; but the Christians still suffered persecutions, and Linus, the first bishop of Rome, was put to death. From the rigorous mode in which he administered the government as prefect and lieutenant of his father, combined with the licentiousness of his private character, the people expected of him a second Nero. But the moment he assumed the imperial government he gave up every private passion and pleasure, and devoted himself wholly to the welfare of the empire. He repudiated Berenice, the daughter of Herod Agrippa, and permitted no secret influence to guide his conduct. In his time (August 23d, A. D. 79), the cities of Herculaneum and Pompeii were destroyed by an eruption of Mount Vesuvius, and the celebrated Pliny was smothered in the ashes. Rome also was devastated by fire and pestilence. The death of Titus was attributed to poison, administered to him (A. D. 81) by his brother and successor, Flav′ius Domi′tian. This prince completed the public works begun by Titus, and for a short time emulated his brother's virtues. The historian Suetonius informs us that Domitian kept in such control the higher class of official personages, of whom the Senate principally consisted, that no one, either in Rome or in the provinces, dared to neglect his duty; and the public functionaries never were more incorrupt than under his government. He cleared away the nuisances of informers and calumniators, forwarded the course of justice, and, during the first years of his reign, was not only free from all imputation of avarice, but splendid and generous. During these years he issued a number of excellent regulations; but found, to his disheartenment, that he made but few friends among the upper classes. This discovery seems to have paved the way for his subsequent change of conduct. He began by endeavoring to win the people by shows, entertainments, and games; and he enormously increased the pay of the soldiery. At length his real character developed itself, and he ultimately launched into the most horrible excesses. His fury was aroused by the repeated disasters sustained by his armies from the Germans. He now gave loose to the cruelty of his disposition, and expelled all philosophers from Rome. The Da′cians, under their gallant king, Deceb′alus, invaded the empire (A. D. 86–91), and Domitian purchased a disgraceful peace by agreeing to pay them tribute. He ordered the second persecution of the Christians (A. D. 95), because they refused to contribute to the rebuilding of the temple of Jupiter Capitoli′nus. It would be useless to enumerate his cruelties, or to describe his malice in inventing tortures. He kept the Senate and all who surrounded him in a continual state of terror: none could approach him but those employed in executing his merciless commands. But these creatures became the instruments of his destruction, instigated by the Empress Domitia, who accidentally discovered the intention of the emperor to put her and others to death, whereupon she caused him to be assassinated (A. D. 96). But the Prætorian guards were so much attached to him that they put to death all those who took part in his murder. The Senate and the upper classes were overjoyed at his death, but the people and the army mourned for him. He was the twelfth and last of the emperors commonly called "the twelve Cæsars". He was succeeded by Marcus Cocceius Nerva, who was elected emperor by the Senate. He was a native of Umbria, and the first foreigner who became emperor. He was an able and wise man, but too aged to encounter the disorders which the soldiers and people indulged in on account of his curtailing their amusements, and reducing the public expenditure. His commands were defied, and his authority disregarded. Under these circumstances he resolved to adopt a young and able colleague in the empire, and selected Marcus Ulpius Trajan, a Spaniard, who was on his way to Rome, having been victorious over the Pannonians. He could not have made a better choice, for Trajan was beloved by the army, and feared by the people. Trajan was elected in October, A. D. 97, and all disorders ceased. He fixed his residence in Rome, with Pliny and Tacitus for his friends, about a year after the death of Nerva (A. D. 98). The latter reigned but 16 months, and Trajan succeeded him as sole emperor without opposition. The persecution of the Christians was renewed: one of the principal victims being Clement, bishop of Rome, who was cast into the sea with an anchor around his neck. Trajan was one of the greatest and best of the emperors of Rome. He reverenced law and order, and was possessed of much goodness of heart. He had been trained in a pure and hardy course of life, and hence he was active and capable of sustaining the greatest fatigue. But his martial education unfortunately led him to imagine that the defence of the empire could be best promoted by extending its limits, and that the public morals could be improved by exciting a passion for military glory. Hence arose the evils of his reign.

A number of eminent literary and scientific men flourished under the Roman sway during this century: L. Annæus Seneca was a native of Cordova, in Spain. He studied rhetoric and philosophy, and became tutor to Nero, whose vicious propensities he endeavored to check. He was, however, a parasite and avaricious. Having amassed a fortune, he was stripped of it by Nero, who also caused him to be put to death. He wrote many essays on philosophical subjects. M. Fabius Quintilia′nus (Quintilian) was born at Calahorra, in Spain, A. D. 40. He became a famous teacher of eloquence at Rome, and wrote a work on rhetoric. He died A. D. 118. Epicte′tus, of Hierap′olis, in Phrygia, was a celebrated philosopher, and the originator of the Stoic philosophy. He lived in the time of Domitian, and did not leave many works behind him. Plutarch, of Chæronæa, in Greece, flourished in the reigns of Nero and Domitian. He wrote the famous work named "Parallel Lives" of forty-six eminent Greeks and Romans, popularly known as "Plutarch's Lives". He also wrote about sixty ethical and other essays. Cornelius Tacitus, the greatest of Roman historians, lived during the reigns of Domitian and Trajan. The date and place of his birth are unknown. His principal works were an account of the German tribes, "Annals of Rome" under the Cæsars, and the life of Agricola. Dion Chrysostom, of Prusa, in Bithynia, an eminent orator, and the author of numerous orations or essays. Velleius Pater′culus (born B. C. 19, in Campania) was the author of a history of Rome. He was, probably, massacred along with the friends of Sejanus. Strabo, of Amasia, in Pontus (born about B. C. 54, died A. D. 24), was a distinguished historian and geographer. Pomponius Mela wrote a treatise on geography. He was a native of Spain, and lived in the reign of Claudius. M. Annæus Lucanus (Lucan), the poet, was born at Cordova, in Spain, A. D. 39. His great work was the "Pharsalia", a heroic poem, in ten books, relating to the war between Cæsar and Pompey. He committed suicide A. D. 65. M. Valerius Martia′lis (Martial), the epigrammatic poet, was born at Bibilis, in Spain, A. D. 43. He wrote upwards of 1500 short poems. Persius Flaccus (born in Etruria, A. D. 34) was the author of many able satires. Petronius (surnamed Arbiter, from his having been constituted director and judge of the imperial pleasures) was an intimate companion of Nero. He wrote a work called "Satyricon", depicting the vices of the age: and committed suicide to avoid being accused of treason. Decimus Junius Juvenalis (Juvenal), the great Roman satirist, flourished at the close of this century. But little is known of his life. Phædrus, a Thracian slave, freed by the Emperor Augustus, was the author of a number of fables composed in verse. Publius Papinius Statius (born at Naples, A. D. 61; died A. D. 96) was the author of poems styled respectively "Sylvæ", "Thebais", and "Achilleis", the last two being heroic poems of considerable merit. Silius Italicus, who flourished under Vitellius, wrote an epic poem on the second Punic war. Valerius Flaccus, a native of Mantua, wrote a heroic poem on the Argonautic expedition. C. Plinius Secundus (commonly called Pliny the Elder) was one of the most eminent literary men of his time. He wrote several works, the principal one being his "Natural History". He perished in the eruption of Vesuvius, which overwhelmed Herculaneum and Pompeii, A. D. 79. His nephew, Pliny the Younger, was a very learned man: his letters to Trajan and others contain most valuable information. Cornelius Celsus wrote a valuable work on medicine: he lived in the time of Tiberius Cæsar. Florus, the historian; Columella, the agriculturist; Frontinus, the author of works on war and architecture; and Apollonius, of Tyana, who pretended to work miracles—all flourished in this century.

What is remarked of the death of Vespasian?—What was the character of Titus?—What of Herculaneum and Pompeii?—Titus's death?—Domitian?—His change of character?—Decebalus?—What cruelties did Domitian commit?—What was his end?—Of what was he the last?—What of Nerva?—Trajan?—His character?

What of Seneca?—Quintilian?—Epictetus?—Plutarch?—Tacitus?—Dion Chrysostom?—Velleius Paterculus?—Strabo?—Pomponius Mela?—Lucan?—Martial?—Persius?—Petronius Arbiter?—Juvenal?—Phædrus?—Statius?—Silius Italicus?—Valerius Flaccus?—Pliny the Elder?—Pliny the Younger?—Celsus?—Florus?—Columella?—Frontinus?

BRITAIN.

NGLAND. — Cymbeline (or Cunob'eline) having banished his son Admin'- this young prince went to Rome, and there made a surrender of the whole ad to the Emperor Caligula (A. D. 40). This was succeeded by a real sion by the Emperor Claudius, instigated by Beric, a British chieftain who been expelled from his native country. The Britons, under the command 'ARAC'TACUS and Togidum'nus, the sons of Cymbeline, offered a brave re- nce to the Romans, who were commanded by the Emperor Claudius in per- but they were forced to submit (A. D. 43). Geoffrey of Monmouth and the r British historians, who have copied him, tell us that the sons of Cymbeline named Guide'rius and Arvir'agus; that Guiderius was assassinated by a y Roman named Hamo, who was subsequently slain by Arviragus at South- ton; that Arviragus submitted to Claudius, and helped him to conquer the ney islands; that he married the emperor's daughter, Genuis'sa; again re- ed; was defeated by Vespasian at Exeter; made peace, and reigned quietly he end of his days, leaving his kingdom to his son, Marius. But nearly the le narrative is fictitious. Claudius returned to Rome, leaving an army under 'tius and Vespa'sian to subdue the island. Vespasian fought 30 battles re he could subdue the southern portion of it; while Plautius was for five s as obstinately resisted by Caractacus, at the head of the Cassii and Silures. rius Scap'ula, the successor of Plautius, moulded the reduced tribes into a an province, and planted colonies of soldiers in different parts of the island D. 50). But the Silu'res, under Caractacus, determined to hold out to the fortified themselves in Shropshire, at a place still remembered by the name 'aer Car'adoc, where a bloody battle was fought, in which the Romans were orious. Caractacus was made prisoner and sent in chains to Rome, where was generously received and restored to liberty. Ostorius Scapula was suc- ed in the government of Britain by Aulus Didius, Vera'nius, and Sueto'nius li'nus. The latter general attacked Mona (Anglesey), the retreat of the ids, whom he there destroyed, and he struck at their power a blow from h it never recovered (A. D. 61). In the same year an insurrection of the i, a British tribe, headed by their heroic queen, BOADI'CEA, broke out. Roman colony at Verulam was destroyed by these insurgents, but they were lly routed at Sunbury; 80,000 were slain, and Boadicea put an end to her life. In this century Christianity was first introduced into Britain. It is that the Apostle SIMON ZELOTES was the first who introduced it, and that uffered martyrdom in England. This is extremely doubtful, but Christian- vas certainly diffused by Christian soldiers in the Roman armies. The coun- was finally subdued by the famous CNEIUS JULIUS AGRIC'OLA (A. D. 78–84), reconciled, by his enlightened government, to the Roman yoke. The island divided by him into six provinces, and civil order was firmly established. don is spoken of as being at this time a flourishing trading city.

OTLAND.—The reigns of Metellan, Carat'acus, and Corbred I., were peace- and prosperous. Dardan, a mad tyrant, was slain after a reign of four years. successor, Corbred II., surnamed "Galgus" or "Gal'gacus" (A. D. 76), was ble prince, and acquired great renown by his valor against the Romans dur- the invasion of Scotland by that people under Agricola. He distinguished self greatly, and even after his total defeat in the battle of the Grampians, contrived to sustain the spirits of his countrymen, and finally expelled the nans from Scotland. He died after a reign of 35 years.

ELAND.—CON'ARY THE GREAT, and CRIM'THAN, were the most eminent mon- s of this century. The island was never attacked by the Romans, though icola had planned its invasion. Under the auspices of CONQUOVAR', king 'lster, a digest of the ancient laws was made, which code was called "the stial judgments". Crimthan and his successor, Fiach'ad, assisted the Picts esist the Romans. On the death of Crimthan (A. D. 90), the Celtic population olted against their Scotic or Milesian masters, and having massacred all the ices and chiefs, they placed one of their own men, named Carbre Cat-can, the throne. He reigned five years. On his death, his son, Moran, refused crown, and reinstated Feredach, the son of Crimthan, in the government. ran was appointed chief judge. To his fame is owing the fable of MORAN'S LAR, which is said to have given him warning, by increased pressure round neck, when he was about to pronounce an unjust sentence.

hat is said of Adminius?—Claudius?—Caractacus?—Togidumnus?—Guiderius?—Arvira- '—Vespasian?—Plautius?—Ostorius Scapula?—What was the fate of Caractacus?—Who ceded Scapula?—What of the Druids?—Boadicea?—How was Christianity introduced? hat of Agricola?—What were the principal events in the history of Scotland?—Ireland?

FRANCE.

THE Roman administration was marked by rapacity and cruelty, notwithstanding the virtues of Drusus. The Gauls served in the Roman armies, and distinguished themselves in the campaigns of Drusus and Tiberius against the Germans, 40,000 of whom were forced to settle in Gaul. After the destruction of Varus and his legions (A. D. 9), Augustus expelled the Gauls from Italy, and Tiberius spent three years in putting Gaul in a state of defence. But the oppression which the Romans were guilty of drove the country into revolt, and JULIUS SAC'ROVIR, an Æduan, and Julius Florus, roused the people to arms. The former was distinguished for his courage and ability, and undertook to raise the centre and the west of Gaul. The latter, an eminent general, raised a revolt in Belgium. Their plans were well laid; but the impetuosity of the Andega'vi and the Tu'rones (two of the revolted tribes) marred the projects of Sacrovir. The Romans, under Acil'ius Avi'ola and Sil'ius, took immediate advantage of this imprudence, and speedily fell upon the half-prepared Gauls near Augustod'unum (the ancient Bibracte), where they gained an easy victory. Sacrovir fled with some companions to his country-house, which he set on fire, and then he and his friends stabbing themselves, their bodies were consumed in the flames (A. D. 21). The Emperor Caligula, the successor of Tiberius, took up his abode for a long time at Lyons, where he was guilty of the greatest extravagances and extortions. The next emperor, Claudius, who was a native of Lyons, abolished Druidism and exterminated its priests (A. D. 43). He also conferred upon the Gauls the right of entry into the Roman Senate, whereby Gaul became assimilated to Italy (A. D. 48). Schools and libraries were established, and Roman literature was very much cultivated in the country. The Narbonnaise produced many men of genius, such as the poets Terentius Varro, Petronius Arbiter, and Cornelius Gallus; the historian Trogus Pompeius; and the orators Votienus Montanus and Domitius Afer. The arts and sciences spread, and vast public works were undertaken. The Gaulish nobility became rich and luxurious, and played an important part in the affairs of Rome.

In the year 64 the beautiful city of Lyons was destroyed by fire. Nero contributed largely to the succour of the inhabitants and the restoration of the city; but his vices and cruelty had so alienated the Gauls, that they, under JULIUS VINDEX, governor of the Lyonnaise, organized a conspiracy to place Galba on the throne of the Cæsars (A. D. 68). The Belgians and Germans, however, set up Verginius Rufus in opposition to Galba. A bloody conflict between the two parties took place at Vesontio, in which the Gauls fell into the greatest confusion, and slaughtered each other to the number of 20,000. Vindex, in despair, destroyed himself, and Verginius might then have made himself emperor, but he refrained from doing so. But the harsh and imprudent acts both of Galba and Verginius discontented the Gauls, and the legions then proclaimed Vitellius emperor. The history of this contest belongs to Rome rather than to Gaul, but the latter country suffered deplorably while it lasted; and, under the inspiration of a Boïan named Maric, the people rose in insurrection. They were, however, soon quelled by the Roman legions (A. D. 69). The subsequent heroic attempt of CLAUDIUS CIVI'LIS, the Batavian, to expel the Romans, was equally unsuccessful. An account of his exploits will be found in the column devoted to the Netherlands (p. 135). The last blood shed for Gaul was that of Julius Sabi'nus, a noble who had set himself up as Cæsar. This youth was violently enamoured of a young maiden named Eponi'na, with whom he lived for nine years concealed in subterranean passages beneath his house. Being discovered, they were taken to Rome, and put to death by Vespasian. Gaul finally submitted to Vespasian (A. D. 70), and became essentially a Roman province. Henceforward, until the irruptions of the Germanic tribes, the history of this country is identified with that of Rome. Gaul was the scene of many conflicts between the rival claimants of the imperial purple; but it flourished in spite of all these scenes of confusion, and became very populous.

There can be little doubt that Christianity found its way into France, as well as into Britain, during this century; for there were converts in the army as well as in the household of Cæsar. There is reason to believe that the Apostle Paul visited France and Spain during the interval between his first and second imprisonment in Rome (A. D. 63–64). It has been supposed by some that he also visited England, but this rests on very doubtful testimony.

What did the Romans do?—What of Sacrovir?—What was his fate?—What were the acts of Caligula?—Claudius?—What men of genius flourished?—What of Lyons?—Nero?—Julius Vindex?—Verginius Rufus?—Vitellius?—Maric?—Civilis?—Julius Sabinus and Eponina?—What happened to Gaul?—What of the introduction of Christianity?—St. Paul?

SPAIN.

The country enjoyed tranquillity and prosperity during the reign of Augustus Cæsar. He conferred many benefits on the people: he made numerous roads and bridges; founded new colonies; reduced the taxes; and advanced many of the natives to the highest offices. His clemency and magnanimity caused him to be adored by them. A remarkable instance occurred in the case of Caracota, a famous robber, who, at the head of a formidable band, had long ravaged the country, and defeated the forces sent in pursuit of him. Augustus set a price on his head; whereupon Caracota waited on the emperor, confessed his own crimes, promised to forsake them, and ended with demanding not only his pardon, but the reward offered for his apprehension. The emperor, struck with his intrepidity, granted what he required.

The reign of Tiberius Cæsar (A. D. 14–37) was a scourge to Spain. This rapacious and remorseless tyrant oppressed the country in the most merciless manner, shedding the blood of the inhabitants and confiscating their property, just as it suited his humor. His prætors were the vile instruments of his crimes. The people revolted, but as the Romans were in military possession of all the strongholds, the revolt was speedily suppressed; but the assassination of Lucius Piso, the governor of Hispania Citerior, whose avarice and cruelty excited general indignation, had a salutary effect on succeeding governors.

The Spanish historian Mariana asserts that the Apostle James the Elder (the son of Zebedee) came into Spain during the reign of Caligula (A. D. 38–41), and preached Christianity; that he founded a church at Saragossa, but had very few followers; also that he then returned to Jerusalem, where he suffered martyrdom (A. D. 42); that after his martyrdom his body was brought by his disciples from Syria to Iria Flavia (now El Padron) in Galicia, and thence transferred to Compostella. There is more reason to believe that St. Paul visited Spain, and preached in Catalonia, Aragon, Valencia, and Andalusia, during his last apostolical journey: he had previously declared his intention of so doing (Rom. xv. 24).

The tyranny of the Emperor Caligula (A. D. 37–41) was worse than that of Tiberius; so was that of Claudius. The cruelties of Nero reached such a pitch that Julius Vindex, governor of Southern Gaul, invited SER′VIUS SULPI′CIUS GALBA, then governor of Spain, to assume the empire. Galba hesitated, but was at length persuaded, by an assembly of the chief men of Spain, convened at Carthagena, to march to Rome. In this step he was greatly influenced by OTHO SIL′VIUS, governor of Lusitania, who supplied him with a large amount of money. Galba accordingly commenced his enterprise; and Nero having destroyed himself in the meantime, the veteran was proclaimed emperor. His reign was very short. His successor, Otho, menaced by the legions of Germany and France, endeavored to conciliate Spain by giving her jurisdiction over Mauretania and Tingitana. Owing to this arbitrary measure, the people of that portion of Africa were forced to resort to the Roman courts at Cadiz for the determination of their lawsuits. The Emperors Vespasian and Titus granted to the Spaniards all the privileges enjoyed by the Italians, and became so popular in Spain that many towns and places adopted the name of their family, FLAVIUS. The celebrated Roman naturalist PLINY was quæstor of Andalusia under these beneficent emperors, and steadily forwarded their views. But on the accession of the tyrant DOMITIAN all was changed, and the people became martyrs to his rapacity and that of his officers.

Spain was at this time divided into three provinces, Bœtica, Lusitania, and Tarraconensis, each governed by a prætor. In each province were several Roman colonies, chartered towns, and courts for determining civil suits. The Christian religion had not yet taken root in Spain; wherefore EUGE′NIUS, the illustrious disciple of Dionysius the Areopagite, bishop of Athens, was sent to preach to the Spaniards. He became the first bishop of Toledo. The converts to Christianity in Spain suffered in the persecution under Domitian, as did others in Italy and Gaul. Eugenius was martyred in the second general persecution under that tyrant. Domitian forbade the planting of any more vines in Spain. He was murdered A. D. 97, and COC′CEIUS NERVA was chosen emperor, who associated with himself MARCUS ULPIUS TRAJANUS (commonly called Trajan), a Spaniard, born near Seville. Nerva died A. D. 99, and Trajan became sole emperor.

Three Spanish poets flourished at Rome during this century, viz., MARTIAL, CAN′IUS, and DECIANUS; and SEN′ECA, Nero's preceptor, was a native of Cordova.

What is said of Augustus Cæsar?—Caracota?—Tiberius?—Which of the apostles visited Spain?—Relate the tradition respecting St. James.—What is said of Caligula?—Claudius?—Nero?—Galba?—Otho?—Vespasian and Titus?—Domitian?—The planting of Christianity?—Eugenius?—Nerva?—Trajan?—What famous Spaniards flourished during this century?

GERMANY.

TIBERIUS was successful in his various expeditions (A. D. 4); and his victories, combined with the wise and humane conduct of Sent′ius, prefect of the Rhine, induced many of the tribes to adopt Roman customs and their useful arts. Sentius was succeeded by VARUS (an able and learned man, and a confidential friend of the Emperor Augustus), who sought earnestly to civilize the Germans. While he remained at his head-quarters, enriched the natives with gifts, and took their sons into his army, they loved and treated him as a guest. But he was induced by Seges′tus, a treacherous chief of the Cherusci, to enforce the Roman laws among that tribe. With 30,000 picked men, Varus encamped among them. But Hermann (or ARMIN′IUS, as the Romans called him), a noble youth of the Cherusci, who had learned the art of war in the Roman armies, secretly instigated his countrymen to revolt, and managed matters with such ability as to draw the Roman legions into the defiles of the Detmold and the Teutoberg forest, where they were surrounded and cut to pieces (A. D. 9). Varus threw himself upon his sword, and Germany was liberated from Roman dominion. Every trace of the Romans beyond the Rhine was effaced, and all their forts and military roads were destroyed. Tiberius, on his accession to the empire (A. D. 14), sent German′icus (the son of Drusus) with a powerful fleet and army against the Germans. Germanicus fell upon the Marsi while they were lying intoxicated at a sacred feast, and slew immense numbers of them. Next year (A. D. 15) he entered the country of the Cherusci, and took prisoner Thusnel′da, the wife of Arminius. At the news of this, all Germany, to a man, rose up in arms. Germanicus boldly advanced to the scene of the defeat of Varus, and there buried the bones of the slaughtered legions. On this spot he was attacked by the whole force of the Germans, headed by Arminius, defeated, and driven to his ships on the Danube (A. D. 16). Next year he was again defeated on the banks of the Weser; so that after a contest of three years Germanicus returned to Rome, leaving only one fort in Germany in possession of the Romans.

Meanwhile the confederation of the Suevi had broken up, and consequently the tribes on the Danube fell a prey one by one to the ambition of Tiberius. Boirebistas, king of the Getæ, having been murdered by his people, MARBOD, uniting the Boii, the Suevi of Upper Germany, and the petty southern frontier tribes, led them into Bohemia, where he was joined by the Getæ. Here he established a kingdom, and his subjects received the name of Marcomanni. Caring nothing for the independence of Germany, he sought an alliance with Tiberius, who was then occupied in crushing the Pannonians, Senones, and Longobardi. This so exasperated the Germans that a league was formed against him by Arminius, and Marbod was entirely defeated. He fled across the Danube, where he lived for 18 years on the bounty of the Romans. In the year 21, the gallant Arminius was murdered by his own relations, who were jealous of his fame. From this moment the Germans ceased to act with unity. The Frisii revolted from the Romans, who had grossly outraged and oppressed them, and they permanently recovered their freedom. The Cherusci, ruined by internal dissensions, ultimately submitted to Fla′vius Ital′icus (A. D. 47). The Catti, crossing the Rhine, were cut to pieces by the Romans (A. D. 50). In the same year, Agrippi′na, the daughter of Germanicus, led a numerous Roman colony to the Rhine, where she erected the great fortress, named after her Colo′nia Agrippi′na (now Cologne). Vast numbers of Germans enlisted in the Roman armies, and greatly contributed to the victories of Titus and Vespasian in Asia.

The history of Germany presents a continual state of warfare amongst the various tribes, who, instead of uniting against the common enemy, destroyed each other, thereby making the war light to the Romans. The Catti fell upon the Cherusci, and dethroned King Chari′omer. Masy′us, king of the Senones, and their famous prophetess, Ganna, fled to Rome. 60,000 Bruc′teri were destroyed by the Chama′vi and the Angriva′rii. The Goths, under Catual′da, the successor of Marbod, king of the Marcomanni, drove out the Suevi, who, in their turn, under Vibil′ius, expelled Catualda. The latter went over to the Romans, and was allotted land in Pannonia. DECEB′ALUS, the brave king of the Getæ, having united the tribes formerly called Pauci′ni, defeated two armies which the Emperor Domitian sent against him. The latter sued for peace, and agreed to pay Decebalus a heavy annual tribute (A. D. 90). The Romans paid this tribute for 10 years, when the Emperor Trajan refused to continue it.

Who was Varus?—What befell him?—And the Roman domination in Germany?—Who was Arminius?—Germanicus?—Relate the incidents of this war.—Who was Marbod?—What befell him?—What was the end of Arminius?—What was the state of Germany after his death?—What is said of Decebalus?

AFRICA.

Ethiopia.—The Emperor Augustus restored to Candace all the towns taken by Petronius, and remitted the tribute, but still considered himself master of the country. It is believed that the only portion of Ethiopia known to the Romans was the kingdom of Meroë, a peninsula adjoining the lower part of Egypt; and even after their invasion the people preserved their independence. Some writers assert that the Christian religion was introduced into Meroë about the 19th or 20th year of the reign of Tiberius (A. D. 34), by the treasurer of Queen Candace, who was baptized by Philip the deacon (Acts viii. 27), and that this convert became the apostle of Ethiopia. It is also asserted that the Evangelist Matthew preached the gospel to the Ethiopians who had settled near the Araxes, and that the Apostle Bartholomew preached to those settled in Arabia Felix. It is very probable that some of the early Christian converts found their way into Ethiopia, and contributed to the spread of the gospel, but there is no certain information on this point. From this period but little mention is made of the Ethiopians in history for more than 200 years.

Mauretania.—Juba was succeeded by Ptolemy, his son by Cleopatra, daughter of the famous Antony and Cleopatra. But the country was not destined to remain long at peace. Tacfari′nas, a native of Numidia, formerly employed in the Roman army, occasioned fresh troubles. He assembled a great number of barbarians, principally robbers and persons of lawless life, formed an army of them, and disciplined it after the Roman manner. He drew over to his side the Masulanians (a wild tribe dwelling near the desert of Sahara), the Cinithians, and a large body of Mauretanians, commanded by their general, Mazippa; and, being confident of success, attacked the Roman legion under Furius Camillus, but was quickly put to flight with the loss of half his army (A. D. 17). Next year he renewed the war, but followed different tactics. Laying waste the country as he went, he moved with such celerity that the Romans could not come up with him. He surrounded a Roman cohort commanded by Decrius, near the banks of the Pazida, killed their leader, and put them to flight. For their cowardice, Lucius Apronius, the commander of the Roman forces, decimated them—every tenth man, drawn by lot, being executed with a club, according to the ancient Roman custom. This rigor appears to have had the desired effect, for shortly afterwards a small body of 500 men routed the whole army of Tacfarinas at Thala. After this the war was carried on in a desultory manner, until an opportunity offered for Apronius to attack the Africans, which he did, routing them with ease. Tacfarinas then had the insolence to send ambassadors to the Emperor Tiberius, threatening him with eternal war if a proper settlement were not made to him and his army. Tiberius, exceedingly incensed, ordered Blæsus, the commander of the Roman forces in Africa, to offer a general indemnity to the Africans, and to endeavor to get Tacfarinas into his hands. Blæsus, by able manœuvres, dispersed the chief's army, and forced him to hide himself in the desert; but being subsequently joined by a large body of Mauretanians, through the connivance or supineness of Ptolemy, Tacfarinas once more attacked the Romans. He was met by Dolabella near the castle of Auzea, and paid for his rashness with his life: being killed, together with a great number of his followers (A. D. 24). This victory restored peace to the Roman provinces of Mauretania and Gætulia. Soon after the death of Tiberius, Caligula, either through avarice or jealousy, caused Ptolemy to be put to death. Thereupon Æd′emon, one of Ptolemy's freedmen, to avenge his death, assembled a large force, and attempted to expel the Romans. But the Roman general, Suetonius Paullinus, ravaged the country, and penetrated as far as Mount Atlas; and his successor, Sidius Geta, drove the Mauretanian general, Salabus, into the desert. But Salabus having been largely reinforced, Geta concluded peace with him on his own terms. It is probable that Mauretania was delivered up to the Romans, for we find it soon after divided into two provinces: the one called Mauretania Tingitana—the other, Mauretania Cæsariensis; and a Roman governor was appointed to each province. Tranquillity was now restored to all the African dominions of Rome.

Arabia.—There is no complete history of the Arabs: from time to time the name of an eminent chief among them appears, and they are occasionally mentioned in the histories of surrounding nations. The Romans, under Gallus, in the reign of Augustus, penetrated as far as Negra, on the Red Sea.

What did the emperor restore to Candace?—What portion of Ethiopia was known to the Romans?—What is said of the introduction of Christianity there?—What were the acts of Tacfarinas?—What was his fate?—What did Ædemon do?—What became of Mauretania?—What is said of Arabia?

SCANDINAVIA.

Sweden.—The annals of the kings of Sweden, during this period, possess little interest. There were a number of petty sovereigns reigning at the same time in the different provinces of Scania, Norway, Denmark, Gothland, and Upsala. Freyer removed his capital from Sigtuna to Upsala, where he built a palace and temple. He adopted the surname of Yngve, hence the sacred race of the Ynglings derived their appellation. His death is placed in the year 19. Of his successors, Fiölner (A. D. 19–24), Svegdir (A. D. 34–48), Vanland (A. D. 48–98), and Visbur, there is little worth recording. Peace and abundance prevailed, and their reigns were the golden age of the North. We may mention that Fiölner was drowned in a vat of mead, into which he had fallen while intoxicated; hard drinking being then, as well as in later times, a royal accomplishment.

Denmark.—The successors of Frode I. were Friedlief II. (A. D. 35–47), Havar (A. D. 47–59), Frode II. (A. D. 59–87), Vermund the Sage (A. D. 87–140), of whom we have nothing of interest to record.

Norway.—Semingve and his descendants reigned, but the annals of this country are so meagre and uninteresting as to require no further notice until the 7th century.

There is reason to believe that before the arrival of Odin, the Danes were divided into many tribes, living independent of each other, and having their own chief. Odin had reduced these into subjection, and placed his own descendants over them. But it was not long before they recovered their right of electing their kings, and other rights essential to national independence. Denmark was for a long time divided into three kingdoms—Scania, Zealand, and Jutland—and the kings were elected by open voting, the electors and soldiers signifying their approval by clashing their shields together. The assembly usually met inside a circle of enormous unhewn stones, having one stone in the middle larger than the rest, on which they made a seat for the king. The remains of these stone circles are still to be seen near Lunden, in Scania; Leyra, in Zealand; and Viburg, in Jutland. In Sweden an oath was reciprocally taken between the new king and his subjects. When the king was elected he was lifted up on the shoulders of the chiefs, that the people might see him.

What events occurred in Sweden?—Denmark?—Norway?—What was the condition of the Danes before the arrival of Odin?—How were their kings elected?

NETHERLANDS.

During this century the Menapii made rapid progress in civilization. They became a maritime people, and carried on considerable trade with England. They even established a colony on the east coast of Ireland, not far from Dublin. The Batavi and the Belgæ, by their intercourse with the Romans, became rapidly Latinized; but those Batavians and Frisians who inhabited Holland retained the manners and language of their ancestors. In A. D. 28, the latter achieved their independence. The Romans had imposed a tribute of ox-hides on them, which was endured until Olennius became prefect of the Rhine. That tyrannical officer demanded not only common hides, but buffalo hides, which were rare in Friesland. The wretched people were forced to sell all they possessed—houses, slaves, cattle, and even their children—to purchase hides of the neighboring nations. At length they rose up and drove the Romans out of their country (A. D. 28). They retained their freedom, for the Romans made no further attempt to subdue them.

In the year 69, Civi′lis, a Batavian, who had lost an eye in the service of the Romans, was thrown into prison by them, being suspected of designs against them. On his release he vowed eternal enmity to the oppressors of his country. During a sacred feast at midnight, in a forest, he appeared among his countrymen, and excited them to open revolt. The people rose at once, and simultaneously massacred the Romans throughout the country. Tribe after tribe followed the example, and the Romans were everywhere defeated. The enthusiasm of the people was greatly stimulated by the exhortations of Vell′eda, a maiden prophetess, who dwelt in a lonely tower in the Bructerian forest, and was regarded with veneration throughout Germany. The Gauls united with the Belgæ, and all went on prosperously through the winter; but in the spring the Emperor Vespasian sent Cerea′lis, a veteran general, into Gaul. That officer speedily subdued the Gauls: the city of Cologne drove out the Germans, and gave up the wife and child of Civilis. That chief was defeated, and, being deserted by his troops, fled to the Batavian islands. But honorable terms being offered, he made peace. Velleda was taken prisoner by the Romans, and carried to Rome.

What progress did the Menapii make?—When and how did the Frisii achieve their independence?—Who was Civilis?—Velleda?—What of their efforts to free their country?

THE CHRISTIAN CHURCH.

At the time of the advent of our Lord, the greater part of the known world was under the dominion of Rome, and almost universal peace prevailed. But mankind were sunk in vice; the most infamous crimes were habitually perpetrated; the ancient religions, or rather superstitions, had become useless for any good purpose; and the necessity for a new Revelation to regenerate the race, coming at the time it did, is to us apparent, but was not so to those amongst whom the Saviour taught. The Jews at this time were the only nation which was not idolatrous: they worshipped Jehovah, the God of Abraham, but had added to the Law of Moses many traditions and observances, which their teachers, or doctors, held to be of equal force with the Law itself. These were recorded in their Talmud, a book consisting of two parts, the *Mischna* and the *Gemara*—the former being the written law, and the latter a collection of traditions and comments of Jewish teachers. Those Jews who taught this, and insisted on the strict observance of the Ceremonial Law, were called Pharisees (from the Hebrew word *perushim*, signifying persons separated from others). Their rivals, the Sadducees (so named from being the disciples of Sadok, the pupil of Antigonus Sichæus, president of the great Sanhedrin about 260 B. C.), were freethinkers and scoffers, who taught that there was no resurrection, neither angel nor spirit (Matt. xxii. 23); that the soul perished with the body; and rejecting all tradition, they preferred the Law of Moses. The sect of the Esse′nes, whose origin is obscure, was composed of men who led a recluse life in caves and deserts, and were unqualified fatalists. These three were the principal sects prevailing amongst the Jews at the time when John the Baptist appeared, preaching repentance, and announcing the immediate coming of the Messiah—a spiritual Messiah, not a temporal monarch—to restore the glories of their nation upon earth, as the Jews expected. John was the son of Zachari′as (a Levite, and priest of the family of Abi′a), and of Elizabeth his wife, a cousin of Mary, the mother of Jesus. He was a man of fervid piety, and lived a solitary life in the desert, when not preaching to the Jews. He was put to death (A. D. 32) by Herod An′tipas, at the request of Salo′me, the daughter of Hero′dias, the wife of Herod Philip (Matt. xiv.). The name "John" signifies "filled with grace".

The precise date of the birth of Jesus (Jehosuah, or Joshua, a name signifying "he who shall save") is uncertain. Historians differ amongst themselves as much as ten years: some fixing it at seven years before the usually received date, and others at three years subsequently. The more recent authorities, including Hales, Blair, and Clinton, fix it at five years before the received era, and this accords better with contemporary history. The use of the present Era was brought into general adoption by the monk Diony′sius Exig′uus, in the reign of the Emperor Justin′ian, A. D. 527.

We will assume, then, that the birth of Jesus took place on the 25th of December, B. C. 5. It occurred at Bethlehem, in Judea. Of the early life of Jesus very few incidents are known. At 12 years of age He was found in the temple disputing with the doctors (teachers of the law). His coming and actual presence had been announced by John the Baptist, whose preaching commenced about the year 26: Pontius Pilate being then the Roman governor of Judea; and Herod Antipas, the son of Herod the Great, being tetrarch of Galilee. About the year 29 Jesus began to teach. His ministry lasted about three years and a half, and was terminated by His crucifixion on the Mount of Olives, near Jerusalem, on the 3d of April, A. D. 33. He left no written instructions for the guidance of His disciples, but confided the promulgation of His doctrines to a band of faithful and heroic men, selected generally from the poorest class, who, during His life, imperfectly comprehended Him; but after His decease, were enlightened as to the true nature of His mission, and were endowed with divine power to preach the gospel ("good tidings") to all nations. Of these disciples twelve were most conspicuous, and were called Apostles (from the Greek word *apostellein*, signifying "to send out"). Those selected were Simon Peter, Andrew, James the Elder, and John (the sons of Zeb′edee), Philip, Bartholomew (or Nathan′ael), Thomas, Matthew (or Levi), James the Less (the son of Alpheus, and brother of Jesus—surnamed "the Just"), Jude (surnamed Lebbeus and Thadde′us), Simon (called "Zelo′tes", and "the Canaanite"), and Judas Iscariot. The last-mentioned apostle, having betrayed his Lord, destroyed himself out of remorse; and the disciples, at the suggestion of Peter, chose Matthias to fill the vacant apostleship. Barnabas was shortly afterwards added to the number of the apostles. The missionary work of Jesus had been limited to Judea, and the apostles for some years confined their labors to that country and Samaria. A period of nearly 12 years from the crucifixion of Jesus elapsed before the gospel was publicly preached to the Gentiles. In the meanwhile it had reached Antioch, through the medium of certain Greeks, amongst whom Lucius of Cyrene was pre-eminent. A number of persons there embraced the new faith, and adopted the name of "Christians" (A. D. 37). The attention of the apostles having been called to this fact, the Apostle Barnabas, taking his friend Paul with him, was deputed by them to that city, and authorized to take the necessary steps for organizing there the first Christian Gentile church (A. D. 40). The Jewish converts had already founded a church at Jerusalem, over which James the Just was appointed *bishop* (a title frequently given in Scripture and early ecclesiastical history, but there is considerable controversy as to the precise duties attached to the office: the word is derived from the Greek, *episcopos*, "an overseer"). Many interesting events had occurred, such as the deaths of Ananias and Sapphira, the martyrdom of Stephen, the conversion of Cornelius, the call of Peter to preach to those Gentiles who believed in the Mosaic dispensation, the conversion of Paul, and the writing of a gospel in Hebrew by Matthew, for the use of Jewish converts. But the dark days of the Church were at hand. The fanatical Jews incited Herod Agrippa to persecute their converted brethren; the Apostle James, the son of Zebedee, was "slain by the sword"; and Peter was thrown into prison (A. D. 42): nevertheless, Christianity spread in defiance of all this. Paul and Barnabas returned to Antioch (A. D. 45), where the former was called to become an apostle for the great work of preaching the gospel to the heathen world, and the two were sent forth from that city on their first mission, accompanied by John, surnamed Mark, the nephew of Barnabas. For seven years these three preached throughout Asia Minor, founding churches in various places; but Mark subsequently left them, and his place was filled by Titus. On their return to Antioch (A. D. 52), they were deputed to Jerusalem to consult the apostles and elders of that church respecting a question which then agitated the Christians at Antioch, viz., the necessity of circumcision for Gentile converts. This question having been answered in the negative, they were deputed to go on a second mission to the Gentiles. On the journey disputes arose between Paul and Barnabas, on account of which they separated. Paul, accompanied by Silas, Timothy, and Luke, accomplished his second apostolical journey, visiting (A. D. 53–55), Cilicia, Phrygia, Galatia, Thrace, Philippi, Thessalonica, Beræa, Athens, Corinth, and Ephesus, where he founded churches. During this journey he wrote his Epistles to the Galatians and the Thessalonians. He then returned to Jerusalem, but remained there only a short time, starting on his third journey (A. D. 55–60), during which he revisited Galatia, Phrygia, Ephesus, Macedonia, Corinth, Philippi, and the Grecian islands, and wrote his Epistles to the Corinthians and the Romans. On his return to Jerusalem the Jews raised a great tumult (A. D. 60), accusing him of sedition and blasphemy. He was thrown into prison, and brought before Felix, the Roman governor, who remanded him to prison. Felix was soon after superseded by Festus, before whom Paul was again brought (A. D. 62). On this occasion he availed himself of his privilege of Roman citizenship, and demanded to be sent to Rome for trial. His request was complied with, and he was sent a prisoner to Rome, accompanied by Timothy, Luke, Aristar′chus, Tych′icus, and Mark. Meanwhile the ferocious Jews, disappointed in making Paul their victim, turned their fury against the Christians at Jerusalem, and stoned to death James the Just (A. D. 62), who had just before written his general epistle to the "Jews in dispersion". After this the Christian church at Jerusalem was broken up for a time, and the apostles dispersed themselves in various directions, preaching the gospel and founding churches. The accounts of their acts and their fate are meagre, and of doubtful authenticity. Tradition says that Andrew went to Scythia, Russia, Sogdiana, Colchis, and Greece; and that he was crucified at Patras, in the Morea, on a cross of a peculiar construction, named after him, "St. Andrew's cross". Thomas visited Parthia and India, where he founded the church known as "the Christians of St. Thomas". He

What was the condition of the world at the advent of Christ?—What were the leading sects among the Jews?—What is said of the Essenes?—Of John the Baptist?—Of his name?—Of the date of the birth of Jesus?—Of his youth?—Of his mission?—His death?—To whom did he confide the preaching of the gospel?

Who replaced Judas Iscariot?—Where and when was the name of Christians first used?—What events occurred before the "dark days" of the Church?—What did Herod do?—State the order of Paul's journeys.—What befell him at Jerusalem?—What were the acts and fate of Andrew?—Thomas?

A.C. 1—100.

THE CHRISTIAN CHURCH.

devoted himself to death to save his church from persecution, and suffered martyrdom by being shot with arrows. JUDE was sent to Ab′garus, king of Edessa, in compliance with a promise alleged to have been made in a letter written by Jesus to that monarch (which is contained in Eusebius's *Ecclesiastical History*, but the tradition, as well as the authority of Eusebius, is of doubtful value). This tradition runs thus: Abgarus had written to Christ to invite Him into his kingdom, and begging to be cured by Him of a distemper with which he was afflicted. To this request Christ sent the following answer: "Abgarus, Blessed art thou, because thou hast believed in me when thou sawedst me not; for it is written of me that they which see me shall not believe in me: that they which see me not shall believe and be saved. Concerning that thou wrotest unto me that I should come unto thee, I let thee understand that all things touching my message are here to be fulfilled, and after the fulfilling thereof I am to return again unto Him that sent me; but after my Assumption I will send one of my disciples unto thee, which shall cure thy malady, and restore life to thee, and them that be with thee." Jude (Thaddeus) was the disciple selected by the Apostle Thomas for this mission; but there appears to be great doubt whether this Jude was the same person as the Apostle Jude. Eusebius states that Abgarus was healed, and that he and a number of his subjects were baptized. The Apostle Jude preached in Palestine, Syria, Lybia, Persia, and Armenia, and is said to have been tied to a cross, near Mount Ararat, and killed with arrows. His general epistle was written about the year 70. BARTHOLOMEW chose India for the scene of his labors, and a copy of St. Matthew's Gospel was found there at the close of the second century, amongst the descendants of his converts. He was flayed alive and crucified at Albanop′olis, in Armenia, on his return from the far East. PHILIP preached in Phrygia, and lived to an advanced age. He settled and died at Hierap′olis, where he brought up his family, which was a large one, in the service of the Church — his daughters becoming deaconesses. SIMON ZELOTES visited Egypt, Cyrene, and Barbary, and is said to have found his way to England, where he suffered martyrdom, but it is more probable that he was crucified at Suanir, in Persia. BARNABAS probably settled in his native country, Cyprus, but all authentic traces of him, after his separation from Paul, are lost. There is a tradition that he lived to an advanced age, and was stoned to death at Salamis. MATTHIAS's destination is not known with certainty: he is said to have preached in Cappadocia, and on the coasts of the Caspian Sea. Some say that he was put to death at Colchis. MATTHEW's fate is equally uncertain: it is supposed that he preached in Persia, and was martyred at Nadabar′. The fate of JUDAS ISCARIOT, JAMES (the son of Zebedee), and JAMES THE JUST, have already been mentioned. Of the fifteen apostles, there remain the three greatest to be mentioned further, viz., Peter, John, and Paul.

PETER probably preached throughout the northern portion of Asia Minor. He went to Rome about the time that PAUL was sent thither a prisoner (A. D. 62). It is most probable that he fulfilled there his peculiar mission to the "proselytes of the gate", or Jewish Gentiles, and founded a church amongst them at Rome. At his request, and under his supervision, Mark wrote his gospel there; and it was at Rome that Peter wrote his general epistles. Paul was tried and acquitted; and having made many friends "in the household of Cæsar", he founded the first Christian Gentile church at Rome, and at his request Luke wrote his gospel and his history of the Acts of the Apostles. Paul wrote at Rome his epistles to the Ephesians, Philippians, Colossians, Laodiceans (now lost), Hebrews, Timothy, Titus, and Philemon. He then preached in Italy and Spain, and thence homeward through Crete and Jerusalem to Antioch, where he ended his fourth apostolical journey. He soon (A. D. 65) resumed his travels; and, on his fifth and last journey, passed through Colosse, Philippi, and Corinth, to Rome. On his arrival there (A. D. 66), he found the persecution of the Christians by Nero in full activity, and this greatest of the apostles became one of its victims. He was beheaded. Peter, after witnessing the execution of his own wife, was crucified with his head downwards (said to have been at his own request, as he deemed himself unworthy to die in the same posture as his Divine Master had died 33 years before him). After their death, JOHN undertook the superintendence of the famous seven churches of Asia Minor (Ephesus, Smyrna, Pergamus, Thyatira, Sardis, Philadelphia, and Laodice′a), which he retained until near the close of his long life. During the second persecution of the Christians, under Domitian (A. D. 95), he was banished to the island of Patmos, where he wrote his "Revelation", addressed to the seven churches in Asia, foretelling what would shortly happen to them, and condemning the doctrines of the Nicolaitans (ii. 6, 15), who held the same doctrines as the Gnostics respecting the two principles of all things, the Æons, and the origin of the world (see next century). The name "Nicolaitan" was probably symbolical: but in the 2d century a sect was founded by one Nicolaus, holding the same doctrines. On John's return from exile (A. D. 97) he wrote his gospel, having previously seen and approved of the gospels of Matthew, Mark, and Luke. He died A. D. 100, at the advanced age of 96, having lived to see the firm establishment of the kingdom of Christ upon earth, and thus "tarried till He came" (John xxi. 23).

TIMOTHY was made bishop of Ephesus, and is said to have been stoned to death there (A. D. 97). TITUS became bishop of Crete, where he died in the 94th year of his age. LUKE preached in Gaul, Italy, Macedonia, Bithynia, and Greece, after the death of St. Paul. He was crucified at Elæa, in the Morea, at a very advanced age. MARK was sent into Egypt, and became bishop of Alexandria. After a successful ministry there of more than twelve years he was seized by the mob, tied to an ox, and dragged about the streets until he died (April 25th, A. D. 68). PHILIP THE DEACON, the same who converted the treasurer of Queen Candace, settled at Cæsarea, where he probably died. His four daughters made a vow of celibacy, and were reputed prophetesses.

Having thus briefly noticed the career of the founders of Christianity, we may now mention some of the circumstances which influenced its progress. The first of these was the appointment, by the apostles, of bishops to preside over the principal churches. At JERUSALEM, the Apostle JAMES THE JUST was consecrated. After his martyrdom (A. D. 62), SIMEON, the son of Cleopas, was ordained bishop. At ANTIOCH, EUODIUS and IGNATIUS were successively ordained. At EPHESUS, TIMOTHY (who was styled an apostle as well as bishop). At CRETE, TITUS. At ATHENS, Dionysius the Areop′agite; and after him, Publius Quadra′tus. At PHILIPPI, Epaphrodi′tus. At SMYRNA, POLYCARP. At HIERAPOLIS, PA′PIAS. At ROME, LINUS, ANACLE′TUS, and CLEMENT. The order of succession between these last three is not easily determined. It is most probable that Clement was appointed by St. Peter to preside over the church of the Jewish converts founded by him at Rome; and that Linus was appointed by St. Paul to preside over that of the Gentiles: that Linus was succeeded by Anacletus; and that Clement, having survived both, at length became sole bishop of Rome. Eusebius asserts that St. Peter and St. Paul were joint founders of the Church of Rome. Clement I. died A. D. 100, and was succeeded by Euares′tus.

The next important event was the destruction of Jerusalem by the Romans, A. D. 70, and the consequent final dispersion of the Jews. With this great event the Jewish polity came to an end: thenceforth all distinction between the various classes of converts ceased, and there was no longer a peculiar law or a peculiar apostle for Jewish converts, proselytes, or idolaters; all the nations were to become members of the Church of Christ. The Jews, in fact, were deprived of their central rallying point.

The third point to be noticed is the early rise of heresy in the Church. A system of philosophy, combining the theories of Plato with the Oriental philosophy, was very popular in the time of the apostles, and was taught in all the great schools, especially in that of Alexandria. Attempts were made to engraft this system on Christianity, and thus originated the heresy called Gnosticism (from the Greek word *gnosis*, signifying "knowledge"). Dosith′eus, Cerin′thus, and others of inferior note, were the promulgators of this heresy during the first century of the Church. A detail of its peculiar doctrines cannot here be given: they will be found in the pages of Mosheim, Eusebius, Neander, and others. Beside the Gnostics there were "false Christs", impostors named Simon Magus and Menan′der, who pretended to be Messiahs, and to work miracles. They had numerous followers. Even so late as the fourth century, believers in their divine mission were to be met with. Simon Magus is said to have broken his neck in an attempt to fly from the roof of the capitol at Rome. Dositheus died of hunger in a cave. It was partly with a view to combat the heresy of Cerinthus that St. John wrote his gospel (Revelation ii. 6, 15).

What is the tradition relating to Abgarus?—What were the acts and fate of Jude?—Bartholomew?—Philip?—Simon Zelotes?—Barnabas?—Matthias?—Matthew?—Where did Peter preach?—At whose request, and where, did Mark write his gospel?—Where did Paul preach?—What was the manner of his death?—And that of Peter?

What did John do?—What is said of the Nicolaitans?—Where and when did John die?—What befell Timothy?—Titus?—Luke?—Mark?—Philip the Deacon?—What bishoprics did the apostles found?—What is said of the destruction of Jerusalem?—The rise of heresy?—Gnosticism and false Christs?

INDIA.

A PRINCIPALITY was founded, A. D. 144, at Ballabi in Gujerat, by Kanak Sena, a prince of Oude. It lasted until destroyed by the Persians (A. D. 524). There were two principal marts in the Deccan at this period. One of them, Tagara, is still well known by name, though its position is forgotten. It is said to have been a very great city; but its site is fixed with so little precision, that we can only guess it to have lain about 100 miles east of Paitan, on the Godavery. The other was Plithana, conjectured to have been identical with Paitan: its locality is as uncertain as that of Tagara. Wherever the latter was situated, it afterwards became the capital of a race of kings of the Rajpoot family of Silar, with whom the ruler of Calian, near Bombay, in the 11th century, and of Parnala, near Colapore, in the 12th, boasted connection.

We have alluded to the schools of philosophy, established among the ancient Hindoos at a very early period. Space does not admit of our examining them in detail. But we may observe that they made considerable progress in logic, and used syllogisms. Their categories, or predicaments, are in some cases similar to those of Aristotle. But one of the most remarkable facts in their system was that they joined a sixth or external sense to the five senses—this sixth sense is the mind, which connects the other five, and answers exactly to the common or internal sense of Aristotle. Dr. Thomas Brown, the Scotch philosopher, has gone a step further, and endeavored to prove that we have a sixth sense, viz., that of resistance to touch. The Hindoos and Greeks overlooked this. Some of their religious and philosophical tenets existed among the ancient Egyptians, whence the Brahmins may have derived them. It is an interesting inquiry which have the prior claims. On this point it has been well observed that our accounts of the Egyptians are found only in books written long after these tenets had reached Greece through other channels; that if they existed in Egypt, they did not form a system, but were held as scattered opinions; that in Greece they were clearly foreign; while, on the contrary, in India they were the main principles on which the religion of the people was founded, and their entire philosophy depended (Colebrooke: *Transactions of the Royal Asiatic Society*, vol. i. p. 579).

Which were the two principal marts in the Deccan at this period?—Where were they situated?—What is said of the Hindoo philosophy?—Of its priority over the Egyptian?

PERSIA.

ON the death of Pacorus (A. D. 106), his brother CHOSROËS (or Khosroo) succeeded. This monarch, on his accession, became involved in a war with the Romans, through attempting to expel Exeda′res, the son of Tiridates, king of Armenia. That prince applied to the Emperor Trajan for aid. The emperor, though advanced in years, led an army into Armenia, and speedily subdued it; and Chosroës was glad to save himself in the recesses of Parthia. Trajan then carried the war into Assyria (A. D. 114), and routing all the armies brought against him, took Ctesiphon and Susa. He was proceeding further, when Chosroës submitted, and Persia was nominally added to the Roman empire. But on the return of Trajan to Rome, the Parthians rose again in arms, and threw off the Roman yoke. The death of Trajan (A. D. 117) put an end to the struggle; for his successor, Hadrian, declared the river Euphrates to be the boundary of the empire, and renounced all claims on the countries to the east of it. The remainder of the reign of Chosroës was devoted by him to alleviating the miseries which the war had brought upon his subjects, and he died (A. D. 121) universally lamented. His son, Volog′eses II., succeeded him. He was a prince of a very mild and beneficent disposition, and had no tincture of the tyranny and barbarity which disgraced so many of his predecessors. The commencement of his reign was an unhappy one, for Pharas′manes, king of the Iberi, stirred up the Alans, or Massag′etæ, to invade Parthia. Accordingly, these barbarians ravaged the northern provinces with fire and sword. They were, fortunately, driven out by the Roman governor of Cappadocia. Vologeses then made complaint to Rome of the conduct of Pharasmanes, but the latter had influence enough to procure a decision in his own favor.

Parthamas′pates, king of Armenia, dying, his son, Achæ′menes, applied to the emperor, instead of to Vologeses, for investiture of his father's kingdom. Resenting this, the Parthian king resolved to destroy the power of Rome in the East; and on the death of the Emperor Antoninus Pius (A. D. 161), Vologeses invaded Syria, where he defeated Attidius Cornelianus, the governor. He then invaded Armenia, and drove out Soemas (who had succeeded his father Achæmenes), and cut to pieces a Roman army sent to the assistance of the latter. These successes alarmed the Roman emperors, Marcus Aurelius and Lucius Verus, and the latter was sent to the East to stop the progress of the Parthian monarch; but he wasted his time in luxurious ease in Syria, and had it not been for the valor and ability of his generals, Lucius Statius Priscus and Avidius Cassius, the Romans would have been driven out of Asia. As it was, Vologeses suffered a series of defeats, and Seleucia, Ctesiphon, and Babylon were taken by the Romans. The Parthians, in despair, drove Vologeses out of the kingdom, and placed Monne′ses on the throne. They did not benefit by this, however; for the Romans, following up their successes, forced them to sue for peace. On which they recalled Vologeses, who, on the conclusion of the war, devoted the remainder of his long reign (as his father had done) to repairing the misfortunes he had brought upon his people. He died about A. D. 167, and was succeeded by his son, Vologeses III., whose reign was marked by another war with the Romans. The Emperor Severus penetrated to Ctesiphon, and nearly took the king prisoner, by surprise. On the death of Vologeses, his son, Artabanes IV., defeating a conspiracy of his brothers, mounted the throne.

The account here given of the history of Persia is extracted from the Greek and Roman historians, and as far as the occurrences of the various wars waged by the Romans with the Parthians are concerned, they are sufficiently reliable. But they give us very little insight into the internal condition of the tribes which composed the Parthian or Persian kingdom. The accounts of this period which we receive from the Persian writers are vague and contradictory, and are unreliable as regards dates. The names they give to their chiefs and princes are different from those given by the Roman historians, and it is not always easy to identify one with the other. From the death of Shahpoor (Sapor), who after a long contest with Antiochus the Great obtained Parthia and Hyrcania (B. C. 212), there is a lapse of two centuries in the Persian annals. They inform us that the successor of Shahpoor was Baharam Gudurz, but if this is the prince whom western writers term Gutarzes, as there is every reason to believe, he was the third prince of the second dynasty of the Arsacidæ, and it was he who avenged the death of John the Baptist upon the Israelites (Malcolm's *History of Persia*, vol. i. c. 5). Shahpoor (or Sapor) was probably the Artabanes of the Greeks. Persian authors inform us that Gudurz was succeeded by his son Volas (or Pallas, as his name is sometimes written): they pass over his son Vonones, who reigned for a short period. Volas was the Vologeses of the Greeks, whose war with the Emperor Nero and embassy to his Court are mentioned (p. 129). From Volas the crown descended to Hoormuz, who appears to have been the Artabanes III. of the Romans; and then to his brother Narsi, who is not noticed under that name by any western writer. At his death another of his brothers, whose name was Firoze (probably Pacorus), obtained the throne. His successor, Khosroo, was the Chosroës mentioned above; but some Persian writers omit even this prince. Hence the student may understand the difficulty there is in elaborating a connected and authentic narrative out of such discrepant and imperfect materials. For this reason we give both the Roman and the Persian accounts.

Khosroo's successors were (according to the Persian historians) Volas and Volasin (the Vologeses II. and III. of the Roman historians), and the latter left his crown to his son, Arduan (Artabanes IV.), who was slain by the celebrated Ardisheer (Artaxerxes) in the early part of the next century. From the death of Alexander the Great (B. C. 323) to the commencement of the reign of Ardisheer (A. D. 226) is a period of nearly five centuries and a half, and the whole of it may be termed a blank in Persian history. Yet the Roman writers record exploits on the part of the Persians of which the vainest nation might be proud; and Parthian monarchs whose names cannot now be found in the history of their own country, were the only sovereigns upon whom the Roman arms, in the very zenith of their power, could make no permanent impression. This may, however, be attributed as much to the nature of the country and to their singular mode of warfare, as to their valor. Lofty and barren mountains, broad and rapid streams, and wide-spreading deserts, characterized Persia from the Caspian Sea to the Persian Gulf. As the enemy advanced the country was laid waste, and the Parthian horseman took unerring aim at his foes while his fleet steed was carrying him away from them.

What is said of Chosroës?—Trajan?—The reign of Chosroës?—Of his successor?—His exploits in Syria?—Their result?—What of Vologeses III.?—Artabanes IV.?—What is the character of the records of Persian history, Roman and Persian?—What of the two centuries after the death of Shahpoor?—Identify some of the Persian with the Roman names.—What of the period between the death of Alexander the Great and the accession of Ardisheer?

CHINA. JAPAN.

Shang-te was a child in the cradle when he was proclaimed emperor (A. D. 106). His mother assumed the regency, and on his death (A. D. 107) she appointed her nephew, Gan-te, a boy 14 years old, emperor. The empire, under her administration, was distracted by the most dreadful inundations and famines; robbers everywhere set her authority at defiance; and the Tartars ravaged the frontiers. The Chinese general, Chang-kiang, penetrated to the Caspian, and brought back the *vine*, which soon became extensively cultivated. The young emperor seized the government, but died shortly afterwards (A. D. 126); and Shun-te, at the age of 12 years, was declared emperor. This prince, as he grew up, showed a sincere desire to render his people happy: he sought out the best counsellors at first, but ultimately gave himself up to the pernicious counsels of favorites, and public affairs fell into confusion. On his death (A. D. 145), Chang-te, a mere infant, ruled for one month, and died. The nobles then chose Chih-te, a prince only 9 years of age, emperor. Young as this prince was, he was sensible enough to decree that all children should be sent to school. He was poisoned by Leang-ke, a brother of the empress, who placed Hwan, their creature, on the throne (A. D. 146). A formidable conspiracy against them was suppressed with some difficulty, and was followed by so dreadful a drought, that more than 100,000 families, of the province Ke-choo, left their homes in search of a better country (A. D. 153).

About this period the Huns began their great movement westward. It is interesting to trace the course of this great inundation of barbarians, which, taking its rise on the western frontiers of China, overspread the countries north of the Caspian Sea, and pouring through Southern Russia, forced forward the Sarmatian and German tribes upon Italy, France, and Spain. Some of the tribes of these Huns submitted to China; others were engaged in warfare with their western neighbors. One branch of them marched towards the Volga and Oxus, and settled in the steppes east of the Caspian, where they became partially civilized. A second division went by the northwest route, and crossed the Imaus, where they encountered and subdued the Alans, a nation as fierce and warlike as themselves. The Alans sought refuge in the mountains of the Caucasus. The Huns continued their progress towards Europe. It is recorded that about this time an embassy arrived in China from the Roman Emperor Antoninus.

Another boy, Sing-te, 12 years old, succeeded to the throne (A. D. 168), but was a mere tool in the hands of the empress dowager and of her favorites. A dreadful plague ravaged the country (A. D. 184), and Chang-keo, a disciple of Laou-keun, raised a rebellion remembered as "the insurrection of the yellow caps", from the badge assumed by his partisans. This rebellion was not put down until several severe battles had been fought. The emperor died soon after (A. D. 189), and his memory is stigmatized with infamy, especially by the learned, of whom he put 1000 to death.

A furious conspiracy now broke out against the favorites of the Court. The mob set fire to the palace, and massacred 2000 of its inmates. The unhappy young emperor, Peen-te, was compelled to drink poison. Another youth, Heën-te, was raised to the throne, but became the blind instrument of Tung-cho, one of the principal generals, a ferocious tyrant, whose conduct filled the whole empire with bloodshed and anarchy. He was at length murdered, and China became a prey to factions. The emperor was a mere cypher, and his whole life a concatenation of misery. The "yellow caps" gained strength, and plundered the country with impunity. Such was the state of this unhappy land during this century!

Japan. — Key-ko reigned 60 years. In his time the island of Tsicuba-sima rose out of the sea, and a temple was built on it. Key-ko died A. D. 131, and was succeeded by his fourth son, Sey-mun. This prince, in the year 137, settled the confines of all the provinces of his empire, and removed his Court to Siggu, in the province of Oomi. He reigned 60 years, and died at the age of 108 (A. D. 192). The next emperor was Tsian-ai, a grandson of Key-ko, who murdered the lawful heir to the throne, but only enjoyed it 9 years.

If we may credit the Japanese account of these early ages, their princes were remarkable for longevity. The average duration of life among the first 14 emperors was 110 years! that of their reigns was 61 years. No other history can show the parallel of this.

Mention some of the incidents in Chinese history during this century.—What is said of the Huns?—Who were the "yellow caps"?—Why do the Chinese execrate Ling-te?—What was the state of the country?—What events occurred in Japan?—What is said of the longevity of the Japanese princes?

ITALY.

One of the first acts of the Emperor Trajan was the discontinuance of the payment of yearly presents to the Dacians. That people retaliated by making inroads on the Roman territories; whereupon the emperor proceeded with an army to the Danube, crossed it, and ravaged its shores. In two years he compelled Decebalus to submit to terms: he retained possession of (what is now) the Banat, and placed a Roman garrison there. He then returned to Rome and celebrated his triumph (A. D. 103). But Decebalus and the Dacians were not disposed to remain subject to him. The Dacian monarch organized a well-disciplined army, and sought to form alliances with his neighbors. Trajan thereupon caused the Senate to declare him an enemy of Rome, and he marched again to the Danube. At Severin he constructed the famous bridge over the river: he levelled roads and turned streams, and hunted Decebalus from place to place, until the latter, rather than fall into his hands, put himself to death. Trajan then planted Roman colonies in the conquered provinces, founded towns, and made Latin the language of the country. Thrace and Mœsia flourished greatly in consequence of these measures. He returned to Rome, where he celebrated his triumph by erecting a column, 110 feet high, with inscriptions recording his victories. He also carried a road across the Pontine marshes; but he wasted enormous treasure in a series of games and festivals, which lasted 123 successive days, wherein 11,000 wild beasts and 10,000 gladiators were exhibited (A. D. 106). He caused the Pontine marshes to be drained, a road to be made from Beneventum to Brundusium, and a harbor to be constructed at Anco′na: he also founded schools for poor children. But he yielded to the clamor of those connected with the heathen temples, whose means of living were damaged by the progress of Christianity, and permitted the Christians to be persecuted afresh. This was the commencement of the third persecution (A. D. 107).

Trajan next conceived the idea of subduing the Persians, who were perpetually troubling the eastern frontier. He accordingly proceeded to Antioch (A. D. 107), where he wintered. In the spring of A. D. 108 he marched into Armenia, and drove out the king, Parthemas′iris, whom the Persian monarch Chosroës had established there. Armenia then became a Roman province. The sequel of this expedition is not known with any certainty; but it appears that he marched into Mesopotamia, took several cities on the Tigris and the Euphrates, and assisted the Persian monarch against his own people. He also attempted to clear and restore the navigation of the canal constructed by the Babylonian kings, which joined the Euphrates with the Tigris. He returned to Rome, where he spent several years, having, as he imagined, securely fixed the boundaries of the Roman empire in Dacia and in the East; the cities of Petra and Bostra, with the surrounding part of Arabia Petræa, having been added thereto by Cornelius Palma, in A. D. 106. But the nations of Asia Minor preferred the Persians to the Romans; and therefore a second expedition to the East became necessary, in order to retain what had been acquired in the first. The emperor started from Rome A. D. 114, and entering Mesopotamia, conquered Seleucia and Assyria, took Ctesiphon, and reached the Persian Gulf. While there, the nations and towns in his rear revolted; the Jews also took up arms; the emperor's generals, Hadrian, Lucius Quintus, Erucius Clarus, and Julius Alexander, devastated the provinces with fire and sword; but the emperor grew weary of the war, and procured from the Senate his recall. He at once set out for Rome, leaving his army and the government of Syria to his kinsman Hadrian, but he died at Seli′nus in Cilicia (A. D. 117) on his way. It is said that he had not named his successor; but Hadrian, aided by Trajan's widow, Ploti′na, pretended that he had, and forged an act of adoption in Trajan's name. The Senate appointed him emperor while he was at Antioch, and he at once assumed imperial authority.

Hadrian was a man of singular character. He professed the deepest veneration for the Senate, and declared that he regarded his powers as solely derived from that body. He possessed wisdom, but was actuated by violent caprices; was at one moment merciful, at another cruel; had much zeal for art and science, but persecuted their professors. Hypocrisy abounded in Hadrian's Court, and his honest advisers, Ta′tian and Sim′ilis, resigned their offices in consequence. He remained in the East until the following year (A. D. 118), for Armenia had revolted, and the Parthians assembled on the Tigris. Perceiving the inutility

What occurred with the Dacians?—What great works did Trajan construct?—What of the third persecution of the Christians?—What were his exploits in the East?—What was the result of his wars?—When and where did he die?—To what artifice did his successor resort?—What was the character of Hadrian?

of extending the empire, he made the Euphrates its eastern boundary; and having quelled the rebellious Jews, he returned to Rome. On his arrival there, he discovered a conspiracy to remove him, and quelled it with great severity. Four senators and many distinguished persons were put to death, and the emperor deliberately set to work to destroy all who might put forth rival pretensions to the imperial dignity. Among the most eminent of these were Lucius Quintus, Cornelius Palma, Celsus, Nigrinus, and the famous architect, Artemido′rus of Damascus. In about two years Hadrian got rid of those whom he considered dangerous. He adopted a system of visiting the various provinces of the empire, keeping strict watch over the armies and their generals, the governors and the other officers, and taking pride in embellishing the provincial capitals with public works and monuments. Rome was left to the care of the Senate, which body comprised members of the best families, and was highly respected. Hadrian visited Mœsia, where he repelled an invasion of the Sarmatians and the Roxolani (A. D. 118); Campania (A. D. 119); Gaul and Germany (A. D. 120), where he ordered the construction of a fortified barrier to protect the open frontier between the Neckar and the Danube; Britain (A. D. 121), where he caused a wall to be built between Newcastle and Carlisle for the protection of the southern portion of the island; Spain (A. D. 122); whence he returned to Rome, and thence passed over to Athens, his favorite city. He spent the winter there, rebuilt a bridge over the Cephi′sus, and ordered other public works, and then crossed over to Asia (A. D. 123). He restored Nicome′dia, Cæsare′a, and other cities which had been destroyed by recent earthquakes; and endeavored by means of treaties and presents to retain what Trajan had acquired by arms. This occupied the whole of the year 124 and part of 125, when Hadrian visited the Greek islands, returned to Athens, and wintered there. He was initiated into the Eleusinian mysteries, and he adorned the city with the Olympeium, theatres, and other edifices. It was at this period that Quadra′tus and the philosopher Aristi′des presented to him an Apology for Christianity; after perusing which he addressed a letter to Minu′cius Funda′nus, proconsul of Asia, putting a stop to the persecution of the Christians. Next year (A. D. 126) he sailed to Sicily, and thence to Rome. He was accompanied on his first journeys by a very beautiful youth, named Antin′ous, who was drowned in the Nile (A. D. 122). The emperor's grief was excessive: he enrolled Antinous among the gods, erected a temple to him at Mantine′a, and founded the city of Antinoöp′olis in honor of him. Works of art of all kinds were executed to his memory, many of which are still extant.

Three years afterwards (A. D. 129), Hadrian again set out for the East, and passed the winter at Athens, where he patronized the learned and enlarged the libraries. In the spring and summer of A. D. 130, he revisited Asia Minor, Syria, Palestine, and part of Arabia. In the autumn he visited Egypt, where sailing on the Nile his favorite Antinous was accidentally drowned. In A. D. 131 Hadrian returned to Syria, where he took a fancy to plant a Roman colony in Jerusalem, or, rather, amid the ruins of that city. Accordingly, a colony was settled there, and the new colony was named Æ′lia Capitoli′na, in the midst of which a temple was raised to Jupiter. This pollution of the sacred site of Mount Zion roused the Jews to fury. That people flocked together from all quarters to Palestine, and rallied round a personage named Barchoch′ebas, or Bar Chozba, who was pronounced by the Jewish priests to be the true Messiah. Under his auspices the Jews revolted, and made as furious a resistance to the Roman legions as they had made in the time of Titus. All the efforts of Ticinius Rufus, the governor of the province, to quell the insurrection proved abortive: at length, Julius Seve′rus, governor of Britain, the ablest of the Roman generals, was recalled and sent to Syria, and the measures he adopted crushed out the revolt. The Jews were forbidden to approach the site of their former Temple; and Severus was made governor of Bithynia.

Hadrian, being childless, resolved to adopt a successor. For this purpose he chose Ceso′nius Com′modus Verus, a person wholly unfit to rule the empire; and in his gloomy jealousy put to death several members of his own family (A. D. 136). Next year he constructed a tomb for himself, called the *Moles Hadriani*, near the Tiber, where the Castle of St. Angelo now stands, and retired to his palace at Tibur, where he was attacked by a fatal disease. Verus, however, died before him; and Hadrian then adopted Ar′rius Antoni′nus, a man specially fitted for the duties of government; but Antoninus was only adopted on condition of declaring Lucius Verus and Marcus Aure′lius his successors. Hadrian soon afterwards died (A. D. 138), detested for his cruelties. On his death the Senate declared null and void all the regulations of the latter years of his reign, and would have deprived his remains of the ordinary honors, had not Antoninus persuaded them to renounce their purpose. He thereby acquired the sūrname of "the Pious". During the reign of Hadrian, the philosophy of the Stoics, as taught by Epictetus and Arrian, became very popular. These men inculcated the insignificance of external evils, the inward dignity of human nature, the duty of acting vigorously one's part in life, and of self-denial and self-sacrifice. The administration of public affairs, and the practical applications of science, had never previously been carried to greater perfection than under the reign of Hadrian.

Antoninus Pius succeeded to the imperial throne without opposition. No complete history of his life or reign has descended to us: all that we know is from fragmentary notices. He adopted (in pursuance of the will of Hadrian) Lucius Verus and Marcus Aurelius (afterwards known as Antoninus the Wise) as his successors. But he soon perceived that Verus would be unfit to be a ruler; nevertheless, he scrupulously obeyed the injunction of the late emperor. He conferred on Marcus Aurelius the title of Cæsar, and gave him his daughter, Faustina, in marriage. His reign was the happiest period of Roman history. Wars were scarcely heard of; some insignificant revolts in Britain, Mauretania, Judea, Greece, and Egypt, were easily quelled; the war with the Germans and Dacians was brought to a close; the princes of the East sought alliance with Rome; and even in Southern Russia the chiefs of the wild tribes appealed to Antoninus as an arbiter. This excellent emperor liberally assisted the erection of public works, and devoted especial attention to the Civil Law. He framed new judicial regulations, employing for that purpose the celebrated jurists Vin′dius Verus, Salvius Valens, Volu′sius Metia′nus, Ulpius Marcellus, and Diabole′nus. The empire enjoyed a mild monarchical government. A love of the arts and sciences was generally diffused, and men devoted themselves to tranquil pursuits. Nevertheless, great corruption of morals prevailed, and the people suffered from heavy taxation. The system of gratuitously distributing corn to citizens entailed great expense. Upwards of 200,000 persons received alms. Trajan had added 5000 children to the number, and Hadrian had increased it still further. This was a very serious tax upon the resources of the emperor, but the early Cæsars who had encouraged and established this system of bribing the people, found the cry of "panem et circenses" (bread and circus shows) too dangerous to be silenced, and their successors continued the evil practice. Antoninus Pius died on March 7th, A. D. 161, in the 75th year of his age, and the 23d year of his reign.

Marcus Aurelius and Lucius Verus became joint emperors on his death. Verus was addicted to pleasure, and being younger than Aurelius, yielded to him in all things. But the peaceful days of the empire were drawing to a close. Those vast national movements among the northern tribes, which had been long fermenting, now began to assume terrible proportions. On the eastern frontier, too, the Parthians renewed their incursions. In the year 162 the Parthian prince, Vologeses, invaded Syria and defeated the Roman governor, Attidius Cornelianus. To repel him, Aurelius persuaded Verus to take the conduct of the war. Aided by his lieutenants, Statius Priscus and Avidius Cassius, Verus went to Syria, where he left the war to their care, and gave himself up to pleasure. Priscus and Cassius conducted matters successfully. Seleucia and Ctesiphon were taken, and the war was terminated A. D. 165. Verus on his return from Syria abandoned himself to frightful excesses. He gave extravagant banquets, one of which is said to have cost $200,000. Aurelius could not restrain him, but contrived to retain all the power in his own hands. In the year 167, the Marcomanni, with other tribes, committed such ravages on the Roman frontiers, that Aurelius found it necessary to take the field against them. Verus was persuaded to go with him into Aquileia, but nothing could induce him to remain. Fortunately for the empire he died suddenly at Alti′num in Venetia (A. D. 169), and thus Aurelius was freed from one cause of anxiety. But he had another in his depraved wife,

How did Hadrian limit the empire?—What were his next acts?—What provinces did he visit?—What public works did he construct?—What effect had the "Apology" of Quadratus for Christianity on him?—Who was Antinous?—What was his fate?—What caused a revolt of the Jews?—Who suppressed it?—What is said of Verus?

How did Antoninus acquire the surname "Pius"?—What of the Stoic philosophy?—Whom did Antoninus adopt as his successors?—And why?—What are the characteristics of his reign?—What famous jurists flourished?—What of public morals?—Of bribing the people?—What events took place on the death of Antoninus?—What is said of Lucius Verus?

Faustina, who shamelessly interfered in public affairs, and so educated her son Com′modus that he subsequently became one of the most sanguinary tyrants that ever disgraced a throne. To add to the emperor's difficulties, a dreadful pestilence brought by Verus from the East desolated Italy, and the German tribes ravaged the northern provinces on the Danube. Hundreds of thousands of persons were carried off by these barbarians, and the Roman legions were disorganized by losses from war and pestilence. The emperor found it necessary to negotiate separately with each tribe, and treaties were made, which the Germans did not hesitate to break almost as soon as made. Aurelius at length set out on a second expedition to the Danube, fully resolved to press the war vigorously. Before leaving Rome, he directed the sale of all the ornaments in the imperial palaces and treasuries. This sale lasted two months, and brought in a large sum of money. The emperor had chastised the Quadi and wholly exterminated two small tribes, when he received intelligence that Avidius Cassius had thrown off his allegiance in Syria, and proclaimed himself emperor. But Avidius was slain by two of his officers (A. D. 175); the Empress Faustina died about the same time; and it was not until after these events that Aurelius proceeded to Syria. He went through Judea to Egypt, and thence through Asia Minor to Athens, giving aid and encouragement everywhere to learned men. He attended the lectures of the philosopher Aristides at Athens, and gave lectures himself. Meanwhile the war raged on the Danube, and the emperor resolved to return to his post there. He gained a decisive victory over the Quadi and the Marcomanni (A. D. 179). But the following year he fell ill, and died before the termination of the war. He was one of the best of the emperors of Rome. From his death, which took place at Sirmium on March 17th, A. D. 180, commences "the Decline and Fall of the Roman Empire". The famous work of Gibbon on this subject protracts the history of it to the destruction of the Eastern or Byzantine branch of the Roman empire at the capture of Constantinople by the Turks in 1453.

Commodus, who was with the army of the Danube at the time of his father's death, concluded a peace with the barbarians as soon as possible. The terms were advantageous to the Romans. The Marcomanni and Quadi promised not to advance their settlements within a league of the Danube, and to hold their popular assemblies only once a month, and that, too, in the presence of a Roman officer; and the Romans razed their forts on the farther side of the Danube, and withdrew the garrisons. The barbarians faithfully observed this treaty for many years. But Commodus inserted an article in it which hastened the downfall of the empire, viz., that 15,000 Quadi and the same number of Marcomanni should enter his legions. This contingent was subsequently made an annual one, and thus the fierce warriors of Germany acquired the art of war, while the luxurious Romans gradually abandoned to them the task of guarding the empire. The emperor was weak and timid, and soon fell into the hands of designing persons, who induced him to plunge into debauchery and neglect public affairs. He thus gradually became merciless and cruel. His sister, Lucilla, and her husband, formed a conspiracy to murder him. The assassin employed to kill him missed his aim, but in so doing exclaimed, "The Senate sends thee this"; and henceforth Commodus conceived a deadly hatred of that body.

After this event the emperor trusted wholly to his guards, and the commander for the time being of that body became all powerful. Perennis, Niger, and Cleander, were the most notorious of these men. Perennis induced the emperor to plunge into all sorts of excesses, but having failed to propitiate the soldiery, the latter, headed by Cleander, sought his ruin. A deputation of 1500 men from the army in Britain marched through Gaul to Rome, and charged Perennis with aiming at the empire. Commodus abandoned him to their fury (A. D. 185), and Cleander soon after obtained the vacant post (A. D. 186). He retained it for three years, during which time Commodus degraded himself by the lowest vices. His favorite amusement was slaying wild beasts, and he celebrated the circus games with fearful extravagance while Rome was desolated by a pestilence (A. D. 189). At the same time Cleander put to death one distinguished person after another; and his cruelty, combined with the famine which prevailed, drove the Romans into insurrection. The troops joined the populace, and a desperate conflict ensued. The emperor was in the greatest danger; but having been induced to give up Cleander to the fury of the people, the tumult was appeased. After this the emperor became more ferocious than ever. He compelled the Senate to worship him in public as Hercules and Mercury: he extorted money from everybody, and put to death any one who offended him, however slightly. The inmates of the palace then resolved to destroy him. The accounts of his death vary: it is believed that they administered poison to him, but that proving ineffectual, a powerful wrestler was called in to strangle him (Dec. 31st, 192).

Helvius Pertinax, an able soldier, was made emperor by the conspirators. But his age incapacitated him from controlling the State; he therefore asked the Senate to choose another ruler. The Senate replied by annulling all the acts of Commodus, and destroying the statues and inscriptions erected to him. The Prætorian guards became furious. Pertinax endeavored to gain their favor by bribery, but was unable to soothe them. A mutiny broke out, and Pertinax was slain, having reigned four months. The soldiers, finding themselves absolute masters of the empire, put it up for sale to the highest bidder. A senator named Did′ius Julia′nus became the purchaser; he promising to pay to each soldier 25,000 sesterces ($100); but he was too insignificant a person to maintain his authority, and the army at once declared against him. Septim′ius Seve′rus in Pannonia, Clodius Albi′nus in Britain, and Pescen′nius Ni′ger in Syria, were proclaimed emperors by their respective legions. Didius took measures to defend himself, but Severus rapidly crossing the Alps at the head of 600 men, boldly entered Rome; the guards and the Senate declared for him, and Didius was beheaded (June 9th, 193).

Severus resorted to stern measures to save the empire. He put to death all who had been concerned in the murder of Pertinax, disarmed and disbanded the Prætorian guard, and marched against Pescennius, who had abandoned himself to pleasure at Antioch. At the same time he pacified Albinus by giving him the title of Cæsar. He defeated the troops of Pescennius near Cyzicus, Nicæa, and Issus. Niger was taken prisoner and put to death (A. D. 194). Severus laid siege to Byzantium, and marched against the Parthians. Crossing the Euphrates, he conquered Adiabe′ne, and added a new province to the empire, which he named Arabia (A. D. 195). Next year Byzantium was taken, and the emperor then marched against Albinus, who had brought his legions into Gaul. The rivals met at Lyons, where Albinus was defeated and killed (Feb. 10th, 197). Severus returned to Rome, and celebrated his victories. He then set off for Parthia, where he gained several victories, and took Ctesiphon (A. D. 198). He made a portion of Armenia into a kingdom for Vologeses (A. D. 199). He also divided Britain into two provinces, and raised his sons, Bassia′nus (also named Marcus Aurelius Antoninus, but better known by his nickname "Caracalla", *i. e.*, long tunic) and Geta, to be colleagues with him in the empire.

Of the literary men who flourished at the beginning of this century, we have already noticed Martial, Juvenal, Plutarch, Epictetus, and Pliny the younger Among those who lived towards the middle and the end of it were:

Arrian of Nicomedia in Bithynia, the great Stoic philosopher, the disciple and apologist of Epictetus, born A. D. 90: he wrote several valuable works on philosophy and history.

Pausa′nias of Lydia, the traveller and geographer, who wrote an Itinerary of Greece.

Dion Cass′ius, the historian, born at Nicæa in Bithynia (A. D. 155). The grammarians Hermip′pus and Nica′nor, and the architect Apollodo′rus.

Hero′des Att′icus, born at Marathon A. D. 104, was a famous rhetorician, and the tutor of Marcus Aurelius and Antoninus Pius. Aulus Gel′lius, the grammarian, and author of a compilation entitled *Noctes Atticæ*, lived in the reign of Marcus Aurelius. Apulei′us of Medaura in Africa, born A. D. 130, author of the "Golden Ass" and of the beautiful allegory, "Cupid and Psyche". Lu′cian of Samos′ata in Syria, born A. D. 120, was the author of "Dialogues of the Gods" and "Dialogues of the Dead". Iam′blichus, the Platonist philosopher, of Chalcis in Syria; Claudius Galen, the famous physician of Pergamus; Claudius Ptolemy, the astronomer; Ap′pian, the historian; and Salvia′nus Julia′nus, the jurist.

What is said of Faustina?—Commodus?—The northern barbarians?—The expedition of Marcus Aurelius to the Danube?—To Syria?—Against the Quadi?—When did he die?—What of Gibbon's "Decline and Fall of the Roman Empire"?—What policy did Commodus adopt?—What of his character?—What is said of Perennis?—Cleander?

What is said of the death of Commodus?—Pertinax?—His end?—The sale of the empire?—The fate of Didius Julianus?—What of Septimius Severus?—Of Pescennius Niger?—Arabia?—Albinus?—The Parthians?—Armenia?—Caracalla and Geta?—Arrian?—Apuleius?—Galen?—Ptolemy?—What other eminent men flourished?

BRITAIN.

ENGLAND.—The Romans introduced many laws and customs which increased the prosperity and happiness of Britain, and the country would have enjoyed profound peace but for the repeated incursions of the Caledonians and Picts, who advanced so far that the Emperor Hadrian came over to the island to repel them. It does not appear, however, that he did much more than construct a ditch and rampart across the island from the Solway Firth to the mouth of the Tyne (A. D. 120), which he left strongly garrisoned. In A. D. 140 the tribes of the Maætæ and Brigantes revolted. The Emperor Antoninus sent Lollius Ur′bicus to quell them. In this he was successful; and, by order of the emperor, constructed a similar fortification across the island from Alcluid, on the Clyde, to Kinneil, on the Forth, which wall he called "the vallum of Antoninus". Nevertheless the Caledonians persisted in their incursions, and in A. D. 180 the Emperor Commodus sent Ul′pius Marcellus to repel them. This general drove them back to their mountains, but was soon after recalled through the jealousy of the emperor. The British legions sent a deputation of 1500 men to Rome to demand the head of the minister, Perennis; and the weak and cruel emperor, meeting them at the gates of the city, surrendered him to their vengeance.

The government of Britain was next (A. D. 190) conferred on Clo′dius Albi′nus, who was made Cæsar by the Emperor Seve′rus. Clodius soon after (A. D. 198) assumed the imperial purple, and led the British legions into Gaul; was met by Severus on the plain of Trevoux, near Lyons, defeated, taken prisoner, and beheaded. Severus divided the island into two governments, bestowing one on Heraclia′nus, and the other on Virius Lupus. According to the British historians the native kings reigned as independent princes, save that they paid tribute to the Romans. Marius, the successor of Arviragus, is described as a man of wisdom and prudence, and as having gained a great victory over a swarm of Picts in the north of England. He was succeeded by his son, Coillus, who was very popular on account of his jovial and munificent disposition, and who, by paying tribute to the Romans, enjoyed his kingdom in peace. Coillus had but one son, Lucius, who succeeded him, and rivalled him in popularity. Lucius sent letters to Pope Eleutherius, desiring to be instructed by him in the Christian religion. The Pope sent two divines, who baptized him, and instructed him in the Christian faith. The king's example was followed by his people, and sundry bishops and archbishops were appointed. The seats of the archbishops were at London, York, and the city of Legions, the ruins of which last are to be seen on the river Usk, in Wales (see Geoffrey of Monmouth's *British History*, ch. xx.). Lucius died at Gloucester (A. D. 156), without issue. Great dissensions thereupon arose among the Britons. The Romans sought to take advantage of these, and additional forces were sent under Severus to subdue the natives. A long contest ensued, wherein Fulge′nius, a British chief, gained several battles, but was subsequently slain.

SCOTLAND.—Galgacus was succeeded by his son, Luctacus, a flagitious prince, who was killed by the people. He was succeeded by his nephew, Mogaldus (A. D. 113), who gave the Romans great trouble, and, after a dissolute reign of 36 years, was slain by a conspiracy, headed by his son, Conary, who succeeded him. This prince was dethroned for his vices. His cousin, Ethodius (A. D. 163), subdued the Hebrides, and was murdered by an Irish harper, after a reign of 30 years. Satrael, who succeeded him (A. D. 195), fared no better, being strangled by his servants after a reign of four years. Donald, the brother of Ethodius, was then elected king.

IRELAND.—The principal event of this century was a popular insurrection, which broke out in A. D. 126, and drove Tuathal from his throne. Having taken refuge in Scotland, he returned with an army of Picts, and, marching to Tara, was re-elected sovereign (A. D. 130). He then convened the General Assembly of the States at Tara, and induced them to swear allegiance to him alone. He also ordained that there should be held, annually, three assemblies of the kingdom. He imposed a cruel fine on the province of Leinster for the misconduct of its ruler. This fine was exacted every second year, and was called "the Boromean tribute": it was the source of continual bloodshed, and was not abolished until the year 693. During the reign of Feidlim (A. D. 164) the criminal code was ameliorated, and municipal courts were erected for the regulation of trade. Feidlim was succeeded by CON of "the hundred battles".

What did the Emperor Hadrian do?—Lollius Urbicus?—Ulpius Marcellus?—What did the British legions do?—What did Clodius Albinus?—Severus?—What is said of Marius?—Lucius?—Coillus?—Who was the first Christian king of England?—What happened on his death?—What were the principal events in Scotland in this century?—In Ireland?

FRANCE.

THE history of France during this century presents little that is remarkable. The country enjoyed peace and prosperity. The emperors founded several cities — Nismes in particular,— and they greatly embellished others. Bordeaux became celebrated for its trade, and Toulouse for its schools. Arras, Langres, and Saintes manufactured cloth and rich robes. The vine was extensively cultivated, and the produce of the grapes of Eastern and Southern France acquired great celebrity. The country had been divided into three provinces by Augustus in the previous century, viz., Belgium, Aquitania, and the Lyonnaise. The city of Lyons became the capital of the country, rivalling Rome in luxury. The city of Trèves, however, was the residence of the imperial lieutenants, and rose to great political importance. The plain of Trevoux, near Lyons, was the scene of the famous battle between the Emperor Severus and the pretender, Clodius Albinus, Feb. 17th, 197, which resulted in the defeat and death of the latter. An account of this contest will be found in the history of Italy.

It was about the year 160 that some Christian priests from Asia Minor, having at their head a bishop named PO-THI′NUS, arrived at Lyons to found a church there. The celebrated IRENÆUS was one of their number, he having been sent as a missionary by Polycarp, bishop of Smyrna. Many of the principal persons of this church were Greeks. Their labors were successful, though the heresy of the Montanists caused them great trouble. This sect was formed by Montanus, of Phrygia, who asserted that he was the promised Comforter, that he had come to perfect the precepts of Christ, and that all polite literature should be swept away. He also inculcated rigid austerity, and abject submission to persecution. But his doctrine had been condemned, and he himself expelled from the Church. The rapid increase of the congregations of Pothinus and Irenæus excited the enmity of the pagan populace, and a violent persecution broke out (A. D. 177), in which many of the Christian leaders and disciples were martyred; amongst others, the venerable Pothinus, then 90 years of age. Irenæus was chosen to succeed Pothinus in the bishopric. On the accession of Commodus (A. D. 180), the successor of Marcus Aurelius, the persecution ceased.

What was the state of France?—What cities became famous?—Who founded the bishopric of Lyons?—What befell him?—Who was his successor?—Who were the Montanists?

SPAIN.

THE history of Spain presents little that is remarkable during this century. The country flourished under the Emperors Trajan, Hadrian, Antoninus Pius, Marcus Aurelius, and Verus (A. D. 100–181). Trajan was the greatest man of his time, and one of the ablest of the Roman emperors. Spain is justly proud of having produced him. Under him, peace and the arts flourished in the peninsula. New roads were constructed by his orders, and the old ones repaired: the beautiful arch of Torre de Barca, in Catalonia; the stupendous bridge of Alcanta′ra, in Estremadura; and the splendid colonnade of Zalamea de la Serena; perhaps also the beautiful circus at Italica (Old Seville), the tower of Corunna, the Monte Ferrada in Galicia, and the celebrated aqueducts at Tarragona and Segovia, attest his patriotism and his magnificence. His successor, Hadrian, was also a Spaniard, and though not so able a man, was not inferior to him in love of his native land, and adorned it with many beautiful works. It is said that the soldiers of the 7th legion founded the city of Leon. Hadrian visited Spain, where he narrowly escaped assassination at the hands of a madman. Spain at this time was divided into three provinces, viz., Lusitania, Tarraconensis, and Bœtica, with which last the Emperor Otho incorporated Mauretania Tingitana. The governors of Hither (citerior) and Farther (ulterior) Spain had supreme control over the civil and military affairs of the nation, and were termed consuls, or prætors. Their office was an annual one, and those who held it longer than a year were termed proconsuls, or proprætors. The governors of Lusitania and Tarraconensis were also styled *Legati Augustales* (Imperial Legates), and each had deputies, or vice-legates.

The Christians in Spain suffered greatly during the persecutions under Trajan (A. D. 103) and Hadrian. In the reign of the latter, Marc, a disciple of Basil′ides, introduced Gnosticism into Spain, where it took root, and spread.

The reign of Antoninus Pius (A. D. 138–161) is almost a blank in history, owing to the suspension of war and violence. Throughout the entire empire of Rome the people enjoyed peace and prosperity. The reign of this emperor, and that of his successor, Marcus Aurelius, are reckoned the happiest period in the history of the human race.

What benefits did Trajan confer on Spain?—What of Hadrian?—Who founded Leon?—How was Spain divided?—Who introduced Gnosticism?—What of Pius and Aurelius?

GERMANY.

The Emperor Trajan conducted the war with such skill that Decebalus (Dezebal) was overcome, but not without great difficulty, and was forced to conclude a shameful peace (A. D. 103). Filled with mortification at his defeat, and with fears for his country, he once more attempted to arm the neighboring tribes against Rome, setting before them the danger to which they were exposed, unless they united against their common enemy. His entreaties were vain, and he was forced to stem the torrent unassisted and alone. A long and desperate struggle ensued, and at length, completely defeated and driven to desperation, he killed himself, after making a vain attempt to poison the emperor. Dacia became a Roman province (A. D. 106); and a stone bridge, of immense length, thrown across the Danube, still records the success of Trajan.

The Emperor Hadrian, the successor of Trajan, followed the plan commenced by Cæsar, and established an immense line of fortified encampments at the most important points, and castles along the left bank of the Rhine and the right bank of the Danube, thus surrounding that frontier with forts. He connected them by high and straight roads, provided with watch-towers at short intervals apart: these roads were carried over the mountains, instead of through the valleys, so as to prevent surprise. He also spared no expense in fortifying the Black Forest, especially that point where it penetrates into Basle; and he constructed a great wall, which extended from Pfarring, on the Danube, to Mittenberg, on the Maine, and is now known as the Teufelsmauer, Heidenmauer, or Pfahlgraben. It was completely fortified from one end to the other. A large number of towns arose near these forts, on the wasted and desolate frontier, which was gradually repeopled and cultivated by Roman colonists, or by poor German fugitives and deserters. These lands were called *agri decumates* (it is uncertain whether on account of a tenth paid by the cultivator, or from a Roman measure for marking out the fields, or from choosing one out of every ten peasants to form the garrison of the fort). Of the cities which thus arose, the most considerable were Trèves and Mentz (Mayence), at the latter of which the remains of a vast Roman aqueduct are still to be seen. The country was placed under military government, the proconsul having unlimited power and authority in the province. The people soon adopted the customs, language, and luxurious habits of their masters. Hadrian and Trajan also planted powerful colonies in Moldavia and Wallachia. The right bank of the Rhine was divided into four provinces, viz., Rhætia, Noricum, Pannonia, and Mœsia; and the left bank also into four, viz., Helvetia, Germania Prima, Germania Secunda, and Belgica.

A long interval of peace had elapsed, when one of those great and mysterious movements amongst the tribes of the East agitated the whole of Germany. A sudden and terrific irruption burst forth, in the year 162, from the interior of Germany, and spread like a torrent over the Roman empire, which was simultaneously attacked on the Rhine and the Danube by these barbarians, and in Asia by the Parthians. The Catti were the first who crossed the Rhine: they were defeated by Pertinax. The Marcomanni, followed by various tribes, next poured into Italy, and laid siege to Aquileia (A. D. 166). The brave defence of this city, and the sudden appearance of the emperor, Marcus Aurelius, with a powerful army, induced them to recross the Danube. The emperor followed them, and, in a desperate battle fought on the frozen Danube, was completely victorious, recovering more than 100,000 Roman prisoners. He afterwards followed the Quadi into their own country, where his army had nearly perished from thirst, when a sudden fall of rain (occasioned, it was said, by the prayers of the Christian soldiers, who thence obtained the name of "the thundering legion") relieved them, and enabled them to subdue their enemies. Marcus Aurelius restored and garrisoned the ruined fortresses on the Danube. His successor, Commodus, however, concluded a shameful peace with the Germans.

During this century the small tribes were gradually fusing together, and many of them now disappear from history. The tribes on the Lower Rhine were henceforth known only as the Catti and the Sicambri; those on the Northern Ocean, as the Frisii, the Chauci, and the Angli; those of Southern Germany, as the Alemanni and the Boioarii; those of Central Germany, as the Hermunduri, the Longobardi, and the Burgundians; those of Eastern Germany, as the Goths, the Gepidæ, and the Vandals. The Franks and the Saxons soon after appear in place of the Sicambri and the Chauci.

What was the fate of Decebalus?—What was the policy pursued by Hadrian?—What is the Heidenmauer?—Where were colonies planted?—How was Roman Germany divided?—What took place A. D. 162?—What great exploits did Marcus Aurelius perform?—Whence arose "the thundering legion"?—What else occurred during this century?

AFRICA.

There is no event of consequence to record in the history of this century. Considerable trade was carried on between Rome and the northern coast of Africa, and even with Ethiopia. The dominion of the emperor of Rome was quietly acquiesced in by the nations dwelling on the shores of the Mediterranean, but the tribes inhabiting the interior of the continent never owned more than a nominal subjection to it. Christianity spread rapidly, notwithstanding the hostility of the pagan priests, and the terrible persecutions permitted by the emperors: the history of its progress will be found in the pages devoted to the Christian Church.

As the speculating Christians of the early ages of the Church assigned to Antichrist, when he should come upon earth, the empire of Egypt, Ethiopia, and Libya, it may not be amiss to notice their traditions and opinions on the subject. "Antichrist" is the name of that Man of Sin, mentioned by St. Paul in 2 Thess. ii., 3, 4, who is expected to precede the second coming of our Saviour. The Mohammedans also expect him, and give him the name of Daggiel (liar, or impostor). The name "Antichrist" has been applied to many persons, especially to Nero, Trajan, Diocletian, Julian the Apostate, and Martin Luther. St. John describes him as having a mark, and a name, with a number expressing it: this number is 666 (Rev. xiii., 17, 18). But it was disputed whether this number was to be discovered in the letters in his name (the letters in the Hebrew, Greek, and Latin alphabets being used as numerals), or whether it was to be understood as simply an arithmetical number. A vast amount of learning has been expended on this subject, but no definite result has ever been obtained. Equally unsuccessful have been the endeavors to fix the time of his coming. The early fathers (Tertullian, Cyprian, Hilary, Basil, Jerome, Chrysostom, and Gregory the Great) thought it was near at hand. Later writers have fixed it variously at A. D. 1026, 1540, 1734, 1789, 1800, and 1994. There was anciently a tradition that he would be born of a Jewish family of the tribe of Dan, settled in Babylonia; that he would become master of Egypt, Ethiopia, and Libya, and then establish himself at Jerusalem for three years and a half: after which the Saviour would reappear on earth, and subdue him.

What was the condition of Africa during this century?—What of Antichrist?—What of his number?—The time of his coming?—His end?

SCANDINAVIA.

Sweden.—The pontiff-kings of the Yngling dynasty, of this century, are Visbur (A. D. 98–130), Domald (A. D. 130–162), Domar (A. D. 162–190), Dyggve (A. D. 190–220), but we know little more of them than their names. The latter was the first that assumed the regal title, his predecessors being merely called Drottar, or lord, and their queens Drottingar. Domald was slain by the advice of his councillors, under the superstitious idea that a severe famine which afflicted the country could only be removed by sprinkling the altars of the gods at Upsala with the blood of their king.

Denmark.—The kings of Denmark—Nermund the Sage (died A. D. 140), Olaf I., surnamed the Mild (A. D. 140–190), and Dan, surnamed Mykillati (or the Magnanimous)—call for no notice, except the last named, who, in the next century, united all the petty kingdoms into which Denmark was divided. Such unions were constantly effected, but they lasted only during the life of the authors of them, and on their decease the monarchy was immediately dismembered. The north swarmed with "kings": we read of thirty being assembled together on one occasion: probably many of them were tributary. When any sovereign of Jutland, or Scania, or Sigtun, or any other place in Denmark, Sweden, or Norway, obtained much celebrity as a warrior, the local chiefs, who always assumed the title of kings, were always ready to seek his protection, and serve under his banner. Though this obedience was temporary, a preference was usually given to such of the more powerful kings as were of the divine race of Odin. They passed their lives in warfare, piracy, and hunting. Their thirst for adventure appears to have been insatiable. The student who desires to learn what exploits were considered honorable, and were attributed to the most renowned of the Scandinavian heroes, should consult Suorro Sturleson's *Heimskringla*, which has been translated into English. The legends of Arngrim, and his magic sword; of Swafurlam, and his twelve sons; of the incantation of Hervör; of Angantyr, and the Berserks; of Sterkodder, the Hercules of the North; of Gorm's wonderful voyage, and the palace of Geruth, are illustrative of these fierce Northmen. They will be found in Dunham's *History of Denmark*.

Who first assumed the regal title in Sweden?—What is recorded of Domald?—The kings of Denmark?—Of Scandinavia?—Their lives?—Their legends?

NETHERLANDS.

The Frisii retained their independence. The tribes, and the provinces into which the country was divided, have already been noticed. The people on the Lower Rhine gradually became known only as the Catti and the Sicambri; and all those on the Northern Ocean, as the Frisii, Chauci, and Angli. The Franks soon afterwards appear in place of the Catti, Chama′vi, Sicambri, Bruc′teri, and Cherus′ci; all which changes prove that the small districts (formerly separate from, and independent of, each other) had everywhere united, and had formed into large communities. This alliance may have been induced by several circumstances, such as common origin, the superiority of a powerful tribe over its weaker neighbors, and finally the necessity of leaguing together on account of the renewal of the war with Rome, which took place A. D. 162. A simultaneous attack on the Roman empire was made by the German tribes. Those on the Rhine were the first in motion. An account of this war is given in the history of Germany (p. 143). The Chauci appeared on the Northern Ocean in their pirate vessels, and ravaged the coasts of Gaul and Britain.

The word Frank signifies "free", and the tribes that confederated for the preservation of their freedom were distinguished by that name. It may be ascribed to Civilis, who, in the preceding century, roused all the Lower Germans in the name of freedom, and is said to have uttered these words to the people of Cologne: "You will be free (*frank*) among the free" (*franken*).

The Saxons consisted of the Chauci, Frisii, and the remnants of the tribes on the Northern Ocean and the Baltic. Their name was derived from the ancient Sacæ (Sikhs) on the Indus, and from *Sachs* (race), and *Sasson* (freeholders). According to tradition, they came by sea from the army of Alexander the Great to Hadel, where they landed, and buying from the Thuringi a gownful of earth, spread it over a large territory to which they laid claim, and then inviting the Thuringian chiefs to meet them unarmed, murdered them during the banquet with knives concealed beneath their dresses. According to their legend, the Saxons, and their first king Ascan, sprang from the Hartz mountains; and the proverb, "There are Saxons wherever pretty girls grow out of trees", is still in use.

What changes took place among the Belgian tribes?—What was the origin of the Franks?—Who were the Saxons?—What is the tradition respecting them?—The legend?

CENTRAL AMERICA.

There can be little doubt as to the high antiquity of the original population of America. The extraordinary number of languages spoken in Central America, at the time of its discovery by the Spaniards, proves either that the country was peopled from a variety of foreign nations, or that the indigenous race must have been established there so long as to enable the laws of Providence, relative to the multiplication and distribution of the human race, to have come into gradual but full operation. There is no evidence that any considerable or varied migration took place from the Old World into the New; although it is highly probable that adventurers from time to time found their way across from Africa to Brazil, and from Asia across Behring's Straits, or through the Aleutian Islands, or from Japan to the western shores of America. We are therefore constrained to adopt the former hypothesis: and we may further assert that no subsequent immigration has been of sufficient magnitude to alter the distinctive character of this indigenous population. The languages of Guatemala, Chiapas, and Yucatan, have their common origin in the Maya idiom. According to Ximenes, the Calchiquel, Quichè, Zutuhil, Tzotzil, Zendal, Chanabal, Conoh, Mamè, Lacandon, Peten, Ixil, Cakchi, Poconchi, and many other languages, are of this class.

American traditions frequently allude to the journeyings of the tribes of the Quichès, who came from the East, from a cold and icy region, across a stormy sea, to a region not less inhospitable on the American continent, whence they directed their footsteps southward. Their march was slow and painful; they encountered terrible privations; but at length they reached Central America, where they settled, and where their descendants are still to be found. The primitive civilization of the southern portion of the continent probably arose in the countries now known by the names of Tabasco, Chiapas, Oaxaca, Yucatan, Guatemala, San Salvador, and Honduras. The multitude and variety of the ruins found there, combined with the traditions of the past, all point to this region as the source of the culture and splendor to which the Mexicans afterwards attained. According to the ancient Tzendal tradition, the banks of the Tabasco and of the Uzumacinta were the scenes of the wondrous works performed by Votan, the most ancient of American legislators, many centuries before the Christian Era. These rivers flow into the Gulf of Mexico from the snowy chain of the Chuchumatanes (Cordilleras of Guatemala). The ruins of Palenquè, the most ancient of American cities, are still to be seen in Guatemala; and, it is said, that even at this day there exist among the Lacandons, dwelling between the Uzumacinta and Vera Paz, populous cities, the last refuge of the ancient civilized Indians of Central America, who preserve their religion and their antique costume. In this region Votan began his labors: he found the people savage, and instructed them in the arts of civilization. That Votan was a real personage there is good reason to suppose, but he has been elevated to the rank of a god, and of a mediator between the Supreme Being and man, and it is impossible to decide whether all the attributes and actions ascribed to him are all his, or due to others of the same name. The analogy in the Tzendal, the Quichè, and the Mexican traditions, relative to the personages presented under the names of Votan, Cukulcan, and Gucumatz or Quetzalcohuatl, leads to the belief that they are one and the same person. Votan was the founder of Palenquè, Paxil, and Cayala, and of those famous temples and palaces whose magnificent ruins still astonish the beholder. The Tzendal tradition says that he came originally from Cuba, with a number of his countrymen; that he first explored the thousand islands of the lagune of Terminos, and then ascended the Uzumacinta, on the banks of which river, at the foot of the Tumbala mountains, he settled; there he founded Nachan (city of serpents), afterwards called Palenquè. He was welcomed by the Tzendals, and became their ruler. In the course of a long reign Votan four times visited his native land; and he wrote a treatise on the origin of the Indians, in which he proved that they descended from Imos, of the race of Chan (the serpent), and originally came from Chivim (wherever that may be: the Spanish historian, Ordoñez, says it means the land of the Hivites, in Canaan). He divided the monarchy which he had established into four parts, and one of them was given to the foreign chieftains: their capital was Tulha, the ruins of which have been found near Ococinco, on the other side of the Tumbala mountains. A curious tradition is still preserved among the Tzendals, that a subterranean road of prodigious length traversed the mountains, and connected the temple of Tulha with that of Palenquè, and that it was dug by order of Votan. He also founded the city of Ghowel, or Tzequil, or Huey-Zacatlan, in a valley of the lofty mountains of Ciudad Real.

As to the era of Votan, there is nothing to guide us; but all American tradition refers it to a very remote period. About the same time another great chief and lawgiver, named Zamna (or Itzamal), arrived in Yucatan, accompanied by a number of priests, warriors, and artists. He established himself there, and founded a kingdom, into which he introduced laws, arts, and sciences. He built the city of Mayapan for his capital; and he divided his territory into large provinces, which he granted as hereditary fiefs to the principal chiefs who had accompanied him, but subordinate to the prince of Mayapan. It is said that he introduced figures or characters for letters. He died at an advanced age, and was buried at a place where subsequently arose the city of Itzmal-Ul (or Itzamal). He was held in equal veneration with Votan in subsequent ages. The descendants of Votan sank into insignificance, and some centuries afterwards succumbed to the Toltecs: the last of them, Chinax, was hung and burnt by the "nagual" (Toltec leader).

The annals of Mexico dwell upon two facts: 1. The arrival of a foreign race, led by an illustrious personage, and coming from the East. 2. The existence of an ancient empire, known by the name of Huehue-Tlapallan, whence the ancestors of the Toltecs (or Nahuas) migrated in consequence of a revolution, and after much suffering established themselves in the Aztec plateau. It is supposed that this last-mentioned Toltec emigration took place either during the first century before, or the first century after, the Christian Era. These emigrants were termed Nahuatl, Nahual, or Nawal (a word signifying wise or skilled), and their language became the predominant one throughout Central America. The illustrious personage who came from the East, heading the foreign colony above mentioned, was styled Quetzalcohuatl (pronounced Ketz′al-whotl), or Gucumatz. Under him they arrived in Tamoanchan, where he founded the city of Xicalanco, which became one of the most flourishing cities in Central America. He extended his influence into the

What is said of the original population of Central America?—Languages?—The Quichès?—The earliest seat of civilization?—Votan?—Palenquè?—Nachan?—The traditions relating to Votan?—And to the temples of Tulha and Palenquè?—Who was Zamna?—What is said of him?—Of the descendants of Votan?—What two leading facts are insisted on in Mexican annals?—When did the Toltec emigration take place?—What of the Nahual language?—Of Quetzalcohuatl?—What city did he found?—What were his exploits?

neighboring empire of Xibalba (Palenquè), and attempted to conquer it; but in this he failed, and he then returned to the land whence he came. On his departure, the four leading chiefs—Oxomoco, Cipactonal, Tlaltetecui, and Xuchicaoaca—convoked at Huehue-Tlapallan the assembly of the Nahuan nation, and established the new calendar for astrological as well as astronomical purposes, which remained in use until the destruction of Mexico by the Spaniards. Oxomoco and Cipactonal assumed the government of the entire empire of the Toltecs. Their sons, Hunhuahpu and Wucub-Hunahpu, having endeavored to gain possession of the empire of Xibalba, were put to death. Another son, Exbalanquè, retired into the mountains of Quichè, where he founded an independent kingdom, of which the sacred city of Utlatlan became the capital. Here we have the old story of barbarous exploits: one king or chief dethrones another. Exbalanquè was driven out of his kingdom, and another Hunahpu replaced him. Chalcatzin and Tlacamitzin succeeded the latter, when a fresh revolution drove the Toltecs to the shores of the Pacific, where they built the city of Tlapallantonco. Thence they removed towards the northwest, and established several kingdoms in Southern California. Some, however, turned towards Yucatan; of these were the Tutul-Xius, who subsequently established their dominion over that country. The epoch of this dispersion of the great Nahuan or Toltec nation has been carefully preserved: it is the first precise date we meet with in the annals of Central America, and is fixed at the year 174 of our era. For a full account of these early ages, and of the national archives whence they are derived, the student is referred to the work of the learned Abbé Brasseur de Bourbourg, entitled *Histoire des Nations civilisées du Mexique et de l'Amérique-Centrale, durant les siècles antérieurs à Christophe Colomb*, to which we are mainly indebted for our information respecting the heroic ages of Central America.

Like all other countries of antiquity, Central America had its giants, the Quinamiès, whose dominion extended over the interior provinces of Mexico and Guatemala, but of whose origin and form of government we are ignorant. They were a brutal race, addicted to the grossest vices; but subsequently became partly civilized by a race whom they styled Olmecs and Xicalancas, and finally were exterminated by them at a solemn festival on the plateau of Huitzilapan. A few escaped, but their descendants were exterminated by the Toltecs some centuries afterwards. The only reminiscence of them left was the name of one of their divinities, Tlaloc (or Tlalotl), who had also been one of their great kings. Contemporary with the Olmecs were the Mixtecas (called also Zapotecas), the Totonacs, and the Othomis. The Totonacs claimed to have been the builders of the great pyramids in Teotihuacan, and to have been the first settlers in Anahuac. They came from Chicomoztoc, while the Chichiecs were still settled there. Some of them settled in Xalpan; others near Lake Xaltocan. The Othomis were a distinct race, speaking a monosyllabic language like the Chinese, which they called Hiang-hiung ("the permanent speech": the name Othomi signifies "never tranquil"). They inhabited Mexico before the Toltecs; and they worshipped one deity, O-kha ("the holy remembrance"): they styled heaven Ma-he-tze. Their principal heroes, whom they worshipped as demigods, were Otomitl (or Othon Tecuhtli), Atetein, and Yoxippa; the last named being the most honored. They shaved their head, with the exception of one tuft or tail, after the Chinese fashion, and it may reasonably be inferred that they were of Chinese origin. But being subdued in turn by the Toltecs, the Chichimecs, and the Aztecs, they became the most abject of men, and their name synonymous with all that is base. Their principal cities were Mam-he-ni (afterwards Tollan), Otompan, and Teotihuacan (their sacred city). Omeacatl is the most famous of the Totonac princes of Teotihuacan. Xatontan, his successor, who lived at the time of the Toltec invasion of Mexico, was buried in one of the vast pyramids of Teotihuacan.

Allusion has already been made to the wearisome migration of the Quichès from Tulan, that distant eastern country whence they came. The particulars are given in the Abbé de Bourbourg's work, above cited (book ii., ch. ii.). The most remarkable incident connected with it is THE APOTHEOSIS OF NANAHUATL, which is constantly referred to in Mexican traditions. The chiefs of the Quichès had vowed that if they ever reached the end of their journey, Teotihuacan, and subdued the land, they would sacrifice one of their number to the gods. Having arrived at the holy city they chose Nanahuatl, who was suffering from a loathsome disease, which became honored afterwards! That chief was accordingly burnt, with his servant Metztli, and they reappeared as a bright sun and moon in the heavens. This is doubtless an astronomical allegory, for it is spoken of with mysterious reverence, and it installed a new period styled Nahui-Ollin (the fourth movement), or of Ollin-Tonatiuh (the sun in movement). It coincides with the Mexican year 1 Silex, and probably commences the era of the calendar of which Oxomoco and Cipactonal were the authors. This apotheosis of the sun and moon gave rise to the erection of the two principal pyramids of Teotihuacan, and the Mexicans observed several festivals in honor of it until the Spanish invasion. It also was the commencement of the horrid practice of offering up human sacrifices to the gods, which in after ages was carried to such a frightful extent.

It has been already stated that the Mayan chronology fixes the year 174 of the Christian Era as the date of the departure of the four Tutul-Xius "from the house of Nonohual and the land of Tulapan, which is to the west of Zuyna (or Zuywa), having at their head Holon-Chan-Tepeuh." This epoch was also that of their arrival in Chacnouitan. After this event the chronology remains silent until the year 268, when a second emigration of the Tutul-Xius took place. But nowhere are we told who were the Tutul-Xius, nor why they left their country. It appears certain that they belonged to the Nahuatl race, and that they powerfully aided the spread of Toltec civilization in Yucatan. We are entirely ignorant as to the length of time which had elapsed since Zamna laid the foundations of civilization in that country, until the appearance of the Tutul-Xius there; and owing to the barbarous fanaticism of the Spanish priest, Diego Landa, bishop of Merida, who destroyed all the native archives and records that he could find, we have no connected history of what occurred during that long period. Nevertheless some traces have been left. We can also ascertain certain particulars with regard to a small number of the deities worshipped by these Tutul-Xius. These gods were kings, who had, in their time, been either good or bad, and to whom altars had been erected either through love or fear, but no dates can be assigned to their existence. The principal deity, or rather demigod, after Zamna, was Kinieh-Kakmô. He dedicated a magnificent temple to the sun in the city of Izamal, where, personifying the god, he received divine honors. After his death his renown increased considerably, and he had the reputation of being able to allay pestilence or famine. The priests in his temple appear to have understood the art of setting fire to objects by directing upon them the sun's rays concentrated in a focus, for we are told that when sacrifices were offered, they brought down the divine fire by the aid of a mirror, and burnt the victims. Kinieh-Kakmô also instituted an order of "Virgins of the Sun", whose duty it was to keep the sacred fire perpetually burning in honor of the great luminary. His daughter was the first who inaugurated the dignity of Ixnacan-Katun (or, Superior of the Vestals). Her chastity and piety caused her to be worshipped after her death, under the name of Zuhui-Kak (or, the Virgin of the Fire), as the protectress of young girls. The rules of this order of Vestals were far more rational than those of the Roman Vestals: for, 1, no one could be compelled to become a member of it. 2. The vows were made for a limited time only; but if they were broken before the expiration of that time, or if the fire should become extinct, the offender was shot to death with arrows. 3. When the time had expired, the Vestals might marry; their lovers merely demanding them of the chief priest, who could not oppose any obstacle to the union, but was expected to give his consent as a matter of course.

Next to Kinieh-Kakmô, in dignity, was Ahchuy-Kak, the god of war. He was, in his lifetime, a famous warrior, but the details of his exploits have not been handed down to us. But among the Tutul-Xius, in time of war, the image of this god was dressed in regal ornaments, and borne before the soldiers by the four most valiant captains in the army, and the greatest honors were paid to it on the march. The Spanish historians, Lizana (*Historia de Nuestra Señora de Izamal*) and Cogolludo (*Historia de Yucatan*), mention other deities; but it is not easy to determine whether these heroes preceded the epoch of the Tutul-Xius, or whether they reigned after that race made its appearance in Yucatan.

What occurred after the departure of Quetzalcohuatl?—Who founded Utlatlan?—What befell the Toltecs?—What of the Tutul-Xius?—The era of their dispersion?—The giants, or Quinamiès?—The Olmecs?—The Mixtecas?—The Totonacs?—The Othomis?—The Othomi heroes, language, and manners?—Who were the most famous Totonac chiefs?

What of the migration of the Quichès?—The Apotheosis of Nanahuatl and Metztli?—The Mexican calendar?—The origin of the two pyramids of Teotihuacan?—And of human sacrifices?—What of the migration of the Tutul-Xius into Chacnouitan?—Of their deities?—Kinieh-Kakmô?—The Vestal Virgins?—Aychuy-Kak?—How was he honored?

THE CHRISTIAN CHURCH.

The Christian religion, in defiance of persecution, had now made great progress. We are assured by the most unexceptionable testimony that it prevailed extensively throughout the whole East, as well as among the Romans, Greeks, Germans, Spaniards, Britons, Gauls, and other nations. Numerous Latin versions were made of the Scriptures, the most valued being that known as the Italic, which was followed by the Syriac, Egyptian, and Ethiopic. Indeed, such progress had Christianity made, that numbers of persons, whose means of living depended on the services of the heathen temples, were thrown out of employment. This occasioned serious outcries against the Christians, and led to the third persecution (A. D. 107-115), which was too readily assented to by the Emperor Trajan. Great cruelties were perpetrated. Amongst the most illustrious victims were Cle′ophas, bishop of Pella, who was crucified at the request of the Jews (A. D. 108). The illustrious and venerable Igna′tius, bishop of Antioch, the disciple of the Apostles Peter, Paul, and John, was condemned by Trajan to be torn to pieces by wild beasts in the amphitheatre at Rome (A. D. 115). But in no portion of the empire did they suffer more than in Bithynia, of which province Pliny the Younger was governor. That officer having applied to the emperor for instructions as to how he was to act towards them, received for answer that "the Christians were not to be officiously sought after, but that such as were accused and convicted of an adherence to Christianity were to be put to death as wicked citizens, if they did not return to the religion of their ancestors." Such was the famous edict of Trajan, under which numbers suffered death. It was renewed and confirmed by the Emperor Hadrian, who was, however, more disposed than his predecessor to protect the Christians, partly owing to the noble refusal of Sere′nus Grania′nus, proconsul of Asia, to encourage the fury of the multitude, and to that officer's remonstrance to the emperor, and partly owing to the *Apology for Christianity*, addressed to him by Quadra′tus, bishop of Athens, a disciple of the apostles. In Judea the furious Barchoch′ebas, the fictitious king of the Jews, vented his wrath against all those Christians who refused to join the revolt which he had raised against the Roman power (A. D. 131). But though the edicts of Trajan and Hadrian afforded some protection to those Christians who were not disposed to avow their faith publicly, and prohibited any malicious search after them, yet their enemies soon found means to evade these edicts; and, under the reign of Antoninus Pius, they invented a new method of attacking them by accusing them of impiety and atheism. This calumny was refuted in an able manner by Justin Martyr (A. D. 141), in an "Apology" addressed to the emperor. The effect of this composition was such that that equitable prince issued an order to the effect that all proceedings against the Christians should be regulated by the edict of Hadrian; and, in order further to stop the atrocities which were practised, he promulgated a fresh edict, denouncing capital punishment against such as should, for the future, accuse the Christians without being able to prove them guilty of crime.

Nevertheless the position of the Christians was not improved by these measures of the emperor. In the reign of Marcus Aurelius they were charged with the most monstrous crimes, and that emperor unhappily lent a willing ear to these calumnies, paying little regard to the Apologies written by Justin Martyr, Athenag′oras, and Ta′tian. Though famed for his humanity, Marcus Aurelius did not display any leniency towards the Christians; but, on the contrary, listened willingly to the accusations brought against them. With his sanction the most cruel torments were inflicted on them: torture, crucifixion, burning, and beheading, were freely used. Thousands of Christians perished; among the most illustrious victims were Polycarp and Justin Martyr. Many churches, particularly those of Lyons and Vienne, in France, were nearly destroyed (A. D. 177). The Emperor Verus was not behind Marcus Aurelius in urging this persecution of the Christians (A. D. 164). During the reign of Com′modus the Christians suffered very little; but at the end of the century, when Seve′rus was proclaimed emperor, Asia, Egypt, and other provinces were literally dyed with the blood of the martyrs.

Numerous heresies, too, sprang up in the Church, the most important of which were those of Basil′ides, Val′entine, and Mar′cion. Basilides was an Egyptian Gnostic. He taught that the Supreme Being produced from himself seven Æons (eternal natures), who, again, engendered 365 angels. These angels made the world, and governed it, until they quarrelled. God then sent his own Son, Christ, the chief of the Æons, to restore peace: he united himself with the man Jesus, who was crucified by the Æon who presided over the Jews. These absurdities were surpassed by Carpoc′rates of Alexandria, who adopted them, and taught that it was lawful for men to give full license to their passions. Valentine, the Egyptian, first promulgated his doctrines at Rome, whence they spread through Europe, Asia, and Africa. His doctrines were very singular, and, as they developed the Oriental philosophy, are deserving of note. He taught that in the "Plero′ma" (immensity of space) there were thirty Æons, half male, half female, and four more of neither sex. These four were Horus, Christ, the Holy Ghost, and Jesus. The youngest of the female Æons, Sophia (wisdom), brought forth a daughter, named Ach′amoth, who being banished from the Pleroma, fell into and arranged the undigested mass of matter; and, by the assistance of Jesus, produced the Demiur′ge (subordinate workman). This Demiurge separated the animal from the terrestrial matter, and out of the former created the heavens, and out of the latter the earth. He also made man, uniting in him the subtile and the grosser matter, but Achamoth added to him also a spiritual and a celestial substance. Valentine further taught that this world is a compound of good and evil; whatever is good in it comes down from God, and to Him it shall return, and then the world shall be destroyed by fire. The sect of the Valentinians became divided into several branches, some of which took the name of the originators. Thus there were the Ptolem′aites, the Secun′dians, the Herac′leonites, and the Marco′sians: some that of their peculiar tenets, as the Ad′amites, who professed primitive innocence; the Serpentin′ians, who held that the serpent which tempted Eve was Christ, and therefore worshipped it.

Marcion of Pontus believed in two principles — one good, the other evil; to these he added a third, or intermediate Deity, to whom he ascribed the creation of this lower world, and the legislation of the Jews. Ammo′nius Sac′chas of Alexandria was of the sect of the Eclectics, or Neo-Platonists. He taught that true philosophy came from the East into Greece, where it was held in all its purity by Plato, but that it had become corrupted, and therefore Christ came to purify it. He considered the Deity and the universe as constituting one great whole, and he maintained the eternity of the world, the empire of Providence, and the government of mankind by demons. He commanded his disciples to mortify the flesh, in order that they might become Theurges, or able to see demons; and he asserted that Christ was the chief Theurge (the workman of God). This new system of philosophy had a most injurious effect on Christianity, for its doctrines became mixed up with all kinds of theories arising out of Platonism, respecting the nature of the soul, the destiny of man, the efficacy of faith, the use of reason, etc.

Besides these sects there arose various others. Prax′eas denied that there was any real difference between the Father, Son, and Holy Ghost: hence his followers were named Monarchians, and also Patripassians, because they said the Father suffered with Christ on the cross. Hermog′enes (the painter), Carpocrates, Bardesa′nes, Elxai, Saturni′nus, and Tatian, were all more or less of the Eclectic school, and had numerous followers; but it is impossible to give here even an outline of their doctrines, which comprehended various degrees of absurdity. But the most audacious of all the heretics of the second century was Monta′nus, an ignorant fanatic of Phrygia, who declared that he was the Paraclete, or Comforter, promised by the Lord; and that he was sent to perfect the precepts of Christ. He taught no new doctrines, but inculcated excessive austerity, and condemned all care of the body and the cultivation of literature. His severe doctrines gained him many proselytes, and his followers afterwards spread over Asia, Africa, and part of Europe, the most eminent being Tertullian of Carthage.

During this century the form of Church government progressed. One *Episcopus* (inspector or bishop) presided over every Christian assembly, and he was assisted by a council of presbyters (elders). Deacons of various classes were subordinate to both. It became customary for the churches to assemble at stated times to deliberate on their common interests. These assemblies were termed Synods by the Greeks, and Councils by the Latins; and the laws enacted by them were called Canons. The authority of the bishops was considerably increased by these Councils, and it became usual to appoint one of the provincial

What progress had Christianity made?—What versions of the Scriptures were made?—What is said of the third persecution?—Of Pliny the Younger?—Serenus Granianus?—Quadratus?—Justin Martyr?—The edict of Hadrian?—Marcus Aurelius?—Verus?—Commodus?—What heresies sprang up?—Who was Basilides?—What were his doctrines?

What is said of Valentine?—What was the Pleroma?—The Æon?—Demiurge?—What were Valentine's doctrines?—Into what sects were the Valentinians divided?—What of the Serpentinians?—What of Marcion?—Ammonius Sacchas?—Praxeas?—What other heresies?—What of Montanus?—Tertullian?—Church government?—What new orders were created?

THE CHRISTIAN CHURCH.

bishops to preside over them. Then, again, as the Church spread, a new order of ecclesiastics was created to superintend the bishops themselves: these were styled Patriarchs. They resided at the capital cities, such as Rome, Antioch, Alexandria, and subsequently Constantinople. The usages in the Church also received some modifications, owing to the adopting of Jewish analogies. Thus the bishops were held to occupy the place of high-priests, the presbyters that of priests, and the deacons that of Levites. Tithes, first fruits, and sacrifices were talked of; and, in imitation of the Greek and Roman mysteries, many terms were introduced which had mystic meanings. Symbols also were used; thus milk and honey were given to converts in token of their regeneration. Turning towards the east, while praying, was a common custom. The religious meetings of the early Christians were held generally on the first day of the week, which hence received the name of "the Lord's day"; though some observed the fourth day, on which Christ was betrayed; and some the sixth, as being that of his crucifixion. The hour of assembly was generally after sunset, or before dawn.

Baptism was celebrated publicly twice a year, viz., at Easter and Whitsuntide (Pentecost), by the bishops. It was performed on adults by immersion, after repeating the Apostles' Creed, and the confession of sins. After immersion they were anointed, and milk and honey were given to them. Great disputes arose between the Eastern and Western Churches as to the time and mode of observing Easter. They both fasted during Passion week, but the Eastern Christians kept the Paschal day (or anniversary of the crucifixion) on the fourteenth day of the first Jewish month, at the time the Jews kept their Passover. Three days afterwards they celebrated the resurrection. But the Western Christians held their Paschal feast on the night preceding the anniversary of Christ's rising from the dead. For so doing they pleaded the authority of the Apostles Peter and Paul. This practice led to severe contentions between the Eastern and the Western Churches. Polycarp, bishop of Smyrna, went to Rome to confer with Anicetus, bishop of that city, upon the subject; but the conference was without effect. Subsequently Victor I., who was bishop of Rome from A. D. 193 to A. D. 201, commanded the Asiatic prelates to celebrate Easter as the Western Churches did. Polyc′rates, bishop of Ephesus, flatly refused to obey him. Some say that thereupon Victor excommunicated all the Asiatic bishops, but was ultimately pacified by the remonstrances of Irenæus, bishop of Lyons. The dispute was not settled until the fourth century, when the Council of Nice abolished the Asiatic practice, and ordained the observance of Easter throughout Christendom according to the Western mode. It may here be observed that the word Easter is of Saxon origin, and imports the Eastern goddess, Astarte (Æstært), in honor of whom sacrifices were annually offered in the spring, about the time of the Passover; hence the two observances of the Passover and of Astarte became confounded, and finally the Saxon word came to represent the Jewish observance.

The sacrament of the Lord's Supper was generally administered on Sundays, and was considered so essential to salvation that it was administered to infants. It was called the "Eucharist" (thanksgiving), because Christ, in the institution of it, gave thanks to God.

We have already seen that the Church founded at Rome by the apostles was presided over at first by Linus, Anacletus, and Clement I. The latter was succeeded by Evaristus (A. D. 100–109), who, it is said, divided Rome into parishes, assigning a priest to each, and seven deacons to attend the bishop. He was martyred at Rome, and was buried on the Vatican mount. The next bishop of Rome was Alexander I., who held the see ten years (A. D. 109–119), and was also martyred. His successor was Sixtus or Xistus I. (A. D. 119–127), of whom little is recorded. It is probable that he was martyred in those sanguinary times. After him came Teles′phorus, a Greek by birth, who became seventh bishop of Rome. He also was martyred (A. D. 139), after holding the see more than eleven years. Hyginus held the see not quite four years (A. D. 139–142), and ended his life peaceably. In his reign Valentine promulgated his famous heresy at Rome; and Cerdo came from Syria to the imperial city (A. D. 140), teaching the doctrines of Marcion. Hyginus was succeeded by Pius I., a native of Aquileia, who excommunicated Valentine and Marcion. It is said that he died by the sword (A. D. 157), and was buried at the foot of the Vatican hill. The first 36 bishops of Rome, down to Liberius, and, excepting him, those who succeeded that pontiff, down to Symmachus, in A. D. 498, are honored among the saints by the Roman Catholic Church; and out of 248 bishops and popes, from Linus to Clement XIII., 78 are included in the Roman martyrology.

The successor of Pius I. was Anice′tus, who has been already mentioned as having a dispute with the Eastern bishops respecting the observance of Easter. His interview with Polycarp, bishop of Ephesus, on the subject, was not productive of good. Anicetus was bishop of Rome more than ten years (A. D. 157–168). He died a natural death, and was succeeded by Soter (A. D. 168–177), of whom few particulars are recorded. The next bishop was Eleutherius, a Greek, who had been deacon of the Church under Anicetus. It is said that Eleutherius was applied to by Lucius, a petty king of Britain, to send some missionaries to instruct the Britons in the Christian faith. The bishop sent several, the two principal being Fuga′tius and Damia′nus (or, as the old Welsh chronicle calls them, Fagan and Dwywan). These two died at Llandaff, and appear to have made many converts. Another act of Eleutherius was his condemnation of Flori′nus, who taught that God was the author of evil; and of Blastus, who maintained that the Eastern mode of observing Easter ought to be observed at Rome. He governed the Church 15 years, and died A. D. 193. His successor was Victor I., a native of Africa, an active and vigilant man, whose pontificate was passed in disputes with heretical teachers, and with the Eastern Churches regarding the observance of Easter. He died a natural death, A. D. 201.

In this century, in addition to the gospels and epistles now generally co[illegible]ered the only authentic Scriptures, there were many others in circulation, whose date, origin, and authenticity are apocryphal (doubtful), viz., 1, an Epistle of Ab′garus; 2, eight gospels, viz., the Protevangel of St. James, the Gospel of St. Thomas, the Acts of Pilate, the Descent of Christ (all four in Greek), the History of Joseph, the Gospel of the Infancy (both in Arabic), the Gospel of the Infancy by St. Matthew, and the Gospel of the Nativity of St. Mary (both in Latin); 3, several acts and journeys of St. Peter and St. Paul; 4, the heretical gospel of Marcion; 5, the Sibylline Oracles; 6, the Book of Ezra; 7, the Book of Enoch; 8, the Testaments of the Twelve Patriarchs; 9, the Ascension of Esaias; 10, Vaticin′ia Hystas′pis; 11, the General Epistle of St. Barnabas; 12, some epistles of Clement and Igna′tius. The other writings attributed to Clement were the Apostolical Canons, the Apostolic Constitutions, the Recognitions of Clemens, and the Clementina. The Apostolic Canons consist of 85 ecclesiastical laws, and contain a view of the Church government and discipline received among the Greek and Oriental Christians in the 2d and 3d centuries. The Apostolical Constitutions are in eight books, and contain rules for Christian worship, to which the author (whoever he was) has prefixed the names of the apostles. The Recognition of Clemens, and the Clementina, were the productions of an Alexandrian Jew, writtten as an answer to the objections brought by the Jews, Gnostics, and Philosophers, against the Christian religion. The Epistles of Ignatius to Polycarp, the Ephesians, the Magnesians, the Trallians, the Romans, the Philadelphians, the Smyrnæans, and the Philippians, are asserted by some to be genuine. Dr. Mosheim says it is not easy to determine the question (*Ecclesiastical History*, vol. i., part ii., ch. ii.). The Epistle of Barnabas is supposed to have been written by a Jew. *The Shepherd of Hermas* was another religious work in vogue at this period; it was the production of Hermas, the brother of Pius I., bishop of Rome. Jerome ranks Seneca, the preceptor of Nero, among the holy writers of the Church, on account of his (alleged) correspondence with the Apostle Paul.

The creed known by the name of "The Apostles' Creed" was not framed by the apostles, although it contains apostolic doctrines; nor did it exist as a creed in their time. Various accounts have been given of its origin. Ambrose of Milan, who lived in the latter part of the 4th century, affirms that it was composed by the twelve apostles, each one contributing a clause. But Luke, who wrote the Acts of the Apostles, makes no mention of so remarkable an event. Many learned writers have discussed this subject: the student is referred to Mr. Justice Bailey's *Common Prayer*, and Sir Peter King's *History of the Apostles' Creed*, for further information.

The first use of the phrase "Catholic (universal) Church" occurs in an epistle from the Church of Smyrna to that of Lyons, written A. D. 170.

What is said of tithes and first fruits? — Symbols? — Religious meetings? — Baptism? — Easter?—Give an account of the dispute between the Eastern and Western Churches.—Whence the name Easter?—What of the Lord's Supper?—What is recorded of Evaristus?—Alexander I.? — Sixtus I.? — Telesphorus? — Hyginus? — Pius I.?

How many bishops of Rome are saints?—How many of them martyrs?—What of Anicetus? — Soter? — Eleutherius? — Lucius, king of Britain? —What gospels and epistles were circulated?—What of the writings of Clement?—Of Ignatius?—The Epistle of Barnabas? — Hermas? — Seneca?—What is said of the origin of the Apostles' Creed?

THE 3D CENTURY

INDIA.

THERE is no doubt as to the progress made by the ancient Hindoos in astronomy. Some of the most eminent of modern European astronomers, Cassini, Bailly, and Playfair, maintain that authentic Hindoo observations of the movements of the heavenly bodies so far back as 3000 years before Christ, are still extant; and it is certain that the exactness of the mean motions which they have assigned to the sun and moon, could only have been attained by a comparison of modern observations with others made in remote antiquity. The strongest opponents of the claims of the Hindoos to this merit, admit that their division of the ecliptic into 27 lunar mansions was made 1442 years B. C. The astronomical rule relating to the Calendar, which is found in every Veda, and is placed there for the purpose of fixing the proper periods for the performance of religious duties, was drawn up in the 14th century B. C.; and Parasara, the first writer on astronomy of whose writings any portion remains, appears to have flourished about the same time. But the priests made astronomy subservient to their own purposes; they invented an extravagant system of chronology, which carried back history millions of years; and they concealed the sources whence their knowledge was derived. As they could have made but little progress in astronomy without considerable knowledge of mathematics, so we find that the ancient Hindoos were far in advance of other nations in this respect, and had discovered much that was unknown in Europe even in the 16th century. In a work entitled "Surya Sidhanta", written in the 5th century after Christ, a system of trigonometry is given which goes far beyond anything known to the Greeks. The Hindoos discovered the proportion of the radius to the circumference of the circle, and they invented the decimal notation. In algebra they excelled all their cotemporaries. Arya Bhatta, one of their greatest algebraists, flourished about A. D. 360. He discovered a mode of resolving equations involving several unknown quantities, and indeterminate problems of the first degree. But he was not the inventor of algebra among the Hindoos: it is evident that the science in his time had been brought to its then state by the labors of the mathematicians of preceding ages.

What was the state of astronomy among the ancient Hindoos?—Who was Parasara?—What is said of mathematics?—What of the Surya Sidhanta?—Who was Arya Bhatta?

PERSIA.

THE reign of Artaba'nes IV. (the last of the dynasty of the Arsacidæ) was marked by an invasion of the country by the Roman Emperor Caracalla. The historian Herodian says that Caracalla endeavored to entrap the Parthian prince in a base manner. He asked his daughter in marriage, and having been betrothed, he invited Artabanes and his Court to a banquet, in the midst of which the Romans fell upon the unarmed Parthians, massacred some and plundered the rest. But according to Dion Cassius, Caracalla made an unexpected inroad into Media, and ravaged the country before the Parthians could prepare for its defence; that he spent the winter in Edessa, intending to renew his invasion in the following summer, but was prevented, having been assassinated by some of his guards at the instigation of Macrinus. The Parthians retaliated by levying an immense army, and pursuing the Romans. The Emperor Macrinus hastened to meet them. Two engagements took place, in which the Parthians got the better of him. They very nearly surrounded him, and so reduced him that he found it prudent to enter into negotiations with them. He was fortunate enough to escape by restoring the year's plunder, and paying an indemnity for the costs of the war. Dion Cassius says the amount was 50,000,000 drachmas (about $213,000,000), but it is scarcely credible that he could have raised such a sum in time. Peace was concluded A. D. 217.

Meanwhile, ARDISHEER (or ARTAXERXES) BAB'IGAN (the son of Babek, a descendant of SASSAN, the grandson of Isfundear), who had risen to eminence by his genius and courage, having resolved to attempt the revival of the Persian monarchy, contrived to make himself master of Kerman, Ispahan', and nearly all Irak, before Artabanes attempted to check his progress. The latter then seeing his danger, resolved to risk all on one battle. The armies met on the plain of Hoormuz, where, after a desperate conflict, Artabanes lost both his crown and his life, and Ardisheer was hailed on the field of battle with the proud title of "Shahan Shah", or king of kings. Following up his victory, he subdued the remainder of the empire, and having thus subverted the dominion of the Parthians, which had lasted 475 years, he firmly established the SASS'ANIDE dynasty of Persian princes on the throne (A. D. 226). The Sassan'idæ occupied it until the conquest of Persia by the Arabs (A. D. 651). From the commencement of the Sassanide dynasty the history of Persia assumes a new character, and there is as fair an agreement between eastern and western writers as can be expected from authors of different nations. The Persian writers have no dates even at this epoch, but the period they assign to the reign of each prince generally accords with the more exact chronology of western authors. With regard to the condition of Persia under the dynasty of the Arsacidæ, the following remarks by Gibbon (*Decline and Fall of the Roman Empire*, vol. i. p. 329) will give the student an accurate idea of it: "The weak indulgence of the Arsacides had resigned to their sons and brothers the principal provinces and the greatest offices of the kingdom, in the nature of hereditary possessions. The *vitaxæ*, or eighteen most powerful satraps, were permitted to assume the regal title; and the vain pride of the monarch was delighted with a nominal dominion over so many vassal kings. Even tribes of barbarians in their mountains, and the Greek cities of Upper Asia within their walls, scarcely acknowledged, or seldom obeyed, any superior; and the Parthian empire exhibited, under other names, a lively image of the feudal system, which has since prevailed in Europe."

After a reign of 14 years, Ardisheer resigned the throne to his son, SHAHPOOR I. (called by the Romans SAPOR) (A. D. 240). He (Ardisheer) was one of the wisest and best princes that ever ruled Persia. But with all his great qualities, Ardisheer was a bigot. He labored to introduce order and uniformity in religion as well as in every other branch of his government: he endeavored to restore the authority of the Magi, and enforced by sanguinary persecutions a strict attention to the orthodox religion (that of Zoroaster). Amid the general confusion into which the empire had been thrown, the established worship, as fixed by Zoroaster, had been neglected, and numerous schisms had sprung up. Several of the Parthian monarchs had inclined to the pagan philosophy of the Greeks, but Ardisheer Babigan was determined to eradicate all heresies, and vigorously enforced the decrees he issued thereupon. The name "Parthia" now disappears from history; it is unknown to Asiatic writers. In the ancient Scythian languages, it meant "exiles", according to some authors. There seems to be considerable doubt, however, as to its origin. Strabo asserts that the Parthians whose territories were upon the banks of the Tigris were formerly called Carduchi: the Carduchi inhabited Carduchia, the modern Kurdistan, and the character of the Kurds accords remarkably with that of the Parthians. The name Parthian is probably identical with Parsi or Farsi, the inhabitants of the Persian province of Fars.

Shahpoor is celebrated for his military exploits. He subdued Mesopotamia and Armenia, took the celebrated fortress of Nisibis, and successfully resisted the Romans under Gordian. He so seriously threatened the Roman dominions in the East, that the Emperor Valerian marched against him; but in an attempt to relieve Edessa, then besieged by the Persians, the Roman emperor was drawn into an ambuscade and taken prisoner (A. D. 260). Valerian was kept in captivity during the rest of his life. Shahpoor set up Cyri'ades, an obscure fugitive of Antioch, as emperor of Rome; but the resistance he met with from Odena'thus, king of Palmyra, caused him to abandon Cyriades and return to Persia. He founded Nishapore, Shahpore, and other cities. His capital was Shiraz, 30 miles from Shahpore. At the same time the great dyke of Karoon was erected for the purpose of fertilizing the plains of Deoful. Shahpoor was beloved for his boundless generosity, and was succeeded (A. D. 271) by his son, Hoormuz (or Hormisdas), who reigned only one year, and founded the city of Ram Hoormuz, where is still shown an orange tree which he is said to have planted. His successor, Ba'haram I., a mild and munificent prince, is remarkable for having put to death Manes or Mani (the founder of the sect of the Manichæans), who pretended to be the Paraclete or Comforter promised by the Saviour while on earth. Ba'haram II. (A. D. 276) was an indolent and tyrannic prince, in whose reign the Roman Emperor Carus nearly subdued Persia. Ba'haram III. reigned four months (A. D. 293). Narsi (or Narses), his brother, subdued Armenia and defeated the Emperor Gale'rius (A. D. 296); but next year (A. D. 297) was in his turn overcome by Galerius, and forced to conclude a disgraceful peace, by which he resigned Mesopotamia and five other provinces to the Romans.

What events distinguished the reign of Artabanes IV.?—What of Macrinus?—Who was Ardisheer Babigan?—What were his exploits?—What change takes place in Persian history?—What does Gibbon say of the Arsacidæ?—What dynasty did Ardisheer found?—What was his character?—What of the religion of Zoroaster?—Of the name "Parthia"?—What were the exploits of Shahpoor?—What cities did he found?—What of Valerian?—The great dyke of Karoon?—Hoormuz?—Baharam I.?—Baharam II.?—Baharam III.?

CHINA. JAPAN.

HEËN-TE was the last of the celebrated Han dynasty, which had ruled for 408 years. This dynasty is remembered for three things: 1. Foreigners from Arabia arrived by sea, bringing tribute to the emperor, and seeking permission to trade at Canton, which request having been granted, the Arabs have the credit of introducing maritime intercourse between the Chinese and foreign nations. 2. The art of printing from blocks was invented. This statement is made upon the authority of the Chinese historians, quoted by Gutzlaff in his *History of China*. It is generally supposed that block printing is a European invention of the Middle Ages, but it is not improbable that the idea was borrowed from the East, as many other notions were, and imported into Europe by the Crusaders, and by travellers from Persia, India, and China. 3. The system of choosing the mandarins from learned men, who should have passed an examination in literature and science, and obtained a degree, was first introduced, and for a time gave great stability to the constitution of the empire. Heën-te died A. D. 220, and Tsaou-tsaou, a man of great talent and wisdom, assumed the reins of government, but died shortly afterwards. He founded the State of Wei, in the north of China. The capital of the empire was at this time Loy-ang, in Honan. Tsaou-tsaou was succeeded by his son Tsaou-pe. Four other princes laid claim to the empire, but Chaou-le assumed the imperial dignity, dethroned Tsaou-pe, and founded the HOW-HAN (or After Han) dynasty. This dynasty lasted until A. D. 263, taking its name from the State of How-han, or Shuh, whose capital was at Ching-tao, in Szé-chuen. The State of Woo was founded by SUN-KEËN, who is celebrated in Chinese history for exterminating the faction known by the name of "the yellow caps". His son, Ta-te, declared himself emperor, and established his Court at Nankin. His dominions comprised the southern provinces of China. Thus the empire was divided into three States, whose history is one of wars waged against each other with unrelenting fury, and is called by Chinese historians "the heroic age of the San-kwo" (or three States). Chaou-le died A. D. 223, and was succeeded by How-te, the last of the After Han dynasty. But the States of Woo and Shuh became so enfeebled by continual wars, that the State of Wei acquired the ascendency. How-te resigned the throne to the prince of Wei, in spite of the remonstrances of his son, Lew-chiu, who exhorted him to fight to the last, and who, when his father had abdicated, took his own wife and children into the hall of his ancestors (a chamber set apart in the palaces of the Chinese emperors and grandees for preserving and recording memorials of their predecessors), beheaded them, and then put an end to his own life (A. D. 265). Thus ended the celebrated How-han dynasty, during the rule of which flourished the greatest literary men that China has ever produced, at least so the Chinese say; but the names of these great writers are not known by the world at large: a few men learned in the language and literature of China are the only persons who are acquainted with them. This period is the heroic age of China. The Han heroes are famous. Haou-han (a good Han) signifies a brave man, and "the Men of Han" is a name in which the Chinese still glory.

Sze-ma-yen, a prince of Tsin, having forced the prince of Wei to abdicate, raised himself to the throne, and founded the second Tsin dynasty (A. D. 265). He endeavored to unite the whole empire under one head,—a work which was accomplished by his successor, Woo-te, after many a hard-fought battle. Woo-te passed the latter years of his reign in debauchery, and left the empire to Hwuy-te (A. D. 290), a youth without any talent, who was entirely governed by his wife, Kea-she, a cruel, vindictive woman, who had murdered several persons with her own hand. She indulged her sanguinary propensities still more when raised to the throne; but her conduct at last caused her to be repudiated by the emperor, and sent into exile.

JAPAN.—Siu-ku-co-gu, a woman, succeeded Tsian-ai. She was the widow of that emperor, and is celebrated as one of the heroines of Japan. She made war on the Coreans, commanding her army in person. She held her Court at Tsi-ku-seu, in Mikassa. She reigned 70 years, and was numbered among the goddesses after her death, by the title of Kassino-day-miosin. Her son, Woo-sin, succeeded her (A. D. 270), and proved a great prince, both in peace and war. He reigned 40 years, and on his death divine honors were paid to him. He was styled Jamata-fatz-man (or, the war-god of Jamata).

Who was the last of the Han dynasty?—For what three things is it famous?—Which city was the capital of China?—Into how many States was the empire divided?—What is said of Lew-chiu?—Of the How-han dynasty?—Of "the Men of Han"?—Of the second Tsin dynasty?—What occurred in Japan?

ITALY.

THE commencement of this century found the Emperor Severus still in Syria with his sons. He remained there until the year 202, when he took a journey into Egypt, visiting Memphis and the Pyramids; after which he returned to Rome. He had raised almost to an equality with himself his friend and countryman Plautia′nus, made him prefect of the guards, and allowed him to indulge in the most arbitrary acts. This man's daughter, Plautilla, was as cruel and arrogant as her father, and spared no violence to gratify her lightest wishes. Such influence had they with the emperor that Caracalla was forced to marry Plautilla, whom he detested. The imperial household became a scene of discord. Caracalla and Geta, completely corrupted by the prevailing licentiousness, hated each other with deadly hatred. Caracalla was animated with like fury against Plautianus, and, to get rid of him, accused him of a plot to murder the emperor. Severus called the accused before him, but while he was listening to his defence, Caracalla suddenly cut Plautianus down, and caused his head to be sent to his mother and wife (A. D. 203). Whatever weakness Severus showed towards his sons and favorites, he was impartial in the administration of justice. Having been bred a lawyer, he presided in the tribunals, and gave judgment with inexorable rigor: he corrected all abuses which had crept in, and selected the ablest jurists to aid him in his decisions and reforms. PAPIN′IAN became the first of the two prefects of the guard, who, in these times, also held the administration of justice; the one taking cognizance of judicial, the other of military matters. Papinian called in, as assessors, PAULUS and UL′PIAN; and all three distinguished themselves in so brilliant a manner by knowledge of law and administration of justice, that in later times Valentinian III. gave the authority of a legislative decision to the opinions of Papinian. Severus displayed equal wisdom in every other branch of the administration, and many instances of goodness are related of him. Never was Rome better governed than during the last years of the reign of Septimius Severus. But the emperor's health began to fail, and his spirits were broken by the wickedness of his sons, especially of Caracalla, who, it is said, made an attempt upon his life. In the year 207 the Highlanders of Scotland made an irruption into Britain. The Roman garrisons were unable to check their incursions; whereupon the emperor resolved to proceed to the spot with a powerful army, and conduct the war in person. He accordingly set out, taking both his sons with him, for he dared not leave them behind him: Papinian also accompanied him. He drove the Scots back into their fastnesses, penetrated into the remotest Highlands, cleared woods, made bridges over rivers, constructed roads over morasses, and turned the course of streams. But the severity of these labors and the ambuscades of the enemy cost him 40,000 men, and so exasperated him that he resolved to extirpate the population of the north of Scotland. He strongly fortified the line between Edinburgh and Dumbarton, erected to protect Britain from the incursions of the Highlanders, and was proceeding to lay waste the north, when Caracalla was detected in an attempt to assassinate him, and to seduce the army from its allegiance. The emperor could not find resolution enough to put his son to death, but sank under grief and bodily afflictions. He died at York (A. D. 211), leaving the succession to the empire to his sons jointly.

CARACALLA and GETA were at once acknowledged emperors by the army. The former was obliged against his will to recognize his brother as his colleague; but he determined to get rid of him, and notwithstanding the watchfulness of their mother, Julia Domna, Caracalla's satellites at last surprised and murdered Geta in her arms (A. D. 212). This murder exasperated the army, and Caracalla was forced to resort to bribery to regain its good-will. He then gave loose to his ferocity, and put to death all who had been in the slightest degree connected with his brother. It is said that 20,000 persons were executed on this pretext alone, Papinian among them. Caracalla having squandered all the public money, caused the rich to be executed, in order to confiscate their property. He plundered the whole empire, and surrounded himself with Sarmatian and German barbarians, whom he attached to his person by sharing in their amusements, occupations, and hardships: he also wore false flaxen hair, in order to resemble them, and he allowed them unlimited license. He marched against the Alemanni, whom he defeated near the river Main (A. D. 214), but he realized nothing by his victory. Proceeding down the Danube into Thrace, he

Where was the emperor?—What is said of Plautianus?—Plautilla?—Caracalla?—Geta?—The death of Plautianus?—The administration of Severus?—Papinian?—Paulus and Ulpian?—Of their decrees?—Of the government of Rome?—The war in Scotland?—The death of Severus?—Of Geta?—And his death?—The cruelties of Caracalla?

attacked the Getæ without success. He then passed over into Asia Minor to Nicomedia, where he wintered. Next spring he went to Antioch, and thence to Alexandria, where he was received with all possible honor and solemnity. In return for this, he assembled the citizens, surrounded them with his guards, and gave orders for the indiscriminate slaughter of all present. The number of the victims was increased by the precipitating of men alive into enormous pits which had been dug for the bodies of the murdered, and many of the soldiers themselves were dragged down along with them. No other known cause can be assigned for these frightful outrages than that at an earlier period, before the emperor visited the city, the Alexandrians had indulged in bitter scoffs at him. The slaughter continued several days and nights. The emperor drove all strangers out of the city, prohibited assemblies and public amusements, and divided the several quarters of the city from each other by walls. On his return from Egypt (A. D. 216), he made a sudden irruption into Media, and perpetrated cruel ravages before the Parthians could prepare for defence. Herodian states that the emperor made a delusive offer of marriage to the daughter of their king, Artabanes; that he gave their chiefs a splendid banquet in his camp, during which he caused them to be massacred; but Artabanes escaped, and levied an army, with which he invaded Syria. Caracalla was preparing to take the field against the Parthians, when he was assassinated at the instigation of Macri′nus, the prætorian prefect, in his camp near Edessa (April 8th, 217).

Macri′nus did not dare to proclaim himself emperor at once, but he secretly gained over to his side the guards who were in Edessa. For four days the empire was without a head; but the troops at Edessa at length proclaimed Macrinus, and their choice was ratified by the Senate. His first concern was to conclude the war with the Parthians. After two unsuccessful engagements, he entered into negotiation with them, restored the preceding year's plunder, and paid them an enormous sum as an indemnity. Peace having been thus obtained, Macrinus returned to Antioch, where he abandoned himself to luxury, and became voluptuous and effeminate. It was in this city and at this time that the unhappy Julia Domna, the widow of Severus and mother of Caracalla and Geta, starved herself to death. The army was offended at the mode in which the Parthian war had been terminated, and provoked by the strict discipline which the emperor attempted to enforce. Mæsa, the aunt of Caracalla, with her two daughters, Mammæ′a and Soæ′mis, took advantage of this to put forward Bassianus, the son of Soæmis, as the son of Caracalla, and as a claimant of the empire. He was young, handsome, rich, and popular with the army. He was a priest of the sun, and pretended to divine favor. Assuming the name of his god, Heliogab′alus, or Elagab′alus, he was hailed by the soldiers as emperor. Macrinus sent troops against him, but they mutinied and killed their commander. He then fled to Antioch, near which city Heliogabalus encountered him. A battle ensued, but the cowardice of Macrinus ruined all. His troops laid down their arms, and acknowledged Heliogabalus as emperor. Macrinus fled to Chalcedon, where he was arrested. He was sent to Cappadocia, and there beheaded, along with his young son, whom he had proclaimed emperor (A. D. 218).

Heliogab′alus was only 15 years of age when he became emperor; and finding himself possessed of unlimited power and wealth, he rushed into every excess of sensuality and vice. In this he was encouraged by his mother, though his grandmother, Mæsa, attempted to check him. When he arrived in Rome, every day was signalized by fresh extravagance. He brought his Syrian idol with him, and passed his time in the most frivolous amusements and the mummeries of the mystical Syrian ceremonies, linked with the most scandalous practices. He sacrificed human victims to Baal and Moloch, caused children to be slaughtered in order to draw presages of futurity from their entrails, and spared no one whom he suspected or took a dislike to. The government was wholly conducted by Mæsa and Soæmis, who even took their seats in the Senate. But Mæsa saw that Heliogabalus must be removed; and she resolved to bring forward her other grandson, Alexia′nus, the son of Mammæa, who had been admirably educated by Julius Fronti′nus and the most eminent philosophers. She induced Heliogabalus to adopt him as his son and present him to the soldiery as his colleague in the empire, though only 12 years old. Alexianus was declared Cæsar under the name of Alexander Seve′rus (A. D. 221). The emperor, vexed at this, tried to depose him, but failed. He then endeavored to procure his assassination, but in this he failed also, for the soldiers took Alexander under their protection. The emperor ordered him to be secluded in the palace, but was forced to retract the order. At length he visited the camp, where Alexander was received with enthusiasm, while he was hooted. Heliogabalus gave orders to punish the rioters, but they turned upon him and his guards, and slew him and his mother, Soæmis (March 11th, 222).

Alexander Severus became sole emperor, under the guardianship of his grandmother; but she dying shortly afterwards, his mother, Mammæa, assumed the government. This great and good woman was, it is tolerably certain, a Christian. All laws emanating from the Imperial Cabinet were discussed in the Senate. The administration of the government was conducted by a council of sixteen experienced statesmen; and that of justice in the capital was confided to fourteen distinguished jurists. The illustrious Ul′pian, the greatest lawyer and most upright man of his time, was the intimate friend of the young emperor. Many good laws were framed by him, and all persecution of the Christians was stopped. But good intentions failed to propitiate the lawless soldiery, and the strict regulations of Ulpian caused them to mutiny frequently. The city of Rome was kept in perpetual tumult, and burnings and massacres took place, in one of which Ulpian lost his life. The emperor's wife, Sulpit′ia Mem′mia, conspired against him, and was banished, and her father was executed. The Persians also became troublesome. Their king, Artaxerxes, laid claim to Asia Minor and Syria, and Alexander undertook a campaign in Mesopotamia to resist him. No decisive result was obtained, and the emperor returned to Antioch (A. D. 232), and thence to Rome (A. D. 233), where he celebrated a triumph. The inroads of the Germans in Gaul next claimed his attention, and he accordingly hastened thither. He found the army attached to Max′imin, a Thracian, a man of gigantic stature and strength, who disputed the orders issued by the emperor. The army forced Maximin to place himself at their head: the Gauls joined them, and Alexander fled to his mother for refuge. Both of them were slain near Mentz (Feb. 10th, 235). Maximin was proclaimed emperor, and this election was confirmed by the Senate and the people.

Maximin was a ruthless barbarian, devoid alike of fear or mercy. He excluded all Alexander's friends from public employment; and despising the effeminacy of the Romans, he suppressed the public games and the doling out of corn to the populace. A conspiracy was formed to overthrow him by Magnus, a Roman noble, but it was suppressed with a slaughter of 4000 persons. Another one, headed by Quartinus in Syria, was visited with like severity. Maximin, however, showed great energy in his campaign against the Germans (A. D. 236), but his ferocious tyranny excited universal horror. A revolt broke out in Thysdrum in Africa, and the people raised to the throne Gor′dian, the proconsul of the province, a man 80 years of age, together with his son, and they slew the friends and servants of the tyrant. But Capellia′nus, governor of Mauretania, an enemy of the Gordians, declared for Maximin; and marching against Carthage, took the city and slaughtered the rebels. The younger Gordian was killed; the elder fell by his own hand (A. D. 238). Meanwhile the Senate declared Maximin the enemy of his country, and prepared to defend Italy. They nominated Clodius Papie′nus Max′imus and Dec′imus Cæ′lius Balbi′nus emperors; but the people, unwilling to obey the tools of the Senate, clamored for a new emperor. Accordingly, Marcus Anto′nius Gordia′nus, grandson of the elder Gordian, a mere boy, was nominated. Maximin marched into Italy, but wasted time by delays, until at last his troops, suffering from severe hardships, mutinied and slew him, with his son. At the same time the tumults in Rome were unceasing: the people were at open war with the Senate, and the Prætorian guards were blockaded in their fortified camp. But watching their opportunity, a party of the latter surprised Maximus and Balbinus in the palace, put them to death, and carried off young Gordian to their camp. All parties now recognized this youth as emperor, and peace was once more restored (A. D. 238).

Gordian occupied the throne but a short time. He was fortunate in having an able and upright prefect at the head of the army. This man, Misith′eus, carried on the government with honor and success, and Gordian married his daughter. The principal event of this reign was the war with the Persian

What is said of the massacre at Alexandria? — Caracalla's subsequent acts there? — The invasion of Persia? — The death of Caracalla? — What of Macrinus? — His exploits and effeminacy? — The fate of Julia Domna? — Mæsa? — Mammæa? — Who was Heliogabalus? — What is said of the death of Macrinus? — The reign of Heliogabalus? — Alexander Severus?

What is said of the death of Heliogabalus? — The character of Mammæa? — Her administration? — Sulpitia Memmia? — The exploits of Alexander? — His death? — Maximin? — His tyranny? — The conspiracy of Magnus? — The Gordians? — Maximus and Balbinus? — The younger Gordian? — Misitheus?

monarch, Sapor. Misitheus conducted it successfully, and recovered Mesopotamia, the young emperor accompanying him. Unfortunately Misitheus died, and Julius Philippus, commonly called Philip the Arabian, succeeded him as prefect. He was a most ambitious and unprincipled man: he patched up a peace with Persia, caused the emperor to be slain, and assumed the purple (A. D. 244).

PHILIP governed wisely, and kept the Germans in check for a short time. But the legions in Syria and on the Danube simultaneously revolting, he sent Decius against the Danubian rebels, who forced that general to proclaim himself emperor, and lead them into Italy. Philip encountered them near Verona, was defeated and slain (A. D. 249).

DECIUS was not more fortunate than Philip. His reign is chiefly remarkable for a violent persecution of the Christians (A. D. 250). The Goths and other tribes conquered Dacia, and under their king, Cniva, marched towards Euste′rium (Novi) and Philippop′olis, where they surprised and routed a Roman army. Decius marched into Mœsia against them, and was there defeated and killed (A. D. 251). GALLUS, the new emperor chosen by the soldiers, paid the Goths a heavy sum to quit the empire, and returned to Rome, where a fearful pestilence broke out, and ravaged Italy for more than 15 years. Other barbarians having invaded Mœsia and Pannonia, were met and defeated by ÆMILIA′NUS, who was saluted emperor by his soldiers. Gallus thereupon marched against the insurgent legions, but was assassinated with his son at Interam′næ (A. D. 253). But Æmilianus was in his turn killed by the troops of VALE′RIAN, who had come to the assistance of Gallus (A. D. 253). Valerian, proclaimed emperor, made his son, GALLIE′NUS, his associate. The Franks ravaged Gaul and Spain; the Alemanni attacked Italy; the Sarmatians invaded Pannonia; the Goths plundered Macedon, Greece, and Asia Minor; the Persians entered Mesopotamia. Gallienus endeavored to check the Franks, while Valerian marched against the Persians, in which expedition he was taken prisoner. Pretenders to the throne started up in all directions. They were named "the thirty tyrants", though their real number was only nineteen. The most distinguished of these were Post′humus, who for ten years maintained his independence in Gaul, and Odena′thus, who, with his celebrated wife, ZENO′BIA, ruled at Palmyra. The latter stopped the progress of the Persians westward, after their victory over Valerian. For his services Gallienus appointed him generalissimo in the East, and gave him the titles of Cæsar and Augustus. Under his rule Palmyra became a flourishing city. Odenathus was assassinated by his nephew, Mæo′nius (A. D. 267), but Zenobia avenged him, and carried on his government with admirable vigor, extending her empire into Egypt. While these events were passing in the East, the empire was rent by factions and civil war. It is difficult to follow the thread of the history. Valerian was suffered to die in captivity. Gallienus, feeling himself unable to regain ascendency in the empire, confined his efforts to preserving Italy. Aure′olus, a pretender to the throne, having raised a revolt, the emperor's general, Claudius, drove him into Milan, where he besieged him. There Gallienus was assassinated (A. D. 268), and Claudius was elected emperor in his stead.

CLAUDIUS was the ablest general of his time. Under his vigorous rule the empire regained its consistency. The revolters were crushed one by one, and the barbarians were driven back. But the great movement which was finally to overwhelm the empire had begun, and Claudius and his general, Aure′lian, could only check it for a time. The emperor routed the Alemanni at Verona, and the Goths at Naissus in Mœsia (A. D. 269). Claudius died of the plague soon after this last victory (A. D. 270). His brother, Quintillus, assumed the empire, but hearing that the army had chosen Aurelian, he put an end to his life.

AURE′LIAN found himself called upon to resist fresh invasions. The Alemanni, Vandals, and Goths poured into the different provinces; and he was glad to make peace with them by giving up Dacia, and taking numbers of them into his pay. These mercenaries filled Italy with terror, and the emperor was compelled to find them occupation. Zenobia reigned independent over Syria and Egypt, and Tet′ricus had declared himself emperor in Gaul. Aurelian resolved to subdue them both. He started for the East in the year 272. Tyana, Emesa, and Antioch surrendered to him. Zenobia's army was defeated near Emesa, and the queen fell back upon Palmyra. But Aurelian pursued her closely, and famine caused the city to surrender. Zenobia attempted to escape into Persia, but was captured. Her friends were treated with the utmost rigor: her chief counsellor, the celebrated LONGI′NUS, was put to death. Aurelian carried off immense treasure, but otherwise spared Palmyra. He took Zenobia back with him to Rome. On his return he set off for Gaul, encountered Tetricus near Chalons, and took him prisoner (A. D. 274). He then celebrated a grand triumph at Rome, in which Zenobia and Tetricus figured; but they were both generously treated, and they passed the remainder of their lives in affluence and peace. Zenobia was one of the most remarkable women of antiquity. She was possessed of rare beauty, great purity of soul, cultivation of mind, eloquence, courage, and wisdom. She had an extraordinary talent for conciliating those with whom she came in contact. Her Court was splendid, but tasteful: her dress was half Greek, half Oriental, and in public she always wore a helmet. She had extended her empire over the greater part of Asia Minor when Aurelian marched against her. The people of Palmyra, however, after her departure, revolted and massacred the Roman garrison. Aurelian instantly returned, took the city at the first assault, massacred its inhabitants, and laid it in ruins. From this blow it has never recovered. The emperor next suppressed a revolt in Egypt, organized by Fir′mius. On his return a revolt took place in Rome, and Aurelian lost 7000 of his best troops in suppressing it. He then started on a fresh expedition to the East, and had reached Byzantium, when he discovered certain frauds committed by Mucapor, his private secretary. To escape punishment, Mucapor caused Aurelian to be assassinated (March 20th, 275). He was one of the ablest of the later emperors, and was adored by the army and the people. After a delay of six months, the army and the Senate elected Tac′itus, an old and respectable Senator.

TACITUS reigned but six months; for, having offended the army, he was murdered while repelling the incursions of the Goths. His brother, Floria′nus, was acknowledged emperor by the Senate; but the army proclaimed PROBUS, whereupon Florianus withdrew (A. D. 276). Probus introduced the strictest discipline into the army, and speedily cleared Gaul of the Franks and Burgundians (A. D. 277); expelled the Goths from Thrace; forced the Persians to make peace (A. D. 278); overthrew the Blemmyes in Egypt (A. D. 279); and crushed the rebellion of Saturni′nus in Syria, and that of Bono′sus and Proc′ulus in Gaul (A. D. 280). But the labors he imposed upon his soldiers excited a mutiny, in which he was slain; and the prefect of the guards, CARUS, was nominated emperor. When the death of Probus was known, the German tribes renewed their inroads, and the Persians attacked the eastern provinces. Carus marched against the latter, and sent Cari′nus, his eldest son, to meet the Germans. Carus died mysteriously in his tent near Ctesiphon (A. D. 283), and his son-in-law, Aper, assumed the empire, but was killed by Diocletian (or Dioclesian), Carus's most distinguished officer, who was immediately proclaimed by the army. Carinus disputed his election, and the struggle between the two lasted several months. But at length Carinus was slain, and then both armies recognized Diocletian as emperor.

DIOCLE′TIAN fixed his residence at Nicome′dia. His reign having been signalized by a furious persecution of the Christians, its commencement (August 29th, 284) was reckoned by them the first day of the ERA OF DIOCLETIAN, or of the martyrs. The empire being too vast and disjointed, Diocletian associated MAXIM′IAN with him, giving him the western portion, and himself retaining the eastern. He subsequently associated CONSTAN′TIUS CHLORUS with Maximian, and GALE′RIUS with himself. Constantius was charged with the recovery of Britain, which he effected (A. D. 296). Galerius was sent against the Persians; and though he at first suffered reverses, he ultimately reannexed Mesopotamia and other provinces to the empire (A. D. 298). Diocletian in person suppressed the formidable revolt of Achil′leus in Egypt (A. D. 297), and the last year of the century was one of tranquillity.

But few names of eminence are met with in literature, science, and art, in this century. PAPINIAN, ULPIAN, and PAULUS have already been mentioned. LONGINUS, the philosopher and grammarian, was the minister of Zenobia: his information was so extensive that he was styled "a living library", and a "walking museum". The historians PHILOS′TRATUS, DION CASSIUS, and Æ′LIAN, also flourished.

What is said of Philip the Arabian?—Decius?—Gallus?—Æmilianus?—Valerian?—Gallienus?—The state of the empire?—"The thirty tyrants"?—Odenathus and Zenobia?—What befell Valerian?—What of Aureolus?—The assassination of Gallienus?—Claudius?—The movement of the northern barbarians?—The death of Claudius?—What of Aurelian?

What is said of Zenobia?—Longinus?—Tetricus?—The revolt of Firmius?—The death and character of Aurelian?—Tacitus?—Probus?—Carus?—Diocletian?—How was the empire divided?—What of Maximian?—Constantius Chlorus?—The recovery of Britain?—Galerius?—What eminent men flourished?—What was said of Longinus?

BRITAIN.

England.—Lupus purchased from the Caledonians a respite from their incursions, and then solicited the presence of the emperor with an army. Seve′rus accordingly set out with his two sons, Caracalla and Geta, and gave the former the command. The expedition (A. D. 211) was a fatal one for the Romans, who lost 40,000 men. They penetrated to the Firth of Cro′marty, and exacted a nominal submission from the natives. Severus, on his return to York, ordered the construction of a stone wall across the island, twelve feet high and eight feet thick, in order to stop the barbarians. This great work was executed, and its remains are still to be seen.

The island was tranquil during the period from A. D. 211 to 284. But, in the year 284, Carau′sius, who was commander of the fleet appointed to protect the coasts from the Saxon pirates, persuaded the Britons to support him in his assumption of the imperial purple. The Emperors Diocle′tian and Maximian for a time admitted him as their colleague (A. D. 293), but at length they sent Constantius against him. Carausius was, however, murdered at York by Allectus (A. D. 294), who for three years enjoyed the fruit of his treachery, when Asclepiodo′tus, prefect of Maxima, reduced the island once more to subjection. Allectus perished in the struggle. Constantius sailed up the Thames, and entered London, where he was hailed as a deliverer, and under his equitable rule the country enjoyed great happiness. During this century the Christian Church in Britain was modelled after the Churches in Gaul and Spain; and bishops were appointed over the principal dioceses, such as London, York, and Lincoln. Britain was divided by the Romans into six divisions: 1. Britannia Prima, which comprised the principal portion of the island, extending from Southampton water to the Humber, and from Wales to the German Ocean. 2. Britannia Secunda, which comprised Wales. 3. Flavia Cæsariensis, which included the counties of Wilts, Dorset, Devon, Cornwall, Somerset, Gloucester, and parts of Hants and Berks. 4. Maxima Cæsariensis, which comprised all England, north of the Humber to the wall of Severus. 5. Valentia, which included the south of Scotland, from the Firth of Forth to the wall of Severus. 6. Vespasiana, the small strip between the Firth of Forth and the Murray Forth. The northern portion of Scotland was called Caledonia, but was never subjugated. Britain was at first a proconsular province. The Emperor Constantine the Great raised Maxima and Valentia to consular provinces, and Prima, Secunda, and Flavia to præsidials. Over the whole island was a deputy governor, under the authority of the prætorian prefect of Gaul. There were also great officers styled "Count of the Britons", "Count of the Saxon coast", "Duke of Britain".

Scotland.—Resuming the legends recorded or invented by Buchanan: King Donald is said to have been converted to Christianity, and to have endeavored to establish it in his kingdom, but the invasion by Severus overturned all his labors. The Scots opposed a heroic resistance to the Romans, and Severus was compelled to be content with their nominal submission. Donald died after an excellent reign of 21 years (A. D. 216). After this the country was the scene of various disorders. Etho′dius II., after a reign of 21 years, was slain in a family quarrel (A. D. 237). His three immediate successors also met with violent deaths. Donald II., who came next (A. D. 264), was dethroned by Donald of the Isles, who was in his turn assassinated by Crathilinth. This usurper aided Carausius in his resistance to the Romans. He died A. D. 301.

Ireland.—"Con of the hundred battles" signalized himself by his wars with the other native chieftains. His successor (A. D. 254), Cormac Ulfadha, was the most learned of all the Milesian princes. He founded three academies at Tara, in which jurisprudence, history, and the science of war were taught. He is also said to have embraced Christianity. His son-in-law, Finn MacCumhal (or Fingal′), the popular Irish hero, was an illustrious warrior and bard, whose name still lives in the traditions of his country, together with those of his son, Oisin (or Ossian), and his grandson, Osgar. Fingal died by the lance of an assassin, A. D. 273. His exploits are the theme of Macpherson's celebrated collection of poems, passing by the name of "Ossian's Poems", and they were achieved in the reign of Carbre, the son of Cormac. In the year 258, Carbre-Ria′da, the son of Conary II., led and settled a colony of Irish in Argyleshire. He named the district Dalria′da. It grew up into a kingdom, and on the destruction of the Picts by Kenneth McAlpine, became the kingdom of all Scotland.

What was done to the Caledonians?—What did Severus do?—Who was Carausius?—What did he do?—What of Allectus?—Constantius?—The Church?—How was Britain divided by the Romans?—How governed?—Who was the first Christian king of Scotland?—Of Ireland?—Who was Fingal?—Ossian?—What of them and other princes?—How was Dalriada founded?

FRANCE.

The Emperor Septimius Severus had little love for Gaul, and was guilty of great cruelty towards its inhabitants. His son and successor, Caracalla, who resided in this country chiefly, took the command of an expedition against the Germans in A. D. 214, in which he was successful, Gaul furnishing him with men and supplies. During the reign of Alexander Severus the Germans invaded Gaul, but were speedily driven out. The Gauls themselves conspired against the emperor, and the legions of the Rhine revolted. The whole country fell into confusion. On the assassination of Alexander, the Gauls rose against the ferocious tyrant Maximin, his successor. This savage, having crushed the German tribes, turned his armies against Gaul, and would have laid it waste, but he was recalled to Italy by the movement against him there, headed by the Gordians. The aid of the Gauls against the tyrant having been solicited by the Senate, they sent a large number of volunteers to assist the latter. The result of the civil war in Italy was the death of Maximin and of the Gordians, and the establishment of Philip the Arabian on the throne of the Cæsars.

Fabian, bishop of Rome, desirous of extending Christianity and the influence of his see into Gaul, sent thither seven bishops: Gatia′nus, Martial, Troph′imus, Paul, Saturni′nus, Stremo′nius, and Dionysius (popularly called Denis). The first preached at Limoges, the second at Tours, Trophimus settled at Arles, Saturninus at Toulouse, Paul in Provence, Stremonius in Auvergne, and Denis on an island in the Seine, where then stood a little village named Lutetia, now magnified into the beautiful city of Paris. Trophimus, however, was weak enough to assist at pagan sacrifices. He was therefore deposed, and replaced by Marcian. The Gallic Church, too, became infected by the Novatian heresy, and on the accession of De′cius, the Gaulish Christians suffered greatly under the cruel persecution which he decreed. Trophimus, the former bishop of Arles, and Saturninus, of Toulouse, were among the victims. The persecution was renewed with great fury under the Emperor Vale′rian. Dionysius (or Denis), the great apostle of the Gauls, was beheaded on the top of Montmartre, and other eminent Christians were sacrificed (A. D. 257). Under the mild administration of Cassia′nius Latin′ius Post′humus, governor of Gaul, in the absence of Aurelian, this persecution ceased.

The piratical Franks now began their incursions on the northern coasts of Gaul, and devastated the country. They were repelled with some difficulty. Posthumus had to defend the Rhine against them. On the death of Valerian (A. D. 269), the army proclaimed Posthumus emperor, and Gaul separated itself from Rome. The new emperor, Gallie′nus, in vain endeavored to recover the province. In this war the celebrated Victo′ria (or Victori′na), and her son, Victori′nus, distinguished themselves. Victorinus was a skilful soldier, and of a wealthy and illustrious family. His mother was a woman of masculine mind and beauty, who had passed her life in camps with her husband and son, and acquired extraordinary influence over the soldiers. She was named by them "*La mère des camps*" (the mother of the camps), and medals, representing her in armor, were struck in honor of her. Posthumus, after gaining a battle with Lælia′nus, a pretender to the throne, was slain by his own soldiers because he would not give up the city of Mayence to plunder. He was one of the greatest men of that age, and was distinguished for his love of justice, his bravery, and his military talents. On his death Victorinus assumed the government of Gaul, but his licentiousness soon provoked the hatred of his subjects, and he was killed in a tumult at Cologne, together with his infant son. The soldiers offered the empire to Victoria, but she declined it, recommending them to choose Aure′lius Ma′rius. That officer was accordingly elected, but having been assassinated soon afterwards, Victoria procured the election of her relative, Tet′ricus, the Roman governor of Aquitaine. Gaul then became split up into factions. Victoria died suddenly (A. D. 268), and was buried with the honors of an empress. The Emperor Aurelian, victorious from the East, marched into Gaul, defeated Tetricus at Chalons, and took him prisoner. He at length (A. D. 273), reunited the whole country to the empire, and founded the city of Orleans. He was soon after assassinated (A. D. 275). Gaul was now overrun by the Germans, and became the theatre of civil war. It was devastated by bands of robbers, called "Bagauds", who were subdued after a bloody struggle by the Emperor Maximian. Under his administration, and that of Constan′tius, Gaul recovered its prosperity.

What occurred to the Gauls during the reign of Septimius Severus?—Caracalla?—Alexander Severus?—Maximin?—What did Fabian do?—What bishops are mentioned?—What of Trophimus?—The persecution under Decius?—And Valerian?—What is said of Denis?—Posthumus?—Victorinus?—Victoria?—Tetricus?—Aurelian?—The Bagauds?—Maximian?

SPAIN.

The Spaniards were well contented with the mode in which they were governed by the Romans, as they made no attempt to shake off the Latin yoke. They had, in fact, become Latinized, and the language of their conquerors superseded the ancient native dialects.

In the reign of the Emperor Gallienus (A. D. 262), the empire was distracted by the rival pretensions of no less than nineteen candidates for the imperial purple. They were nicknamed "the thirty tyrants". One of them, Pesu′vius Tet′ricus, set up the standard of revolt in Spain, but not being cordially supported by the Spaniards, he had recourse to the Suevi, the Franks, and other fierce tribes from Germany for aid. Responding to his invitation, these barbarian auxiliaries poured into Spain, and laid several flourishing towns in ashes. During twelve years this destroying flood overspread the wealthy but defenceless country, and so great was its fury that a century of peace hardly sufficed to obliterate its ravages. Tetricus maintained his authority while it lasted; but at length the barbarians were overcome by Posthumus, the rival of Gallienus, and driven across the Strait of Gibraltar into Mauretania, and Tetricus was vanquished by the Emperor Aurelian at Chalons in Gaul (A. D. 272), taken prisoner, and exhibited in triumph at Rome, along with Zenobia, queen of Palmyra. Tetricus was generously treated by the emperor, and died in peace and opulence.

The introduction of the Christian religion into Spain softened the ferocity of a fierce people; but its progress was gradual, and it had to encounter every species of opposition before its truth was recognized, and its authority established. None suffered more than the Christians in Spain did during the fearful persecutions under the Emperor Severus (A. D. 202–3), Decius (A. D. 250), Valerian and Gallienus (A. D. 254–276), and Diocletian (A. D. 284–304); and nowhere was greater heroism displayed by martyrs to the faith. In the persecution under Gallienus an edict was published by Æmilianus, the governor of Hither Spain, commanding the Christians, under pain of death, to sacrifice to the gods. This order was openly disobeyed by Fructuo′sus, bishop of Tarragona, who, with his deacons, Augurius and Eulogius, was accordingly condemned to be burned. The three met their fate with the utmost calmness, astonishing even the savage Æmilianus. But it was under Diocletian that the persecution raged with most fury in Spain. The emperor's most sanguinary agent was Publius Dacia′nus, long remembered for his ferocious attempt to destroy the entire Christian population of Saragossa. Having promised a free pardon to all who should quit the city on a certain day in search of another abode, a great multitude of men, women, and children assembled, and marched forth; but the troops of Dacianus, which had been placed in ambush, fell upon them, and massacred every individual. The most illustrious victim of the persecution was Vincent of Saragossa, deacon to Valerius, bishop of that city. A description of his sufferings will give the student an idea of the cruelty and ferocity of the times, and the perils to which the Christians were exposed. Dacianus committed Valerius and Vincent to a dark dungeon, heavily fettered, where they were kept for some days without food. They were then brought before the tyrant, and exhorted to sacrifice to the gods; but Vincent, in a speech of surprising eloquence, denounced the absurdities of paganism, and vindicated the superiority of Christianity. Dacianus thereupon gave orders that his limbs should be dislocated; but this failing to extort a groan from the victim, he ordered that the flesh should be torn from his bones: he was then laid upon an iron bed covered with sharp spikes; boiling liquids were poured into his wounds; his bones were crushed by blows with iron bars, and his body was then thrown upon a heap of flints. As he was not quite dead, the fiendish tyrant had him placed upon a comfortable couch, and directed that every effort should be made to restore him, so that he might be subjected to fresh torments; but in a few hours Vincent expired, his tormentors having been throughout unable to extort from him a single cry of pain. The fame of his superhuman constancy spread throughout Christendom; but we may well doubt whether the legend has not greatly exaggerated the sufferings of the Christian martyr. Lauren′tius, Oren′cius, Eula′lia, Patien′tia, Narcissus, and Felix, also acquired celebrity by their heroism under torture. Basil′ides, bishop of Astorga, having been deposed by a council for heresy, applied to Stephen, bishop of Rome, who commanded the Spanish bishops to restore him, which they refused to do, and they were sustained in their conduct by Cyprian, bishop of Carthage.

What is said of this century?—Tetricus?—The Suevi?—Their ravages?—The effects of Christianity?—The Spanish martyrs?—Fructuosus, Augurius, and Eulogius?—Dacianus?—The massacre at Saragossa?—Relate the torments inflicted on Vincent of Saragossa.—What is said of the legend?—Name other eminent martyrs.—What of Basilides?

GERMANY.

The Alemanni now appear prominently in history. They first appeared in Suabia after the great war of the Marcomanni. The Emperor Caracalla took them into high favor, but suddenly vented his mad ferocity on them. On one occasion he sent for a number of young Alemanni, under pretence of enrolling them in his army, and then ordered them to be put to death. A general insurrection followed, but Caracalla was victorious, and after his victory caused the captive women to be brought before him: having asked them which they preferred, death or slavery, he was answered by their killing their children, and then themselves (A. D. 213).

During the campaign of the Emperor Alexander Severus in Parthia, the Germans crossed the Rhine, and spread universal terror (A. D. 234). Severus died before he could reach the seat of war. Max′imin, his successor, collecting an immense army, crossed the Rhine, and carried war and desolation into the very heart of Germany. He marched 400 miles in different directions through the land, burning and destroying all before him. A great battle took place in a now unknown morass, in which the emperor narrowly escaped with his life. To him is ascribed the transplanting of 11,000 British maidens into Gaul, who on their way were killed by the arrows of the wild Saxons, near Cologne, on the Rhine. There is reason to doubt the truth of this popular legend, with which the name of St. Ur′sula has so long been identified. The basis of this story is a false translation of an ancient Latin manuscript, wherein "MD.XI. (*undecimilla*) *virgo* (the eleven thousandth virgin), was construed into eleven thousand virgins." It was subsequently pretended that a revelation from heaven, made in the year 1163, pointed out their bones to a company of monks.—(Hase's *History of the Christian Church*, period 1, div. ii., ch. i., sec. 56.)

In A. D. 253 the Alemanni invaded Gaul. In the course of six years sixty Gallic cities were utterly destroyed, not one stone being left on the other. But in Italy they were defeated with severe loss near the lake of Garda, where, it is said, 300,000 of them were routed by 12,000 Romans. In A. D. 265 the Emperor Aurelian repelled a fresh invasion of Gaul by them, and in A. D. 273–277 they were again unsuccessful against the warlike emperor, who, for a short time, even restored the Heidenmauer and the fortresses of Hadrian; but after his death they again crossed the frontier, and attacked the Emperor Maxim′ian at Treves, where they met with a sharp repulse. The emperor, however, ceded to them the waste lands lying on the frontiers, and entered into an alliance with them, thereby laying the foundation of their future importance.

Christianity meanwhile progressed in Germany, notwithstanding the persecution to which the Christians were subjected. But strict reliance is not to be placed in the accounts that have come down to us of the sufferings of these martyrs. It is said that Maximian caused a whole legion, called "the Theban legion", with their leader, Maurit′ius, to be cut to pieces (A. D. 287) on account of their profession of the Christian faith, with which he feared they might infect the rest of the troops. This event took place at Sitten (or Sion), in the Valais, on the spot where the large monastery of St. Moritz now stands. About the same period, at Augsburg, which was then a Roman city, St. Afra, a dissolute female, who had been suddenly converted to Christianity, zealously preached the new faith; for this she suffered martyrdom, and was afterwards canonized.

The intestine feuds of the Germans alone saved the Roman empire, which was now hastening to decay. The efforts of Maximian and Diocletian to stem the threatened dangers were of little avail; but the Goths and Vandals, pressing forcibly onwards, were opposed in a bloody struggle by the Thuringi, Burgundians, and Alemanni, and extorted from the Roman, Mamer′tius, the exclamation: "Holy Jupiter, at length they bathe in their own blood!" But the exultation of the Romans was only momentary. Helvetia was soon invaded by the Alemanni, who, during this irruption, destroyed all the works of the Romans, particularly the magnificent cities of Vindonis′sa and Aven′ticum, which were so completely razed to the ground that, fifty years later, a forest, known as "the Helvetian wilderness", covered their sites.

The Franks also now come prominently forward. In A. D. 260 they invaded Gaul and Spain. Probus caused several thousand of them to be transported to Asia. But they seized a Roman fleet at Constantinople, with which they plundered the coasts of the Mediterranean, and returned home laden with booty.

What is said of the Alemanni?—Maximin?—St. Ursula and the 11,000 virgins?—The invasion of Gaul?—The progress of Christianity?—The Theban legion?—St. Afra?—The intestine wars?—The exclamation of Mamertius?—The subsequent exploits of the Alemanni?—The Franks?—Their expatriation?—And how they returned?

AFRICA.

There is little to record of Africa during this century. In the beginning of it there was extensive intercourse between Rome and Ethiopia. About the year 270 the Emperor Probus undertook an expedition against the Blem′myes, a tribe of banditti in the Theb′ais, in Upper Egypt, and vanquished them; but, though subdued for a time, they remained a constant source of trouble to the emperors. They were so wild a looking race that the inhabitants of Rome were greatly surprised at their appearance when exhibited in the triumph of Probus. Towards the close of the century the Blemmyes and the Noba′tæ, a people inhabiting the banks of the Nile in Upper Egypt, committed great depredations on the Roman territories; and the adjacent part of the Thebais being, probably on this account, but thinly peopled, the Emperor Diocletian found his revenue from that province so reduced as to be scarcely sufficient to maintain the garrisons placed there to keep the Ethiopians in check. He therefore assigned to the Nobatæ lands in the Roman dominions, and gave both them and the Blemmyes a considerable annual sum to desist from their plundering. But notwithstanding their assurances to the contrary, they continued pillaging the Roman subjects down to the time of Justinian (6th century).

Christianity spread rapidly throughout the north of Africa during this century. Alexandria and Carthage were two of the most important bishoprics in the Church. The celebrated Cyprian, bishop of the latter city, asserted an authority equal to that of the bishop of Rome, with whom he frequently differed, especially with regard to receiving back into the Church those who abandoned heretical sects. The Eastern Christians established a law that all heretics were to be rebaptized before their admission to the communion of the true Church. Stephen, bishop of Rome, therefore broke off communion with the Asiatics, and excluded them from the Church of Rome. Cyprian assembled a council, which adopted the opinion of the Asiatics. Stephen then threatened Cyprian with his displeasure, who replied by calling a second council at Carthage, wherein it was declared that baptism, administered by heretics, was void of all efficacy. Stephen thereupon excommunicated the African bishops, who had acted with moderation throughout, but his death put an end to the controversy. Sabel′lius, bishop of Ptolemais, an African by birth, taught certain doctrines with regard to the Trinity. Origen and Dionys′ius of Alexandria were also distinguished ornaments of the Church in Africa during this century.

Arabia.—Although the vast peninsula of Arabia properly belongs to Asia, some brief notice of its history here will not be amiss. The first division of the peninsula was into Kedem and Arabah—the former comprehending the eastern, the latter the western portion. Ptolemy, the geographer, divided it into Arabia Petræ′a, Arabia Deserta, and Arabia Felix. The first contained the most celebrated localities, such as Mount Sinai, the wilderness of Sin, the desert of Sinai, the cities of Petra, Bostra, and Moca. The second comprised the region bordering on Babylonia. The third comprised the southern portion, between the Red Sea, the Indian Ocean, and the Persian Gulf. Arabia was peopled in ancient times, as it is now, by independent tribes. They traced their origin to the remotest antiquity, and some of them appear from time to time in the histories of the neighboring nations. The Midianites, the Amalekites, the Horites, the Hadarites, the Casluhim, the Caphtorim, the Ishmaelites, were all Arab tribes. They worshipped the sun, moon, and stars as deities, but as being inferior to the Supreme Being, whom they styled "Allah Taâla" (the Most High God). Some believed in a future state; others did not. A few idols were worshipped under the names of Wadd, Sawâ, Yaghûth, Yaûk, and Nasr, who, it is said, were men of great piety and repute in their time. Jupiter Ammon and Bacchus also were worshipped in later ages. An account of the ancient Arabian kings and princes, with their exploits, will be found in the *Universal History*, vol. xviii., book iv. Christianity was introduced into Arabia by the apostles and their disciples, but speedily became corrupted by heresies. The Jews fled into Arabia after the destruction of Jerusalem by Titus (A. D. 70), and became very populous and influential there. In after times they persecuted the Christians with great fury. One of their leaders, Dhu Nowas, burnt 340 in the city of Najran alone, and offered large sums for their destruction in other places. At the instigation of the patriarch of Alexandria, the king of Ethiopia invaded Yemen, and deposed Dhu Nowas.

What is said of the Blemmyes?—The Nobatæ?—The spread of Christianity?—Cyprian?—His controversy with Stephen?—Baptism by heretics?—What other African prelates flourished?—How was Arabia first divided?—How did Ptolemy divide it?—How was it peopled?—What religion prevailed?—What of Christianity?—The Jews?—Dhu Nowas?

SCANDINAVIA.

Sweden.—The kings of Sweden in this century were Dyggve (A. D. 190–220), Dag Spaka the Wise (A. D. 220–260), Agne (A. D. 260–280), Alrek and Erik (A. D. 280–300). On the death of Agne (A. D. 280) the kingdom was divided between his two sons, Alrek and Erik, which very much weakened it. Sweden was exposed to the occasional attacks of the kings of Denmark and Norway, but the Swedes faithfully adhered to the sacred race of the Ynglings, and expelled the invaders. The history of this barbarous period is entirely devoid of interest.

Denmark.—Dan (surnamed Mykillati, or "the Magnificent") reduced all the provinces of Denmark under his sway. The marriage of his sister with Dyggve, king of Sweden, is the first matrimonial alliance recorded between the two crowns. After a very long reign he died, A. D. 270, and was succeeded by Frode III., surnamed "the Pacific", from his peaceful disposition, the like of which was very rarely met with in those barbarous times, and among the fierce Northmen, who delighted in war. He must have been a man of singular wisdom to have maintained his position for 40 years. The list of the kings here given is extracted from the Danish historian, Suhm, by Mr. Dunham, in his *History of Denmark*, who makes the following remarks on the subject: "No two chroniclers agree as to the series of the kings. All differ, not only as to the order of succession, but as to the names themselves. Whence this difference? Doubtless from a variety of causes. In the first place, the title of 'King of the Danes' was applied to the governors of Jutland no less than to those whose seat was in Zealand and Scania. As either became the more powerful he claimed a place among the descendants, or at least the successors, of Skiold. In the second place, it frequently happened that Jutland, or Zealand, or Scania, was subdued by the neighboring kings of Norway and Sweden, and they were without hesitation admitted as kings of Denmark. Add the number of revolutions inseparable from such a lawless state of society—where king after king was driven into exile, or put to death, or forced to bend for a while before the torrent of invasion—and we can scarcely be surprised at the difference, extreme as it is, between the lists of Scandinavian kings."

What events in Sweden are mentioned?—What in Denmark?—What of Frode III.?—What of the Danish chroniclers?—What are the three reasons assigned for their differing?

NETHERLANDS.

The Franks now appear in two great divisions. Those dwelling near the river Saal are distinguished as the Salic Franks; those on the banks of the Rhine, as the Riparian, or Ripuarian Franks (from the Latin word *ripa*, signifying "a bank"). Their history more properly belongs to that of France and Germany than to that of the Netherlands, but as they acquired power and territory in the Low Countries, they must be noticed here. They had among them many petty leaders, or dukes, who were oftener at war with each other than with their neighbors.

The first half of this century passed without any remarkable occurrence. But about the year 250 the Salian Franks crossed the Rhine and the Meuse, and settled in the neighborhood now occupied by the cities of Antwerp, Breda, and Bois-le-duc. All the tribes, except the Menapians, subdued by the Romans, opposed the invaders. The Menapians took part with them, and fought against the Romans and their allies. They were defeated by the Emperor Gallienus (A. D. 256). Subsequently (A. D. 260) the tribes made an irruption into Gaul, and thence penetrated into Spain, where they maintained their position for twelve years, when they were driven back by the Roman general Post′humus. The Emperor Aurelian repelled a fresh invasion of Gaul by them in A. D. 265; and in A. D. 273 the Emperor Probus successfully resisted a third invasion, and he defeated both them and the Alemanni (A. D. 277). Numbers of the captive Franks were transported to Asia. The contest lasted nearly half a century, and the Romans sustained many reverses. Carausius, originally a Menapian pilot, but promoted to the command of a Roman fleet, made common cause with his follow-citizens, and proclaimed himself emperor of Britain (A. D. 287). Having possession of the sea, he was enabled to aid the Franks very materially in their struggles with the Batavians and the Romans. The Emperor Maximian, having subdued Gaul, prepared another fleet to attack Carausius. This fleet was completely destroyed by the latter, who also took Boulogne, and deprived the Romans of their naval resources. Having seized on the islands of the Batavians, and massacred nearly the whole of their inhabitants, he there established his faithful friends, the Salian Franks.

Into what two great divisions were the Franks formed?—Where did the Salic Franks settle?—What wars did they carry on?—Who was Carausius?

CENTRAL AMERICA.

One of the great obstacles to mastering the history of Central America will be found in the difficulty of pronouncing the names of its localities, cities, and public men. The youthful student cannot readily remember such words as Ixtlilxochitl, Quetzalcohuatl, Tetzcatlipoca, Mixcoatepetl, Nonohualcatl, Tlamacazqui, Tlacatlacuilolli, Huexotzinco, etc., chiefly because he cannot pronounce them. A few simple instructions may, perhaps, remove some of this difficulty. The ancient languages of Central America, especially the Mexican, were symbolical or hieroglyphic (like the Egyptian), phonetic (sounds expressed by signs), and oral. The roots of the words were monosyllabic; but as the languages were not copious, it became necessary to compound these roots and their derivatives, in order to express abstract ideas or complicated descriptions: hence the length of the words. For example, the word Teocaltitlan is compounded of the words *Teotl* (God), *calli* (a house), *ti* (used as a grammatical link between two words, but frequently omitted), and *tlan* (the teeth); it signifies "near the temple". The Mexican language has no *b, d, f, g, j,* or *r*, and no word begins with *l*. The *x* is pronounced like *sh;* the *z* like *s; ch,* as in *church; uh, hu,* like *w,* in *wood; qu,* like *k; ç, z, s,* and *c,* before *e* and *i,* like *ss; u,* like *oo.* Thus, Ixtlilxochitl is pronounced *Ish'tlil-shochitl';* Quetzalcohuatl, like *Ketz'al-whotl;* Huexotzinco, like *Weshotsinco;* Mexico, like *Meshico';* etc. The Mexicans had a complete system of hieroglyphics, many of which have been deciphered. Had the ruins of their temples been less fragmentary, it might have been possible to obtain from these inscriptions as complete an insight into the ancient history of that singular people as has been obtained into that of Egypt, by the researches of Dr. Young, Champollion, and their successors. As it is, considerable progress has been made in investigating it, thanks to the labors of the Abbé Brasseur de Bourbourg, M. Aubin, and others, who have discovered many documents of the ancient Mexicans. These chronicles consist mostly of a series of dates, with a summary of corresponding events. Sometimes are added the remains of oral traditions or historic songs. It was the custom of the Mexicans to learn these by heart, and to recite them in public: they were taught in the schools and colleges for the training of orators. M. Aubin is of opinion that the *tlatolli,* or harangues, so frequently recited from memory by the Indians in modern times, are the remains of these ancient orations; and that this origin is sufficiently indicated by extreme conformity to the literal language, the modern dialects of which seldom preserve more than a third of the words, and by the certainty that the dialogues are derived from ancient native compositions, dramatic or oratorical, adapted to Christian subjects by monks since the Spanish conquest.

The year 258 is the epoch of a fresh emigration of the Tutul-Xius, and of their establishment in the province of Zyan-Caan, to the southeast of the peninsula of Yucatan. It was then that they left Chiapas, and, ascending the Uzumacinta, entered the mountains which separate Vera Cruz from Peten-Itza and Yucatan. Across these inhospitable regions they took their way to found the first kingdoms of Guatemala, to which succeeded those of the Quichès and the Cakchiquels. The Tutul-Xius had at their head a prince named Ahmécat Tutul-Xiu (a title signifying "head of the family of Tutul-Xiu"). In a few years they made themselves masters of all the territories situated between Bakhalal and Chichen-Itza. The inhabitants of the last-named city, driven out by the victorious Nahuans, took refuge in Potonchan (now Champoton), on the Gulf of Mexico. It appears that the cause of quarrel between the people of Chichen-Itza and the Nahuan Tutul-Xius was a difference of religious opinions; and on this occasion the Tutul-Xius applied to the king of Mayapan for aid, offering at the same time to become his subjects. The king accepted this offer, sent them assistance, and established them in Chichen-Itza, where they became faithful feudatories; he also invited them to establish a colony in the metropolitan kingdom, and accorded to them the same privileges as those possessed by the nobles of Yucatan. From this alliance dates the foundation of the city of Mani, in the plain which extends to the north of the mountain of that name. It increased in prosperity so rapidly that in a few years it became one of the most important settlements of the Tutul-Xius. Tradition also says that at this same period they founded the city of Tihoò, upon the site whereon the Spaniards afterwards built Meri'da, the present capital of Yucatan. There, in the most ancient times, was worshipped a god named Ahchun-Caan, and another named Baklum-Chaam, answering to the Pria'pus of the Romans. An artificial hill of considerable extent occupied the centre of the city, and upon its broad surface was erected the sanctuary of Baklum-Chaam, which equalled in magnificence the temples at Izamal. It bore the title of Yahau-Kuna (the great temple), and was renowned for the delightful groves which surrounded its base. The Spaniards, on their arrival, found a number of vast and sumptuous edifices in Tihoò. Cogolludo, the historian, gives the following extract from a letter to Philip II. on this subject: "The city (Tihoò, or Merida) is thirty leagues in the interior. It is called Merida. It received this name on account of the magnificent edifices which it contains, for, throughout the entire extent of the country which we have discovered in the Indies, we have found none so beautiful. They are well built of stones of an immense size. We know not who erected them. It appears that they must have been built before the birth of Jesus Christ, for there were trees above as tall as those which grew below at the foot. These buildings are five toises (32 feet) in height, and are made of hard stone. At the summit of these edifices are four apartments, divided into cells like those of monks, twenty feet long and ten broad: the jambs of the doors are of one block, and the ceiling is vaulted. The monks have established a convent of St. Francis in the edifices situated in the part we have discovered. It is right that that which has served for the worship of the devil should be transformed into a temple for the service of God. It is in this sanctuary that we have celebrated the first mass that has been heard in the country."

We have previously noticed the Apotheosis of Nanahuatl and of Metztli (symbolical of the rising and the setting of the sun), and of the institution of human sacrifices in honor of the divinity. These abominable sacrifices continued more than a thousand years, notwithstanding the resistance from time to time offered by the disciples of Quetzalcohuatl. But this resistance occasioned only momentary interruptions, the triumph of these sectaries having rarely been of long duration. Among the solemn ceremonies instituted to the glory of the sun and the moon, the Tuetleco was one of the principal: blood then flowed in torrents. On the evening of the day whereon it was supposed that the gods had made their entrance into Teotihuacan, it was the custom to go in procession to wash the feet of those who were charged to represent them at the festival, and the night was passed in festivities of every kind. For this occasion a large number of captives taken in war were reserved: these unfortunate beings were burnt alive, in huge fires made of logs of wood prepared for the purpose. Troops of young men, dressed in a fantastic and monstrous manner, pretending to be companions of the gods, danced around the flames, throwing into them from time to time one after the other of the miserable captives. These horrible practices remind us of those of the ancient Canaanites.

History and tradition are both silent as to the destinies of the Nahuas and of the city of Teotihuacan. Up to the moment of the arrival of the Toltec tribes on the Aztec plateau we meet with nothing but dates and names more or less obscure, indicating their march across the countries which lie between Chicomoztoc and the valley of Anahuac. It may here be noticed that all the traditions in the Nahuatl language invariably give the name of "Chichimecs" to the nations or tribes who invaded the soil, whatever may have been their distinctive characteristics. In the eyes of the invaders of Anahuac, this title, instead of being a subject for contempt, was, on the contrary, consecrated as a title of nobility. The Chichimec was the stranger who had come from another country, who had conquered with his bow and arrows the soil whereon he came to fix his dwelling, or hunt the game: he gloried in it, while the more ancient possessors saw in it nothing but a title of repulsion and hatred. It is thus we may obtain an idea of that mistrust with which the population of certain modern colonies receive foreigners. Hence the pride of the Chichimec, who, after long years of residence among these native inhabitants, often refused to mix his blood with theirs, for fear of spoiling its purity; hence that nobility of which he was so proud, and which was held in such high esteem in later ages by the population of the Aztec plateau. We are thus reminded of the "sixteen quarterings" of the Germans, and the "sangre azul" (blue blood) of the Spaniards.

What is the chief difficulty as regards Mexican history?—What of the Mexican language?—Its pronunciation?—Hieroglyphics?—Traditions and historical songs?—Tlatolli?—The year 258?—What route did the Tutul-Xius take?—What of Chichen-Itza?—The foundation of Mani?—Of Tihoò?—What city did the Spaniards build there?

What god was worshipped at Tihoò?—What is said of the temples of Tihoò?—What description is given of the city?—When and where was the first mass celebrated?—Describe the ceremony of the Tuetleco.—What became of the Nahuas and Teotihuacan?—What of the Chichimecs?—Of Aztec pride?

THE CHRISTIAN CHURCH.

In the beginning of this century the Church suffered calamities of various kinds throughout the provinces of the Roman empire. These sufferings were increased in a terrible manner in consequence of a law made A. D. 203, by the Emperor Severus, by which every subject of the empire was prohibited from changing the religion of his ancestors for that of the Christians or Jews. This edict became an additional instrument of torture in the hands of corrupt magistrates, and many disciples of Christ were put to death. Yet the emperor showed the Christians many marks of favor; it is even said that he paid a certain sort of worship to Christ. He was influenced, probably, by his mother, Julia Mammæa, who had a very favorable opinion of the Christian religion, and had on one occasion sent for the celebrated Origen to instruct her in it. From the death of Severus to the reign of Maximin (A. D. 211–235), the condition of the Christians improved, and became even prosperous. In the army, and at Court, were many Christians who lived quite unmolested, and who even assembled together for public worship, with the connivance of the magistrates. But with the accession of the Emperor Maximin affairs changed. That unworthy emperor caused the bishops to be seized and put to death, and the Christians suffered in a barbarous manner. Fortunately his reign was brief; and his successors, the Gordians and Philip, were protectors of the Christians; the latter emperor is said, indeed, to have embraced Christianity. The accession of Decius Trajan to the imperial throne (A. D. 249) raised a new storm, which fell with the utmost fury on the Church; for this emperor issued the most cruel edicts, commanding the prætors everywhere, upon pain of death, either to extirpate the whole body of Christians without exception, or to force them by tortures of various kinds to return to the pagan worship. Hence, in all the provinces of the empire, multitudes of Christians were, during the space of two years, put to death by the most horrid methods that human ingenuity and cruelty could invent. Fabian, bishop of Rome, was amongst the martyrs. This dreadful persecution had the effect of causing many to fall from the profession of the faith, and save themselves by offering sacrifices to the pagan gods. This defection of so great a number of Christians produced great commotion in the Church on the cessation of the persecution; for those who had lapsed from their profession were desirous of being restored to the Church communion without submitting to the penitential discipline which the ecclesiastical laws required. The bishops were divided in opinion on the subject, some being willing to show lenity, some insisting on rigidly observing the law. In Egypt and Africa many of the lapsed, in order to obtain pardon, procured from the martyrs "letters of reconciliation and peace", wherein they (the martyrs) declared in their last moments their belief that the lapsed were worthy of being readmitted into the Church. Upon the authority of these letters, some of the bishops and presbyters received back many of the apostates.

To this period (A. D. 250) is referred the memorable legend of "The Seven Sleepers of Ephesus". The story is that, during the persecution, seven Christian youths took refuge in a cave near Ephesus, were thrown into a trance, and miraculously preserved until the year 447, when they were awakened by the opening of the cave by the proprietor. One of them, named Iamblichus, was sent into the city to buy bread; but his antique dress and language caused him to be arrested. The cave was visited by the authorities, and the seven sleepers, having related their story, bestowed their benediction on their visitors, and expired (Gibbon's *Decline and Fall*, c. xxxiii). The account given by Butler, in his *Lives of the Saints*, is that they were seven grown up persons, named respectively Maximian, Malchus, Martinian, Dionysius, John, Serapion, and Constantine, who, having confessed the faith before the proconsul at Ephesus, were walled up in a cave in which they had hid themselves, and their remains were accidentally found in the year 479. Another famous Christian legend is that of the Theban Legion. This legion was raised in the Theb'ais, in Upper Egypt, and consisted entirely of Christians; Mauricius (or Maurice), Exuperius, and Candidus being the commanding officers. It numbered 6600 men, and was one of the legions sent by Diocletian out of the East to compose his army in Gaul. In crossing the Alps they arrived at Octodurum (now Martignac), where Maximian ordered the whole army to sacrifice to the gods. The Theban Legion thereupon withdrew to Agacenum (now St. Maurice), three leagues off. The emperor ordered them to be decimated; but they still refusing to sacrifice, he surrounded them with his army and massacred them, not a man of them offering resistance, but each one encouraging the other to suffer with fortitude and faith in Christ.

Gallus, the successor of Decius, rekindled the fury of the persecution, which was beginning to flag. The Christians again fell victims to the blind rage of the heathens; moreover, a fearful pestilence desolated the Roman empire, and the pagan priests persuaded the people that it had been sent by the gods on account of the lenity shown to the followers of Christ: thus the measure of their sufferings was filled up. But when Valerian ascended the throne (A. D. 253), he stopped the persecution, and restored tranquillity. This interval of repose, however, was of short duration; for, in A. D. 257, at the instigation of Macrianus, he issued an edict prohibiting the Christians from assembling together, and sent their bishops and doctors into banishment. Next year numbers were put to death in the most cruel manner: amongst those who suffered were Cyprian, bishop of Carthage, Stephen, bishop of Rome, Vincent of Saragossa, and Laurentius (or Lawrence), a Roman deacon, who was consumed by a slow fire. The taking prisoner of Valerian by the Persians (A. D. 260), placed his son, Gallienus, at the head of the empire, and peace was subsequently restored to the Church. Matters went on tolerably well until the fifth year of Aurelian (A. D. 275), who prepared a tremendous attack on the Christians; but he was fortunately murdered before his edicts were published throughout the empire. Few therefore suffered martyrdom, and during the remainder of this century the Christians enjoyed considerable ease and tranquillity. Christianity now numbered in its ranks the most wealthy and influential persons, and the profession of it was no bar to public preferment.

The form of the government of the Christian Church became more defined in this century. At the head of each local church was a bishop, assisted by a presbytery, both being elected by the community; and in each province one bishop was invested with a certain superiority over the rest in rank and authority, but his powers were not accurately defined, nor does it appear that this authority was always conferred on the bishop of the metropolitan church. The bishops of Rome, Antioch, and Alexandria, as rulers of primitive and apostolic churches, had a kind of pre-eminence over all others, and were not only consulted frequently in affairs of a difficult and momentous nature, but were also distinguished by peculiar rights and privileges. These privileges appear to have been, the right of presiding in general assemblies, of calling councils and presiding therein, of admonishing their brethren in a mild and fraternal manner, and of executing such offices as these ecclesiastical meetings required. Thus Cyprian, bishop of Carthage, called a council of bishops in that city, A. D. 252, and another, A. D. 256, in which the questions of the readmission into the Church of those who had apostatized during the terrible persecution under Decius, and of the baptism of heretics, were discussed. In this controversy, Cyprian treated the opinions and the arrogance of Stephen, bishop of Rome, with the most perfect contempt. But the government of the Church was fast degenerating into a monarchical form; the clergy were becoming arrogant, ambitious, and domineering; and notwithstanding the danger attached to the episcopal office, the increasing wealth and importance of the hierarchy made it a subject of fierce contention. In this century minor or inferior orders were added to the bishops, presbyters and deacons. *Sub-deacons* were appointed to assist the deacons in their smaller duties, such as preparing the sacred vessels of the altar, and delivering them to the deacons in time of Divine service; to attend the doors of the church during the communion service; to carry the bishop's letters and messages, etc. They were considered so inferior that the Council of Laodicea forbade their sitting in the presence of a deacon without his leave. *Acolytes* (attendants) were employed to light the candles of the church, and to attend the ministers with wine for the Eucharist. *Ostiarii* (doorkeepers) were appointed to open and shut the doors, and to give notice of the times of prayers and of assemblies. *Readers* were appointed to read the Scriptures in the church. *Exorcists* were employed to drive evil spirits out of persons possessed: this class of ministerial assistants had long been known in the Church, but were first made an ecclesiastical order in this century. *Copiatæ*, or *fossarii* (sextons),

What calamities did the Church suffer?—What was the law of Severus?—His sentiments?—What of Maximin?—The Gordians and Philip?—Decius?—Fabian?—What was the effect of the persecution under Decius?—What controversy arose?—What of the Seven Sleepers of Ephesus?—Of Maurice and the Theban Legion?

What took place on the accession of Gallus?—What distinguished men were martyred?—What of Gallienus?—Aurelian?—The position of the Christians?—The government of the Church?—The three principal bishops?—The corruption of the clergy?—What inferior orders were created?

THE CHRISTIAN CHURCH.

were instituted to take care of funerals and provide for the decent interment of the dead. The use of exorcisms and spells, fasting, making the sign of the cross, burning incense and preaching long sermons in church, and the practice of celibacy, became general. Marriage was generally allowed amongst the clergy of all classes, but many advocated celibacy, and thereby acquired a higher reputation for sanctity.

A mystic theology arose in the early part of the century, maintained principally by the celebrated ORIGEN, a presbyter and catechist of Alexandria, who taught that there was a mystical and spiritual, as well as a natural, mode of interpreting Scripture. He was a man of vast ability, piety, and learning, and exercised immense influence in the Church. He drew a prodigious number to his views, and it was he who brought into prominent notice the controversy respecting the Millennium, and the baptism of heretics. Next in celebrity to him was JULIUS AFRICANUS, the greater part of whose writings is lost. Hippolytus, Dionysius, bishop of Alexandria, Methodius, Tertullian, Cyprian, bishop of Carthage, Minucius Felix, Arnobius, Cyril, Clement of Alexandria, and Lactantius, were much esteemed Christian writers of this century; but most of their works are lost. Gregory, bishop of New Cæsarea, acquired the title of *Thaumaturgus* (wonder-worker), on account of the miracles he is said to have wrought. For a full account of these writers, and of the doctrines and writings of Origen, the student is referred to Mosheim's *Ecclesiastical History*, Century 3d, Part II. In the year 228, Origen, on his road from Alexandria to Achaia, was ordained presbyter by the bishops of Cæsarea and Jerusalem. This gave great offence to Demetrius, bishop of Alexandria, who declared Origen unworthy of the priesthood, because he had mutilated himself, and asserted that the two bishops had exceeded their jurisdiction. A violent controversy arose in the Church on these points: Origen was obliged to leave Alexandria (A. D. 231), and two councils were called at that city, — one of which condemned him and deprived him of his office, and the other degraded him from the sacerdotal dignity. A full account of this celebrated controversy will be found in Eusebius's *Ecclesiastical History*.

A new sect was founded by MANES (or MANICHÆ'US), a Persian, and a Magian priest, who asserted that he was the Comforter promised by Christ, and taught a system of doctrines which was a mixture of Christianity with the ancient religion of the Persians. He also insisted on the mortification of the body, and the suppression of all the natural appetites. These Manichæans were among the most remarkable of the heretics who troubled the Church at this period. Their general assembly was headed by a president who represented Christ; with him were joined twelve rulers representing the twelve apostles; and these were followed by seventy-two bishops, representing the seventy-two disciples. These bishops had presbyters and deacons under them, and all the members of these religious orders were chosen out of the class of "the elect", or perfect Christians; the other class, or imperfect Christians, styled "hearers", being ineligible. The Manichæans were at one time very numerous, especially in the East, and caused much disturbance to the orthodox Christians. Manes himself was put to death by Var'anes I. (Baharam), king of Persia, at the solicitation of the Magi, because he had mixed up Christian doctrines with those of Zoroaster; but some authors say he was punished for having attempted to cure the king of a painful disease by miraculous power, and failed (A. D. 272).

The sect of the Hieracites was founded by Hierax, a bookseller of Leontium, who taught that all indulgence of the outward senses was abrogated by Christianity; that Melchizedek was the Holy Ghost; that those who died while children did not go to heaven; and that there was no resurrection of the body.

The controversies relating to the Trinity, which originated in the Gnostic and Platonic Christianity of the preceding century, now began to spread extensively and cause fresh dissensions in the Church. NOËTUS of Smyrna affirmed that the Supreme Being, whom he styled "the Father", had united himself to the man Christ, and was born and crucified with him, thus making it out that the Father had suffered on the cross. For this opinion Noëtus and his followers were termed "Patripassians". About the middle of the century, SABELLIUS, an African presbyter, taught that it was not the person of the Father, but a certain energy only, proceeding from Him, was united to Jesus; and that the Holy Ghost was a portion of the Father. These doctrines were condemned by Dionysius, bishop of Alexandria. But Sabellianism prevailed extensively. PAUL OF SAMOS'ATA, bishop of Antioch, founded a sect called "Paulians" or "Paulianists", who held that Jesus was a mere man, but that the wisdom of God descended upon him and enabled him to work miracles; and on account of this union of the Divine power with human nature, Christ might be called God. For teaching these doctrines Paul was condemned by a council held at Antioch (A. D. 269), and degraded from the episcopal order. A variety of minor sects sprang up, which cannot be noticed here; but there was one sect which gave rise to the most deplorable divisions, and made an unhappy rent in the Church. This was founded by NOVA'TIAN, a presbyter of the Church of Rome, a man of great learning, but of austere character, who bitterly opposed the readmission into the Church of those who had separated from its communion during the persecution under the Emperor Decius. The other presbyters differed from him, especially Cornelius. The latter was chosen to succeed Fabian as bishop of Rome, but Novatian opposed his election with great bitterness, and after Cornelius had occupied the pontifical chair, he withdrew from his jurisdiction. Thereupon Cornelius called a council at Rome (A. D. 251), and cut off Novatian and his followers from the communion of the Church. Novatian being joined by Novatus, a Carthaginian presbyter, founded a new society, of which he became the first bishop. This community flourished until the 5th century, under the title of "Novatians", though there was no difference in point of doctrine as between them and the orthodox Christians; but pretending to hold the faith in greater purity, they compelled all who joined them to be rebaptized.

The bishops of Rome during this century require notice. Victor, who occupied the See from A. D. 193 to A. D. 201, has been already mentioned. He was a native of Africa, and was distinguished for his zeal in suppressing the numerous heresies which had crept into the Church, especially those of the Montanists, the Patripassians, and the followers of Tatian, who taught that marriage was criminal, and the use of wine unlawful, even in the Lord's Supper. These fanatics were termed Encratitæ (the continent). Victor died peaceably A. D. 201. His successor, Zephiri'nus, held the See more than 17 years, but there is nothing remarkable to record of his administration of the affairs of the Church. Calix'tus (or Callis'tus) I. (A. D. 219–222) instituted the four fasts called Ember days; and he bestowed much care and money in beautifying the ancient cemetery at Rome wherein the Christian martyrs were buried. The catacombs were used for this purpose by the Christians, who never burnt the bodies of their dead, as the Romans did, — nor preserved them, as the Egyptians did, — nor cast them to wild beasts, as the Persians did. The origin of the catacombs of Rome appears to be attributable to the caverns and pits dug by the ancient Romans to get sand and other materials for building; and the Christians availed themselves of these for cemeteries, digging lodges on each side, in each of which they deposited a corpse, and then walled up the entrance of that lodge. The Roman Christians gave up the native custom of burning the dead, and adopted the Jewish custom of burying them, believing that the body must return to dust until the general resurrection (Butler's *Lives of the Saints*, vol. x. p. 280).

Callistus was put to death (probably in some tumult) at Rome, on Oct. 12th, A. D. 222. Urban I., his successor, died peaceably A. D. 230. Pontia'nus, the next bishop, was banished by the tyrant Maximin to Sardinia (A. D. 235), where he died. Ante'rus, or Ante'rius, held the See only one month and ten days, and was martyred. Fabian was elected his successor. He governed the Church 15 years, and perished in the persecution under Decius (A. D. 250). The See remained vacant 16 months. At length, while the emperor was absent from Rome, Cornelius was elected by the Roman clergy. He condemned the Novatians, and called a council to confirm the readmission of the "lapsed" Christians into the Church. He was banished to Centumcellæ, where he died (A. D. 252). Lucius held the See for a few months only. Stephen I., his successor, was beheaded (A. D. 257). Sixtus II. held the chair for a few months. The See remained vacant a year: Dionysius was then elected. He governed the Church with great wisdom for 10 years, and died A. D. 269. His successor, Felix I., was martyred A. D. 275. Eutych'ian (A. D. 275–283), Caius (A. D. 283–296), Marcelli'nus (A. D. 296–304), occupied the See during the rest of the century.

What is said of marriage?—What did Origen teach?—What of Julius Africanus?—What other Christian writers flourished?—What was the controversy relating to Origen?—What is said of Manes?—The Manichæans?—Their government?—The fate of Manes?—The Hieracites?—What controversies sprang up?—What did Noëtus teach?—Sabellius?

What is said of Paul of Samosata?—What contest was provoked by Novatian?—What step did Cornelius take?—What is related of Victor?—Tatian?—Zephirinus?—Callistus I.?—The Christian mode of burial?—What of Urban I.?—Pontianus?—Anterus?—Fabian?—Cornelius?—Lucius?—Stephen I.?—Dionysius?—Felix I.?—Eutychian, Caius, Marcellinus?

THE 4TH CENTURY

INDIA.

In their chronology the ancient Hindoos surpass all other nations in absurdity. According to their system a calpa, or day of Brahma, consists of 4,320,000,000 years, at the expiration of which time a complete revolution of the nodes and apsides of the earth's orbit will have taken place. In this period are included fourteen manwantaras, or periods, during each of which the world is under the control of one Menu. Each manwantara consists of seventy-one maha-yugas, or great ages, and each maha-yuga contains four yugas, or ages, of unequal length. The first, or satya-yuga, extends through 1,728,000 years, and answers to the golden age of the Greeks. The second, or treta-yuga, extends through 1,296,-000 years, and answers to the silver age. The third, or dwapar-yuga, endures 864,000 years, answering to the brazen age; and the last, or cali-yuga, 432,000 years, answering to the iron age. Of the last age (or cali-yuga) of the present manwantara, 4960 years have elapsed, and within this period most historical events have occurred, but some are carried much farther back: thus the "Surya Sidhanta" was revealed in the satya-yuga, about 3,000,000 years ago; the Institutes of Menu were written more than 4,320,000 years ago; Rama lived 1,000,000 years since. These are some of the absurdities of the Hindoo chronology.

Of their literature in these ancient times we know but little beyond the works already mentioned, namely, the Vedas, the Ramayana, and the Mahabharata. The first two are evidently of remote antiquity. We have already spoken of Vyasa, author of the Vedas (p. 26). Valmiki, the author of the Ramayana, lived some time after the epoch of Rama, but at what precise period is not known; at all events the poem is very ancient. The Mahabharata is attributed to Vyasa, the author of the Vedas; but it was put in its present form by Sauti, in a more recent age. Internal evidence proves that part of it was written in the 4th century B. C., and it was in familiar use in the 3d and 2d centuries B. C. The general characteristics of ancient Hindoo literature are poverty and diffuseness of style, deficiency of ornament, and incessant repetition: according to Mr. Colebrooke and Sir William Jones there is no sign of imagination or of vigor of thought in the Vedas.

What are the divisions of Hindoo chronology?—With what ages do the yucas correspond?—What of the ancient literature?—When were the three great works composed?

PERSIA.

Narsi resigned the throne (A. D. 303) to his son, Hoormuz II. (Hormisdas), in whose reign no events of importance occurred. On his death he left no children born, but one of his wives bore a son shortly after his death (A. D. 310), who was named Shahpoor II. (Sapor), and whose long and splendid reign lasted 71 years. It is stated by some historians that he was not crowned until he was born, and that the crown was then suspended over his infant head; others, as already noticed, say that the crown was suspended over his mother before he was born, in token that the infant about to come into the world was to be the future sovereign of the country. But the difference between the two accounts is of little consequence, the principal fact to be noticed in reference to it being the loyal and wise conduct of the nobles of Persia. In order to preserve the country from the evils of a disputed succession, they gave to their resolution to sustain the rights of the infant monarch all the impression that it could receive from the strictest observance of outward forms. They either were, or pretended to be, satisfied with the assurances of their priests that the child would be a male; and when he was born they unanimously gave him the name of Shahpoor. The same wisdom which led them to preserve the crown for the infant prompted them to give him an education worthy of the future sovereign of Persia, and their care was well rewarded. During the minority of Shahpoor the empire was invaded by most of the neighboring nations, especially by the Arabs, who carried fire and sword into the most fertile valleys of Persia. But the young king, as soon as he was able, took terrible vengeance on the invaders for their cruelty, and acquired the title of Zoolaktaf (or "lord of the shoulders"), from his causing the shoulders of the Arab prisoners to be dislocated by a string passed through holes pierced in the shoulder-blades. He then commenced his celebrated expeditions against the Romans by laying siege to the famous fortress of Nisibis (A. D. 338). This war with the Romans lasted with varying success for half a century. Eastern historians have narrated many marvellous tales relating to Shahpoor II. One of them is dwelt upon by them with great zest, perhaps on account of its improbability. It is said that the proud and powerful Persian monarch left his kingdom to go as a spy to Constantinople, where he was detected, at a royal feast, through the striking resemblance which he bore to a portrait of himself in the possession of the emperor; that while a captive he suffered every degradation that could be inflicted on him; that he was carried, harnessed like a horse, with the Roman army, to witness the most dreadful scenes of pillage and devastation committed upon his kingdom; that he made his escape while his guards were enjoying themselves at a feast; and that he retaliated upon his enemies all the disgrace inflicted on him, by capturing the Roman emperor, keeping him ten years in close confinement, and forcing the Roman prisoners to repair by their labor the injury they had done in Persia, even to the replanting of the smallest trees which they had destroyed. (Malcolm's *History of Persia*, vol. i., p. 108.) But reliable history gives us a different aspect of affairs. Twice was Shahpoor obliged to raise the siege of Nisibis, though at the battle of Singara he totally defeated the Emperor Constantius (A. D. 348). A third time he failed in his attempt on Nisibis (A. D. 350). He next invaded Mesopotamia, and besieged and took Amida, Singara, and Bezabde (A. D. 359–360), and became the terror of the Eastern empire. Julian (surnamed the Apostate), the greatest military genius of the age, resolved to humble the pride of the Persians, and led an immense army into their country. He encountered Shahpoor near Ctesiphon, and so completely routed him that the Persian king barely saved his life by flight with a few followers (A. D. 363). The sudden death of Julian allowed Shahpoor to recover himself, and, raising a fresh army, he pursued the retreating Romans, who were glad to make terms with him. By the treaty of Dura the Emperor Jovian ceded Nisibis to Persia. Shahpoor caused this city to be colonized by a body of Persians. Mesopotamia and five other provinces were restored to him. The Romans also abandoned Armenia, and Shahpoor soon annexed it to his empire. He seems to have been a prince exactly suited to the Persians, who justly account him one of their greatest monarchs. Of all the princes of the Sassanide dynasty, not one caused greater terror to Rome than Shahpoor did; but he was a cruel persecutor of the Christians, who suffered severely during his long reign. He died A. D. 381, aged 71 years. He was as remarkable for his wisdom as for his valor. Some of his sayings have been handed down, for instance: "Words may prove more vivifying than the showers of spring, and sharper than the sword of destruction;" "The point of a lance may be withdrawn from the body, but a cruel expression can never be extracted from the heart that it has once wounded." Shahpoor, however, did not always merit the high encomiums which the Persian historians bestow upon him, for he occasionally resorted to treachery, as was the case in the mode in which he annexed Armenia to his dominions after the Romans evacuated it. It is said that he persuaded Tiranes, the king of that country, to come to his court; that he seized him at a festival, and threw him into a dungeon, where his life soon terminated (Gibbon, *Decline and Fall of the Roman Empire*, vol. iv., p. 312). Such acts as these, however, tended little to diminish his glory in the eyes of his subjects; and subsequent generations of Persians have been so inured to perfidy on the part of their rulers that these shortcomings of one of their best and greatest monarchs appear very small.

Ardisheer II. (Artaxerxes) succeeded Shahpoor, and reigned four years, during which no event of any importance occurred. He was deposed by Shahpoor III. (A. D. 385), the son of Shahpoor II., a virtuous prince, who, after a reign of five years, was accidentally killed by the fall of his tent, the cordage of which was broken by the violence of a whirlwind, and the pole struck the monarch as he slept. These whirlwinds were, and are still, very common in Persia. He was succeeded by his brother, Baharam IV., surnamed Kermanshah, from having been ruler of the province of Kerman, and from founding the city of Kermanshah, now a large and prosperous town. Baharam is the Varanes IV. of Roman history. He reigned 15 years, and was killed by an arrow while endeavoring to quell a tumult in his army (A. D. 404). Some of the sculptures at the Tauk-e-Bostan, near Kermanshah, are the work of this prince; for a description of them, see Malcolm's *History of Persia*, vol. i., ch. vii. The tomb of the prophet Daniel is still shown at Susa; and that of Mordecai and his adopted daughter, Hadassah (or Esther), the beautiful queen of Xerxes, is yet visited by pilgrims to Hamadan.

What is said of Narsi?—Hoormuz II.?—Shahpoor II.?—What remarkable circumstances attended his birth?—What were his first acts?—What title did he acquire?—What of his wars with the Romans?—What curious tale is related of him?—What reverses did he meet with?—What were his subsequent exploits?—His character?—His conduct to Tiranes?—What of Ardisheer II.?—Of Shahpoor III.?—Baharam IV.?—What was his end?—What sculptures are mentioned?—What of the tombs of Daniel, Mordecai, and Esther?

CHINA. JAPAN.

Hwae-te, a wise and intelligent prince, did his utmost to restore peace to the empire, but the king of Han, Lew-tsung, drove him from the throne, took him prisoner, and, after subjecting him to the grossest indignities, put him to death (A. D. 313). Ming-te, another prince of the Tsin family, was set up as emperor, but, after vainly contending against Lew-tsung, he surrendered to the conqueror in a novel manner, *i. e.*, seated on a cart drawn by oxen, with a coffin by his side. However, he fared no better than his predecessor, and was ultimately put to death (A. D. 317). The year 315 is memorable for the introduction of the tea plant into China from Assam and Yunnan. On the death of Ming-te, Sze-ma-juy was chosen emperor by the unanimous voice of the people, and with him begins the Tung-tsin (or Eastern Tsin) dynasty. On his accession he adopted the name of Yuen-te. He was a kind and affable prince, well versed in ancient literature, but he proved wholly incapable of checking the ferocious excesses of his nobles. The details of their atrocities on this occasion will give a faithful picture of the state of China under the Tsin dynasty. The nobles, having resolved to avenge themselves upon the Han family for all the crimes they had committed, assembled a body of soldiers, and entering the palace, drove them into the street, and massacred them without distinction of age or sex. Kin-chun, the leader of this movement, then proceeded to the tombs of Lew-yuen and Lew-tsung, and severed their heads from their bodies. But the friends of the Han family mustering a strong force, slaughtered Kin-chun with his whole family, and burnt the palace and all the public buildings at Ping-yang. This engendered retaliation on the part of the nobles, in the midst of which confusion Yuen-te died of grief (A. D. 322). His successor, Ming-te, ultimately subdued the rebels, but died A. D. 325. A child of five years old, named Ching-te, was now placed on the throne, and another general rebellion broke out. Some of the nobles made themselves emperors in their respective provinces, and particularly in the Chaou principality, where Chih-le had established himself. Here his successor, Shih-hoo, erected a magnificent palace, wherein more than 10,000 persons lived. He was attended wherever he went by a body-guard of tall ladies on horseback, splendidly attired and armed; but he was a heartless tyrant, and his extortions reduced the country to such distress that many of his subjects committed suicide to escape starvation.

The history of the empire during the remainder of the century is but a repetition of the same scenes: children placed on the throne; the government in the hands of women and priests; the powerful nobles proclaiming themselves emperors, and at feud with each other and with the crown; while the distressed people were crushed under foot, starved, massacred, and tortured, just as it pleased the fancy of their merciless oppressors. To Ching-te succeeded Kang-te, a youth (A. D. 344); and after him, Muh-te, a babe two years old (A. D. 344). The next prince, Gae-te (A. D. 362), gave himself up to the dreams of the Taou sect, and was persuaded to live upon a mixture called "the liquor of rejuvenescence", by which his health and mind were ruined, and he died a miserable, lingering death (A. D. 365). His brother, Te-yih, the next emperor, reduced the State of Yen to obedience (A. D. 372). After him, Keen-wan, who died in the year of his accession to the throne. Heaou-woo was 10 years old when he began to reign (A. D. 373), and at 14 he assumed the reins of government. He began by contending with the northern Tsin princes, whom he finally overcame. He then gave himself up to drinking; but in a drunken fit he was strangled by one of his wives (A. D. 397). His son and successor, Gan-te, took no part in the government, but remained in his palace entirely ignorant of the state of affairs. It was under his reign that Lew-yu, the founder of the celebrated Tsung dynasty, became known. His parents were very poor: his mother died at his birth, and his father deserted him. He was adopted by a charitable woman, and he displayed great intelligence as he grew up. He gained his living by selling sandals, but subsequently enlisted as a soldier, and raised himself to eminence by extraordinary valor.

Japan.—Woo-sin was succeeded (A. D. 313) by Nin-to-ku, who was also a great and good prince. He reigned 87 years, and died A. D. 400. A temple was built to his honor in Tsino-kuni. If these Japanese annals can be relied on, the climate of the country must have been eminently favorable to longevity in those times.

Mention some particulars of the history of the early part of this century.—What dynasty was founded?—What is recorded of the prince of Chaou?—Of the state of the empire?—Of Gae-te, and the liquor of rejuvenescence?—Of Heaou-woo?—What is recorded of Lew-yu?—What of Japan?

ITALY.

This century commenced with the most furious persecution of the Christians that had yet taken place. It was decreed by Diocletian, at the instigation of Galerius. Much doubt exists as to the motives which induced the two emperors to act thus, but there is none as to the fact that the 23d of February, A. D. 303, was fixed upon as the last day of Christianity. The persecution commenced at Nicomedia, where the churches were destroyed. On the next day appeared the edict of Diocletian, decreeing that the Christian churches throughout the empire should be demolished; that all persons who should hold secret assemblies for religious worship should be put to death; that the bishops should deliver up their sacred books to be burnt; that the property of the Church should be confiscated; and that its communicants be placed out of the pale of the law. This barbarous edict was savagely enforced, the fury of Diocletian having been increased by the fact that his palace was twice set on fire. Further edicts were issued from time to time, increasing the severity of the persecution. It lasted ten years (A. D. 303–313), and such multitudes of Christians suffered death that the emperors believed they had completely extirpated Christianity. Rome witnessed, in A. D. 302, for the last time, the ceremony of a triumph, which was awarded to Diocletian and Maximian. Diocletian celebrated the twentieth year of his reign (A. D. 303) by festivities at that capital; but being disgusted with the freedom of manners which prevailed there, he quitted the city abruptly on the eve of his ninth consulship. A severe illness followed his return to Nicomedia, said to have been occasioned by vexation at the ill success of his attempts to extirpate Christianity. Soon after this, Diocletian resigned the empire (May 1st, A. D. 305), and retired to his country-seat at Salona, where he amused himself with gardening, and died nine years afterwards. Maximian also abdicated on the same day at Milan, and retired into Lucania. This joint abdication of the two emperors of the world is the most remarkable instance recorded in history. Constan′tius and Gale′rius became emperors, assuming the title of "Augustus"; and they made Seve′rus and Max′imin their associates, with the title of "Cæsar". Constantius and Severus took the western provinces; Galerius and Maximin, the eastern. Constantius went into Britain to quell an invasion of the Picts, and died there at York (July 21st, A. D. 306), where he was buried. The humanity of this great man, during his administration in Gaul and Britain, greatly alleviated the sufferings of the Christians in those countries. The principal officers of his household were Christians; and he instituted a noble system of toleration, which was adhered to by his son and successor, Constantine (afterwards surnamed "the Great"), who had accompanied him to Britain, and, on his decease, was proclaimed emperor by the army. At the same time, Maxentius, the son of Maximian, caused himself to be proclaimed emperor in Gaul, and persuaded his father to remount the throne. Severus led an army against them, but being deserted by his troops, was taken prisoner at Ravenna, and put to death there. Galerius then marched against them, but failing in an attempt to take Rome, he ignominiously returned to Greece, and conferred the title of emperor on his friend Licin′ius; he also acknowledged Constantine as Augustus, and allowed the same title to Maximin in Syria. Thus the empire was shared by six sovereigns, viz., Galerius, Licinius, Maximian, Maximin, Maxentius, and Constantine, though Maximian held only nominal power in the Court of his son-in-law, Constantine. This state of affairs, however, did not last long. Maximian, having conspired against Constantine, was made prisoner at Marseilles, and put to death (A. D. 311). The following year (A. D. 312) Galerius died. The cruel Maxentius was the next to succumb to the rising fortunes of Constantine, who, called into Italy by the voice of the people, defeated and cut to pieces the army of the tyrant (Oct. 27th, A. D. 312), at Saxa Rubra, on the Cremera, nine miles from Rome, a spot where, 789 years before, the Fabii had perished (see page 85), the tyrant himself being drowned in the Tiber while attempting to make his escape. It was during this campaign that Constantine is said to have seen a miraculous vision of a luminous cross in the heavens, a little before sunset, and to have been warned in a dream to take this sacred symbol as his standard. His first acts, on becoming master of Rome, were to disband the Prætorian guards, restore the authority of the Senate and magistrates, recall the exiles, revoke all edicts against the Christians, and patronize their clergy. Galerius had done the same in the East, towards the Christians,

What event marked the commencement of the century?—What of the edict of Diocletian?—The sufferings of the Christians?—What did Rome witness for the last time?—What of the closing events of the reign of Diocletian?—Of Maximian?—Constantius and Galerius?—Severus and Maximin?—Maxentius?—Licinius?—Constantine?—The Christians?

shortly before his death (May, A. D. 311). This toleration on the part of the two emperors increased the hostility of Maximin to the Christians, and he persecuted them with greater fury in the East. He also conceived the idea of dethroning Constantine and Licinius; the latter, however, met him near Adrianople (A. D. 313), and so totally defeated him that he fled to Nicopolis, where he died of rage. Licinius now became sole master of the East, and Constantine of the West. Licinius married Constantine's sister, Constantia; and an edict was issued, in the year 313, relieving the Christians of many disabilities. In the same year died their greatest persecutor, Diocletian. The ambition of Licinius led him to attempt the acquisition of the whole empire, and for this purpose he made war upon Constantine, but he was unsuccessful. He was defeated at Cibalis in Pannonia, and at Mardia in Thrace; after which he agreed to a peace, by which he ceded to the conqueror all his provinces in Europe (A. D. 314). Constantine, in an edict issued in A. D. 315, further favored the Christians by condemning to be burnt alive all Jews who should persecute or ill treat converts from their sect to Christianity. The Donatists also appealed to him as an arbitrator. In the year 317 he conferred upon his sons, Crispus and Constantine, and on his nephew, the younger Licinius, the title of "Cæsar". He, in conjunction with Crispus, carried on successful operations against the German tribes, the Goths, and the Sarmatians, on the Danube (A. D. 319–322). Hostilities were soon after renewed between Constantine and Licinius. They met in hostile array at Maritza, near Adrianople, where Licinius succumbed to the all-conquering Christian emperor (July 3d, 323). The fallen monarch fled to Byzantium, where he was immediately besieged. Thence he passed into Asia. Crispus destroyed his fleet in the Hellespont, and Licinius, finally overcome at the battle of Chrysopolis (Sept. 28th, 323), resigned his imperial dignity, and surrendered himself to Constantine. At the intercession of Constantia, the emperor promised to spare his life; but he shortly after put him to death (A. D. 324).

The controversies in the Church, between the respective followers of Arius and Athanasius, led to the convening of a general council of Christian bishops at Nice, in Bithynia (A. D. 325), at which the emperor was present. At this celebrated council the Nicene Creed was framed, and was sanctioned by the emperor. The doctrine of the Trinity was authoritatively laid down and defined; Arius was banished; his writings publicly burned, and all those in whose possession they were found capitally punished. The Empress Helena, the mother of the emperor, was a zealous convert to Christianity, and visited Palestine, where she founded many churches. For his great services to the Church, Constantine was fanatically admired (we might say idolized) by the Eastern Christians. On this point the great German historian, Niebuhr, remarks: "His motives in establishing the Christian religion appear to have been very strange. Whatever religion was in his head must have been a confused mixture. On his coins he has the *Sol invictus* (unconquered sun); he worships pagan deities; consults the *haruspices* (professors of divination); holds heathen superstitions; and yet he shuts up the temples, and builds churches. As president of the Nicene Council we can only look upon him with disgust: he was himself no Christian, and would never be baptized until he was at the point of death. He had taken up the Christian faith as a superstition, which he mingled with his other superstitions. When, therefore, Eastern writers speak of him as an *isapostolos* (equal to an apostle) they do not know what they are saying, and to call him a saint is a profanation of the term" (*Lectures on Roman History*, vol. iii., p. 303). The emperor was induced by jealousy of the popularity of his eldest son, Crispus, to murder him on false accusations; to which crime he is said to have added that of the murder of the empress, on discovering his error. His unpopularity with the Romans on account of abandoning the ancient religion, and also on account of the murder of his wife and son, made him resolve to quit Rome, and give a new capital to the empire. For this purpose he selected Byzantium, to which he gave the name of Second or New Rome, but the people named it Constantinop′olis, or city of Constantine, which it has ever since retained. Thither he removed his Court, and he lavished immense sums in beautifying his new capital. He divided Constantinople into fourteen departments or regions, bestowed on its municipal council the title of Senate, gave to its citizens the privileges of Rome, and raised numerous edifices of public utility. The festival of dedication was held May 22d, 330. To whom the city was dedicated is not quite evident: the Christians assert that it was consecrated to the Virgin Mary; but from that time Constantinople took its place among the great cities of the world. Constantine also changed the form of the government of the empire, converting it into a simple despotism. He divided the empire into four great prefectures, viz., that of the East, of Illyricum, of Italy, and of Gaul. Rome and Constantinople had prefects of their own. These officers had control of the civil government of their respective provinces. Constantine also appointed new great officers of State, and reconstituted the army and the system of taxation. He instituted "The Indictions", so important in fixing the chronology of the Middle Ages. The emperor subscribed the Indiction, which was fixed up in the principal city of each diocese, imposing the amount of taxation required for the pay of the army. The period of service for the soldiers being fifteen years, a new assessment of property was made at the expiration of every cycle of that duration, and the public accounts were regulated accordingly. The Council of Nice ordained that years should be reckoned from the Indictions, to commence Jan. 1st, 313. Christianity became the established religion of the empire, revenues being appropriated to the endowment of churches and the support of the clergy. Constantine, when dying, received the sacrament of baptism from Eusebius, the Arian bishop of Nicomedia, and expired May 22d, A. D. 337.

Constantine left three sons — Constantine, Constantius, and Constans — to inherit the empire. The three met and settled the extent of their respective jurisdictions,—Constantine taking the capital; Constantius, Thrace and the Asiatic provinces; and Constans, the Western provinces. Constantine II. began by causing the massacre of all his kinsmen of the Flavian family; the only two who escaped being Gallus and Julian, the youngest sons of Julius Constantius. A sanguinary war broke out with Sapor (Shahpoor), king of Persia (A. D. 339), which lasted nine years, and led to no decisive results, but occupied all the attention of Constantius. Meanwhile Constantine, having wrested Africa from Constans, invaded Italy (A. D. 340), where he fell into an ambuscade, and was slain, whereby Constans became master of two-thirds of the empire. But the latter disgraced himself by his vices, residing usually in Gaul, and addicting himself to hunting and to the most rapacious extortion. A revolt at Autun, headed by Magnentius, commander of the imperial forces, caused Constans to flee towards Spain, but he was overtaken and put to death. Constantius returned from the East to put down the new pretender to the crown, and met him on the plains of Mursa (Essek), where a dreadful battle ensued, in which 54,000 men were slain, and Magnentius was defeated. It is said that this battle absorbed the strength of the empire, for it was found that no such noble bands of veterans as fell in it could ever afterwards be collected. Magnentius destroyed himself; and Constantius, freed from rivals, gave way to all kinds of excesses. Julian, the only surviving descendant of Constantius Chlorus (except the emperor), was appointed governor of the northern provinces, then harassed by the Germanic tribes. He acquired a brilliant reputation by his military achievements against the barbarians, whom he nearly subdued; and by his able government, by which he raised Gaul to unexampled prosperity. In the East, Sapor renewed his attacks on the empire (A. D. 359), and Constantius was called away to resist him. During his absence the army in Gaul proclaimed Julian emperor, and escorted him in triumphal procession through the streets of Paris. Julian at first refused the crown, but ultimately accepted it, and entered into negotiation with Constantius for the recognition of his elevation to the empire, at the same time he prepared for war. Constantius commanded him to return to his allegiance, but Julian in reply publicly declared that he committed his own safety to "the immortal gods", thus renouncing Christianity, although he had a few weeks previously celebrated the festival of the Epiphany: he was hence styled "the Apostate". The new emperor hastened to his eastern capital by a daring journey through Germany, and down the Danube. On his arrival, the whole population of Constantinople went out to meet and welcome him. Constantius had started from Antioch with an army to encounter him, but he fell sick on the march, and died near Tarsus (A. D. 361), having, it is said, named Julian his successor.

Julian the Apostate began his reign by reforming the abuses prevalent in the Court, and abolishing its luxury. He restored and beautified Athens, Corinth,

What befell Maximin?—What of Licinius and Constantine?—The edict of the latter?—The Donatists?—Crispus?—The fate of Licinius?—The Council of Nice?—The Nicene Creed?—The punishment of Arius?—The Empress Helena?—The murder of Crispus?—The foundation of Constantinople?—Its privileges?—Dedication?

What changes were made in the government of the empire?—What of the Indictions?—What did Christianity become?—What did Constantine do when dying?—Who succeeded him?—What were the first acts of Constantine II.?—Of the war with Sapor?—The fate of Constantine?—Constans?—Magnentius?—Constantius?—Julian?—The acts of the latter?

ITALY.

Argos, Delphi, and Elis, but he revoked the edicts against idolatry, and closed the schools kept by the Christian clergy. He disliked the Christians, and was an enemy to Christianity, although he proclaimed universal toleration. He decreed the rebuilding of the city and the temple of Jerusalem, in order to prove the falsity of the prophecy that they should never be raised again. The work was commenced with ardor, but was arrested by the untimely death of the emperor. The Christian writers of that period alleged that it was stopped by the bursting forth of subterranean fires, or by the ignition of foul air, which so alarmed the superstitious workmen that they refused to continue their labors (A. D. 363). Julian was summoned to take the field against the Persians, who, under Sapor, had invaded Assyria. He displayed unusual valor and ability, but was killed in a desperate battle which proved favorable to the Roman arms. His death occurred after a brief reign of twenty months. He was the most able and accomplished man of his time, and was the author of an elaborate work against Christianity, composed amid the preparations for the Persian war: fragments of this work have been preserved by Cyril of Alexandria. He was succeeded by Jovian, the chief of his attendants, who was saluted emperor by the army (A. D. 364). This prince saved his famishing forces by concluding an ignominious peace with the Persians. He speedily restored the Christian religion to its supremacy, although personally indifferent to it. His career was short, for, after a reign of eight months, he died on his way to Constantinople. During ten days the empire was without a sovereign, but at length Valentinian, who had held important commands under Julian, was elected. He was the son of Count Gratian, a native of Cibalis, in Pannonia, who had raised himself from obscurity to distinction. Having been acknowledged by the army, Valentinian divided the empire with his brother, Valens, to whom he gave the East, reserving to himself the West, and making Milan the seat of government. He found full occupation in checking the Germans in Gaul during the commencement of his reign. He sent Theodosius, one of the ablest generals of the age, to repel an invasion of Britain by the Picts and Scots (A. D. 369), and that officer having been successful there, was also employed against the Germans in Gaul, and in suppressing the formidable revolt of Firmius in Africa (A. D. 372). Valens nearly lost his empire in the East through the revolt of Proco'pius, a kinsman of Julian the Apostate, which was put down with difficulty (A. D. 373). Soon afterwards (A. D. 375) Valentinian died suddenly from the effects of passion. He was an able though severe ruler, and he protected the Christians from the persecutions of his brother, Valens, who took part with the Arians, and was guilty of great cruelty to the orthodox clergy. Valentinian was succeeded by his sons, Gratian and Valentinian II., the latter a child only five years old, who was added as a colleague to Gratian by the general council of the army. Gratian stained the beginning of his reign by putting the illustrious Theodosius to death on false accusations. He enacted several laws for the advancement of the interests of the Church, and the punishment of heterodoxy.

The whole empire was now at peace (A. D. 376), when the Huns, a people more ferocious than any that had yet appeared, attacked the northeastern provinces, and, crossing the Don and the Sea of Azof in innumerable hordes, swept the territories of the Goths and Visigoths of their inhabitants. Joined by the Alans, and other barbarous tribes whom they had conquered, they drove all before them. The Goths were forced into the Roman provinces. Athan'aric, their king, fortified himself on the Pruth, and his people obtained leave of the emperor to settle in Thrace. It is computed that a million of persons established themselves in that province. At the same time Arianism was implanted among them by their bishop, Ulphilas, who edited the Gothic Alphabet, and translated the Scriptures into their language. The officers appointed by Valens to superintend the settlement of the Goths in Thrace practised the greatest extortions, and even attempted to murder the Gothic chief, Fritigern. This caused a revolt, and Fritigern, at the head of his barbarians, ravaged Thrace, Macedon, and Thessaly, and having obtained aid from the Ostrogoths, threatened the very existence of the empire. Valens, attempting to check them, was defeated near Adrianople (A. D. 378). Having been wounded, he was carried to a neighboring cottage, but the enemy pursuing him, set fire to it, and the emperor was burnt to death. Gratian having, by the death of Valens, become master of the East and West, associated with him in the empire Theodosius, afterwards surnamed "the Great", the son of the Theodosius whom he had put to death. This able prince not only defeated the Goths, and suppressed the revolt, but converted these fierce foes into friends. He then summoned a council of bishops at Constantinople to repress heresy, and issued several edicts thereupon. Meanwhile Maximus, governor of Britain, revolted against Gratian, who, abandoned by his troops, was taken prisoner and put to death (A. D. 383). His body was claimed by Ambrose, bishop of Milan, and honorably interred in the Cathedral there. Theodosius suppressed the revolt of Maximus, who was given up by his own soldiers, and put to death (A. D. 387). Valentinian was murdered by Arbogastes (A. D. 392), a Frank, whom he had taken into favor, and who now set up one of the royal secretaries, Eugenius, as emperor. Theodosius, however, defeated the forces of Eugenius, who was murdered by his own soldiers (A. D. 394). Arbogastes committed suicide, and the empire was then, for the last time, united in the hands of one sovereign. Theodosius divided the empire between his two sons, Honorius and Arcadius, and died universally lamented (A. D. 395).

Roman history henceforth diverges into two parts, distinguished respectively as the Western and the Eastern Empire.

The Western Empire was fast hastening to destruction. Honorius, the younger son, left the cares of empire to his celebrated minister, Stilicho, who had been expressly named by Theodosius as the fittest person to be intrusted with the administration of both empires. An attempt was made to carry this out with regard to the Eastern Empire, but as it threatened to bring on civil war, it was abandoned. Stilicho then devoted himself to the affairs of the West. His first act was to suppress a revolt in Africa, led by Gildo, the brother of Firmius, which was put down through the agency of Mascezel, another brother of Gildo. Stilicho's next exploit was to repel, with the forces of the Western Empire, the Goths who had invaded Greece. By his masterly manœuvres he drove Al'aric, their king, into a corner of Elis (A. D. 397). Alaric, however, made his escape, and not only made his peace with the Emperor Arcadius, but obtained the appointment of governor of Illy'ricum; whereupon Stilicho returned to Italy (A. D. 398), which he was soon called upon to defend from an invasion by Alaric (A. D. 400).

The Eastern Empire was, as we have seen, bestowed upon Arcadius (the elder son of Theodosius the Great), who was a feeble and indolent prince, and resigned all power into the hands of his minister, Rufinus, a wretch stained with every species of crime, who tried to force him into a marriage with his daughter. The courtiers, however, persuaded him to marry Eudoxia, the most beautiful woman of the age. Rufinus was murdered by the contrivance of Gainas, commander of the forces, who, with the grand chamberlain, Eutropius, and Eudoxia, obtained complete control over the feeble emperor, and excluded Stilicho, the minister of Honorius, from the administration of affairs. Yet to that extraordinary man Arcadius was indebted for the salvation of his empire from Alaric, who, on the refusal of the emperor to pay the tribute promised by Theodosius, led his soldiers into Greece, as above mentioned. The concluding years of this century are stained with the atrocities of Eutropius, who had obtained possession of the principal influence in the State. The career of this wretch was cut short by an invasion from the Goths, under their king, Tribigild (A. D. 399), in which the imperial forces fared badly, and by an insurrection headed by Gainas, who, combining with Tribigild, extorted from the emperor the destruction of the unworthy favorite. They filled Constantinople with their troops, but the citizens suddenly falling on them, expelled them with great slaughter (A. D. 400).

The same poverty of intellect which characterized the preceding century also marks this. The Christian Church produced the men who most distinguished themselves and influenced the world. Such were Lactantius, Porphyry, Eusebius, Jerome, Cyril, Augustine, Basil, Martin, Hilary, Chrysostom (who are emphatically styled "the Fathers of the Church"), Epiphanius, Gregory of Nazianzen, Gregory of Nyssa, Ambrose, Ulphilas, Arius, and Athanasius. The historians, Eutro'pius, Ammia'nus Marcellinus, Aurelius Victor, and others of less note; the mathematicians, Theon and Diophantus; the geographer, Pappus; and the grammarian, Donatus — were the most distinguished literary and scientific men of the age.

Why was Julian styled "the Apostate"?—What was his fate?—Who was his successor?—What of Jovian?—Valentinian I.?—Valens?—Milan?—Theodosius?—Gratian?—Valentinian II.?—The Huns?—Athanaric?—For what is Ulphilas famed?—What was the fate of Valens?—Whom did Gratian associate with him?

What is said of Theodosius the Great?—Gratian?—Ambrose of Milan?—Valentinian?—Eugenius?—Arbogastes?—The division of the empire?—And of Roman history?—Honorius?—Stilicho?—Gildo's revolt?—Alaric?—Arcadius?—Rufinus?—Eudoxia?—Gainas?—Eutropius?—Tribigild?—The Goths in Constantinople?—What eminent men flourished?

BRITAIN.

England.—Asclepiodotus, who recovered Britain for the Romans, was "præfectus pretoris" under Constantius Chlorus, but he is scarcely mentioned in the authentic history of the period. Geoffrey says that Asclepiodotus crowned himself king, and governed the country in justice and peace for 10 years. Coel, duke of Caer-colvin, or Colchester, revolted against Asclepiodotus, and killing him in a pitched battle, took possession of the kingdom. The Romans sent Constantius, the illustrious Senator, to subdue Coel, but the latter made submission, and was allowed to retain his kingdom on payment of tribute. Coel died very shortly afterwards: he is the hero of the old popular ditty, "Old King Cole was a merry old soul". Geoffrey also asserts that Constantius married Helena, the beautiful daughter of Coel, and that she became the mother of Constantine the Great; but this does not tally with the Roman account.

The Christians in Britain suffered greatly during the persecution under Diocletian (A. D. 303–306). This was principally owing to the cruelty of Maximianus Herculius, general of the Roman army, who ordered all the churches to be pulled down, and all the copies of the Scriptures that could be found to be burned in the public markets. The priests were put to death, and many females were tortured and killed. The most distinguished of the martyrs was Alban of Verulam. His confessor, Amphibalus, having been pursued, Alban concealed him in his house, and then offered himself to die for him; thus becoming THE FIRST BRITISH MARTYR. On the accession of Constantius, religious freedom was restored. This excellent prince died at York (A. D. 306), and his son Constantine (afterwards surnamed "the Great") assumed the government of the island. When he became sole emperor, he placed Britain under the jurisdiction of the prefect of Gaul, and appointed subordinate ministers called the vicar of Britain, the two consulars of Valentia and Maxima, and the three presidents of Flavia, Britannia Prima, and Britannia Secunda, to administer the affairs of the island. Under Constantine and his sons, Britain enjoyed more than 50 years of tranquillity and prosperity, and exported annually great quantities of corn to the continent. The Picts and Scots gave great trouble during the reign of Valentinian, who sent Theodosius to quell them (A. D. 367). This great man was eminently successful, and restored peace to the island (A. D. 379). Maximus, an ambitious officer, contrived to gain the affections of the soldiers, and made himself master of the country; but his defeat and death in Pannonia, in A. D. 388, again restored it to the empire.

Scotland.—The persecuted Christians from Britain took refuge in Scotland, and the purity of their lives contributed largely to the spread of Christianity. In the list of kings (authentic or otherwise) furnished by Buchanan, we find in this century the names of Fin-Cormac, Romach, Angus, Fethelmach, and Eugenius, nearly all of whom met with violent deaths. The history of the period is filled with bloody disputes between the Picts, Scots, Britons, and Romans,—the latter of whom, under Maximus, in conjunction with the Picts, expelled the Scots from the island, and drove them to take refuge in the Hebrides, Ireland, Norway, and Denmark. Maximus then reduced the country of the Picts to a Roman province.

Ireland.—The native chiefs made alliances with the Picts, and harassed the western shores of Britain. The Irish joined the Picts and Scots in their famous invasion of England, which was repelled by Theodosius (A. D. 367), who followed them to their own shores. Towards the end of the century the throne was usurped by Huas Colla, one of three brothers bearing the same name. The rightful monarch, Fiach, lost his life in the great battle of Dubcomar, where the "fighting Druid" was slain. The usurpation had lasted five years, when the three Collas fled to Scotland. Next year they returned, and assisted the king, Muredach Tiry, in an invasion of Ulster. The princely palace of Emania was entirely destroyed, after a battle which is said to have lasted six days, and not a trace of its glories was left. In the year 396 an invasion of Britain on a grand scale was undertaken by NIAL "of the nine hostages", one of the most gallant of all the princes of the Milesian line. After plundering Lancashire and Wales, he was compelled to return, leaving marks of ruin everywhere. It was against him that the Roman minister, Stilicho, took those precautions which so excited the admiration of the poet Claudian. The Attacotti, a fierce tribe of Irish, greatly distinguished themselves in this invasion.

What is said of Asclepiodotus?—Coel?—Constantius?—The persecution under Diocletian?—Alban of Verulam?—Constantine the Great?—The Picts and Scots?—Maximus?—The history of Scotland during this century?—Of Ireland?—Of the palace of Emania?—Of the invasion of Britain by Nial?—Of Stilicho?—And of the Attacotti?

FRANCE.

THE opening of the century was marked by the continued persecution of the Christians under Diocletian. On the abdication of that prince (A. D. 305), Constantius was made Augustus. His son, the illustrious Constantine the Great, was promoted to the empire by the army of Britain on the death of his father. The history of his career will be found in that of the Roman empire. On his embracing Christianity, the Gauls flocked enthusiastically round his standard, and materially contributed towards making him master of the empire. With him ceased the persecution of the Christians by the pagan emperors, and Christianity became the State religion. Constantine's son, Crispus, was appointed Cæsar of Gaul—an office which he held until his murder by his father (A. D. 326). On the death of Constantine the Great (A. D. 337), the empire was divided between his children, and Gaul fell to the lot of the eldest, Constantine. This young prince declared himself the protector of the Catholic faith, and the Church of Gaul became the centre of orthodoxy. Constantine took an active part in the great Arian controversy, and reinstated Athanasius in Egypt. But in endeavoring to deprive his brother Constans of his share in the empire, he was slain in Italy, and Constans became master of Gaul, where his depravity and mal-administration soon rendered him odious. A conspiracy was formed against him; and MAGNEN′TIUS, a native of Armorica, and an ambitious soldier, was encouraged to set up as emperor. Constans attempted to escape, but being overtaken was slain by the conspirators (A. D. 350). Magnentius took energetic measures to sustain his own authority, which was speedily acknowledged throughout Gaul and Italy. He persuaded Vetranio, prefect of Illyricum, to join in the revolt; and in this he was seconded by Constantina, the sister of the murdered Constans. Ambassadors were sent to Constantius in the East, to propose a treaty of friendship—an offer which was indignantly rejected. With great ability, Constantius detached Vetranio from the conspiracy, and being joined by his legions, he marched against Magnentius. After a decisive campaign, in which the usurper sustained severe reverses, the revolt was crushed, Magnentius destroyed himself, and Gaul was once more annexed to the Roman empire.

Constantius declared himself an Arian, and began a persecution of the orthodox Christians. Hilary, bishop of Poitiers, was banished into Phrygia, and the Church suffered greatly. At this period the northern and eastern portions of the country were ravaged by the Alemanni, the Franks, and the Vandals; and Constantius appointed Julian (afterwards emperor, and surnamed "the Apostate") governor of Gaul. The great military abilities of Julian soon restored peace to the country: he obtained a brilliant series of victories over the barbarians, and drove them across the Rhine (A. D. 355–359). Under his administration, agriculture, manufactures, and commerce revived, and national prosperity began to develop itself. Julian was particularly attached to the city of Paris, which he styled his "beloved Lute′tia" (the ancient name of the subsequent metropolis of France, which in this century was styled "Lute′tia Parisiorum", from the Parisii, a tribe which occupied that part of Gaul). He fixed his winter residence there; but at that time the city was confined to the small island in the Seine, and was accessible only by two wooden bridges. A forest covered the northern bank of the river, but on the southern side a palace, an amphitheatre, houses, baths, and an aqueduct were constructed, and a field of Mars was laid out for the exercise of the Roman troops. Julian was so beloved in Gaul, that he was proclaimed emperor. He was escorted in triumph through the streets of Paris, and soon after started on his memorable expedition to Constantinople. The death of Constantius (A. D. 361) left him master of the empire.

During the remainder of this century, the country was distracted with incursions of the German tribes, and with the political convulsions occasioned by the candidates for the imperial throne. The Arian controversy added fury to all parties. HILARY of Poitiers (restored by Constantius), MARTIN of Tours, and AMBROSE of Milan, ultimately acquired dominant influence in the West. The rulers of Gaul were Gratian, who was assassinated; the usurper Max′imus (defeated and slain by Theodosius); and Valentinian II. The last reaction of paganism took place in the year 392, when Arbogas′tes of Toulouse raised a revolt and proclaimed Euge′nius of Trèves emperor. This movement was promptly suppressed by Theodosius, who issued edicts against paganism, and the empire became definitively Christian.

What marks the opening of the century?—What is said of Constantine the Great?—Crispus?—Constantine II.?—Constans?—Magnentius?—What followed the suppression of the revolt?—What were the exploits of Julian the Apostate?—What of his administration?—Arianism?—Hilary?—Ambrose?—Arbogastes?—The edicts of Theodosius?

SPAIN.

On the division of the Roman empire, consequent on the abdication of Diocletian and Maximian, Spain fell to the lot of Constantius, the father of Constantine the Great. He died in A. D. 306, and Constantine succeeded to his dominions. About this time flourished the native poet, Pruden′tius; Rufus Festus, the historian; and Ho′sius, bishop of Cordova, one of the most learned men of that age. When the Arian controversy broke out, the emperor sent Hosius to Alexandria to reason with Arius, and endeavor to put a stop to the dispute. Hosius failed in this embassy. He afterwards was called upon to preside at the great Council of Nice, by which Arius and his doctrines were condemned. Another council was held at Ilib′eris (Grena′da) soon after, in which other weighty matters were discussed. Some authors, however, place the Council of Ilib′eris before that of Nice, in point of time. If this be correct, this is the most ancient council whose acts have come down to us. It consisted of 19 bishops, 36 presbyters, and a still greater number of deacons. Its 81 canons treat of baptism, confirmation, the Lord's Supper, penance, holy orders, matrimony, celibacy, fasting, and many matters of doctrine and of discipline.

Constantine divided the empire into four prætorian prefectures, one of which included Italy, France, and Spain. The residence of the prætor was established in France, and under him a vicar governed Spain. Constantine also separated Tingitana from Bœtica, and severed the governments of Carthagena and Galicia from Tarraconensis: hence he formed six provinces, viz., Tarrago′na, Carthage′na, Galicia, Lusitania, Bœtica, and Tingitana. The Emperor Theodosius the Great subsequently added a seventh, viz., the Balearic Isles. It is said that Constantine the Great owed his conversion to Christianity to a Spaniard. On the death of Constantine, the empire of the West was given to his son, Constans. In the year 337, Magnentius having made himself master of France and Spain, set up a claim to the imperial throne; but his defeat put an end to his ambitious schemes. He fled to Lyons, where he killed himself. Constans having been murdered, Constantius became emperor of the West, and the empire was for a time reunited under one head.

Nothing calls for mention respecting Spain during the reigns of Constantius, Julian the Apostate, Jovian, Valentinian I., and Valens, except the elevation of a Spaniard, Dama′sus, to the bishopric of Rome. Gratian and Valentinian II. were princes of no ability. Gratian appointed Theodo′sius (a Spaniard, afterwards styled "the Great") to the chief command of the Roman armies. This celebrated man proved himself qualified for the position. The Romans had sustained a sanguinary defeat from the Goths, who, exulting in their victory, were threatening to destroy Rome. But Theodosius gained two signal victories over them, and forced them to conclude peace (A. D. 382). In the following year Maximus, governor of Britain, having assumed the imperial purple, invaded Gaul. The Emperor Gratian, in opposing him, was slain; and Maximus was acknowledged emperor in Spain, Gaul, and Britain. In 387 Maximus endeavored to expel Valentinian, the brother of Gratian, from Italy; but Theodosius espoused the cause of the latter, and marched into the West at the head of a powerful army, defeated Maximus in Pannonia, and drove him across the Alps to Aquileia. There Maximus was surrendered to the victor and put to death. Theodosius now became sole emperor. He died A. D. 394, and divided the empire between his sons, Arcadius and Honorius; the latter becoming emperor of the West, the former of the East.

The Church in Spain was much disturbed by the teachings of Priscillian, a native of Galicia, who was joined by many followers. Having been cited to appear before a synod at Saragossa, he refused to attend. He was accordingly excommunicated, and he and his followers were expelled from their churches. They then had recourse to the Emperor Gratian, and procured an edict for their restoration. Not succeeding in getting reinstated, they appealed to the usurper Maximus, who, instead of befriending them, ordered them to be tried at Trèves. There Priscillian and his friends were sentenced to death, and executed. His doctrines were formally condemned by the Council of Toledo, held A. D. 400. This was the first council held at that city: it was attended by 19 bishops, and a corresponding number of inferior ecclesiastics. These bishops seem to have been equal in power, and independent of one another. They were elected by the people. The Spanish Church had as yet no primates nor archbishops.

What is said of Constantine the Great?—Hosius?—The Council of Iliberis?—What changes did Constantine introduce?—What other incidents occurred in succeeding reigns?—Who was Damasus?—What is said of Theodosius?—Gratian?—Maximus?—Priscillian and his followers?—The Council of Toledo?—The Spanish hierarchy?

GERMANY.

The Alemanni rose again in great force and ravaged Helvetia (A. D. 303), and Con′stantine the Great owed his elevation to the throne to the friendship of their leader, Crocus, who assisted him with troops (A. D. 306). This aid he repaid with base ingratitude. They aided his successor, Constantius, in his war with the Franks; but after the latter were subdued, the faithless emperor turned against his allies (A. D. 353). The Alemanni were defeated at the Bodensee (A. D. 355) and at Strasburg by Julian (afterwards emperor, and surnamed "the Apostate"), where their king, Chnodemar, was taken prisoner. Julian forced the nation to submit to his arms (A. D. 359). On his departure the Alemanni again rose, but were routed by Jovi′nus (A. D. 360). They were not subdued, however: on the contrary, under their leaders, Vitica′bius and Macria′nus, they defied all the efforts of the Emperor Valentin′ian to reduce them to obedience. Macrianus was murdered by the Franco-Roman commander, Mellobau′des (A. D. 375), who cut to pieces a large army of the Alemanni at Colmar, and forced the remainder to quit Gaul. They then turned to the Alps and settled in Helvetia, where their descendants, the Swiss, still dwell.

The Franks play an important part in the history of Germany and of Gaul in this century. Constantine the Great labored hard to subdue them. Having instigated them to revolt, he attacked and overcame them, and threw several of the noblest prisoners to the wild beasts in the amphitheatre. The Germans, Franks, and Alemanni, enraged at this cruelty, united against the emperor, who, entering their camp in disguise, gave them false information of his departure, and of the place and time when he would be most open to attack. This stratagem completely succeeded, and the allied Germans were entirely routed (A. D. 310). In a subsequent expedition (A. D. 318) he suddenly crossed the Rhine at Cologne, and unexpectedly attacking the Franks, he gained another important victory over them. Yet they aided him in his war with Licinius! Magnen′tius, who contended for the imperial throne, was a Frank, as was also Arbogas′tes, who aided the Romans against his own countrymen. In A. D. 388 they invaded Gaul and aided Arbogastes in setting up Euge′nius as a candidate for the empire. The Goths sided with his rival, Theodosius, and the Franks were completely routed at the battle of Aquile′ia. Arbogastes fled to the Alps, and put an end to his own life (A. D. 394). The Franks then became closely allied with the Romans, and this alliance contributed materially to alter their character.

The Goths also now become prominent in history. Extending their migrations from Norway to the Volga, they had in the preceding century carried terror and desolation throughout Thrace, Asia Minor, Greece, Illyria, and Italy. In this century, under their king, A′raric, they resisted and defeated Constantine the Great (A. D. 331). The emperor then incited the Vandals against them, but this attempt failed also. The Goths were early converted to Christianity, and several Gothic bishops took part in the Council of Nice (A. D. 325). Araric and his successor, Geb′eric, subjugated the Alani, the Vandals, the Gepidæ, and the Burgundians. Their successor, Her′manric, also subdued the Heruli, the Visigoths, and several Slavonian tribes; and he extended his empire from the Baltic to the Black Sea. He made an alliance with Rome, and spread his conquests far into Russia. But a new and terrible enemy now appeared on the scene. The Huns, an immense swarm of misshapen barbarians, from the far east of Asia, appeared on the frontiers of his kingdom. Distracted by domestic troubles, the old king put an end to his life in his 110th year. Bal′amir, prince of the Huns, subdued both the Ostrogoths (or Eastern Goths) and the Visigoths (or Western Goths). The latter fled into Thrace, where, being ill treated by the Romans, they raised a revolt. Having invited the Alans and Huns to join them, they annihilated the Roman army under Valens at Adrianople (A. D. 378). This disgrace was avenged by Theodosius the Great, who, aided by the Franks, drove the Goths across the Danube. The Visigoths settled in Thrace, and elected Al′aric their king. This celebrated man planned and executed the most daring enterprises. Suddenly invading Greece, he plundered and destroyed the most considerable cities (A. D. 396), sparing Athens alone. Alaric fixed himself in Illyria, where, being half-way between Rome and Constantinople, he threatened both. In the year 400 he invaded Italy, at the head of numerous German tribes, and attacked Aquileia; and notwithstanding the efforts of the celebrated Stil′icho to arrest his progress, he pressed gradually onward.

What befell the Alemanni during this century?—And the Franks?—Who was Magnentius?—Arbogastes?—What is said of the Goths?—Of their kings, Araric, Geberic, Hermanric?—Whence came the Huns?—Who was Balamir?—And Alaric?—Mention some of his exploits.—What were the Ostrogoths?—The Visigoths?

AFRICA.

In the year 335, Frumen'tius, a native of Tyre, undertook to convert the Ethiopians to Christianity, and having obtained leave of the queen of Ethiopia, and been appointed bishop of Axu'ma by Athanasius, he proceeded on his mission. He met with the greatest success, and founded many churches. Being a zealous disciple of Athanasius, he refused to tolerate Arianism, and all the efforts of the Emperor Constantius to introduce that heresy into Ethiopia were vain. At this time there reigned in that country Abra and Asba, as joint kings, between whom the harmony was so great as to become a proverb. We have but few details of the history of Ethiopia during this century. The Abassines (or Abyssinians, as they are now termed) were the leading tribe.

The incidental notices of the Arabs are likewise scanty. We find them mentioned as ravaging Mesopotamia in the time of the Emperor Constantius, and as joining the Persians against Julian, because the latter had discontinued the pension which his predecessors had paid for the maintenance of a body of Arab troops for service in the Roman army. An Arab queen, named Mavia, sent a force to aid Valens against the Goths, who were besieging Constantinople.

The history of the Roman provinces in Africa is intimately connected with that of the Christian Church. They suffered severely during the persecution under Diocletian and Maximian (A. D. 303–313). After the abdication of Diocletian they were governed under the name of Severus, and were exposed to the implacable resentment of Galerius. The revolt of Maxentius immediately restored peace to the Church in Africa, and this tyrant, so merciless to his other subjects, was humane towards the Christians, even when they gave him provocation. This was illustrated in the case of Mensu'rius, bishop of Carthage, who had shielded from the officers of justice a deacon of the Church who had published a libel on the emperor, for which offence he was summoned to Court, but instead of being punished, was permitted to return to his diocese.

The Donatist schism, in the African Church, afflicted the country above 300 years, and was extinguished only with Christianity itself. The origin of this memorable schism was a double election for the bishopric of Carthage. The candidates were Cæcilia'nus and Majori'nus; the ordination of the former was performed in the absence of the Numidian bishops (seventy in number), who, on their arrival in Carthage, condemned Cæcilianus, and consecrated Majorinus. The latter died soon after, and the party of Majorinus then elected and consecrated Dona'tus, a man of great ability. Cæcilianus claimed supremacy because of priority of ordination, but the other party contended that he had been illegally elected and ordained in the first instance, and refused to recognize him. A violent controversy arose, which was tried in five successive tribunals appointed by the Emperor Constantine, and the whole proceedings, from the first appeal to the final sentence, lasted over three years (A. D. 312–315). Judgment was at length pronounced by the emperor himself, in his sacred consistory, in favor of Cæcilianus, and the latter was universally acknowledged by the civil and ecclesiastical powers as the lawful primate of Africa. But the Donatist faction obstinately refused to acquiesce in the decision, and the emperor found it necessary to banish some of the leaders. The Donatists then became more violent than ever. They excommunicated Cæcilianus and his supporters, denounced the rest of the Church throughout the world, and in numberless ways outraged the feelings of the orthodox Christians. They concentrated their strength in Numidia, where they had 400 bishops; and having acquired complete ascendency over the ignorant and ferocious population, they set at defiance the attempts of the Roman emperor to restore peace to the Church. Styling themselves "Circumcellio'nes" (wanderers from cave to cave), and arming themselves with huge clubs, which they called Israelites, they ravaged the country. Attacking the Roman troops at Bagai, hundreds were slaughtered; those that were taken were put to death, but these fierce Africans were not subdued, and they gave continual trouble for many years.

The peace of the provinces was broken by the revolt of Firmius, a Moor, occasioned by the rapacity of Romanus, the governor. This revolt was suppressed by the elder Theodosius (A. D. 373). A more formidable one occurred A. D. 386, headed by Gildo, the brother of Firmius, who maintained his sway over Africa for twelve years, but was at length defeated and deposed by an army sent from Italy under his younger brother, Masce'zel. Gildo destroyed himself (A. D. 398).

Who preached Christianity in Ethiopia?—What is said of him?—What accounts are there of the Arabs?—What are the principal events in the history of the Roman provinces?—What of Mensurius?—The Donatist schism?—Who were the "Circumcelliones"?—What befell them?—What of the revolt of Firmius?—And of Gildo?

SCANDINAVIA.

Sweden.—Alrek and Erik I. were succeeded by Yngve and Alf, but the divided authority was restored to one ruler in the person of Hugleik, who was subsequently expelled by Hakon, a Norwegian pirate. Towards the end of the century two kings ruled jointly, viz., Jorunder and Erik II., who were succeeded by Aun-hinn-Gamle the Old. The manners and religion of the people were ferocious and licentious. Captives, slaves, children, and animals, were sacrificed to the gods: wizards and diviners abounded, and the most grovelling superstition prevailed.

Denmark.—Halfdan I. succeeded Frode III. (A. D. 310). This prince subdued Sweden. He defeated the king in many battles, and having driven him from the throne, fixed his residence in Upsala, where he died after a reign of 25 years. Friedlief III. occupied the throne after him.

The study of a list of kings is profitless enough, but it is all that is left of this early period. We will turn for a moment, therefore, to the legend of Hamlet, immortalized by Shakspeare. It is given in full in Saxo Grammaticus' *History of Denmark*, book iii., but is too long to be extracted here. The outlines of it are as follows: Hamlet was the son of Hor'mendil', governor of Jutland, a famous pirate and vassal of Ruric, the son of Hoder, who exercised sovereignty over a portion of Denmark in the days of Odin (1st century B. C.). Hormendil and his brother, Fengo, held joint sway over Jutland, and the former married Gertrude, the daughter of Ruric. The envious Fengo murdered Hormendil, and married Gertrude. Hamlet, aware of the facts, assumed madness, in order to disguise his intention of avenging his father's murder. The succeeding incidents of the legend are introduced in the play, and need not be recapitulated. On his return from England, where he had married the daughter of a British king, Hamlet killed Fengo in his bedroom, and not in public, as Shakspeare has represented it. The people elected Hamlet their governor. He then revisited Britain, married the widowed queen of Scotland (his first wife having died), and returned to Jutland; soon after which he waged war with Wiglet, a king of Denmark, the successor of his grandfather Ruric, and fell in battle — his wife becoming a prize to the conqueror.

What is related of Sweden?—The manners of the people?—Denmark?—The legend of Hamlet?—Wherein does it differ from the play?—What befell Hamlet?

NETHERLANDS.

We may now trace an entirely new population in the Netherlands. The Batavi (or Batavians), who inhabited the island formed by the Rhine, the Waal, and the Maas, were annihilated, almost without resistance, by the Salian Franks. The Menapians, under the name of Armoricans, united themselves with their people who bordered the channel. The Frisii (or Frisons) joined the tribes settled on the shores of the German Ocean, and formed with them the famous Saxon league. Thus was framed on all points a union between the maritime races against the inland inhabitants, and their mutual antipathy became more developed as the decline of the Roman empire ended the former struggle between liberty and conquest (Grattan's *History of the Netherlands*, ch. ii.). The Salian and other Franks occupied the high lands. Between the Saxon tribes and the Franks the ancient feuds were renewed. In the year 355 the Varni, a race of Saxons from Denmark, made a descent on the ancient isle of the Batavians, then inhabited by the Salians. They expelled the latter completely, notwithstanding the efforts made by Julian the Apostate to save them. From this time the Salians disappeared from the Low Countries, and joining the other Franks, passed into Gaul, where they established themselves, their numbers being recruited by continual emigration from Germany and the Netherlands. The Varni remained settled near the mouth of the Rhine, where they remained until near the year 500, when they became lost in the general emigration of the Saxons. The latter spread themselves over the shores of the adjoining countries, and as their numbers increased they carried out expeditions beyond the sea, where they settled. Some established themselves near the mouths of the Loire; others, subsequently (in the next century), settled in Britain.

Paganism was the prevailing religion among the tribes of this country. Many attempts were made to introduce Christianity, but none of these took permanent root; at all events, no extensive conversion of the people was effected. The western portion of the Netherlands was laid desolate by Clovis and his Franks from Gaul, at the close of the next century; but the eastern portion was exceedingly prosperous, and the land was well cultivated.

What became of the Batavians?—What is said of the Menapii?—The Frisons?—The Salian Franks?—The Varni?—The progress of Christianity?—The state of the country?

CENTRAL AMERICA.

In the absence of authentic history during this and the following century, we may notice some of the early myths of Guatemala. It is remarkable that all primitive nations have a tradition of a deluge. The Quichès, who, so far as has yet been ascertained, were the earliest inhabitants of that portion of Central America, are no exception. They have their cosmogony, or sacred account of the creation of the world, which probably veils under symbolical language the primitive events of their history. According to this "Genesis", the Supreme Being employed several agents in the work of creation. The first portion of the universe that was made was Heaven. The language of the legend will give an idea of Mexican reasoning. "When its angles were laid down, its limits fixed, its lines and parallels put in their respective places, it received its name from the Creator and the Maker, the father and mother of life and of existence, through whom everything acts and breathes, the father and the preserver of the peace of nations, the father of his vassals, the master of thought and of wisdom, the excellence of all that is in heaven and upon earth, in the lakes and the sea. It was named when all was tranquil and calm, when all was peaceful and silent, when nothing as yet moved in the void of the heavens. There were then neither men, nor animals, nor birds, nor fish, nor crabs, nor wood, nor stones: neither valleys, nor herbs, nor forests: there was nothing but heaven. The image of the earth had not yet appeared. There was but the sea, surrounded on all sides by the sky: nothing had a body, nothing which moved from place to place: nothing had motion, and not the least breath agitated the air: there was but the calm and peaceful sea: nothing but the sea, which was calm. In the midst of this calm and tranquillity, there was but the Creator and Maker, Tepeu-Gucumatz, in the obscurity of the night: there were but the fathers and generators upon the whitening water, and they were clad in azure vestments, whence the name of Gucumatz (literally, plumed serpent) has been bestowed upon these illustrious sages, these great masters of science. It is owing to them that Heaven exists, that in like manner exists The Heart of Heaven, and this is the name of God."

The legend then reveals the creation of man, and the existence of a Trinity in the Supreme Being. It thus continues: "Then the word came to them from Tepeu-Gucumatz in the darkness of the night, and said, It is time to consult together, to understand and unite and hold counsel among yourselves, to unite your speech and your wisdom, in order to light your path and become mutual guides. Then they saw men appear: they distinguished what had been formed, what existed, all that had received life and existence in the obscurity of the night from the hands of the Creator of the heavens. And His name is 'A Voice that roars', Hurakan; the first is the Voice of Thunder; the second is the Lightning; the third is the Thunderbolt: and these three are The Heart of Heaven: they descended near Tepeu-Gucumatz when he was considering the work of creation, and how the seeds would be made when the day should appear, and who should be the servants and sustainers. 'Know that this water will retire and give place to land, which will exist and be everywhere. There will be seeds to make: there will be light in heaven and upon earth: but as yet there is no being fashioned and formed by us, who shall respect and honor us.' They spake, and the land immediately existed. Like a cloud and a fog was its being; and like lobsters extended in the water appeared the great mountains. Then came the plains, and on them cypresses and pines: the streams divided themselves, winding at the foot of the hills; and the lofty Cordilleras arose."

Then came Man, not from the hands of the Deity, but from those of inferior agents: he was made out of mud, to render homage to them. The names of these agents (supposed to be those of the first rulers or legislators of the Quichès) are Hunahpu Wueh, Hunahpu Utiu, Zaki Nima Tziz, and Tepeu-Gucumatz. In the legend the Supreme Being and his agents are sometimes confounded. The Mexican Genesis says that when heaven and earth were created, man had already been formed four times (evidently alluding to the four attempts at civilization mentioned in the earliest annals); that God made man out of ashes on the seventh day, Ehecatl (a word signifying "the breath of life"), but that Quetzalcohuatl perfected him. There are several points in which this cosmogony resembles that of Moses.

State the particulars of the Quichè myth of the Cosmogony.—Of the creation of man.—The Trinity.—In what order did the various portions of nature make their appearance?—What is said of the creation of man?—How many agents aided?—What do the Mexican legends add?

THE CHRISTIAN CHURCH.

This century opened with a furious persecution of the Christians, set on foot by the pagan priesthood and by Galerius, who persuaded Diocletian to issue an edict (A. D. 303) directing the pulling down of the churches of the Christians, the burning of all their books and writings, and the depriving them of all their civil rights and privileges. This was followed by another, commissioning the magistrates to force them all, without distinction of age or sex, to sacrifice to the gods, condemning them to be punished as incendiaries if they refused to do so; and by a third, which directed that all ministers and bishops should be cast into prison, and that all sorts of torments should be employed to induce them to renounce their religion. Thousands perished under these cruelties. It has been computed that in this tenth persecution, as it is commonly termed, not fewer than 17,000 Christians were put to death in one month. It lasted ten years, and during that time no fewer than 150,000 persons, in Egypt alone, died by the violence of their persecutors. Five times that number perished through the fatigues of banishment, or in the public mines wherein they were condemned to labor. Gaul, which was then under the mild rule of Constantius Chlorus, was happily exempted from these horrors. The accession of Constantine the Great in the West (A. D. 307) checked the persecution there, and soon afterwards the death of Galerius (A. D. 311) and the defeat of Maxentius (A. D. 313) restored tranquillity to the East. Shortly before his death, Galerius, desirous of repairing the mischief he had done, published in his own name, and in those of Licinius and Constantine, an edict by which, admitting that he had failed in convincing the Christians of their folly, he permitted them the free exercise of their religion, and added: "We hope that our indulgence will engage the Christians to offer up their prayers to the Deity whom they adore, for our safety and prosperity, for their own, and for that of the republic." This edict was issued at Nicomedia on April 13th, 311; but Galerius did not long survive its publication, for he died in the beginning of May, in the most excruciating torments. Constantine and his colleague, Licinius, subsequently issued edicts (A. D. 313) granting to the Christians the full power of living according to their own laws and institutions, and the former prince embraced Christianity. Universal toleration now prevailed. Licinius some years afterwards made an attempt to free himself from the authority of Constantine, and, excited by the heathen priests, he persecuted the Christians in a cruel manner, putting to death many of their bishops; but aspiring to become sole emperor, his enterprise proved abortive: Constantine was everywhere victorious, and Licinius was ultimately obliged to submit to the conqueror, who ordered him to be strangled (A. D. 325).

The reign of Constantine the Great is one of the grand epochs in the history of Christianity. Its external troubles and trials were now over. It was firmly established as the religion of the Court, and soon became predominant throughout the Roman empire. Henceforth, the foes of the Church were those of its own household. An exception must, however, be made as to the reign of Julian the Apostate, who abandoned the principles of Christianity in which he had been educated, and exerted himself to restore the heathen worship. This apostasy was, doubtless, mainly owing to his aversion to the family of Constantine, who had murdered his father, brother, and kinsmen. He did not resort to open violence to destroy the Church, but tried stratagem. He revoked the privileges granted to Christians and their spiritual rulers; he shut up the schools in which they taught; and he not only encouraged sectarians and schismatics, who brought the Church into disrepute, but wrote books himself against the Christians. He would have proceeded further, had not his sudden death freed the Church from its most dangerous enemy, after a reign of 20 months. The Emperor Theodosius the Great exerted himself vigorously to extirpate pagan superstitions, and enacted severe laws against such as adhered to them. Honorius and Arcadius pursued the same course; so that at the conclusion of the century the Gentile religions irrecoverably lost their authority and splendor.

But while the Church was thus prospering in the West, sad reverses attended it in Asia. A most dreadful series of persecutions of the Christians was ordered by Sapor, king of Persia. Three times were they subjected to incredible cruelties in that country. The last persecution, which began in the year 330 and lasted 40 years, proved almost destructive to Christianity in the far East. Incredible numbers of Christians perished: those who escaped took refuge in the

What of the persecution under Diocletian?—How many perished?—What stayed the persecution?—What of Constantine the Great?—Licinius?—Julian the Apostate?—What course did he adopt?—What did Theodosius attempt?—What became of the Gentile religions?—What did Christianity become?—What happened in the East?

inaccessible mountain regions of Armenia and Georgia. Their descendants subsequently embraced the doctrines of Nestorius, and these are now the prevailing tenets among the modern Armenians.

In the internal history of the Church there occurred many most important events. The first was the Meletian Controversy, occasioned by the deposition of MELE′TIUS, bishop of Nicop′olis, by the bishop of Alexandria, on a charge of having lapsed into idolatry (A. D. 302)—a measure which was treated with contempt by Meletius, who was supported in his opposition by many other bishops. This dispute caused a breach in the Alexandrian Church which lasted more than a century. The second was the institution of the MONASTIC SYSTEM in Egypt by ANTONY (about A. D. 307), an illiterate man, a native of Coma, a village in Upper Egypt, and born A. D. 251. His parents were Christians, and very rich, but they neglected his education. From early youth he had been addicted to solitude, penance, and contemplation; and in the year 285 he took up his abode in the ruins of an old castle on the top of a mountain, where he secluded himself for 20 years, seeing only one man, who brought him bread and salt. His fame spread abroad, and at length, having been importuned to quit his solitude, he came down from the mountain (A. D. 305), and founded his first monastery at Phaium. During the persecution of the Christians (A. D. 311) Antony went to Alexandria, courting martyrdom, but he was not harmed, and he returned to his monastery (A. D. 312). Soon afterwards he built another near the Nile; but he himself withdrew with his disciple, Maca′rius, to a cell in a mountain of difficult access. In A. D. 355, being 104 years old, he went to Alexandria to preach against the Arians. He died A. D. 356, in his lonely cell, attended only by his disciples Macarius and Amathas. Legends say that the disease called the "sacred fire", which raged violently in Europe in the 11th century, was stayed through his prayers; hence it was called St. Antony's fire. The monastic system founded by him spread rapidly. Fifty monasteries were planted to the south of Alexandria by his disciples. A Syrian youth named Hila′rion took up his abode on a sandy beach about seven miles from Gaza, where he persisted in austere penance for 48 years. His example found numerous imitators, and monasteries were established all over Palestine. Martin of Tours founded a monastery at Poictiers, and thus introduced the system into France; and so numerous did monks become there, that it is said 2000 of them attended his funeral. Every province of the Roman empire was filled with them. The disciples of Antony penetrated into Ethiopia. In Britain the monastery of Bangor was established, and soon held 2000 devotees: thence a number crossed over to Ireland, to spread their practices there; and Iona, one of the western islands of Scotland, became celebrated as the abode of learned and pious recluses. Females also began to retire from the world, and devote themselves to solitude and devotion; and the practice was sanctioned by the Council of Carthage (A. D. 397). They were strictly secluded from worldly intercourse, and subjected to severe discipline. There were several classes of monks, as the Anchorites, the Eremites (or hermits), the Sarabaïtes, etc.

The third great event was the contest between Cæcilia′nus and Majori′nus for the bishopric of Carthage (noticed in the history of Africa), which gave rise to the DONATIST CONTROVERSY; so called from DONA′TUS, bishop of Casæ-nigræ, who made himself conspicuous in the dispute. The Donatists espoused the cause of Majorinus, and appealed to the Emperor Constantine, who referred the case to Melchiades, bishop of Rome, and to three bishops of Gaul. These referees decided against Majorinus; but the emperor again, at the request of the Donatists, called a council at Arles (A. D. 314) to settle the dispute. The decision of this council was also against the Donatists. They now appealed to the emperor in person, who inquired into the whole affair, at Milan (A. D. 315), in presence of the contending parties, and decided against the Donatists. The latter, becoming furious, loaded the emperor with invectives; whereupon he deprived them of their churches in Africa, and banished their seditious bishops; some of them he put to death. But worse disorders ensued (see history of Africa), and at last the emperor repealed the edicts against the Donatists.

But the most furious schism which ever rent and disgraced the Church, in this or any other age, was the ARIAN CONTROVERSY. This celebrated dispute originated in an assembly of presbyters at Alexandria (A. D. 320), when Alexander, bishop of that See, expressing his sentiments on the subject of the Trinity, maintained that the Son was not only of the same dignity but of the same essence with the Father. This doctrine was opposed by ARIUS, one of the presbyters, who maintained that the Son was totally distinct from the Father; that He was the first of beings whom God had created, and by whom He formed the universe, and therefore was inferior to Him in every degree. Great uncertainty prevails as to the real tenets of Arius on other points, but on this there is none. He soon had numerous followers, especially among the learned and influential classes. Alexander, at the instigation of his secretary, ATHANA′SIUS, called a council at Alexandria (A. D. 321), wherein Arius was condemned and expelled from the Church. In the same year, the Emperor Constantine issued an edict prescribing the observance of Sunday (*Dies Solis*). This was followed by another inflicting punishment on all who should exact from Christians the observance of heathen ceremonies. Meanwhile Arius retired into Palestine, where he wrote letters to the most eminent men of the time, demonstrating the truth of his opinions, with such surprising success, that vast numbers were drawn over to his views. The controversy reached such a height at last, that in the year 325 Constantine assembled the famous COUNCIL OF NICE, in Bithynia (also styled "the first general council"), whereto the deputies of the Church universal were summoned. It was attended by 318 bishops, under the presidency of HOSIUS, bishop of Cordova; the emperor himself also attending. The council began their discussions on June 19th, and ended them on August 25th. After many keen debates, and a great display of virulence from Athanasius, the doctrines of Arius were condemned by the majority. Arius was banished to Illyria, and his followers were compelled to assent to the creed which was drawn up by the council (thence called "the Nicene Creed"), and sanctioned by the emperor. This summary of the orthodox faith may be found in the epistle of Eusebius to the Cæsareans, and runs thus:—"We believe in one God, the Father Almighty, Maker of all things visible and invisible. And in one Lord Jesus Christ, the Son of God, the only begotten; begotten of the Father, that is, of the substance of the Father; God of God; Light of Light; true God of true God; begotten, not made; *consubstantial* with the Father, by whom all things were made, things in heaven, and things on earth; who for us men, and for our salvation, came down and was incarnate and became man, suffered and rose again the third day, and ascended into the heavens, and comes to judge the quick and the dead. And in the Holy Ghost. And the Catholic and Apostolic Church doth anathematize those persons who say there was a time when the Son of God was not; that he was not before he was born; that he was made of nothing, or of another substance or being; or that he is created, or changeable, or convertible." This creed was sent to Sylvester, bishop of Rome, who, in the Thirteenth Council of Rome, which was attended by 275 bishops, solemnly confirmed it. The Nicene Creed, as it then stood, therefore became the established exponent of the articles of the Christian faith. Eusebius of Nicomedia and 16 other bishops rejected the word "consubstantial"; but finding that the emperor was determined to enforce the decisions of the council, they all (except four) subscribed the creed. The writings of Arius were publicly burnt, and it was decreed that all persons in whose possession they should be found should be capitally punished. But the controversy was not put down; and the question as to whether Christ was of the same nature (*homoousios*) with God, or of a similar nature (*homoiousios*), occasioned furious contests. These two Greek words differed from each other only in one letter, but that fact was enough to excite the bitterest enmity between the Homoousians and the Homoiousians. This celebrated Council of Nice also settled the Meletian and Novatian schisms, and the disputes as to the time of observing Easter. It defined the jurisdiction of the greater bishops, and very nearly imposed celibacy on the clergy.

Soon after this the Empress Helena, the mother of Constantine, visited Palestine, where she was baptized: she founded many churches there. Athanasius was elected bishop of Alexandria (A. D. 326). The penal laws against the Arians were relaxed, and the exiles were recalled (A. D. 328). But the most important event was the transfer of the imperial capital from Rome to Constantinople, and the establishment of a metropolitan See there (A. D. 330). This caused that rivalry between the two Sees which terminated in a permanent breach between

What was the first important event in the internal history of the Church?—Who was Meletius?—What was the second important event?—Who was Antony?—State some particulars of his history.—His death.—What of his system?—Of Macarius?—Hilarion?—Martin?—Female recluses?—Other monks?—What was the third great event?

What is said of the Arian Controversy?—What did Arius teach?—Who was Athanasius?—What edicts did Constantine issue?—What of the Council of Nice?—Its decree?—The Nicene Creed?—The opposition to it?—Its ratification?—What was done to Arius?—What else was settled?—What of Helena?—Athanasius?

A.C. 300—400.

THE CHRISTIAN CHURCH.

the Eastern and Western Churches. The emperor leaned towards Arianism; and the restored Arian prelates held councils at Cæsarea, Tyre, and Jerusalem, and voted the deposition of Athanasius, who consequently was ordered by the emperor to retire to Trèves (A. D. 335). Next year Arius died suddenly, not without suspicion of poison. Constantine also died (A. D. 337), having previously been baptized by Eusebius, the Arian bishop of Nicomedia.

No character has been exhibited in more contrary lights than that of Constantine. Christian writers have exalted him, while the pagans have blackened him. Convinced of the impiety of paganism, he exhorted his subjects to embrace the gospel, and employed all his authority to abolish heathen worship. The story of his conversion to Christianity has been much disputed. According to his own account, he was marching against Maxentius, oppressed with the critical importance of success, and reflecting that he needed a force superior to arms for subduing his adversary: he therefore anxiously invoked the aid of some deity. About noon, while praying for this aid, a luminous cross above the sun was seen by him and his army, inscribed with the words, *In hoc signo vinces* ("In this sign shalt thou conquer"). Amazement overpowered all beholders. Constantine continued to ponder on the event until night, when, in a dream, Christ appeared to him, confirming the vision, and directing him to adopt the cross as his symbol. Eusebius, who received the account from Constantine himself, and wrote the life of that emperor, did not credit it, though Constantine attested it by an oath. No date nor place is assigned for the occurrence, nor is there any evidence that any one in the army save the emperor saw the phenomenon. The opinions of the different writers on the subject will be found in the appendix to the first volume of Dr. Gregory's *History of the Christian Church.* Constantine in one of his edicts commanded that places of worship and other effects should be restored to the Christians; in another, he restricted the edict to "The Catholic Church". Upon this "grant" great pretensions were based in after ages.

Athanasius returned to Alexandria, but was again deposed (A. D. 341) by a synod held at Antioch. He fled to Rome, where a synod was held (A. D. 342) to support him. The Arian bishops met at Antioch (A. D. 345), and published a confession of their faith; and the bishops of the West did the same at Milan (A. D. 346), declaring their adherence to the Nicene Creed. This was followed by a general council at Sardica, wherein the Athanasian party were triumphant; but the majority and minority mutually excommunicated each other. Terrible tumults occurred at Alexandria (A. D. 349), in which Bishop Gregory was killed. The Emperor Constans threatened to restore Athanasius by force: this threat caused him to be reinstated in his See. Dreadful commotions also took place at Constantinople respecting the rival claims of Paul and Macedonius to that See. Paul was banished and put to death (A. D. 352), and Macedonius was installed by force. The whole Church was a scene of scandalous confusion: bishops mutually excommunicated each other, and their deposition became quite common. The Councils of Arles and Milan (A. D. 355) deposed Athanasius and his supporters, and he was expelled by violence from Alexandria. Liberius, bishop of Rome, was amongst those treated in like manner by the Arians; but having subsequently, it is said, conformed to Arianism, he was reinstated in his bishopric (A. D. 358). Athanasius afterwards returned to Alexandria; his predecessor, George of Cappadocia, having been killed there by the people, in consequence of his odious tyranny. He was a man of infamous character; but the Arians honored him as a Christian martyr. He became revered in Palestine and Armenia, and after the Crusades his popularity spread over Europe. The English adopted him as their patron saint. A full account of him will be found in Dr. Heylin's *History of St. George* (see also Gibbon's *Decline and Fall*, ch. xxxiii.). Athanasius closed his turbulent career in A. D. 373. The Arian controversy continued to rage after his death. In 380 a council was called at Antioch to depose the Arian bishops. At one held at Constantinople the bishops quarrelled and *fought:* Gregory of Nazianzen, one of the bishops present, was so disgusted that he resigned his bishopric. The power of the Church was shown in the conduct of Ambrose, bishop of Milan, who refused to allow the Empress Justina even one church for Arian worship at Rome, and enjoined penance on the Emperor Theodosius for a massacre committed by his orders at Thessalonica. The Emperor Constantius (A. D. 343) exempted all ecclesiastics and their property from new imposts, and the Emperor Gratian (A. D. 377) accorded them extensive immunities. On the other hand, the Emperor Valentinian issued an edict (A. D. 370) prohibiting the arts practised by the ecclesiastics to obtain wealth, and Gregory of Nazianzen inveighed against their pride and luxury. The growth of hierarchical power kept pace with the decay of intellectual energy, and education was generally neglected. Among the controversies and heresies which disturbed the Church during this century, may be mentioned the controversy respecting Origen; that set on foot by Ærius, a semi-Arian presbyter of Asia Minor, who condemned the ceremonial observances that had crept into the Church; that of Jovinian; the heretical teachings of Eustathius, Meletius, Lucifer (bishop of Cagliari), Ætius, Eunomius, George of Laodicea, Basilius, Apollinaris the younger, Marcellus of Ancyra, Photinus, Macedonius, Ardæus, the Messalians or Euchites, the Antidico-Marianites, and the Collyridians. Priscillian, who taught that sensual pleasures were sinful, was condemned by the Councils of Saragossa (A. D. 380) and Bordeaux (A. D. 385), and beheaded with his followers at Trèves.

Many ceremonies were introduced into the Church during this century. Some of the rites of the heathens were now adopted, with alterations. Robes, mitres, tapers, crosiers, images, and gold and silver vases, were used. Churches were everywhere erected and consecrated with great pomp; and the "right of patronage" (or of appointing ministers) was accorded to those who founded them. The worship consisted in hymns, prayers, reading the Scriptures, a sermon, and the celebration of the Lord's Supper, but a variety of liturgies were in use. The Psalms of David were sung as hymns: during the sermons, the audience testified their satisfaction by clapping of hands and loud acclamations: the first day of the week (Sunday) was the ordinary time for religious assembling: Christmas day was observed as a holy day, and festivals and commemorations of saints and martyrs were multiplied. Fasting was much practised, but consisted merely in abstaining from meat and wine. Baptismal fonts were erected in the porch of each church, and baptism was administered during the vigils of Easter and Whitsuntide: in some places salt was thrown into the mouth of the person baptised, as a symbol of purity and wisdom, and he was obliged to wear white garments for seven days after the ceremony. The Lord's Supper was administered in church on Sundays and sometimes during the week, and at the tombs of martyrs and at funerals; but catechumens, penitents, and those supposed to be possessed by evil spirits, were not allowed to partake of it.

The government of the Church underwent modification. Constantine the Great modelled it according to the civil form. There were four pre-eminent bishops or "patriarchs", viz., those of Rome, Antioch, Alexandria, and Constantinople: — "exarchs" were appointed to inspect several provinces each: — "metropolitans", to govern one province each: — archbishops, to rule over a district: — bishops, over one or more churches. The administration was divided into external and internal. The former related to the discipline, possessions, and privileges of the Church, and was assumed by the emperor; the latter related to controversies, worship, offices of the priests, &c., and was committed to bishops and councils. The bishops of Rome during this century were Marcellinus (296–304); the See vacant (304–308); Marcellus (308–310); Eusebius (310–311); Melchiades (311–314); Sylvester I. (314–336); Marcus (336–337); Julius I. (337–352); Liberius (352–366); Damasus I. (366–384); Siricius (384–398); Anastasius I. (398–402). They call for no particular notice, except Damasus, whose election was the cause of bloody strife in Rome—a rival, Ursicinus, having been set up by another party. As yet the bishops of Rome had not acquired that pre-eminence they afterwards enjoyed; and none of the other bishops acknowledged that they derived their power from the Apostolic See.

The most eminent men in the Church during this century were: Eusebius Pamphilus, the ecclesiastical historian, bishop of Cæsarea; Basil of Cæsarea; Cyril of Jerusalem; John Chrysostom (John, the golden-mouthed), bishop of Antioch, afterwards of Constantinople, renowned for his eloquence; Epiphanius; Gregory Nazianzen; Gregory of Nyssa; Hilary of Poictiers; Lactantius; Jerome, a monk of Palestine, and a voluminous writer; Augustin, bishop of Hippo; Optatus, Paulinus, and Rufinus.

What is said of the removal of the capital to Constantinople?—What was its result?—What did the Arians do?—What of the death of Arius?—Of Constantine?—His character?—His conversion to Christianity?—His grant to the Church?—The confusion in the Church?—St. George?—The death and character of Athanasius?

What more of the Arian controversy?—What of Priscillian?—Ambrose of Milan?—The wealth of the Church?—What of minor heresies?—What new ceremonies were introduced into the Church service?—What of Divine worship?—Fasting?—Baptism?—The government of the Church?—What eminent men flourished?—What of the bishops of Rome?

THE 5TH CENTURY

INDIA.

This century is the epoch of the highest degree of perfection in Indian science. We find the Brahmins, at this early period, discussing the subject of the precession of the equinoxes, and the diurnal revolution of the earth, which last doctrine, though suggested by Heracli′tus of Ephesus, in the 6th century B. C., was not revived in Europe until the time of Coper′nicus, in the 16th century. There is no doubt that the Brahmins were well acquainted with the astronomy and mathematics of the Greeks, and it is very probable they made use of both to improve their own knowledge. They appear to have had considerable skill in medicine. They used metals and minerals, as well as herbs, in the treatment of diseases, and understood how to prepare oxides, sulphurets, and carbonates; they administered mercury and arsenic, the first in the form of calomel and corrosive sublimate. Their knowledge of surgery was remarkable, and they were able to perform some of the most difficult operations. In music and painting, the ancient Hindoos never attained to a high degree of excellence, nor did they ever approach the Greeks in sculpture and architecture.

The history of India at this period furnishes but few details. A dynasty of princes, styled the Andras, reigned in the valley of the Ganges over the kingdom of Magadha. The accession of this race to power dates from the beginning of the Christian Era, and they continued to reign until the year 436, when a period of confusion ensued, and different parts of India were seized by different races, of whom nothing further is known. The Andra dynasty is mentioned by the Roman historian, Pliny, as being a powerful one. The ancient kingdom of Magadha existed as far back as the war of the Mahabharat, or about 1450 B. C. Nanda (about 400 B. C.) and Sandracottus (about 320 B. C.), who have been already noticed, were the two most famous kings of this nation. The Chinese annals mention the arrival, in the year 408, of ambassadors from Yajna, the last king of the Andra dynasty. There was also a dynasty of the same name in the Deccan. After the period of confusion above referred to, a dynasty of princes, called the Guptas of Magadha, ruled along the valley of the Ganges to Prayaga, from the 5th to the 8th century.

What was the state of science at this time?—What of medicine and surgery?—The fine arts?—Who were the Andras?—What incidents are related of Magadha?

PERSIA.

Baharam IV. was succeeded (A. D. 404) by Yezdijird I. (the Isdigertes of the Greeks), surnamed Ulathim (or "the sinner"), a prince described by the Persian historians as devoid of every virtue, and abandoned to luxury; but the Greek historians represent him as a wise and good man, so much so that the Emperor Arcadius appointed him protector of his young son, Theodosius, a trust which Yezdijird fulfilled with the greatest fidelity. The truth of this story has, however, been doubted (Gibbon, *Decline and Fall of the Roman Empire*, vol. v., p. 413). But whether true or not, it proves that the reputation of the Persian monarch was high among the Western nations, and perhaps this circumstance has caused his name to be execrated by the bigots of his own country. Some of his sayings have been preserved, which show a lofty sense of morality. One was: "The wisest of monarchs was he who never punished when in a rage, and who followed the first impulse of his mind to reward the deserving." Another was: "Whenever a king ceases to do good actions he necessarily commits bad; and the thoughts of eternity cannot for a moment be absent from the mind without its verging towards sin." After his death (A. D. 420), his son, Baharam V. (who had been educated by Noman, an Arab chief), ascended the throne, and became one of the best and greatest sovereigns that ever ruled Persia. There was opposition to his succession, however, for the nobles dreaded a monarch who had been raised among the Arabs, and they set up Khosroo, a prince of the royal family, but Baharam made good his claim without much difficulty. The romances of Persia say that he proposed that the crown should be placed between two lions, and that he and his competitor should try which could get it from them; that Khosroo shrunk from the challenge, and that Baharam then killed both lions, and was proclaimed Shah. His munificence is the theme of Persian historians of every subsequent age. He encouraged music, and went to great expense to induce musicians to come into Persia. His reign commenced with troubles. First (A. D. 422) came a war with Theodosius, which was remarkable for failures on both sides, and was inglorious to both Romans and Persians. It ended in a truce for a hundred years. It was during this war that Aca′cius, bishop of Amida, sold the plate of his Church to redeem 7000 Persian captives. Then the Khan of the Transoxiana tribes of the Hiatilla, or White Huns, invaded Persia (A. D. 430) at the head of 25,000 men, and spread terror over the country. Baharam disappeared, and, concealing himself, secretly raised a small army, while the Persians crowded in to submit to the conquerors, believing resistance to be useless. The Huns, thrown off their guard, were surprised one dark night by Baharam, at the head of 7000 chosen warriors, and cut to pieces, and the country was thus freed from them. The use he made of this great victory was to establish peace with all his neighbors, and after this was concluded he returned to his capital. Baharam's ruling passion was a love of the chase, and particularly of the wild ass, or "gour", whence he was surnamed Baharam-gour. In pursuit of one of these animals he lost his life: having in the chase come suddenly upon a deep pool, in a valley between Shiraz and Isfahan, into which his horse plunged, and neither the animal or his rider was ever seen again. He had reigned 18 years. Yezdijird II., the worthy son of a worthy father, succeeded him (A. D. 438). In his reign Persia enjoyed prosperity and tranquillity, with the exception of a short dispute with the Romans, which was soon settled amicably. This prince was surnamed Sipahdost (or "friend of the soldier"), so popular was he with the army. He died A. D. 456, and was succeeded by his younger son, Hoormuz III.; but his eldest son, Firoze (the Peroses of the Greeks), enraged at being thus set aside, fled across the Oxus into Turan, and solicited Khoosh-Nuaz, king of the White Huns, to place him on the throne of Persia. That monarch sent an army of 30,000 men to the assistance of Firoze, whereupon the Persians deserted the weak Hoormuz, who was speedily dethroned and put to death (A. D. 458).

A drought of seven years' duration followed the accession of Firoze. It is said to have been so severe that there was not even the appearance of moisture left in the beds of the Oxus and the Jaxartes. During the dreadful famine which ensued, it was mainly owing to the care of Firoze that his subjects were saved from total destruction. But his other acts show him in the most disadvantageous light, notwithstanding the eulogiums of Persian historians. This prince showed the basest ingratitude towards Khoosh-Nuaz, who had so generously aided him. He invaded Tartary with the intention of dethroning his benefactor. There he was led into a snare, and his whole army perished. Firoze himself was taken prisoner, but was generously pardoned, and sent back by the victor. He did not, however, profit by this lesson, but invaded Turan a second time, when he was defeated and killed (A. D. 484).

His son Pallas, or Palasch (the Valens of Roman history), succeeded him. No event of any consequence occurred during his reign, which lasted four years. On the death of Pallas (A. D. 488), his brother Kobad became Shah, or king. It was in the tenth year of Kobad's reign (A. D. 497), that the religious impostor, Mazdak, began to propagate his creed. He is sometimes called Mozdek, and was a native of Istakhar (or Persepolis). He forbade the use of flesh, and, clothed in coarse woollen, gave in his own person an example of an abstemious life. He taught that, as all things belonged to God, it was impious in man to claim property in anything, even in his wife; therefore all things should be in common. He would probably have sunk into obscurity, had he not, by a pretended miracle, acquired complete ascendency over Kobad. This miracle consisted of conversing with the sacred flame in the temple of fire, and was managed by means of a confederate skilfully concealed. His doctrines were embraced by the Shah, but they soon became most pernicious in their effects, producing anarchy everywhere; for the votaries of Mazdak seized the wives, daughters, and property of others without hesitation, and the king could not punish them, he having adopted their creed. Under these circumstances the nobles combined against both Kobad and Mazdak. The latter was too powerful to be seized, but the former was dethroned, and put in prison; and his brother, Jamasp, was raised to the throne. Kobad, however, was released, through the address of one of his sisters, and escaped to Tartary. By the aid of the Tartar king he regained his throne, and Mazdak and his doctrines were allowed full sway, but they gradually fell into disrepute, and became obsolete.

During this century the great migration of the Huns, from the north of China into Europe, took place. Persia suffered little, as the barbarians went round by the north of the Caspian Sea.

What are the accounts of Yezdijird I.?—Repeat his memorable sayings.—What occurred on the accession of Baharam V.?—What was his character?—His exploits?—What of Acacius?—The White Huns?—What was Baharam's passion?—His end?—What is said of Yezdijird II.?—Hoormuz III.?—Firoze?—Khoosh-Nuaz?—The drought and famine?—The fate of Firoze?—What of Pallas?—Kobad?—Mazdak?—What miracle did he pretend to perform?—What were the effects of his doctrines?

CHINA. JAPAN.

This century is one of the darkest in the annals of China: the country was a scene of rapine and crime, scarcely any emperor having either the power or the wish to put a stop to anarchy. The infamous religion of Budha had greatly increased; the temples were very numerous, and the priests swarmed; but though some of the northern princes prohibited this superstition, their decrees were unavailing. Lew-yu, who had greatly distinguished himself against the northern Tartars, was declared protector of the empire. His first step was to cause Gan-te to be strangled (A. D. 419), and his brother, Kung-te, to be placed on the throne. But he soon forced Kung-te to abdicate, and having murdered him, and almost all the imperial family, he put an end to the Tsin dynasty (A. D. 420), and ascended the throne, under the name of Kaou-tsoo, being the first of the Northern Sung dynasty. Kaou-tsoo died soon after (A. D. 422). He was gifted with splendid talents, but was capable of any crime. His son, Shaou-te, who succeeded him, gave himself up to hunting. The nobles therefore dethroned him, and placed his brother, Wan-te, on the throne (A. D. 424). This prince erected colleges, and encouraged literature. He also improved the calendar, and patronized all useful arts, so that the country began to revive under him, but his career was cut short by domestic feuds, and he was assassinated by one of his sons (A. D. 454), who, in his turn, was murdered by his brother, who seated himself on the throne under the name of Woo-te. Having exterminated the partisans of his late brother, this prince gave himself up to debaucheries, which soon ended his life (A. D. 465).

His son and successor, Fe-te, was so cruel and abandoned that the Chinese historians are loath to assign him a place in the line of emperors. This ferocious monster murdered every one around him, but was himself murdered while consulting the Taou priests as to exorcising evil spirits (A. D. 466). His successor, Ming-te, seeing himself surrounded by rivals, killed fourteen of his nephews, and waged a war of extermination against all of the imperial blood. A revolt of the entire nation was stopped by his timely death (A. D. 472), but the people were no better off with his successor, Tsang-woo-wang, who associated with the dregs of the populace, and often amused himself by running through the streets with a drawn sword, killing every one who came in his way. One day, however, coming home drunk, some attendants cut off his head (A. D. 477), and proclaimed the brave general, Seaou-taou-ching, emperor. This man appointed Shun-te, the adopted son of Ming-te, to the throne — an arrangement which lasted but a short time. Shun-te was forced to abdicate in favor of Seaou-taou-ching (A. D. 479), who ascended the throne under the title of Kaou-te, and founded the Tse dynasty, which took its name from the State of Tse, belonging to the new emperor. Shun-te was shortly after put to death, and thus the Northern Sung dynasty ended.

The reign of Kaou-te was disturbed by the usual amount of rebellion. He died in the year 482, and his son, Seaou-tse, succeeded him, under the name of Ou-te: he decreed that the mandarins should hold office for three years only, and give an account of their stewardship. His passion for hunting induced him to leave the affairs of the empire to one of his sons, who died A. D. 493. The emperor grieved so for his loss that he died immediately after. His grandson, Seaou-tchao-ye, succeeded him, but soon manifested so vile a disposition that his relative, Seaou-loun, formed a conspiracy to dethrone him. The emperor was put to death, and the young prince, Seaou-tchaou-ouen, was decorated with the imperial title for a few days. He, in his turn, was murdered, and Seaou-loun placed himself on the throne by the title of Ming-te (A. D. 494). Continued cruelty and civil war stain the wearisome annals of China. To-pa-hong, the prince of Oueï, deprived Ming-te of a large portion of his domains, and the emperor died of rage (A. D. 498). His son and successor, Hoen-hoen, took the name of Pao-kuen: he was as licentious and cruel as his predecessors.

Japan.—The reigns of the Japanese princes during this century were remarkably short. They are: Ritsin (400–406), Fan-sey (406–414), Inkioo (414–454), Ankoo (454–457), Jurukia (457–480), Se-nei (480–485), Gen-soo (485–488), Ninken (488–499), Buretz (499–507). Jurukia was the first who coined the putzies (round copper coins, with a hole in the middle for stringing). He also enacted a law, valid to this day, that the children of such one of the Dairo's (emperor's) wives as should be declared empress, should be lawful heirs to the crown.

What is said of this century?—What befell the Tsin dynasty?—What of the Northern Sung dynasty?—Wan-te?—Fe-te?—Mention some of the acts of the emperors.—What of the Tse dynasty?—Mention some of the remaining incidents in Chinese history.—And in Japanese.—What coins and laws were made?

ITALY.

The close of the career of the once mighty Roman empire now draws near. We have seen that the Emperor Theodosius divided his dominions between his two sons, Honorius and Arcadius: the former receiving the western portion, which comprised Italy, France, Germany, Spain, Britain, and Africa; the latter receiving the eastern portion, comprising Greece, Asia Minor, Syria, and Egypt. Had either of these princes possessed ordinary capacity this division might have prolonged the life of the empire, by enabling them to devote their attention to a more limited sphere of action. Unfortunately they were both youths of feeble intellect, and easily swayed by favorites. The Roman people, too, had become thoroughly effeminate; the most shameful profligacy was everywhere indulged in; the soldiers became unequal to the fatigues of war, and laid aside their defensive armor, whereby they were exposed to easy defeat whenever brought into the field. The only reliable forces were the German and Gallic mercenaries. Theodosius had appointed Stilicho guardian of both empires during the minority of Honorius and Arcadius, and we have seen how ably he checked the progress of Alaric in Greece, and crushed the revolt of Gildo in Spain. His vigorous and impartial administration for a time saved the empire from becoming a complete wreck. At the opening of this century he was again called on to meet his old antagonist, Alaric, who had long cherished the scheme of invading Italy, and now carried it out. At the head of a powerful army he marched upon Milan. Honorius fled in dismay to the fortress of Asta, in Piedmont, where he was besieged by the Gothic king. Meanwhile Stilicho collected an army, suddenly fell upon Alaric at Pollentia, and dispersed his troops. He then offered to the Goth a pension, and permission to retreat from Italy: Alaric accepted this offer, peace was concluded, and Italy was saved. Honorius celebrated the victory at Pollentia by a triumphal procession at Rome, and by the celebration of public games on a magnificent scale. This was the last occasion on which the inhuman combats of gladiators were allowed to pollute the amphitheatre. The Emperor Theodosius had previously issued an edict forbidding them; but it was reserved for a Christian poet, Prudentius, and for a monk, Telemachus, to be the means of putting a final stop to them. Honorius listened to their remonstrances, and issued an edict abolishing gladiatorial exhibitions forever. The incensed Romans stoned Telemachus to death, but submitted to the edict.

The recent danger to which Honorius had been exposed led him to fix his residence at Ravenna. That city owed its origin to a colony of Thessalians who settled there in the 7th century B. C., and afterwards (B. C. 520) resigned it to the Umbrians. The Emperor Augustus had established a naval arsenal there, for the nature of the surrounding country made it almost impregnable; but in the time of Honorius the sea had receded, and the port of Augustus had become converted into orchards. This situation was now strongly fortified, and, amid the walls and morasses of Ravenna, Honorius and his feeble successors sought safety from the political and social storms which from time to time devastated Italy (A. D. 404). Ravenna remained the capital until the 8th century.

In the year 405, Radagai′sus (or Rhad′agast), chief of the Obot′rites (a tribe of Germans inhabiting the territory now known as Mecklenberg), led a horde of barbarians into Italy. 200,000 warriors followed his standard, accompanied by a like number of women, children, and slaves. This vast host was composed of Vandals, Suevi, Alans, and Burgundians, collected on the shores of the Baltic. Leaving their homes, they poured down on Southern Europe, and one-third of this immense number entered Italy. Stilicho with difficulty collected an army of 40,000 men, whom he assembled at Pavia; but he was unable to stop the progress of Radagaisus, who pillaged and destroyed many cities. Florentia (Florence) was the first that offered serious resistance. This celebrated city owed its origin to the triumvirs, in the 1st century B. C., who planted there a colony which soon became *florens* ("flourishing"), and had become an important trading republic in the days of Honorius. Its Senate and citizens defended it to the last extremity, but Stilicho contrived to relieve them. With consummate skill he hemmed in the barbarians with long lines of fortifications, and, cutting off their supplies, he starved them into surrender. Radagaisus was beheaded, and his followers were sold into slavery (A. D. 406). Thus a second time had Stilicho earned the title of "Deliverer of Italy". He made an alliance with the Franks and the Alemanni, and purchased the silence of Alaric by a treaty, in

What were the characteristics of Honorius and Arcadius?—Of the Romans of that time?—What were the exploits of Stilicho against Alaric?—What of the gladiators?—Where did Honorius fix his Court?—What is said of Ravenna?—The invasion by Radagaisus?—Florence?—Stilicho's exploit and title?

which that chief was formally declared master-general of the Roman armies throughout the prefecture of Illyricum. But it soon became evident that the Gothic king had designs on the empire, though professing allegiance to Honorius. Stilicho assembled the Roman Senate in the palace of the Cæsars, and submitted to it the condition of affairs. That body, thus suddenly called back to life, condemned the purchase of a truce with a barbarian king; and one of them, Lampa′dius, declared that "it was not a treaty of peace, but of servitude." At the same time, Olympius, a crafty attendant of Honorius, poisoned the mind of the emperor against Stilicho, and a conspiracy was formed against him. His friends at Pavia were massacred: he fled to Ravenna, and took sanctuary in the Christian church there, but was dragged from thence by Heraclian, a servant of Honorius, and put to death. His son, Eucher′ides, was also slain; and the emperor divorced Maria and Therman′tia, the two daughters of Stilicho, both of whom he had married. Such was the gratitude shown to the deliverer of Italy.

Alaric now threw off the mask, and having no Stilicho to oppose him, entered Italy with a large army. He marched direct to Rome, plundering and exacting ransom from the cities on his route. The Romans closed their gates, and defended themselves for a time, showing their barbarity by causing the pious and amiable Sere′na (the widow of Stilicho, and daughter of Theodosius) to be strangled. Famine at length compelled them to surrender, and Alaric granted them their lives on condition of their paying 5000 pounds of gold, 30,000 pounds of silver, 4000 robes of silk, 3000 pieces of scarlet cloth, and 3000 pounds of Indian pepper. This last-named article was expensive, but much used by the Romans in their cookery, and at that time was sold at about $2 a pound. The Romans complied with the demands of the conqueror, who compelled his troops to refrain from pillage and insult, and to respect the sanctity of the Christian churches (A. D. 409). Having been reinforced by a body of Goths and Huns, under Adolphus (or Ataulph), the brother of his wife, Alaric marched into Tuscany. He then declared himself the friend of peace and of the Romans, and persuaded the Senate to send three of their number to Honorius as ambassadors, stipulating for himself the provinces of Dalmatia, Noricum, and Venetia, with the rank of master-general of the armies of the West. But Honorius, by the advice of Olympius, rejected these terms. Popular indignation thereupon became irresistible. The attendants of the emperor transferred the government of Honorius and the empire to Jovius, the Prætorian prefect. Olympius was flogged to death at a subsequent period. The Court of Honorius was a scene of corruption and anarchy. Instigated by Jovius, the guards mutinied, and demanded the heads of two of their generals; the great chamberlain was beaten to death with sticks in the presence of the emperor; and Jovius obtained the free disposal of the public money. But the demands of Alaric were insultingly refused, and that prince now resolved to take summary proceedings. He marched to Rome, took possession of the port of Ostia, and summoned the Romans to surrender at discretion, which they did. He then declared Honorius deposed, and he bestowed the purple on At′talus, prefect of the city (A. D. 409). The greater part of Italy submitted to the new emperor, and troops were sent into Africa to secure the obedience of that province. Alaric marched to Ravenna to negotiate with Honorius, but the latter obstinately refused to communicate with him. The expedition to Africa proved unsuccessful: the troops of Attalus were defeated; the supply of corn and oil was cut off from Rome; and both Alaric and the people complained. Attalus acted in defiance of both—wherefore he was publicly deprived of his crown, in the presence of an immense multitude at Rimi′ni (A. D. 410). Alaric now made another attempt to negotiate with Honorius at Ravenna, but his advances were repelled, and a body of his troops cut to pieces by his old enemy, Sarus, whom the emperor had taken into his pay. The exasperated Goth thereupon marched to Rome, and delivered that city up to pillage by his barbarous troops. 40,000 slaves were liberated, and permitted to gratify their vengeance without remorse. It is not known how many thousands of Romans perished in this fearful scene, which lasted six days. It has been computed that Rome, at this period, contained about 48,000 houses and 1,200,000 inhabitants.

After the sack of Rome, Alaric marched to Capua and Nola, and meditated crossing into Sicily, when death put an end to his projects. He died at Consen′tia (now Cosenza), A. D. 412. A splendid sepulchre, adorned with trophies, was constructed in the bed of the small river Busenti′nus, the waters having been diverted from their course. The remains of Alaric were then deposited in it, and the river was restored to its natural channel; and in order that the grave might never be discovered, the prisoners who had dug it were put to death. Adolphus was elected the successor of Alaric. He at once declared his intention of befriending Italy, made terms with Honorius, and accepted the chief command of the Roman army. He married the emperor's sister, PLACID′IA, so famed for her beauty. Peace was restored to Italy; beneficent laws were passed; and so great was the change in the administration of affairs, that, in less than seven years, the traces of the great Gothic invasion were almost obliterated. Adolphus became in reality emperor, though not assuming the title. He marched into Gaul against some revolted tribes, and thence into Spain, where he was assassinated (A. D. 414). Placidia was detained a prisoner.

The peace of the empire had in the meantime been disturbed by sundry revolts. Herac′lian, count of Africa, landed with an army near Rome, but having been boldly encountered, fled ignominiously. Con′stantine, governor of Britain, proclaimed himself emperor of that province, and of Gaul and Spain (A. D. 409). He extorted from Honorius a recognition of his title, promising to deliver Italy from the Goths. But Geron′tius, the usurper's lieutenant in Spain, set up Max′imus, and, suddenly marching into Gaul, attacked the unprepared Constantine and his son, Constans. The latter was taken, and put to death. Constantine was besieged in Arles, but was unexpectedly relieved by an army sent by Honorius, under the command of Constantius, a general of great ability. Gerontius fled to the confines of Spain, where he killed himself. Constantine was induced to open the gates of Arles, when he and his son were made prisoners, sent to Ravenna, and executed (A. D. 411). The revolt of Jovi′nus and Sebastian, in Germany, was suppressed by Adolphus at the request of Placidia, and their heads were sent to Honorius (A. D. 413). But their followers, the Goths, the Franks, and the Burgundians, permanently settled in Gaul.

The death of Adolphus was avenged by his successor, Wallia, and by a Roman army under Constantius. Placidia was honorably restored to her brother; the Spaniards, after three obstinate campaigns, were reduced to nominal obedience to Honorius (A. D. 419); and Constantius was subsequently rewarded with the hand of Placidia, and made emperor. But he died in the seventh month of his reign, and was followed to the grave soon after by Honorius (A. D. 423). That miserable tyrant had grossly insulted his sister, Placidia, who had consequently fled to Constantinople; but on hearing of his death, she hastened back to Italy to secure the empire for her son, Valentinian III., then only six years old. During her absence, John, the *primice′rius* (or private secretary) of Honorius, usurped the throne. But Theodosius II., who had succeeded Arcadius in the Eastern Empire, sent an army under Ardabu′rius and Aspar to maintain the claims of the young prince. Ravenna was entered by stratagem, and John was taken, and put to death. Placidia was appointed regent of the empire. She reigned 25 years in the name of her son, and is supposed to have purposely enervated his character by a dissolute education. The person who principally shared her confidence at first was the celebrated Æti′us, the son of Gauden′tius, an illustrious citizen of Scythia, and master-general of the cavalry. He became her minister, having previously acquired a brilliant reputation by his military exploits. He and Boniface, count of Africa, another equally distinguished officer, have been styled "the last of the Romans". The two became rivals for the imperial favor, but Ætius being present at Ravenna, had great advantage over Boniface. The former was, however, called away to take up arms against Theod′oric, king of the Visigoths, who was besieging Arles. Successful in his expedition, he returned to Ravenna to thwart the intrigues of Boniface, who had been recalled from Africa by Placidia. The artful Ætius persuaded Boniface to resist the imperial orders, and to call in the aid of the Vandals from Spain (A. D. 429). The African general followed this advice, but found too late that he had ruined himself by so doing. The Vandal king, Gen′seric, whom Boniface had invited into the Roman provinces in Africa, kept possession of them. All efforts to expel him were fruitless, and at last Boniface returned to Ravenna. On hearing this, Ætius, who was occupied in repelling an invasion of the Franks in Gaul, hastened with his army into Italy. Boniface, with the imperial troops,

What treaty was made with Alaric?—What of the Senate?—The fall of Stilicho?—And of his friends?—What of Olympius?—The invasion by Alaric?—The siege of Rome?—The negotiations with Honorius?—Of his Court?—Of the second siege of Rome?—The size and population of the city?

What of the death and burial of Alaric?—Who succeeded him?—Whom did he marry?—What of his administration?—His death?—What commotions troubled the empire?—What became of Placidia?—Constantius?—What of Honorius?—John, the *primicerius*?—Theodosius II.?—Valentinian III.?—Placidia's regency?—Ætius?—Boniface?—Genseric?

encountered and defeated him, but received a wound of which he died. Ætius fled to the Huns, and by their aid regained his power (A. D. 432).

The greater part of Africa was ceded by treaty to Genseric (A. D. 435). The provinces of Gaul and Spain were perpetually harassed by the barbarians. Spain was lost to the empire, but the great military talents of Ætius for a time preserved Gaul. He gained a series of victories over the Burgundians and Visigoths, but for many years his utmost vigilance was required to resist their encroachments. He was forced to withdraw the Roman troops from Britain, which province was finally abandoned by the Romans (A. D. 442). At length the illustrious Roman was called upon to roll back the fearful tide of barbarism from the far West. AT′TILA (or Etzel), king of the Huns, who was at the head of 500,000 barbarians, and styled himself "the Scourge of God", moved to the West to plunder Germany and Gaul. Ætius, having formed alliance with Theodoric, king of the Visigoths, and Merovæ′us, king of the Franks, assembled their united forces, and encountered Attila on the plains of Châlons-sur-Marne. One of the most terrible battles recorded in history ensued, and Attila was defeated with immense slaughter (A. D. 451). He then withdrew into Pannonia. This great victory, which saved France and Spain from devastation, was purchased with the life of the brave Theodoric. Next year Attila recruited his army and entered Italy. He laid siege to Aquileia, which held out for three months. He then marched to Rome, but was dissuaded from attacking the city by Leo the Great, bishop of Rome, who boldly visited the fierce king in his camp, and remonstrated with him. Attila recrossed the Alps towards the end of the year 452, and died soon afterwards.

The power and influence of Ætius excited the jealousy of Valentinian III., who caused him to be murdered (A. D. 454). In the following year the emperor himself was killed by Petro′nius Max′imus, whose wife he had outraged. Petronius assumed the imperial purple, but three months after was stoned to death by his subjects. At the same time Rome was plundered by Genseric, who carried off many thousands of its inhabitants. By the assistance of Theodoric II., king of the Visigoths, Avi′tus was made emperor. After a year's reign he was deposed by RI′CIMER, commander of the barbarian auxiliaries in Italy, who placed Majo′rian on the throne (A. D. 456). Majorian made vigorous efforts to remedy the disorders of the empire, but it was a hopeless task. He made vast preparations for attacking the Vandals in Africa, but the immense fleet he had collected for the purpose was destroyed by them in the harbor of New Carthage, in Spain (A. D. 460). He thereupon concluded peace with Genseric; but his popularity excited the jealousy of Ricimer, who forced him to resign. Majorian then committed suicide (A. D. 461). Ricimer was *de facto* emperor, but it pleased him to place Seve′rus on the throne. After a reign of four years Severus died a natural death (A. D. 465), and a nominal interregnum ensued. The increasing power of the Vandals induced Ricimer to consult the Eastern emperor, Leo; and, with his concurrence, Anthe′mius was named emperor (A. D. 467). After a time, disagreements sprang up between Anthemius and Ricimer. The latter laid siege to Rome, and Anthemius was killed on the capture of the city (A. D. 472). Ricimer, still refraining from assuming the title of emperor, conferred it on Olyb′rius, who died three months afterwards. Ricimer died about the same time. Glyce′rius then became emperor, through the assistance of Gundebald, the Burgundian. But the Eastern emperor refused to acknowledge him, and proclaimed Julius Nepos emperor. Glycerius was dethroned by his rival (A. D. 474), and forced to become a priest. From an obscure soldier he was raised to the dignity of bishop of Salona! Julius Nepos did not long enjoy the imperial sceptre. Orestes, commander of the mercenaries, deposed him, and proclaimed himself regent for his own son, Romulus (called, in derision, Augus′tulus, or "little Augustus"). Nepos fled into Dalmatia, where he was assassinated some years afterwards by his former rival, the bishop of Salona. But the end of the Roman empire had now arrived. It had been founded by a Romulus, and was destined to end with a Romulus, after a duration of 1229 years. ODOA′CER, at the head of a promiscuous horde of barbarians called He′ruli, entered Italy. Orestes encountered him at Placentia, but was defeated and killed. Romulus was deposed, but allowed to live in retirement; and Odoacer, assuming the title of king of Italy, declared THE ROMAN EMPIRE AT AN END (A. D. 476).

What was the fate of Boniface?—What of the abandonment of Britain?—Attila?—The battle of Châlons?—Leo the Great?—The fate of Ætius?—Of Valentinian III.?—Petronius?—Genseric?—Avitus?—Ricimer?—Majorian?—Severus?—Anthemius?—Olybrius?—Glycerius?—Julius Nepos?—Orestes?—Romulus Augustulus?—Odoacer?

We have thus traced the rise and fall of the most remarkable empire the world has yet seen. Founded in violence, its whole career was distinguished by unprincipled aggression and remorseless lust of conquest. Its annals are derived chiefly from its own historians; but had we the accounts which its victims could give, a different story would doubtless be told. A system of domination, based solely upon force, fitly gave way to force. The Romans, after having subdued all that portion of the world extending from the Atlantic shores of Europe to the Euphrates, including England, France, Spain, Portugal, Morocco, the North of Africa, Egypt, Italy, Greece (as far north as the Danube), Asia Minor, and Syria, gorged themselves with the spoils of those countries, and gradually sank into effeminacy and debauchery. The state of society in Italy under the emperors, as depicted by the satirists, Juvenal, Martial, and Petronius, was frightful. The wonder is that the fabric raised to such a height by Julius and Augustus Cæsar, and brought so low by the vices of Commodus, should have been so long in falling. For more than five centuries after the death of Julius Cæsar did the name of Rome carry *prestige* with it, and to the last there were men anxious to secure the dangerous and empty title of emperor. Yet with all its violence, faults, and vices, the Roman republic had a great mission. This was to bring the myriads of small and discordant States, into which the world was divided, under one vigorous sceptre; to civilize them by a central and enlightened system of jurisprudence; to expand commerce by grand public roads and buildings; and to lay the foundation of future empires by implanting its beautiful language and literature among the conquered countries of Europe. From this source are derived the modern Italian, French, Spanish, and Portuguese languages, and a large portion of the English language is borrowed from it. The Roman literature is inferior to the Greek, for the Roman mind was deficient in imagination. From Greece was drawn the inspiration of the great writers of Rome. Her philosophy, arts, and science, came from the same classic soil, and Athens was her chief university. In a word it may be said that, except in the departments of jurisprudence and military science, Rome was inferior to Greece. But from these two empires of antiquity we derive much of our modern civilization.

Odoacer ruled Italy for many years with prudence and humanity. He maintained the laws of Rome, and the country began to recover from the anarchy which had so long prevailed. He also added Dalmatia and Nor′icum to his dominions. But in the year 488, the Eastern emperor, Zeno, threatened by Theod′oric the Ostrogoth, diverted the attention of that chieftain from Greece to Italy. Theodoric was induced to abandon his projects on Constantinople, and march westward. At the head of an immense force he entered Italy. Odoacer bravely met him, but was defeated in two severe battles — one at Aquileia, the other at Verona. Milan surrendered to Theodoric (A. D. 489). Next year Odoacer sustained a final defeat on the Adda. He then retired to Ravenna, where he fortified himself. Theodoric besieged him for three years in that city. At length, moved by the sufferings of his soldiers and the liberal offers of Theodoric, Odoacer surrendered (A. D. 493). But a few days afterwards he was treacherously stabbed at a banquet, and all the foreign mercenaries were massacred, by order of Theodoric. Master of Italy, though nominally a subject of the Byzantine emperor, Theodoric founded THE ITALIAN KINGDOM OF THE OSTROGOTHS. Great prosperity attended his administration, and his fame for wisdom and munificence spread far and wide. The barbarism of the age overlooked his treacherous murder of Odoacer. He married Audefle′da, sister of Clovis, king of the Franks, and he strengthened himself by other alliances. He visited Rome, and stopped the demolition of the works of art there, causing many of them to be restored, and appointing an officer to take care of them.

The inhabitants of Venetia, who had fled from Alaric and his Visigoths to the numerous islands in the north of the Adriatic, there founded the little town of Rialto (A. D. 421). Thirty years later the towns of Grado, Palestrina, Caorlo, and Malamocco were founded by them. These little towns were the beginning of the famous REPUBLIC OF VENICE.

Literature and art were almost extinct. The Christian Church contained what light was left. JERO′ME, AU′GUSTINE, CYRIL, HIL′ARY, PATRI′CIUS (Patrick), PELA′GIUS, and EU′TYCHES were the most prominent teachers and writers of the age. CLAU′DIAN, the friend of Stilicho, was the best poet of this degenerate epoch.

What are the characteristics of the Roman empire?—What was its mission?—What of its literature?—Its excellencies?—Wherein was Rome inferior to Greece?—What of the rule of Odoacer?—His fate?—What kingdom did Theodoric establish?—What is said of him?—Of Venice?—What eminent men flourished?

THE EASTERN EMPIRE.

After the death of Gainas, the Emperor Arcadius resigned himself to the sway of his wife, the beautiful Eudoxia. The first years of this century are marked by the tumults occasioned by the persecution of the celebrated Chrysostom, archbishop of Constantinople. The fearless preaching of that prelate against the corrupt practices which prevailed in the Church raised up against him a host of enemies, especially among the ladies of the Court, but his immense popularity rendered it dangerous to attack him openly. The empress, inviting the aid of the hostile bishops, especially of Theoph′ilus, archbishop of Alexandria, formed a plan for his destruction. A body of Egyptian marines was sent to Constantinople to encounter the populace, while a synod of bishops was convened in a suburb of Chalcedon, surnamed "the Oak", in order to condemn him. Chrysostom, having refused to attend this synod, was arrested; but the people fell upon the monks and the Egyptians, and slaughtered them without mercy in the streets of Constantinople. The terrified Eudoxia implored the emperor to recall the archbishop, and Chrysostom was accordingly reinstated in triumph (A. D. 403). But this triumph was of short duration. A council of the Eastern prelates was called, and his deposition was decreed. A body of troops was introduced into Constantinople: Chrysostom was arrested, but not without strong opposition from the people, who set fire to the cathedral, the Senate-house, and other buildings, and was banished to Caucasus, a small town in Lesser Armenia. There he lived three years, and was then removed to the desert of Pityus, where he expired (A. D. 408). Soon after this event Eudoxia died, leaving an infant son, Theodosius. The emperor also died (A. D. 408), having previously requested Yezdijird, king of Persia, to act as guardian of the young prince — a trust which he honorably fulfilled.

The actual administration of affairs was assumed by the prefect, Anthemius, who, by his superior abilities, obtained the ascendant over the minds of the people. One of his first measures was to expel Ul′din, king of the Huns, from Thrace. Half of these barbarians were exterminated; the remainder were taken prisoners, and sold into slavery. New fortifications were erected around Constantinople, and a strong fleet was stationed in the Danube. But the rule of Anthemius was terminated by the assumption of the government by Pulche′ria, the youthful sister of the Emperor Theodosius II. She was two years older than her brother, and was then but sixteen (A. D. 412). This extraordinary woman governed the empire nearly forty years. She and her two sisters, Arcadia and Marina, dedicated themselves to perpetual celibacy, though Pulcheria subsequently nominally married Marcian, the senator. Her palace was converted into a monastery, from which all males, except the clergy, were excluded. She and her ladies formed a religious community, renounced the vanities of dress, and lived on spare diet, fasting and praying incessantly. She built numerous churches, founded extensive charities, and zealously combated the heresies of Nestorius and Eutyches; yet she did not neglect the government of the empire, which enjoyed peace and prosperity under her administration. The emperor was a weak-minded youth, who passed his time in frivolous amusements, and acquired the epithet of *Callig′raphes* (or, fair writer), from the elegance with which he transcribed religious books. At the instigation of Pulcheria he married Athenaïs, the daughter of Leontius, the Athenian philosopher. This lady on her marriage renounced paganism, and was baptized, receiving the Christian name of Eudoxia. She composed several literary works, among them a poetical paraphrase of the first eight books of the Old Testament, and of the prophecies of Daniel and Zachariah; verses on the life and character of Christ; the legend of St. Cyprian; and a panegyric on the Persian victories of Theodosius, alleged to have been gained in a war occasioned by the fierce persecution of the Christians by Baharam, the successor of Yezdijird. But in truth no decisive successes of any kind were achieved on either side, and the contest was terminated by a truce for a hundred years (A. D. 422).

The Empress Eudoxia visited Palestine, where her munificence exceeded that of Helena, the mother of Constantine the Great. On her return she aspired to the government of the empire, but the influence of Pulcheria was too powerful. The principal adherents of Eudoxia were executed or disgraced, and she herself was exiled to Jerusalem, where she died sixteen years afterwards. The affairs of the Western Empire next occupied the attention of the Court. At the request of Placidia, the sister of Honorius, a powerful armament, under the command of Aspar, was sent to Italy, and thence to Africa, against the Vandals (A. D. 431); but the latter proved victorious, and the Roman legions returned discomfited. A new danger threatened the Eastern Empire: this was the advance of Rugilas, king of the Huns, who menaced the provinces, and even Constantinople, with an attack (A. D. 433). The meek-spirited Theodosius was glad to avert the danger by stipulating an annual payment of 350 pounds of gold. But the impatience of the barbarians, and the intrigues of the Court, created disputes which might have led to disastrous results, had not the emperor listened to the voice of the Senate, and sent ambassadors to negotiate with the king of the Huns. Rugilas had died, but his nephews and successors, At′tila and Ble′da, consented to receive the envoys, which they did on horseback, in a plain near the city of Margus, in Upper Mœsia. They dictated the terms of peace, viz., an increase of the tribute to 700 pounds of gold; a fine of eight pieces for every Roman captive who had escaped; the renouncement of all treaties with the enemies of the Huns; and the surrender of all fugitives from justice. At this time Attila was ruler of all the country between the Rhine and the Volga, and it was said that he could bring an army of 700,000 men into the field. He was, therefore, the terror of the Eastern as well as the Western Empire, and it was not long before he found a pretext for making war upon the former. By the treaty of Margus a free market had been established on the northern bank of the Danube, near the Roman fort, Constantia. A troop of barbarians violated the commercial security, killed or dispersed the unsuspecting traders, and levelled the fortress with the ground. The Huns justified the deed as an act of reprisal for an alleged attempt of the bishop of Margus to steal the treasure of their kings, and demanded the surrender of that prelate. Theodosius refused to comply with this demand. The Huns at once swept through Illyria, destroying the cities of Sir′mium, Singid′unum, Ratia′ria, Marcianop′olis, Naïs′sus, and Sar′dica: they spread across the whole breadth of the country between the Euxine and the Adriatic, and desolated it with fire and sword (A. D. 441). Theodosius recalled the army of Aspar from Italy, and the garrisons from the Persian frontiers, and sent them to meet Attila. But they were defeated in three several engagements, and the emperor was left to such protection as the walls of Constantinople could afford. Theodosius then solicited the clemency of Attila, who dictated humiliating terms of peace. The conditions were: 1. The cession of a strip of territory between Belgrade and Novæ, in Thrace. 2. The augmentation of the tribute from 700 pounds of gold to 2100 pounds, and the immediate payment of 6000 pounds of gold to defray the expenses of the war. 3. The release, without ransom, of all the Huns taken prisoners, and the payment of 12 pieces of gold for the redemption of all Roman captives. Theodosius consented to these terms (A. D. 446), but in order to raise the necessary funds he was forced to levy heavy contributions on his nobles for the payment of Attila's demands. That terrible Hun continually imposed fresh demands upon the feeble Theodosius, and several embassies took place between the two monarchs. In one of these the unworthy favorite, Chrysa′phius, who had acquired complete ascendency over the weak emperor, endeavored to bribe one of the Hunnish envoys to assassinate Attila; but the faithful Ed′econ revealed the plot, and the result was a demand for more money, and for the head of Chrysaphius. With difficulty the emperor raised the first, and obtained a remission of the second. A few days afterwards he was thrown from his horse while hunting, and so much injured that he died (A. D. 450). His sister, Pulcheria, at once ascended the throne, and her first act was to cause the execution of Chrysaphius without trial, and the confiscation of his ill-gotten wealth. She then married Mar′cian, a senator sixty years of age, who was accordingly invested with the imperial purple. He was a man of ability, mild disposition, and useful talents. He reigned three years as the husband of Pulcheria, and after her death (A. D. 452) he remained to the close of his life the undisputed sovereign of the East. He promulgated some severe edicts against heretics, for which he received great encomiums from the Catholic writers. Yet he quietly endeavored to repress the ambition of the priesthood. Under his auspices the Council of Chalcedon reversed the acts of the "robber Synod" of Ephesus; deposed Dios′corus, the violent primate of Egypt; and restored Theod′oret and the other bishops who had been expelled.

What was the conduct of Arcadius?—What befell Chrysostom?—When did Eudoxia and Arcadius die?—What was the last act of Arcadius?—Who succeeded him?—What of Anthemius?—Pulcheria?—What was her character?—That of Eudoxia?—And of Theodosius?—What of the war with Persia?—The fate of Eudoxia?

What of the expedition of Aspar?—Of the Huns?—How did Theodosius act?—What of Attila and Bleda?—The treaty of Margus?—Its violation?—The results?—What did Theodosius then do?—What were the terms granted by Attila?—What of the plot of Chrysaphius?—The death of Theodosius?—What of Pulcheria?—Marcian?—His principal acts?

THE EASTERN EMPIRE.

The death of Marcian (A. D. 457) would have exposed the empire to the danger of a popular election, if the influence of Aspar, the patrician, had not been sufficient to incline the balance in the favor of any candidate who might have been named. Being unable to assume the crown himself, in consequence of being a heretic (Gibbon's *Decline and Fall of the Roman Empire*, ch. xxxvi.), he nominated Leo the Thracian, a military tribune, and the principal steward of his household, for emperor, who was accordingly elected.

Leo I. (also styled "the Great") was a man of singular firmness and prudence. Aspar had hoped that he would have proved a mere instrument to carry out his own designs, but Leo soon undeceived him, and having secretly introduced a body of Isaurian troops into Constantinople, he disarmed and expelled Aspar and his adherents. Having freed himself from this obstacle, he turned his attention to the Western Empire, which was then in the throes of dissolution. The Italians had implored his aid against the Vandals, and Leo now declared Anthe′mius, the son of the patrician general, Proco′pius, his colleague and emperor of the West (A. D. 467). Anthemius had married Euphemia, the daughter of the Emperor Marcian, and had distinguished himself by gaining a victory over the Huns on the Danube. Accompanied by a splendid retinue and a strong guard, he left Constantinople and marched to Rome, entering that city in triumph, and being welcomed there by all parties. Great rejoicings took place; his daughter married Ricimer, the Gothic prince, and the nuptials were ostentatiously celebrated — the poet and orator, Sido′nius, pronouncing a panegyric thereon, for which he was rewarded with the prefecture of Rome. Leo professed great affection for Anthemius, and resolved to deliver Italy and the Mediterranean from the Vandals. The troops of Egypt, Thebais, and Libya were assembled, and embarked under the command of Herac′lius, prefect of Constantinople. Heraclius landed on the coast of Tripoli, and surprised and subdued that province. At the same time another grand expedition, consisting of an army of 100,000 men and a fleet of 1113 ships, sailed from Constantinople for Carthage, under the command of Basilis′cus, the brother of the Empress Veri′na, wife of Leo. This force joined that of Herac′lian and the troops from Italy under Marcelli′nus, who had (A. D. 464) expelled the Vandals from Sicily; and the combined armies landed at Cape Bona, 40 miles from Carthage. The Vandals who opposed them were successively vanquished, and if Basiliscus had boldly advanced on Carthage, that city must have surrendered, and the kingdom founded by Genseric would have been extinguished. Genseric, however, saw his danger, and offered to submit himself and his dominions to the will of the Emperor Leo, and obtained a truce of five days. During this interval he manned his largest ships of war with his bravest Moors and Vandals, and sent them against the Roman fleet. Towing after them large barks filled with combustible materials, they attacked their enemy in the night, and burnt or sank half their fleet. Basiliscus fled disgracefully at the beginning of the engagement, and returned to Constantinople with the remains of his army (A. D. 468), and took sanctuary in the cathedral of St. Sophia, where he remained until his sister obtained his pardon from the incensed emperor. Heraclius effected his retreat through the desert to Libya, and Marcellinus returned to Sicily, where he was assassinated. Thus ended this great enterprise, which cost the empire about $26,000,000. After its failure Genseric again became the tyrant of the sea: the coasts of Italy, Greece, and Asia were exposed to his depredations, and Tripoli was reannexed to his dominions.

After the death of Anthemius (A. D. 472), Olybrius, the senator, was elected emperor of the West, with the secret connivance of Leo. But meanwhile the election of a new colleague in the empire was seriously agitated in the council of the Eastern emperor. The Empress Verina was anxious for the selection of Julius Nepos, prince of Dalmatia, who had married one of her nieces; but while the matter was under discussion, Glycerius, an obscure soldier, was invested with the purple by his patron, Gun′dibald, the Burgundian king. But the latter not sustaining him, Julius Nepos easily displaced him, and was acknowledged emperor of the West by the Senate, the Italians, and the provincials of Gaul. His triumph was but brief, for next year (A. D. 475) the barbarians under Orestes advanced to Rome. Nepos fled to Dalmatia, where he was assassinated five years afterwards by Glycerius. Orestes then placed his son, Romulus, on the throne of the West, but the barbarians under his command mutinied for increased pay and privileges, and, under the leadership of Odoacer, finally extinguished him, and along with him, the Western Empire (A. D. 476). In the East, the empire, on the death of Leo the Thracian (A. D. 474), devolved on his grandson, Leo II., whom he had associated with him. This prince survived but a few months. The patrician Zeno then procured his own elevation to the throne, but he was destined not to occupy it without a struggle, for Verina, the widow of Leo I., persuaded her brother, Basiliscus, to take up arms, and assert his claim. Zeno fled into Isauria, whither he was pursued by an army sent from Constantinople. Three years he remained in exile, but at the expiration of that time he contrived to gain the good will of the troops, and being likewise encouraged by Theodoric, king of the Ostrogoths, he marched back in triumph to Constantinople (A. D. 477). He was at once reinstated on the throne, and Basiliscus was banished to Cappadocia, where he died. Verina fled to Syria, and thence to Egypt, where she raised a revolt which she maintained to the close of her life. All her relatives and friends were subjected to the most cruel tortures, and their property was confiscated.

Meanwhile Theodoric, who had contributed so much to the restoration of Zeno, and had been profusely rewarded by him, suddenly spread the flames of war to the very gates of Constantinople, devastating Thrace with merciless severity. Zeno was unable to resist these ravages, but at length succeeded in persuading him to try his fortune in Italy, agreeing that if successful there he should rule as the emperor's lieutenant. Theodoric accordingly led his swarms of barbarians into that unfortunate country, and effected its subjugation after a severe contest with Odoacer. Zeno died in the year 491, and his widow, Ariadne, giving her hand to Anasta′sius, an aged domestic of the palace, raised the latter to the throne amidst the exclamations of the people. This prince issued an edict granting liberty of conscience in religious matters, and he remitted many oppressive taxes; but his reign was disturbed by the rebellion of his brother-in-law, Longi′nus, in Isauria. This convulsion lasted six years, and was terminated by the capture and death of the rebel. The most remarkable portion of the history of the reign of Anastasius is that relating to the circus factions of Constantinople. The descriptions transmitted to us of the scenes of tumult and violence which disgraced the capital in consequence of the rivalry of these disorderly parties, almost exceed belief. They represented in a striking light the fearful degeneracy of the Eastern Empire, which was in fact but the decrepit remains of the once mighty empire of Rome, and lingered on in a life of feebleness and decay for nearly a thousand years. We cannot do better than conclude this portion of its history with an extract from Gibbon's great work, *The Decline and Fall of the Roman Empire* (to which we have already been so much indebted), descriptive of these horrors of the Hippodrome:

"The games (of the circus) were exhibited at the expense of the republic, the magistrates, or the emperors, but the reins were abandoned to servile hands; and if the profits of a favorite charioteer sometimes exceeded those of an advocate, they must be considered as the effects of popular extravagance, and the high wages of a disgraceful profession. The race, in its first institution, was a simple contest of two chariots, whose drivers were distinguished by white and red liveries; two additional colors, a light green and a cerulean blue, were afterwards introduced; and as the races were repeated twenty-five times, one hundred chariots contributed in the same day to the pomp of the circus. The four factions soon acquired a legal establishment and a mysterious origin, and their fanciful colors were derived from the various appearances of nature in the four seasons of the year: the red dog star of summer, the snows of winter, the deep shades of autumn, and the cheerful verdure of spring. Another interpretation preferred the elements to the seasons, and the struggle of the green and the blue was supposed to represent the conflict of the earth and the sea. Their respective victories announced either a plentiful harvest or a prosperous navigation, and the hostility of the husbandmen and mariners was somewhat less absurd than the blind ardor of the Roman people who devoted their lives and fortunes to the color which they had espoused. Such folly was disdained and indulged by the wisest princes; but the names of Caligula, Nero, Vitellius, Verus, Commodus, Caracalla, and Elagabalus, were enrolled in the green or blue factions of the

How was the successor of Marcian elected?—What is said of Leo the Thracian?—Of Aspar?—Anthemius?—What great expedition did Leo fit out?—Relate the particulars of its exploits.—What did it cost?—What of Genseric?—Olybrius?—Julius Nepos?—Glycerius?—Orestes?—And Romulus?

Who succeeded Leo the Thracian?—What is said of Zeno?—Basiliscus?—The restoration of Zeno?—The fate of Basiliscus and Verina?—What of Theodoric?—How was he got rid of?—What of Ariadne and Anastasius?—Of Longinus?—What was the condition of the empire?—What of the circus factions?

circus; they frequented their stables, applauded their favorites, chastised their antagonists, and deserved the esteem of the populace by the natural or affected imitation of their manners. The bloody and tumultuous contest continued to disturb the public festivity till the last age of the spectacles of Rome; and Theodoric, from a motive of justice or affection, interposed his authority to protect the greens against the violence of a consul and a patrician, who were passionately addicted to the blue faction of the circus.

"Constantinople adopted the follies, though not the virtues, of ancient Rome; and the same factions which had agitated the circus raged with redoubled fury in the hippodrome. Under the reign of Anastasius this popular frenzy was inflamed by religious zeal; and the greens, who had treacherously concealed stones and daggers under baskets of fruit, massacred, at a solemn festival, three thousand of their blue adversaries. From the capital this pestilence was diffused into the provinces and cities of the East, and the sportive distinction of two colors produced two strong and irreconcilable factions, which shook the foundations of a feeble government. The popular dissensions, founded on the most serious interest or holy pretence, have scarcely equalled the obstinacy of this wanton discord, which invaded the peace of families, divided friends and brothers, and tempted the female sex, though seldom seen in the circus, to espouse the inclinations of their lovers, or to contradict the wishes of their husbands. Every law, either human or divine, was trampled under foot; and as long as the party was successful, its deluded followers appeared careless of private distress or public calamity. The license, without the freedom, of democracy, was revived at Antioch and Constantinople, and the support of a faction became necessary to every candidate for civil or ecclesiastical honors. A secret attachment to the family or sect of Anastasius was imputed to the greens; the blues were zealously devoted to the cause of orthodoxy and Justinian, and their grateful patron protected, above five years, the disorders of a faction whose seasonable tumults overawed the palace, the Senate, and the capitals of the East. Insolent with royal favor, the blues affected to strike terror by a peculiar and barbaric dress: the long hair of the Huns, their close sleeves and ample garments, a lofty step, and a sonorous voice. In the day they concealed their two-edged poniards, but in the night they boldly assembled in arms and in numerous bands, prepared for every act of violence and rapine. Their adversaries of the green faction, or even inoffensive citizens, were stripped, and often murdered by these nocturnal robbers, and it became dangerous to wear any gold buttons or girdles, or to appear at a late hour in the streets of a peaceful capital. A daring spirit, rising with impunity, proceeded to violate the safeguard of private houses; and fire was employed to facilitate the attack, or to conceal the crimes of these factious rioters. No place was safe or sacred from their depredations; to gratify either avarice or revenge they profusely spilt the blood of the innocent; churches and altars were polluted by atrocious murders; and it was the boast of the assassins that their dexterity could always inflict a mortal wound with a single stroke of their dagger. The dissolute youth of Constantinople adopted the blue livery of disorder; the laws were silent, and the bonds of society were relaxed; creditors were compelled to resign their obligations; judges to reverse their sentence; masters to enfranchise their slaves; and fathers to supply the extravagance of their children. The despair of the greens, who were persecuted by their enemies and deserted by the magistrates, assumed the privilege of defence, perhaps of retaliation; but those who survived the combat were dragged to execution, and the unhappy fugitives, escaping to woods and caverns, preyed without mercy on the society from whence they were expelled."—(ch. xl.)

In one of these riots the hippodrome was burnt, great damage was done to the city, and the statues of the Emperor Athanasius were thrown down and destroyed (A. D. 491).

Such was the deplorable condition of Greece and its new capital at the close of the fifth century of the Christian Era, and of the first century of its existence. We have not mentioned all the horrors that were perpetrated, for they cannot be described without offence to propriety. The succeeding centuries of the Eastern Empire present the same sad picture of licentiousness and utter want of principle on the part of both rulers and people.

How long did the tumult continue?—What of the hippodrome?—What increased the discord in the time of Athanasius?—Give an outline of the conduct of the factions?—To whom were "the greens" and "the blues" respectively attached?—What befell "the greens"?—What occurred in A. D. 491?

ENGLAND.—This was an eventful century for England. The Roman legions were withdrawn, and the natives established petty States under kings whose violence soon filled the island with confusion. The Picts and Scots renewed their incursions; the disunited Britons, unable to resist them, vainly implored aid from Ætius, the Roman general in Gaul. Vortigern, king of Kent, then invited the Saxons to aid him, and a body of them, under HENGIST and HORSA, landing at Ebbsfleet, in Kent (A. D. 446), were cantoned in the Isle of Thanet. For six years they served Vortigern faithfully. He married Rowena, the beautiful daughter of Hengist, whereby he forfeited the love of his people. About the same time, ST. GERMAIN, bishop of Auxerre, and Lupus, bishop of Troyes, arrived in England, and preached the gospel, combating especially the Pelagian heresy, which had infested the Christian Church in Britain. Hengist invited numbers more of his countrymen over. The Britons, perceiving their object, refused to supply them with provisions. Moreover, they deserted Vortigern, and set up his son, Vortimer, as king. This was the signal for war. A battle was fought at Aylesford, on the Medway (A. D. 455), in which Horsa and Catigern, another son of Vortigern, killed each other. The remarkable monument, called "Kit's Cotty house", still marks the grave of Catigern. Vortimer drove the Saxons to their ships, and they returned to Germany. The British hero having been poisoned by Rowena, Vortigern was reinstated in his kingdom, and Hengist was invited to return, which he did with a large number of followers. An assembly of the British chiefs was convened at the monastery of Ambrius (Ambresbury) to treat with the Saxons; but at a given signal the latter fell upon the former, slew 460 of them, and took Vortigern prisoner. Another disastrous battle was fought near the Cray, and Kent was abandoned to the invaders. The last struggle was at Wyppedsfleet, in which twelve British chieftains were slain (A. D. 473). Hengist and his followers contented themselves with the possession of Kent, where they founded the first Saxon kingdom in Britain.

In the year 477, ÆLLA, another Saxon chief, landed with his sons at Selsey, and established himself there after vigorous opposition. He founded the kingdom of the South Saxons (Sussex). In the year 495, CERDIC and his son CYNRIC landed at Charmouth, in Dorsetshire, and founded the kingdom of Wessex (or West Saxons), the third of the Heptarchy (or seven kingdoms). But he met with the most determined resistance from the Britons of Cornwall and South Wales, under their native princes, Natanleod, Aidan, Brochvael, Geraint, Cadwallo, Ambrosius, and Uther Pendragon. The Britons believed that Uther was aided by the enchanter, AMBROSE MERLIN, whose prophecies were often cited in the middle ages. They are given in Geoffrey of Monmouth's *History of England.* Uther was the father of the famous King ARTHUR, whose exploits belong to the next century. AURELIUS AMBROSIUS was elected king of Britain (A. D. 484).

SCOTLAND.—Fergus, son of the last king of the Scots, had taken refuge in Norway, whence, having acquired great fame, he was invited to return to Scotland. Assembling a vast number of Scottish exiles and Danes, he landed in his native country, united his forces with those of the Picts and the Britons, and attacked the Romans. One of their chiefs, named Græme (or Graham), broke through the wall of Severus. Fergus and Durst, the Pictish chief, were both slain, and Graham was appointed regent (A. D. 404). He divided Scotland into districts, and recalled the exiled monks. The next king, Eugenius, fell in battle against the Saxons (A. D. 449). It was in his reign that Palladius was sent from Rome to Scotland to preach against the doctrines of Pelagius. That legate created the first Scottish bishops. The successors of Eugenius were Dungard, Constantine I., and Congal I.

IRELAND.—The great event of the century was the preaching of Christianity by PATRICIUS (or PATRICK), a native of Scotland, whose family name was Succoth. Aided by his disciples—Benig'nus, Ailbe, Declan, Ibar, and Secundi'nus—he rapidly converted the Irish, and established churches and bishoprics. He landed in Dublin, A. D. 432, and died March 17th, 465. King Nial was succeeded by Dathy, the last of the pagan kings of Ireland. Leogaire, to whom St. Patrick preached, embraced Christianity. He was succeeded by Olill Molt, who was killed in the great battle of Acha (A. D. 483), whereby the family of the Nials became masters of all Ireland. Lugard was the first king of the race of the Hy Nial. At this time the Irish poet Sedulius (or Shiel) lived.

What of the withdrawal of the Romans?—What of Vortigern?—The Saxons?—Rowena?—St. Germain?—Hengist and Horsa?—Vortimer?—Catigern?—Ælla?—Cerdic and Cynric?—What kingdoms were founded?—What of the British chiefs?—Merlin?—Arthur?—Ambrosius?—What of Scotland?—Ireland?—St. Patrick?

FRANCE.

This country formed part of the dominions of Honorius on the partition of the Roman empire. In the year 406 the Vandals devastated the land: Constantine, governor of Britain, crossed over thence, and defeated them at Cambray; and having been joined by the Franks and Burgundians, made himself master of Gaul. About this time, Conan Meriadec, who in 385 led a band of adventurers into the country, founded the kingdom of Brittany (Bretagne or Armorica), then peopled by the Cimbri, a nation identical with the Cymry or Welsh. In the year 409 he formed a league with the Salic Franks, and in conjunction with their king, Theodomir, inflicted a severe defeat on the Vandals, who lost their king, Gundegisil, in the battle. After this the Gauls leagued themselves with the Franks, and Constantine formed the design of dethroning Honorius. He marched into Italy; but finding himself unsupported, returned into Gaul, where he was put to death by order of Honorius. Meanwhile, Jovinus had been proclaimed emperor by the Belgians (A. D. 411). He was at first supported by Adolphus, the successor of Alaric; but the latter afterwards caused him to be put to death, and resolved to re-establish the authority of Honorius in Gaul. The war was a fierce one, both Gauls and Franks fighting ardently for liberty. The Romans recovered the south of Gaul, but left the northern portion of it to the Franks. The Romans divided (A. D. 418) their portion into seven provinces, making Arles the capital, and Agricola prefect. The emperor subsequently (A. D. 419) put Wallia, king of the Visigoths, in possession of Aquitaine. On the death of Wallia, his successors, Theodoric and Euric, made themselves masters of the south of France, fixing their royal seat at Toulouse.

At this time, it is alleged, Pharamond, a chief of the Ripuarian Franks, was elected king by those who had settled in Gaul. He is said to have died in A. D. 428, but as nothing is known of him but his name, the account is scarcely worthy of credit. Clodion the Hairy, the next king of the Franks, resided beyond the Rhine, and endeavored to make himself master of Roman Gaul; in which attempt he was foiled by the celebrated Roman general Ætius. He, however, established himself at Amiens, which he made his royal residence. His successor, Merovæ′us (A. D. 447), was the next chief elected king after the manner of the Franks, and became the founder of the Merovingian dynasty. He was soon called upon to defend his kingdom against Attila and his Huns, and, joining with the Romans under Ætius, and the Visigoths under Theodoric, took part in the ever-memorable battle of Châlons (A. D. 451). After the defeat of Attila, and the murder of Ætius, the Franks established themselves permanently in Northern France.

On the death of Merovæus, his son, Chil′deric, was chosen his successor (A. D. 458). The debauchery of this prince soon disgusted the Franks, who elected Ægidius (Giles), the commander of the Roman militia, for their king. Childeric, however, regained his throne, with Paris, Orleans, Angiers, and Beauvais. The reign of Childeric I. ended in A. D. 481, when Clovis, the young chief of the Franks at Tournay, was elected king. He is generally considered the founder of the French monarchy. In A. D. 485, he attacked Syagrius, governor of Soissons, and took possession of his territory and capital. Soon after this he married Clotilda, niece of Gundibald, king of the Burgundians, a Christian princess, by whom he became instructed in the Christian religion. In a desperate battle with the Alemanni at Zulpich, in A. D. 496, he vowed to become a Christian if he proved victorious. Being successful, he was baptized, with the greater number of his followers, by Remigius (or Saint Remi), bishop of Rheims, an orthodox prelate; and the king, being supported by the clergy of Gaul, who were hostile to the Arians, received the appellation of "Most Christian King" —a title borne by his successors, kings of France, down to the most recent times. He first held his Court at Soissons, but afterwards transferred it to Paris. His kingdom, however, was not very extensive; for Euric, king of the Visigoths, was master of all the south of France. Nor was his authority very despotic, for the Franks assembled in council every spring in their Campus Martis, or Champ de Mars, where they deliberated on public affairs, and controlled them by their votes. The kingdom or duchy of Burgundy was founded in A. D. 413 by Gundicar, or Gunthacar, who, with 10,000 men, fell heroically resisting Attila. His successors, Gunderic (436–466), Chilperic (466–491), and Gundibald, call for no particular notice. This kingdom comprehended Alsace and Lorraine.

What is said of Constantine?—Conan Meriadec?—Jovinus?—How was Gaul divided between the Romans and the Franks?—What of Pharamond?—Clodion?—Merovæus?—Childeric I.?—Clovis?—Clotilda?—The conversion of Clovis?—His new appellation?—The extent of his kingdom?—The Champ de Mars?—The duchy of Burgundy?

SPAIN.

After the destruction of the army of Radagaisus by Stilicho in Italy (A. D. 407), the Vandals under Gunde′gisil, the Alani under Respen′dial, and the Suevi under Her′manric, crossed the Rhine into Gaul—whence, unsuccessfully combating the Franks, they suddenly turned south, crossed the Pyrenees, and entered Spain. There they were well received. The Basques and the Iberians willingly submitted to them, and the three great tribes found no difficulty in acquiring possession of the land, and making terms with the Romans, whose dominion in Spain was now limited to a small portion of the country.

The Vandals, under Gun′deric, the successor of Gundegisil, ruled at Seville, and gave their name to the province of Andalusia. The Suevi settled in Castile and Galicia, and the Alani on the Ebro and in Lusitania. The latter, a more fierce and restless tribe than the others, drove the Vandals out of Bœtica, and the Romans out of Celtiberia. Adolphus, king of the Goths, was the next invader of Spain (A. D. 417); but his career was cut short by assassination at Barcelona, and his successor, Sigeric, shared the same fate (A. D. 418). Wallia was chosen in the place of the latter. This prince subdued the Alani and incorporated them with the Goths, which gave rise to the Gotho-Alanic nation and the province of Catalonia. Wallia held his Court at Toulouse, which became the capital of the kingdom of the Visigoths. He died A. D. 419, and was succeeded by Theod′oric. On the death of Wallia, Gunderic, king of the Vandals, aspired to the sovereignty of all Spain. Attacking the Suevi, he drove them into the mountains of Leon; but he died suddenly at Seville. His brother, Gen′seric, having been invited by Boniface into Africa, led an army of 80,000 men into that country, and founded a kingdom there. This movement relieved the Suevi from their difficulties, and they soon recovered their power. Hermanric, their king, died A. D. 440, leaving the government to his son, Rech′ila, who added the provinces of Toledo, Lusitania, and Carthagena to his dominions. His son and successor, Rech′iar (A. D. 448), was the first Christian prince of the Suevi.

Theodoric, king of the Visigoths, eager to extend his dominions into Spain, attacked the Suevi, but was called away to resist the terrible advance of the Huns under Attila, who threatened to desolate France and Spain, as he had done Eastern Europe. The victory at Châlons (A. D. 451), gained by Ætius and Theodoric, cost the life of the latter. His death was bloodily avenged by his son, Thorismund, and the Huns were driven out of France. Thorismund was murdered by his brothers, Theod′oric and Fred′eric, the former of whom became king of the Visigoths, and embraced Arian Christianity. His great ambition was to make himself master of Spain. He accordingly invaded it with a powerful army (A. D. 456), and overpowered the Suevi, whose king, Rechiar, perished in the struggle. After the death of Theodoric (A. D. 467), his brother and successor, Euric, completed the conquest of Spain, with the exception of Galicia, which was still held by the Suevi; and the Roman dominion in the Peninsula was finally extinguished.

Euric was the founder of the Gothic kingdom of Spain. Bœtica and Catalonia had submitted to his father, and he resolved to subdue the Suevi. This he accomplished, leaving them in possession of Galicia, Leon, and part of Portugal; but they were thoroughly humbled by his prowess. He then extinguished the remains of the Roman colony of Tarraconensis, with Lusitania and the centre of Spain. Being then master of the Peninsula, he invaded Gaul, and made such rapid and extensive conquests there, that the Emperor Julius Nepos was glad to make terms with him. Subsequently, Odoacer, king of Italy, gave up to him all the Roman provinces beyond the Alps, as far as the Rhine and the ocean. Euric established his seat of empire at Arles, where he died (A. D. 483), having induced his subjects to elect his son Alaric as their king. Euric was the first legislator of his nation, and originated and collected the code of laws called the *Forum Judicum*, or *Fuero Juzgo*. He was undoubtedly a great prince. Being an Arian, he persecuted the orthodox Christians. Alaric had not the ability of his father: he was of a less warlike temperament, and labored to purchase peace on terms which would have been rejected by his predecessors. With the infusion of this Gothic element into Spain, the history of that country assumes a new character. The Roman laws were altered or abrogated, and those rude principles of liberty common to the Northern barbarians were introduced. The era of romantic adventure began, and the Spanish character was considerably elevated.

What nations invaded Spain?—What of Adolphus?—Wallia?—Theodoric?—Genseric?—The invasion of Africa?—Hermanric?—Rechiar?—The battle of Châlons?—Thorismund?—Euric?—What kingdom did Euric found?—What were his principal acts?—Where did he establish himself?—What of Alaric?—What was the effect of the irruption of the Goths?

GERMANY.

The exploits of Alaric are referred to in the histories of the Eastern and Western Empires. Having been foiled in his invasion of Italy and Greece by Stilicho, he retired into the mountains (A. D. 403). Radagaisus, at the head of the Alemanni, having poured into Italy (A. D. 405), met with a similar fate at the hands of Stilicho. This famous general, being suspected by the Emperor Honorius of carrying on a secret understanding with Alaric, and even of aiming at the imperial crown, was put to death, together with the wives and children of 30,000 Germans in his service. This insane proceeding of the emperor at once roused the fury of these mercenaries, and Alaric, being joined by them, suddenly reappeared, marched to Rome, and forced the city to pay a heavy ransom. He then attacked Ravenna, but being foiled there, returned to Rome, which he took and plundered (A. D. 409). Yet the city was not destroyed, and the defenceless ones were spared. The church of St. Peter, and the valuables deposited therein, were left untouched. The Goths even joined in a solemn procession to the cathedral, and in the religious services. Leaving Rome, Alaric marched into Lower Italy with the intention of visiting Africa, but his fleet was wrecked off Messina, and he died suddenly in his 54th year. The river Busentinus (Baseno) was diverted from its course, and the Gothic monarch was buried with an immense treasure in its bed; after which the stream was restored to its natural course, and the secret of his burial-place was sealed by the murder of the laborers.

In A. D. 407, the Vandals, Alans, and Suevi entered Gaul, and, passing thence into Spain, established themselves there. In A. D. 412, the Franks and Burgundians having joined in proclaiming Jovinus emperor, Honorius, emperor of the West, persuaded Adolphus, the successor of Alaric, to march against them, which he did, and having been victorious, took possession of the south of Gaul and north of Spain. The motive which mainly actuated Adolphus in following the advice of Honorius, was the passion entertained by the Gothic monarch for Placidia, the beautiful and talented sister of the emperor, who had been taken prisoner by Alaric at Rome. After the conquest of Northern Spain, the nuptials of Adolphus and Placidia were celebrated at Narbonne (A. D. 414) with barbarous magnificence. Adolphus was murdered at Barcelona (A. D. 415), and Sigeric usurped the throne, but was in his turn slain by Wallia, who fixed his Court at Toulouse, and founded the province of Catalonia. Theodoric, his son and successor, greatly extended his dominions.

The Emperor Honorius allotted to the Burgundians the territory of Alsatia as a fief of the empire. The ancient Helvetians no longer existed as an independent people, the fierce Alemanni and Suabians being sole possessors of the country. The worship of Odin prevailed exclusively amongst these tribes, from the Alps to the Northern Ocean. The Franks and Salii settled in Gaul, where they founded the kingdom of France.

About this time there arose a powerful leader amongst the Huns, called, by the Romans, Attila, and by the Germans, Etzel. He united beneath his rule all the Huns and the Ostro-Germanic tribes, whose kings were his servants. He was one of those mighty spirits, born to rule millions, and was called "the Scourge of God", from the devastation which he caused. He laid waste the whole of Greece: Constantinople was saved by ransom (A. D. 451). Attila, with his brother, Bleda, then ravaged Germany, putting men, women, and children to the sword. One attempt only to arrest his progress was made, and that was by 10,000 Burgundians, under Gunthachar, on the right bank of the Rhine, who fought and fell like a second Leonidas, with all his gallant followers. Attila continued his route to France, and was met on the plains of Châlons by the combined Roman, Frank, and Gothic armies, under Ætius, and there, in one of the most fearful battles which history records, he was utterly defeated: 200,000 Huns were slain, and the tide of barbarism westward was stayed. Attila then passed into Italy, and marched against Rome, intending to pillage it, but he was induced to spare the city, by an unlooked-for incident. Pope Leo, an aged and dignified man, set forth to meet the Huns, at the head of the Roman clergy in their priestly robes, and chanting hymns. He and they were received with marked respect by Attila, who promised to spare the city, and retire from Italy. This ferocious tyrant died on his way back, some say from the bursting of a blood-vessel, others from the dagger of a maiden named Ildegunda. He was buried with great pomp, but those who buried him were put to death, that the place of burial might never be known. His sons quarrelled among themselves, and the Germans threw off the yoke of the Huns, who were defeated on the banks of the Nelad and the Danube, and driven beyond the Black Sea.

Genseric, the Vandal, established an empire in Africa; and Ricimer, king of the Visigoths, became master of Italy. The latter dying in A. D. 472, Odoacer, prince of the Heruli, accomplished the destruction of the Roman empire in the West, dethroning Romulus Augustulus, the last of the emperors, and causing himself to be proclaimed king of Italy (A. D. 476). He made Ravenna his capital (see Italy, page 171).

At this period of history, Germany was inhabited by a number of tribes formed into confederations, the principal of which were the Teutonic races of—1. The Franks, on the Rhine and in Gaul, which gave their name to the country. 2. The Alemanni, on the eastern bank of the Rhine, and thence to Lake Constance and Bohemia. 3. The Saxons, in Bremen and Holstein, Saxony, and Hanover. 4. The Vandals, in Mecklenburg, Pomerania, and as far as the Oder. 5. The Goths, who were divided into the Burgundians, dwelling on the confines of Germany and Poland; the Heruli, who dwelt near Palus Mæotis; the Lombards, in the north of Pannonia; and the Gepidæ, also in Pannonia. 6. The Thuringians, from the Mein to the Harz forest. There were also Slavonian tribes in Bohemia, Lusatia, Mecklenburg, and Misnia. The Heruli and Lombards penetrated into Italy; the Suevi, Alans, and Vandals traversed Gaul, and entered Spain; the Burgundians settled in the east of France; the Franks settled in Gaul and the Netherlands. The Suevi and Alemanni united, and settled in Switzerland and Rhætia, and were afterwards called Suabians; while the Boii settled in Bavaria. The Franks were divided into two great confederacies, the Salian and the Ripuarian (from *ripua*, the bank of a river). The former, under Clovis, founded the French monarchy (A. D. 481). Clovis extended his sway over the Suabians, Thuringians, and Bavarians, and married Clotilda, niece of Gundibald, king of the Burgundians (A. D. 493), by whom he was converted to Christianity.

Who was Stilicho?—What befell him?—What did Alaric do?—Did he spare Rome?—How was he buried?—Describe the movements of the various tribes.—Who was Adolphus?—Whom did he marry?—What befell him?—Who were his successors?—How did the Burgundians acquire Alsatia?—Who was Attila?—What great battle stopped his career westward?—What incident saved Rome?—What was the mode of Attila's death and burial?—Who was Genseric?—Ricimer?—Odoacer?—How was Germany peopled at this epoch?

AFRICA.

This century is memorable in the history of Africa for the establishment of the kingdom of the Vandals in Mauretania and Numidia. Count Boniface, the Roman governor of those provinces, having conspired against the party of Ætius in Italy, who was all-powerful with the emperor, called in the aid of Genseric, king of the Vandals in Spain. In the year 428 Genseric crossed into Africa at the head of a large army; but Boniface, having in the meantime made his peace with the emperor, requested Genseric to return. The Vandal king returned him a disdainful answer, and in a very short time expelled him and the Roman forces from the province. The enterprising but cruel Vandal in eight years made himself master of all that country now called Barbary. Being an Arian, Genseric savagely persecuted the orthodox Christians. He also destroyed all the works of art of the Romans in Africa, and devastated the country in a horrible manner. The Eastern emperor, Zeno, made peace with him, and yielded up the Roman provinces to him. Genseric became more tolerant towards the orthodox Christians at the close of his reign, but on the accession of his son, Huneric (A. D. 477), they suffered more cruelly than ever. The horrors of this reign surpass anything in African history. Huneric died mysteriously (A. D. 484), and was succeeded by a grandson of Genseric, named Gutamund, a generous and amiable prince, who immediately stayed the persecution, and, although an Arian, restored the African Church to its pristine state. Unfortunately he died after a reign of eleven years (A. D. 496), and was succeeded by his brother, Thrasamund, a prince of an opposite temper, who quickly revived the persecution against the Church, banished the orthodox Christians, shut up their churches, and sequestered their monasteries. 120 bishops, at the head of whom was the learned Fulgentius, were banished to the island of Sardinia.

Ethiopia.—In the reign of Alamid, vast numbers of monks and Anchorites came out of Egypt, and settled in Ethiopia, and Christianity flourished for a time. But the nation (or, at least, its rulers) relapsed into paganism, and the Christian faith was then forcibly restored by Aidog (or Adad), king of Axuma (A. D. 521), in pursuance of a vow made by him previously to a severe battle with the Homerite Arabs.

State the particulars of the establishment of the Vandals in Africa.—What of Genseric?—Huneric?—Gutamund?—Thrasamund?—Christianity in Ethiopia?

SCANDINAVIA.

Sweden.—Aun-hinn-Gamle (or, "the Old") was king for many years, but was twice expelled from his kingdom,—once, after an obstinate contest, by Halfdan I., king of Denmark, who reigned at Upsala 25 years, and again by Ole-hinn-Frækni (or, "the Active"), the son of Friedlief III. Aun immolated nine of his sons to the gods, in order to obtain what he most desired, viz., extreme old age, and after an immensely long reign he died A. D. 448. His successor, Egill, had to contend with insurgents, one of whom, named Tunni, defeated him in eight battles. Egill, however, slew him with his own hand, whence he took the name of Tunnadolgi. He died A. D. 456. His successor, Ottar, fell in a naval action with Frode IV. of Denmark, in the Linn Fiord, after having ravaged the district of Vendila; whence he is surnamed by Danish historians Vendilkraka. Adils, the next king, was involved in a protracted quarrel with the Norwegians, which was at length terminated in his favor by a pitched battle on the ice, on Lake Wener.

Denmark. — Frode IV. succeeded Friedlief III. Of Ingild, Halfdan II., and Frode V. little need be said. Halfdan's sons, Roe and Helge, inherited the kingdom and agreed to divide it between them. Roe built the city of Roskilde, but gave up his patrimony for the Danish possessions in England, where he established himself. Helge invaded Sweden, plundered Upsala, and carried off the queen, who became his wife, and mother of the famous hero, Hrolf (or Rolf) Krake. To Helge and Roe succeeded Frode VI., whose reign extended into the next century. These barbarous chieftains of an equally barbarous people passed their time in piratical and plundering excursions, rude field sports, and carousing. The history of one century is very nearly that of another, for a long time to come, and is involved in the greatest uncertainty. The student will find in the introduction to Dunham's *History of Denmark*, an interesting discussion of this obscure portion of history, and notices of the original races of Scandinavia, the Suiones, Gettones, Dankiones, Jutes, Lapps, Finns, and Quens, with their mythological kings and heroes who lived long prior to the time of Odin. Among these there was one named Ju'binal, who is still invoked by the Lapps. But space cannot be devoted to further mention of these topics here.

Mention the incidents in the history of Sweden.—And of Denmark.—What of Roe?—Hrolf Krake?—What were the original races of Scandinavia?

NETHERLANDS.

The history of this century is nearly a blank. It is in fact compounded of that of the Saxons, who were pouring forth their colonists over the northern shores of Europe and into Britain, and that of the Franks, who under Clovis and his successors had established the kingdom of France, and were extending their empire to the Rhine. The inhabitants of the Western Netherlands were involved in perpetual contests with these fierce and lawless conquerors, and appear to have been brought to such a state of subjugation and despondency as to wish to denaturalize themselves, and become as though they were foreigners, even on their own soil. The Frank (or French) nobles appear to have considered the district of the Ardennes, and the beautiful region of the Moselle and the Herbesthal, as their own peculiar hunting grounds. The land in those days was covered with dense forests, abounding in bears, and it was to indulge in their favorite sport of bear hunting that they made it uninhabitable. We are told that those parts of the Netherlands which belonged to France resembled a desert, and the monasteries which were there founded were established, according to the words of their charters, amid immense solitudes. Under this new rule not a vestige of the ancient nations of the Ardennes was left: the civilized population either perished or was reduced to slavery, and all the high grounds were added to the previous conquests of the Salians.

A different fate awaited the Eastern Netherlands. The Alemanni in the Gallic territories, having acknowledged the superiority of the Franks, were permitted by the conquerors to enjoy their peculiar manners and institutions, under the government of official and, at length, of hereditary dukes. After the conquest of the western provinces, the Franks alone maintained their ancient habitations beyond the Rhine. They gradually subdued and civilized the exhausted countries as far as the Elbe and the mountains of Bohemia.

It has been supposed that the expedition of Hengist and Horsa, the celebrated Saxon chieftains, for the conquest of Britain, sailed from the Netherlands. Certain it is that the shores of the Northern Ocean were inhabited by the hardy Northern tribes who owed no allegiance to the Franks, but lived in perpetual enmity with them.

What was the condition of the Western Netherlands during this century?—What did the French nobles do?—What of the Eastern Netherlands?—Hengist and Horsa?

CENTRAL AMERICA.

The Quichè legend adds, that when Gucumatz and the gods made man they first made him of clay, but that the rain having spoilt him, they called to their aid Xpi-Yacoc and Xmucané, the chiefs of magic, who advised that the man should be made of wood and the woman of cibak (the Quichè name for the marrow of a species of sword-grass out of which matting is made). From these two sprang ungainly children, devoid of intelligence, but capable of speech to praise their creator. But having failed to glorify Hurakan, they were destroyed in a flood: a heavy rain of bitumen and rosin fell from heaven upon them: wild birds and beasts devoured them: but a few were saved, and their descendants are those apes which inhabit the woods. Then a new creation took place, and a race of intelligent beings was formed, which praised God and obeyed His laws. Such is the mythical account of the creation of man which prevailed among the ancient people of Guatemala.

The traditions collected by Las Casas, the Spanish historian, have something like history in them. According to them, in the ages anterior to the Deluge, the Grandfather and Grandmother who dwelt in heaven were adored in Guatemala; and for a long time afterwards the Deity was invoked by these two names, until a woman of great authority taught them to address Him otherwise, having learned by a special revelation His true name. This tradition undoubtedly refers to a queen much celebrated in the antique legends of the Guatemalians, and whose memory is connected with a number of places in Central America. She was called Atit (grandmother). The volcano Atit-al-huyu was named after her. According to the legend, Atit lived four centuries, and from her descended all the royal and princely families of Guatemala. This probably refers to the period during which her dynasty or family reigned. She married Copichoch, who was the first that established his dominion in Guatemala. According to the chroniclers, Copichoch, the son of Tamub, had previously reigned at Tulha, whither he had come from the East, after having crossed the sea with other chiefs named Cochochlam, Mahquinalo, and Ahcanail. They brought with them from that distant country the famous black stone, since worshipped in the temple of Cahba at Utlatlan. Their descendants, having settled in Guatemala and multiplied exceedingly, founded those kingdoms of which Utlatlan, Atitlan, and Iximché (or Quanhtemalan), were subsequently the capitals. The race of Tamub, to which the later Quichè princes traced their origin, is undoubtedly the most ancient in the annals of Guatemala: that of Ilocab (which name comes after that of Tamub) appears to have succeeded it in power, or to have reigned conjointly with it over some of the neighboring provinces. Exbalanqué, who has been already mentioned (p. 145), came from the city of Utlatlan when he marched against Xibalba. Whatever may have been his claims to the sceptre of the Quichè States, and whether acquired by violence or not, he went to reign over other countries; and it was, according to all appearance, the race of Tamub or of Ilocab which obtained or resumed the crown of Utlatlan after his departure. But he was worshipped afterwards in Guatemala, and down to the time of the Spanish conquest, the people continued to pay him divine honors, and to sacrifice human victims to him, of which hideous custom he had been the founder. This is all that tradition furnishes respecting the primitive epochs of the history of Guatemala. It is not until a later period that the first Toltec emigrations appear, of which formal mention is made. They are those of the populations known afterwards by the name of Xuchiltepecs and Pipiles, which coming from Chollulan established themselves on the shores (now desert) between Tehuantepec and Soconusco (anciently Xoconochco). We know not the motives which induced them to abandon the Aztec plateau; but the tradition which relates to them appears to coincide with that of the taking of Chollullan by Huemac in the 9th century.

Through the mists of tradition, it may reasonably be inferred that the ancient civilization of Central America was introduced by some enterprising European or African adventurers. We know that the Phœnicians and the Carthaginians fitted out expeditions for the purposes of discovery and colonization; that they were acquainted with the Northern Ocean; and that they sailed round the Cape of Good Hope. Some of these navigators may have anticipated Columbus, or been driven by storms and tides across the Atlantic, and thus been the means of introducing the arts and sciences of the Old World.

What more is said of the creation of man?—Of the first race of human beings?—Of other traditions of Guatemala?—Of Queen Atit?—Of Copichoch?—The race of Tamub?—Exbalanqué?—Subsequent traditions?—What may be inferred as to the origin of the ancient civilization of Central America?

THE CHRISTIAN CHURCH.

The Church being now the State religion of the Eastern and Western Empires, it made great efforts to spread Christianity amongst the heathens. The Burgundians readily embraced the faith: the Vandals, Suevi, and Alans were likewise converted, but by whom and at what precise time is unknown. The Germans and Goths had already been partially converted. The Roman pontiff, Celestine, sent Palladius into Ireland to preach to the savage people of that country, but his labors were not very successful. He was of more use in Scotland, where he combated heresy. The same pontiff sent Succoth, a native of Scotland, who had studied in Gaul, under the famous Martin of Tours, to Ireland in the year 432. This eminent man, better known by his assumed name Patricius (or Patrick), was completely successful in planting Christianity in that island; and in the year 472 he founded the archbishopric of Armagh, which has since remained the metropolitan See of Ireland. The convents he established, until some time in the 7th century, were the centres of a fervent ecclesiastical activity for the island, which was thence styled "the Isle of Saints". He has been justly called "the Apostle of the Irish". In Britain, however, Christianity was nearly exterminated by the idolatrous Saxons, who, on the abandonment of the island by the Romans, invaded and settled in it, and finally made themselves masters of it. The British Church continued only in Wales and in the mountains of Northumberland, and the national hatred between the Britons and the Saxons was too intense to allow the latter to receive the gospel from the former. In Gaul, the Franks committed the greatest cruelties on the Christians, and it was not until the year 496, when Clovis embraced Christianity, that these persecutions ceased, and France became Christian. The conversion of Clovis was mainly owing to the zeal of his Christian wife, Clotilda. At the battle of Tolbiacum (Zulpich), when he saw his ranks give way, he raised his hands in supplication to the God of the Christians; and having gained the victory, he was baptized at the cathedral of Rheims by St. Remigius (Remi): he was saluted as a Christian king and a second Constantine. He soon distinguished himself by his zeal for the Catholic faith, and being then the only orthodox king, he professed to feel bound in conscience to obtain possession of the territories of the Arian princes, and in his attempts to do so received much assistance from their Catholic subjects. The Franks and Alemanni followed his example; in consequence whereof Arianism began to decline, and in the 8th century, when the Lombard kingdom was overthrown, its independence as a national religion was entirely lost.

In the East, Simeon, a Syrian, persuaded the wild inhabitants of the Libanus and Northern Arabia to adopt the Christian religion, by imitating that kind of penitence or penance practised by the fakeers of India. When a boy, he had been more than once saved from fanatical suicide in the convent wherein he had taken refuge; and when of mature age, he passed his life on the tops of pillars, alternating between one and another, they being respectively 9, 18, 33, 54, and 60 feet high, in the neighborhood of Antioch. He asserted himself to be a mediator between heaven and earth, and preached repentance to the astonished multitude. For 37 years (A. D. 420–457) he lived in this manner, his food being conveyed to him in a basket. He was much venerated, and became an umpire and an apostle to the Arabs. The Greeks gave him the appellation of "Styl′ites" (from *stylos*, a column). He had many imitators, even down to the 12th century, in the East; but these "pillar saints" (*sancti columnares*) never acquired influence in the West. But in Persia the imprudent zeal of the bishop of Suza, who pulled down one of the temples erected by the worshippers of fire, drew down upon the Christians in that country a fierce and inhuman persecution, and their churches were levelled to the ground (A. D. 414). This persecution was renewed in 421, and continued for a great number of years, during which time a prodigious number of Christians were tortured and put to death, and the faith became all but extinct in Persia.

The internal history of the Church shows the increasing development of the power of the hierarchy. The influence of the bishops was much augmented, especially of the patriarchs of Constantinople, between whom and the Roman pontiffs the direst hostility existed. The latter were gradually building up the great fabric of Papal power which was soon to enslave the western world. A variety of circumstances contributed to this. Among them were the inroads of barbarians, the supineness or feebleness of distant bishops, and the policy of the western kings, who advanced their own interests in co-operating with the bishop of Rome. Leo the Great, who filled that See from 440 to 461, asserted with great vigor and success the pretensions of the See of Rome; but he met with much resistance, especially from the African bishops. The vices of the clergy were carried to enormous lengths, and the licentiousness of the monks became proverbial. The practice of invoking the spirits of departed Christians, and of praying for their intercession, became habitual. Images were worshipped, and the relics of saints and martyrs were eagerly sought after and enshrined. Public processions and pilgrimages to holy places became extremely common, and were sometimes carried to ridiculous extremes; for instance, some Christians journeyed to Arabia in order to see the dunghill on which Job sat, and to kiss the ground which had absorbed his blood (see Chrysostom's *Homily to the Antiochians*). The doctrine of the purgation of souls by fire after death also became prominent, and was elaborately discussed by Augustine. It was held that all mankind have to pass through this fiery purification to judgment, and will suffer more or less, individually, in proportion to the degrees of iniquity waiting to be burnt out. In time, this hypothesis was displaced by the belief in a permanent purgatory, in which the process of burning out worldly pollution is constantly going on. New rites were introduced into the Church service; such as, perpetual hymns, which were chanted day and night; the adoration of images of the Virgin Mary with the Child Jesus in her arms; the addition of a vast variety of ornaments to the sacerdotal robes; and the confession of sins privately to a priest, instead of publicly before the congregation, as had been the practice heretofore. The Roman festival of the Birth of Jesus, on the 25th of December, was adopted in the Eastern Churches. Love feasts, which had originated in the charitable feelings of the early Christians towards their needy brethren, and had subsequently taken the form of repasts for the poor provided by the whole Church, fell into disuse during this century. The *tonsura Petri* (shaving the crown of the head) was adopted by the clergy of the Roman Church. The building of churches became a desire as well as a necessity, especially after the establishment of Christianity as the State religion. They were generally erected over the graves of martyrs, in the form of the Basilica (imperial palace or court of judicature). This was an oblong parallelogram, divided lengthwise by double or quadruple rows of pillars, and terminating in a semicircular hall (or sanctuary). On these pillars rested a beam, on which rested a second row of pillars with arcades, and above these a rather flat gable-roof. Before the entrance was a quadrangular court surrounded with colonnades, and with a fountain in the centre. In the sanctuary, separated from the other parts by lattice-work and curtains, stood the main altar, behind which were the seats for the priests, with the episcopal throne in the centre. Before the altar was an elevated chair for the singers, by the side of which was a pulpit, sometimes two. Such was the style of the principal churches in the 5th century.

The controversy respecting Origen raged with great fury (see 2d and 3d centuries), and Jerome, Rufinus, Theophilus, and Chrysostom distinguished themselves in it. Efforts were made (A. D. 401) to expel the latter from Constantinople; and by a synod held at Chalcedon (A. D. 403) he was banished, but was soon recalled, through fear of a popular tumult. The faction of the Donatists still troubled the Church by their obstinacy, and the brutal violence of their soldiery. Councils were held at Carthage in 404 and in 407, which sent deputies to the Emperor Honorius, requesting him to enforce the laws against them. He accordingly fined those who refused to return into the Church, banished their doctors, and issued stringent edicts against them; but he allowed them to plead their cause before his tribune, Marcelli′nus, who was sent expressly into Africa to settle these unhappy disputes. The hearing lasted three days, and Marcellinus pronounced in favor of the Catholics, chiefly through the exertions of Augustine, who took the principal part in the controversy. After this the greater number of the Donatists returned to the Church, but many remained obstinate, and suffered fines, imprisonment, and even death; and though they were afterwards aided by Genseric and the Vandals, who invaded Africa in A. D. 427, they never recovered their former influence. The Arians, also, oppressed by the imperial edicts, took refuge among the Goths, Suevi, Vandals, and Burgundians.

What is said of the spread of Christianity?—Palladius?—St. Patrick?—What title did Ireland acquire?—What of Christianity in Britain?—The conversion of Clovis?—The decline of Arianism?—Simeon Stylites?—The "pillar saints"?—The persecution in Persia?—The power of the hierarchy?—The influence of the bishops?

What were the leading causes of the increase of the Papal power?—What of Leo I.?—What new practices grew up?—What of the doctrine of purgatory?—What new rites were introduced?—What of love feasts?—Shaving the crown?—The building of churches?—Chrysostom?—The Donatists?—The Arians?

A.C. 400—500.

THE CHRISTIAN CHURCH.

A new sect, which became the source of the most fatal divisions in the Church, was formed by NESTO′RIUS, bishop of Constantinople, a man remarkable for his learning and eloquence, as well as for his unbounded arrogance. Apollina′ris, bishop of Clermont in France, having taught that Christ was not endowed with a human soul, but with the Divine Nature, which was substituted in its place, and performed its functions, Nestorius vehemently opposed this doctrine, and sought to exterminate its supporters. He contended that the Divine and human natures in Christ were entirely distinct; and he commanded his disciples to distinguish carefully between the actions and perceptions of the Son of God, and those of the Son of Man. As this doctrine favored the notion of there being two distinct persons in Christ, and as Nestorius also taught that the Virgin Mary ought not to be styled "Mother of God", but "Mother of Christ", he was furiously attacked by CYRIL, bishop of Alexandria, who, joining with Celestine, bishop of Rome, assembled a council at Alexandria (A. D. 430), and issued no less than 12 anathemas against him. Nestorius treated these fulminations with contempt, and charged Cyril and Celestine with heresy. To settle the controversy, the Emperor Theodosius called a council at Ephesus (A. D. 431), over which Cyril presided. Nestorius was cited to appear before it. This he refused to do, because it was proposed to decide the matter before the arrival of the Eastern bishops. He was therefore judged without being heard, deprived of his bishopric, banished to Petra in Arabia, and thence to the oasis in the great desert of Africa (A. D. 435), where he died about the year 450. This celebrated Council of Ephesus, the proceedings of which were conducted without the least fairness or decency, established the doctrine which has since been adopted by the majority of Christians, viz., "that Christ was one Divine Person, in whom two natures were most closely and intimately united, but without being mixed or confounded together"—a doctrine which many have thought was in reality the same as that of Nestorius. Be this as it may, the progress of Nestorianism was prodigious in the East. All the Oriental provinces of the empire embraced it: the Persian Christians adopted it with ardor. The celebrated school of Edessa translated from the Greek into Syriac the works of Nestorius, and instructed youth in them. Thus his doctrines spread throughout the East, and were afterwards carried into Tartary and China, where they flourished for many centuries, and to this day they form the tenets of the Armenian Church. His most ardent disciple was Barsu′mas, who preached with great zeal, and persuaded the Persian monarch to appoint him to the bishopric of Seleucia—a post which the patriarch of the Nestorians has since always filled. Barsumas also founded a school at Nisibis, whence issued those Nestorian doctors who, in this and the following century, spread their tenets throughout Asia.

Further contests were occasioned by EU′TYCHES, an abbot of Constantinople, who taught that there was but one nature in Christ, viz., "that of the incarnate Word". For this he was excommunicated: he thereupon appealed to the decision of a general council. Accordingly, the Emperor Theodosius convened one at Ephesus (A. D. 449), which was conducted with such turbulence and want of decency, that it was called by the Greeks "an assembly of robbers". Eutyches, however, was acquitted, and Flavia′nus, one of his opponents, was publicly scourged. The latter then appealed to Leo, bishop of Rome, who with great difficulty procured of the Emperor Marcian the convoking of the Council of Chalcedon (which is reckoned the fourth general council), (A. D. 451), in which the acts of the Council of Ephesus were revoked and annulled, and its president, Dioscorus, condemned and banished. But this Monoph′ysite (or one nature) controversy became the cause of incredible discords, and even of civil war. The Emperor Basiliscus, having espoused the cause of the Monophysites, summoned all the bishops to condemn the Synod of Chalcedon. The restoration of Zeno to the throne changed the posture of affairs. In 482 that emperor issued his "Henot′icon" (or one nature dogma), to be subscribed by the contending parties; but many of the Syrian bishops refused to sign it, and were displaced. The Western bishops offered the most determined opposition to all union with the Monophysites. Felix II., bishop of Rome, issued an anathema against Acacius, patriarch of Constantinople, and all communion between the Eastern and Western Churches was broken off (A. D. 484). Attempts were subsequently made to renew it, but the breach was never healed.

What is said of Nestorius?—Apollinaris?—The Council of Ephesus?—What doctrine did it establish?—What of the progress of Nestorianism?—Of Barsumas?—The bishopric of Suza?—The heresy of Eutyches?—The second Council of Ephesus?—The Monophysite Controversy?—Zeno's Henoticon?—The schism between the two Churches?

Another controversy was raised by PELA′GIUS and CELES′TIUS, the former an English monk, the latter an Irish one, who about the year 410 went into Sicily from Rome, and taught that the doctrine of the original corruption of human nature and the necessity for Divine grace to restore it, was false. Several councils were held to suppress this heresy, and by dint of edicts and penal laws, the Catholics demolished this sect in its infancy. In the course of the controversy, AURELIUS AUGUSTINE, bishop of Hippo (now Bona in Algeria), promulgated his famous doctrine of Predestination. This celebrated man was born at Tagaste, in Numidia, in November, A. D. 354. His father was a pagan, but his mother, Monica, was a Christian. He became a Manichæan, but was subsequently converted to orthodox Christianity. His works are voluminous, and much esteemed —the most remarkable of them being his treatise *De Civitate Dei*, or history of the visible kingdom of God, from the creation to his own times. This doctrine of Predestination was the occasion of further controversy, especially in Europe; and the Western Church was divided by the contest between the followers of Augustine and those who were called Semi-Pelagians. The latter had for some time the advantage, especially in France, owing to the unpopularity of the doctrine of the absolute decrees of God; but in Rome and Africa the doctrines of Augustine were zealously upheld.

The patriarchs of Alexandria and Antioch were now fast losing their importance, and the patriarch of Constantinople absorbed supreme authority in the East. He styled himself "the Universal Bishop."—a pretension which was fiercely resented by Gelasius I. and the succeeding bishops of Rome, especially by Gregory I. (surnamed "the Great"), towards the close of the 6th century. But though Gregory refused to assume the title, his successor, Boniface III. (A. D. 605), obtained from the Emperor Phocas the privilege of bearing it, and of transmitting it to his successors. The emperor at the same time declared the Church of Rome to be the head of all other Churches, and Boniface assumed to himself alone the appellation "Papa" or "Pope", which had formerly been applied indiscriminately to all bishops; and from this period (A. D. 606) dates the rise of the Papacy, which will be more fully discussed in the second part of this work, comprising Mediæval History.

The bishops of Rome during this century were: Anastasius I. (A. D. 398–402); Innocent I. (402–417); Zosimus (417); Boniface I. (418–422); Cœlestinus (422–432); Sixtus III. (432–440); Leo I. (440–461); Hila′rius (461–468); Simplicius (468–483); Felix III. (483–492); Gela′sius I. (492–496), who abolished the observance of the Lupercalia, the last remnant of idolatry; Anasta′sius II. (496–498); Sym′machus (498–514).

A considerable number of controversial and of didactic writers flourished in this century. Among the Greeks and Orientals the most distinguished were CYRIL, bishop of Alexandria; Theod′oret, bishop of Cyprus; Isidore, bishop of Pelusium; Theoph′ilus, bishop of Alexandria; Palladius; Theodore of Mopsuestia; Nilus; Basil of Seleucia; Theod′otus, bishop of Ancyra; Gelasius of Cyzicus; Synesius, bishop of Ptolemaïs; Nestorius, bishop of Constantinople (already noticed); Eutyches; and others. Among the Latin writers were Leo the Great, Symmachus, Innocent I., Boniface I., Gelasius, and Felix, bishops of Rome; Orosius; Sidonius Apollina′ris; Vigil′ius of Tapsus; Arnobius; Zos′imus; Isidore of Cordova; HILARY, bishop of Arles; PATRICK, the apostle of Ireland; and others. One of the celebrities of the 5th century was HYPA′TIA, the daughter of Theon, a famous mathematician of Alexandria. She was born at the close of the 4th century, and was educated by her father, whom she soon surpassed in celebrity. Her beauty and genius attracted crowds to her school, where she taught mathematics, and gave lectures on science. She refused to be converted to Christianity, obstinately adhering to paganism. This excited the anger of Cyril, bishop of Alexandria, who attributed to her influence the persecutions which the Christians endured from Orestes, governor of the city. The partisans of Cyril seized her as she was going to her school, dragged her from her carriage into a neighboring church, stripped her, and beat her to death. They then cut her body into pieces, which they carried about the streets, and finally burnt publicly in a place called Cinaron (March, 415). Hypatia wrote several works, but they have not come down to us. An interesting account of her will be found in Kingsley's beautiful tale, "Hypatia".

What is said of Pelagius and Celestius?—Augustine?—His doctrine of Predestination?—The position of the patriarchs of Antioch and Alexandria?—What title did the patriarch of Constantinople assume?—What of that of "Pope"?—Who were bishops of Rome during this century?—What eminent men flourished?—What is said of Hypatia?

SUMMARY.

We have now completed the sketch of the history of that restless period in the life of the human race which has, by common consent, been designated "Ancient". It corresponds with the infancy and childhood of man. At the commencement, all is vague and uncertain; what is known is but a dim, shadowy outline of events, imperfectly remembered, whose significance is not perceived nor understood. The early traditions of mankind resemble those obscure impressions which have been left on the mind of a child by passing events, which he beheld but did not comprehend. The primitive races found "the world all before them where to choose", and, either by destiny or by chance, located themselves in the lands wherein we first meet with them. India, Persia, Asia Minor, Chaldea, and Syria testify to the presence, at a period far beyond our knowledge, of the great Aryan (or Indo-Germanic) race, upon whose language have been erected the structures of the classic tongues of antiquity and of modern Europe. Their native land was the eastern portion of the Persian empire. India was the scene of their first exploits, yet there they found a still earlier race of men, whom they subdued. Their influence extended through Asia into Egypt. The root, Ar, of their name (signifying "noble"), is traced in the words *Ar*amæan, *Ar*ab, *Ar*oer, *Ar*arat, *Ar*menia, and in a multitude of other words in the Persian, Chaldee, Greek, and Latin tongues. We may consider them the fathers of the great Caucasian race, with its stock of kindred languages. But what affinity, or whether there was ever any, between them and the Mongolian and the Negro races, the present state of our knowledge does not enable us to discover. In the "Ante-historical period" this subject was mentioned, and we need not dwell on it further now. We may observe, however, that as regards races of men, all ancient traditions, except those of the Hebrew, inculcate the belief in the appearance and disappearance of a succession of them, rather than the idea of one common origin for all nations. This has been shown in the histories of India, Persia, and Egypt.

We have traced the development of this Caucasian family of nations from the earliest dawn of history to the formation of great empires. Egypt, Babylonia, Assyria, Persia, India, and China claimed our first attention. Obscure, imperfect, and even contradictory as their annals sometimes are, we found abundant evidence of their having attained to a high degree of material prosperity and power, under forms of government suited to the infancy of the race, the will of one man being accepted as the rule of right. We may here notice the curious fact that the names of the first king, or lawgiver, of these different nations strongly resemble each other. Thus in Egypt we find Menes; in Phrygia, Manis; in Lydia, Manes; in India, Menu; in Crete, Minos; and in Germany, Mannus. It is not an unfair inference that these personages are one and the same being, who, at a very remote period, framed laws for the Aryans in their native regions, and that they carried these laws, together with the remembrance of their author, with them into the new lands which they colonized. If it be allowable for a historian to indulge in surmises, we should say that The Institutes of Menu were the great original code of Asia, whence the other codes were derived, and that the antiquity of this code should be carried back to a far more distant age than has been assigned to it (see page 51). The recent researches of the great philologists of Germany have already thrown much light upon the primitive history of Asia, and will probably throw more; we may, therefore, without presumption, doubt the accuracy of the conclusions of Sir William Jones and other Oriental scholars of the last century.

We traced the rise of Egypt, whence the ancient world drew its store of wisdom. For a thousand years—perhaps more—this extraordinary nation was the predominant power of the world as it then stood: its people had become ancient when the first Assyrian empire arose. The old Persian empire yielded to the enterprise of the followers of Ninus, and two rival powers appeared on the stage. Syria became their battle-field, but no permanent results followed from their desolating wars. A few monumental inscriptions are all that remain of the grand expeditions of Sesostris and of Semiramis. Nineveh and Babylon survived to compete in luxury and splendor with Memphis and Thebes. Unnoticed by the powerful despots of the Nile and the Euphrates, an upright man, scorning the prevailing idolatry, went out from the midst of its abominations to worship The One True God on the plains of Syria. There he planted that little germ of faith which one thousand years afterwards developed itself in the form of The Hebrew Theocracy, and the wealth and wisdom of Solomon. Yet another thousand years, and the work of Abraham was crowned by the appearance of THE MESSIAH. But much had taken place in the interval. Eighteen centuries before the Christian Era were laid the foundations of Grecian power and intelligence; small was their beginning: the petty Hellenic tribes formed themselves into little communities, and remained ignorant of their strength until there arose a great conflict between the barbaric power of Asia and the intellect of Europe. This conflict is popularly known by the name of The Siege of Troy, and has been consecrated by the genius of Homer. In it the Greeks acquired the knowledge of their power. We soon find them sending out colonies, and bending their energies to the ridding their land of the obstacles to its proper cultivation. These labors are typified under those of Hercules. The Phœnicians extend the wings of commerce to remote regions, and the Celtic race, having already overrun Europe by land, now invests it by sea; carrying with it, however, that most horrible form of idolatry known as Druidism. The distant coasts of Britain, Ireland, and Scandinavia, are explored by these merchants. The great continent of Africa is circumnavigated by sailors from Carthage, which has now risen up a prosperous Phœnician colony. Hints are thrown out that another and more westerly continent has been visited, but the penalty of death is laid upon him who utters them. Yet it must have been about this time that Votan and Zamna arrived in Central America, bringing with them a new form of civilization. The foundations of Rome are laid, and we soon become occupied with listening to the march of nations contending for empire or for liberty. Races more energetic are in the field. Egypt subsides into fatuity under the later Pharaohs; but it is still the land of wonders, the region of the dead. Nineveh expires with Sardanapalus, and Babylon with Belshazzar. Cyrus, with his Persians, establishes a mightier empire on their ruins, and his successors add Egypt and Asia Minor to their dominions. Their career of conquest is, however, checked at Marathon; and a second struggle between the barbaric power of the East and the intelligence of the West takes place. It lasts two centuries, at the expiration of which the Macedonian empire has extended over Asia, and swallowed up the liberties of Greece. The fabric raised by Alexander the Great falls to pieces under his successors; but a show of power is left in the Seleucidæ and the Ptolemies for a time. While these events are passing in the East, Rome and Carthage are contending for mastery in the West. The star of Romulus prevails over that of Dido, and Carthage is blotted out from the page of history. But the Roman eagle has also fixed its talons on Spain and Greece, and the latter dies, bequeathing to her destroyer her literature, her science, and her arts. After this, the conquest of the known world becomes a mere question of time with the Romans. Julius Cæsar and Pompey plant their standards in the far East and the far West. Having subdued the world, the Romans have but to enjoy it, and they accordingly abandon themselves to sensual pleasures, become too indolent to govern their empire, and therefore confide the task to the Cæsars.

How these rulers fulfilled their trust has been shown in the latter centuries of this work. In the height of their arrogance they failed to perceive that a Power far higher than their own was supplanting them, and that it would in time issue its edicts from their palace. We have traced the rise of Christianity until it became an engine of State in the hands of Constantine the Great and his successors, and we leave it at the close of this first portion of our history about to become the ruling power of the Western world. We have also pointed to the gradual overrunning of Europe by tribes pressing each other forward from Central Asia: they are fresh incursions of the Indo-Germanic race, whose mission was to extirpate the feeble remnants of Roman power, and lay the foundations of the leading nations of modern times. The Anglo-Saxons have settled in Britain, which now becomes Anglo-land, or England; the Franks have converted Gaul into France; the Bavarians, Saxons, Burgundians, and others, have laid out the map of Germany; and the Goths are masters of Spain and Italy. Here Ancient History terminates. The childhood of the race has come to an end: it now enters on its youthful career with higher aspirations. Its achievements and crimes will form the theme of the second part of our history.

What is said of primitive history?—The Aryans?—Their name?—Their first exploits?—Ancient traditions?—What empires first arose?—What of their government?—Of the names of the first lawgivers?—The Institutes of Menu?—Egypt?—Assyria?—Syria?—The results of their wars?

What is said of Abraham?—The foundations of Grecian power?—The siege of Troy?—The labors of Hercules?—The Phœnicians?—Druidism?—Africa?—America?—Rome?—Egypt?—Nineveh and Babylon?—Persia?—The second contest?—The Macedonian empire?—Carthage?—The Roman empire?—Christianity?—The irruptions of the barbarians?

INDEX.

[Note.—Where there is a difference between the accent or the spelling given in the text and that given in the index, the latter is to be preferred; and where the strictly classical pronunciation differs from the customary, the latter has been preferred, as in "Alexan'dria", instead of "Alexandri'a".]

INDEX.

INDEX.

D.

INDEX.

INDEX.

INDEX.

INDEX.

INDEX.

INDEX.

INDEX.

END OF PART I.

www.ingramcontent.com/pod-product-compliance
Lightning Source LLC
LaVergne TN
LVHW011222110826
845150LV00006B/1515

* 9 7 8 1 4 2 5 5 1 5 8 8 1 *